# The
# AMERICAN
# SCHOLAR
# Reader

# The AMERICAN SCHOLAR Reader

Hiram Haydn and
Betsy Saunders, editors

With a new introduction
by Irving Louis Horowitz

Transaction Publishers
New Brunswick (U.S.A.) and London (U.K.)

Library of Congress Catalog Number: 2011041343
ISBN: 978-1-4128-4295-2
Printed in the United States of America

Library of Congress Cataloging-in-Publication Data

The American scholar reader / editors : Hiram Haydn and Betsy Saunders ; with a new introduction by Irving Louis Horowitz.
    p. cm.
"Originally published in 1960 by Atheneum Publishers."
ISBN 978-1-4128-4295-2
    1. American essays. I. Haydn, Hiram Collins, 1907-1973. II. Saunders, Betsy.

AC5.A56 2011
808.4--dc23

2011041343

# Contents

# CONTENTS

# CONTENTS

# Searching for the American Scholar

IRVING LOUIS HOROWITZ

*T he American Scholar Reader* is a fine collection from a previous period that was written by outstanding people now nearly all gone from earth. The anthology deserves not only to be reread as an antique, but imitated for the qualities that it stood for: intellectual content on important items, literary styles that differed in form, but were united in a sense of the English language as a precious legacy from Great Britain, and a sense of probity that in the words of George Santayana's moving statement on American philosophers, "do not attempt to drive other people to think as I do, let them be their own poets."

The contents of this volume glisten so that they need few adumbrations. What does require some explanation, or at least expansion, is its morphology, the structure of the book in terms of time and space, from 1933 to 1959, or if you will, the rise of Nazism and fascism, the force of communism, and the cloud of a Great Depression followed by the dust of a Great War. It is intriguing to note that in a work of 425 pages; only 125 pages are taken up with the period ending in 1945, or the close of World War II. For if this volume painfully highlights the distance from whence we have come since 1960, more than a half century ago, it now also serves notice on how warfare itself changes the cultural complexion of even the biggest and more powerful of nations.

The fine editor, Hiram Haydn, was a man of quiet courage. I dare note he was kind enough to publish the works of a very young academic—me—on the war game that lead to the first major war in our history—in Vietnam—that ended neither in glory nor in shame, not in victory or defeat, but rather in a shocking demonstration that not every war is unconditional, and not every result is a triumph for the march of progress. He took on the dogs of McCarthyism by a side door rather than a frontal assault—by making certain that the editorial board was representative of a wide panoply of scholars representing the American scholars on the ground as well as in print. Nonetheless this volume while giving a few glimpses of what was to follow—from environmental values at home to political diversity abroad—is a story for later volumes to cover. This anthology tells us a good deal of *The American Scholar* and the path of *Phi Beta Kappa* in an age of great change with a story to tell of its own time.

There were cross cutting influences that reflected an America that emerged with the New Deal, and no less a New England past that saw America in just such terms: Columbia and Harvard, Boston and New York, and what E. Digby Baltzell well termed the Protestant Establishment. Indeed, it might well be that *The American Scholar* in its formative period captured that last hurrah of an older tradition. Columbia University itself is represented by Lionel Trilling, Richard Rovere, John Dewey, Jacques Barzun, Richard Hofstadter, Margaret Mead, Charles Frankel, John Herman Randall, Irwin Edman, and even Paul Tillich who happily served as visiting professor during my stay at Columbia during 1951-1953. Harvard runs a close second. The quarterly read like a literary reflection of the Saul Steinberg famed *New Yorker* cartoon picturing a map of America in which New York represented a solid fifty percent of the American nation, with New England and California another forty percent, and the rest of America neatly tucked into the remaining ten percent.

But the handwriting was on the wall. African Americans and Jewish Americans changed the cultural character of the nation, and its gilded literary estate. David Riesman, Max Lerner, and David Daiches from one side, and Paul Robeson, Saunders Redding, and C. Vann Woodward from the other. In 1954, Phyllis McGinley could write a poem to open the volume entitled "In Praise of Diversity"—long before the term was transformed into a movement. Haydn captured this well in noting that "after the war years there is a perceptible return to catholicity, together with a resurgence of interest in religion and psychology." Those trends were themselves part of the diversity movement, but at the same time indicated a tremendous movement toward understanding the private person subject to the battering ram of a public world.

Many of the figures represented in this volume are part of the dusty bins of unread works gathered in library depositories and archives at major universities. That does not signify a lack of relevance or even less an absence of talent. But it does indicate that the theme and topics of an earlier time are not always the same as what now dominates our culture. Especially notable is the absence of media studies, the American way of crime and corruption, and even less, recognition of technology as a driving force of modern times. It was a gentle world in which literary manners still dominated. Essays on Thornton Wilder and John Dewey prevailed, and "mass culture" was a field disparaged by conservative sociologists like Ernest Van der Haag. The writings of Sigmund Freud socialized by Erich Fromm and privatized by Norman Kelman, was the order of the times. It was an age in which reflection quickly changed into self-reflection. The old romanticism of Europe turned into the new eroticism of America. There was a disquieting feeling that some of these contributors held that the old order was vanishing, but had very little sense of what the new order was to bring in its stead.

What such ruminations indicate is that while there is at least an implicit sense of what is worth preserving in such an anthology, the issue for our time period is what, among the essays selected, remains worth reading. More bluntly, what makes an article, a book, or for that matter, ideas as such, worth recalling if not entirely compelling, is a question of note. What is worth preserving in 1959 is not necessarily the same as what should or might be read in 2012. The greater the distance between the production of a work and the present, the fewer the number of articles can be considered memorable. My own belief is that the extent to which a piece expresses the quotidian moment linked to the historical tradition being examined is a key to the essay as a literary form. That is easily said than done. Into the mix one must pour a sense of continuing urgency and policy risk.

It must be said that not every contribution to *The American Scholar Reader* meets such rigid, admittedly subjective, standards. Some of the essays reveal a precious sense of cultivated people in search of the clever. Even brilliant statements on Catholic Ireland, Nazi Germany, and rural America seem in retrospect as hesitant in content. They represented an older tradition of people in high places examining the review of people in low places with empathy, but not always with a sense of intimacy one found for example in James Agee's *Let Us Now Praise Famous Men* or *A Death in the Family*. The Depression and then World War II impacted different strata within American society in profoundly disparate ways. The massification of academic life that fueled changes in attitudes and orientations had not quite taken hold.

*The American Scholar* became the testing point and touchstone for quality in smaller, literary publications. *Partisan Review, Antioch Review, Hudson Review,* and a host of regional and state-based journals clearly looked to *The American Scholar* as a model to be emulated. But the model itself changed dramatically with struggles not only in the character of overseas conflict or domestic violence, but with intense conflicts within university life itself. This volume well offers the reader a sense of struggle among academic elites.

Having introduced such cautions and caveats, it remains a fact that this reader is emblematic, as well as symbolic, of some fine writings about American scholarship. It is hardly possible to not appreciate brief essays by the likes of Jacques Barzun, George Santayana, Reinhold Niebuhr, and a goodly number of other snapshots of America that illustrate the conversion of the United States and its intellectual classes from observers and emulators of European culture to the creators of a tradition of their own. Indeed, Robert Gorham Davis' essay, "The New Criticism and the Democratic Tradition," done in 1949, well illustrates this basic shift from aristocratic to populist inspiration. This volume is a sober reminder of a nation that changed its class colors, but somehow remained true to its democratic character. Perhaps this is an augury of the American future as well as its past.

September 25, 2011

# Foreword

## HIRAM HAYDN

To ATTEMPT to include, even in a large book, a sufficiently comprehensive number of representative essays and articles to do justice to the publications of thirty years is a staggering task. Miss Saunders and I found that we suffered even in cutting down the possible inclusions to two hundred. But what we were faced with was the need to cut again to the final fifty! We achieved the result to be found in this book with the feeling that we might well have another and equally good collection of fifty other pieces. To mention the names of only a few of those painfully eliminated from the final one hundred is to give some hint of the problem:

| | |
|---|---|
| Ruth Benedict | Van Wyck Brooks |
| Harrison Brown | Albert Guérard |
| Aldous Huxley | Alvin Johnson |
| Alfred Kazin | Dwight MacDonald |
| Archibald MacLeish | Perry Miller |
| Herbert Muller | Richard H. Rovere |
| Bertrand Russell | Harlow Shapley |
| Lionel Trilling | Wendell Willkie |

Confronted with so difficult a problem, we did not, I think, succeed in solving it with any impeccable logic or with the confident use of an arbitrary yardstick. We groped and felt our way along, knowing only that, in so far as we could, we wanted to have these elements in the final selection: (1) A selection of quality (those included must be *among* the best several hundred); (2) a diversity of subject matter and approach (the "invocation" by Phyllis McGinley suggests the conscious striving of the magazine's editors for diversity and balance); (3) a selection representative of the different interests stressed in the magazine's history, and of how they reflected the prevailing intellectual and cultural currents of the times.

Let me explain this last point: in the selections from the first half of the thirties there is a greater emphasis on economics than in other periods of *The Scholar*'s history. This is illustrated by the inclusion here of two such articles out of the five chosen from the first five years of the magazine. Similarly, though perhaps not quite so clearly, in the second half of the decade of the thirties the magazine reflected the general concern with the impending world crisis. I say "not so clearly" because we have not included as large a proportion of these articles in this final gathering together, but they were there in the magazine.

Again, after the war years there is a perceptible return to catholicity, together with a resurgence of interest in religion and psychology.

The selections from the third of the three decades, I think, indicate the full restoration of diversity. If there are any emergent trends discernible, they are to be found in a new interest in general social and cultural matters and in a semi-new kind of writing on nature, embodying a growing awareness of ecology and the importance of conservation.

I offer these generalizations both tentatively and diffidently. When only fifty selections are made from the work of thirty years, the statistical evidence that it is possible to present is so slight, I am sure, as to satisfy no statistician and perhaps no one else. I would like to add only a word. The appearance in this volume of the pieces about William Allan Neilson, Christian Gauss and Irwin Edman commemorates only three of the dozen or so outstanding figures who became over the years symbols, as well as exponents, of what *The Scholar* was and is striving for. And that is a magazine written by highly qualified and expert people who nonetheless are not writing in a specialized way for their peers, but lucidly for an unspecialized audience—attentive, curious and intelligent.

# A Note on the History of
## *The American Scholar*

### BETSY SAUNDERS

PERHAPS THE DAY of the quarterlies is gone by, and those megatheria of letters may be in the mere course of nature with-
drawing to the swamps to die," James Russell Lowell brooded
almost a century ago, after his initial experience as editor of a
quarterly magazine. Neither his extensive knowledge of magazines
nor the fortification of Charles Eliot Norton as coeditor seems to
have cheered him. But even in a moment of discouragement Mr.
Lowell retained his sharp imagery when he cast the quarterlies as
"those megatheria of letters." The Megatherium was the largest of
the ground sloths found in the Pleistocene of America. Too heavy-
bottomed to run, too slender and loose-jointed in the fore limbs to
fight, even its skin was unarmored. And to add insult to the in-
juries that finally did it in, the Megatherium was the victim of
one of nature's cruelest oversights—it had no front teeth. It could
chew endlessly on crude molars, but it could not bite. Even devotees of quarterly magazines cannot fail to grasp the parallel.

The quarterly has never fared well in America. Its pace always
has been too slow for a people excited by and dedicated to the contemporaneous. The first one in this country, launched at the beginning of the nineteenth century with high hopes, was buried
quietly two years later. The case history has been repeated many
times since. In 1852 the *Literary World,* a weekly publication devoted to the discussion of books, commented: "It has been the
fashion to write of 'the poor old Quarterlies,' and attribute to
them the same degree of influence which grandmothers possess in
modern society." That this vigorous publication expired the following year does not invalidate the statement. The fact remains
that no matter how stalwart and optimistic their parents might be,
quarterlies have remained the delicate offspring of the magazine
family, with a mortality rate unknown among the other members.
They have never developed an immunity to the chief diseases encountered by the first American magazines, as diagnosed by Frank

Luther Mott in his *History of American Magazines:* the indifference of possible authors and readers, inadequate means of distribution, and the inability to collect subscription accounts. These progressive symptoms are then followed by the death rattle—the inability to meet publishing costs—and another quarterly passes on. The sequence is the rule rather than an exception.

We hope, therefore, that it will be understood and pardoned if *The American Scholar* goes about the preparation for its thirtieth birthday with a delighted disbelief. Modesty would not become it at this time, for the magazine not only has survived, it has become the beneficiary of the largest paid subscription list known to a general quarterly in the history of American magazines.

*The Scholar* was started by the United Chapters of Phi Beta Kappa in 1931, a year that did not rush forward to embrace new babies or magazines. But perhaps it should not be surprising that an organization founded in 1776, and rooted in scholarship, would maintain its aplomb during the Depression.

The magazine actually began to take shape in the mind of William Allison Shimer, as he trained to become the new executive head of the United Chapters during the winter of 1930. Mr. Shimer recalls that while writing obituaries of deceased Phi Beta Kappa members, to be printed in the Society's house organ, he realized the need for investing time and energies in a scholarly publication to challenge the interest of the intelligent reading public. (Would that all history might be so frank.) And even after the obituary notices were up to date, Mr. Shimer's ideas for a new magazine persisted. In the early spring of 1931 he discussed them first with Will D. Howe, an editor and director of Charles Scribner's Sons, and then with John H. Finley, an editor of *The New York Times.* As their enthusiasm grew, they expanded their discussions to include John Erskine, Christian Gauss, Alvin Johnson, Adam Leroy Jones, John Herman Randall and Frederick J. E. Woodbridge.

On May 11, 1931, *The Scholar* became an entity, like so many other American institutions, over lunch. The magazine was given its name that day by John Erskine, with the unanimous acceptance of the group and with full credit to Mr. Emerson, who had delivered a noble address on "The American Scholar" almost a century before. Now it remained to convince the Senate, the governing body of Phi Beta Kappa, and the Council, composed of delegates from each of the Phi Beta Kappa chapters, of the need for a magazine that would exhibit American scholarship rather than just talk about it.

In some future utopia all children may be loved and anticipated before and after conception, but this was too much to hope for in the early thirties. Information about the plans for a new magazine was sent out to members of the Senate, and replies came back promptly, among them the following:

*June 9, 1931*

DEAR DR. SHIMER:

I have just read with some dismay your letter suggesting that Phi Beta Kappa inflict upon a long-suffering and patient people another "scholarly" and "different" magazine.

The proposition should have mature reflection before being placed before the Council. I wonder if you have recently examined the magazines which are on the racks in any large library? I do not now recall a single field of inquiry and thought which does not have its special magazine—all designed "to promote scholarship"—and most of them doomed to starvation, except for some "angel" willing to sink some thousands in its publication.

What is the need for another one? Each comes out as "different"—each, within a few months, is compelled into a standardized style by the insistent demand of critics and readers— if any body of readers is found. Why should Phi Beta Kappa enter this crowded field, already pre-empted by universities and technical societies?

The questions posed were legitimate ones. Although they were given serious thought and investigation, they seemed to have one answer: Scholarly reading and writing, as excellent as pieces of it might be in isolation, remained a mosaic without design; a magazine such as the proposed *American Scholar* was needed.

Further plans were developed throughout the summer of 1931, with the founding group agreeing to serve on the first Editorial Board, adding to its number William Allan Neilson, Ada Louise Comstock and Harry Allen Overstreet. In September the Senate and the Council of the United Chapters of Phi Beta Kappa met at Brown University, and after reviewing a prospectus of *The American Scholar*, they voted to authorize its publication. The first issue of the magazine appeared in January, 1932.

William Allison Shimer was the first editor of *The Scholar*, carrying out his editorial duties in addition to those of the Executive Secretary of the United Chapters of Phi Beta Kappa. When Mr. Shimer resigned in 1943, Marjorie Hope Nicolson edited the magazine for a year until Hiram Haydn arrived in the fall of 1944. The unique contribution of each of the three editors is clearly evident in the past issues of the magazine.

During its almost three decades *The American Scholar* has played a contented Ruth to Phi Beta Kappa's Naomi. The Society has always made room for the magazine in offices that have moved through a small apartment and a loft over a bakeshop in New York City, to the burnt-out shell of Phi Beta Kappa Hall and a dormitory of the College of William and Mary in Williamsburg, and finally to permanent quarters in Washington. It is not likely that some future Boaz will make much impression, for the United Chapters consistently has remained a good provider, giving this offspring encouragement, financial support and complete freedom even to make its own mistakes. The president of the Society sits on the Editorial Board of the magazine, ex-officio, as Consulting Editor; and the Senate retains the right to give final approval of the members elected to serve on *The Scholar* Editorial Board. These controls, if they can be called such, have proved to be blessings rather than hindrances.

Elsewhere in this volume is a list of the men and women who have served on the Editorial Board of *The Scholar*. An examination of it will make a rather obvious explanation of the strength and success of the magazine. At least three times a year twelve to fifteen of these members come together to discuss general business and to criticize past and future issues. If records of these meetings are ever released they will delight posterity, for, as Marjorie Hope Nicolson has said, they are "evenings of wit and badinage, of serious business handled lightly." And between meetings, each member of the Board reads, criticizes, votes for or against the publication of the manuscripts submitted to him or her by the Editor. There can be no question that the quality of *The American Scholar* has grown out of the group deliberation and judgment of its Editorial Board. For it is this working Board that has held the magazine to the middle line between lightness and learning, that has opposed pedantry as a stultifier of knowledge, and that has made of the hazardous inability of quarterlies to consider the contemporaneous a strength rather than a weakness.

It should be noted here that an integral part of the structure and the system that have aided *The Scholar* in its growth and added to its depth and fiber has been its staff. Every magazine has its assistant editors, its typists, salesmen, proof readers, file clerks, subscription processors and copy editors. But *The American Scholar* has had more than God's plenty of people who, by doubling in all these roles, were willing to hold up the hands of the prophets.

Here in this volume are presented portions of *The Scholar's* past. Although the present health and vitality of the magazine are reassuring, it is to be remembered that thirty years is only a moment in the evolution of ideas and no proof of durability. If it is able to maintain its vision, *The Scholar* will continue to record and interpret the uncertain weather of intellectuals in a democracy, with the firm belief that this is the only atmosphere in which truth and its sister freedom can be found. But because *The Scholar* is a barometer rather than a crusade, it will never surpass or excel the imagination and the influence of American scholars.

Predictions for the future of anything are highly speculative affairs, but they are better based on the facts of the past than on present hopes. In 1941, as America prepared for another war and *The Scholar* entered its second decade, a distinguished historian serving on the Editorial Board of the magazine commented on its future. The past twenty years, with all their seismic shifts and tremors, have not altered Crane Brinton's prophecy:

> In these excited times, when all the really respected prophets are prophets of doom, when mankind is perpetually at a crossroads or on the brink of a volcano or tottering toward a *Völkerdämmerung*, this modest prophecy for the future of *The American Scholar* may seem most unlikely to come true. Of course if the prophets of doom are right, and civilization goes to smash, *The American Scholar* will go with it. But if the prophets of doom are wrong—and how wrong they have been in the past every historian knows—then we may foresee that in the next few years the magazine will go its steady, quiet way, avoiding extremes, even when they are picturesque extremes, seeking the new, the striking, the provocative, but never seeking these qualities only, and never seeking them at the expense of truth, accuracy and sense. To believe that a periodical with such a policy has not an assured future in this country would indeed be to despair of America.

# ACKNOWLEDGMENTS

The Editors give grateful acknowledgment for permission to reprint the following.

"In Praise of Diversity," copyright 1953 by Phyllis McGinley. Reprinted from *The Love Letters of Phyllis McGinley*. By permission of The Viking Press, Inc., and J. M. Dent & Sons (London).

"Impression of Ireland" by Irwin Edman, copyright 1940 by the United Chapters of Phi Beta Kappa. By permission of Mr. and Mrs. Lester Markel, representatives of the Estate of Irwin Edman.

"Music for the Man Who Enjoys Hamlet," copyright 1944 by the United Chapters of Phi Beta Kappa. Later appeared in *Music for the Man Who Enjoys Hamlet*, by B. H. Haggin, published in 1944 by Alfred A. Knopf, Inc., and in 1960 by the Modern Library Paperback series. By permission of the author.

"The Best of Two Worlds: Some Reflections on a Peculiarly Modern Privilege," copyright 1950, 1951, 1953 by Joseph Wood Krutch. Reprinted from *The Best of Two Worlds*, by Joseph Wood Krutch. By permission of William Sloane Associates.

"Freud, Religion and Science," copyright 1951 by the United Chapters of Phi Beta Kappa. Amplified version appeared in *Individualism Reconsidered*, by David Riesman, published in 1954 by The Free Press and in 1955 by Doubleday-Anchor. By permission of the author.

"Liberal Education and a Liberal Nation," copyright 1952 by the United Chapters of Phi Beta Kappa. Parts of this article later appeared in *Educational Wastelands*, published in 1953 by the University of Illinois Press, and in *The Restoration of Learning*, published in 1955 by Alfred A. Knopf, Inc. By permission of Alfred A. Knopf, Inc.

"Christian Gauss as a Teacher of Literature," copyright 1952 by Edmund Wilson. Reprinted from *The Shores of Light*, by Edmund Wilson. By permission of Farrar, Straus and Cudahy, Inc.

"The Turn of the Tide" by H. M. Tomlinson, copyright 1953 by the United Chapters of Phi Beta Kappa. Later appeared in *A Mingled Yarn*, published in 1953 by The Bobbs-Merrill Company. By permission of the Society of Authors.

"America and Art," copyright 1953 by the United Chapters of Phi Beta Kappa. Later appeared in *Company Manners*, by Louis Kronenberger, published in 1954 by The Bobbs-Merrill Company. By permission of the publisher.

"Alaskan Summer: Leaves from a Candid Journal," copyright 1953 by the United Chapters of Phi Beta Kappa. Amplified version appeared as "To Alaska" in *Pelican in the Wilderness*, by F. Fraser Darling, published in 1956 by Random House, Inc. By permission of Random House and George Allen & Unwin, Ltd. (London).

"A Glimpse of Incomprehensibles," copyright 1954 by the United Chapters of Phi Beta Kappa. Later appeared in *Anatomist at Large*, by George W. Corner, published in 1958 by Basic Books, Inc. By permission of the publisher.

"The Pseudo-Conservative Revolt," by Richard Hofstadter, copyright 1954 by the United Chapters of Phi Beta Kappa, based on an address delivered at the second annual Barnard College lecture series in American Civilization, devoted to "The Search for New Standards in Modern America." By permission of Basil Rauch, chairman, American Civilization Program, Barnard College.

"The Present Human Condition," copyright © 1955 by Erich Fromm. Excerpted from the last chapter of *The Sane Society*, by Erich Fromm, published in 1955 by Rinehart and Company, Inc. By permission of Holt, Rinehart and Winston, Inc.

"The Judgment of the Birds," copyright © 1956, 1957 by Loren C. Eiseley. Reprinted from *The Immense Journey*, by Loren C. Eiseley, published in 1957 by Random House, Inc. By permission of the publisher.

"Equality: America's Deferred Commitment," copyright © 1958 by the United Chapters of Phi Beta Kappa. Later appeared in *The Burden of Southern History*, by C. Vann Woodward, copyright © 1960 by the Louisiana State University Press. By permission of the publisher.

*The*
*American Scholar*
*Reader*

# In Praise of Diversity

PHYLLIS MCGINLEY

(*1954*)

Since this ingenious earth began
    To shape itself from fire and rubble;
Since God invented man, and man
    At once fell to, inventing trouble,
One virtue, one subversive grace
Has chiefly vexed the human race.

One whimsical beatitude,
    Concocted for his gain and glory,
Has man most stoutly misconstrued
    Of all the primal category—
Counting no blessing, but a flaw,
That Difference is the mortal law.

Adam, perhaps, while toiling late,
    With life a book still strange to read in,
Saw his new world, how variegate,
    And mourned, "It was not so in Eden,"
Confusing thus from the beginning
Unlikeness with original sinning.

And still the sons of Adam's clay
    Labor in person or by proxy
At altering to a common way
    The planet's holy heterodoxy.
Till now, so dogged is the breed,
Almost it seems that they succeed.

One shrill, monotonous, level note
    The human orchestra's reduced to.
Man casts his ballot, turns his coat,
    Gets born, gets buried as he used to,
Makes war, makes love—but with a kind
Of masked and universal mind.

3

*His good has no nuances. He*
  *Doubts or believes with total passion.*
*Heretics choose for heresy*
  *Whatever's the prevailing fashion.*
*Those wearing Tolerance for a label*
*Call other views intolerable.*

*"For or Against" 's the only rule.*
  *Damned are the unconvinced, the floaters.*
*Now all must go to public school,*
  *March with the League of Women Voters*
*Or else for safety get allied*
*With a unanimous Other Side.*

*There's white, there's black; no tint between.*
  *Truth is a plane that was a prism.*
*All's Blanshard that's not Bishop Sheen.*
  *All's treason that's not patriotism.*
*Faith, charity, hope—now all must fit*
*One pattern or its opposite.*

*Or so it seems. Yet who would dare*
  *Deny that nature planned it other*
*When every freckled thrush can wear*
  *A dapple various from his brother,*
*When each pale snowflake in the storm*
*Is false to some imagined norm?*

*Recalling then what surely was*
  *The earliest bounty of Creation:*
*That not a blade among the grass*
  *But flaunts its difference with elation,*
*Let us devoutly take no blame*
*If similar does not mean the same.*

*And grateful for the wit to see*
  *Prospects through doors we cannot enter,*
*Ah! let us praise Diversity*
  *Which holds the world upon its center.*
*Praise* con amour *or* furioso
*The large, the little and the so-so.*

4

Rejoice that under cloud and star
    The planet's more than Maine or Texas.
Bless the delightful fact there are
    Twelve months, nine muses, and two sexes,
And infinite in earth's dominions
Arts, climates, wonders and opinions.

Praise ice and ember, sand and rock,
    Tiger and dove and ends and sources;
Space travellers, and who only walk
    Like mailmen round familiar courses;
Praise vintage grapes and tavern Grappas,
And bankers and Phi Beta Kappas;

Each in its moment justified,
    Praise knowledge, theory, second guesses;
That which must wither or abide;
    Prim men, and men like wildernesses;
And men of peace and men of mayhem
And pipers and the ones who pay 'em.

Praise the disheveled, praise the sleek;
    Austerity and hearts-and-flowers;
People who turn the other cheek
    And extroverts who take cold showers;
Saints we can name a holy day for
And infidels whom saints can pray for.

Praise youth for pulling things apart,
    Toppling the idols, breaking leases;
Then from the upset apple-cart
    Praise oldsters picking up the pieces.
Praise wisdom, hard to be a friend to,
And folly one can condescend to.

Praise what conforms and what is odd,
    Remembering, if the weather worsens
Along the way, that even God
    Is said to be three separate Persons.
Then upright or upon the knee,
Praise Him that by His courtesy,
For all our prejudice and pains,
Diverse His Creature still remains.

5

# Economists and the World Crisis

## ELMER DAVIS

### *( 1933 )*

Known for his lucid, shrewd and often droll interpretations of the news, ELMER DAVIS became for millions of radio listeners the voice of his time. Mr. Davis died in 1958. Those who remember his terse analyses and political affiliations will be amused by a comment in this article: "I am no passionate admirer of the incoming president, but one thing about Mr. Roosevelt enlists my confidence—he does not seem to know what to think about the tariff—and I note that even experts are by no means of one opinion."

I AM not an economist—only a member of that humble but occasionally useful class, the popularizers. But by ancient privilege a cat may look at a king, and in virtue of that same large tolerance a layman may perhaps be permitted to scrutinize a group of savants, and offer some commentary on their behavior in the past few years; especially if the layman happens to be an average specimen of a very large group—the ordinary citizens whose knowledge of economics goes no farther than the obligatory college freshman course; who in times past never had any particular understanding of that science or any particular interest in it; who regarded such matters as the money question, and the theory of value, with the same respectful incomprehension that they felt about the doctrine of the Trinity; who supposed, until the autumn of 1929, that they had nothing to do with economics, and that economics had nothing to do with them.

The average citizen knows better now, but there remains between him and those who are supposed to know, a gap, not only in knowledge but in attitude, that needs to be bridged. In the complex society of the present and the future, a good understanding

between the average man and the expert is of tremendous importance; and in no field is this more true than in economics. If we are
ever to have a sanely ordered society—if our present society is to
hold together—the economists must be among the most responsible advisers of our rulers. And in a democracy we must have not
only leaders fit to lead, but followers who are convinced that the
leaders are worth following.

It cannot be said that either of these conditions has been ideally
fulfilled in the past four years. The administration which is
soon to pass out of office did often enlist experts of various sorts
to find facts; but it usually employed them only to find supplementary arguments, on the plane of reason, in support of doctrines already received by revelation, and not to be altered if it
turned out that they were not in accord with the facts. The most
conspicuous of many instances was of course the protest of 1028
economists against the Smoot-Hawley tariff bill. Granted that this
was not a purely spontaneous demonstration, that somebody
drummed up this protest, none the less it was a most remarkable
occurrence; more than a thousand men whose professional reputation was their chief asset were willing to stand up and be counted,
as experts, on a controversial political issue. Nothing that the
economists have done in recent years has been so creditable—and
this is true whether you happen to believe that they were right,
in this instance, or not. That is the sort of thing that must happen,
more and more frequently, if a complex society is to be conducted
at all; the men who know must say what they know, even if they
are aware that somebody will be offended.

A corollary, of course, is that the men who know must really
know; and another corollary is that the men who govern must be
willing to listen to expert advice, even if it happens to be unpalatable. In this particular case the mass protest of experts was worse
than futile. The President signed the Smoot-Hawley Act; and
while he did so, apparently, without any great enthusiasm, his admiration for that measure increased month by month, in direct
ratio to the decline of customs receipts under the new rates; until by the time he was campaigning for re-election he seemed to
regard this latest tariff as the greatest document ever struck off at
one time by the brain of man.

Criticism of an administration already repudiated is shooting a
dead duck. The point is worth mentioning only because Mr.
Hoover is superior both in intellectual capacity and in range of
information to the average of our recent presidents. He certainly

qualifies as an intellectual in at least the ordinary sense of that term; and since his qualifications were not minimized by his publicity there is some real danger that his failure may discredit intelligence as such. He failed, not because he was too intelligent but because he was not intelligent enough; because, at critical moments, he was governed by metaphysical concepts whose truth he did not question, no matter how much the facts might contradict them.

I am no passionate admirer of the incoming president, but one thing about Mr. Roosevelt enlists my confidence—he does not seem to know what to think about the tariff—and I note that even experts are by no means of one opinion. We are more likely to be served well by a president who does not know what to think, and may possibly end by taking the best professional opinion, than by one who regards all controversial issues as closed by the infallible pronouncement of a party platform.

Whether or not the next administration is properly hospitable to expert opinion, the only chance of making modern society work at all lies in getting a government which will be guided by expert opinion. This will entail both a change of heart among men who are elected to public office, and a much livelier and more continuous interest in the whole matter on the part of the average citizen; and it will further entail—with all respect be it said—a higher degree of dispassionateness, of trustworthiness, among the experts, notably so among the economists.

Economics is, of course, a social science; or at least is so counted. Mr. George Soule has observed that it "is not yet a science" at all; and some of us indeed are pessimistic enough to feel that all the branches of learning which are politely called the social sciences might be better described by some other name. But whatever you call them they deal, as Professor Taussig has remarked, not with the precise quantities of the physical sciences (even these are by no means as precise as they used to be) but with "man and his wavering and incalculable behavior." Furthermore, they deal with matters of present urgency, affected in consequence by present emotions; not only the emotions of the average man who is at once the material of the science, and the heathen to be converted by the scientist's conclusions, but the emotions of the scientist himself. If the economists have made grave blunders it is not only because they deal with the wavering and incalculable behavior of man, but because they are themselves men, whose behavior is likely to be wavering and incalculable.

Astrophysics deals with matters of vital importance to the human race, and it appears to be the most inexact of sciences. In successive seasons we learn that space is curved, that it is not curved; that the earth is two billion years old, that it is ten billion years old; that the universe is finite and more or less stable; that the universe is expanding and contracting like an accordion. No wonder that minds which crave a sense of order and stability in life revolt against the levity of the astrophysicists, who are willing to tear up one universe after another and throw them into the wastebasket, to begin again with confidence that this time they will come somewhat nearer the truth than they did last year or the year before.

Economists, as a class, are somewhat more flexible than theologians but considerably less so than astrophysicists. It cannot be said that they deal with graver matters. Nothing is more important to the human race than the question whether the second law of thermodynamics is or is not valid, whether the universe of which we are residents is or is not inexorably running down. But this problem is not of immediate urgency; and whether the answer is pleasant or unpleasant there is in all probability nothing we can do about it. The economist deals with present problems which can often be affected by human action; he reaches conclusions whose validity can often be tested, not a billion years from now, but next month or next week. This ought to make him at once more humble and more flexible than the astrophysicist, less dogmatic in pronouncing his opinions and readier to admit it when the evidence proves them wrong.

Economists are not the only men who have made mistakes; all we like sheep have gone astray, and if we laymen can say that at least our mistakes have harmed no one but ourselves, that is not particularly to our credit. But the experts are paying for their reputation. People who believed them when they were wrong are now in the mood to disbelieve them, even if they happen to be right.

It would be ungracious as well as unnecessary to recite the mistakes of eminent economists in the past four years; nor is there any need here to offer the case for the defense. That was done in *Harpers Magazine* for last August by Professor Taussig, who compared the situation of the economists in the face of the crisis to that of the doctors in dealing with cancer. They know a good deal about it, they are doing their best to learn more; but they do not know yet what causes the disease or what will cure it. It is perhaps appropriate here to point out some reasons why great men have gone astray and to suggest not only how these men may be a little

9

more trustworthy in the future, but also how they may convince the average man of their trustworthiness.

This latter objective may seem ignoble to the more austere of the scientists. A year ago last June Sir Josiah Stamp remarked in an after-dinner speech to some of his colleagues that "it is not the duty of the economist to be an amateur politician, and regulate himself by the gullibility of the public. He must ascertain the truth and teach it, regardless of what the voter can stand or understand." In the modern democratic world, however, the destiny of nations—the course that organized society is to follow, with ineluctable consequences to all of us, great and small, expert and inexpert—is determined, not always, but now and then, on certain critical occasions, by the voters. It is hardly the part of wisdom, therefore, to disdain to make oneself, and one's expert opinions, intelligible to the masters of one's destiny. Despise the arts of the politician, but they are about the only practical means of getting things done. If a man will not use them to get done what he thinks necessary, somebody else will use them for the attainment of very different objectives.

The scientist is a bad scientist if he regulates himself by the gullibility of the public; but he is a bad citizen if he does not try to mitigate that gullibility—if he does not try to teach the public what he thinks is the truth, even though that entails a wearisome reiteration of the elementary; if he does not try to make the average man, whose vote may determine even the exceptional man's destiny, understand that certain things are likely to work, and certain other things almost certainly will not work. And now and then there is evidence that public intelligence in politics, low as it often is, may sometimes be rather higher than that of the politicians who think they are playing down to it. But before the pure scientist attempts to educate the public he ought to make sure there is no beam in his own eye. The layman may not always see that protruding timber beforehand; but he can see it afterward. The average citizen may not know a great deal about economics, but after reading the papers for the last four years he feels he knows a good deal about economists; and he inclines to believe, until convincing disproof is offered, that even experts are men of like passions with himself.

Probably no recent book on economics is more renowned than Mr. Keynes's *Economic Consequences of the Peace*. In the twelve years since its appearance many of its scientific theories—not all, but many—have come to seem sound to people who rejected them at the moment. They were, of course, rejected at the moment by such a large fraction of society because men are emotional more often than they are rational—not only men who read books, but men who write them. Mr. Keynes argued for a cancellation of war debts which would have meant, in connection with his reparations proposals, substantially that Great Britain should pay almost as large an indemnity as Germany, and that the United States should pay one considerably larger. The course of events has shown that on the whole this was good realistic reasoning. But such a suggestion, made immediately after the close of the War, was not only inequitable but unpalatable, and it is not surprising that it failed to gain much favor with American opinion. A further reason for its rejection is implicit in the book itself. Mr. Keynes's intense dislike for the French and the Poles—or at any rate for the personified national concepts of France and Poland—was not concealed; and his arguments against the French and Polish points of view lost some weight in consequence. The argument appeared to the reader, however it may have been intended by the author, as an antithesis between Keynes's emotions and other people's emotions.

When President Hoover addressed the Chamber of Commerce of the United States on May 1, 1930, he told his hearers that "all slumps are the inexorable consequences of the destructive forces of booms," and went on to give an interpretation of the events of the past six months which I think any economic expert would approve as sound, on the basis of the evidence then available. Five months later, speaking to the convention of the American Bankers Association, he repeated that "whatever the remote causes may be, a large and immediate cause of most hard times is inflationary booms." Continuing, he observed that "the economic fatalist believes that these crises are inevitable, and are bound to be recurrent. The same thing was once said of typhoid, cholera, and smallpox. This is not the spirit of modern science. Science girds itself with painstaking research to find the nature and origin of the disease, and to devise methods for its prevention." This, again, is unexceptionable. Yet President Hoover in action (or rather in inaction) was then, and for almost a year afterward, not only devising no methods to prevent a recurrence of the disease, but was making no effort to cure its present onset; he was relying on time, luck, the *vis medicatrix naturæ*. And when he was a candidate for reelection he had revised his opinions as to the nature and origin of the disease. No longer did it have anything to do with inflationary booms as such. It all went back to causes whose inexorable oper-

11

ation was under way a dozen years before he took office; it was something for which he could not have been blamed.

Obviously even a politician in office can view the course of events with a dispassionate scientific coolness, when no election is at hand; yet when compelled to get out and fight for his job he can bring himself—from the loftiest impulses of public service—to repudiate the good sense he has shown in the past. The good done by President Hoover in the past year was accomplished largely by the institution of a limited type of socialism. It was limited in extent and was meant—how successfully no one can say—to be limited in duration; none the less it was socialism, or at any rate collectivism, as far as it went. In spite of this, the man who had introduced it, and probably averted still more serious disaster by so doing, was denouncing socialism right up to the end and de-claiming rhapsodies of praise about the old-fashioned individu-alism which in practise he had rejected.

Some allowance may be made—or at any rate commonly is made —for careless dealings with the truth on the part of candidates for office. But we expect something better from the universities. Usually, it should be said, we get it; but there have been some con-spicuous instances, in very high places, of experts whose business it is to deal with the wavering and incalculable behavior of man, who yet were totally oblivious of the effect their doctrines were almost certain to have on the human mind.

In May 1927 one of the most distinguished of American econo-mists, a man who has rendered high service both to the theory and to the practise of economics, published a book which began with the complaint that certain writers had been talking about the "bankruptcy of economics," on the ground that the economists had failed to make a scientific study of one of the outstanding phenom-ena of the new era of Coolidge prosperity. The book in question was an answer to that complaint, and offered the scientific study that had been demanded. The author described the century of diligent research and hard thinking that following the industrial revolution had gone into the rebuilding of the science of eco-nomics; and went on to say that as a consequence of the new de-velopments the author had been considering, "we now stand on the brink of another revolution in economic science and economic life, scarcely inferior to its predecessor."

That was in 1927. We have since then experienced a revolution in economic life and a revolution, not to say a disintegration, in economic science; but not in either case—unfortunately—the one

12

forecast in the passage quoted. For surely no book ever laid down more attractive blueprints of a new and brighter economic era. The abolition of poverty had not yet been officially promised; but its whole economic and metaphysical framework was already present in this announcement of a millennium which still remains around the corner.

In times past it had been supposed that there was a regrettable but inescapable antithesis between spending and saving; one could either have a good time with money or invest it for future profit, but the same money could not be applied to both uses. But in 1927 we heard that "in the broader sense there is really little difference between production and consumption." Both are utilization of wealth. Production is not merely the growing of crops, the manufacture of things, but "the creation of the productive efficiency which renders future wealth more easy of attainment." In other words, in having a good time one does more than have a good time; one increases productive efficiency and thereby makes a due contribution to the welfare of society. So far as I know, this was the first time it had been announced by an economic authority of the very first rank that a man could eat his cake and have it too. The author drew a clear enough distinction between productive consumption, and consumption that is destructive or merely neutral; but the criterion of utility must be the result. The species of productive consumption primarily considered by the author was the driving of automobiles purchased on the instalment plan. For the book in question was Professor Seligman's *Economics of Instalment Selling*. If I use it as a text for some observations, it is with no lack of respect either for his great authority, or for the lofty idealism with which his work is informed.

At that time (as Mr. Coolidge was presently to note in his final message to Congress) the American standard of living had passed beyond necessities and into the realm of luxury. That luxuries had become such necessities that a man who had all he needed might still be considered poor, and might so consider himself, was not regarded in the excitement of the moment; any more than anyone conceived the possibility that in another four years the bare necessities of 1928 would have become luxuries which few could afford. In those days the American people were just about to enter the Promised Land. "It is no longer necessary," Professor Seligman wrote, "for the individual to skimp and save, to look with apprehension to the future, to endeavor at all costs to make provision for the days to come." Indeed, as a multitude of respected authorities were telling us in those days, the individual who did that was not only a fool but a bad citizen; it was his duty not only to spend all he made but to sign up for all he hoped to make the next year. Again, Professor Seligman made the requisite reservations; but in the popular version of his doctrine these were usually overlooked. There are, he observed, two kinds of poverty. We are poor in the old sense "if we have not enough money to satisfy our wants"; but in 1927 this familiar form of poverty was about to be abolished. In its place a new kind of poverty had been invented; as Professor Seligman put it, "we are also poor if we have not enough wants to induce us to live a civilized life." Every advertising page of the period shouted that same doctrine simplified, made cruder, but in its essentials the same doctrine proclaimed by the high authority of Seligman. The man who did not want an automobile or a radio, who thought he could get better value out of his money somewhere else, was a bad citizen. Skeptics, even then, suggested that if this year's commodities continued to be bought with next year's income, the increase of the nation's productive plant would outrun the consumer's capacity, and that some day, consequently, there would remain no unmortgaged income to buy with. But this, said Professor Seligman, was "entirely erroneous." Increased production increases income; and "the productive utilization of wealth" (that is, more golf, more radios, more automobiles) "makes men more efficient." The spiral was to move forever upward. "If the possibilities of output are boundless, the possibilities of consumption are still more so."

So far as the layman can discern, the facts set down in the book are correct, and the inferences drawn from them are, in most cases, at least, defensible. One direct attack, however, can be made on this doctrine—which was also the doctrine of most of America in 1927, 1928, and 1929; but this attack can hardly be made on economic grounds. "There are no limits to the growth of demand," wrote Professor Seligman, "save those which depend on the physical and economic restrictions on production." He evidently never envisioned the possibility that some members of the human race might grow tired of being mere consuming machines, of working harder and harder in order to have more and more money to spend for the things someone else had to sell. A man who had been for many years professor in a great university should at least have realized that some people might not regard consumption as the whole, or even the primary, duty of man. But this, after all, is aside from economics.

Since the chief effect, if not the chief purpose, of this doctrine was to stimulate the sale of automobiles, the statistics of automobile production since 1929 would indicate that something was wrong with it, from the purely economic standpoint. In the first place, a confusion between the possible and the necessary; what we should all (or most of us) have liked to have had happen, and what might conceivably have happened under certain circumstances, was set down as already happening. True, the author, in the spirit of the scrupulous scientist, set down his provisos, his qualifications, his reservations. There must be an adequate distribution of purchasing power (but, by implication, there was); productive consumption differs from wasteful and destructive consumption (but by implication American consumption is generally productive). An examination of the whole book, qualifications and reservations included, and some knowledge of what was going on in the world and the sort of people living in it might have led to the conclusion (even in 1927) that the thesis was attractive but not wholly plausible.

But most people did not read Professor Seligman undiluted and entire. His doctrine was announced at a dinner given by General Motors and most people learned the doctrine from the column or two which the newspapers published about that dinner, or they got it at still another remove from somebody who had heard about it. And here the doctrine was not accompanied by the qualifications which might have warned the cautious and reflective reader of the book. Was that the fault of the author? He might, since he has lived a good many years, have guessed how his doctrine would be taken by the average man and the average woman, always avid to believe that what is agreeable is true. Here was one of the most agreeable prospects ever set before the human race, and it was presented on the authority of one of the most distinguished living economists. I do not believe that any book was ever published in the United States which so strongly tended to corrupt the mentally and emotionally immature of all ages as *The Economics of Instalment Selling*.

It is a pleasure to turn from this flagrant instance of how a scientist should not behave—especially a scientist attached to a university, one who might be expected to feel a somewhat higher sense of responsibility than the salaried economist of a bank, an investment trust, or a public-utility corporation—to the behavior of the general run of economists in the past two or three years. They cannot be accused of concealing what they know, or even what they surmise. If their views of the causes and the cure of economic crises, or their opinions of the possibility of cure, are by no means in accord, that is no more than was to be expected, and creates a greater confidence on the part of the general public. I can here note only one detail, applying to only one aspect of contemporary economics, though that is a fairly conspicuous one—the discussion of economic planning.

If America falls it will not be for lack of a plan but more probably because of a surplus of them. Plans have been offered by the dozen in the past two years, yet nothing has been done about them. The outgoing administration was opposed to the whole idea of a planned economy, though its policy of the past year, its only record of successful achievement, was an acceptance of the idea even if the planning was on a modest scale. What the incoming administration will do depends apparently upon which of Mr. Roosevelt's somewhat changeable moods may happen to dominate him at the moment of action.

Professor Taussig has remarked that "no one can say what is the best way of organizing for planning, and still less can one say what will be its results." No one knows—certainly not an amateur—which is the best of the many plans that have been suggested; but even an amateur can see that the idea of planning has not been sold to the class whose conversion is most important. The economists, the statisticians, the engineers may be for it by an overwhelming majority; but one would not get many votes for it, yet, among the owners of industry.

Those who believe in the class struggle may not care to waste time in trying to convert the owner class, for by dogma the owners will hang on stubbornly till the aroused workers in their overwhelming numbers dispossess them. I do not believe this is true; at least I do not believe there is any earthly necessity for things to work out in that way. What used to be called the profit system has for three years past been the deficit system; and even the blindest can see that if we let things go on in the old way, after the next period of greater or less prosperity the profit will be the deficit system again. A couple of years ago the emotional attachment of the average industrial capitalist to the old system was so strong that he could not be reasoned with; but this has considerably weakened by now, and will be weaker still before anything that can be called prosperity comes back. A systematic attempt to persuade the owners of American industry that a planned economy would be, in the long run, a good thing for them as well as for their workers and consumers might at last have some chance of success.

If the orthodox Socialist theories are correct there is no need to bother with the owners; but a good many owners are also managers and if one considers American industry as a whole, it is very largely the owners who would have to run it under a planned economy—even, perhaps, under a Socialist economy. It is obviously to the general interest to have the plan operated (once it is adopted) by men convinced of its desirability and practicability, rather than by reluctant die-hards submitting, under protest, to an act of Congress; besides which, of course, the more people who are converted in advance, the more chance there will be that a change, once enacted in law, could be actually accomplished with a minimum of economic disturbance.

Economic planners have given most of their attention to the technical details of their plans, and very little to the selling of their ideas. It may seem irrational to criticize the planners for not being evangelistic enough, when I have criticized Professor Seligman for preaching an evangelist's sermon in the vestments of a scientist; and perhaps the answer is that I believe in planning and did not believe (even in 1927) in Professor Seligman's deferred-payment millennium. But aside from that I believe the thing can be done properly and decently, with due recognition and acknowledgment of arguments on the other side. Mr. Simeon Strunsky has lately been contending that scientists should never be allowed to rule because they must follow truth wherever it leads, without any consideration of the social utility of their conclusions. So they must; but if they happen to reach conclusions which they think will be socially useful, it ought to be possible to set forth those conclusions persuasively.

But the man who does that must be sure that his conscience is clean and his heart is humble. I have spoken of the salaried economists attached to corporations, and I do not question their integrity. But a man who works for a bank or a manufacturing company can no more publicly assail the interest of his employer than a lawyer can attack the case of his client, or a clergyman can impugn the doctrines of his church. For the detachment and impartiality we need we must look to the universities—where many men have already displayed it, and others now chastened are likely to display it in future; and to the newspapers, whose financial editors have on the whole made a better showing than any other class of economists in the past four years. Less than any other

17

group have they let their own hopes, their own pride, stand in the way of a disinterested effort to ascertain the truth.

We are likely to need expert knowledge and cool reasoning even more in the next administration than we did in the last one. Industrial planning may or may not become an urgent issue, but there remains the question of the tariff which we hope, at least, may at last be considered as a scientific problem rather than a religious dogma; there is the disturbing and perhaps insoluble problem of farm relief; and there is, and not only on the farm, the question of the practical possibility of deflation of indebtedness to meet the deflation of everything else. The candidate for whom I voted last November thought (and with the support of some expert opinion) that this could best be accomplished by a capital levy. There are grave practical objections to that, but still graver objections, I believe, to any other course. All the knowledge, all the capacity for honest and self-forgetful thinking that the nation possesses, will not be too much to deal with the issues of the next four years.

If economics is not yet a science, at least a good deal of scientific thinking has been applied to it, and a good many men of the true scientific temperament are practising it. But they will better serve society if they realize that the old definition of economics as "the science of wealth" is a misleading abstraction. It is a social study; that is to say, the science—if it may be called one—of human beings as they are affected by wealth, the lack of wealth, or the hope of wealth in future. Grave errors in this and other branches of social study could be avoided if experts would only remember that the world is inhabited by the human race, and that even experts themselves partake of human passions and human failings.

# Teaching and the Spirit of Research

## JOHN LIVINGSTON LOWES

## ( *1933* )

Here is a discourse about learning by JOHN LIVINGSTON LOWES, an American scholar who applied the spirit of adventure and inquiry to a teaching career of more than fifty years. Mr. Lowes, who died in 1945, insisted that learning is not dull, that it is only learned men who make it so: "It is salutary to remember that the dullest, most utterly benumbing teachers may be, and sometimes are, the most erudite."

MAY I begin by stating clearly the limitations which I have imposed upon my theme?

It is to the members of a Graduate School of Arts and Sciences that what I mean to say is addressed. And the primary end of such a School is to train scholars who are also teachers, or teachers who are also scholars, as you please. It is, then, the relations of research to that desideratum, and to that alone, of which I mean to speak. The great field of pure research lies outside my purpose here.

I wish there were another word than "research" which I might use. For to most of you the associations of the term are chiefly, if not wholly, with doctoral dissertations and all that in them is. And that is not the association which I have in mind at all. For in linking *teaching* with research I am thinking of something far more deeply interfused than that (if I may put it so) with the activities which soon enough will face you. What I have in view is rather an attitude of mind, an openness to hints, suggestions, intimations— from the fall of an apple at Woolsthorpe, to a flash from a page in a book taken down from the shelf—a responsiveness to suggestions which may come unbidden, and beckon along untravelled roads to regions which are new to us, and (it may be) even to our little

19

world. It is, in a word, something to be thought of rather as an adventure than as a task imposed—something which, through calling us at times from our beaten paths, may on occasion save our pedagogical souls alive. That, then, is what I mean to talk about. Your professional training, except by implication, it is not my business to discuss.

What underlies that training is, however, both my affair and yours. For that winged thing, intellectual discovery, is no footless bird of Paradise. It must have a *pou sto* from which to spring. I have spoken of hints and suggestions which lead one into fresh fields. But there has to be something for one's hint, one's intimation to connect with, before new *aperçus* can be born. There must be two poles to a battery before a spark can flash. Things have meaning only as they associate themselves with other things, and they take on added meaning only as those associations multiply. It is only when one's mind is already a storehouse of impressions that it will possess the focal points on which fresh impressions will converge. A page from a travel-book will not set up relations with a poem, or a phrase in a medical treatise leap across centuries to illuminate *The Anatomy of Melancholy,* or a volume taken down by chance suggest questions to which we may turn in our so-called leisure hours for months, unless we first know our poet, and our Burton, and unless we have the trick of ranging far afield. It was because Newton's apple fell into a reservoir already stored with the observations and ponderings of years that human thought about the laws of the universe was revolutionized. For it is not in the spiritual world alone that "unto him that hath shall be given, and he shall have abundance." And it is just that preliminary storing of the cells which much of the training which you have been undergoing is designed to initiate. But your life will not suffice to complete the enterprise.

I am not just now much concerned with what we call our additions to the sum of human knowledge. That in the end may be your happy fortune. It is rather the effect of a habit of mind upon one's *teaching* that is the point. And teaching is effective—if one must be axiomatic—only when the one who teaches is intellectually alive. May I draw for a moment upon first-hand experience? Through the accident of having years ago shifted from one field to another, I suffered—to paraphrase the Scriptures—many things of many teachers in one undergraduate and three graduate or professional schools, over a period of eleven years. And out of the scores of teachers under whom in consequence I sat, two tower

head and shoulders above the rest. And the reason for that pre-
eminence is to the point. It was because, through their vividness
and their vitality, and through their gift of bringing to bear at will
on the subject they were treating whatever was pertinent in the
whole wide range of their learning, they awakened intellectual
curiosity and stirred to emulation. One felt one's self *kindling*—to
use Dorothy Wordsworth's word about her brother—under their
influence. And they were men who thus stirred intellectual curiosity—and this is my point—because they were endowed with it
themselves. For they were both of them inveterate explorers in
their respective fields. Much of what they said has been in the lapse
of years forgotten. It was their *spirit*, their *vivida vis animi*, which
after one's kind one caught. One thinks—with a difference—of
what Goethe said of Winckelmann: *"Man lernt nichts, wenn man
ihn liest, aber man wird etwas"*—You learn nothing when you
read him, but you *become* something. In their case one learned,
and learned enormously. But that, as one looks back, was as nothing to what, through their power of awakening, one became. And
the fact that they were among the most learned men whom I have
ever known is not without significance. For it is not learning that
is dull. It is only learned men who sometimes make it so. And since
you are by way of becoming learned yourselves, and teachers to
boot, the implicit caveat is not impertinent.

For it is salutary to remember, too, that the dullest, most utterly
benumbing teachers may be, and sometimes are, the most erudite.
You cannot know, let me say at once, too many facts, unless—and
there's the rub—you ossify in them. We can ossify, you know. Like
Mephistopheles, *"Ich habe schon in meinen Wanderjahren Krys-
tallisiertes Menschenvolk gesehn"*—men fossilized like pterodac-
tyls (which once had wings) under their accumulations. There are
minds—to shift the figure—which are crowded reservoirs of facts,
but the reservoirs are stagnant. I have just referred to two great
teachers. Their power lay in one's sense of the immediacy, the pungent freshness of their knowledge, drawn from the fountain-heads
themselves. But I have also sat under teachers—they are most of
them, like Chaucer's Petrarch, "now deed, and nayled in hir
chestes"—through whose teaching no streams flowed: learned men,
who year after year rehearsed essentially what they had said the
year before, not even always *"mit ein Bisschen andern Worten."*
No spark disturbed one's clod. One learned from them little which
one could not better have learned one's self from the sources of
their information. And "to sit"—as Carlyle observed of Coleridge's

21

talk—"to sit as a passive bucket and be pumped into . . . can in the long run be exhilarating to no creature." Learning, even erudition, will be quickening or dulling, alive or dead, according as its possessor has or lacks the adventuring mind.

There is a remark of G. K. Chesterton which the late Stuart Sherman used to quote: "There are no uninteresting things; there are only uninterested people." Now things are interesting when they excite our desire to know more, when they stir us from a passive to an active frame of mind; when, in a word, they awaken intellectual curiosity. And the possession of that, and the power of kindling it in others—for it is contagious—are the earmarks of the scholar who is a teacher too. There is a queer notion abroad that in the field of scholarship, "interesting" and "superficial" are apt to be synonyms. On the contrary, it is only when one has steeped one's self in one's subject, and ranged it from end to end, that the full power of its fascination (I am using the word deliberately) can ever be exerted. That is what leads us on, and it is the communication of that spell which makes great teaching. And the case for intellectual curiosity, imaginative vision—call it what you will —is essentially the case for culture in Matthew Arnold's famous dictum. For the value to a teacher of the discoverer's bent of mind is precisely this: that through its alert responsiveness to suggestion, and its keenness in following where suggestion leads, it does vivify, like a freshly flowing stream, masses of knowledge which otherwise lie leaden and inert. One's individual explorations may or may not have momentous consequences for learning. That for the moment is not the point. The thing is that the spirit of one's expeditions, minor exploits though they may be, into the territory of the unexplored will permeate one's whole attitude toward the body of knowledge handed down from the explorers and the builders of the past. And it will also pervade and vitalize one's teaching. It is quite on the cards that the results of our personal excursions may never directly enter that teaching at all. It is the attitude of mind which they stimulate that is the vital thing. What you know and don't teach permeates and fecundates what you teach. And if you want to find supremely stated the essence of the spirit which I am trying to express, reread the sonnet "On First Opening Chapman's Homer," and ponder that.

To have, then, if we're lucky enough, our own adventure which may lead us along untrodden ways into undiscovered lands, and keep our eye alert and our sense of values keen—that good fortune may enhance the very powers which lend life to teaching. But what

I have called the spirit of research will far more directly quicken what we teach. You obviously cannot, when you begin, have first-hand knowledge of everything with which you have to deal. But if you are to keep your mind alive, you dare not rely, nor will you, on knowledge gained at second hand. Your training, whatever it may have been, in formal research is useless, except in so far as it develops a bent of mind which instinctively strikes for the fountain-heads. Let me use the simplest possible illustration of what I mean. And I must draw, for obvious reasons, upon my own field. The principle is common to all fields.

Take, as a single one of countless instances, the great Ode on "Intimations of Immortality." Of what experience *is* that the imaginative projection? How can you know? Every book about Wordsworth discusses the Ode, and you may take that short and easy way. If you have the instinct which strikes for the heart of things, you will turn to Dorothy Wordsworth's *Journal*. And you will find between March 14 and March 27, 1802, in a sensitive and revealing personal chronicle, the records of a veritable nest of poems. And four of them stand in intimate connection through their expression of a common mood—a mood first stirred by vivid recollections of childhood, awakened by the sight of a butterfly. On Sunday morning, March 14, Dorothy Wordsworth writes: "While we were at breakfast . . . [William] wrote the poem 'To a Butterfly.' . . . The thought first came upon him as we were talking about the pleasure we both always felt at the sight of a butterfly"; and then follow charming childhood reminiscences. Nine days later Dorothy wrote: "William worked at 'The Cuckoo' poem." Two days later: "William wrote to Annette,"—the entanglement of Wordsworth's soul with the world during just those days was acute—"then worked at 'The Cuckoo.' . . . While I was getting into bed, he wrote 'The Rainbow' "—the lines, that is, beginning: "My heart leaps up when I behold A rainbow in the sky." And the next day's entry begins: "A divine morning. At breakfast William wrote part of an ode." I am tearing, as I must, the bare entries from the graphic context which gives them life. But each of those four poems, written within less than a fortnight, is the expression of one dominating mood, called up by the glimpse of a butterfly, the call of the cuckoo, the sight of a rainbow—the mood from which the first four stanzas of what Coleridge called "The Immortal Ode" one morning at breakfast sprang. And if one read these four stanzas in conjunction with "The Butterfly," "The Cuckoo," and "My Heart Leaps Up," one gains a conception of their meaning such as all the critics, commentators, and biographers together cannot give.

Moreover, the last seven stanzas of the Ode, written almost three years later, after the tragic death of Wordsworth's sailor brother John, form again one of a group of four poems, of which the great "Elegiac Stanzas" and "The Happy Warrior" are two. And only by reading together these four, in the light of the family letters, can one feel the significance of the new and lofty mood in which profound personal grief is lifted into the atmosphere of "calm of mind, all passion spent," and in which the earlier stanzas are taken up and wrought with the later ones into a splendid and consistent whole. And if one further observe that Wordsworth, when he finally brought all his poems together, set, after "Poems written in Youth," "The Rainbow" at the beginning and the Ode at the end, one recognizes that to him their common theme epitomized his deepest thought. Nothing on earth will make all that *real*, save saturation in those intimately interrelated poems themselves. And the ardency of mind which leads one to that is what I call the spirit of research. And that ardency lends in turn contagious quality to one's teaching.

Or poems may spring not only from the contacts of a poet's mind with cuckoos and butterflies which in the end may lead him to "truths that wake, To perish never," but also from the stimulus of provocative personal relations. And I wish I dared stop to illustrate the thing I am trying to clarify, from that brilliant conjunction of Byron, and the Shelleys and Claire Clairmont, and John Cam Hobhouse, and "Monk" Lewis, and Dr. Polidori, and Madame de Staël, on the shores of Lake Geneva between April and October in 1816. *Manfred*, conceived and largely written then, is the most copiously discussed of all Byron's dramas. You will never begin to understand it—and I think I know—until you have thrown overboard your baggage of second-hand critical apparatus and have read, for those months, Mary Shelley's diary, and Shelley's letters to Peacock, and Byron's to John Murray and Augusta Leigh, and Byron's and Hobhouse's journals of their expedition into the Bernese Oberland, and Polidori's journal and the Countess Guiccioli's book, and the storybook called *Fantasmagoriana*, and *The Vampire*, and *Frankenstein*—a collection of human documents seldom matched for their vividness and their absorbing interest. Read those—and *Manfred*, from being dead, will come alive. And out of that welter of human documents a question may thrust up its head, like Proteus rising from the sea—a question so provocative that one's attempt to answer it may metamorphose one's whole conception of the drama. But whether that be so or not, the spirit which leads you instinctively back to the life itself from which poem or drama springs will vivify, when you teach, your interpretation of the imaginative projection—ode or drama —of that experience.

For literature is *life taking form,* and only your own imaginative projection of yourself into that human experience will reveal to you the coalescence, in a work of art, of raw stuff and imaginative energy. The trouble too often is that the people who know the facts don't use their imagination; the people who have imagination don't trouble with the facts. It is the combination, in whatever field, which is the rare, the priceless thing.

Now that, and not set tasks, is what I mean by research in relation to teaching. It is a response to that spirit of the discoverer which one's teaching should animate, not dull. For, like the quality of mercy, it is twice bless'd. Not only does it lend life to our teaching, but our teaching may quicken it. Often in the very act of teaching—as every one who truly teaches knows—when the effort to reach other minds kindles and clarifies one's own, one's perceptions strike suddenly into unforeseen relations, and old problems fall into fresh perspective, or new quests are born. But that will come only when the cells are stored. And if you wish a brilliant and provocative study of the relation between that storing of the cells and those flashes of vision which may issue in discovery, and which do lend wings to teaching, read Henri Poincaré's great chapter on "Mathematical Discovery" in his *Science et Méthode.* For what I have been saying of literature is true, *mutatis mutandis,* of every field.

It may be that I am giving the impression that research, as I am treating it, is a thing merely of happy chances, flashes of inspiration, lucky *aperçus.* If so, I have not made my meaning clear. I am assuming, as axiomatic, rigorous exactness in both the employment and the presentation of one's facts; scrupulous verification of every statement resting on authority; wise caution in drawing inferences; a vigilance which overlooks no evidence—in a word, the inexorable demands of scientific method in the conduct of research. But that once for all understood, the gift of the utmost value to teaching and to one's research alike is the faculty which we name *vision.* Call it imagination, if you will, so that you keep the sense of a power which sees relations where the eye sees only facts; which sees the lines of form that strike through seeming chaos; which sees in phenomena apparently diverse, their underlying unity. But the facts must first be mastered before their relations may be seen; one must make one's way, like Satan, through the "strait, rough, dense, or rare" of chaos, before its elements fall into form; one can never reach the underlying unity of disparate phenomena save when one has come to grips with the phenomena as they appear. And that exacting business is not, in old Thomas à Kempis's words about another matter, *opus unius diei, nec ludus parvulorum*—it's a long trick, and a man's job. Vision is a gift—a free gift of the gods, if you will. But its exercise demands knowledge arduously acquired. For vision—which is seeing with what lies behind the eye—is not something independent of knowledge, or somehow superadded upon knowledge when it is acquired. It is a faculty which works *through* knowledge. And knowledge without vision is barren, as vision without knowledge distorts. It is only when we have won our way through our chaos of obdurate facts that *"die guten Einfälle"* —flashes of insight, happy conjectures—come and stand before us *"wie freie Kinder Gottes,"* as Goethe says, and cry out "Here we are!" But it is we who must build the road by which they reach us.

And the road by which they reach others too. I have thus far been speaking of the bearing of all this upon your teaching. But many of you will some day have to communicate the results of your explorations to what we love to call the learned world. It may even occur to you that beyond those sacred precincts there are readers of no less intelligence and of equally inquiring minds. In our attempts at exposition, in a word, we face a problem as delicate and difficult, and as absorbing in its interest, as any which our research itself can raise. And the fine art of marshalling one's chaos of facts into lucid order is worth infinite pains to master.

We do not always take the pains, and one of the crying needs of scholarship is that they should be taken. Why, to be explicit, are doctoral dissertations, and articles in learned journals, and even books addressed *ad clerum,* with notable and distinguished exceptions, so often deadly reading? They often are, and one need make no bones about it. Just why the academic mind should be regarded as less susceptible to boredom than the lay mind, I do not know. I do know that I, whose mind, *ex hypothesi,* is academic, am sometimes moved to tears, if I could only shed them, by the flatness and lack of distinction and facile professional lingo of some of the things I am compelled to read. Yet a piece of learned exposition may, in its kind, be as luminous and urbane as a chapter of Cardinal Newman, or an opinion handed down by Mr. Justice Holmes.

There are few things in the world more interesting than the disclosure of facts which illuminate and throw into fresh perspective a mass of other facts. And the results of research, however learned, may be presented, without shallowness or artifice, in lucid order, and with clarity of phrase, and even may at times possess the fascination of a tale. Our fatal blunder is to sit down, when our problem is solved, and let (as we say) the facts speak for themselves. There are few more mischievous fallacies. To us who have mastered their meaning, our facts do speak for themselves. To those for whom we are writing, their speech, which we have learned, must be interpreted. "There are," said the Apostle Paul, himself a past master of exposition—"there are so many kinds of voices in the world, and none of them without signification. Therefore if I know not the meaning of the voice, I shall be unto him that speaketh a barbarian, and *he that speaketh shall be a barbarian to me.*" That indictment is sometimes terribly pertinent, I fear, to us. "They order this matter better in France," and in English the mathematicians and physicists are beating the humanists at their own game. To apply to results obtained through the rigid methods of science the principles of an art—that is a contribution never more needed than now. And it is a contribution infinitely worth our pains to make.

One of the very best books about that art—to be practical for a moment—was written about fifty years ago by a physiological psychologist. Few people seem to know it now; I wish more did. It is by George Henry Lewes, whom one first thinks of in connection with George Eliot, and the book was originally a series of articles in the *Fortnightly Review,* with the unappealing title: *Principles of Success in Literature.* In it occurs this sentence: "The greatness of an author consists in having a mind *extremely irritable,* and at the same time *stedfastly imperial."* And Lewes, being a biologist, is using "irritable" in its physiological sense of "responsive to stimuli." What has his phrase to do with our problem of exposition?

Precisely what it had to do with Shakespeare, or Coleridge, or Keats, or Darwin, or has to do with Eddington or Jeans. It means, with its "extremely irritable," the utmost susceptibility to impressions; it means, with its "stedfastly imperial," a sovereign molding of them into form. You have first to *discover,* and then to *translate.* And the problem of exposition is a challenge to the exercise of your keenest faculties, and an adventure comparable both in its difficulty and in its engrossing interest to the enterprise of discovery which precedes it. For the essence of what I have called discovery is the perception of some clarity or order implicit in the confusion of phenomena; the business of what I have called translation is to impose another clarity and order upon the chaotic mass of observations and impressions through which we have reached our end. And that it is which is too often scamped.

I have just quoted a natural scientist and an apostle. It was a poet who more than a century ago stated succinctly why we fail. "We want," Shelley wrote in 1821, speaking not of poetry, but of political and economic problems ("concealed," as he says, "by the accumulation of facts") —"we want the creative faculty to imagine what we know." Translated into concrete terms that means, for us —I meet the problem in doctoral dissertations every year—this. Here we are, with our chaotic mass of facts, through which, in the sweat of our brow, we have slowly learned our way. We have lived with them, become saturated with them, until they are as familiar to *us* as the streets we daily walk. And our problem is to make them intelligible—and lucid, if we can—to readers who are not, as we are, permeated with the implications and associations of our particular congeries. But when we have lived with our own particular chaos for months, it may be for years, we forget with fatal ease that our readers are unfamiliar with the landmarks of anybody's chaos but their own. And the first requisite of effective exposition is the power of seeing with another's eyes—the eyes of our students or fellow scholars—the things which we have been seeing only with our own. We must possess, in a word, that creative faculty which *imagines* what it knows—the ability to stand outside the mass within which we are ourselves at home, and to see it, if not *sub specie æternitatis,* at least from our readers' or our hearers' point of view.

There is a pregnant remark of Amiel's—to add, now, to scientist, apostle, and poet, a professor of philosophy—which is much to the point. "To understand things," says Amiel, "we must have been once in them and then have come out of them. . . . He who is still under the spell, and he who has never felt the spell, are equally incompetent." Very well! To stand outside the chaos of massed observations in the implications of which you are steeped, and think through them with that intellectual detachment which alone permits their reduction to clarity and order, is an achievement beside which the arduousness of the research is sometimes as child's play. But the one may be an adventure as engrossing as the other. And, to speak frankly, unless one can catch in one's researches, and even in the effort to impart them, something at least akin to the spirit of adventure, the thing is dead. And the glory of teaching, in its turn, lies in the opportunity it offers to awaken and direct inquiring spirits.

There are eight lines of Goethe into which is compacted the essence of what I have tried to say. And I shall leave you them as an expression of the breath and finer spirit of the high enterprise before you.

> *Weite Welt und breites Leben,*
> *Langer Jahre redlich Streben,*
> *Stets geforscht und stets gegründet,*
> *Nie geschlossen, oft geründet,*
> *Aeltestes bewahrt mit Treue,*
> *Freundlich aufgefasstes Neue,*
> *Heitern Sinn und reine Zwecke:*
> *Nun, man kommt wohl eine Strecke——*

"Well, one gets ahead a bit"—and one *does*.

# The Humanity of Mathematics

## CASSIUS J. KEYSER

### ( *1933* )

Mathematics is revealed here as the perfect guide and clue to the pursuit of all other learning. Many of the ideas set forth by CASSIUS J. KEYSER, who died in 1947, are now being explored and emphasized in modern mathematics.

No ONE, I hope, will be deterred from reading this essay by the mere presence in its title of the term mathematics, for to follow the discussion understandingly demands neither an extensive knowledge of mathematics nor the rare gift of special mathematical aptitude. All that is required is a little logical acumen and a moderate degree of disciplined attention.

Any great Form of human activity—mathematics, science, art, philosophy, literature, religion, and so on—reveals, in some measure, what is most characteristic and most significant in the distinctive nature of Man; and any such Form at the same time serves as a more or less potent agency for guiding the conduct of human life. The measure in which it performs the twofold function of revelation and guidance is the measure of what I call its humanity. In respect of that measure, it is commonly held, rightly or wrongly, that the cardinal enterprises of mankind differ greatly, occupying different levels in a hierarchy of human significance and human worth.

My present task is that of appraising the humanity of mathematics. To perform it completely I should have to deal with sheer Mathematics, with mathematical Applications, and with what I call the Bearings of mathematics: three things which, though interrelated in many subtle ways, are yet radically distinct. To handle the three themes adequately in a brief essay is impossible. It seems best to treat but one of them and I have chosen the third one. There is a special reason for the choice. The other two themes have been treated often and are the subject of an extensive literature, while the *bearings* of mathematics, though the subject is a highly important one, have never, so far as I am aware, been accorded the distinction of serious and systematic consideration.

By the bearings of mathematics I mean a certain rich manifold of light-giving relations that connect mathematics with those great human interests and human concerns in which there is, properly, no question of establishing mathematical propositions or of making mathematical applications to one or another kind of subject-matter. Such interests and concerns human life has always had and continues to have in greater and greater measure. We are to see that many of them can be much clarified, deepened, and advanced by study of the relations in question.

Our theme is the humanity of mathematics as revealed by the bearings of mathematics upon the universal concerns of mankind. From among such bearings I select for initial consideration a very grave one, one that shows the significance of mathematics as at once a function and a representative form of human culture. The bearing in question was discerned for the first time only a few years ago by Oswald Spengler, who has signalized it with much repeated emphasis in his truly momentous work, *The Decline of the West*. Briefly stated, it is this: The peculiar type of mathematics found in the mature culture of a given people is a clue to the essential character of that culture taken as a whole. To set the idea in clear light it must be disentangled from certain other ideas with which, despite its independence of them, it is enmeshed in Spengler's discourse. And therefore a brief preliminary discussion is necessary.

In Spengler's great work one encounters certain very striking conceptions, assumptions, or theses which, though they are there closely interwoven with the idea above indicated, have nevertheless nothing whatever to do with the question of its own validity. For that reason and despite their own intrinsic interest and importance they are to be entirely excluded from consideration in this essay. One such thesis is that the culture of a people always comes to birth as a living organism—not figuratively but literally speaking—and that, like any other organism, it grows and develops, arrives at maturity, declines, and dies. Another of the theses is that the existing culture of the West—the so-called Faustian culture of Europe and America—has already passed the climax of its development and is now rapidly declining to the doom of destined extinction. A third one of the theses is, in effect, that culture history is a history, not of culture, but of cultures—the Hindu, the Egyptian, the Classical, the Arabian, and others—constituting no continuous stream of development but appearing only as magnificent episodes, loosely scattered over the space-time map of human life, and differing essentially in *kind.*

With these theses, utterly irrelevant to my present purpose, I am not here concerned. The matters with which I am concerned are far less debatable; indeed, once they are rightly understood, they are not debatable at all. Succinctly stated, they are these:

1. In the course of its growth and development every culture gradually shapes and expresses itself in a variety of cardinal Forms: literature, religion, ethics, architecture, painting, sculpture, music, mathematics, science, philosophy, jurisprudence, and others. That is obvious.

2. Although all such major expression-forms are common to all of the great cultures in the sense that religion, for example, or philosophy, or architecture is found in all of them, yet each of the forms as seen in one culture differs profoundly from its kind as seen in another. That, too, is obvious, and is highly significant. To see it one has only to note that the religion or the drama or the science or other expression-form of (say) the Classical culture differs from its correspondent in the culture of the West as profoundly as a Greek temple differs from a Gothic cathedral or as Æschylus from Shakespeare or as Thucydides from Gibbon. Not less profoundly does the Classical geometry, well represented by Euclid's *Elements,* differ from that of the West. The former, confining itself to the properties and mutual relations of only *finite* figures, like ordinary familiar triangles, circles, cubes, cylinders, and so on, knows nothing of *infinite* elements, and never dreams of exploring space as such. (Indeed there is no word for space in Euclid or even in the Greek language.) In the sharpest contrast therewith, Western geometry has infinity for its dominant theme, and, not content with the endless reaches of ordinary space, creates and geometrizes spaces of higher and yet higher dimensionality. No wonder that two such geniuses as Hermann Weyl and the late Henri Poincaré, both of them imbued with the spirit of Faustian culture, have agreed in saying that "Mathematics is the science of the infinite"—a statement that would have seemed to Euclid or Archimedes to be quite meaningless or absolutely false.

3. Notwithstanding the vast difference between an expression-form as found in one culture and that form as found in another, all

of the forms as found in a given culture are spiritually so congruous with one another, so marked by a family likeness, that they together constitute, like the features of a face or a landscape, a single unitary picture—the *physiognomy* of that culture. No informed and sensitive intuition can fail to discern the deep congruity of Greek mathematics, Greek science, Greek architecture, Greek religion, Greek drama, and so on, as beheld in the physiognomy of Classical culture, or fail to discern the like similitude of the mathematics, the science, the architecture, the religion, the drama, and so on, together making up the immensely different physiognomy of the Faustian, or Western, culture.

4. In virtue of that principle of inner congruity or family likeness, each of the expression-forms of a given culture essentially bears the image of every other such form, represents it, tells virtually the same tale, revealing in and of itself what is distinctive in that culture's soul. And therefore, were a culture completely lost save for a single one of its expression-forms, it would be theoretically possible, and in a measure practically so, to determine from that sole survivor what the lost forms and the total culture itself were like.

The reader has doubtless perceived that the subject I have been delineating in this section is both big and grave. Further elaboration of it, were there room for that, would but confirm a conclusion already so evident as to require nothing additional save final formulation.

One thing is a *function* of another if the two be so connected that the former changes whenever the latter does. It is obvious that whatever is a function of human culture is laden with human significance. Mathematics, we have seen, is such a function. What are the salient aspects of the functional relationship? As already said, they are these: mathematics is an integral component of each and every one of the great cultures; the type of mathematics found in one culture differs from the type of it found in any other, there being as many such types as there are cultures; mathematics is among the cardinal expression-forms of each and every culture; like any other one of the major expression-forms of a given culture, mathematics is a *clue* to the distinctive character of that culture taken as a whole—a clue to its soul.

Those functional aspects merit and will amply repay prolonged meditation upon them. The more they are pondered, the more profound their significance is seen to be. I hardly need add that they are among the ways in which the humanity of mathematics can be made to disclose itself to any one whose mind is open to such considerations.

The humanity of mathematics reveals itself with almost startling brilliance in the fact that mathematics sets before us in perfect light the essential nature of those spiritual phenomena, at once so strange and so familiar, which are everywhere known as *ideals*.

What is an ideal? What does the great term properly signify? The question is important. For, as every scholar knows, it is a common fortune of all great terms to acquire a variety of vague, misleading, sometimes incompatible, and frequently false connotations. The term ideal has not escaped that fate. Since in vulgar usage it has come to signify things that in point of kind are actually separated by an unbridgeable chasm of difference, in the interest of clear thinking one is obliged to say that ideals are of two radically different kinds: the *spurious* and the *genuine*.

What is a genuine ideal? What is a spurious one? And what is the principle discriminating them? The questions can be answered with perfect precision. The necessary and sufficient means thereto are found, as we are to see, in the mathematical notion of Limit, but not elsewhere. It would not be easy to exaggerate either the mathematical and scientific power or the subtle refinements of meaning represented by that little five-letter word. But for the purpose of the present discussion, designed primarily for laymen, a sufficient grasp of the momentous concept can be gained by looking keenly at two or three simple examples of it, so simple indeed that for any scholar to shy away from them would be a bit disgraceful.

Think of a 10-foot line. In thought cut off half of it, then half of the remainder, then half of the new remainder, and so on unceasingly. Let $S$ be the sum of all parts that have been cut off at any stage. $S$ is a variable that grows as the cutting goes on, gets to differ from the length 10 by as little as you please, by less indeed than any prescribed amount however small, but it never reaches 10. Here 10 is the limit of the variable $S$.

Again, let $R$ be the ratio of $100 + x$ to $2 + x$. If $x$ changes in value, $R$ changes also; that is, $R$ is a variable. Now let $X$, starting with some definite value, shrink to half the value, then to half the new value, and so on endlessly. $R$ thus gets nearer and nearer, as near as you please, to 50, but never can reach it. Here 50 is the limit of the variable $R$.

As another example, let $C$ be a given circle. If $r$ be its radius, its *area* is $\pi r^2$, and its circumference is $2\pi r$. Now think of the regular polygons that may be inscribed in $C$—first a triangle, next a square, then a pentagon, then a hexagon, and so on forever—an *endless* sequence of them. Let $A$ be the area and $P$ be the perimeter of any one of the polygons. As we pass in thought along the sequence or succession of polygons from the very beginning of the sequence, both $A$ and $P$ continually increase; $A$ grows more and more nearly equal in value to $\pi r^2$, coming to differ from it by less than any pre-assigned amount however small, but never reaches it; while $P$ similarly approaches, without ever attaining, the value $2\pi r$. In the one case, $\pi r^2$ is the limit of the variable $A$, and in the other, $2\pi r$ is the limit of the variable $P$.

The reader knows that many variables are limitless. An obvious example is *time* reckoned backward or forward from any chosen date; another is *distance* measured along a Euclidean straight line from any chosen point on the line; a third is the *volume* of a sphere whose radius increases unceasingly at the rate of (say) a mile a minute; and a fourth is the numerical variable $N$ if its law of variation requires it to take on, in the order indicated, the values 1, 2, 3, . . . , in the unending series of integers.

Regarding any variable that *has* a limit, it is essential to note carefully two facts: first, in the endless course of its variation, the variable comes to differ from its limit by less than any prescribed amount however small; second, the variable never reaches its limit—after any stage of approximation there always remains a further course to run.

Such, briefly described and simply exemplified, is the mathematical concept of limit. In it we behold in perfect light the precise pattern to which any ideal, if it be a genuine one, conforms. No matter whether an ideal be one of justice or of injustice, of freedom or of tyranny, of beauty or of ugliness, of happiness or of misery, of wisdom or of folly, of moral good or of moral evil, of power or of impotence, of clarity or of obscurity, of skill or of un-skill, of piety or of impiety, or of any other distinction, it will be a *genuine* ideal, if and only if, like a mathematical limit, it admits of being approached through an endless sequence of closer and closer approximations, and is, again like a mathematical limit, incapable of being actually attained. It is obvious that many ideals, commonly so called, do not conform to that pattern; they fail to conform to it because they are attainable. All such ideals I describe as *spurious*, not to imply that they are ignoble, for often they are of great worth, but in order to distinguish them sharply from genuine ideals, from which they differ infinitely. I say infinitely because the difference between being attainable and being unattainable, is, quite strictly, an infinite difference. Think of any attainable degree of excellence in no matter what activity or art, and of perfection in the same. Obviously the two are separated by an endless series of intermediate gradations, as are, for example, any given degree of rational plausibility, however high, and flawless reason.

To any one who has clearly seen, as above, precisely what it is in a genuine ideal that makes it such, the following facts cannot fail to be evident:

1. A genuine ideal is not, like a spurious one, a goal, a post that can be reached, but is, as Emerson said, an "ever-flying perfect," not to be overtaken by any pursuit however prolonged, but admitting of an endless series of closer and closer approximations.

2. Neither does a genuine ideal, as many seem to think, essentially signify something having *moral* perfection, something infinitely desirable but desirable solely or mainly on grounds of ethical worth. On the contrary, the idea of an ideal evil no more involves an internal contradiction than does that of an ideal good. Evidently a specific ideal may be infernal or supernal, satanic or divine, or something between such poles.

3. Nor does a genuine ideal denote or connote, as many have thought, something visionary, hazy, merely utopian, wildly or sentimentally romantic, unreal, without significance or worth in a workaday world. Very far from that, genuine ideals are not what would be left if that which is hard in reality were taken away; they are themselves, in the realm of mind, to which they belong, the very flint of reality—hard, cold, logical, austere.

Had the mathematical concept of limit been known in the days of Plato, the great thinker's shining Absolutes—absolute justice, absolute beauty, absolute truth, absolute good—whose "perception by pure intelligence" brings us, said he, "to the *end* of the intellectual world," would not have appeared to him as "ends," or final terms, of any sequences or progressions within the intellectual world, but rather as limits, or ideals, above and beyond it, as downward-looking aspects of an over-world.

The role of ideals in the life of mankind is too vast a subject for treatment here. Suffice it, in this connection, to say two things, of which one is this: that every art of men, every sort of human activity, however common or rare, humble or high, begets in the minds of those devoted to it some vision of the possibility

of reaching in it higher and higher degrees of excellence, culminating in an appropriate dream of perfection, which, though
not attainable, admits of an unending sequence of approximations
thereto; so that ideals are not the peculiar fortune or the special
prerogative of a few elect men and women, but, in one way or another, now consciously and now unconsciously, constantly figure
and function in the lives of all.

The second thing to be said is that, because genuine ideals cannot be realized, a certain philosophy, now much in vogue,
condemns them and counsels us to eschew them, on the alleged
ground that, because they are unattainable, they dishearten, de-
press, and devitalize. But that philosophy lacks *vision* and *wing*.
It is the philosophy of a burrowing mole guided solely by the
immediate pressure of the soil upon its nose. It does not perceive
that among genuine ideals, the nobler ones, far from depressing,
are as "angels of progress leaning from the far horizon, beckoning
man onward and upward forever." It does not perceive that it is
the lure and the light of such unattainables that have made possible the great triumphs of the human spirit in every zone of life.

Let us pass from the highly abstract and general to something
more concrete and particular. From a consideration of the
mathematical revelation of that which, because it is essential to
each of them, is common to all genuine ideals, I now turn to the
bearings of mathematics upon certain grave ideals of a specific
kind.

Genuine ideals are shining things—stars, so to say, in a psychic
sky—and, like the physical stars, they differ in glory. They differ,
too, almost or quite immeasurably, in respect of complexity. A
perfectly simple ideal, if the thing exists, would be hard to
identify as such.

Obviously the ideal of human education is at once among the
highest and among the most complex, involving in its composition
innumerable ideals which, though perfectly genuine themselves,
are yet, in comparison with the other, subordinate and auxiliary;
for the ideal of human education may be characterized by its aim,
and its aim is nothing less than that of qualifying men and women
to realize in fullest measure, and to represent worthily, in their
lives, their personalities, and their work, the potential dignity of
man.

Because human education contemplates human beings in their
full integrity as humans and not as mere followers of specialized

human pursuits, it demands discipline and orientation of our human faculties in their relation to all the great enduring massive facts of life and the world. How can such discipline and orientation be achieved—not perfectly, of course, for that is impossible, but more and more approximately? There is one and only one way—through progressive cooperation of the mighty disciplines—history, philosophy, physical science, social science, religion, aesthetics or art, and the rest.

Now consider what it is that, in ultimate analysis, each and every one of the great disciplines deals with, not indeed exclusively but mainly. It is mainly with ideas that they deal. Ideas own a genuine kind of reality peculiar to themselves; they have a being and character of their own; they are mental things, and their ways are not ways of matter but ways of mind. To deal successfully with ideas as ideas it is necessary to deal with them in accordance with what it has long been happily customary to call "the laws of thought." And the long-established fame of mathematics rests upon the practice of dealing with ideas in conformity with the laws of thought. Logical rectitude is itself an ideal of immense human significance and worth. In nearness of approach thereto mathematics has far outstripped every other intellectual enterprise—a fact disputed by none. In respect, then, of logical rectitude, mathematics is a well-nigh perfect model, or exemplar, for all other educational disciplines in so far as these have, ultimately, for their main concern, the handling of ideas as such. Thus it is evident that the bearing of mathematics upon the ideal of human education is the bearing of one great ideal upon another.

But, in view of the fact that the ideas with which most of the major disciplines are obliged to deal have not attained sufficient precision to admit of logically rigorous handling, must it not be said that the standard of logical rectitude is of very limited availability? The right response is an emphatic negative. Certainly it requires no extraordinary acumen to see that the truth is this: no matter how remote, or seemingly remote, a given field of ideas may be from that of mathematics or that of mathematical applications, just in so far as our thinking in the given field departs from the standard of logical rectitude, our discourse sinks down towards the level of prehuman or subhuman chattering.

Perhaps no other bearing of mathematics is more helpful than its clear revelation of what is most distinctive in the nature of our human kind. For such a revelation we have long been schooled to look to the so-called humanities, which have been commonly spoken of as if mathematics (and science, too) were alien to them. The foregoing considerations seem to indicate that, on the contrary, mathematics is itself one of the great humanities, and the evidence will grow. What is the test? None, I believe, will deny it to be this: those subjects or enterprises are best entitled to rank among the humanities which (*a*) disclose most clearly the most significant defining mark of man as man, and (*b*) best serve to guard and guide human life. Let the two parts of the double criterion be applied severally.

What is it that most significantly distinguishes the race of man from that of animals? The answer is found, I think, in what Count Alfred Korzybski a few years ago happily called the *time-binding* capacity of man. The time-binding power is that highly composite innate human endowment which enables each human generation to employ its inheritance of the accumulated achievements of all preceding generations as *living capital* for the achieving of yet greater and greater things. Without that inborn endowment humans might, perhaps, have initiated what we call civilization, but they certainly could not have advanced it.

The power in question is more or less discernible in the development of every great subject, but, and this is the decisive consideration, mathematics is the only subject in whose history the thing presents itself at every stage and in *stark nakedness*. That surpassing revelation of what it is that most significantly sets man apart from, and immeasurably above, all such artful creatures as the fox, the beaver, or the bee, strongly supports the claim of mathematics to membership in the assembly of the humanities.

This conclusion is confirmed by a glance at mathematics regarded as a guardian and guide. Native to man are a propensity and a power for *idealization*. In virtue of that dowry there hovers above each cardinal type of human activity a corresponding ideal of excellence, serving as a kind of muse to beckon and woo us upward along the endless steep towards perfection. One of the great types is that of logical thinking. Its muse, the muse of mathematics, is Logical Rigor, an austere goddess, demanding, though never quite securing, absolute precision; demanding, though never quite securing, absolute clearness; demanding, though never quite securing, absolute cogency.

But mathematics is far from being the goddess' sole care. Her authority, as before pointed out, extends to all provinces of thought as thought. In her empire the distinction of mathematics is only that of an exemplary agent, operating as a model, guardian, and guide.

What has been said touching the humanity, as disclosed by the bearings, of mathematics is hardly more than a suggestive beginning of what might be said. A full discussion would expand to the proportions of a large volume, for not one among the universal interests of mankind could be excluded from the purview of such a work. The reader is invited to join in glancing quickly at an additional series of prime concerns.

1. *Relations* pervade our human life in all its dimensions, for not only are relations of one or another kind denoted, directly or indirectly, explicitly or implicitly, by a great majority of the words in any language; but there are countless hosts of nameless relations, since, as it is reasonable to assume, every thing in the world has named or unnamed relations to all other things. As an object of possible knowledge or as a field of research, the universe is a boundless locus of relations, for, as the late Henri Poincaré used to say, science cannot know "things" but only "relations." *Being* itself, said Lotze, consists in relations. Relations seem to be both infinitely numerous and infinitely diversified, and they are literally omnipresent. Relations are used by everybody all the time. For these many reasons, the understanding of relations, the gaining of relation-knowledge, is a matter of necessary, perpetual, and universal interest and concern.

The bearing of mathematics thereupon is twofold: It is a certain unique relation—called logical implication—that has rendered possible the very existence of mathematics; and second, the understanding of relations is precisely what mathematics, at first unconsciously, at last consciously, has been pursuing from time immemorial.

And just because the relations investigated by mathematics are *abstract* while those conditioning life in our concrete world are *concrete*, the bearing in question is effective; for, as Professor A. N. Whitehead has said, "The utmost abstractions are the true weapons with which to control our thought of concrete fact."

2. *Change* is a second prime concern. Of things found out by humans, many are discovered by only a few, but some are discovered by all, and of these, one is the stupendous fact of change— fertile mother of all phenomena—creator of all our problems, concrete and abstract.

Were all the processes of change chaotic, or lawless, no problems could be solved. That all changes whatever, including those of very minute submicroscopic individual elements, conform to precise laws, the present state of science enables no one to affirm. But speaking macrocosmically—having reference, that is, not to individual elements themselves, but to masses or bodies or systems of them—it is possible to say with confidence that the changes which *they* undergo are *lawful*. To deal successfully with lawful changes it is necessary to know their laws; and to afford such knowledge is the characteristic aim of science. For the pursuit of that aim, mathematical applications furnish science with an indispensable *pattern*. For such applications always essentially involve the study of *functions,* and the study of functions is just the study of the ways in which changes in one or more variable things beget changes in related things. It is true that in the mathematical theory of functions the changes investigated are always highly ideal and abstract. But that is the reason why, as before said, they are so nearly perfect as patterns for the investigations of concrete change in the concrete world.

3. *Invariance* belongs in this series. Permanence and change are the poles of the world, but the idea of invariance is the idea of permanence-in-the-midst-of-change. In the realm of ideas that idea is sovereign. Is it only a dream, or is it realized in the universe of concrete fact? To find it so realized has ever been at once the supreme desire and the supreme striving of men. In that sense, "The Quest of Man for Abiding Reality" is the greatest of themes. Will it at some time be worthily handled? The task evidently demands a critical evaluation of all the great enterprises of the human spirit, and whoever undertakes it will need to have the genius and the universal attainments of a Leibnitz; for science, mathematics, art, philosophy, jurisprudence, ethics, theology, and religion, however much they have differed in their methods and their findings, are but diverse forms of *one* emprise—that of our human search for things everlasting, for realities that keep their integrity amid all the mutations of the world.

What is here the bearing of mathematics? In a chapter of his charming little book, *The Queen of the Sciences,* Professor Bell has delightfully sketched for laymen the development of a certain doctrine that, starting as an acorn, has attained, in recent generations, the proportions of a giant oak. That doctrine is the mathematical Theory of Invariance, wherein one is permitted to behold innumerable things—properties, relations, forms, configurations—that remain quite unaltered despite the storm and stress of literally infinite hosts of transformations. And thus it appears that the bearing in question is, in both content and manner, that of a luminous archetype or pattern.

4. *Infinity* is a fourth prime concern. In a poignantly beautiful letter recently written, at the age of ninety-one, by Oliver Wendell Holmes, great jurist and great man, are found these words: "Life seems to me like a Japanese picture which our imagination does not allow to end with the margin. We aim at the infinite." We do aim at the infinite in manifold ways—in our endless conceptual extensions of time and of space; in our arts of commemoration; in our searchings for eternal verities and goods everlasting; in our hopes and dreams of immortality; in the boundless soarings of "bodiless music"; in the limitless recessions of background in many a great picture; in our outreachings and inreachings for Deity; in the "God-feeling" expressed and evoked alike by the interior and by the exterior of a "Faustian Cathedral." Professor David Hilbert, a world-famous mathematician, has recently said: "The infinite. No other great question has ever moved the spirit of man so powerfully, no other has stimulated his intellect so fruitfully." Under one or another of its many forms the idea of infinity has significantly figured both in scientific thought and in philosophical speculation, East and West, from remote antiquity.

In modern mathematics and not elsewhere that momentous concept has at length attained precision. Very recently, as before noted, Hermann Weyl, eminent mathematician, physicist, and philosopher, has written in italics that *"Mathematics is the science of the infinite."* For the most part mathematics has dealt and deals with infinity only implicitly but there is a large mathematical literature dealing with it explicitly. It contains many things to astonish and to edify, but no answer to the question: If a man die, shall he live again? Yet in that literature one may find muchneeded help in trying to discover what it is, intellectually, that the idea of immortality essentially involves. And that should seem a precious service to all those who, once they have made their yearnings articulate, ardently desire to ascertain what their words really mean.

5. *Religion*, finally, belongs in this series of prime concerns. Regarding the bearings of mathematics upon religion I may refer to Professor David Eugene Smith's recent address on *Religio Mathematici* as affording a helpful clue. Because of its sheer ideality Plato's great concept of a world of ideas transcending the world of sense has been specially congenial to the temper and

habit of mathematical minds. Perhaps the concept originated in mathematics. At all events, shortly after its rise, it was both much clarified and greatly reinforced by Euclid's *Elements,* for this soundest of all the works that have come down to us from antiquity deals with *pure* ideas and not with objects in the world of sight and touch. In such thought many have found a deep source of religious consolation for, because sheer ideas are wholly unaffected by temporal vicissitudes, one feels, in contemplating them, that one is literally in touch with things eternal.

Theology, too, has been thereby deepened and fortified. One recalls that Pythagoras, for whom the essence of the cosmos is Number, was the founder of a religion in which mathematics was held as sacred; and that Nicolaus Cusanus (1401–1464), Bishop of Brixen, who, in the competent judgment of Professor Weyl, "was one of the epoch-making minds in both Theology and Mathematics," held that the only way to an understanding of the divine is the symbolic way of mathematics. For Cusanus, as for Spinoza, the true love of God was an intellectual love.

Obviously the series of topics that have now been briefly discussed could be readily extended to include others of hardly less importance—such, for example, as the bearings of mathematics upon the art of logical criticism, upon psychology, upon metaphysics, upon expository style, upon the nature and limits of pragmatism, upon crises in the development of methodology. It is not less evident that the foregoing discussions could, without exhausting their several themes, be so expanded as to make up a large volume. I believe, however, that what has been said is sufficient, for all those whose minds are not closed against the kind of considerations adduced, to vindicate the claim of mathematics to rank second to none among the prime humanities.

# The Germans: Unhappy Philosophers in Politics

## REINHOLD NIEBUHR

### ( *1933* )

REINHOLD NIEBUHR is one of the leading spokesmen in the United States for Protestant orthodoxy. An intense concern with the significance of human history and social change has motivated him to study and interpret the relation of religion and philosophy to social and political problems.

THE fascist movement in Germany is, in certain of its aspects, merely a figure in the general pattern which is being woven in the whole of modern civilization and with which events in Italy and Japan have made us familiar. Even the nationalist victory in Britain in 1931 and the Rooseveltian program in our own country reveal elements roughly analogous to Hitler's movement, the elements of increased national sentiment, of the abrogation of democracy, and of stronger state control upon industry. What is distinctive and unique in the Nazi movement of Germany is derived in part from the political temper of a defeated nation and in part from unique characteristics in the German nature. The Germans are philosophers and they have the intellectual's unhappy penchant for consistency. They are therefore particularly inept and unhappy in the game of politics, for the complexities of politics demand improvisation and compromise.

Fascism, as a general movement, is the characteristic defense of an imperiled social system. Most of the Western nations are developing fascist tendencies because the poverty and the disillusionment of the post-War period have given the radical political parties sufficient strength to challenge the established order. One method of meeting this challenge is to identify national peace and social unity with the established order and thus to place those who

44

wish to change the system under the disadvantage of threatening social peace. Fascism exploits national and patriotic sentiment in favor of the present organization of society. This was done by the British Tories in 1931 no less than by Hitler. The difference is that the British appealed to the patriotic sentiment of the man in the street without being under the necessity of establishing a cult in nationalism and racialism. The Germans, with their passion for consistency, met the Marxian doctrine of the class struggle with a highly elaborated philosophy of *Volk und Rasse,* of nation and race. Hitler was of course not the philosopher who developed this philosophy. He was the demagogue who exploited the resentments of a defeated nation and the apprehensions and discontents of a divided people in terms of that philosophy. But once Hitler fanned the flames of racialism there were dozens of philosophers, historians, and theologians who fed the flames with tinder gathered from everywhere. If they were philosophers they reconstructed Hegelian thought in order to give dignity to the new emphasis upon *Staat und Volk.* If they were theologians they rediscovered Luther's theory of the *Schöpfungsordnung,* of "God's order of creation," to give pre-eminence to the organic relations of life, race, family, nation, and vocation against the more "rationalistic" social constructions of the class and the international order. "Rationalistic equalitarianism" and "rationalistic internationalism" are thus at a complete discount in Germany today. Whether the philosopher uses Hegel or the theologian appropriates Luther, the results are remarkably similar. The state and nation is affirmed as the community of most significant loyalty against the competing communities of the class and the international order. This is a general tendency in the whole of modern civilization; but in Germany it is given a consistent elaboration unknown in other countries and therefore makes for a fanatic state absolutism.

The philosophic temper of the Germans may hardly seem to be the cause of the kind of public hysteria which Hitler, with the aid of Dr. Goebbels, his genius for technicized propaganda, has been able to create in support of his program. Yet the two are related. Intellectualism divorces the intellect from its organic relation to the emotions. The intellect does not come into a fuller control of the passions by that divorce. It becomes enslaved to them. The emotions, in this case the fever of patriotic sentiment, are fanned by an arch-demagogue like Hitler and an expert propagandist like Goebbels, and the professors, thinking in an atmosphere created by this artificially aroused emotion, invent, elaborate, and redis-

45

cover theories of state and nation which establish the cult of nationality to its final consistency and absurdity.

Only by such cooperation between demagogues and philosophers is it possible for Hitler to attempt a state absolutism more unqualified than any ever attempted by monarchical autocrat. Bismarck respected the particularism of the South-German states. Hitler appoints governors to administer the affairs of Bavaria and Wuertemberg. The Kaiser was forced reluctantly to grant freedom of organization to the trade unions. Hitler brings trade unions totally under the ægis of the state and completely destroys the bargaining power of the laborers. Every kind of trade association, cultural organization, religious institution, and trade union must submit to the passion for "coordination," i. e., must sacrifice its autonomy to the monolithic state.

One has the feeling that the kind of state which Hitler is creating is the typical handiwork of a man lacking the necessary shrewdness of a real statesman. It does not do justice to the complexities of modern life and it is not fitted to relax tensions where they threaten to reach a breaking point. Hitler's state is the product of a demagogue suffering from megalomania and not certain enough of his power to qualify its exercise. But the personal weaknesses of a Hitler could not result in such a personal creation if the cultural and economic factors of the nation did not play into his hand. The economic factors which make for fascism are given in the whole disintegration of the economic structure of Western civilization and therefore affect other nations as well as Germany. The cultural factor peculiar to Germany is its intellectualism which permits the development of one theory of government and politics to a degree of consistency which renders it absurd.

The anti-Semitism of the fascist movement is intimately related to the extravagant nationalism which it is developing. If the state and the nation are to be absolutized as the Nazis are doing, the concept of state and nation must stand for something more than a political order. It must be "spiritualized." It must stand for an organic fellowship, not for a technical political cooperation. Thus it is *Volk* rather than state which is apotheosized by the Nazis. The blood brotherhood of the race, the *Volksgemeinschaft,* is what is arousing all the sublime passions of the frustrated young men of Germany. The reverse and darker side of that passion is anti-Semitism. The poor Jews must pay in misery and poverty for the rediscovery by German youth of their "Germanic" unity. Anti-Semitism is, of course, something more or less than the dark side of

46

the rediscovery of *Volk*. Since fascism is the political tool of the impoverished professional and middle classes and since it does not propose significant economic measures to restore these classes to prosperity, it will supply this defect by destroying the business of Jewish merchants and vacating the positions of Jewish professionals and bureaucrats. Thus it will create the illusion among some thousands of its followers that it has actually provided a "new deal." Furthermore anti-Semitism is a handy instrument of the anti-liberal and anti-radical purposes of fascism. Since Jews are prominent in the leadership of both the liberal-democratic and the communist-socialist movement the program against the Jews is a powerful thrust at radicalism and liberalism. Anti-Semitism is in short an instrument of the class struggle in Germany. The brutal vigor with which that instrument is being used would revolt the souls of the more decent Germans, however, were it not for the fact that they are completely obsessed with their new cult of race and nation. They recognize the brutality but regard it as an inevitability in the struggle of Germany for racial solidarity. They are inclined to answer misgivings in the words of Southey's famous poem, "After Blenheim," "Things like that, you know, must be in every famous victory." Anti-Semitism is not a vice peculiar to the Germans. It still flourishes in every nation which has a considerable body of Jews within its national boundary. But most of the cultured nations manage by both honest effort and dishonest and hypocritical pretension to qualify and to obscure the fact of race prejudice. Only philosophers like the Germans can work themselves into a state of mind in which they regard race conflict as one of the inevitabilities of a world which must cherish racial solidarity. Thus, again, its demagogues operate in an atmosphere created by innumerable pedants and their pedantic elaboration of the cult of *Volk und Rasse*.

The anti-democratic creed of Hitler is unique only in the consistency with which it is stated and even in that it is very similar to Mussolini's ideas. But here again the Germans give the general development of modern politics, with its preference for dictatorship over democracy, a passionate avowal which threatens to destroy every democratic safeguard. The destruction of democracy is a part of the pattern through which the whole modern era expresses itself politically. There are many reasons for this. Democracy presupposes the willingness of a minority to acquiesce in the policies of a majority. Such a presupposition holds only as long as the differences between minority and majority are not too great. When

47

the differences between them represent the differences between two diametrically opposed social systems, capitalism and socialism, it cannot be assumed that either the one or the other will yield the power over the state without making an extra-constitutional and non-parliamentary effort to maintain itself. The most parliamentary of all socialist parties, the British labor party, has been steadily moving to the left in the past two years and is no longer as sure as it once was that it can establish socialism unless an effort is made by capitalism and the old order to maintain itself against a parliamentary socialist venture. Thus British socialists, even when they insist on constitutional means, are no longer certain that their enemies will abide by the constitution. Harold Laski has written a book, *Democracy in Crisis,* to prove that labor ought to be constitutional in its bid for power but that it ought not to expect its enemies to abide by the constitution, once they are confronted with a resolute socialist majority in parliament, irrevocably intent upon nationalizing industry. Even as comparatively mild a laborite as Sir Stafford Cripps recently declared: "If, when labor gets power, the other people want to cause a revolution, I want to have control of the armed forces and the police before the revolution starts." In other words there are doubts and apprehensions in the motherland of constitutional democracy about the ability of parliamentary democracy to resolve the ultimate conflict between capitalism and socialism.

If such doubts can arise in England it is, perhaps, not surprising that the social struggle should have led to the abrogation of democracy in Germany. That fascism finally developed from the right rather than a dictatorship from the left is due partly to the fact that the socialists were wedded to the democratic creed and piously disavowed every non-parliamentary procedure. In 1919 the socialists had 46 per cent of the votes and a corresponding prestige. They wrote the Weimar constitution in its essential outline. They could have taken power and could have destroyed the Junkers who conspired fourteen years later to destroy them. But the socialists had given up their rigorous Marxism before the War. A man by the name of Kautsky had transmuted Marxian determinism into a sleepy kind of fatalism and had persuaded the socialists that the self-destruction of capitalism and the victory of socialism were so certain that the socialist party need only wait for the inevitable. Consequently the socialist party waited and meanwhile participated in the innumerable inter-party maneuvers by which liberals, Catholics, and socialists tried to maintain parliamentary government and through which parliamentarism became ultimately discredited. In the end it was discredited because it was unable to resolve the conflict between two almost equally powerful camps of reaction and radicalism. The power of the comparatively small Catholic party through all the post-War years rested upon its ability to work out *ad hoc* compromises between conservatism and radicalism. The socialists meanwhile had made such a fetish of the Weimar constitution that they could do nothing but make futile appeals to its authority even when it became apparent that their enemies would no longer abide by it. Thus Von Papen destroyed the socialist-Catholic government of Prussia by non-constitutional means and the socialists countered his move by an appeal to the supreme court. The impatient younger generation meanwhile had become convinced that democratic procedure could not resolve the impasse of the social struggle and give the political life of Germany a clear direction, either to the right or to the left.

Parliamentary government was furthermore discredited in the eyes of the resentful young men of Germany because the liberal and socialist parties who maintained it were also responsible for the various policies of *Erfuellung,* of conciliation with the victorious allies. Acceptance of the Dawes plan, the Young plan, the Locarno agreement, etc., were expected by the liberals and socialists to emancipate their country gradually from the thraldom of an unjust peace. To the young men of Germany it seemed as if their nation was being more and more completely enslaved to the outside world. The stage was thus set for the fascist venture. In it the fears of the privileged classes, the nationalistic resentments of an entire nation, and the impatience of the young people of all classes were compounded to create a tremendous driving force. The fascists did what the socialists might have done in 1919 but lacked the courage and resourcefulness to do. They used the democratic method to carry them as far as possible to power. They negotiated the rest of the distance by non-parliamentary and non-constitutional means and then destroyed the instrument of democracy so entirely that their enemies could not avail themselves of it.

The success of fascism depended upon the possibility of welding the impoverished middle classes into one political party with the richer industrialists and landed aristocrats. Only a demagogue could perform a task like that. For this very reason Hitler rather than Von Schleicher is ruling Germany today. Von Schleicher wanted a semi-fascism which would be "neither capitalistic nor socialistic." In attempting to establish a basis for his fascism broad enough to include the world of labor he lost the support of the landowners and industrialists who, through Von Papen, undermined his influence with Hindenburg, at that time the only key to state power. In his place came Hitler, who talked with more demagogic skill about the unity of the nation but who actually had a narrower basis for his authority, the basis being the money power of the wealthy and the votes of the impoverished middle classes. Thus Hitler used the democratic instrument of the vote more successfully than Von Schleicher to abrogate democracy more completely than Von Schleicher had intended.

Fascism is, in other words, an instrument of the social struggle in Germany, as it probably will be in every other Western nation. But no fascist demagogue will ever have as many philosophers and pedants to support his creed as Hitler is able to claim in his support. A whole new school of political thought has been developed in recent years with the avowed purpose of discrediting democracy. Democracy, it is declared, is an illusion of the "Age of Reason" and nothing is so completely at a discount today in Germany as the thought of the eighteenth century. According to this new school, democracy is rationalistic and individualistic. It believes that society is established by a social contract between individuals who conceive of themselves as atomic individuals; whereas, in fact, the individual is organic to society from the beginning. This organic relationship of the individual to society cannot be expressed in terms of democracy. It can be expressed only in the symbolism of the leader's authority over his people. Logically this thought leads to monarchical conceptions and to the theory of "divine right." Practically it is being used at the moment to maximize the authority of the man who throughout Germany is being hailed as "The Leader." In this whole development theologians are cooperating with philosophers, the theologians using Luther as the philosophers use Hegel to discredit democracy.

There are no doubt weaknesses in the creed of the nineteenth-century democrats which these wise men of Germany are uncovering. It may be that modern democracy has been too much the development of middle class life and has therefore been too individualistic and too little appreciative of the organic character of social life. It may also be true that communism substitutes a rationalistic mechanistic collectivism for a rationalistic mechanistic individualism and that both the individualism of capitalism and the collectivism of communism fail to do justice to important aspects of social life. Some modern German social thought is really very illuminating in exploring these defects of both democratic and socialistic thought.

But again the passions which demagogues arouse and the consistencies in which pedants indulge have been combined to discredit democracy so completely that it will not be available to the German people when they have need of it. Democracy is after all a peaceful method of arbitrating conflicting interests. If it should be true, as it probably is, that conflicts of interest may become too sharp to be amenable to democratic arbitration, it does not follow that democracy has become a useless tool.

Every society must either resolve the conflicts of interest within its communal life by the methods of democracy or it must use force to subject the interests of one group to those of another. It is of course true that democracy may be the means of oppression as well as a method of arbitration. That is why the disinherited classes of Western civilization are so cynical about the pretensions of democracy, and it may be necessary therefore on occasion to challenge the pretensions of democracy with force. But it must be clear that pure force is always a method of warfare and not a method of arbitration. It may be used to gain a victory for the proletarian class over the middle classes or of the middle classes over the working class. It cannot be used to harmonize the conflicting interests of various classes or functional groups. The pretensions of the German fascists that they have abrogated democracy for the sake of creating a unified people are therefore worse than any pretensions ever made in behalf of democracy. Every indication is that German labor, having lost both the vote and the bargaining power of collective industrial action, will have its living standards increasingly debased. German industry will become a vast sweatshop for the world by the very policies which were to redeem the German people from their slavery. Since no amount of fascist oppression will be able to destroy the opposition of German labor to this ruthless effort to reduce it to permanent slavery, fascism can maintain itself in Germany only until its oppressions have ripened the resentments and the vehemence of the labor world and have healed the breach between socialism and communism.

It may be that fascism will be in power in Germany for several decades to come. But it must count on a stronger opposition than it faced in Italy, for Germany is a more highly industrialized state and the power of the industrial worker is correspondingly greater. When the day of reckoning comes there will be no method for the dissolution of the old order and of reconstruction but through a

51

bloody civil war. It may be that a similar fate awaits every Western nation. But that is not absolutely certain for other nations and it is practically certain for Germany. Her fascist venture has blocked the way to any peaceful resolution of the difficulties which Western industrial nations face. The very consistency of her awakened nationalism will breed an internationalism as consistent among her dispossessed. Fascism and communism must face each other in fratricidal conflict; and in that conflict many of the values which German social philosophers think they have saved in the present development will be irretrievably lost.

The Germans are in short too consistent in their thought and action to be able to deal advantageously with political problems. They could learn a great deal from the English who are not as intellectual but more sane in their approach to human and social problems. "What governs an Englishman," declares Santayana, "is certainly not his intelligence." The British maintained their organic conception of society even while they perfected the instruments of democracy. They take the organic character of national life for granted while the Germans engage in passionate arguments to prove that a nation is more than a conglomerate of individuals. British socialism has been a hodge-podge of ideas and never consistently Marxian. But experience is driving it more and more to the left where the more consistent Marxian socialism of Germany was fifty years ago. British socialism, learning slowly by the experience of history, arrives at this left position at a time when German socialism is practically annihilated under the heels of a victorious fascist foe. British labor is united and German labor was divided into socialist and communist camps. That division was one cause of its undoing. The German socialists were doctrinaire parliamentarians and the communists insisted on the pattern of the Russian revolution for the complexities of German political life. The British socialists will probably lose some of their confidence in pure parliamentarism and will move in the direction of pragmatic radicalism with a united front. Thus political doctrines grow directly out of experience in British life. That is possible because the British are sane rather than intellectual, i. e. they apply their intelligence directly to the situations in which they stand and they are thus able to gauge and apprehend the imponderables of politics in a way which no consistent political theory is able to do.

Furthermore there is a possibility that the privileged classes of Britain may yield before the tensions of modern industrial society result in civil war. They do not yield easily. No dominant class does. But they usually do yield just a moment before it is too late. That is their policy in India and that is what they have done in the long struggle of the middle classes against the landed aristocracy. The decline of capitalistic civilization will create some crises which may demand too much even of the dominant classes of Britain. There is in other words no certainty that modern civilization will evolve a social system adequate to the necessities of a technological civilization without social convulsion and confusion. But if it is possible at all, political muddlers like the British are more likely to succeed than philosophers like the Germans.

The Germans will probably always produce more interesting philosophy than the British. They explore the heights and the depths of life more fully. The greatest philosophers of Britain were significantly empiricists like John Locke and David Hume. In the field of philosophical idealism, more typically the field of philosophic generalization, the English have had to borrow from the German Kants and Hegels. Nor have the English had an optimist as consistent as Leibnitz or a pessimist as thoroughgoing as Schopenhauer. No one has expressed as ruthless a revolt against Christian morality in England as did Nietzsche; and the most consistent philosophy of rebellion against a bourgeois civilization was developed by a German Jew, Karl Marx. In as far as the catastrophic element in Marxism did not seem congenial to workers, who were beginning to reap some benefits from industrial civilization, it was revised by another German Jew, Eduard Bernstein and the revision was more consistent than the semi-socialism of English Fabianism. In Germany every social strategy is supported by a complete *Weltanschauung* or world view and every political attitude is developed into a religion. The German socialists had a completely irreligious and *Vaterlandslose Weltanschauung*. They did not live up to their revolutionary faith and they proved themselves in the War and after to be as patriotic and nationalistic as their British fellows. But their creed aroused and seemed to justify the nationalism which has now destroyed them.

The Germans arm the warriors of every political camp in the rest of the world with weapons of the spirit. They are so adept at sharpening these weapons to a razor edge and feel so obligated to experiment with them upon each other that their body politic bleeds from many wounds and betrays scars as numerous as those found on the youthful faces of a German *Studentenschaft*. Thus the Germans develop a strategy of political reaction to a consistent

53

fascism and will probably be the first to dissolve this fascism into an equally consistent communism. But they will probably continue to be without peace or serenity in their political life and will be last to bring peace to a tormented world. If they could only be as unintellectual, or even unintelligent, as the British, they might be a saner and certainly a happier people. The social problems of the modern world must be solved by the guidance of clear and unambiguous principles; but when principles are applied to the actual complexities of a specific situation the clairvoyant intelligence of the statesman is more helpful than the philosopher's passion for consistency.

# Private Property or Capitalism

## HERBERT AGAR

### (*1934*)

The illusion that capitalism is a system of private property was viewed as a deterrent to the solution of the economic tension and instability that enveloped the United States when HERBERT AGAR wrote this article. His proposal for the resolution of the dilemma was a return to conservatism, meaning property ownership by "the many." A versatile thinker and a prolific writer, Mr. Agar now lives in England.

THE first period of liberalism in modern American politics, the Progressive Era, came to a sordid end in 1921. The "Square Deal" of Theodore Roosevelt and the "New Freedom" of Wilson gave way to the "normalcy" of Harding. Liberalism failed because it did not correctly analyse the problem it sought to cure. A famous *New Yorker* cartoon shows two men drifting about on life-preservers in an angry sea, one of them remarking, "fundamentally the ship was perfectly sound." That is the root error of liberalism, as it showed itself in the first two decades of the century. The liberals were convinced that fundamentally America was perfectly sound, that with a little tinkering at the laws and a little more honesty of administration all would be well. In fact there was already grave danger that all might be ill. The American people were already at the crossroads and had to choose their way for good or bad. We are still at the same crossroads today, but not being gypsies we cannot camp there for ever.

The United States, when Theodore Roosevelt became president, had a democratic form of government suitable to a nation of property-owners in which a majority of families had a real stake in the country. But the United States was rapidly becoming a country in which the large majority of the citizens were proletarians—a word that has been defined as meaning "a man politically free,

55

that is, one who enjoys the right before the law to exercise his energies when he pleases (or not at all if he does not so please), but not possessed by legal right of control over any useful amount of the means of production." In a country where a few people own most of the means of production and the majority of people is proletarian, democracy has always been and must always be a farce. There is no good, in such a country, in calling the rich men names or in passing laws prohibiting them from buying a controlling interest in the government. The most that such laws can do is to make the buying somewhat more complicated, and somewhat more gratifying to the rich men's lawyers. But democracy cannot be saved in a country in which a small group controls the means of production. If the forms of democracy are kept they will merely become a soiled screen for plutocracy. The honest choice before such a country is either to let the rich own the government openly, just as they own everything else, or to prevent them from owning everything else, either by restoring the institution of private property or by creating the institution of communism. It is this choice which the liberals of yesterday failed to face—a failure which explains why the Progressive Era of Theodore Roosevelt, Taft, and Wilson came to nothing, or rather why it came to Harding, who may fairly be described as worse than nothing.

The friends of "normalcy," of course, were even further from facing the facts than were the Progressives. They therefore led us steadily and enthusiastically to 1929 and to the subsequent débâcle under Mr. Hoover. As a result in 1932 the country turned again to a liberal. On the evidence of the speeches and articles collected in his book, *Looking Forward,* Mr. Franklin Roosevelt in 1932 was a traditional American liberal, full of humanitarianism and of zeal for reform, but unaware that a vital change was required. The collapse of February and March, 1933, made him revise his views, and plan for a more thorough reorganization of the United States. It appears, however, that this reorganization is still being carried on from the liberal point of view, that is, from the point of view of one who holds that democracy and capitalism can somehow be made to work together—that the existing American system is fundamentally sound. And it is hard to see how the new liberalism can be more successful than the old.

This is not to suggest that Mr. Roosevelt himself will fail. Mr. Roosevelt appears to combine the adaptability of Proteus with the wile of Ulysses, and if his present purpose is indeed unrealistic he will doubtless change it in time. The point of this essay is not to discuss Mr. Roosevelt's chances but to try and suggest that the liberal approach to the American problem will not lead to a stable solution today any more than it did yesterday. (And at the same time I hope to suggest that the conservative approach could lead to a solution both stable and agreeable.)

If all we had to do was to cure abuses in a system that is healthy at root, liberalism would be what we need. But our task is not to repair the existing system and then administer it with more conscience and more humanity; our task is either to build a new system or to restore the old one that is almost destroyed. The job, in other words, calls for revolution or else for true conservatism.

One error underlying American liberal thought is the belief that the United States is now engaged in a struggle to preserve a system of private property against the menace of communism. In fact the traditional American social order, which was based on the institution of private property, has already been largely supplanted by thoroughgoing capitalism. And the essence of capitalism (and this has been true ever since its origins in the 16th and 17th centuries) is that property in significant amounts is not owned by the ordinary citizen. Everybody in America may still own *something*. But only a small proportion of the population owns a share in the means of production—land, tools, natural resources. It is only when private property in this real sense is widely distributed that the institution of private property can be said to exist; it is only then that the benefits of that institution (such as responsibility, enterprise, family stability) can be expected. But when the means of production are owned by a very small percentage of the population it is vain to expect the watching millions to be filled with enterprise or endowed with responsibility or hope. It is this latter state to which America has come today. And the name of this state is capitalism. And capitalism is the negation of private property. But the liberal continues to talk and plan as if capitalism *meant* private property, which explains why the liberal finds it hard to solve the problems raised by capitalism. An amusing example of this lack of realism was offered by Mr. William Wirt when he complained that members of the President's Brain Trust were out to destroy "the America of Washington, Jefferson, and Lincoln." Mr. Wirt might just as reasonably have been shocked if some rash youth had suggested destroying the America of Pocohontas.

This confusion between capitalism, which means the denial of private property (in any significant amounts) to the vast majority of the nation, and the true system of private property which capitalism is supplanting, has persisted in America for reasons that are not hard to find. During the first generations of its life the United States really was a nation of property-owning citizens; that is, a large proportion of American families owned something real (such as land, or a store, or a machine shop, or a small factory) , with the result that such ownership was the basic institution of American life and set the tone of that life. Americans were proud of this institution and they have naturally been slow to notice its disappearance. Also, during the generations after the Civil War, when capitalism encroached more and more fatally upon the old America, the steady settling of new groups of farmers in the West meant that there were still many Americans of modest financial status who were genuine owners of property. Those whose hearts still lay with the America of Washington and Jefferson could avert their eyes from the heavily populated districts and dream that the "real America" was still a land of free farmers, that the United States was still based on private property. It is this dream, and the failure of analysis which this dream encourages, which defeated the liberalism of the Progressive Era.

The time has now come when it would be fatal to persist in a false analysis of our plight. It may not be too late to make a modern version of the America of Washington and Jefferson in which it will once again be normal for American families to own real property. But it will very quickly become too late unless we notice what is going on around us and act accordingly. Everyone knows that the thing which is going on around us is called capitalism but strangely few people know what capitalism means. It is therefore worth repeating that capitalism, in its pure state, means that almost all productive property is owned by a very few and that almost nothing is owned by the very many. The great difference between modern capitalism and the classical slave state is that under modern capitalism the propertyless majority is politically "free."

The best that can be said for modern American capitalism is that it is not quite capitalism in its pure state. It is capitalism tempered by humanitarianism—by rather more humanitarianism under a liberal administration, by rather less under a reactionary administration. But we have reached a state of tension and instability in which no amount of tempering, or of temporising, is of any benefit. A real solution is demanded. And there are only three real solutions logically possible.

The first solution is communism. Take the means of production away from the few and let the state administer them for the good of the many. This is at least an honest system which admits what it is doing and can give a moral basis for its action. And perhaps in the long run communism may prove to be compatible with true democracy. Those of us who think that this is highly unlikely base our view on the belief that the institution of private property is deeply rooted in human desire and that the communist solution for the dilemma of capitalism, though logical, will always have to be maintained by force. But if communism were the only alternative to what we have, it might at least be a better and a more stable social order.

The second solution may be described as an American version of fascism. This would lead to a confirmation of the few in their ownership of the means of production, while at the same time definite minimum rights and a definite status are conferred on the many: the capitalist proletariat, during a time of slump, has nothing to fall back on except the vote (which under capitalism is a fake) and "liberty" (which under capitalism is a myth). The fascist proletariat would have a right to a decent living at the community's expense in return for an abandonment of its "liberty" and an acceptance of the obligation to work when work is given it. Obviously this would be the negation of the old American system. It would, in a sense, be the modern world's version of the classical slave state. But it would be stable and it would be realistic, and again it would be better than the present disheartening pretense. Under fascism the national income would be more fairly distributed but ownership of the national resources would remain the prerogative of the very few. Although the fascist state would probably be more obnoxious to liberals than to any other group it is toward just such a state that liberalism tends. For liberalism, by refusing to go boldly to the right or to the left, prolongs the present disequilibrium. In the course of time, under such a policy, fascism will become the one alternative to a smash.

The third solution is conservatism: a return to the original American system under which the ownership of property is the normal expectation for a family. The word "conservative" is usually applied, in the United States, to the politics of Big Business. This is a misuse of language, for it is the politics of Big Business which has been destroying traditional America. If any return to that America is possible it will be by the policy known as "distributism"—the revival of the common ownership of real property. Consequently it is reasonable to annex the word "conservative" for this policy.

59

The fact that these three solutions were the only possible outcome of capitalism was foreseen as long ago as 1912 by Mr. Hilaire Belloc. "To solve capitalism," wrote Mr. Belloc, "you must get rid of restricted ownership, or of freedom, or of both." Conservatism, as I have here used the word, would do the first: it would get rid of restricted ownership. Fascism would do the second: it would get rid of freedom. Communism would do the third: it would get rid of both. Liberalism is an untenable attempt to keep both, to find some way of making restricted ownership and freedom live side by side. It cannot be done. The longer the effort goes on, the greater will be the tension and the instability of our social order. Restricted ownership will make freedom, for the propertyless majority, more and more of a fraud. In good times this may not be resented but in bad times it breeds a revolutionary situation, sooner or later destroying the society based on these two incompatibles.

If liberalism—if the present combination of restricted ownership, humanitarianism, and democratic forms of government—is too unstable, the American people must choose between the possible ways out. If the choice be put off too long communism will come from the sheer force of economic determinism. But that danger is still in the future. For the present the choice lies between what I have called conservatism and what I have called fascism. Fascism can make a fairer distribution of the national income than is now known and can guarantee a decent living to the proletariat if the proletariat will accept permanently a working-class status. Conservatism, slowly and with difficulty, can redistribute ownership and not merely income. It offers risks and responsibilities rather than bread and circuses. But it also offers the only realistic way of reviving that much-mentioned America of Washington and Jefferson. Which course will the American people choose?

There is a popular delusion which tends to obscure the issue by making the conservative choice sound impractical. According to this delusion the industrial revolution (and still more the power revolution of the past few decades) has made small property-holdings impossible, since nowadays the economic production of most goods requires machines that are too costly for the ordinary owner to possess. There is only one ray of truth in this argument— namely, that in a society which does not intend to cherish the institution of private property, a society which is perfectly willing to let things rip according to the laws of economic determinism, the tendency in the modern world is for the means of production to get into fewer and fewer hands. But to say that this tendency is a law of nature and that it cannot be thwarted is to say a lie. If the American people made up their minds that they really wished to return to a system of private property it would be quite possible for the modern tools of production to be owned on a share-system by companies whose shares had a real meaning. The first step toward such a system would be to break the existing credit-monopoly, which gives finance the power to make all so-called ownership a joke. The second step would be to pass laws to foster and protect the small owner, creating artificial disadvantages in the path of enormous concentrations of ownership. The details of such a program have been worked out and can be found in the copious literature of distributism; they need not be repeated here. But what does need constant repetition is that there is nothing about modern machine technique which makes the system of distributed private property impossible. It may be true that the system would cost something, that it would be slightly "uneconomic" as compared with the capitalistic concentration of ownership. But if the American people decide they want to own real property there is no reason to believe they lack the fortitude to pay the price. Heaven knows they have a potential abundance out of which to pay it.

The real reason why modern industrialism has tended to destroy private property and to be a curse instead of a blessing is that the industrial revolution took place in eighteenth-century England, which was already a capitalist country, a land where most of the means of production were owned by a very few people and where control over the national credit had already been taken away from the Government and made the monopoly of a tiny group. In such circumstances, as Mr. Belloc and others have repeatedly pointed out, the effect of the machine was to aggravate an already nasty state of affairs, to increase the already unpardonable gulf between the Two Nations. Had the machine first come to a nation in which private property was widely distributed, it could have increased the common wealth, increased the amount of property that the normal family held. Instead, it led rapidly to the state described with ferocious indifference by nineteenth-century economists, who spent evil hours proving the obvious falsehood that it was "scientifically" impossible for the proletariat ever to get more than a bare subsistence wage. Indeed, said these economists, if the proletariat was unwary enough to breed too fast its wage would have to fall below subsistence level until starvation had re-established "the army of unalterable law."

It was under such auspices and with such bad example that industrialism spread to America. It is no wonder that here too it worked hand in hand with the growing system of capitalism for the death of private property. But the fact that it did so work is no proof that it had to or that it must be allowed to go on working in that fashion to the end. The instinct for private property is still a live thing in America; it is the task for conservatives to foster it. To accomplish this task they must do three things. First, they must destroy the illusion that capitalism is a system of private property; second, they must destroy the illusion that industrialism is incompatible with private property; third, they must strive to rouse an active, conscious demand from the American people for a return to a state of things wherein most families may reasonably hope to hold a share of the nation's means of production.

If they can do all this they can preserve America, not only from communism, the threat of the future, but from fascism, the threat of today. For it is quite in the cards that just as the old liberalism of the Progressive Era died away into Harding and the Ohio Gang, so the new liberalism, if unalleviated by conservative thought, may die away into fascism and the modern slave state.

# Catholics and Other People

## GEORGE N. SHUSTER

### ( *1937* )

GEORGE N. SHUSTER, who recently retired as president of Hunter College, is well prepared to discuss the relationship of American Catholics to the secular community. As a leading lay representative, he has written numerous books and articles on the subject and was at one time managing editor of *Commonweal.*

D URING several years past the following scene has been enacted in a great number of American communities. A Protestant clergyman, a Catholic priest and a Jewish rabbi appear together before an audience which—due allowance having been made for the merely curious—consists of people who feel (a) that religious prejudice is a calamitous and outmoded disease, and (b) that the ethical imperatives respected by all monotheists are of such value to society they ought to be fully utilized. On matters of doctrine, the speakers insist, the various faiths are as separate as the fingers of a hand, but on fundamental tenets of the *lex aeterna* they are "as united as a clenched fist."

Are such programs testimonials to the existence of any genuine reality or are they merely echoes of a pious wish that would be father to a purpose? I can imagine many a citizen thinking as he weighs the question that although educated Protestant dislike of bigotry is sincere the Catholic Church remains uneasy over any display which assumes that it can meet dissident or disaffected groups on a plane of theoretical equality. No one can speak "for" even the 20,000,000 Catholics of the United States but it is quite possible to write scientifically "about" Catholic views on cooperation because these are determinable things.

The trend towards religious unity which has to some extent characterized the recent past grows out of two quite different conceptions. The first is based upon the feeling that the chaotic disarray which confronts the observer of organized Christianity is the

63

result of historical conditions which matter to present-day human beings only in so far as they have produced several distinct types of worship. We are powerless to change either the conditions or their fruits. Our proper task is therefore to inculcate mutual respect and a measure of interest in common effort, and our hope must be that after some generations the desire to make concessions will be stronger on all sides. The second conception is derived from fear lest a rising tide of secularism uproot all religious authority and abrogate all freedom of conscience, and its exponents struggle to form a united spiritual "front" against the enemy. This anxiety is the outgrowth of a somewhat panicky fondness for liberalism. It is normally less concerned with what religion might accomplish than with what the state may do if unchecked.

That the Catholic Church considers itself the sole true form of the Christian communion is at once obvious and difficult to understand. The phrase "outside the Church there is no salvation" must not be taken to mean that for a Roman theologian every "heretic" or "unbeliever" is doomed to bathe in brimstone. It merely formulates from orthodox premises the relatively common-sense conclusion that the sacramental system is the Divinely or-dained means through which human salvation is to be effected. Since this system is held to be non-existent outside the Catholic Church it follows that no one can profit by it unless he be inside that Church. Taken in this sense the *extra ecclesiam nulla salus* doctrine may sound bad but is quite logical. But—salvation can be effected otherwise, either through sacramental institutions bor-rowed and conserved outside (e.g. Protestant baptism) or through Divine Providence. Since it is the soundest of teaching to assert that the bounty of this Providence is endless, it follows that every human being of good will shall find peace.

No doubt much of what has just been said appears to be woe-fully formalistic. One may just as well admit that anyone unwill-ing to think in terms of the most rigid theological logic will make a poor student of the Catholic position. That is why gentlemen like Harry Elmer Barnes, whose minds operate on gusts of turbulent intellectual emotion, seem so dreadfully naive when they speak of Rome or Medievalism. I shall therefore illustrate the point of view stressed above. If we suppose that a priest is not baptized and, quite unaware of the fact, takes orders and ministers to others he will be (a) as definitely outside the Church as any heathen Patagonian and (b) incapable of administering the sacraments to those who rely on him. It is therefore hypothetically possible that a Catholic community might in good faith be really "without a priest" during the whole of a man's mature lifetime. And here again, of course, the Providence of God would be relied upon to correct or supply what had been left undone through human error.

If this fundamental Catholic position could somehow be conceded by those not in the Church, purely religious cooperation with the Catholic organization would naturally be a good deal easier. That is, however, quite impossible. The point has been seen and described so clearly by Professor Karl Barth, the great Swiss Protestant theologian, that one need only refer to him. It will not help to act as if the difficulty did not exist and those who do so are wasting their time. Catholic authority would rather disappear from the public scene and face real persecution than ignore this issue because its vision of the Christian life has its origin here. By comparison dozens of things currently deemed important are of no practical significance whatever.

Well, you will say, can anything be done? A good deal, fortunately. In so far as religious discussion is concerned let me quote the opinion of a very able American canonist, the Reverend Joseph P. Donovan, C.M., of Kenrick Seminary, St. Louis. He writes:

> There is only one prescription in the Code dealing with religious cooperation and that deals with it only indirectly. Canon 1325 declares that Catholics are to take care not to enter into debates or conferences, especially of a public kind, without the previous permission of the Holy See, or in case of emergency without the permission of the ordinary. I conceive this to mean procedures such as the Purcell-Campbell and the Hughes-Black debates were, and also such undertakings as the Congress of Religions at the Chicago World's Fair of 1893 and the more recent conversations at Malines between Cardinal Mercier and representatives of the Anglican Church were. I think an incidental debate would not come under the prohibition. Much less, as authors point out, would apologetic talks, even if difficulties and objections were aired. But all organized efforts to present the evidence for the Catholic faith certainly require the approval of the local bishop.[1]

The essential fact in this ruling is not prohibition but prudence. It is imperative, as the good Baron Von Hügel used to say so fre-

[1] In a letter to the author.

quently, not to minimize or soft-pedal the tenets of the Catholic faith lest it seem too easy and attractive a belief. Quite as necessary is the curbing of the zealot whose idea of orthodoxy is rabid over-statement. Against these perils ecclesiastical authority is often alert to the verge of timidity, but it seems to me that such caution is preferable to loosing the floodgates of aimless chatter. Bishops are human beings dwelling in an inconstant world and their conceptions of prudence naturally vary a good deal. There are two countries in which the problems of inter-faith fellowship are particularly vital and to them one may turn hopefully for enlightenment. In the United States there has been emphasis on the practical aspects of the truth that a working agreement with other Christian groups is desirable. Catholic leaders in a large number of dioceses have sought to work with Protestants in prayer for coveted blessings, in fostering religious education and in meeting the challenge of youth, though the absence of an underlying program or theory has greatly hampered progress. Until we have a generally acceptable philosophy according to which the protagonists of co-operation can steer their course mutual aid is bound to remain haphazard. By comparison Germany has been a country in which the theory of cooperation has made rapid progress while the art of applying that theory to everyday life is still in its infancy. Before the Hitler upheaval a brilliant review (*Una Sancta*) published endless impressive papers on the subject and in the Catholic camp younger Jesuits in particular were very active. Some of these men openly regretted that it had proved impossible for the Church to take part in the Stockholm Oecumenical Congress and they made earnest efforts to appreciate the drift of Lutheran theology. More recently Paul Fechter phrased a Protestant appeal for greater solidarity between the Churches, and Catholic contributions to the discussion which followed are worth a good deal of study. Professor Alois Dempf, Father Max Pribilla, Dr. Ernst Michel all expressed the deepest respect for Protestantism and commented on methods of liaison.[2]

It seems to me that if some first-rate student of the problem were to conjoin German theory with American experience he might advance the whole cause a goodly step further. Unfortunately little equally favorable news can be reported from other

[2] For the benefit of those who may be interested the following indications are given: for Professor Fechter's article see *Deutsche Rundschau*, February 1936; for Professor Dempf's see *Hochland*, March 1936; and for Professor Michel's see *Hochland*, April 1936. Various discussions of the theme by Father Max Pribilla, S.J., may be read in the files of *Stimmen der Zeit*.

countries. The Latin nations for the most part find Protestantism incomprehensible and conversely most Protestants find Latin religiousness incomprehensible. We should have been far less unprepared for the civil war in Spain if the average author of five or ten years ago could have grasped the nature of anticlerical revolt in that country. There, at least until recently, the man who sacked convents and jailed priests during his heyday usually sent for the vicar on his death bed and made sure of the beyond. How can such actions be explained? The best one can do is to say that the Latin regards both the priestly function and the supernatural as quite objective realities. Accordingly both have a practical value, and conflict arises when this value is confused with others. Whatever may happen in Spain I am sure it will never be a Protestant country and that its people will, barring a few exceptions, never be dissuaded from associating the Catholic faith with birth and death at least.

On the other hand the average Latin or indeed the average Hispanic ecclesiastic has a very hard time making head or tail of a Protestant. It has been difficult to persuade some of them to concede liberty of conscience to "heretics" because of their disinclination to believe that heretics have consciences! If the priest's real reason for being is his control over certain spiritual functions held to be of vital importance it follows that the most dangerous enemy is the man who denies the validity of those functions while proclaiming himself at the same time a possessor of the Christian religion. To all this Great Britain would seem an antithesis but there the situation is so beclouded with racial, social and historical resentment that the possibilities of cooperation are realized by few.

Under such circumstances hopes for a world-wide reunion of Christendom (or for the adoption of an ethical program embodying principles by which all set store) appear to be rather futile. Yet it is impossible to deny that many Protestants are sincerely in favor of both things or to doubt that the reigning Pope and his immediate predecessor have been very much more "liberal" in their attitude towards cooperation than were the Sovereign Pontiffs of the 19th century. Recent Encyclicals have gone far beyond recognizing the existence of "our separated brethren." [3] In dealing with the Oriental Churches, which are looked upon as schismatic, Rome has come a long way. German resistance to the threat of Nazi paganism has found Catholics and Protestants ready in a measure to share the perils of defense. When the full fury of the

[3] See for example the Encyclical on Motion Pictures (1936).

attack upon the dissident Lutheran pastors was unleashed Bishop Nicholas Bares of Berlin petitioned the faithful to remember these men in their prayers. The diocesan authorities of Munich and Cologne likewise expressed their admiration of the Protestant leaders. Cardinal Faulhaber declared that there was no longer any conflict between Catholics and Protestants, both standing united against a common enemy of religion. Nor was the believing Jew spurned. Outside and inside the Third Reich religious periodicals have explored the ground shared in common by orthodox Catholic and Protestant foes of an anti-Christian political and social order. The work of *Der Deutsche* in Polen is an example.

There is no prohibitive ruling whatsoever against Catholic participation in cultural and civic effort. A priest is wholly at liberty to associate with Congregational clergymen and Unitarian professors in any enterprise he adjudges likely to benefit the community of that hazy entity the human mind. Henry Fairfield Osborne has left a record of his fruitful comradeship with priest scientists and the Vatican itself has issued works by noted Protestant scholars. John Milton was on friendly terms with Vatican librarians and the records of the once-famous Metaphysical Society, to which both Cardinal Manning and John Huxley belonged, would suffice to indicate that even philosophy can be an excuse for amiable intercourse.

But there are real difficulties. In the United States, where religious differences have meant so much, a strange though doubtless natural uneasiness is often manifested when the Catholic participant in a discussion shows up. He may find himself credited with the oddest persuasions and desires. If the Catholic is a priest he is likely to find that offering prayer is on the list of events. This is intended to be a courtesy towards him but it immediately raises the question of common worship—the activity for which he must have authorization. If he be a layman he often finds himself being maneuvered into a "representative capacity" which is bound to render him very uncomfortable since he cannot "represent" anybody except himself. Why cannot civic and intellectual cooperation proceed without these deplorable if well-meant addenda?

Naturally there are some kinds of effort repugnant to the Catholic ethos. I shall say nothing about such expedients as social welfare through contraception for the reason that a separate essay would be required. If a priest, however, were to acquire such a job as that which during the last national campaign descended upon Dr. Stanley High he would get himself soundly and raucously laughed at. The thought of solemnly delivering the "church vote" to Mr. Roosevelt or any other presidential candidate is one which is either ironed out by Catholic seminary training or would find the going tough if it emerged later on. The idea of standing at Armageddon and battling for the Lord on the second Tuesday in November has for most clergymen of my creed in the United States a comical implication. Nobody will ever get all Catholics into one political party, not even the Democratic. The effort to direct political affiliations is not considered evil in itself but there is no mandatory obligation to conform.

Similar in character is the so-called "Common Front." This term was evoked by the triumphs of Fascism and implies that since Catholics suffer from dictatorial governments they must strongly welcome an invitation to pool their resources with other similarly victimized groups. To some Catholics the vision of cordial relations with a more or less faddish Left is to be sure attractive, and there are also Catholics who subscribe to the Socialist creed in everything but name. Nevertheless a Christian religion cannot foster intimate partnership with a movement avowedly non-religious and historically, at least, anti-religious. This truth may well be disadvantageous to Catholics from the temporal point of view. It almost automatically creates a drift toward social theories hostile to Marxism and therewith an alignment in *practice* which is not consonant with *theory*. For there can be no doubt that the traditional ethical urge of the Church has far more in common with the Labor Party, for example, than with fascism, even of the Italian variety.

These difficulties are considerable but they are less weighty than the problem of disparate Catholic points of view. Just when the outsider (who normally supposes that all members of the Roman communion are drilled into absolute conformity) thinks he has at last hitched the wagon of the Church to his star the spokes fly out of the wheels, the chassis tumbles in a heap and he is left to survey as well as he can the bedraggled team. What has he failed to take into account?

Simply the fact that the absolutism of the Church extends only to the religious life proper or to the moral code which renders that life possible and is even here far more dependent upon quasi-parliamentary discussion than is generally imagined. On all humanistic topics a greater relativism is encouraged by the Catholic system than by any other. The sons of the Church are profoundly skeptical about philosophical, historical and scientific dicta. They

69

have produced arguments for every conceivable kind of aesthetic. There are Catholic vitalists and mechanists, conservatives and liberals, golfers and scoffers at gold. The average Catholic convention is an unparalleled display of disagreement. To a certain extent these phenomena result from a supra-national point of view. Few Catholics, especially among the intellectual, give their all to the culture of their people or country. Their contacts and their training engender a measure of universalism so well symbolized by the Latin language. The normal priest has studied medieval philosophy, French pietistic literature, German church history, British apologetics and Irish poetry. He may sometimes appear to be out of the swim but he is seldom to be caught in a corner.

Accordingly there is just no use trying to corral "Catholic support" for some favorite idea or scheme. All that can be done is to accept individuals as friendly individuals and to rely on their standing in the community for a certain resonance. Usually they will belong to a circle of like-minded people all of whom have profited from the united effort demanded by the Church. I believe it is not generally realized how many such groups can be found. Many Protestants, misled by names and attitudes which are prominent in the daily press, are greatly surprised when chance brings them together with other Catholics whose very existence they have not suspected.

Perhaps one ought to conclude by saying that the cooperationists have a right to be proud of their achievement to date. Community Chest and other efforts to raise money for charity work, interfaith interest in religious education for public school children, related endeavors to popularize concepts of social reform and of peace morality have enabled good men in various groups to appreciate one another. Hundreds of local meetings throughout the United States have lessened prejudice and released pent-up energies useful to the community. The larger organizations for the development of good will (notably the National Conference of Jews and Christians) can point to undertakings particularly interesting for the light they throw upon growing Catholic participation in general religious or moral activities. It is true that "common worship" has no appeal for more than a handful but "common betterment," if intelligently and realistically understood, can be an effective solvent of prejudice and the will-to-be-alone.

If we now turn to surmisals that autocracy is destined to become the form of our political institutions unless religious men form a common front to protect liberty of conscience the outlook

CATHOLICS AND OTHER PEOPLE

is somewhat less encouraging. For my part I do not believe that any such amalgamation of forces could stave off dictatorship if it were really impending. During somewhat more than a century and a half the Christian Churches, Catholic and Protestant, reluctantly adapted themselves to a liberalistic society. In Europe this society was the creation of the bourgeoisie, a group which most religious leaders persistently opposed not merely because of their latent admiration for royalty and its retinue but also because they deeply distrusted the "rugged individualism" of bourgeois enterprise. The Church—even the most loosely organized Church—is either a community aware of intertwining responsibilities or it is a hollow shell. And how could there be any community in a veritable sense where "self reliance" was the universal slogan?

The Catholic Church did not lose the struggle with individualism. It merely sloughed off tens of thousands over whom it exercised a merely nominal control. The sincerely religious in every 19th-century generation were doubtless more intimately united than the congregations of earlier times. But there came a time when the zest for battle died down on both sides, and then religion widely capitulated to the age and said Amen to individualism, just as it had conceded the sacredness of kings after the long struggle of the Middle Ages had led to an impasse. During the conflict with liberalism many issues had been confused and beclouded. Men identified outer forms with inner values, clinging to royalism, for instance, when they should have emphasized solidarity. Then, in their haste to recognize the legitimacy of the outer forms they swallowed part of the latent heresy itself. Today there are thousands of churchmen who uphold the bourgeois order as zealously as their predecessors of a century or two ago argued for the Divine right of kings.

It may be that the malady of unbridled individualism—the theory that the one can relinquish his responsibilities to the many without blame—can be cured without any radical alteration of the social structure. Or it may be that some kind of revolution is inevitable. I do not know. But surely past experience indicates that overt ecclesiastical action is powerless to ward off the relentless attack of historical destiny. Words of Newman now nearly a hundred years old treat this subject with a contemporaneousness which makes them decidedly worth looking up. His thought may be restated as follows: the mission of the Church is to build up its own community or kingdom. This it must do regardless of time, of ease or of difficulty. And such a kingdom or community cannot

71

be erected on the assumption that what goes on in the outer world is of primary importance. As soon as that happens religion is infected with the prevailing disease and ceases to be the regimen with which disease can be prevented.[4]

Under existing conditions a union of Churches to ward off dictatorship would only lead—if it led anywhere—to the ultimate identification of the Churches with *one form* of dictatorship. Accordingly it seems to me such a front ought to be shunned. Religious leaders should seek intensification of their own effort and leave politics alone. This is naturally a personal view the hurry to adopt which will occasion no stampede. During 1930 I wasted a good deal of time urging that the Churches undertake the relief of all the needy among their members. My feeling was that if the essential Christian mandate of charity were revived in this country on a determined and voluntary basis Christianity might hope to accomplish three things: to live up to its own fundamental principles; to convince the destitute that faith is not just all words; and to prevent government from acquiring a collectivistic grip upon the lives of its citizens. We are living in times when ministering to human need has become the primary function of the state, requiring the time and energy of a vast bureaucracy—a fact anomalous in Christian history. If such an attitude had been adopted during early centuries the faith enshrined in the New Testament would never have obtained the allegiance of mankind. Moreover the manner in which destitution is being dealt with visibly challenges the Christian conscience.

Perhaps the trend to collectivism which seems to be fostered by present social needs will go on until the state fashions a society which in character is the antithesis of individualism. Certainly the Churches are powerless to curb the state by merely banding together for the sake of opposition. But if their own communities are sincerely formed and aroused to full consciousness of their import the state will have nothing comparable to offer. And a society whose energies would be derived from a family of cooperating Christian communities seems so utterly feasible and so wonderfully beneficient that the Catholic, for his part, can only long for its realization.

[4] Cf. "The Christian Church an Imperial Power," in *Sermons on Subjects of the Day.*

# On the Importance of Being Unprincipled

## JOHN HERMAN RANDALL, JR.

### (*1938*)

Author of numerous books on philosophy, religion and the history of ideas, JOHN HERMAN RANDALL, JR., is Woodbridge Professor of Philosophy at Columbia University. At the time Mr. Randall submitted this article to THE AMERICAN SCHOLAR, he wrote: "The conclusions embodied in this paper are the results of long experience and observation and study and reflection, which have forced me from an original addiction to the drug of principle to my present wisdom; and I am prepared to support them by a metaphysics, a logic, a theory of knowledge and an axiology, all of which are so authoritative as to be positively stupefying."

S URELY there are more political principles in active circulation today than for many a long year. One has only to open the morning paper to be caught in a barrage of them. They volley from the Right, they thunder from the Left; and even peaceable citizens, anxious to go about their business undisturbed in the broad Center, have had to lay in a generous stock in self-defense. When we look across the seas we find the atmosphere from Moscow to Madrid so cluttered up with eternal principles in irrepressible conflict that it is hard to discern any merely human beings. Even the British Lion is going through contortions in the endeavor to put on the unaccustomed armor of principle. We are all in a fighting mood today. Mere name-calling, though satisfying for a time, soon exhausts our stock of epithets; and then, grasping a principle firmly in either hand, we sally forth bravely to the fray.

Side by side with this strife of principles has gone a marked decline in what we used to regard as political intelligence. At least the political intelligence that was once enough to adjust our differences seems no longer adequate now that we disagree so much more violently and, we are sure, so much more fundamentally. Indeed we have thought up elaborate if not wholly respectable philosophies to convince ourselves that the intelligence we are certain the other fellow doesn't possess has really no place in our political quarrels and that we have got to fight it out with him, the sooner the better. In the old days when one group of us disagreed with another about what ought to be done we managed in the end to effect some kind of working compromise with them. Today it has come to be the fashion, in Europe at least, to shoot them instead. Why waste time trying to argue? Direct action is so much simpler and more expeditious! America has so far proved a notable exception to this new fashion. Under a consummate compromiser, a leader quite gratifyingly unprincipled, it seems to be displaying more political intelligence than any other major country. And wonder of wonders, that intelligence has made its appearance even in the steel industry!

Now there seems to be a very close connection between this decline in political intelligence and the rise of the appeal to principles. In fact most of the world's political difficulties today focus in men's preference for laying down principles and fighting over them rather than engaging in the give and take of discussion and eventual compromise. So it seems worth while to emphasize the importance of being unprincipled in political action. In political action, mind you—for in themselves principles are fine things. In their proper place of course they are quite indispensable. But that place is not to regulate the group activities of men. Men can live together and succeed in accomplishing things cooperatively only if they have the patience and the intelligence to compromise. It would of course sound less unconventional if instead of speaking of unprincipled action I spoke of "the principle of compromise," meaning thereby the principle of acting without regard to one's principles in the interest of acting with other men. And should some dialectician object that I too am advocating a single principle of compromise against all others I could not demur. For what is at issue, against all the new political faiths and certainties flying about in our world, is very close to what I conceive to be the American way. It is commonly known, in fact, by a more familiar name. It is not the name but the political method I am concerned with; I want to make clear what is really involved in what Americans conceive political intelligence to be.

74

Now anybody who is at all capable of learning anything from experience knows that the only way to get along with people, the only way to do anything together with anybody else, is through compromise. You don't need exceptional brains to realize that; you need only to be married or to have a friend. Cooperation between human beings is possible only if they are willing to compromise; and politics, the art of cooperation, of group action, is at bottom nothing but the practical application of the method of compromise. Only two kinds of men can really afford the luxury of acting always on principle: those who never act at all, who live in a sort of social vacuum, who never try to get other men to do anything; and those who have so much power they don't have to regard the wishes or habits of other men but can just give commands. These are the two kinds of men who know nothing about the art of cooperation, the impotent and the omnipotent—the college professor and the Supreme Court Justice, for example.

But of course no one ever really does act on principle alone, with complete logical consistency. For no man is so omnipotent, not even a dictator, that he does not have to resort to all kinds of compromises with his followers to secure the power to shoot those who disagree with him. And no man is so impotent that he never tries to cooperate with his fellows at all. Should he begin to act that way we have a special institution made for him in which we lock him up—the insane asylum. Even college professors, who often have the brains to think up all kinds of principles and the irresponsibility to advocate them, are likely to forget all about them, blithely and intelligently, when it comes to college affairs where they have some power and some responsibility for action. They become good college politicians. And should they rise to be "administrators," deans and presidents, they are notoriously likely to become the most unprincipled of men. To be sure they are apt to retain the bad habit of talking about principles. This is a little unfortunate, for it makes them seem hypocrites. It is really only an occupational disease, shared by most intelligent administrators who happen also to be intellectuals.

In general it is only intellectuals, those who think but don't have to act, who may understand things clearly but never really try to do anything about it, that can afford to have political principles. It is preachers, teachers, writers and literary men who can get down to the roots of things and really understand them. They are free to be political radicals. The only action such men ever have to engage in is to protest, in the name of their principles, at what other men are doing. Principles are great things for protesting. That is in fact about the only kind of action you can really accomplish with them. Such intellectuals are never faced by the problem of getting something done, of cooperating with other men. It is significant that radical intellectuals, those who have the firmest and often the most penetrating principles, are notoriously incapable of cooperating with each other; and that groups which begin by protesting against things in general are apt to end in bitter protest against each other's principles. That is at bottom why practical men, trade unionists for example, are so suspicious of intellectuals; they have too many principles which seem quite irrelevant to the problems faced in daily living. They are so unable to compromise—they have never been forced by experience to learn how! They have so little political intelligence.

A friend recently returned to university teaching from Washington where he had been engaged in several of the many enterprises there going on. "Now that you're back again," a colleague remarked, "you can afford to be radical once more. You have no further responsibility for getting anything done." "Yes," the ex-scholar in politics replied, "now I can get back to criticizing. Why, there in Washington I was too busy trying to set up and get those important agencies going ever to ask whether what I was doing was really consistent with my principles."

The reason why principles are irrelevant to any political or cooperative action lies in the very nature of principles. Principles, as defined by Aristotle, who discovered them, are those ideas in terms of which something is understood. They are the set of concepts and axioms which make it intelligible to us. When once we see them then everything else falls into a consistent pattern; it all makes sense, we say. Just what ideas will make a thing intelligible to us, Aristotle pointed out, depends on our experience; and we have found out since Aristotle that the same things can be understood in a great variety of ways, depending on what our experience of them has been—that is, that a single thing can be made intelligible in terms of a number of differing sets of principles, as our experience of it has varied.

Principles are accordingly instruments not of action but of understanding. Their place is not in the practical art of politics but in the knowledge that is science. The history of our science has been the history of the change and modification of the principles that enabled men to understand as their experience has been changed and enlarged. Now science or organized understanding has built up a kind of cooperative experience shared by all scientists. Therefore there is a fair measure of agreement, at any one time, on the principles in terms of which the subject-matter of any one science is to be understood, though notoriously it is these principles of explanation—the way in which the observed facts are to be understood—that form just that aspect of science about which there is most difference of opinion. There is in fact no science in which there are not various "schools," so far as "theory" goes, various principles entertained; though on the experimental findings there is substantial agreement.

But what is a minor factor in science is the prevailing rule with practical problems. There are no two men who understand a given situation in precisely the same terms, for there are no two men whose previous experience has been precisely the same. Anyone who has ever served on a committee knows that if there are 15 members, 15 really informed men, 15 experts, there will be 15 different slants on the committee's problem, 15 different sets of principles through which it is approached. Especially is it true that there are no two economic groups, whose adjustment and cooperation furnish the major task of present-day politics, which see problems in the same light or which have had the same experience. How could one expect Kansas farmers, Detroit auto-workers, Lawrence mill-hands and New York bankers to understand anything in the same terms? Each group has found for itself different principles; and even should they all agree that they want the same thing—security for example—it would inevitably mean something different for each group.

In such political problems there is no possibility, that could be more than verbal, of agreement on principles, no possibility of really understanding the problem in the same way. You can never hope to get two groups, two parties to a controversy, to see it in the same light, to have it make sense in the same way, for such parties never look out on the world through the windows of the same experience. What you can hope to get agreement on is some specific measure, some concrete program of action. That program will not completely satisfy anybody or any group and each will understand it and criticize its shortcomings in the light of its own principles. But if it is a successful compromise it will give all of them enough of what they want to make them support it.

The way it actually works is familiar enough. A group, let us say a committee, meets to tackle a problem. Each member begins by laying down his principles, how it shapes up for him, his slant upon it. This takes a lot of talking. Then, if the members are good politicians and possess political intelligence, they stop talking about principles and get down to the real business of working out a compromise measure which will meet the major objections and do something to satisfy the most insistent demands. The result is finally laid before the groups concerned, who, not having been present at the previous discussion, repeat the same objections that were there dealt with. There is a new outburst of principles and criticism. If this keeps up too long the plan is modified to satisfy the loudest protests and then put into effect. In its actual operation it will have certain consequences that no one foresaw and there will be more roars. Something then has to be done to appease them; and so it goes on. This is the political method, the method of compromise at work. It is obviously a never-ending process. It is the only way of getting men to work together, the only way of really enlisting their cooperative interest and effort, no matter what principles they may severally have or think they have. We call this method "democratic" according to how early in the process the different groups concerned have a chance to talk, to make their wants known and to object. Under any scheme of organizing human action they will do so in the end, and if they are strong enough they will make their demands felt and have to be given something.

If the members of our committee are not good politicians, if they are intellectuals without much intelligence, they will naturally keep on talking about principles a lot longer. Each will try to convert the others to his own. That will probably result in a deadlock and nothing will be accomplished. If something simply has to be done there are two chief ways out. Either the talk will go on until everyone manages to understand each other's principles and there is general agreement that each is right from his own point of view. The committee will then be able to compromise on a practical plan. Or else somebody will propose a new principle, more general than those previously argued for—so general, in fact, that each can accept it with his own private interpretation. Then they will get down to business. In either case the committee will never begin to get anywhere till the principles have been removed from discussion by some means or other. The easiest way of dealing with such principled men is to agree immediately to all their principles. It is in fact the only way of getting a man with no political sense whatever to compromise. Usually, after everybody has grown tired of talking about principles

—or rather after everybody has grown tired of hearing the others talk about theirs, for no man ever wearies of expounding his own —and it is clear that the discussion is getting nowhere somebody will remark, "Now that we are all agreed in principle"—and then the real compromising begins.

This is the method of politics. Of course if you don't really want to get men to do anything, if you don't have to solve the problem, you can stick to your principles and refuse all traffic with compromise. This will normally be either because you don't want to act at all, because you are irresponsible and don't have to, and prefer to be free to criticize; or else because you want to fight. Now principles are perfectly grand for fighting. You can't really fight well without them; at least you can't fight very long without acquiring a set. For a principle is by definition a postulate, an assumption: it is an idea that cannot be proved by anything else or it would not be a principle. Nor can it be verified by an experience different from your own. Since you can't therefore prove it if it is questioned you can only support it by fighting for it. To call a thing a principle means that the case is closed and the argument over. You are going to act, no matter what the consequences; you are going to fight to the bitter end. It has become "a matter of principle" with you. Those words are uttered when faith burns bright and you are resolved to turn from words to deeds. And when you have made such a resolve of course you have to formulate principles to justify your intransigence.

In practical matters no particular problem is ever solved by an appeal to principles. To make such an appeal leads to a fight and is intended to lead to a fight. When the fight is over and the principle "established," or when both parties have finally got tired of fighting for their principles, the problem still remains to be solved, and to be solved by the political method of compromise and adjustment of conflicting interests and demands, in an atmosphere now made doubly difficult by the fighting psychology and the passionate devotion to principles that have been generated. The really big fights, like revolutions, usually give rise to a situation in which political intelligence, the ability to compromise, is quite destroyed. And the successful revolutionists normally start fighting among themselves over their principles until they are kicked aside by some politically-minded man who knows how to get men to compromise and work together on their problems. The most famous man of resolute principle in the world today is Leon Trotsky.

Of course there is often nothing to do but fight if political intelligence be so lacking that some entrenched group refuses to admit this political method, refuses to meet and discuss and bargain and compromise. Industrial corporations have been known to act thus unpolitically toward their employees. Then the political method becomes itself a principle that has to be fought for. In fact the only thing that fighting does seem to be able to win is the adoption of a certain method, and it can achieve permanent gains only if that method be the method of politics. Experience reveals that the only principle really worth fighting for is the extension of the principle of compromise to a new area in which it has not prevailed before—to the field of industrial relations, for example, or to those problems where the Supreme Court says political compromise mustn't be applied. It is significant that our politician president has seemed willing to compromise on anything and everything except the refusal to allow compromise or to permit the political method to be employed. He seems willing to fight to enable political intelligence to function.

It is the politician who is the expert in the method of compromise. He possesses the art of getting conflicting groups and interests together in some working balance of effective forces. He helps them think out some plan to which none will object too violently. Inevitably the measures that result from his efforts are likely to be inconsistent when judged by any principle. They are always faulty, in the sense that they never do everything that any group wants; they never do all that any clear principle would demand they should. They stand always in need of amending and re-amending. They are a register of the effective demands of those concerned, worked out by pressure groups pressing and lobbyists lobbying and a final slow process of compromise. Men with principles, especially if they are irresponsible and don't have to take part in the complex process, are always prone to exclaim: How much better if we had real leaders with clear principles, able to force through what is so obviously desirable! If some groups don't want what I see is needed they should be made to take it and like it.

Other nations today have found such Leaders. They have swept away the politicians and substituted coercion for compromise. To be sure, even such leaders have to be politically minded and have to compromise with any really insistent demand. But most Americans would agree that there is a genuine difference. These Leaders are pretty ruthless about coercing minority groups, or larger groups that are weak and get the worst of the official adjustment of conflicting interests. Politicians and the method of politics have their virtues in comparison with Dictators and Storm Troops and the Gestapo. Perhaps the most important function of politicians is to act as a buffer in our group conflicts. They soften bitter passions and moderate the storms that without them might so easily lead to the violent coercion of weaker groups. Politicians may on occasion be less than wholly honest and veracious but they don't shoot us—and what is still more important, they keep us from shooting each other. They give us enough of what we demand to keep our principles slightly below the boiling point. With politicians in charge the way, we know, is always open to compromise. The danger begins when anything is definitely removed from politics and made a matter of principle, for then the shooting is likely to begin.

Politicians can perform their function of effecting compromises and softening clashes only if they have no principles of their own. Their most engaging quality, in fact, is that they are so largely unprincipled themselves and can therefore get down to business so easily. At least they keep their principles for their speeches and rarely let them interfere with their work. And the whole political process can go on only if men are willing to grant that every group knows its own problems and its own needs better than anyone else and is therefore entitled to get as much of what it wants as it can. Once get the idea that you know better than other men what is really good for them, once get faith in some principle which will tell you just what the nation must do to be saved and just what every man ought to be working for, and you will have little stomach for the political method. What you see clearly as the one thing needful will seem so important that you will have no patience with those who see incorrectly. If you have the virus of political principles you will always be losing your patience with the fools or the rascals who see something else. Impatience is the characteristic mark of the over-principled. They cannot wait to persuade or educate—or learn. They have to act right away, on principle. They have to get other people to act; they have to force them to act. Any means and any method will be justified by your principle: that is where single-minded devotion to political principle always ends up. Such a man will naturally hate the very thought of compromise; he will much prefer to shoot or even to get shot. Europe is full of just such men of principle today; and with so many principles and such intense faith in them it will be very lucky to get off without fanatical religious wars on a grand scale. It has very little political intelligence left: it has lost the ability to compromise.

In America we have not reached such a desperate state as yet. We do not take up arms after an election because our side has lost or won. It seems that not even the Liberty League believed in its principles. The nearest approach to such intensity of faith is probably to be found in some of our Communist friends. But I have never known a Communist in this country who seemed really capable of shooting; and if they persist in their present policy of a united front (that is of politic compromise in action) they are bound sooner or later to lose their principles—though it is too much to expect that they will ever stop talking about them.

What we Americans are prone to call our "principles"—such things as freedom, security, equality, democracy and the like— are really not so much ideals to be debated and fought over as problems to be worked out by political methods in particular instances. Absolute freedom and absolute security are not given to mortal man. Human freedom and human security are specific problems to be dealt with in specific cases. They can be solved only if they are made questions of fact, of inquiry about the means of securing them, of getting compromises not too unsatisfactory to those concerned. They can be solved only if the conditions are established that will transform conflict and debate into inquiry into a problem: only, that is, if the political method of compromise is enabled to function. Any solution of our social and industrial difficulties will therefore depend on our becoming as a people more politically minded, on our developing more political intelligence. We need more actual experience in compromising on measures for dealing with particular problems under particular conditions; we must become less rather than more content to take refuge in general principles, to sit back, criticize, protest and fight.

There is great hope for the spread of such political-mindedness in the countless boards and committees of the agencies set up by the present administration. The A.A.A. was peculiarly successful in this political education but even the N.R.A. played its part and the training it gave seems to have had a good deal to do with the political intelligence recently displayed by both the C.I.O. and employers. The spread of labor organization, especially along industrial lines, in which countless locals and boards really face the problems of their industry as a whole, cannot but be a factor in generating further political intelligence. Only with such political-mindedness can America hope to escape the devastating effects of the essentially unpolitical class struggle that has afflicted Europe. That is the very antithesis of the method of politics, the method of compromise and political intelligence: it is the method of fighting for principles and of ruthless coercion for the vanquished. And lest some troubled soul rise at this point to ask whether America really can escape the fate of Spain or Germany let me anticipate his query by insisting that I do not know and that I know that he does not know, nor does anyone else. But I do know that to act on the principle that America cannot escape is the surest way to destroy political intelligence. There will doubtless be many particular fights to establish the conditions of political compromise; there will be a general fight only if both sides abandon politics for principles.

What I have been calling "political intelligence" and "the method of compromise" is usually called "democracy." I have preferred not to use that term, for democracy is usually taken as an ideal, a goal, a principle—that is, as something quite meaningless and irrelevant to political problems. I have been considering what is implied in democracy taken concretely as a method, a method of dealing with particular problems by the active participation of as many as possible of those concerned and there hammering out a working solution to be revised in the light of further experience. The democratic method does not consist in sending men to Washington with a majority to install some scheme which will usher in the millennium. That is not the democratic method at all; that is the method of Hitler, all except the millennium.

In our struggling world the problems are largely set for us—set by what different groups of men want and by the opportunities and the limitations of the natural and technical materials we have to work with. We possess the technical skill to give men what they want in abundance. We already possess a surprising amount of economic intelligence: we know how to go far in relieving our economic insecurity. The great problem is how to get men to apply this skill and intelligence, how to get them to agree to use the intelligence now available in our society. Our pressing need is for political intelligence. The means which Americans have the chance to employ is the method of democracy—the method of politics, of compromise on particular measures, in disregard of our principles, however dear.

# The Century of the Child

## GEORGE BOAS

## ( *1938* )

Twenty-two years ago, GEORGE BOAS noted and deplored the childlike qualities that characterized twentieth-century man—his lack of reason, his extremism, his passion for "cuteness." The passing of time does not seem to have invalidated Mr. Boas' interpretation or to have matured his subject.

Mr. Boas has recently retired as a professor of philosophy at Johns Hopkins University.

WHEN Ellen Key prophesied that the 20th century would be the century of the child she little knew in what sense her prophecy would be true. She thought it would be the epoch when children would be given their rights at last, be studied as true individuals having interests different from those of adults and satisfied as such. But she did not realize that the Child would become not only the focus of all our thought but also the model for our behavior. She foresaw a benevolent paternalism in which all the sweetness and innocence of childhood would bloom; what eventuated has been on the contrary a maleficent paidocracy in which with the usual flattery of the governed, adults have imitated their real rulers not only mentally but in some cases physically.

Those of us who have children have no illusions about their sweetness and innocence. Children are much less on the side of the angels than on that of the devils; their souls are dark and treacherous; illusion is their realm and, born of lust, their god is appetite. But lest I succumb to rhetoric let us list the most prominent characteristics of children and see whether or not we have a composite photograph of contemporary man.

Children, lacking reason, rely on phantasy and like the savage have no power of grasping facts for what they are. Shadows are not the interception of light but ghosts, spectres, portents, things

84

to fear and frighten others with. Flowers have faces; trees sigh, dance, shiver and laugh; clouds are dragons, ships, beasts; every possibility of committing the pathetic fallacy is actualized. They are typical Neo-Platonists, believing that everything is something else. They are good Wordsworthians in their common detestation of Peter Bell: the child does not exist who would look at a primrose and see it only as a primrose. The flower in the crannied wall when pulled out of its cranny—and what child would dream of not pulling it out?—inevitably turns into God and Man. Nothing is simply what it is—all must be something else.

The process of growing up is precisely the opposite of this. The rational man knows that primroses are primroses and when he meets one on the river's brim enjoys its visual beauty, may mutter *"Primula vulgaris"* as a concession to pedantry, and passes on. Clouds, mountains, trees, rivers are something to enjoy the sight of and utilize, not something to be edified by. The Neo-Platonic—or the Wordsworthian—way to him is simply confusion and he finds no sense in confusion. If everything is something else sooner or later one gets back to where one started from. For if flowers in the crannied wall have to be God and Man, what in the world are God and Man to be? Such people, like Stevenson when he wrote his *Child's Garden of Verses,* are made happy as kings by sheer multiplicity but unless there is an actually infinite number of things they are going to give out sooner or later and the process of confusion will have to end. The man of reason knows this and therefore is willing to admit that things are themselves and nothing more.

But the modern man is not a man of reason. Neo-Platonism has won out and we are all childlike and innocent. This is seen most clearly in our political innovations. When historians come to write the story of our times they will be wrong unless they point out as its most remarkable characteristic its revulsion against democracy. Democracy is a regime which to be successful demands the greatest intellectual maturity, for not only is it based upon reasoning but upon the willingness to let others reason. Parliaments, that is—and I am equating the parliamentary system with democracy—exist not only to represent the electorate but to discuss and debate issues whose conclusions are not self-evident. But there is no debate where there is only one side and in order to have more than one side there has to be freedom of discussion, which in principle admits that the other fellow may be right and you wrong. Such a principle has no charm for a child. A child always knows that he, his gang, his street, his school, his church, his city, his state, his country, whatever can be identified with him, are right and there's no sense in denying it. If you do deny it you're crazy and he's willing to fight you to prove that you're crazy, mental weakness being characteristically confused with physical. When the question is not one of appetite he is willing to go beyond the limits of his own experience, but only to appeal to what Dad says, or all the fellers or my teacher. Thus if the question concerns the relative merits of Little Orphan Annie or Buck Rogers his say-so is enough; but if it's a question of who's going to get the pennant then his say-so requires backing—but the backing is always someone else's say-so.

Every substitute for democracy is similar; each is anti-intellectualistic. Away with parliaments, for they are merely debating societies. Away with discussion; we want action. Down with professors, we want practical guys who get things done. A Duce, a Fuehrer, a leader—the head of the gang, to whom unquestioning loyalty is due and by whom it is exacted—such is our ideal. If you have doubts they are answered not by argument but by mob violence—the logic of persuasion (according to which only castor oil or tar and feathers have value as evidence) having taken the place of the logic of conviction.

The logic of persuasion is the logic of the brute, and the child is of course as close to the animal as any human being other than an idiot can get. The brute is not a Neo-Platonist, so far as I know, but the child is both an animal and a Neo-Platonist. There is one trait of the infra-human world which we all admire—its dumbness; this is its one trait which children have not taken over. The ruthless cruelty of animals, self-centered in the solitary beasts, herd-centered in the gregarious, this is the characteristic which children most perfectly exemplify. They will go to any lengths to torture others whom they suspect of being weaker than they. The schoolboy who is a bully is acting, in his sphere, exactly like the cat who tortures a mouse before killing it. There is doubtless some deep biological necessity for both but we are not discussing causes. The child who cannot bully another physically, being too ineffectual in his muscles, does it mentally, by ridicule, slander, or sophistry. But it is peculiarly interesting that the victims of bullies are usually the most valuable members of society: those who are imaginative, inventive, artistically talented, intellectually gifted. They are nuts, in other words, and no child likes a nut. All of us can remember the agony of having been made to wear a cap or a suit or a tie which made us a little different from the other fellows; all of us can remember the punishment meted out to the boys who were obedient or who got good marks or who were good in drawing or music. Such children instead of exciting the admiration of their fellows invariably excited their contempt, a contempt which was expressed in the usual forms of cruelty.

After a century in which humane impulses were cultivated, in which altruism was lauded to the skies, in which the highest ambition of young people was "social service" of some sort or other, we come to a time when humanitarianism is despised as the philosophy of the milksop. The very term "liberal," which used to be a term of praise, is now one of derision. One must be an extremist, whether red or white makes very little difference, but to be able to give each man his due, admitting the diversity of human nature, this is the great modern vice. Extremism is typical of the child-mind, which believes in the universal applicability of the law of the excluded middle. To exclude the middle facilitates brutality for it divides the world at once into good and bad, i.e. my kind and the other kind, and nothing is too bad for the other kind. Hence we find political, social and racial minorities treated with a cruelty which would not have been tolerated in the 19th century when statesmen found the preaching of altruism, not national egoism, the best means of arousing public sympathy. I do not say that nations in the 19th century were really more altruistic than they are today; I merely say that altruism was at that time an effecive means of propaganda. It would be laughable today.

A Neo-Platonic brute when he has to excuse his behavior does it, not by saying that his victims are weak and therefore appointed by destiny to be his victims but by saying that they are evil. This is the technique of the literary "realist" who maintains that only discreditable motives are true ones. The wave of debunking that has washed up into our libraries so many absurd biographies, so much psychoanalytic fiction, so many "economic interpretations" of acts not economic in their nature, is symptomatic of this trend. One need not have many illusions about the human race to realize that some people—perhaps only enough to have saved Sodom and Gomorrah—are really brave when they seem brave, really honest when they seem honest, really faithful when they seem faithful. One can, if one is mature, recognize the existence of hypocrisy, indeed of insanity, without maintaining that all men are hypocrites or crazy. One can, in other words, recognize the unusual, the "unnatural" if one likes the term, the abnormal, without immediately concluding that it is the standard from which all things deviate. A simple mind is made uneasy by deviation; it is helpless when confronted with statistics and insists that "beneath the surface" of deviating individuals there must be some fixed and immutable reality by which the deviations can be tested. Thus one finds the argument that, for instance, since the line between sanity and insanity is hard to draw it doesn't exist. (So is the line between hot and cold, moist and dry, but any fool knows when to pull up the blanket or put on a raincoat.) When one goes only so far as this one is simple-minded; one becomes childish when one insists that the worse end of a scale is necessarily the real end. There are cases, to be sure, where goodness is an illusion but there is no universal law from which we can deduce the unique reality of evil. A child has a kind of cacotropism which not only turns him automatically to the bad but which on that very account leads him to believe that only evil is real. That is why he sneers at every act whose evil motive is not apparent.

That attitude is explicable enough in childhood. The process of education is a refinement upon nature made by human nature. It substitutes a way of living which has been developed with difficulty and has been imposed upon the animal regimen into which we relapse when the restraints of civilization are loosened. The original condition of man was apparently found unsatisfactory some thousands of years ago but since experience is not inherited every child has to begin the ascent afresh. He has no way of knowing that the process is worth while and sometimes by inertia, sometimes by open rebellion, tries to avoid it. To him brutishness is innate—it is the condition which if he could talk he would say is "natural." He does not see that our problem is to thicken the coat of civilization, not to remove it. But it is an error which is pardonable in his case.

It is not pardonable in adults. They are not permitted to reason that because the muscles exist to move our bones man is therefore essentially a skeleton. They ought to be able to see things in their proper relation to one another, however destructive that may prove to neat system-building. It ought to be automatic with an adult to recognize a fact when he sees it; in reality the facts that hardened realists say they see are usually dreadful fictions. Thus all the shadows of the unconscious, the sight of which is held to be especially revelatory of human motives, can be seen only through the glasses of theory—yet a thinker who remains on the conscious level of experience is said to have no eye for facts. He is being condemned, however, not by the falsity of his findings but by his infidelity to metaphor. Were his accusers able to speak in literal language not even they would think themselves profound. It sounds superficial to state that when a person says whatever comes into his head he is likely to make some remarks usually considered indecent; it sounds profound to say that free association releases the verbal inhibitions of the Censor. Who could resist the glamor of such phrases as "the depths of the mind," "the roots of consciousness," "the source of human motives"?

The child, whose education is a farewell to savagery, falls easily into resentment and fear. His appetites are checked by fear of consequences: if he does this he will get sick; if he does that he will break his Mother's heart; if he does the other he will disgrace the family name. He begins to dwell upon the terrors that surround our unhappy race and takes a special delight in ghosts, witches and hobgoblins. His heroes are great athletes or great criminals. He talks of gangsters, murderers, crooks. His imagination moves in a kind of Gothic darkness.

When we read the *Castle of Otranto* today we think of *Northanger Abbey* and laugh. We pity the poor imbeciles of the 18th century who for all their wit and reason could find recreation in such nonsense. Yet we too have our Gothic novels, only in ours the ruined castle is the Southern plantation and the ghost is the pervert—we find our horror in human ruins; the 18th century found its in architectural. But the fascination of decay is as strong for us as it was for our forefathers nor is it any the less childish. One has only to think of *Tobacco Road, Sanctuary,* most of *Eyeless in Gaza,* to wonder how an age which delights in such things can have the stamina to perfect the physical sciences. The achievement of the authors of these books has been in part to have discovered a human degeneration which needed articulation, in part to have dished it up as fiction so that we may actually enjoy it without any feeling of responsibility for changing it. A more heroic age would be interested in lessening human misery; a childish age takes horror for normal, dwells upon it as a spectacle interesting in its own right. This appetite is, I suppose, the same kind of coprophilia which babies are supposed to have. The youth turns from the colon to the genitalia.

A child, however, does not want to stay a child; he usually wants to grow up. We who have grown up so hanker after childhood that we openly deny our years. Has there ever been a period when adults so brazenly have pretended to be young? No matter what their age, our women dress and act like girls, our men like undergraduates. The greatest compliment you can pay a person is to remark upon his youthful appearance. Everything is done to conceal the fact that human life lasts longer than 25 years. We have not only prolonged our infancy but what we foolishly imagine to be the tastes of infancy. Hence the passion for "cuteness." We have cute little houses with peaked roofs and picket fences, with cute little casement windows and diamond shaped panes; we have cute little gardens with earthenware gnomes and elves fishing in cute little fishponds; we have cute little table decorations, glass animals and imitation flowers; cute little movie stars and animated cartoons; cute little pets—Scotties and wire-haired terriers and Pekinese; cute little apartments with cute little kitchenettes and a cute little terrarium on the window-sill; it's all just too cute for words. No real child ever wanted to be cute; no adult that wanted to be a child ever failed to. Cuteness has the charm of make-believe; children make believe because they cannot have reality—adults because they are afraid to have it.

This passion for cuteness is stimulated by our schools. Thanks to the pedagogues of those two nations which have given us fascism and national socialism the rights of immaturity and free expression have been given full license. There can be no question but that progressive education has freed the elementary and secondary schools of much of the cruel discipline and formalism of the olden days. No one is going to deny that making school interesting was a blessing and that the elimination of subjects whose only recommendation was their difficulty needs no excuse. It is also granted that adjusting education to individual aptitude was a necessary reform in a society where education is compulsory. At the same time it had two great weaknesses. Like the elective system its administration requires psychological knowledge which few teachers possess and frequently it mistakes laziness for inaptitude. As its practitioners are now beginning to realize, if it is to work some way must be found to instil self-discipline to take the place of that formerly administered by the teachers. That unfortunately has not been done in the past, with the result that children educated to believe their desires and personalities are sacred continue to demand of life that same consideration which their teachers are accustomed to give them. When they grow up those children retain their childish ideals for the very reason that they have never heard of any others. If, when they emerge into a world which is not so cute as they have been taught to expect, they consider active work futile, why wonder that they continue the tradition of the kindergarten? Just as they go pottering round a golf course hitting a ball, so they hang up their stockings on Christmas Eve until the day of their death, expecting Santa Claus to come down the chimney and bring them what every grown man knows they can only earn for themselves.

Confusion, brutality, pessimism, fear, all translated into terms of cuteness—these are the marks of modern man. What wonder that we are unhappy and incapable of self-government. In what were formerly two great nations, Italy and Germany, Youth holds the reins and, as a German recently told me, a man of 40 is an old man. Why this general arrested development has overtaken us I have no means of knowing; that it has overtaken us is proved daily by the papers, the movies, the museums, by all the effluences of what inner life we have. It is not sufficient to grumble about it; it is the decided duty of every teacher to act upon his knowledge that it is so and to correct it. And by "teacher" I do not mean merely those who hold positions in schools.

# The Challenge of Our Times

## HAROLD J. LASKI

### *(1939)*

Tyranny is the challenge to which HAROLD J. LASKI here refers. At a time when the vested interests of such self-styled
dictators as Hitler, Mussolini and Franco were threatening
the privileges and opportunities of free men, Mr. Laski ad-
monished his readers to try to understand why the challenge
arose. Never satisfied to be an armchair theorist on economics
and political affairs, Mr. Laski was teaching at London University when he died in 1950.

NOT even the years before the War of 1914 have imposed so
tense a strain upon men's minds as the period since the advent of Hitler to power. The conventions upon which our civilization has been built are challenged at their foundation. The burden of suffering has become so wide and deep that we everywhere
encounter the horror of becoming accustomed to horror as part of
our normal way of life. We have accustomed ourselves to assume
that conflict is inevitable. We embark upon the politics of power
with hardly a thought of the way in which habituation transforms
means into ends.

The danger of our time is, above all, a failure to see it in its
proper perspective. We have given new names to old things and
unless we are careful we run the risk of forgetting the claims of
reason in our bewilderment at the re-emergence of the old in new
forms. For, after all, what we are confronted with is tyranny; and
the habits of the tyrant are as old as history itself. Our business,
when tyranny challenges us, is not to beat our breasts and bewail
our fate but rather to understand why the challenge has come. At
bottom there is nothing unexpected in its onset. A large part of the
19th century is a warning of its arrival; our error is to have neglected the warning. And the clue to the process in which we are

involved is in our hands. The issue is whether, realizing this, we have the courage to follow it to its appointed end.

The clue, I say, is in our hands. The outstanding feature of our time is insecurity. Epochs of this character—witness the Reformation and the French Revolution—have always been unfavorable to reason and tolerance; they have therefore been epochs in which dictatorship has its opportunity. And men always feel insecure when their privileges are challenged. They are not prepared to accept the invasion of their wonted routines. They seek to make their private claims universal rights; and those who provide them with the means of enforcing their claims are regarded as their saviors. The limits of men's faith in a reason which disturbs their established expectations are more narrow than we care to admit. Yet such disturbance always comes in an age of economic contraction. Whenever, historically, the economic forces of society cannot contain themselves within the political forms—as, once more, in the Reformation and the French Revolution—we have moved into an epoch of war and revolution. And these have always led to an adjustment of the proportion, the discovery of a new social equilibrium which makes possible the renewal of an epoch of economic expansion. In such an epoch, reason and tolerance resume their empire because we are again able to satisfy the established expectations of men.

Political democracy was successful in the 19th century because it coincided with an age of immense economic expansion. Roughly its effect was to bring the middle class to power; and the reign of the middle class was accepted because the wealth that its rule made accessible permitted a wide extension of material benefits to the masses. But the middle class won its victory only by alliance with the working class. The price of its victory—a price which in Great Britain it took over a century to exact—was political democracy based upon universal suffrage. The middle class paid that price without undue alarm so long as political democracy did not challenge its economic and social privilege. And this the political democracy did not do so long as economic well-being was continuously extended. As soon as the extension ceased, however, the masses inevitably used the political power conferred upon them to reopen the issues of privilege concealed from view in the heyday of expansion. Exactly as in the three centuries after the Reformation the middle class, in its effort to secure a form of state suited to its needs, had met (and overthrown) the landed aristocracy; so, in our own day, the masses challenge the middle class and seek, not the overthrow of political democracy but its extension to those economic and social fields from which its consequences had been excluded after the victory of the middle class had been won. And exactly as the feudal aristocracy thought the claims of the middle class (and therefore of political democracy) inadmissible, so in our own day the middle class regards as inadmissible the claims of the masses to the extension of the democratic idea. It prefers rather to fight for its privileges than to give way, exactly as its predecessor in power preferred to fight. Its enthusiasm for democracy as a form of government wanes as the consequences of democracy make imperative a sharing of privileges with those who have previously been excluded from them. On every hand it is evident that this is the root of the matter. It is apparent in the attitude of business men to social equipment. They welcome it when their economic position is undisturbed by its cost; they fear and resist it whenever it threatens their power to dominate the state. Their attitude is apparent in the different reception which they accorded the dictatorship in the Soviet Union and the dictatorships of Mussolini and Hitler. The one, from the outset, was treated with passionate indignation; it altered fundamental rights of property for the benefit of the masses. The others were treated, at their inception at least, with tolerance if not with favor. For, far from disturbing the rights of property, they seemed to make them more secure by striking at the trade unions, the cooperative movement and the socialist parties—the weapons developed by the working class in the 19th century to push forward the frontiers of democracy into those spheres of economic and social life from which it had previously been excluded. It seems that the forms of private property, as these have been evolved in a society dominated by middle-class business men, must not be touched by the normal operations of political democracy. Any effort to change them is regarded as something contrary to the inherent structure of the universe. And if a change in them is part of the immanent logic of democracy, then business men will cooperate in the destruction of democracy as ardently as they cooperated in the destruction of feudalism in the centuries between the Reformation and the French Revolution.

All those who speculated seriously about politics at the end of the 18th and the beginning of the 19th centuries knew well what, at bottom, we have got to make up our minds to accept—that equality is of the inner essence of democracy, and that the alternative to equality is the ability in any society to make continuous concessions of material well-being to the masses. This choice was concealed from most Americans until 1932 because the infinite resources of the United States enabled those concessions (above all in comparison with Europe) to be made. As soon as depression made their continuance a threat to the economic privileges of business men, widespread doubt emerged as to the validity of the democratic principle. It is reasonable that this should be even more true of Europe, where opportunity on the American scale has never been known and where social equality has never advanced to the point where, as in the United States, it had served to conceal many of the graver consequences of economic inequality.

The flaw in the 19th-century system, Professor Albert Murray has said, was the principle of national sovereignty. There is a sense in which that is a vital truth. But it is even more important to emphasize that the principle of national sovereignty was, in its turn, a necessary consequence of the class structure of our imperfectly democratic society. For the maldistribution of income in a society dependent on the profit-making motive demanded, in the long run, a system of protective tariffs at home and of imperialism abroad. This meant that war, as a weapon of national policy, was rooted in the economic system by which we lived. And the decline in the power of that economic system to expand intensified both the height of tariffs and the urgency of imperialist adventure. Given the technological background, the strain which the cost of preparation for war imposed upon national economic systems has at each stage of its advance made less possible the conferment of those material concessions which, as I have said, the logic of democracy requires. This, in its turn, has two effects. By sharpening social conflict within, it weakens the faith of the middle class in the implications of democratic government; while by intensifying national rivalries, it increases the chances of war and thus compels the governments of states to organize against the advent of armed conflict. And the price of that organization has everywhere been a replacement of solutions of consent by solutions of coercion. Neither in the national or in the international sphere is that replacement compatible with democracy.

The validity of this analysis can, I suggest, be corroborated on every hand—particularly by the recent history of Great Britain. Everything—the abandonment of free trade, the acceptance of the principle of universal military service, the development of a situation in which one-eighth of the total national income (as compared with about one-fortieth before the War of 1914) is devoted to defense preparations, the necessity for organizing an entire society for civilian defense against attack from the air—points to the outline of a society utterly different in its basic pattern from anything the 19th century could have conceived, still less adjudged desirable. A democratic society involves government by discussion and therefore free play for discussion. But the experience even of a pre-war period like that in Great Britain (the classic Rome of free speech) during the past few months reveals a limitation of free discussion, less by outright than by obscure and often obscurantist techniques of control. And these were avowedly only the precursor of a rigorous censorship in wartime. The liberal society of the epoch before 1914 is unthinkable in our age.

From our experience since the War there emerges the simple lesson that the survival of political democracy depends upon substantial agreement between different classes about the objects to which the system of government is to be devoted. When the society is expanding economically there is little difficulty about this agreement. But there is the gravest difficulty in securing it once the society is economically contracting over any considerable space of time. The society then confronts a dilemma: the price of the reforms demanded by the underprivileged is more than the privileged are willing to pay; whereas the methods urged by the privileged as the price of recovery—as Dr. Brüning learned during his period as German Chancellor—drive the underprivileged into a frenzy of discontent with the fruits of political democracy. It is characteristic of such a period of contraction that the cleavage between political parties grows wider and more intense. Seen from this angle the virtual disappearance of the Liberal Party in Great Britain and the breakdown of the Popular Front in France are portents of great importance. It is significant also that the opposition to the New Deal in the United States is not confined to Republicans but so permeates the ranks of the Democratic party as to make the main lines of difference in political outlook those of income rather than of party alignment. In a word, the crisis of capitalist democracy has fulfilled the prophecy made by de Tocqueville after the *annus mirabilis* of 1848. It has brought into the foreground of discussion the central problem of the ownership of the means of production. It has made the central debate of our time the question whether this ownership can be left in private hands without disaster.

Nothing, I think, is gained by saying that this is an issue the people should decide. In a democracy, at least, they can choose their rulers, and the will of the majority will prevail in so far as those rulers, when chosen, carry out their mandate. This, clearly, is excessive simplification. It assumes that the people are, as a whole, interested equally in the result of the political process in a democracy; since the society is in fact unequal this is, of course, not true. It assumes, further, that men are interested in the forms of government for their own sake whereas men are interested in them for what they do rather than for what they are. An American has only to read the evidence given before Senator La Follette's committee on civil liberties to realize that this is the case. When employers engage private armies, armed with most of the lethal weapons of modern warfare, to fight against the principle of unionization, it is at least unlikely that they will easily accept a complete transformation in the basic principles of social organization. Our society is not a unity in which men have an equal and common interest. It is a system of class interests in which, when there is an economic crisis, the well-being of the privileged is purchased and maintained at the expense of the underprivileged. That is the necessary consequence from the capitalist system. The marriage of that system to political democracy is, therefore, a contradiction in terms at the point where the economic system ceases to expand. For the logic of capitalism denies the purpose of democracy. It demands of the underprivileged the subordination of needs, grimly felt, to the requirement of profit. By the use of their voting power the underprivileged naturally seek to prevent this subordination. The privileged then become aware that the enemy is the democratic principle which threatens the economic and social principles whereby they maintain their position. They could, of course, abdicate by cooperating in their own erosion. But history, so far, has given us no example of a class that has preferred abdication to conflict.

That, indeed, is natural enough unless we assume that reason has a complete empire over men's minds. It would be a betrayal of reason itself to make such an assumption. Our ideas are largely the outcome of our interests; no task is more difficult or more complicated than that of transcending them. The history of 300 years has taught the middle class to identify its needs with the common good. It is not likely, except in terms of geological time, to deny that identification. For its own ends it has made the law what it is. Those ends color the whole of the administrative process, the educational system, the instruments of propaganda, even the

97

teaching of the churches. The true faith of our society is, the Soviet Union apart, the religion of private property. Every change in the most minute of its dogmas—witness the abolition of child labor—has been stoutly resisted, and usually resisted with a complete sincerity that the dogma was an essential element of social well-being. The middle class is just as accustomed to rule as its predecessor, the feudal aristocracy. It would regard its displacement from privilege as a no less momentous disaster to society. For what I describe as "privilege" it regards as "right." An alternative method for the regulation of ownership seems to it morally wrong and economically mistaken. Because it lives differently it thinks differently from those whom its economic power enables it to control. In a period of crisis, like our own, it thinks so differently that it is unable to speak the same language. Its notions of right and wrong, good and bad, wise and unwise, have an utterly dissimilar content. To give way to the will of a majority would seem to the members of the middle class equivalent to the acceptance of social ruin.

It may be said that this is an unfair view to take of men who hate the dictatorship of Mussolini or of Hitler as sincerely as any of the underprivileged. Now that Mr. Chamberlain, for example, is driven to repel German aggression by force he is said to be fighting for the principle of democracy against the principle of dictatorship. That is, I suggest, an excessive simplification. Mr. Chamberlain does not concern himself with the methods of government in Germany. He has constantly manifested his goodwill to Hitler. What he is fighting is aggression; and he would fight it if its objectives were pursued by the United States no less than when they are pursued by Hitler. The democracy Mr. Chamberlain defends is the capitalist democracy of Great Britain. And it is at least reasonable to argue that in his estimate of its interests, the capitalism is fully as important as the democracy. It is notable that men of his outlook thought quite differently of the Soviet dictatorship and the dictatorships of Germany and Italy until the interests of the latter clashed with those of Great Britain. Chamberlain showed no special interest in the preservation of Spanish democracy. He sacrificed the democracy of Czechoslovakia to Hitler almost with the air of one who had won a triumphant victory. Accident rather than design makes a Conservative Prime Minister in Great Britain (whether Mr. Chamberlain or another) the embodiment of the democratic principle. I recognize it is to the interest of the democratic principle that a fascist dictator should be defeated. But I am arguing, first, that the victory of Mr. Chamberlain in such a conflict, being the victory of both capitalism and democracy, would leave unresolved the problem of their future relationship; and, second, that the meaning of that victory can only be assessed as the constitutive principle of the society which emerges from the conflict is determined. On any showing a capitalist democracy is, I think, a better society than a fascist dictatorship; insofar the defeat of the latter would be definite social gain. But capitalist democracies all over the world, not least in the United States, leave uncertain the future of the political form of government. Their victory in the kind of conflict now under way would not insure the survival of the principle of democratic government if there were an internal effort to transform the economic basis of society from the private to the public ownership of the means of production. Nothing in Mr. Chamberlain's record indicates that his enthusiasm for the form of state is so much greater than his zeal for the content enshrined therein that he will insist on respecting the will of the majority in all cases.

There are those, of whom Professor C. M. McIlwain is a distinguished example, who trace the crisis of our time to the breakdown of the rule of law. "The present danger," he has written, "is despotism. It must be prevented, and by legal limitations on government . . . We must preserve and strengthen those bounds beyond which no free government ought ever to go, and make them limits beyond which no government whatever can ever legally go. We must make *ultra vires* all exorbitant acts of government." [1] Few people will disagree with this desire. But Professor McIlwain has not explained why the rule of law, whether in domestic or in international affairs, has broken down. He has not explained how we are to place legal limitations on government. He has not defined those "limits beyond which no government whatever can ever legally go." He has not given us a list of those "exorbitant acts of government" which are to be made *ultra vires* or of the methods by which this end can be achieved.

He has not done so because he refuses to analyze the causes behind the political phenomena he describes. At the back of his mind is the notion of a fundamental law conditioning the validity of all particular acts of law for which a government makes itself responsible. But in any society such a fundamental law is no more than conceptual unless the members of the society agree to regard

[1] McIlwain, C. H., *Constitutionalism and the Changing World*, Macmillan Co., New York (and Cambridge University Press), 1939.

it as fundamental and, thereby, willingly to accept the imposition of its content upon themselves. The outstanding characteristic of our time is the absence of such an agreement. I have argued here that it is absent because what the middle class regards as fundamental does not so appear to those excluded from the privileges which the middle class enjoys by virtue of its ability to maintain the rules that secure to it those privileges. And the only way to win that agreement is to attain the conditions under which there is a renewal of economic expansion. Germany and Italy do not violate international law for the sake of violating it. They do so because, in an age of economic contraction, they cannot reach the ends they desire within the rules sanctioned by the past traditions of international law. So, similarly, in the municipal sphere. A prosperous Germany would not violate most of the rules we have come to regard as essential to civilized living. But the new Germany is compelled to break them because, granted the ends its rulers desire, the rules are incompatible with their purposes. Until Mr. McIlwain and those who think with him realize that, historically, means and ends cannot be divorced from one another, they will be building a juristic theory of the state without root in the actual conditions we confront.

The same difficulty applies to theories like those of Mr. Walter Lippmann who seeks, in his *Good Society*, a state which is to act as the neutral arbiter between conflicting interests. For the state (which in everyday life means its government) is by nature incapable of neutrality unless the interest of its members in the result of its processes is equal. But since, in a capitalist democracy, that interest is, by definition, unequal, the state-power is necessarily biased in its incidence. The impact of that bias is obscured in an age of economic expansion. In such a period men are largely agreed about fundamentals because the general position of all is usually one of continuous improvement. But so soon as contraction supervenes, agreement halts because the result of policy bears so differently upon various classes in society. This becomes evident when major social reforms are embarked on in any period of contraction. If such reforms are reflected in the scheme of taxation, men with privileges to lose become fearful of their position and withdraw their confidence from the proposals of the government. The attitude of Wall Street to the New Deal is one instance of such a withdrawal; that of General Franco and his supporters toward the Spanish Republic is another. The formula of majority rule will not be respected by any class in society if it believes those interests which it regards as fundamental to be threatened, and if it considers itself in a position to fight for them with the prospect of success.

I am not arguing about the rights or wrongs, the wisdom or the unwisdom, of this outlook. I am arguing only that the constitutive principle of a democratic government involves, by its own inherent logic, the idea of a democratic society, above all in the economic realm. It therefore follows that a truly democratic society (which is the necessary consequence of relating democracy in politics to capitalism in economics) can be evaded only so long as capitalist democracy is outstandingly successful in the economic field. Once the constitutive principles of each group in a society are diverse the interests of each will be in contradiction; and the ideologies of men in society will broadly (though only broadly) follow the interests with which they believe themselves to be most closely connected. They will identify those interests with the high name of the common good; and they will fight for the victory of their interests in the confident and sincere belief that they are battling for the common good.

The same holds true in the international sphere. The state requires sovereignty so long as men assume that what is to be protected is a matter about which there can, ultimately, be no judgment superior to that of the state; and the state will have no difficulty in assuming that denial of its judgment is a threat to fundamental interests which it must protect. Its power to make the assumption will be immensely strengthened by the relation of the state to the nation in the modern world, for by using the psychological unity of nationhood it can gloss over the real interests it is protecting as a state. In this context British imperialism looks quite different to Germans or Italians from the way it looks to British citizens. An attempt to share the spoils of imperialism seems "national development" to the Germans and Italians while it seems "aggression" to the British. The principle of consent to change in international affairs has no validity so long as the interests of each nation-state in the results of change are as divergent as they are in the present economic configuration of society. The state requires sovereignty to protect those interests it considers (rightly or wrongly) to be fundamental. It deems that interests are fundamental by reason, above all, of their economic consequences to its citizens. These consequences, in their turn, are judged by governments which are bound predominantly to reflect the immanent logic of the relations implicit in the property system over which they preside. For, at bottom, judgment is the expression of interest; and our emotions of approval and disapproval, and the actions based on these emotions, will follow the interest which the government protects by its constitution. Its fundamentals are what Mr. Justice Holmes called the "can't helps" of its property relations. Sovereignty in international relations has become the protective armament of what is implied in those relations.

No nation-state in the modern world wants war; and no class in the modern state wants revolution. But both nation-states and classes seek ends which they cannot attain without either war or revolution. That is the basic dilemma of our age. We have reached a term in the evolution of our social institutions because we are no longer able, within the framework of existing economic relations, to satisfy the demands we encounter. If we preserve the basis of our present framework, we cannot continue to maintain a democratic principle, whose logic is in contradiction to it. If we maintain the democratic principle then we must adjust the framework of existing economic relationships to the consequences of the democratic principle. Our difficulty is a tragic one in that the dilemma reveals how small is the area of common conceptions of the common good when vested interests are in jeopardy.

This makes pitifully small our power to proceed by consent. And historically, whenever that power is as small as it has recently been, the danger is always great that men without principle will seize the instruments of authority, thus still further reducing our capacity to proceed by consent. Having seized power they seek to maintain it at all costs and therefore subordinate the traditional means of government to ends which, both within and without, they are able to impose only by coercion. So acting, they abridge those only elements in human nature through which reason has an opportunity to exercise its influence. They rule by fear; for they cannot otherwise maintain their rule. Fear is compelled to strike blindly, for it is the supreme enemy of reason. Unprincipled men are thus compelled to attack the basic values of civilization. They provoke challenge because they are unable to live in the atmosphere of rational discussion. When that stage is reached in the history of a culture it has to discover a new basis for property relationships if it wishes to survive.

# Impression of Ireland

## IRWIN EDMAN

### ( *1940* )

Professor of philosophy at Columbia University until his
death in 1954, IRWIN EDMAN was not content with the pursuit
of abstract theory alone; his first concern was for its application as a vital human impulse. Mr. Edman brought wit, insight and erudition to all the essays he wrote for THE
AMERICAN SCHOLAR, many of which appeared in his department "Under Whatever Sky."

I KNOW quite well that the way I am going to write about Ireland
is not an analysis of the civilization in that bemusing island.
I should, I know, be concerned in detail, or with profound speculation, however hypothetical, with the racial strains, the heritage
of folklore, the intellectual and religious cross-currents which have
made Ireland. Nor do I propose a contribution to sociology. I
remember once meeting a radical Irish-American author in
Dublin during my brief—and enchanted—stay there. He had
been in the city scarcely any longer than I. He was already filled,
even to the statistics, with the agricultural backwardness, the
ecclesiastical family skeletons, the political morasses, of Irish
life. He was depressed by all these things and so obsessed by them
that he had failed to notice the green of the grass in Ireland, the
cadences of its speech or the humor and poetry that played over
the surface of its life, however tragic. He was doubtless more mature in his observation than I. He deserved a Guggenheim Fellowship for a project on The Condition of Ireland at the Present Time.

That condition has certainly grown worse. I know, by the time
these lines are printed, that the Ireland in the newspapers will
not be the one I am trying, from a few weeks' delighted experience, to recapture in memory. It may be an Ireland filled with

parachutist German soldiers and the Gestapo may be established in the General Post Office or on O'Connell Street.

The Ireland I remember is something different, perhaps only a sentimental fragment conjured up from the memories of a month of soft mist and soft rain and the briefest bursts of soft sunshine, gilded, too, with the colors of previous expectation. But it is the Ireland I do remember, and remember as one of the singularly gracious oases of travel in a world where travel and delectation have become impossible.

Of course one comes to a country expecting to find certain things and if the country or one's own imagination is susceptible of creative fiction one finds it. My expectations were, I confess, formed on literary fragments and on an acquaintance with a few Irish people—not many and certainly not typical.

Maria who keeps house for me is, I suppose, not typical. Not altogether, that is. But there are authentic Irishisms in her after 35 years in New York, and not only in speech, though Ireland lives on in her language. When guests come unexpectedly I hear her remark that they have come over the bog, or when I get up particularly early that I'm early to Briney's with my wheel. It lives, too, in her pagan and material Catholicism, in her enjoyment of sudden deaths and of well-attended funerals, in her general kindness and her gusts of dark irrational moodiness, inexplicable and, for the moment, incurable.

Norah is, perhaps, not typical either, or not altogether so. A cultivated lady who has lived all her life in New York, her imagination has lived all its life in Ireland. Her conversation was dotted with affectionate references to parts of Dublin which, up to a few years ago, she had never seen. She has at her tongue's end a ceaseless stream of anecdotes about the clergy and the peasants, stories always testifying to their quickness and their imagination if not always to their reasonableness or integrity. Now that Norah has actually been to Dublin there are even more stories and the old ones have acquired an exact and documented setting. It was Norah, I think, who made me finally decide I must see Ireland; and the decisive thing was her account of the blessing, a whole torrential page long, that a beggar in Dublin shouted after her when she gave him sixpence, a benediction which she remembered word for word, or, since she is Irish too, may have invented. A country where one could be blessed that long and that vividly for sixpence! It was no wonder when, one summer in England, having to make up my mind whether I would go to see Sweden the Middle Way, or Denmark the Cooperative Commonwealth, or Ireland, I chose the last. I had a prophetic feeling that Ireland was eternal and that the middle way and the cooperative commonwealth were not. For Hitler was already threatening Czechoslovakia. I chose, perhaps unwisely, the eternal.

But it was not only Irish friends who made me wish to see Ireland. Who that has heard the liquid and wistful cadences of the Abbey Players or read Yeats or George Moore, or Joyce, has not wished to see it, or, better, to hear it at home where it lives? The comic-stage Irishman had long been exiled from my memory by the transcendental Irishman, compounded of poetry and lustiness, of squalid realism tinctured with the eeriness and magic one comes to know in Irish literature. Celtic twilights and the winds wailing over the West Country, peasants standing against the rocks or by a hut in the moors, a gleam of merriment in a house of tragedy, all these went into the complex of my expectations as at Euston Station I boarded the Irish Mail.

Even the name of the train had childhood associations. For had I not once had a child's handcar, painted red, with which I had coasted down Morningside Park in New York and had not the little red handcar been called the Irish Mail? I remembered having inquired what was meant by that. I had inquired of a policeman whose childhood had been spent in Dublin. He described the train that came west in England to the coast at Holyhead and the Mail steamer across to Kingstown and the great Westland Row Station in the heart of Dublin itself.

And here I was already, in spirit and by virtue of my fellow-travellers, in Ireland. There was one Englishman in the compartment and I expected that constrained and courteous suspicion with which English passengers generally, or at least before the War, regarded strangers; the others were Irish. One detected at once from the accent, that singing blend of gaiety and melancholy which is Irish speech, that these were Irish people. One detected it, too, from the atmosphere of a house-party current ten minutes after we left London. Long before we got to Holyhead everyone knew everyone else's destination, family history, psychological problems, financial status; and all had enlightened me with pleasant competitive opinions on what was most worth seeing in Ireland. Only the Englishman was primly still.

But Ireland itself began for me at Westland Row Station. I am quite prepared to believe there is an international race of taxi-drivers, and that there is a closer ethnological relationship be-

tween hackmen in Chicago and Singapore than between a Middle-
Western American passenger and his taxi-man. None the less I do
not think anyone save an Irishman could have said exactly the
words, or lighted on the thought, uttered by the driver I encountered as soon as I left the train at Dublin. "The Shelburne
Hotel" I said. And within something like a minute and a half, for
it was only just around the corner, I was there. "How much?" I
said. "Three shillings" replied the driver. "But it's only just
around the corner." The driver looked at me with an expression
compounded of pity and scorn and a sighing despair that there
was no more reasonableness current in this absurd world. "And
me," he said, "waiting three hours here at Westland Row Station
for a customer, and you complaining about a few shillings more
or less!" It was an answer nicely calculated to promote in me or in
anyone a feeling of meanness and, what was even worse, of having
been utterly silly.

For weeks thereafter one of the pleasures of Ireland for one
academic wanderer was the delicious unexpectedness of conversation, cropping up at the most routine occasions and from the most
commonplace persons. One had but to ask a policeman where one
could post a letter, for instance, to be looked at firmly with a tinc-
ture of good-natured contempt and curiosity and to receive the reply "And what," pointing to the huge building across the street,
"would be wrong with the General Post Office?" One had but to
ask the hotel porter "Is the afternoon train to Galway a good
train?" to have him reply "A good train, sir? It's fit for King
George the Sixth himself, or the President of *your* United States!"
One would only have to bemoan a cloudy day to be assured that
"It was a fine day surely, for if the sun were shining, it would
mean that it was going to rain."

And one discovered in this charming people, sometimes in the
shabbiest of surroundings, the expected but somehow always unexpected gift for poetry and laughter in the midst of the prose of
life and its grimness. A question would not bring an answer but a
soliloquy, and the soliloquy was more often than not something
that with not very much editing might have gone into one of
Synge's plays. It cropped up, the fanciful flow of rhetoric, the
turn of humorous paradox of phrase or thought, in every class of
society. One heard it at a gathering of authors in Dublin, from the
country priest or the waitress at a village inn in Connemara or
from the professor of medicine at Trinity College. One could not
help speculating on the origins and the implications of this passion

for speech in Ireland and the delight in it. How did it happen, I kept asking myself, that this love of words and their deployment, the obvious delight in the music made by phrases and the pleasant counterpoint one might play upon meanings and associations, was a game enjoyed not simply by the men of letters in Ireland? How did it happen that so many *were* by instinct men of letters? I heard grave men, deeply versed in the tragic history of Ireland and concerned for its future, speculate on this very thing. "It's a joy to you, a visitor," they said, "but it's been one of the curses of Ireland. More than anywhere in the world the mind runs away in Ireland. It is seduced by images and caught up by the stream of words. The internecine bitterness has often been a quarrel over slogans, or a quarrel for the sake of the rhetorical excitement of controversy, a rhetoric that has often been paid for in blood."

I was reminded of all this a week or more later in Galway. I had gone off to the West Country on the suggestion of Sean O'Failon, the Irish novelist, who said to me "You'd better see the West of Ireland if you really wish to say you have seen this island. That's Ireland; here in Dublin we're all corrupted; we are Anglo-Irish. We're uneasy colonials. Go west."

I was at first disappointed, for the town of Galway itself is at first glance marked chiefly by gray squalor. The women look very picturesque with their shawls wound round their heads. But they look older than one suspects them to be and there is misery in their eyes. The shops are dirty and sullen looking and the houses are, most of them, grimy tenements.

In a squalid side street I came upon a little shop with a captivating array of Irish lace and embroidery framed in a forlorn dirty window. I saw one piece I was sure Norah would like. Behind the counter was a half kindly, half belligerent looking, middle-aged woman. She reminded me of Maria in one of her less expansive moods. "How's business?" I could not help asking when I had made my purchase. I had learned that one question in Ireland sufficed often to yield an oration. The woman of the shop looked at me almost angrily. "And how's business, you're asking? How's business!" she repeated, almost contemptuously. "How would it be?" she said. "Terr-ible. And it's been terrible," she added, leaning over the counter and shaking an expository forefinger at me, "it's been terrible ever since the blackguards brought us our freedom."

"But," I said, "I thought the Irish wanted their freedom?" "Did they now?" she said. "Did they now! Listen to that! Wanted their freedom, did they? And wasn't it a great country here in the West of Ireland, full of English toffs and lords and swells, spending their money like gentlemen and helping all the country roundabout with their hunting and fishing and their great houses and the hordes of servants they had. There was Lady L— and a grand lady she was too. *That* important," she stretched her arms out as wide as they would go, "you would have to get a parchment that long and signed with all the important names of East and West to get to see her at all. And what a blessing she was to the countryside, with her parties and the grand shenanigans during the hunting season and her graciousness to all the people in the whole county of Galway. And what did those blackguards do now? They burned down her house. And don't you think," she said, looking at me intently as if to see if I followed closely the logic of her argument, "and don't you think, now," she repeated with that sense for rhythm no less than for reiteration that I had repeatedly observed in this country, "don't you think, now, she'd be moving away?" She did not wait for assent. "Well, she did!"

Part of the real Ireland I had been urged to see in Galway was a Professor Michael Moriarty of Galway University. He was Professor of English literature in Galway but that was accidental, I was told, rather than essential to him. He really should have been teaching Gaelic, for no one could better have embodied, so I had been forewarned, intense Irish nationalism. Had he not lived through the Trouble and in 1922 had his house not been a center of the Irish Republican Army? And had he not been sent to Galway as a perfectly fitting emissary of the specifically Irish Nationalist movement in education? It was with pleasurable anticipation that I sought out the Professor a mile out of town. Did I mind waiting? he began, his head close to the radio, until the football match between Galway and Cork was ended. It was a beautiful game and it was being beautifully announced (as indeed it was) by one of his former students; and the championship of Ireland, Southern Ireland, the Ireland that counted, was dependent on the issue. The game ended, we settled down to an enormous tea during which I was instructed that to see the real Ireland I had to go still further. The Eire I had been hearing about for an hour seemed real enough. It was the Ireland of the Trouble, and "Mind you, all incriminating papers had to be hidden in the crib of this young lady here," pointing to his sixteen-year-old daughter. "It was a lively world we lived in in 1922. Ireland was full of passion, then, and of hopes. We were all a little crazy, surely, but it's crazy we were for an ideal. We're soberer now, and a little dead.

"But you must have a look at the real Ireland; you haven't seen it yet. It's not in the green Southern counties or in the pretty speech of the women of Cork. You must go to Connemara. There it is lonely, it is clear, it is beautiful. Pity my young son isn't here to go with you. He's a poet, the lad is. He tries to keep it from us. He tears up his poems and throws them in the wastebasket. But his mother here has pieced them together and some of them are very lovely. I wish my son, the poet, were here, for he could guide you well."

I rather wished during the succeeding days in Connemara that I had had a poet with me. Not that one needed a poet, even an Irish one, to point out the melancholy loveliness, the spacious tragic charm of the hills and moors of Connemara. There were many things I had been told I should find on this island: relics of ancient superstitions, medieval Christianity, the pitiful and the picturesque poverty bequeathed from the days of the absentee landlords, squalor and comedy, dirt and magic. Nobody had told me I should find Greece, transposed into a Celtic key. But here it was, the same clear bare outlines of mountains, and a lonely clean-cut peasant boy standing by his cart against a sky in this August light, almost, though I had found out by this time how briefly, a Mediterranean blue. I could not help thinking of how long, during the Middle Ages and the Renaissance, Ireland had been an outpost of European, that is to say of Greco-Roman, culture. It was a long way from Sunion on an Aegean headland, to Connemara; but here, on an Irish headland above the sea, one could imagine a Greek temple beckoning mariners from the West as the one at Sunion beckoned those from the East. And, as the evening mist settled down over these gray rocks and gray sea, one thought of the singular transpositions and modulations Greek thought and feeling had gone through, in Ireland at least. One thought of the Celtic accent of magic and mystery that the Irish scholar, Stephen McKenna, had given Plotinus in his great poetic translation; of Dublin University, the center of classical studies. Here, in the West of Ireland, it was not too surprising to find a magically transmuted image of Greece.

My Dublin friends smiled a little at my enthusiasm for Ireland, though not without pleasure. They would not believe even my notebook when I recited to them turns of phrase or of thought I had picked up in my wanderings, South and West and in Dublin itself. They would deny with a music and picturesqueness of which they themselves were completely unaware that the Irish, peasant or professor, spoke as vividly as I insisted they did or that their imaginations had any idiosyncrasy of enchantment. They aired the troubles of Ireland, the bog of disillusion in which the romantic nationalism of the early 20's had left the intellectuals. I would speak with delight of the atmosphere of an 18th-century town, dignified and intimate, which was Dublin at its best. They would reply despairingly of the Puritan provincialism, the backwater of culture Dublin had become. I would mention the Abbey Theatre and they would say its best days were over. I had but to speak of the warmth and graciousness with which the Irish, priests and poets, farmers and doctors, received a stranger. "But you have not been here long enough," they would say, "to see, and you apparently do not remember how the Irish have treated each other." There was indeed only one point at which I could elicit an agreement; that was about the green of Ireland. And they agreed about that chiefly because I had been complaining about the rain. "But," said my novelist friend, "if it did not rain so much it would not be Ireland and if it did rain so much it would not be so green."

Staring through the window at that almost unbelievably intense green I apologized. Could it be, I wondered, that it required a land so bathed in vividness to produce a people so bathed in vivid images and vivid speech? This was a race of poets, surely, bred on intensities. The air of this island made the tragedy of this people. It nourished their passions as the rain bred their melancholies, and the mists clouded their minds with historic bitterness. Perhaps by the time these lines appear, I repeat, the Gestapo may be in O'Connell Street. I do not think they will be able to erase the color on St. Stephen's Green or the music of Irish speech or the free flights of their imaginations. Not England or the Church or famine have been able to do that.

# Music for the Man Who Enjoys Hamlet

## B. H. HAGGIN

## (1944)

The only way to understand music is to listen to it, insists B. H. HAGGIN, well-known music critic. This essay introduced Mr. Haggin's book, *Music for the Man Who Enjoys Hamlet*, which has been reprinted in the Modern Library Paperback Series.

You reach home, let us say, with expectations of a quiet dinner, of slippers, easy chair, a much-read copy of *Hamlet* to take your mind far from the wearying details, arguments, and vexations of the long day at the office. And you learn with dismay that this is the night of the third concert of the city's major series, that your wife is going, and you are going with her.

"Schnabel is playing!"—and it is evident that your eyes should light up in anticipation; but instead you groan in recollection. Later, after a hurried change of clothes, a rushed dinner, seated uncomfortably beside your wife in the concert hall while a gray-haired man plays something called Sonata in B flat major by Schubert, you think, as you fold and unfold your program: "It seems to mean a lot to Schnabel; and I suppose it means something to all these other people; but it doesn't make sense to me." But by the time Schnabel is playing Beethoven's Sonata Opus 111 your boredom has given way to irritation; and savagely throwing away the shreds of your program you think: "I'll bet it doesn't mean any more to the others or to the old boy on the stage than it means to me. It *doesn't* make sense; and they're only pretending it does."

Some of them may be pretending; but the music Schnabel is playing does make sense—to him, and to others; it makes as much sense, and the same kind of sense, as *Hamlet* makes to you. You don't see that; but you will, I think, if you consider what *Hamlet* is and what it does.

To begin with, *Hamlet* is an example of the employment, on a very large scale, of an artistic medium. The nature of this employment we may see more easily in a small-scale example—in one of the *Sonnets:*

> *Full many a glorious morning have I seen*
> *Flatter the mountain-tops with sovereign eye,*
> *Kissing with golden face the meadows green,*
> *Gilding pale streams with heavenly alchymy;*
> *Anon permit the basest clouds to ride*
> *With ugly rack on his celestial face,*
> *And from the forlorn world his visage hide,*
> *Stealing unseen to west with this disgrace:*
> *Even so my sun one early morn did shine,*
> *With all-triumphant splendour on my brow:*
> *But, out! alack! he was but one hour mine,*
> *The region cloud hath mask'd him from me now.*
> > *Yet him for this my love no whit disdaineth;*
> > *Suns of the world may stain when heaven's sun staineth.*

Other men have had thoughts and emotions about the love they have possessed and lost; what they have not done is to elaborate these thoughts and emotions into the complex form of words, rich in rhythmed sound, in images, in overtones of sense and feeling, in which Shakespeare makes *his* thoughts and emotions on the subject articulate. The articulateness in words in metrical patterns is common enough: it produces huge quantities of worthless poetry by children, adolescents, adults. In Shakespeare's sonnet, however, the quality of the mere articulateness in the medium is itself uncommon; and its complexities and splendors represent in addition the workings of an uncommonly complex and rich mind and personality. Involved, that is, with the articulateness, operating through it, crystallized in the completed poem, are Shakespeare's personal resources—what he is in character, mind, feeling, what he has lived through, what his experience has done to him, what insights it has given him. This is true even of the sonnet; and it is true more obviously, more richly, more excitingly, of *Hamlet.*

If you are moved, excited, exalted by *Hamlet,* if for a time afterwards the real world appears to you wonderfully changed, that is because for several hours you have been looking through Shake-speare's eyes at an imagined world created between the covers of a book or on the stage of a theater—a world in which the natures of the human beings who inhabit it, the situations in which they are placed, the things they do and say, all express significances which life has come to have for this man with perceptions and insights that you and I do not possess. If *Hamlet* leaves you with an impression of greatness, that impression is one of the greatness of mind and spirit which Shakespeare reveals in his play. And if the insights of that mind and spirit impress you as much as they do, that is because of the richness of the poetic form in which they are embodied and presented to you.

Which brings us to this important fact: that if you are affected by *Hamlet* it is, first of all, because you have the personal resources which enable you to appreciate the insights it conveys; but it is also—and this is the important thing for our discussion—because you have the susceptibility to the poetic medium which enables you to be affected by the poetic form in which these insights are conveyed. I say this is the important thing for our discussion because similar insights are conveyed in Schubert's B flat Sonata and Beethoven's Opus 111, but through a different artistic medium; and if they do not get through to your mind it is because the *medium* is one to which, at the moment, you are not susceptible.

"Perhaps even Shakespeare never reached that final state of illumination that is expressed in some of Beethoven's late music," says Sullivan in his excellent book about Beethoven. If the state of illumination that is conveyed to you by Shakespeare is not conveyed by Beethoven in his second movement of the Sonata Opus 111, the reason is that you are susceptible to Shakespeare's medium of artistic communication but not to Beethoven's; and you will understand how this might be so, if you consider how long and how much you have read Shakespeare, who uses the words that are your own medium of communication and expression, and how few encounters you have had with Beethoven, whose musical idiom is not that of the folk songs or school songs or Broadway songs which you may be familiar with.

Understanding this, you may be disposed to try an experiment —which is to listen to the opening passage of that movement of Opus 111 at least once every evening for a couple of weeks, in order to become thoroughly familiar with it, and to see whether, as you come to know it, you begin to get from it some communication of what a man like Beethoven might feel at the end of his life

—the sense of experience mastered, of profound lessons learned, of resignation, inner illumination achieved. You can hear the passage on side 3 of the Columbia recording of Egon Petri's performance (play it to the point about one and a half inches from the first groove; and for the present resist the temptation to go further than that point).

You will be serving the purpose of the experiment and increasing its chance of success if you listen in the same way to another passage—the opening statement up to the faint rumble in the bass, in the first movement of Schubert's Sonata in B flat, which in a different way also communicates the sense of profound lessons learned, inner illumination achieved. By this time Victor may have issued the English recording of Schnabel's performance.

And listen also to two other passages for what they may communicate to you. One is the beginning of the third movement of Beethoven's Trio Opus 97—the two statements of the piano that are echoed by the violin and cello, which you can hear on side 6 of Victor's recording of the Rubinstein-Heifetz-Feuermann performance or on side 5 of the old Victor recording of the Cortot-Thibaud-Casals performance. The other is the statement of the piano with which the first movement of Beethoven's Piano Concerto No. 4 begins; and hear it as it is played by Schnabel on the Victor record, not as it is played by Gieseking on the Columbia record.

I have suggested a couple of weeks; but obviously the experiment doesn't have to stop after two weeks. Give yourself all the time you may need to find those passages of music acquiring significance for you, or on the other hand to satisfy yourself that music is not for you the medium of artistic communication which you are willing to believe it is for others.

## II

If now those passages convey significance to you, we can go on —first of all to get a more precise idea of this significance and how it is conveyed.

In the sonnet I quoted, or in one of Hamlet's soliloquies, we see a complex form of words embody and communicate a complex synthesis of thought and emotion. And if anyone were to ask "What thought, what emotion?" the answer would be "The thought and emotion expressed and defined by that form of words." One can say that the sonnet is concerned with the love which is given and then withheld; one can say further that this love is compared with the sun which lights the earth and then is hidden by clouds; but to do this is not to convey the rich overtones of sense and feeling that are expressed by

> *Full many a glorious morning have I seen*
> *Flatter the mountain-tops with sovereign eye,*
> *Kissing with golden face the meadows green,*
> *Gilding pale streams with heavenly alchymy;*

and the rest of the poem. The only way of conveying those overtones is to state the precise form of words that Shakespeare himself devised for this purpose.

A painter, too, may be aware only of choosing a bit of paint and placing it on the canvas in relation to a number of other bits; but the choice, the placing, the relation, involve exercise of judgment —which is to say that they involve the whole man; the sum at that moment of his experience, thought, emotion, insight. What is involved in the choices and uses of the bits of paint reveals itself through them; and in the end the completed integrated arrangement of lines, colors, planes, masses, and forms is a visual embodiment and communication of a particular synthesis of that experience, thought, emotion, insight.

Roger Fry has described the process of a Cézanne still-life, in which bottles, pears, and apples, so commonplace as to have no emotional associations in themselves, are "deprived of all those specific characters by which we ordinarily apprehend their concrete existence," and are "reduced to pure elements of space and volume" which are then "coordinated and organized by the artist's sensual intelligence." He refers to Cézanne's own conception that it was out of these relations of formal elements that emotion was to emanate; and he says: "One may wonder whether painting has ever aroused graver, more powerful, more massive emotions than those to which we are compelled by some of Cézanne's masterpieces in this genre." And these emotions to which we are compelled—not by the subjects of the paintings, but by the pictorial treatment of the subjects—these grave, powerful, massive emotions are something we have no way of knowing or defining or conveying, other than by those relations of formal elements on the canvas that were Cézanne's way.

So with the piece of music that is a formal organization of sound —or sounds—in time. The sounds have no external references to objects or ideas; what they have is the internal coherence of a kind of grammar of their own; and the relations in which they are placed—in a texture of horizontal lines of sounds in sequence (melody) and vertical sounds in simultaneous combination (harmony), articulated by duration and stress (rhythm), and colored by the timbres of instruments or voices—are governed basically by this grammar, which is used in an individual style by each composer, in obedience to the laws of his own being. He too, that is, may be aware only of choosing a sound and placing it in relation to a number of others; but the choice, the placing, the relation, involving exercise of judgment as they do, involve the sum at that moment of his experience, thought, emotion, insight—of which a particular synthesis is finally embodied and communicated in the completed formal arrangement of sounds. If anyone were to ask about the second movement of Beethoven's Sonata Opus 111 "What thought, what emotion, what insight?" one could say, as I did earlier, "The sense of experience mastered, lessons learned, resignation, inner illumination achieved." But one would have to use the same words about the opening of Schubert's B flat Sonata, to describe experience mastered, lessons learned, resignation and illumination achieved that are different from Beethoven's and expressed in different musical terms. This demonstrates the inadequacy of the words, and the fact that here again we have no way of knowing or defining or conveying the synthesis of experience and emotion that is embodied in each piece of music, other than by the formal construction in sound that each man used for the purpose.

One might, for that matter, find no other words than "experience mastered, lessons learned, resignation and illumination achieved" for other pieces of music by Beethoven himself—that is, for the same synthesis of experience and emotion that embodies itself in different constructions of sound. From this we realize that in dealing with a work of art we are concerned not with meaning but with meaning as embodied in form. We read Shakespeare not merely for his profound insights, but for these insights as made explicit and affecting in his rich poetic forms; and so with Cézanne's powerful emotions, and the inner illumination and exaltation of Beethoven in his last years. We are, then, interested in each different formal construction on canvas from which we get the impact of the same powerful emotions, each different construction of sound which conveys to us the same inner illumination and exaltation.

### III

I have gone into all this to get you to see that just as the way to understand Shakespeare's poem is to read it, and the way to understand Cézanne's still-life is to look at it, so the way—the only way —to understand Beethoven's or Schubert's sonata movement is the one you have already used successfully with its opening passage— to listen to it. It was natural for you, when the music made no sense, to ask to be told what its sense was, and to ask to be told in words, since you were accustomed to think of sense as expressible in words. And it was necessary for you to learn to apprehend from a phrase of music a sense which was not definable by words— which was defined solely by the particular organization of sounds in that phrase of music. You may say that I did use words to describe it and help you apprehend it; but they did not really describe what in the end you had to apprehend from the music and would have apprehended even without my words; and you will discover, when you are accustomed to the medium, that the meaning of a phrase of Beethoven or Schubert is grasped immediately with the sounds, and that if there is any difficulty, what is needed is not explanation of the phrase in words but repeated hearing of it. And you cannot get a wrong idea by listening to Beethoven or Schubert himself, but you will get some very wrong ideas by listening to the people who undertake to speak for him.

It was natural for you also, when the music made no sense, to think that you might understand it if you were told things about it—about the man who wrote it, the period in which he lived, the ideas, tendencies, forces, which influenced him. But when you have experienced the joyousness, buoyancy, and exuberant playfulness embodied in Beethoven's Eighth Symphony you may be surprised to discover the vexations and turmoil that filled his daily life at the time he was writing this work; and you will learn from this that the biographical and historical background of a work of art may be quite irrelevant to it. For it is the inner core of personal qualities, emotions, and insights created by a lifetime of experience that governs the artist's selection and arrangement of words or paints or sounds in a poem or picture or symphony; and although this inner core is constantly altered and developed by his continuing experience, it is not affected by any and every happening of the day. When this inner development in Beethoven had reached the emotions and attitudes we are made aware of by the Eighth Symphony, they pressed for expression in the sounds of this symphony, unaffected by the external turmoil that was irrelevant to them. Earlier, too, it was the heroic emotions and attitudes that Beethoven had developed in the face of disaster which operated through his articulateness in his medium to produce the *Eroica* Symphony; if there had been no French Revolution there would have been no dedication to Napoleon to tear up when he made himself emperor, but there would have been the same *Eroica* Symphony. And Ernest Newman once pointed to the striking differences in the three great symphonies that Mozart wrote in those two months of wretchedness and despair in the summer of 1788, as evidence of the fact that "creative imagination of a great artist functions too deep down within him to be greatly affected by anything that may happen on the surface of his life or his being." It is not, then, the biographical or historical background that gives us a clue to the meaning of the music; it is instead the music that often gives us our only clue to what was going on inside the composer.

But to know even relevant biographical and historical details *about* a work of art would not make the relations of elements *in* the work of art clearer and more significant. It is true, as we have seen, that the whole man was involved in the process which produced the Cézanne still-life; and it is further true that with the man there must have been involved, more remotely, the influences which had operated on him—the general ideas, the social and political conditions of the time. But when you knew these things that were involved in the process you would still have to perceive and feel the impact of the formal relations of space and volume that are the result of the process; and for this the things you knew about Cézanne's life would be neither necessary nor helpful. And so with Beethoven's or Schubert's sonata.

Nor do you need the technical knowledge of the professional musician. A piece of music is, to begin with, an organization of sounds; experiencing it begins with hearing the sounds and the way they are related in each phrase, the relation of one phrase to the next in the progression; and learning to hear these relations is at the same time a process by which you learn to follow the grammar and logic of musical thought, the operations by which it proceeds; but you can do all this without knowing the technical facts and names of what you are hearing. For one of those opening passages to acquire significance for you it was necessary to hear the sounds and their relations, for which you did not have to know that the tonic of C major was followed by a second inversion of the dominant seventh—any more than you have to know that a particular brown which you see in a painting is called burnt umber, and another which is placed in relation to it is called yellow ochre. What is true is that when you have heard something you will find the name of it convenient to use in referring to it; and someone else will find the name convenient to use to refer to it when talking to you about it. But a great many matters which the professional musician is concerned with, and the terms which he uses in discussing them—these you don't have to know anything about.

And now go on to hear what comes after those opening passages.

# The Problem of the Liberal Arts College

## JOHN DEWEY

## (*1944*)

JOHN DEWEY, long considered dean of American philosophers, died in 1952 at the age of ninety-two. As active in education as he was in philosophy, Mr. Dewey presented these
comments as part of an AMERICAN SCHOLAR forum on "The
Function of the Liberal Arts College in a Democratic Society." Other participants were Alexander Meiklejohn, Scott
Buchanan, Arnold S. Nash, Kenneth C. M. Sills and Ernest
Earnest.

NOTHING is more striking in recent discussions of liberal education than the widespread and seemingly spontaneous use of
*liberating* as a synonym for *liberal*. For it marks a break with the
traditional idea that a certain group of studies is liberal because of
something inhering in them—belonging to them by virtue of an
indwelling essence or nature—as opium was once said to put persons to sleep because of its dormitive nature. This latter view of
the liberal arts has the merit, for some writers and educators, of
rendering it unnecessary to inquire closely into what the subjects
actually accomplish for those who study them. If a particular
group of studies is "liberal" in and of itself, such an inquiry is
irrelevant. Failure to exercise a liberating educative effect in given
cases is not the fault of the studies but of external conditions, such,
perhaps, as the inherent incapacity of some students to rise to a
truly "intellectual" level. To define liberal as that which liberates
is to bring the problem of liberal education and of the liberal arts
college within the domain of an inquiry in which the issue is settled by search for what is actually accomplished. The test and

justification of claims put forth is found in observable consequences, not in an *a priori* dogma.

The concrete significance of the foregoing generalities in locating the present problem of the liberal arts college is found in outstanding historic considerations. The theory that certain subjects are liberal because of something forever fixed in their own nature was formulated prior to the rise of scientific method. It was consonant with the philosophical theory which was once held about every form of knowledge. For according to that doctrine if anything is knowable it is because of its inherent nature, form or essence, so that knowledge consists of an intuitive grasp by pure "intellect" of this nature. This doctrine is completely repudiated in the practices which constitute the scientific revolution.

In the second place, the traditional doctrine was embodied in educational institutions in a period that was pre-technological as well as pre-scientific. The liberal arts were sharply contrasted with the useful arts. This contrast had its basis in social and cultural conditions. The useful or industrial arts were acquired by means of sheer apprenticeship in fixed routines in which insight into principles played a negligible part. The industrial revolution which marks the last few centuries is the result of the scientific revolution. Only the most backward "useful" arts are now matters of empirical routine. They are now technological, a fact which signifies that they are founded in scientific understanding of underlying principles.

In the third place, and most important of all, social organization has also undergone a revolution. The distinction between "liberal" and "useful" arts is a product of the time when those engaged in industrial production were mechanics and artisans who occupied a servile social status. The meaning attached to the traditional doctrine of liberal arts cannot be understood except in connection with the social fact of division between free men and slaves and serfs, and the fact that only the former received an "intellectual" education, which under the given conditions necessarily meant literary and linguistic training. At the time in which a scientific revolution was radically changing the nature and method of knowledge, understanding and learning, and in which the industrial revolution was breaking down once for all the wall between the hand and the head, the political revolution of the rise of democracy was giving a socially free status to those who had been serfs. It thereby destroyed the very foundation of the traditional separation between the arts suitable for a "gentleman" and the arts suited to those engaged in production of useful services and commodities: that is to say, the separation between "liberal" and "useful" arts.

It is not possible to grasp and state the present dilemma of the liberal arts college, and of the function it should undertake in our society, except as they are placed and seen in this context of irreversible historic movements. Nothing can be sillier than attributing the problems of the contemporary liberal college in this country to the activities of a number of misguided educationalists, instead of to the impact of social forces which have continually gained in force. If there is anything equally silly, it is the assertion (by those who would resolve these problems by a return to an outworn identification of "liberal" with the linguistic, the literary and metaphysical) that their opponents are complacently satisfied with the present situation. For, in fact, the latter anticipated the former by many years in pointing out the confusions, conflicts, and uncertainties that mark present collegiate education.

When the situation is viewed in historic perspective (a kind of view quite foreign to the victims and adherents of an exclusively literary and metaphysical training) it is seen that scientific studies made their way into the college against the resistance of entrenched orthodoxy because of their growing importance in the conduct of social affairs, not because of intrinsic love of scientific knowledge—much less because of widespread devotion to scientific method. When Latin lost its monopoly as the universal language of communication among the learned, living languages were added to the curriculum. Not only were the degrees of S.B. and Ph.B. added to the old A.B. (or else the latter extended to cover the new studies), but the curriculum became congested and its aim wavering and unsure.

The new modes of social pressure did not stop at this point. A large number of new callings and occupations came into existence. They competed vigorously with the three traditional "learned" professions, and the effect of this competition found its way into the colleges. At the same time, two of the learned professions, medicine and law, were undergoing great changes. New discoveries in chemistry and physiology so changed medicine as to render it virtually impossible to crowd preparation into the time previously allotted. Studies which in effect, if not in name, were premedical found their way into the college. The great changes that were going on in industry and commerce together with their social effects affected the practice of law. The consequences for college education were less overt than in the case of medicine, but they are genuinely present.

The net result of the alterations produced by the social changes here briefly noted has been to render the name "liberal arts college" reminiscent rather than descriptive when it is applied to many of our collegiate institutions. Under these circumstances it is hardly surprising that representatives of the older literary and metaphysical point of view who have been on the defensive have now taken the offensive. Consistently with their view that certain subjects are inherently liberal, they are proclaiming that other subjects, notably those that are scientific and technological, are inherently illiberal, materialistic, and utilitarianly servile, unless they are kept in strict subjection. Social revolutions rarely if ever go completely backward in spite of reactions that occur. I do not believe that there is great likelihood that the American undergraduate college will, in any large number of cases, return to the literary and metaphysical course of study of the traditional liberal arts institutions. I seem to notice that those who are verbally active in this direction are not discouraging receipt of funds to add still more new scientific and semi-vocational courses to an already swollen curriculum.

The danger, to my mind, lies elsewhere. It is possible to freeze existing illiberal tendencies and to intensify existing undesirable splits and divisions. At a time when technical education is encroaching in many cases upon intelligent acquaintance with and use of the great humanistic products of the past, we find that reading and study of "classics" are being isolated and placed in sharp opposition to everything else. *The problem of securing to the liberal arts college its due function in democratic society is that of seeing to it that the technical subjects which are now socially necessary acquire a humane direction.* There is nothing in them which is "inherently" exclusive; but they cannot be liberating if they are cut off from their humane sources and inspiration. On the other hand, books which are cut off from vital relations with the needs and issues of contemporary life themselves become ultra-technical.

The outstanding need is interfusion of knowledge, of man and nature, of vocational preparation with a deep sense of the social foundations and social consequences of industry and industrial callings in contemporary society. On the face of this need we have urged upon us a policy of their systematic separation. I lately received from a man distinguished in public life, not a professional educator, a letter in which he writes: "Millions of our soldiers are coming back reactionaries of a kind through their lack of cultural education to appraise their surroundings and the events that are taking place." I would add that there are at home many other millions who are confused and bewildered, at the mercy of drift and of designing "leaders," because of their lack of an education that enables them to appraise their surroundings and the course of events. The present function of the liberal arts college, in my belief, is to use the resources put at our disposal alike by humane literature, by science, by subjects that have a vocational bearing, so as to secure ability to appraise the needs and issues of the world in which we live. Such an education would be liberating not in spite of the fact that it departs widely from the seven liberal arts of the medieval period, but just because it would do for the contemporary world what those arts tried to do for the world in which they took form.

# Vertical and Horizontal Thinking

## PAUL TILLICH

## (*1945*)

Formerly professor of philosophical theology at Union Theological Seminary and now a University Professor at Harvard University, PAUL TILLICH is a stanch and persuasive interpreter of Christian existentialism: "Whatever the relation of God, world and man may be, it lies in a frame of being."

Participating in an AMERICAN SCHOLAR forum on "The Future of Religion," with Raphael Demos and Sidney Hook, Mr. Tillich explained the relation between the temporal and the eternal in terms of two basic forms, the horizontal and the vertical.

THE first statement I want to make about the future of religion is the expression of a profound discomfort about the phrase "the future of religion." For this phrase conveys the idea of a product of history which may or may not have a future, whose future may be shorter or longer, which may be destroyed or merged with something else and disappear in one way or another. Such a view is logically possible, as it is logically possible to look at a man as a stimulus-response mechanism and to treat him accordingly. But the man will raise a furious protest; he will denounce this view as a denial of his human nature, of his dignity as a person. In the same way those who identify themselves with religion consider the phrase "the future of religion" as an implicit denial of its true nature, of its transcending of the modes of time.

Religion as a living experience does not ask the question of its own future. It is only interested in its content, the eternal and our relation to it. Religion cannot imagine any past or future in which man has lived or will live without an ultimate concern, i.e., without religion. Man is that being which by his very nature is ultimately concerned and therefore essentially religious. He may not accept this situation; he may fight against it. He may try to escape the shaking experience of being grasped by an ultimate concern. He may express the ultimate in mythical, theological, philosophical, poetic, political, or any other terms. He may avoid "religious symbols" in the narrower, traditional sense of the word. But he cannot avoid religion in the larger, more profound and more universal sense. Religion lasts as long as man lasts. It cannot disappear in human history, because a history without religion is not *human* history, which is a history in which ultimate concerns are at stake.

This is the first reaction of religion to the question of its own future. If this reaction has been expressed religion can accept the question of its future development. Indeed, religion itself asks this question, whenever a religious interpretation of history is attempted, or the contemporary situation is religiously analyzed, or the theoretical and practical needs of the Church are discussed. Without some anticipation of the future no acting in the present is possible.

The relation between the temporal and the eternal takes on two basic forms, the "vertical" and the "horizontal" one. Both belong to every religion. But it makes a great difference whether a religion emphasizes the vertical or the horizontal element. It is the thesis of this article that religion (in the sense of "ultimate concern") will return towards the "vertical" element after it has been "horizontalized" in the preceding period.

Vertical and horizontal are spatial metaphors for qualities of our religious experience. "Vertical" points to the eternal in its presence as the ground of our being and the ultimate meaning of our lives. It points to our ability to elevate ourselves over the inescapable anxiety of finitude and over the destructive despair of guilt, in our personal and social existence. The religious cult, including prayer and meditation, the aesthetic intuition and the philosophical eros, mystical union and the "quiet of the soul" in face of the vicissitudes of existence, are expressions of the vertical element in religion. "Horizontal," on the other hand, points to the transforming power of the eternal whenever it manifests itself. "Horizontal" is the prophetic fight for social justice and personal righteousness, the struggle against the structures of evil in our souls and our communities, the work for the formation of men and the world. Sacred and secular ethics, education and politics, healing and the control of nature are expressions of the horizontal element in religion. Wherever an ultimate concern expresses itself, both elements—the vertical and the horizontal—do appear. For we are ultimately concerned about what has ultimate being, and, consequently, is the ultimate good for those who participate in being. What is and what ought to be are united in the ground of all being. A religion which relates itself to the "ultimate" in terms of "being" only results in a world-defying, static mysticism, without ethical dynamics and without a world-transforming will and power. A religion which relates itself to the "ultimate" in terms of "ought to be" only results in a world-controlling technical activism, without a spiritual substance and a world-transcending will and power.

The five hundred years of Western civilization which we usually call the modern period—ending in the first half of the twentieth century—are characterized by man's largely successful attempt to gain the control over nature and society through rational analysis and construction. The more man dedicated himself to this attempt and the more actual control he gained, the more he lost the vertical element in his interpretation of life; he moved horizontally from one conquest of reality to the other. The ultimate concern of man expressed itself in terms of scientific and technical progress, of moral imperatives, educational norms and social ideals. The eternal became the background of man's horizontal activities: God was degraded to a "boundary-concept" and removed from the realm of real existence. The ultimate, that which gives meaning to life, is ahead and not above. This was a great and courageous attempt, especially in the fighting period of the modern mind. Prophetic wrath rings in the passionate words of Voltaire and Marx against the demonic distortion of the established churches, who used the vertical element in religion for the conservation of social injustice and tyrannical power, who used the eternal as a brake against the progress of the temporal, who identified the vertical element with conservatism and reaction. In this situation the horizontal protest was not only justified, but necessary for religion itself; it was a religious protest though it often appeared in antireligious terms; it was prophetic, even when it attacked the belief of the churches.

But the prophetic spirit disappeared from the secular mind when the victory was won. It was replaced by a self-complacent immanentism which produces means without ultimate ends, which sets purposes without an ultimate meaning, which has innumerable concerns without an ultimate concern. The expulsion of the vertical element (though historically understandable) deprived the horizontal element of its depth and its spiritual foundation. An atmosphere of unconquerable anxiety, a feeling of meaninglessness, of cynicism about principles and ideals, a despair of the future developed. Often this was covered by a normalized, conformistic existence in routine work and routine pleasure; sometimes it was alleviated by remnants of the optimistic expectations of the past. But it could not be removed any more; it became more and more typical for individuals and masses. The fact that the smashing victory of the Allied Nations and the discovery of the atomic power have not created anything like the enthusiastic hopes of the years after the first World War, but just the opposite, shows the change of the spiritual climate during the last twenty-five years. A tragic feeling about the limits of man's spiritual power—in contrast to his almost unlimited technical power—has spread all over the Western world. The transformation of our existence has ceased to be our ultimate concern and is replaced by the foundation of our existence as the content of our real concern: the pendulum has started swinging back to the vertical element in religion.

Not everything, of course, which seems to prove this movement is a real proof. The fact that the immediate presence of death for millions of people during the war has turned their minds towards the eternal does not necessarily mean a change of the basic trends in religion and culture. More significant may be the increasing influence of the Christian churches on the social and political life of the nations, as in the case of the churches of resistance in Europe, of Roman Catholicism, especially in the United States, and even (though with great restrictions) of the re-establishment of the Orthodox church in Russia. But these events could be explained either in terms of the natural reaction which follows revolutionary catastrophes, or in terms of political expediency. They do not give a clear evidence of a religious trend towards verticalism. Neither does the increase in enthusiastic groups which try to return to old mystical traditions. Things like that have always happened in periods of great insecurity and deep-rooted anxiety.

But there are genuine symptoms which give evidence that a trend towards a more vertical expression of our ultimate concern does exist in all realms of life. Much could and should be said about these symptoms and their significance for the understanding of our time. Here I can only point to them.

The vertical element in religion appears in two main types, the mystical type and the faith type. Although they do not exclude each other they must be distinguished. Both of them have reappeared—long before the world wars—with new power and meaning. Theology as well as philosophy of religion has rediscovered the meaning of the mystical experience, partly in connection with a deeper understanding of the Asiatic religions. It has become obvious that mysticism is not darkness and irrational emotion, but that it is a special way of looking at world and soul, which has its own right and its own perfection. Faith as a possible and meaningful attitude has been rediscovered by the prophetic-revolutionary movements of our period as well as by recent interpretations of religion by "Existential" philosophers and radical Protestants. It has become obvious that faith is not the belief in something which has a low degree of evidence but that faith is the state of being grasped by the eternal when it breaks into the temporal, reversing the expected course of things.

The mystical and the faith experience belong to the vertical element in religion. In correlation with them a new understanding of man has emerged. It has become visible that man is largely dependent on unconscious, individual and collective forces of an ambiguous character, that his conscious decisions have roots in preconscious levels, that he is not free for good and evil, but dependent on universal structures of evil and good for which he is the battlefield. It is not only theology but even more depth-psychology and sociology which have opened our eyes to this predicament of man. They have shown the tragic structures in human existence which refute any kind of utopianism, progressivistic as well as revolutionary. There is no doubt that the new emphasis on the vertical element in religion is very much strengthened by such a self-interpretation of man.

Symptomatic of the same trend are some changes in the doctrine of the Church. Its nature is not so much understood in terms of its purpose—the horizontal line—as in terms of its foundation—the vertical line. It has become obvious that receiving (the eternal) must precede acting (the temporal). Liturgical reforms in Protestantism, as well as in Catholicism, are expressions of this feeling. The "Ecumenical" movement tries to find the common principles on which all activity in all Christian churches must be based. The question of the foundation begins to overshadow the questions of operation.

The problem of the future of religion is not the problem of its relation to science, as it was in the "modern period" which also in this respect has come to an end with the beginning of this century. Historical criticism, natural sciences and recent psychology have been accepted without restriction by the predominant forces in Protestant theology. The sciences, on the other hand, have learned to distinguish their prescientific presuppositions and philosophical visions from their scientific insights. Both sides have recognized that the symbols in which our religion, i.e., our ultimate concern, expresses itself do not lie on the level of statements about the existence or non-existence of beings or a highest being. The religion of the future will be free from the more and more sterile conflict between "faith and knowledge."

The pendulum is swinging back to the vertical element in religion, and the danger is that it will swing too far. That this may happen is the justified fear of many liberal Protestants and humanists. They are afraid that Protestantism as well as humanism may disappear in this process of "verticalization." They certainly will disappear if their leaders do not understand the longing of the man of today for the eternal, from which he has been more and more cut off by the exclusive emphasis on the transformation of the temporal. The future of religion is dependent on a new, creative union of its vertical and its horizontal element.

# Neilson of Smith

## MARJORIE HOPE NICOLSON

### *( 1946 )*

Drawing on the recollections of a seventeen-year professional and personal association, MARJORIE HOPE NICOLSON wrote this sagacious portrait of William Allan Neilson after his death in 1945. Miss Nicolson, who is now chairman of the Department of English and Comparative Literature at Columbia University, served as dean of Smith College for eleven years during Mr. Neilson's presidency.

IT SEEMED to me natural and right that the obituary notices of William Allan Neilson, even in metropolitan dailies and weeklies, should have been personal and lively rather than formal. Perhaps some had been written in advance for the "morgue" by men or women who had known him; others must have been compiled at the last moment from records, for his death was unexpected. At all events even these anonymous editors realized that here had been a force to conjure with, a man who must not be sent to his grave merely with bald facts gleaned from *Who's Who*. In a way he wrote his own obituaries, for the columns sparkled with the quick wit of Neilson of Smith, who had been Neilson of Harvard, of Columbia, of Bryn Mawr, most of all Neilson of Scotland.

Even in his own lifetime he became a legend. Stories about him grew as in sagas and eddas. Day unto day uttereth speech, and one generation of college students hands down to the next tales which grow like snowballs. Usually Neilson was amused by *Neilsoniana*. Many a time I have caught his eye when a presiding officer was introducing him with a supposed "Neilson story." After the event, I would challenge him: "You never said that, did you?" "No," he would reply with that infectious twinkle of his, "but I wish I had."

But on other occasions he was irritated, as was I when I read in the papers some of the stories to which he most objected, particularly the oft-repeated but entirely unfounded tale that he, the President of Smith College, discovering a girl who was attempting to get into her dormitory after hours via the fire escape, gave her a gentle boost. Such stories he imperiously denied, as well he might, for they were out of character. Swift of wit, readier on the intellectual trigger than anyone I have ever known, he had one basic quality which gave the lie to such stories: he was a man of such inherent dignity and taste that he could not do or say anything fundamentally cheap.

For more than ten years I was his Dean at Smith College. During that period I saw him constantly in Northampton and in many other places among other groups of men and women. We were fellow editors of THE AMERICAN SCHOLAR, of which he had been a founder. Indeed the last time I ever saw him—with no presage that it was to be the last time—I walked with him after our meeting from the Biltmore Hotel to the Grand Central Station, where he was to take a train for home. It had been the kind of evening in which he always delighted, as AMERICAN SCHOLAR meetings are likely to be, an evening of wit and badinage, of serious business handled lightly. His old friend Will Howe was absent that evening, but Neilson and another fellow-founder, Christian Gauss, had teased each other as usual. Dean Gauss was just retiring from his long and distinguished deanship at Princeton, and Neilson occupied himself with giving his junior lessons on "how to be a good emeritus—a real art, I assure you, Gauss." He had sat next to Irita Van Doren, as he always tried to, for he was a rare judge of charming women. ("I ought to be," he would say, "surrounded as I have been by two thousand of them every day.") He bandied words with Irwin Edman, whom he greatly admired. And while Harlow Shapley, who fascinated Neilson—I suspect because he was even more fertile in ideas than Neilson himself—spent most of that evening on the long-distance phone trying to persuade Congress to make the world safe for the atom bomb and the bomb for the world, he had managed between calls to say one or two Shapleian things of the sort that always made Neilson chuckle.

It was a good evening which led Neilson to reminiscence in the station about the days, fifteen years ago, when he and Christian Gauss, Will Howe, John Finley, Dean Woodbridge and others had founded this magazine. Those early days of the SCHOLAR I know only at second hand, yet I seem to remember them well, for after each meeting he used to talk to me about them, so that somehow those dinners became in my mind a sort of Mermaid Tavern:

> *What things have we seen*
> *Done at the Mermaid! heard words that have been*
> *So nimble and so full of subtile flame*
> *As if that every one from whence they came*
> *Had meant to put his whole wit in a jest. . . .*

As I write about him, phrases from the Elizabethans keep coming to my mind, for he was himself a belated Elizabethan. I do not mean only that he was an Elizabethan scholar, though he was that of course. He edited Shakespeare; he taught the period to generations of students. The last formal class he ever conducted was a graduate seminar in Elizabethan literature at Smith College, which he relinquished reluctantly when his duties became too heavy and his absences too frequent. "Dean," he said to me, "when the time comes that young graduate students are more up-to-date on 'discoveries' and 'recent scholarship' than the professor, it's time the professor got out." But he remained, as he had always been, an Elizabethan in his immense zest for life, his gusto, his vitality, his exuberant personality. He seemed to me the last of those Renaissance men who knew everything.

I should, I suppose, write a judicious appraisal of Neilson the scholar, Neilson the administrator, Neilson the man of public affairs. But all that is being done by others. Tributes have poured into the college and to his family; "minutes" and "resolutions" will be written for months. I am writing about him personally, in part for Smith alumnae who knew him in Northampton but not abroad, in part for those who sat with him upon such boards as that of THE AMERICAN SCHOLAR, who knew him abroad but not at home. Most of all I am writing because of my pleasure in remembering the years during which I was privileged to work with him so closely.

Well as I knew Neilson in Northampton—and I saw him every day for more than a decade except when one or the other of us was "on the road"—I remember best the many occasions when we went off together on trips for the college. Sometimes we went by train, more often, when the distances were not too great, by car. On those trips I was the chauffeur, and Neilson sat beside me smoking his interminable cigars. Paradoxically—he was a creature of paradox—he had a car and he had a driver's license, but he never drove. I well remember the period when he earned that license with sweat and tears. He had no mechanical ability, and, so far as I could tell, was quite devoid of the sense of rhythm and timing necessary for a good driver. That lack always seemed to me strange, because his sense of rhythm and timing in other aspects of life was so nearly perfect. For some reason—I suspect it was the Scotch Presbyterian in him coming out—he felt it his duty to learn to drive because he had bought a car.

I remember one afternoon in early summer when I saw him in the deserted quadrangle—one of the world's worst places to practice—grimly piloting his car around the curves. It was not a hot day, but he was sweating like a wampus, whatever a wampus may be. I hailed him, but with an instinct for self-preservation, leaped to the greensward before he stopped.

"What on earth are you doing?" I asked.

"Dean," he said, "I'll learn to drive this thing and I'll get my license if it kills me, but when I do," he savagely loosened his collar, "I'll be darned if I ever touch the wheel of a car again."

Members of our faculty who did not know us well used to say to me, "How nice that you and the President go off on so many trips together! It must give you such a good chance to talk over college affairs." They little knew. Rarely did we speak of Smith College on those trips. We might spend our time arguing about Shakespeare, Milton, Bacon. Sometimes he would spend a whole day talking about Masson's lectures on Milton at Edinburgh, which he recalled with a combination of respect and amusement. Perhaps our conversation might be about Neilson's experiences at Bryn Mawr or Columbia, or about our many acquaintances in the academic world. During the years when he was editor-in-chief of Webster's Dictionary, I heard about his work over at Springfield, where he spent every Tuesday morning. He seldom came back from those weekly visits without something of interest, whether a previously unnoticed derivation, a new tendency in pronunciation, another "expert" called in on a technical problem. I learned more philology from him than ever I learned in a graduate school.

Most often his talk was of Harvard, for Neilson was as loyal a Harvard man as if he had been born to the crimson. One of the great pleasures of his last years was his election to the Harvard Board of Overseers. He would talk at length of earlier Harvard professors whom I had not known. He often spoke about President Eliot, sometimes in connection with the "Five Foot Bookshelf," sometimes about his own opposition to Eliot because he stayed too long.

"Dean," he would say abruptly, "don't let me stay too long. It was easy to talk when I was young, but as I get on, I know there is a great temptation to stay in harness. It's hard to lay down the reins, hard not to finish the story."

This became a reiterated motif in his later years. When he and I attended the funeral of Ellen Pendleton at Wellesley, he said again, "She stayed too long for her own strength. Don't let me stay too long."

He didn't stay too long at Smith—not long enough for any of us. To be sure, he put off his retirement for a year or two after the date he had originally settled upon, in part because of the immense pressure of trustees, faculty, alumnae; in part, because his younger daughter was in the Class of 1938, and, with true Scottish sentimentality, he wanted to give her her diploma. Yet he was still to have nearly seven years of activity. They were good years for him, and invaluable to the many organizations to which he devoted his efforts.

On those trips I came to realize the extent to which Neilson of Smith, a very loyal American, always remained Neilson of Scotland. Scots are good colonials, and Neilson settled down happily, at first in Canada, then in the States. He did not wish to return to Scotland to live. All the living members of his family were in this country: "Mr. Bob," his older brother who died a few years ago in Orange, Connecticut, "Miss Lizzie," and "Miss Jean," his sisters, who lived with "Mr. Bob." Yet he was never more proud than when Edinburgh called him back for an honorary degree, the regalia of which added much to the somewhat sombre academic processions at Smith College. What graduate will ever forget that gaudy red robe which so became him, the velvet cap, which worn at his own rakish angle, made him look still more like Mephistopheles?

Little by little I learned a great deal about his early life, though he was never one to unlock his heart or wear it on his sleeve. His mother, whose picture he showed me more than once, looked as I had always imagined Barrie's Margaret Ogilvy. He had begun his "professional career," I remember, at the age of ten, when he substituted for his father, the local schoolmaster. I learned from casual remarks that he had lived on a pittance when he attended the University. One day as we started off on a trip he was irritable because Smith students were demanding some privilege, which they undoubtedly called a *right*. This was in the period of inflation when America was at the high.

"Dean," he said suddenly, "did I ever tell you that when I was at the University, 'Meal Monday' still meant something?"

I knew "Meal Monday" only as an Edinburgh holiday, but I had learned to wait.

"On 'Meal Mondays'," he said, "the 'members of the University'—as I suppose our privileged brothers at Oxford and Cambridge would say—went home to get the bags of meal on which they lived during the next term. They walked home and they walked back. I was more fortunate than many of my generation." For a time there was silence; then he said abruptly: "Eleven of my classmates died of tuberculosis; actually, if you put it bluntly, they died of malnutrition. These girls have enough and too much. I won't have it."

I have forgotten now what he would not have, but I am willing to take my oath they did not get it. Not for nothing did we call him "Willy Nilly."

Because I was a Scot, though at a generation removed, he often let himself relapse into the vernacular with me. Ordinarily, except for the slight burr he never lost, his speech was the purest English, but when he was reminiscing, it could become so broad that I had difficulty understanding him. "Degenerate woman," he would tease me, "you whose grandfather had the Gaelic!" But his lapses into the vulgate with me were nothing compared with the conversations I heard him carry on when Sir Herbert Grierson was a visiting professor at Smith College. The two men had been at Edinburgh at about the same time, though Grierson, I think, was slightly senior to Neilson. Those conversations you could have cut with a butter knife—but it was the very best butter!

Neilson was a lowlander, and it both amused and touched me to see that sometimes he was on the defensive with highlanders. He need not have worried. Where *that* Macgregor sat was always the head of the table! I remember how he used to squirm with acute discomfort when Americans insisted on singing "Auld Lang Syne"; it was not our sentiment but our accent which offended him. When any of his colleagues taught the Romantic poets, Neilson could be depended upon to come to our classes and read Burns—if only to save the Scottish bard from the blasphemies to which we subjected him. Only recently did I learn that during his Columbia days his nickname was always "Burns."

The fact that Neilson was and remained a Scot throws some light, I believe, upon two important matters. When he was appointed to the Smith presidency, many of his academic colleagues wagged their heads, saying that he was a professor and not a businessman. Neilson surprised them, as he amazed his trustees. Not only did he balance the budget even during the Depression, but he made money for the college. His finance committee found in him no rubber stamp, but a shrewd business manager. He had a sense for finance which, had he chosen to use it for personal ends, might have enabled him to die a millionaire instead of the recipient of the sadly depleted Carnegie pension.

I do not discount his remarkable business acumen when I say that the real secret of his success as the business head of a college lay in his un-American sense of *thrift*. Generous to a fault with his family and friends, the Abou ben Adhem of our community in contributions to charities, he probably never balanced his personal budget. Yet profligate though he was with his own income, he saved the college pennies whenever he could. A story which illustrates this virtue is one about which he loved to tease his sisters. Upon one occasion, driving from New Haven to Northampton the sister "bated at noon," as Milton would say, when they noticed the road sign of a famous New England inn. They went in; they looked at the menu; they came out, still hungry, and climbed upon stools in the local drugstore, where they satisfied the pangs of nature, murmuring, "Something nearer thruppence!"

"Something nearer thruppence!" That was Neilson's motto. He would spare no expense when it came to important developments. But he never adopted qualities of the typical busy executive of American movies and stories. Not for him a telegram if a three-cent stamp would do—as it usually will. Not for him the long-distance telephone except in emergencies. When he was abroad—he used to go to Europe nearly every year in the old days—I sometimes needed to communicate with him on matters of importance. You may be sure I justified a cable in my own mind before I sent it. Once I remember getting back a message so terse— because he was counting the words—that I was not sure of his meaning. I did not send another cable to find out!

He hated extravagance as much as waste. He would not have the president's office redecorated and refurnished, though it was shabby enough; we had to put pressure upon him to order a more comfortable chair, though nearly every office in College Hall was better equipped than his. He teased the President of Wellesley (I think this was still in Miss Pendleton's time) when the new Administration Building was opened, and he found himself entering through an elaborate series of offices "into the presence," as he

137

said. On that occasion, I remember, he and I had gone to Wellesley by train; when we were ready to start back, our hostess was disturbed to find that we were casually taking an accommodation train that had no Pullman. "We're doing it on purpose," he told her. "The Dean and I must make the descent to Avernus one way or another, and the day coach will help us get used to living at Smith again!"

Often Neilson and I waited for over two hours in the Springfield station when we missed a Northampton connection. For reasons far beyond anyone's comprehension, our little local train made a point of pulling out three minutes before the express arrived from Chicago or St. Louis. Once when we were sitting in the station, having arrived on the Southwestern Limited to find the "dinky" gone, Neilson looked up from his book.

"Dean," he said, "we're a pair of obstinate Scots. When you think what our time is supposed to be worth, it's hard to justify our spending two hours here because we won't pay seven dollars for a taxi to Northampton."

My favorite story about his feeling against extravagance has to do with Yale. As he was a Harvard man, I was a Yale woman, and he loved to tease me about my "Alma Pater." Before the Sterling Library at Yale was opened, Neilson went down to see it. I had so often insulated him about *his* Widener Library that he could hardly wait to get back to Northampton to insult me about *my* Sterling Library. He dropped into my house, as so often, using my back door which he passed on the way home, to tell me about the spacious halls of Yale. A special kind of stone had been ordered for the main entrance, he said, because regular marble wasn't expensive enough to use up the whole sum of the gift.

"It's grand," he declared. "Of course the library attendants must wear choir robes and carry censers, sprinkling incense before the readers, who should wear academic dress. To be sure, they're worried about operating the place; they'll probably have to close up at four o'clock because they can't afford light and heat. It cost six million dollars, your new library down at Yale. When I'd looked it all over, I said to the President, 'Well, Angell, you haven't done so badly. You've managed to build a building with the whole endowment of Smith College, on which I annually educate two thousand young women—and educate them pretty darned well!'"

As his Scottish characteristics were to be seen in his business acumen, so, I think, his racial background was in part responsible for the toleration and liberalism of which so much has been rightly said. He was, as everyone knows, one of the great liberals of his generation, a stalwart champion of the underprivileged, of all racial minorities. He always stood out against restrictions which had to do with race, creed, color. I well remember a meeting of a group of college administrators at which the agenda called for a discussion of quotas. All colleges had been asked to submit figures covering a period of years. Neilson's quick eyes ran over one set of statistics; then he turned to the President.

"Is it," he asked with characteristic irony, "by chance, coincidence, luck or Special Providence that the Jewish applications at your college have remained for seven years at exactly seven per cent and that you have never had a Negro applicant?"

Only a week before he died, one of my former colleagues was discussing the whole problem with him. After he had had his say, she remarked, "Mr. Neilson, you are without doubt the most tolerant person I have ever known."

He hesitated, then replied with his usual humility, "If I am, it's because I was a Scot before I was an American. Scots don't talk much about democracy, because they are really democratic. Scots don't have racial prejudices, because they don't have racial problems of the sort you have in America. Of course"—the twinkle appeared for a moment—"Scots don't like the English! But I never knew anything about Jewish or Negro problems in my youth, and so I never developed the kind of prejudice which surprised me so much in America."

"But," my colleague pursued, "your attitude is different from the intellectual and abstract 'theory' of toleration one often finds. You really *haven't* any race-prejudice, have you?"

"No," he replied, "I can't remember ever feeling any prejudice against a race or a group. I guess it's because I think of them not as tribes but as people, and you know I like people." That was Neilson in a nutshell—he *liked people*.

He was ever a fighter for his principles. In his stand on the Sacco-Vanzetti case he opposed some of his staff and a large majority of his townsmen. He was frequently criticized for making so many appointments of "foreigners" to the faculty. As the situation in Europe became more and more acute, he incurred opposition by opening our doors to many refugees. I do not mean to imply that he encountered widespread opposition in the college itself on these matters, for our faculty as a group was liberal, tolerant and democratic, and the majority were in agreement with

Neilson's principles and policies on all these matters. There were occasional malcontents among the faculty and more among the alumnae, yet Neilson stuck to his guns on these matters as he did in his persistent stand on the perennially difficult issue of "academic freedom." I well remember those periods when the local postman used to make special trips to College Hall, loaded down with fat bags of letters which were certainly not "fan mail"!

Much of Neilson's life at Smith College was spent in attempts to convey to students his own ardent feeling for liberalism, democracy, toleration. More and more these became the themes of his "chapel talks," famous among many generations of students. For several years after I began my work with him, chapel was held every day, and Neilson often spoke four or five times a week. During the last years, after a college chaplain had been appointed, he spoke every Monday morning.

Neilson was the most consistently satisfactory public speaker I have ever heard and one of the finest. To be sure, the greatest of Winston Churchill's speeches surpassed the best of Neilson's, because the provocation was greater; apart from that Neilson was, I think Churchill's equal. As public speakers, they had much in common. Both had high regard for the English language and used it superbly. Both had great feeling for the sound as well as for the sense of their phrases. They could play upon the emotions as well as upon the intellect, could adjust themselves to the mood of the audience they found. Both had that sense of "theatre" essential in great public speakers. Each had a happy sense of exit, never talking overlong, stopping just when the audience was most eager that he continue.

I never heard Neilson give a poor speech; I often heard him give a magnificent one. Ordinarily he spoke without a manuscript and usually without notes. Indeed he was the *bête noire* of publicity directors, for he would not send a manuscript in advance. "Publicity," he would say impatiently, "it's the curse of our time and is having a pernicious influence upon public speaking. How do I know what kind of audience I'm going to face six weeks from Tuesday? I have to wait and size them up before I'm sure just what I'm going to say." Even his most formal speeches seemed to come so easily that many of his audience were unaware of the hours of thought that lay behind them, and perhaps did not sufficiently appreciate the art and craft which went to make him the superb speaker he was.

Only one kind of talk ever bothered him—the "vesper sermon"

which he had to give twice a year. On such occasions he was always ill at ease, though he never showed it. It was not because this was a "sermon," for Scots are natural born preachers. His restlessness was the result of his realization that he was the first lay-president of the college and that the earlier trustees—and many of the older members of our faculty—had doubted his ability to "lead" Smith students in their religious life. Those doubting Thomases need not have feared: chapel continued at Smith, without compulsion, long after it was dead or dying at neighboring institutions. It continued because of Neilson. Generations of Smith students of all denominations came to know the Bible as living literature as they heard him read it, day after day. It used to amuse me to see that visiting ministers often insisted on having a marker placed in the "lesson" they had chosen from the Scriptures, while Neilson the layman, Neilson the "suspect," never bothered about markers, secure in his knowledge of that great Book, which he loved even more than he loved Shakespeare and Chaucher and Milton.

Phrases from both the Old and the New Testaments, I know, still echo in the minds of his students—Protestant, Catholic, Jewish. They listened eagerly for his first words, knowing that the passage he had chosen for the day's "lesson" would give them a clue to the "sermon" that would follow. "Let us now praise famous men": Smith alumnae will never forget that familiar prologue to the anniversary of a great leader, as they will not forget Neilson's reading on Lincoln's birthday of Whitman's "O Captain! My Captain!"

Yet if, on the anniversary of a great man, he praised the king and counselors who sit in the seats of the mighty, he was likely to remember at the next chapel those nameless sons—and daughers —of Martha, who have left no memorial, yet who now, as in Biblical times, "maintain the fabric of the world"—for in their work is their strength.

Again and again he led services for our college dead. Whenever one of our members had died ripe with years, Neilson read the Ninetieth Psalm. Only once have I heard his reading of that great utterance on human mortality equalled. At his funeral, his successor spoke those words over his coffin. Had anyone read them less perfectly, it would have been unbearable; as President Davis said them, they were reminiscent, poignant, comforting.

Neilson's range in his chapel talks was extraordinary. Upon occasion he could be Moses, Jeremiah or Isaiah, Lewis Carroll or

141

W. S. Gilbert. He could cajole, tease, scold, reprove, encourage, praise, exhort. He might take a text anywhere. One morning he would turn from Proverbs—"Hast thou a word in thy throat? Hold it. It will not choke thee,"—to a *diatribe* on student gossip, satirical as Pope or Swift. On another morning he might use as text a sentence from Dorothy Sayers' *Gaudy Night*, "Three years of your life which ought to be different." He had been visiting dormitories with the superintendent of grounds to see what changes were essential, and had been depressed by finding many students playing bridge in the afternoon.

"College is a place to grow up in," he announced abruptly on another occasion, when he delivered one of the finest defenses I have ever heard of the American liberal arts college, with its emphasis upon the whole personality of the student rather than merely upon professional training. In that sentence was contained much of Neilson's philosophy of education. The primary function of a college was the training of the mind; Neilson the intellectual never discounted that. But Neilson the educator did not believe that this was the sole object of an American college. He never forgot that students are adolescents: "You come to us children, you leave us young women—even qualified voters," he used to say.

He wanted his graduates to be well-rounded women, whose college experience had made them more capable of seeing and thinking clearly, of applying to everyday modern life the wisdom they had gained from great thinkers of the past. If he was sometimes discouraged when he came back from visits to alumnae clubs, wondering what had happened to those alert and eager young minds he had seen unfolding before him, he still believed that the college had an important function, that it was a place in which students "grew up."

Yet he refused to take the whole responsibility for the process. College years are built upon the years of youth, and no college can produce a complete transformation of personality. I well remember his reply to one irate mother who wished to lay upon the college all the responsibility for the shortcomings of her daughter, who had not "grown up" well in our community. "Madam," he said, "you had your daughter for eighteen years; I have had her for eighteen months. Which of us is responsible?"

During the latter years, when he spoke only at Monday chapel —and occasionally at Wednesday assembly—the students missed something of his vast range. They did not know their president as well as earlier students had known him, for they did not see him in all his moods. Theirs was a more serious president, for as the clouds grew darker over Europe, Neilson devoted more and more of his chapel talks to international affairs. He did his best to make the younger generation realize that a day of reckoning was coming.

It was not Neilson's fault if war caught any Smith alumna of his generation unprepared. For years he did his best to chart the course of Europe and America and the Orient. A pacifist at heart, he spent the years of the '30's attempting to make his students averse to war, and indeed, we had a great wave of student pacifism at that time. But Neilson knew it was only an intellectual pacifism, a youthful adherence to a cause which was not yet real to those who espoused it. "They'll send the white feather to their young men," he used to say, "just as the generation before them did." Nothing in their experience had prepared that generation for what happened to them. Born when war seemed already a thing of the past, they had grown up in abnormal times: they spent their childhood in a period of abnormal inflation, their youth in a period of abnormal depression.

He knew he was fighting for a cause already lost, but he was ever a fighter, and he doubled his efforts as the lights began to go out in Europe. During those last years at Smith, he was a much more somber president than in the earlier days when he had been all fire and spirit, when he had bubbled over to his students and they knew him for the myriad-minded man he was.

Those were happy days—brief years between two periods of war, when he could laugh and tease and cajole, rather than exhort and instruct—happy for him, happy for us. During those years he did his best work for the college, less distracted than he afterwards became by outside activities in international relations and on racial problems. He had taken on the presidency of Smith when women's colleges were, if not entirely disparaged as "finishing schools," somewhat overlooked in the total picture of American education. During his administration, Smith College took its proper place in the sun. Whatever he found it—that was before my time—he left it on a par with leading universities of the country.

Indeed, under Neilson, Smith had always a "university" rather than a "college" flavor—if the tastes are different, as I think they are. He raised the standards of entrance and graduation until many alumnae protested. He reformed the curriculum more than once, attempting to find a true basis for what is now called "general education." He expanded the work in art and music, both of which he believed as legitimate parts of a liberal arts curriculum as work in literature or history. He inaugurated the "Special Honors" program for superior students—protested by many alumnae but loved by the students who followed it—by which we turned out B.A.'s on a par with M.A.'s in many institutions. He constantly emphasized "scholarship" in his talks to students, though he knew that the number of women who will ever proceed with "scholarship" will always be limited. That did not deter him from preaching the scholars' gospel. He believed that basic attitudes of scholarship may and should be carried over into everyday life.

With one kind of "scholarship" alone he had no sympathy. He hated pedantry as he hated other forms of ostentation and display. If our students learned nothing else from him, they learned, I hope, to carry their learning lightly. The best of them wore their rue with a difference, for the acquirement of highest honors at Smith was fun and excitement in Neilson's day.

Ardent though he was for women's rights, Neilson always insisted on a balanced faculty of men and women at Smith College. Coeducationally trained myself, I like to tease him by telling him that he was a coeducationalist at heart. When Harvard introduced coeducation—though Harvard still denies it—he thought it a salutary change. His policy in regard to the faculty at Smith College was clear enough to me, though it was often misunderstood by my women colleagues. Men were promoted at Smith more rapidly than women. That, I believe, is inevitable since a man has more "market value" than a woman. Even first-rate women on a women's college faculty usually expect to spend their lives in one place, but men do not, and, because of frequent calls from outside, they go up more rapidly.

Neilson had a well-defined policy about men at a women's college: "Get them young; get the best ten or fifteen years of their teaching and research; then let them go reluctantly, for women's colleges cannot compete with men's colleges or with coeducational universities. Their endowments are too low, since most wealthy women"—I can still hear his ironic voice—"insist on leaving their money to their husbands' colleges, rather than to their own."

The roster of Neilson's "faculty graduates" is a distinguished one. Many men who served us well for ten to fifteen years are scattered all over the land. Wherever they are, whatever their salaries, I know that many of them look back to those years they spent under Neilson's liberal administration as the happiest period of their academic lives.

I have called him "Neilson of Smith." So he will go down in academic history. If posterity writes no other epitaph, he will be content, for he fulfilled himself at Smith and deliberately chose to stay there. Yet a women's college, no matter how good—and he made Smith very good—did not offer the fullest scope for his great abilities. Last year I was told that some eighty American institutions, large and small, were seeking presidents. They found much "lumber" but far too little presidential "timber." Neilson was seasoned timber, the greatest college president, I believe, of his time. I have sometimes resented the fact that many alumnae took for granted that he remained at Smith because he had reached the *ne plus ultra* of all careers. That of course is not true. Neilson knew his abilities, as he knew his limitations, and he was quite aware that he could have fulfilled himself even more completely had the scope of his activities been greater. But I have done him less than justice if I have not indicated that his principles always came before his preferences. The reason he did not accept the presidency of a great university was a simple one. He disapproved profoundly of our American emphasis upon extramural athletics, our tendency to exalt the football coach above the professor. He would not accept the presidency of any institution committed to an extensive athletic program.

I confess that I have often wondered what would have happened had the Harvard presidency fallen vacant when he was younger. Many of us remember his wry smile when he read a clipping from a Boston newspaper, at the time reporters were guessing about the succession. After a long list of imposing names, the writer added: "There is also the able but aged President of Smith." Knowing him as I did, I believe he would have stuck to his guns even in the case of Harvard, but I am glad he did not have to make that particular choice.

So far I have described him, as most of us will remember him, as if he had been a paragon of all the virtues. But his quizzical eye is upon me. He would not wish to be embalmed and treasured up to posterity as a glorified mummy. In that minor classic which William Allen White wrote many years ago about his dead daughter, he said, "She was as full of faults as an old shoe and just as comfortable." Neilson had no aura of saintly perfection; he had plenty of faults, but like young Mary White, he was a most comfortable person to live with. He had his little vanities.

For example, he was always sensitive about his height. Not under the average masculine stature, he was only a little above it, and as he grew older he stooped so that he seemed shorter than he was. He hated to be paired in academic processions with tall men or women, and would go out of his way to rearrange the line of march when he could.

He liked praise, even adulation, for, as he liked people, he wanted people to like him. His successor was somewhat appalled when, at the time of his appointment, he received a telegram from the Alumnae Association saying, "Twenty-two thousand women welcome you." Neilson could take twenty-two thousand women in his stride, even when at his last Commencement they threw before him hundreds of paper hearts, symbolic of the place he held in their affection. Like all great men, he was a bit of an exhibitionist. Many a man would have quailed at that Ivy Day custom at Smith College, when the President walked down the long path between lines of cheering alumnae to meet still another group of women, the seniors and juniors. But Neilson ran the gauntlet jauntily, with a gay smile and a wave of his hand. Actually he loved the occasion.

Others of his "faults" could have been much more serious. I told him more than once that he had the strongest sense of mercy I had even known, but not so marked a sense of justice. His quality of mercy was never strained. He was so kindly, so human, that if someone wept on his shoulder—and it was frequently mildewed!—he was likely to capitulate, forgetting an analogous case of another member of the staff who had been more restrained. For a seasoned administrator, he remained curiously innocent, peculiarly unsuspicious of human motives. I came to realize that he was not a very good judge of people, often overestimating them when he made appointments, excusing them when they did not live up to his expectations, attributing to chance or circumstance the failure of some he had appointed with enthusiasm. As a member of various fellowship and scholarship boards outside the college, I found that his recommendations were not dependable. They always erred on the side of praise. I do not remember ever seeing a really adverse criticism.

Even more serious was another "fault"—if you wish to call it so. Ardent as he was for the causes to which he devoted his efforts, he did not always discriminate between just and less just causes, and he sometimes fought doggedly and even obstinately for a cause or a person not worth his defense. I said to him once: "You are so ardent for the underdog that you will never believe that an underdog can be a yellow dog." But these "faults" were only the defects of his great qualities. Had he been less kindly, more suspicious of human beings, less ardent for lost causes, he would not have been the great personality we shall always remember. We are richer in humanity, perhaps, because of his faults than because of his undoubted virtues.

Nothing in his life more became him than the leaving of it. I am back to the Elizabethans, as I knew I should be. As I have said, he had a happy sense of exit, never speaking too long, never staying long enough. He was always among the first to leave a party, just when everyone most wanted him to stay. As if by the sheer force of personality, he seemed to control even destiny. The end came swiftly, as he would have wished. As always, before he started on a trip, he had cleaned up his desk. The day before he was taken ill he had written the last words of the *History of Smith College,* on which he had been engaged since his retirement. In another way, too, it almost seemed as if he had deliberately chosen the time of his departure.

Neilson always hated to give people trouble; he would not have wished his trustees and alumnae to disturb their schedules, to take long trips to attend his funeral. And so he slipped away while all the trustees and alumnae officers were in Northampton for their regular midwinter meeting. As I sat in the hall in which I had heard him talk morning after morning, during so many years, and thought of that campus, much of which he had planned with eagerness and affection; as I watched the men and women he had chosen to help him build a great college—I could feel no regret for him. My sadness was only for those of us who are left without him. He had fought the good fight, he had finished his work. He had lived a rich, full, rewarding, and a happy life. Over the casket where lay that good grey head that all men knew, someone should have spoken words which he had often read over others who did not merit them so fully:

> *Nothing is here for tears, nothing to wail*
> *Or knock the breast, no weakness, no contempt,*
> *Dispraise, or blame, nothing but well and fair,*
> *And what may quiet us in a death so noble.*

"When a great man dies," his countryman James Barrie wrote in his tribute to George Meredith, "the immortals wait for him at the top of the nearest hill." What a goodly fellowship must have waited for Neilson that night on the summit of Mount Tom, our little peak above Paradise Pond, which on clear days seems almost in the President's front yard. Neilson had lived beyond the Biblical three-score years, even by virtue of strength beyond three score and ten, and many he had loved had gone before him. The immortals who swarmed down our easy mountain pass that night were not Plato and Aristotle, Homer and Virgil. Even Neilson would have been ill at ease with those highlanders! These were lesser fry, men he had missed during his last years as they must have missed him, waiting eagerly for reunion.

Neilson always boasted that, because of his long experience with a feminine community, he could seat two ladies at table at once. All of us who knew him well remember how he could greet two friends at once, his right hand extended to one with that quick firm clasp, his left arm about the shoulders of another. I like to think that, as his spirit went up Mount Tom that night, one hand reached out to John Finley, one arm was a moment across Dean Woodbridge's shoulders. Woodbridge had his persistent pipe, Neilson, with a last chuckle at the doctors he need never mind again, lighted one of his interminable cigars. And what "grand clacks" they're having now, those three great men and great conversationalists, in some other Mermaid Tavern in the empyrean!

> *No pyramids set off his memories,*
> *But the eternal substance of his greatness,—*
> *To which I leave him.*

# Ritual and Reality

## LEO STEIN

## ( *1947* )

Leo Stein spent most of his life in Europe. He was an early patron of many of the painters who became the masters of modern art, including Picasso and Matisse, although he was savagely intolerant of Picasso's later work. Mr. Stein wrote two books, *Appreciation: Painting, Poetry and Prose* and *The A-B-C of Aesthetics*. A posthumous book, *Journey into the Self*, consisted of his autobiographical writings.

SOME years ago there was published a book that caused a deal of discussion. It was in French and called *Le Trahison des Clercs*—that is, *Betrayal by the Intellectuals*. It is long since I read the book, and the particular contents do not concern me. My concern is with the question raised—in what respect do the intellectuals fail?

First, one must define the intellectual. In general one may say he is a man of superior intelligence debauched by a false education. So one must define a right education. A right education is one that progressively enlightens *and* integrates. Enlightenment is not difficult to understand. It means becoming operatively acquainted with facts, their relations, their meanings, and their values. Integration is not so easy to understand, because that is generally lacking and so is not a familiar notion. It means that this enlightenment is not compartmented—that one's religion, one's philosophy, one's science, one's art and one's way of living go together; that when facts, their relations, their meanings and their values are incompatible, one does not believe them all, effecting this result by preventing them from mixing, but that one either holds them to be in part false, or keeps them in abeyance while looking for further coordination.

It is commonly supposed that religion and philosophy in

especial serve to secure coordination. I believe this to be radically untrue. There are many religions and many philosophies which are entirely incompatible with each other, and which are held in belief by men of equal moral and intellectual standing. This is a commonplace. What is the state of mind of a critical person—and of course, one who is not simply credulous must be critical—who ignores this fact? He is certainly not integrated, since he evades the assimilation of something that is sure and incontrovertible. Of course, one may hold, as Moses Mendelssohn did, that all religions are merely symbolic expressions of common ineffable truths; but in that case why does one so commonly accept one formula in which one is more or less rigidly encased, and so become estranged from others who, according to this, believe the same vital truths? In such a case, the definite religions with their dogmas and rituals are certainly a pest and a strait jacket, and an enemy to integration.

No one pretends that all philosophies are no more than symbolic expressions of ineffable truths. Their reason for being is that they are logically adequate and genuinely explicatory. If one philosopher is convinced of the truth of an explanation which another, equally competent, rejects, the right question to ask, so it seems to me, is not what is the matter with the philosophy but what is the matter with the philosopher. Is he an integrated person, or is it that he will have a ritual of thought at any price? The question about philosophies has been asked *ad nauseam*. It is time to ask seriously the question about the philosopher.

The treason of the intellectual lies in this: that he is grotesquely credulous, while pretending to be discriminatory and critical. He takes himself for granted, an extravagant assumption. He has never taken this central question of integration seriously, and inquired into his own state. He is, in the current slang, a wishful thinker who has certain preferences in beliefs, and simply discounts those who are otherwise inclined.

Of course, being ostensibly open-minded, he goes through the forms of considering the views of others and finding out what is the matter with *them*—but this is a mere form. It is a familiar fact that no mature philosopher ever changes his views as the result of all the critical study he devotes to the work of others. I know only one exception to this law. Russell, a professor at Williams College, was converted to pragmatism when he could not meet the challenge of William James to give some other meaning to the notion of truth than that given by the pragmatists.

But this is not really an exception, as pragmatism is not really a philosophy. Intellectuals are, like other men, moral cowards, and are afraid to let go the supports to which they are used to cling. They go far enough away from them to peek at other things, but when there is a threat to them, a danger of having to stand alone without the protection of their opinions, they scurry back. So at this moment markedly, when there is a greater felt threat than at any time in many generations, a condition unequalled perhaps, since the fall of the Roman Empire.

In philosophy, as in religion, the situation is to an unprejudiced observer, grotesque, even comic. When I was in college it was taken for granted that the valid philosophical line ran through Kant. James was admittedly a great psychologist, and otherwise amusing, but Royce was the *real* philosopher. The prevailing view at Harvard was well expressed by the student who said in class, "But Professor James, to be serious for a moment . . ."

The Berkeley-Hume-Kantian paradoxes which, at best, are brilliant *jeux d'esprit,* were taken with preternatural solemnity by people who wanted to go through somehow, though there was no certain thoroughfare. James heretically declared the right way of philosophy to be around Kant, not through him; Santayana treats him despitefully; Whitehead barely mentions him. It seems to me more probable that the right way is around the whole subject.

James said, and this is unquestionable fact, that philosophies are not disproved but outmoded, which tells the true story and confutes the notion of their intellectual seriousness. They are attempts to allay the disturbance that the heterogeneity of things impinging on us causes; but, as with sedatives, the effects are not enduring, and after a while we want some other drug. Just now there is an unusual demand for an old comforter, the neatly articulated platitudes of the Aristotelian-Thomist tradition. There are philosophies as there are drugs—for all temperaments, all diatheses, all seasons.

A mind divided between the desire for belief and the desire for proof is in a bad way. It ranges in type from one who tries to explain away the flagrant infidelities of his wife, one like Lord Augustus in *Lady Windermere's Fan,* easily convinced, to the hero of Cervantes' story, who, wanting absolute proof of his wife's inviolable chastity, drives her into infidelity. Something of this division is common. James has much to say of it in the preliminaries of his *Pragmatism*. One wants to explain nature in such a way that desire and proof accord, and in order to escape from obvious credulity or scepticism, one makes a mixture that seems palatable.

That very sceptical philosopher Francis Bradley, ironical, acutely critical, who stepped on vermin with a heel of iron, said that philosophy should satisfy all sides of our nature, and that he would not finally accept the result unless it did. Why it should do so, he cannot say; he wants it that way, and that is all. Margaret Fuller said simply, "I accept the Universe," and Thomas Carlyle, with his raucous prophetical voice, said, "Gad, she'd better." From this one would hardly guess that the contorted, irascible, vociferous prophet of "Silence" never did accept it.

I agree with Margaret Fuller, but I find it necessary to pose conditions, not on nature but on myself. Man is either a part of nature, an animal with consciousness, or he is outside nature. If he is a part of nature, then it is natural that nature should satisfy essential demands. If he is outside nature, then this is not at all evident. The testimony of the intellectual over thousands of years from the Solons, the Jobs, the Siddarthas, to the Lawrences, the Eliots and the Huxleys, is that man is not satisfied. Whatever he may speculatively think, he feels that the universe should somehow be adapted to him. But, if man is really to be at one with nature, then man must, like other creatures in nature, be ready to eat or be eaten as the case may be. All animals do their best to eat and avoid being eaten, and man has superior means at his command to control events. But to interpret things so that his *right* to eat is greater than his *liability* to be eaten, is to take him out of nature.

The philosopher expresses his will to believe, disguised under a mask of logic, but the religious person tries rather to expand his will to believe, like the frog in the fable. "Help thou my unbelief." What he can't believe by himself, he believes with the aid of those who have a bigger swallow.

"I can't believe that!" said Alice.

"Can't you?" the Queen said in a pitying tone. "Try again: draw a long breath, and shut your eyes."

Sometimes the method of Mark Twain works best: "I couldn't lie, so I told Harris to do it." Philosophers and religious leaders do all they can to keep the world the troubled confusion that it is by solving the essential problems with fictions instead of facing the facts.

What are these facts? The first is that man is the only animal, so far as we know, that habitually lies. Other animals have their ruses, their stratagems to gain their ends, but man is the only animal, probably, that lies for the repose and comfort of his soul. Lying and integration have as much affinity as chalk and cheese. The honest philosopher who is not satisfied till nature has consented to his essential demands, should first try to learn how far these demands are valid, and how far they result from the fictions with which he has nursed his mighty youth. It may be that he is so little accustomed to truth that he cannot distinguish it from fiction. He may feel honest, just as he may feel that he has proved a case which another with equally strong feelings and equal capacity finds absurd. But feelings of honesty do not answer serious questions.

The real question can be posed in these terms: man is the conscious animal; there is no intellect or specific human feeling without consciousness. Is the intellectual fully conscious, or isn't he? Emerson said, "There is a crack in everything God made." The crack in the intellectual is his imperfect consciousness. Can he look himself squarely in the face, and can he look at himself all around as he would look at another who supposedly included himself? That is, as if he, at one and the same time, knew what he knows of himself, both clearly and as in a glass darkly, and see it as an object in the round, impartially, as another might see it? Until he has done this, his honesty has never been put to the ultimate test. He has not proved his readiness to give up all that is untrue. He may be a sufficient juror for an ordinary trial, but these trials of philosophy and religion, which purport to go beyond the ordinary, require all or nothing. We are not satisfied, even in such an "inferior" discipline as physical science, if the seeker does not come into the open with everything that is relevant. The first demand to be made in religion and philosophy is that the man have nothing up his sleeve. So far as we know he always has.

Animals have developed all sorts of societies, all sorts of symbioses, complex relations of many kinds, without developing man's peculiar type of mendacity. Man appears to believe that without lying there can be neither philosophy, religion, communities, commerce or society. Here comes the second fact. Instead of truth, he has rituals, sacred and profane; and with these, as we all know, he makes an awful mess of things. Some fatuous people believe that at some remote time, in Greece or in the Middle Ages—times of which we know little, and nothing, of course, at first hand—he made less of a mess with these. That gets us nowhere. There is a call here and now to look for something other than a reconstruction of what perhaps never existed —to look toward a reformation of what is, to make an advance, and not to make a turn backward.

If man lived on the animal level, though with more knowledge of outward things than the animals have, he would probably get along as they do with their ups and downs. And in truth, men do so live on their merely practical side. But it is the business of the intellectual not to be satisfied with this, but instead to be concerned for validity and truth. Cleansing the inside of the cup has got to have another meaning from what it had in the good old days, when to mean well was evidence. The ritual-ridden world is to my eyes very much like the king in the fable who wore the magic garments admired by all till the child said, "But he hasn't anything on!" In fact, this world is garmented in fictions.

A brave new world can date only from Freud. He did not get very far, but he threw more light on mendacity than even the Jesuit casuists, and mendacity is the central difficulty. Mendacity and secrecy go together, and mendacity cannot be cured until secrecy is abandoned. In no way can it be cured out of hand; it will take generations and more generations, but the price must be paid. Essential change and improvement in the future will depend on this.

This article is not a *Trahison d'un Clerc*, it is not the product of speculation or fantasy. The results I have come to were come to the hard way. Starting with the treatment of a severe neurosis, I have continued unceasingly through the years, a full quarter of a century, to find out how thoroughly honest one could be with oneself. I developed a special technique for this, far more drastic than the technique of psychoanalysis, and too difficult in application to be practicable. It has not obliged me to believe things that are probably not true, to wrestle with absurd problems of evil, to reconcile a god of love with the Nazi regime, or to explain why Brahma created a world of illusion and how he is related to it; and yet it works out as a continuous conversion. From month to month, from week to week, sometimes from day to day I am reborn, and for this I need no revelation. The process goes on

154

without halt even now—when according to the calendar I am an old man, soon to be seventy-five; and as long as I live and retain my faculties, it will keep going on. It will keep going farther from ritual toward reality, from the confusions of "sin," "guilt," "shame," "anxiety," and the complexes of inferiority and superiority, toward untangled relations with events—and for all this I need no revelation. My obligation is to nothing except intellectual honesty, but that is absolute. In this article I for the first time speak out on the subject. It was written, one might say, with blood and iron, though literally the iron was all in my typewriter and haemoglobin.

With the progress of this work, I lose more and more my feeling of possessiveness. When I was younger I had it very strongly. Now to possess anything that does not serve a real interest seems to me absurd. But this applies as much to intellectual and spiritual possessions as it does to material ones. An explanation that does not explain, a belief not validated by its context, a work of art whose interest is nominal, gives me as much satisfaction as a pair of shoes I can't wear, though all may have merits of workmanship. Simplification is progressive when integration is insistent, and I shall not believe the fifty-seven varieties of religion and philosophy to have other than anthropological interest until they have been tried in the fire of an integrative process. Follows the credo that has grown out of this work.

I believe in the life of everyday, which is, in a more complex way, the life we share with the other animals. I believe in knowledge and appreciation—the first, especially the realm of science; the other, of art. I believe in logic, which is, implicitly, the core of functional activity. I do not believe in philosophy, which I consider an invalid and messy mixture of art and logic. It is poetry distorted. I believe in religion as the consciousness of life, of living. Christianity and Buddhism have reversed this. They negate life and substitute for it fantasms which have their valid place in the symbols of the poets.

I believe, furthermore, that it is not true, as usually assumed, that the man we know is the normal man. He is not. He is a hybrid between the conscious and the unconscious, and the product of this hybrid state is the repression which produces the secondary and pathological unconscious. The unconscious impulses should work out as the full consciousness of experience and make man sane. As he now is, he is a nuisance and should disappear. He may, like the great saurians, come to an end, but, unlike them, be himself a main agent of his own destruction; or he may grow out of his barbarous half-consciousness and become the normal, or conscious, man—not through evolution, but by a slow process of education carried through many generations. So he may become viable, but he may meanwhile devastate irremediably the earth.

I believe finally, that the influence of mendacity, including wishful thinking, makes any serious progress in human affairs impossible. Science provides information and creates instruments, but until for applying these we have honest conscious men instead of those who think that a ritual in affairs, in thought, in culture and in worship, can take the place of wide-awake honesty, we must stay where we are. We may spin like a whipped top, faster and faster, but going faster will be the only change.

# The Devil Is Dead, and What a Loss!

## GERALD W. JOHNSON

## ( *1947* )

Historian and journalist, GERALD W. JOHNSON is best known for his pungent and reflective observations on the American scene. For almost half a century he has examined and consistently dismantled the sacred cows of his time.

O PTIMISTS among us have cherished the delusion, in recent years, that the United States has attained a level of intellectual maturity at which public opinion will no longer tolerate attempts by magistrates to set themselves up as censors of morals, as far as literature and the arts are concerned. But their optimism has been rudely jarred since the day of Japan's collapse; for the last two years have seen a veritable epidemic of attacks on books, plays and other forms of expression—even a statue was removed from one show in New York, although that was done by private, not public, censors. The number and violence of the assaults almost equal those that followed the collapse of the Kaiser in 1918.

Plainly, a recrudescence of Puritanism—meaning, of course, not the theology and ethics of Cromwell and Cotton Mather, but the tyrannical Bluenose—has developed in the United States, and some examination of its nature and origin is essential to an understanding of the prevailing mental climate of the country. There are indications that it differs in important respects from the old Puritanism with which we are familiar; for one thing there is no evidence that it is based upon a revival of belief in theocracy, for there has been none. If you question its strength, though, you should consult one of the publishers who has fought his way through the courts, or a radio commentator suddenly cut off the air, or any script writer in Hollywood. They all know that not in many years has free expression of opinion in America been so dangerous.

In the absence of religious fanaticism, the only explanation of tolerated censorship is fear. Superficially, it would seem to be preposterous to suggest that the United States is terror-stricken. Never before in its history has it possessed military strength so prodigious, absolutely or relatively. Our navy is by long odds the mightiest afloat. Our army has recently proved that its high mechanization, rather than the number of its soldiers, has made it capable of shattering simultaneously two of the most powerful armies that the world has ever seen. A hideous war lasting six years has broken down and destroyed the efficiency of every other military power in the world except one, and that one is a land power far removed from contact with our borders except at a single remote point, the extreme tip of Alaska.

Strategically, therefore, the United States would seem to be safer than it has been at any time since 1776.

Economically, the wealth of the United States, as measured in money, is greater than at any previous time, and this in spite of frightful expenditures during the war. The national debt of 260 billions is almost all held by our own people. Paying it will be simply a matter of transferring money from one pocket to another. If every dollar were paid off tomorrow, practically no money would leave the country. Our industrial equipment is enormously greater and more efficient than ever before. Our labor force is larger and better trained than ever before. The productivity of our soil per acre has been increasing, not decreasing, especially since the Soil Conservation Program began to work in a big way. Our forests and mineral resources have been depleted by the war, but intelligent effort can easily restore the forests within one generation. Only in minerals have we suffered anything that can properly be called a permanent economic loss.

Economically, the country is in a far sounder position than it was in, say, 1933.

Politically, the divisions among our people have been eroded and erased to the point at which since 1946 we have had virtually one-party government. The really sharp differences now are not between the parties, but between factions within the parties— between Northern Democrats and "Rankin Republicans" from the South, and between Old Guard Republicans and Sons of the Wild Jackass. Emphatically, there is no danger that the parties will resort to violence to settle their differences, as there was in 1876, when the Hayes-Tilden dispute threatened civil war.

Politically, there is less danger of a *coup d'état* today than at almost any other period in our national history.

Strategically, economically, politically, the United States enjoys in 1947 a security the like of which it has never attained before. Yet terror is the order of the day. Vice societies prosecute authors, even poets, as they have rarely prosecuted them before. Business interests purge the radio. Congress offers to make membership in the Communist party a crime. If this were done, there are grounds for fear that membership in the Socialist party would soon be condemned, and then suspicion of adherence to the New Deal would be enough for an indictment. The President of the United States demands an appropriation of $25,000,-000 to delouse the government service of traitors, who must have been put there by his own party, since it has been in power for fourteen years.

Since neither military power, money power nor partisan rancor offers any threat to our safety, it is evident that the threat must be of an intangible kind. Indeed, this is evident from the form our precautions take. Censoring books, gagging radio comedians, purging the civil service, are not defenses against armed enemies, nor against business competitors, nor even against politicians run mad and turned Populist. Such a program, if it is effective against anything, can be effective only against what the Japanese police called "dangerous thoughts." What we fear desperately is not the Russians, or the cartels, or the Republicans. The real fear is that the American people are about to get out of hand.

This is something contrary to the old tradition. Time was when it was the fashion to rejoice that no one could control the American people—in their morals, in their speech, or in their political ideas.

A proposal to censor books could once draw from Jimmy Walker the scornful comment, "I wish the honorable gentleman would cite one instance of a woman's being seduced by a book."

A proposal to purge the list of government employees could once draw from Thomas Jefferson the remark, "If there be any among us who would wish to dissolve this Union or to change its republican form, let them stand undisturbed as monuments of the safety with which error of opinion may be tolerated where reason is left free to combat it."

A proposal to "knock Mr. Bryan into a cocked hat" once drew

Woodrow Wilson's approval, but only on condition that the means to that end should be both "effective and dignified." Failing that, he was against the project.

From Jefferson to Jimmy, in short, it was assumed as a matter of course that the people were never in hand and never would be. Now it is assumed that unless we get them and keep them in hand, ruin is just around the corner. So Edmund Wilson and the concocter of *Forever Amber,* whose name I forget, are haled into court charged with using naughty words. So Fred Allen is cut off the air for making unseemly jests about his sponsor. So we are to spend $25,000,000 purging the public payrolls. The nephews of Uncle Sam are to think none but decorous and immaculate thoughts. They are not to have a mind to sport with Amaryllis in the shade. They are not to giggle in the Cathedral of the Holy Dividends. They are not to suspect that there can be other political parties than the existing Janus-faced organization, Democan on one side, Republicrat on the other.

What in the name of all that is preposterous is the basis of this frowsy idiocy?

I suppose there is no short and simple answer. National hysteria rarely results from a single cause, and usually from a complex of many factors. In the instant case, a number come to mind at once—nervous exhaustion following the emotional orgy of a great war, apprehension at finding ourselves suddenly thrust into the leading role among the nations, mass miseducation conducted by able propagandists, the latent but ever-present fear of freedom in the human heart, resentment at having to solve problems set by others, and the reaction following a moment of intense fright.

There is one element, however, to which analysts of public affairs rarely pay much attention, but which may be more important than they suppose. This is sheer boredom following the death of the Devil.

For the spirit of Puritanism has never been wholly eradicated from the American mind, and it is characteristic of Puritanism that while it may get along comfortably enough without God— witness the host of Puritanical agnostics, from Bob Ingersoll to Clarence Darrow—it has always found the Devil indispensable. He is Protean in his manifestations, of course, but he must exist in some shape if the Puritan is to live comfortably.

Beginning in 1933, we had a highly efficacious Devil in the person of Adolf Hitler, whom we hated with a satisfaction that rose in a steep crescendo into frenetic exultation at the end of a dozen years. But then the inconsiderate Russians shot down his capital about his ears and buried him in its flaming ruins. By the rules of the game we had to thank them, of course, and we did; but it really left a great vacuum in our lives. The Mikado served briefly as a substitute, but he soon bowed himself out of the role, and there we were left, all wound up to hate furiously, and with nobody to hate.

It has taken us nearly two years to perceive the obvious and elect Stalin to the vacancy. In fact, we have not been able to make it unanimous even yet, for Henry Wallace is still howling a contrary vote up and down the land, and until we corral him and his following in concentration camps there will always be doubts that Stalin is the real thing. But time passes. We have no really effective Devil, and the high-pressure hatred generated within our bosoms must have an outlet or we shall choke.

In the circumstances, it was perhaps inevitable that the blushful books, the impudent jokesmiths and the always vulnerable bureaucrats should come in for a vigorous fustigation. It may be, indeed, that it is fortunate that these became the victims, for otherwise we might have vented our uneasiness on Negroes and Jews, with results infinitely more damaging socially. After all, jailing a few authors and turning a few radio comedians and jobholders out to starve is not nearly as bad as murdering an indefinite number of persons belonging to racial and religious minorities.

For it is characteristic of the Puritan that he cannot live at ease with his own conscience unless he is persecuting somebody. He has never really accepted the Pauline doctrine of the Vicarious Atonement; in theory he adheres to it, of course, but in actual fact his philosophy parallels the Hindu doctrine of Karma—that is to say, the theory that he must atone for his own sins. He diverges from Hinduism in holding that this is not to be accomplished through reincarnation, but by the neater and simpler process described by Samuel Butler—

> *Compound for sins they are inclined to,*
> *By damning those they have no mind to.*

Censorship of books, for example, is an advantageous catharsis for the semi-literate. Discreetly administered, it may compound for a vast deal of lechery actively practiced. Similarly, cropping the ears of comedians undoubtedly affords relief to the humorless who are troubled by knowledge of their own tendency to extortion and excess. As for applying the bastinado to jobholders, that has been regarded as a manifestation of civic virtue from time immemorial, and none is more vociferously in favor of it than the man who never takes the trouble to vote.

It is rather hard on the novelists, the clowns and the clerks, but if their pains and penalties serve to divert the Puritan rage into channels less murderous than those it would otherwise follow, perhaps they suffer in a good cause. In any event, there is reason to believe that their present disability will not be of long duration.

They are, in fact, rather poor substitutes for a real Devil. They matter so little. If literature and dramaturgy were completely abolished, the lives of huge masses of the citizenry would be affected not at all. As for jobholders, nobody has ever proposed to abolish them; the sport is merely to throw the present ones out and put others in their places. It is for the entertainment of seeing them jump that we propose to spend $25,000,000—not for the abolition of the species.

Once we have a Mephistopheles of real stature, thoroughly established as the orthodox object of hatred for all well-conducted persons, nobody will waste much time and energy pursuing mere scriveners and mimes. Present indications are that this consummation is about to be effected. Stalin is obviously to be the archfiend, whose damnation will compound for all our agreeable sins. Presumably it will not be the authentic, but a synthetic Stalin, one of our own design, a creation much better adapted to the purpose than the somewhat prosaic, matter-of-fact individual who inhabits the Kremlin. His construction is in progress now, and apparently nothing will be taken from the biological Stalin and incorporated in the psychological Stalin except the fact that he represents communism.

As for communism itself, it has long since undergone a metamorphosis that would bewilder Karl Marx. Communism, American style, seems to be the theory that whenever the consumer is robbed, the wage earner should have a large cut of the swag. Old-fashioned Americanism, on the contrary, holds that it should be split between management and the stockholders in the proportion of 60–40 (or, as the progressives insist, 80–20) in favor of management. To the suppression of the current form of communism, all right-thinking men are now being summoned as to a Holy War. And it seems likely that they will soon be so violently engaged in it that books, plays and statues, if not jobholders, may hope to escape in the confusion.

This is not, it must be admitted, quite the ideal solution. In the first place, there is a group of eccentrics who hold that the consumer should not be robbed at all. But these are, at best, only a splinter faction—in numbers and influence comparable to the Dukhobors in the religious world. They are not practical men, and most of them are under suspicion of adherence to the memory of F. D. (Antichrist) Roosevelt, so they may be disregarded.

A more serious objection is the fact that the biological Stalin may get the idea that the epithets we apply to the psychological Stalin are intended to apply to him and so grow peevish. This is serious, for he can hit hard. It is authoritatively stated that he already has at least one atomic fission pile now in operation—which means that he has the material of the atomic bomb. All he needs now is to learn how to detonate it, and he will be in position to come over the Arctic and knock Chicago into the middle of Lake Michigan.

The flat truth seems to be that it is by no means certain that the election of Stalin as Devil-in-chief will be an improvement, even though it may mean a better chance for American novelists to wear their stripes vertically, instead of horizontally. As long as soulful descriptions of fornication and funny business men remain, in American opinion, the most flagitious of all crimes, the pursuit of artists, literary and other, might engage the Puritan almost to the exclusion of the pursuit of Russians; and censorship at its bitterest cannot have repercussions that would vaporize Chicago.

But it cannot be. The artist is, at best, but a bush-league Devil—an Azazel, perhaps, or a Mammon, but certainly not a Beelzebub, still less a Lucifer. The proud Puritan spirit is not satisfied to contend with such; our sins cannot be compounded by belaboring anything less than an out-sized, jet-propelled, supersonic Satan, and Stalin seems to be the only candidate in sight who meets the specifications. There is little hazard in the flat prophecy that he is It.

There are, indeed, now as always, certain antinomians who scoff at the necessity of erecting any Devil at all. Having got rid of Hitler, they are content to do without. Puritanism, they point out, is a religion that prevents nobody from sinning, but does prevent anybody from enjoying it. Since America is obviously bent upon sinning in flagrant and scarlet fashion anyhow, they would have us relax and enjoy it. But this is as impractical as the gift of milk which Mr. Wallace did not recommend for the Hottentots. Puritan we are, and Puritan we shall doubtless remain indefinitely. If that involves us in any unnecessary war, the fact is to be regretted. But to suggest that at this late date we should bend our energies to the elimination of Puritanism from our mental make-up is certainly un-American and perhaps unconstitutional. The Devil is dead, and we must speed the search for another.

For until one is found we cannot hope to return to our normal state of terror and misery. At best, we can only be afraid of a moral collapse, which is not much of a terror, and lament the deterioration of manners and taste, which is no real misery. The Devil that censorship belabors is only *papier-mâché*. We need one that can be worked on by the F.B.I., the Ku Klux Klan, the American Legion, and the heroic taxi-drivers of Greenville, South Carolina. Until we find him our lives will be somewhat empty, somehow lacking in savor.

# The New Criticism and the
# Democratic Tradition

ROBERT GORHAM DAVIS

( *1949* )

With this indictment of the New Criticism as antidemocratic, ROBERT GORHAM DAVIS, formerly professor of English at Smith College, and now on the faculty of Columbia University, launched a controversy that reached seismic intensity both in and outside THE AMERICAN SCHOLAR. The volume of plaudits and invectives convinced Hiram Haydn that both sides of the discussion should be given a hearing. Therefore, in August of 1950, Mr. Haydn brought together five of America's most distinguished literary critics: William Barrett, Kenneth Burke, Malcolm Cowley, Allen Tate and Mr. Davis. A verbatim record was made of the four-hour session that followed, and it was later published in the Winter, 1950–51, and the Spring, 1951, issues of the magazine.

ALTHOUGH his influence has enjoyed a succession of revivals in France in the years since his death in 1821, Count Joseph de Maistre, author of *Du Pape* and *Soirées de Saint-Petersbourg,* is little known in this country. His works are not available in English, and when he is mentioned, it is usually simply as the supreme champion of clerical reaction. It was De Maistre who celebrated the headsman with his axe as the chief support of civilized society. Personally, De Maistre was an amiable and courageous man, and in his treatises on the developments of constitutions and of dogmas, he anticipated some of the most important ideas of Taine and of Cardinal Newman. But his experience of the French revolution made him a bitter enemy of all the "errors" he held responsible for it: not only Protestantism, rationalism and the Enlightenment, but the whole English philosophic and scientific tradition running through Bacon, Hobbes, Locke and Hume.

"To despise Locke is the beginning of wisdom," De Maistre wrote. He wished *"absolument tuer l'esprit du dix-huitième siècle,"* and restore to France an even more absolutist and Papist regime than she had known during what he considered her best period, that of Louis XIV and the rather Gallican Bossuet. To the progressive, perfectionist illusions of Rousseau and Condorcet, De Maistre opposed the dogma of original sin, *"le péché originel, qui explique tout, et sans lequel on n'explique rien."* For De Maistre, the manifestations and punishment of original sin made the pattern of human history.

It is hard to imagine anyone more remote from the America of Franklin Roosevelt and Harry Truman than this somberly reactionary envoy from Sardinia to the court of Alexander I. We have, it is true, a party opposed to the Democrats, but when the Republicans speak, it is not in the name of reaction, the Church, *l'ancien régime,* but of a sounder liberalism, a greater individual freedom. The place to find the values and views of De Maistre, during these sixteen years of liberal-democratic presidencies, has been the critical quarterlies. The vocabulary of some of our academically most influential critics—critics who have taught and edited textbooks and written good poetry as well as criticism, and who knew each other at Vanderbilt or Louisiana State—has been the vocabulary not of Locke or Mill or Emerson or Whitman, but of the author of *Du Pape.*

Over the last two decades, in the journals of the New Criticism, *authority, hierarchy, catholicism, aristocracy, tradition, absolutes, dogma, truths* became related terms of honor, and *liberalism, naturalism, scientism, individualism, equalitarianism, progress, protestantism, pragmatism* and *personality* became related terms of rejection and contempt. As programmatic social movements, the New Humanism and Agrarianism seemed short-lived. They elected no senators or representatives, and had no influence on the popular culture of the mass media. These latter became, indeed, as a result of the war and the later rivalry with Russia, much more active propagandizers for democratic freedoms and minority rights. And during the thirties, the humanist-agrarian philosophy lost out in most of the colleges to the Marxian social-consciousness which became fashionable in that period. But during the forties, with the intense reaction against Stalinism, the socio-historical patterns of acceptance and rejection established by the humanist-agrarian movement quietly triumphed on the higher literary levels, and became the required postulates, curiously enough, for the proper evaluation of literature as literature. In an article in the *Sewanee Review* in the winter of 1946–47, Robert Heilman contended that holding liberal-democratic-progressive views with any conviction made one incapable of appreciating imaginative literature at all.

The development of this complex of ideas is well-documented through the thirties, and easily studied. It is found in the New Humanist symposia at the beginning of the decade, in the Agrarian manifestoes, "I'll Take My Stand," and "Who Owns America?"; in the "reactionary" criticism of Allen Tate and Yvor Winters; "God without Thunder" by John Crowe Ransom; in the files of the Southern quarterlies, of Eliot's *New Criterion,* and especially of Seward Collins' Catholic-distributivist *American Review*—for which G. R. Elliott, Donald Davidson, Norman Foerster, Yvor Winters, Cleanth Brooks, Allen Tate, Mark Van Doren and Austin Warren continued to write, even after it became openly pro-Franco and pro-fascist. In the forties, their pattern of attack was strengthened by the very explicit criticism of scientific, progressive and liberal attitudes in the Catholic novels of Graham Greene and Evelyn Waugh, and in the Anglican-orthodox thrillers of C. S. Lewis. Lionel Trilling made the inadequacy of the liberal imagination the central theme of his influential study of E. M. Forster. W. H. Auden, in *For the Time Being,* imagined Herod a fussy, futile, murderous, self-bemused Liberal, trying to oppose his ideas of reason and progress to the fact of the Incarnation. Protestant neo-orthodoxy, as vigorously preached by Reinhold Niebuhr, joined with T. S. Eliot in *The Idea of a Christian Society,* and with anti-Stalinists who still retained their Marxian frame of reference, in identifying liberalism with an "age of free exploitation which has passed."

This general intellectual assault on the assumptions of democratic liberalism at a time when the United States is contending with Russia for world leadership in the name of democratic liberalism has caused a spiritual expatriation in the approach to literature which goes much deeper than the physical expatriation of the twenties. And it represents a much greater alienation than the Marxist criticism of the thirties, which professed itself the heir of the democratic tradition. It caused the contradictions and uncertainties which appeared in the most responsible comments defending the award of the Bollingen prize to Ezra Pound. What was brought into question here was not so much the matter of recognizing as a good poet a man with reprehensible social views. What was brought into question was a complex of ideas which made poetic sensibility, purity of language, and the integrity of art inextricably involved with ideas of authority, aristocracy and reaction, and at odds with the ethos of a liberal democracy. The character of this complex may be seen more clearly if we put beside Pound a man who was convicted in a French court at Lyons shortly before Pound was imprisoned at Pisa, a man who was also an admirer of Mussolini and a great hater of Jews, the academician and poet of *Musique Intérieure,* Charles Maurras.

Pound, a Protestant from Indiana, is still a pretty unorthodox American individualist. Maurras represents the union of classicism, clericalism and reaction, in a much purer form. And Maurras, through Pound's friend T. E. Hulme, and through T. S. Eliot, had a much more direct and explicit responsibility than Pound for many of the ideas that pervade American criticism today. This combination of ideas is not peculiar to this country or this century. The basic premises go back to De Maistre, whom Maurras called *"le type et le chef"* of the *"maîtres de la contre-revolution."* A critical revaluation of cultural history back to the thirteenth century is required, with a series of rejections which include a good deal of the Reformation and the Renaissance, and even the criticism of Scholasticism by the English rationalist-anti-traditionalists, Duns Scotus and Occam. An extreme rendering of this thesis may be found in the essay, "The Southern Quality," by the Canadian, Herbert Marshall McLuhan, in *A Southern Vanguard* (1947).

The central question is of the nature of man, and from its answer the religious, literary and political conclusions follow. Here orthodoxy finds itself contending with two persistent heresies, the Pelagian and the Calvinist. The first results in the faith of the Savoyard vicar, romanticism, Deweyanism and democratic progressivism. The second results in scientific determinism, the naturalist novel, the ethos of capitalist self-interest, and the Hobbesian-Stalinist state. McLuhan, for instance, finds both heresies characteristic of a rationalist-individualist New England mind in rebellion against the patristic established church of the Stuarts. He opposes the Calvinist Edwards and the Pelagian Emerson to the organic traditionalism of the South. "The *essential* impatience and rebellion of the New England mind disqualifies it for political and artistic functions, so that the defection of Henry James and T. S. Eliot was a trauma necessary to the preservation of their talents." Both De Maistre and Maurras explain Rousseau by his origin in the Geneva of Calvin, and with Robespierre's dictatorship the circle is made complete.

The orthodox view of human nature as essential postulate for literary criticism was introduced into recent Anglo-American literary controversy by Irving Babbitt and T. E. Hulme. Both explicitly acknowledged the French sources of their ideas. All the most important doctrines of *Rousseau and Romanticism* and *Democracy and Leadership* are to be found in the quotations from reactionary French writers in *Masters of Modern French Criticism,* a book which shows how thoroughly most of the questions which have agitated American criticism in the last two decades had already been fought out in the French nineteenth century. Hulme's influential essay, "Romanticism and Classicism" firmly links classicism, the Church and the dogma of original sin. Hulme denies the truth of the Rousseauist-progressive faith in man as an "infinite reservoir of possibilities," as against the classical view of man as "an extraordinarily fixed and limited animal whose nature is absolutely constant. It is only by tradition and organization that anything decent can be got out of him." Those for whom this distinction is most vital, Hulme wrote, are "Maurras, Lasserre and all the group connected with *Action française.*" Hulme's essay had been written in 1913 and Babbitt's *Masters* published in 1912, the period dramatized in Martin du Gard's *Jean Barois,* when French intellectual youth was turning against the Republican régimes brought into power by the Dreyfus victory. Under the leadership of the *Camelots du Roi* they beat up Jewish and liberal professors in the Sorbonne and fought for the cult of Joan of Arc. Among them "republican" was the same sort of pejorative that "liberalism" has become in our own reviews.

Critic of Rousseauist progressivism and scientific naturalism though he was, Babbitt retained his New England individualism and an affection for Emerson. He preached an abstract higher will, rather than orthodox tradition and the church. And Hulme was attracted by thinkers like Bergson and Sorel. Though Hulme's theory of discontinuity and Babbitt's "law for thing and law for man," both helped to preserve the distinctions among religion, art, science, society and history which scientific naturalism and romanticism were accused of destroying, T. S. Eliot and those who followed him identified themselves much more positively with the dogmatic and clerical elements in the tradition to which Hulme and Babbitt introduced them.

Eliot's lectures at the University of Virginia in the first year of the New Deal, published as *After Strange Gods: A Primer of Modern Heresy,* make the most useful text. They are not outdated, for the same principles are found in *The Idea of a Christian Society* and *Notes toward the Definition of Culture.* In the earlier lectures, addressed to a society "worm-eaten with Liberalism," Eliot expressed his sympathy with the new Agrarians of a South which, as compared to New England, was further from New York, "less industrialised and less invaded by foreign races." Of his general literary-religious thesis Eliot said, "I doubt whether what I am saying can convey very much to anyone for whom the doctrine of Original Sin is not a very real and tremendous thing," and of the evangelical heresies but sound anti-democratic insights of D. H. Lawrence: "That we can and ought to reconcile ourselves to Liberalism, Progress and Modern Civilisation is a proposition which we need not have waited for Lawrence to condemn." We need not have waited, for in the same words, in reference to the Pope, this had been the final proposition anathematized in the *Syllabus of Errors* of 1864.

This *Syllabus,* attached to the *Quanta Cura* of Pius IX, condemned liberalism in precisely the terms made familiar by our contemporary reviews. A compilation of eighty modern "errors" attacked in papal documents of the period immediately preceding, it had its inception in the year 1849, as did the preparation of the Bull, *Ineffabilis Deus,* which re-emphasized the dogma of Original Sin. Both resulted from Pope Pius' extreme reaction against liberalism after the events of '48, and both prepared for the definition of papal infallibility, the doctrine so strongly advocated in De Maistre's *Du Pape.* The papal decrees of Pius IX, Professor Soltan says, represent "the political philosophy of De Maistre as re-edited by Louis Veuillot."

In the year 1851, also reacting to the revolutions of '48, the critic St. Beuve wrote a very favorable piece on De Maistre, admitting that recent events had justified a good many of his theories. And in the same year, also reacting against his brief Republican enthusiasm of '48, Charles Baudelaire discovered a significant relationship between De Maistre and Edgar Allan Poe. *"De Maistre et Edgar Poe m'ont appris à raisonner,"* he wrote. In his two prefaces to his translations of Poe, Baudelaire opposed Original Sin to progress, and aristocracy to democracy, in the manner now so familiar to us. He made Poe the martyr of Northern commercialism, *"quelle odeur de magasin, comme disait J. de Maistre à propos*

*Locke.*" Andrew Lang, in *Letters to Dead Authors,* speaks of "your translator, M. Charles Baudelaire, who so strenuously shared your views about Mr. Emerson and the Transcendentalists, and who so energetically resisted all those ideas of 'progress' which 'came from Hell or Boston.' " Baudelaire found most pertinent the passage from *Colloquy of Monas and Una* which ends: "He grew infected with system and with abstraction. He enwrapped himself in generalities. Among other odd ideas, that of universal equality gained ground; and in the face of analogy and of God—in despite of the loud warning voice of the laws of *gradation* so visibly pervading all things in Earth and Heaven—wild attempts at an omni-prevalent Democracy were made."

It is this passage which Charles Maurras used as the epigraph for *Trois idées politiques,* the first book to come out of the movement, *Action française.* "*Cette idée de hierarchie, salutaire et nourricière a été reprise longtemps plus tard, par les Italiens du fascisme—Gerarchia—selon les purs échos de Baudelaire et de Poe. . . . L'aristocrate virginien proclame la contradiction radicale et complète entre toute démocratie et les archétypes supérieurs auxquels le monde doit sa vie, sa durée, son progrès, sa beauté.*"

Maurras, born in Provence in 1868, was himself a Southern regionalist, interested in Provençal poetry, and expecting a Southern renaissance that would restore the national character. His federalism, like the States' rights program of our own South, was intended to preserve provincial cultures from destruction by a powerful, commercial North which had been their enemy ever since the Albigensian crusades. Maurras' review of Barres' *Les Déracinés* developed into a book on decentralization. Maurras was converted to classicism by a visit to Greece, and to anti-Semitism by Drumont's *La France Juive.* The Dreyfus affair turned him into a militant clerical nationalist, who opposed the rationalism, romanticism and Protestantism of Germany and England to the traditional, classical Latin Catholicism of France and Italy. Maurras' favorite period was that of Louis XIV, Bossuet and Racine, just as Eliot's was that of the Stuarts, Andrewes and Donne. It was not only from De Maistre, whom he frequently cites, that Maurras got his idea of a traditional order based on the family, the region, the monarch and the church, but also from Comte, Renan and Taine, who were, respectively, a positivist, a sceptic and a determinist.

Comte had urged the alliance of Catholics and Positivists

against the disintegrative spirit of Protestantism. In thirty years
of philosophical writing, he had always represented *"la souve-
raineté du peuple comme une mystification oppressive, et l'égalité
comme un ignoble mensonge."* Renan and Taine both reacted
strongly after the Commune and the defeat of '71 in the direction
of tradition, discipline and monarchy. In *"Les Origines de la
France contemporaine,"* Taine attacked the Rousseauist alienation of the individual, with all his rights, from the community,
and the Jacobin attempt to force real men and real communities
into their abstract molds. "Nothing," Taine wrote, "is more
dangerous than a general idea in narrow and empty heads." The
error of '89, Maurras said in his *"Enquête sur la Monarchie,"* was
perpetuated in the nineteenth century only by "purely sentimental and romantic geniuses, Hugo, Lamartine, Michelet, Sand
and Quinet, while the stronger minds, not only Bonald and De
Maistre, but also Balzac, Le Play, Taine and Renan emphatically
repudiated this error." *"Leurs doctrines puissantes et précises ont
lentement et profondement penetré dans l'âme et dans le coeur
des jeunes generations intelligentes."*

This emphasis on the superior precision and truth of traditional
orthodoxy, quite apart from the matter of faith, is now a familiar
theme in American criticism, which opposes it to the abstractions
of liberalism and to the devaluative and depersonalizing effects of
secular science. For Eliot, the Church is the great repository of
wisdom, and in the essay on Pascal he describes the logical steps by
which one finds oneself inexorably committed to the dogma of the
Incarnation. "The organized meaning of the encounters of man
and nature, which are temporal and concrete, is religious tradition," Allen Tate wrote, "and its defence is dogma." According
to the theories of the New Criticism, a poem is comparable to
traditional orthodoxy in providing the most responsible and complete version of our experience. If it avoids a list of heresies parallel to those of theology, poetry becomes a form of knowledge superior to that of science. And, like the dogmas of orthodoxy,
poetry is not conditioned, but absolute. To this sense of poetry,
which he held, Maurras, like John Crowe Ransom, applied the
term "ontological." *"Ontologie serait peut-etre le vrai nom, car la
Poésie porte surtout vers les racines de la connaissance de l'Être."*

The indebtedness of the New Critics to Maurras, through Eliot,
is a direct one. Maurras was an atheist, but he supported the
Church, not only as the essential basis of a classical and aristocratic
society, but also as, in its dogmas, coming close to the truths of hu-

man nature. This was consistent with a French reactionary clericalism from De Maistre to Brunetière, which valued the Church primarily for the way in which it shaped and organized an anti-democratic culture of hierarchy, authority and tradition. It was this attitude which permitted Eliot to contrast the orthodoxy of the unbeliever Joyce with the heresies of Yeats and Lawrence who, though strongly anti-democratic and anti-rationalist, were misled by their Protestant individualism into magic and primitivism rather than into the Church. When *Action française* was finally condemned by the Pope, and Maurras accused of leading young men away from faith, Eliot came to his defense in two pieces in the *Criterion,* and said, "I have been a reader of the work of Maurras for eighteen years; upon me he has had exactly the opposite effect." Later, in a group review of books on fascism, Eliot wrote, "Most of the concepts which might have attracted me in fascism I seem already to have found, in a more digestible form, in the work of Charles Maurras." In his essay on Babbitt, Eliot said that if Babbitt could only come to accept the Church, "his influence might join with that of another philosopher of the same rank— Charles Maurras—and might, indeed, correct some of the extravagances of that writer." Under the influence of Jacques Maritain, however, who had been an earlier supporter of *Action française*, but who accepted the Papal condemnation, Eliot came to realize the spiritual dangers of what was basically a pragmatic support of the Church, even in the interests of culture and of a traditional, aristocratic order.

Eliot's church is the Established Church of England, but in this country there is no established church, and the founding fathers were determined that there should not be. Though Ransom, Tate, Brooks and Warren, following Eliot's emphasis, have all discussed religion in relation to literature and the South, they have had as much difficulty in finding a native orthodoxy as in finding acceptable political and literary American ancestors. All John Crowe Ransom could suggest at the end of "God without Thunder" was, "With whatever religious institution a modern man may be connected, let him try to turn it back towards orthodoxy." But obviously neither the rationalist, Protestant neo-orthodoxy of Reinhold Niebuhr nor the Romanism of the American Catholic Church are really compatible with the complex of ideas which underlies the New Criticism.

The truth is that there is no such relation between orthodox religion in the United States and conservative or reactionary politics as that we associate with the name of Burke in England or De Maistre in France. And despite the Civil War, there are not two Americas like the two Frances, red and black, consistently opposed in religion, politics and ideas, the two Frances which Renan compared to the twins fighting in the womb of Rebecca. The French pattern cannot be made to fit ours. The Southern founding fathers were sons of Locke and the Enlightenment, and the greatest works of the moral imagination, in Hawthorne, Melville and James, have come from the commercial and Calvinist North. But even in France, where the reactionary movement has been so pragmatic and romantic in nature, it has had a very dubious social base. France has no king, and the aristocracy lost its regional independence and responsibility long before its terrible abuse of privilege brought on the violence of the revolution. The Catholic Church of Montalembert and Leo XIII, recognizing that France's future lay with republicanism, did come to terms with it. Maurras' dream was finally realized, under Marshall Pétain, only by surrendering France to the Germany Maurras hated. In 1939 and 1940, Maurras used his still very considerable prestige in reactionary and military circles to help bring about this betrayal.

Nothing is more fantastic than the application of the ideas of De Maistre and Maurras to America, even though they are linked by dubious and derivative logic to a very impressive body of poetry and criticism. The neo-traditionalists are guilty of exactly the error of which they accuse the idealogues of the Enlightenment, the attempt to impose ideas which have no roots or source in the traditional way of life. There is a distinctively American character which, as foreign visitors report it, has remained remarkably stable in the last hundred and fifty years, and which has been deepened and complicated, but not changed, by the "influx of foreigners" which it has successfully assimilated. This character has been developed by a way of life, a received tradition, which has increasingly realized the ideas of those philosophers most under attack at the present time for their rationalist abstractions. This tradition, too, represents preserved experience, including experience with established churches, privileged orders, absolutism and dogma going back to the thirteenth century. Every circumstance in this country has tended to the strengthening of this tradition, and no social basis exists for a rival tradition of serious cultural significance. That there are deficiencies in the prevailing culture, in the character of its customs, its imaginative symbols, its commercialized mass media and its image of the ethical self, the New Criticism has helped to make emphatically clear. But, on the other hand, the debate in *Partisan Review* last spring over "liberalism," and the debate over the Pound award in the *Saturday Review* last summer, showed the alienating and paradoxical results of the pattern of social rejection underlying the New Criticism. They increased the sense that the New Criticism, even in a purely literary way, has completed its corrective purpose. What these debates prepared us for, as we enter the literary fifties, is a new assumption of cultural responsibility by the intelligentsia but within the terms of the democratic society, and a new restorative effort that finds its materials within the imaginative and historical resources of the democratic tradition itself.

# The Best of Two Worlds

## Some Reflections on a Peculiarly Modern Privilege

### JOSEPH WOOD KRUTCH

### ( *1950* )

JOSEPH WOOD KRUTCH is one of those rare individuals who are twice-blessed—he has been able to partake of the best of the two worlds that he here describes. For many years he was professor of dramatic literature at Columbia University. Now retired, he lives at the edge of the desert in Arizona.

IF ALL my days were spent as the majority of them are, they might not give me as much pleasure as they do. Nearly two-thirds of my time is passed in the country, and that does not always seem enough. But it may be that I am more aware of country life than I should be if I lived it all the time.

Your pure countryman, born and reared, is often satisfied with his life, and often would choose no other. But he is also very often a man whose interests and satisfactions are very different from those of us who have been transplanted. It is said that Mr. Bryce, for whom Bryce Canyon was named, left concerning it only one recorded utterance: "A terrible place to lose a cow in."

Country schools now give courses in "nature study" to the farmers' children, and they often need them almost as much as those bred in the slums. Your farmer frequently grows up in an ignorance (the maintenance of which it seems difficult to understand) of everything in nature not immediately relevant to his profession. More than once—and plainly rather out of politeness to me than because of any genuine curiosity—I have been summoned to wonder at some creature described as strange, horrendous, and undoubtedly extremely rare, only to have it turn out a prevalent insect or, perhaps, one of the commonest of the salamanders. And how sinister everything not a regular part of his daily life seems to be! Every milksnake is a copperhead, every spider is deadly, nearly every weed is poisonous. I should be willing to bet that the famous brave man who first ate an oyster came from inland and that it was not a farmer who exploded the legend of the noxious tomato.

One friend who read something I wrote about the pleasures of living with some awareness of other living things, rebuked me for assuming that city dwellers did not know that pleasure. He spoke of the geranium on the tenement window which is all the more admired because it seems so improbable. He spoke even of Wallace's spider, and he might, though he did not, have gone on to speak of that stuffed owl, which, according to Wordsworth in his most solemn mood, brought comfort to a young girl long in city pent.

How such things may be, I know too well to question them. Indeed, I am prepared to go much further in making concessions about the city. It is more than merely the sense of contrast which gives me and many like me some kind of awareness of the natural world not common in those who have always lived close to it. We are really a new breed. When we speak of "returning" to something, we are using a wrong word. If we move wholly, or for a part of our time, from the city into the country, we are not resuming a kind of life which was once the usual one. The whole economic foundation of that life rests upon a complex urban civilization. And what is more important, our kind of sensibility, or at least our awareness of it and our articulateness concerning it, are different from anything which ever existed, even in Arcadia.

"I walk," said Thoreau, "as one possessing the advantages of human culture, fresh from the society of men, but turned loose into the woods." His was the best of two worlds, and he knew it as well as I do. We have that smattering of science which makes nature more wonderful, and we have also been trained in sensibility by reading. It was Thoreau, also, who proclaimed that "decayed literature makes the richest soil," and the man who made that statement was not one who was advocating any mere primitivism. To say that few men would fall in love if they had never read any poetry is true in exactly the same degree, and to exactly the same extent, whether one is speaking of the love of woman or the love of nature. Without thought and without culture, one might take a kind of animal delight in either, but he could not experience much more.

Certainly I feel no need to apologize either to myself or to others when I bring with me into the country whatever I may have learned from men or from books. Neither do I see any inconsistency in introducing into country life whatever from a different world may seem to enrich it. I see no impropriety in returning from an inspection of my marsh or from a walk in the snow to listen to Mozart's G minor quintet on the phonograph. To me, at least, it sounds better than it would in a concert hall, and even those much more absolute than I in their condemnation of the gadget are only biting off the nose to spite the face when they refuse to accept whatever advantages may accrue from it while still being compelled, willy-nilly, to pay the penalties entailed. What I bring from the country into the city is perhaps less obviously important, though I am not sure that it is not equally so. I once used something I had learned from a mouse—she was a wartime refugee from Cambridge, by the way—to demonstrate in a review the unreliability of a certain biographer. But this is hardly the place to talk about that.

I have met few men or women wholly country-bred and completely without experience of life in cities, with whom I felt entirely at home. About them there is nearly always something *farouche*, if not actually savage. At some time in the course of his experience, every man should rub shoulders with his fellows, experience the excitement of a metropolis' nervous activity; live close to the great, the distinguished, the famous, and the merely notorious—if for no other reason than because only so can he learn properly to discount them, or at least learn in what ways they are, and in what ways they are not, to be taken at their own and the world's valuation. Those who, for example, have never seen an author are likely to take books with the wrong kind of seriousness! Urbanity seems to be literally that: something impossible to acquire except in cities. But one need not, and one should not, I think, spend a lifetime in getting it, for in that respect, as in so many others, the city pays a diminishing return. The years between eighteen and thiry should be amply sufficient to polish anyone capable of being polished. If he is not urbane by then, something more drastic than mere residence in a city would seem to be called for. And if I have never felt entirely at home with anyone who had never had any experience of cities, I can say much the same of those who have never had any other kind.

What seems to me so terribly, perhaps fatally, wrong with the present stage in the evolution of the human spirit is not its tend-

178

ency to go beyond a mere "life in nature," but its tendency to break completely the connection which it cannot break without cutting off its roots; without forgetting with desperate consequences that the human arises out of the natural and must always remain to some extent conditioned by it.

Beauty and joy are natural things. They are older than man, and they have their source in the natural part of him. Art becomes sterile and the joy of life withers when they become unnatural. If modern urban life is becoming more comfortable, more orderly, more sanitary, and more socially conscious than it ever was before —but if at the same time it is also becoming less beautiful (as it seems to me) and less joyous (as it seems to nearly everyone) — then the deepest reason for that may be its increasing forgetfulness of nature. She is often none of the good things which the city is, but she is almost always, nevertheless, somehow beautiful and somehow joyous.

Joy is the one thing of which indisputably the healthy animal, and even the healthy plant, gives us an example. And we need them to remind us that beauty and joy can come of their own accord when we let them. The geranium on the tenement window and the orchid in the florist's shop, the poodle on the leash and the goldfish in the bowl, are better than nothing. In the consciousness of the city dweller, they ought to play a part no less essential than that of the sleek chrome chair and the reproductions of Braque and Miro. For me, however, I found them not enough.

## II

Here, on the other hand, I have, literally, God's plenty. I am glad that the neighbors are not too near, that my little lawn and my brief paved walk end soon. Everything reminds me that man is an incident in nature rather than, as one comes to suppose in the city, that the natural is, at most, an incident, surviving precariously in a man-made world. If I do on my own a little of that peeping and botanizing which Wordsworth scorned, I think that I profit less from what I learn *about* nature than I do from what I should prefer to call the example she sets me—the example, I mean, of confidence, of serenity, and, above all, of joy. In the city, perhaps especially in the city of today, one may pass whole weeks without meeting a single joyous person or seeing a single joyous thing. One may meet laughter there, and wit—sometimes, perhaps, a fragment of wisdom. These are all good things which I would not willingly do without. But joyousness, as distinguished from diversion and amusement and recreation, is so rare that a whole philosophy has been developed to make a virtue out of its absence.

The world, we are told, is a terrible place, and it is wicked not to be almost continuously aware of the fact. Diversion in limited quantities is permissible as a temporary relaxation, but moral indignation should be the staple of any human life, properly spent. Yet it seems to me that Joy and Love, increasingly fading from human experience, are the two most important things in the world, and that if one must be indignant about something, the fact that they are so rare is the thing most worthy of indignation.

The limitations of the animal mind and the animal sensibility are no doubt so great that we can hardly conceive them. But no behaviorist's theory that the bird's song is merely a "sex call" or, as the more recent and therefore more depressing theory has it, that it is the male announcement of his claim to a hunting territory, can conceal the fact that the sex call or the "keep-out" cry is joyously given. From such phenomena I should like to learn, and I think that to some extent I have learned—though not very completely or very well, I confess—the natural way of making the processes of living joyous rather than troubling.

My very cats set me an example, for though they have taken on many human traits—though they can, for example, be bored, and sometimes irritated—I think that they have made little or no progress in what some seem to think the most praiseworthy of human accomplishments: the ability, I mean, to worry. They can be very impatient for food but, unlike men, they never seem concerned over where the next meal after that is going to come from. That is one of the reasons why I always feel more serene after a conversation with a few friendly animals than I do after an evening with even the most brilliant of my human acquaintances.

Or consider again the case of the birds. The most convincing explanation which has ever been given of the fact that so many species migrate to the north in summer to raise their families is not that food is more abundant—actually it isn't—but quite simply that there are more hours of daylight; more working hours, that is, during which the appalling amount of food necessary to feed the young can be collected. Now the spring just past happens to have been an unusually early one. Before the end of May, I noticed that my robins, their beaks already to the grindstone, were digging worms out of my lawn from dawn to nightfall. The summer was no vacation time for them. But they seemed not in the slightest degree resentful; in fact, they seemed quite happy over the whole business. What we call the cares of a family appear to be, for them, the pleasures of it. I think it is no mere pretty sentimentality to say that nature has remained joyful and that man, who has so much enriched his capacity for variety and experience, has lost a great deal of that capacity for joy, without which all the other capacities seem such dubious boons.

To anyone merely country-bred, I should certainly not speak of nature's superiority over art, nor should I tell him, if he happened to long for concert halls or art exhibits, that the wood thrush is in certain ways as much worth listening to as Isabelle Baillie, and the song sparrow is habitually in much better voice than a certain still-popular coloratura whom I had better not name. That would be worse than fatuous; it would be, for him, positively untrue. Whether one is inclined to say: "Nature I love, and next to Nature, Art," or whether one reverses the order of precedence, may quite properly depend largely upon how many opportunities one has had to experience his love for the one or the other.

But what I would not say to the merely country-bred, I should not hesitate to say to the bigoted metropolitan. If he asked me whether I did not feel seriously the lack of those opportunities for artistic enjoyment which, by the way, only a very few of the very largest cities abundantly afford, I should ask him to take a look at the fresh new moon above the tree on some clear, crisp evening, or even merely to compare the drive home through country roads from some sortie into the village with a return by subway—or even by taxi, if he happened to be one of those whose economic status permits him to remain most of the time above ground.

### III

"But you do not seem to realize," many will immediately object, "how exceptional your circumstances are. Even among the rich, there are few who can escape the burdens imposed by their riches sufficiently to lead your kind of life as much of the time as you do. And among those who, like you, have a living to make, still fewer can arrange to make it as you do. Even granting for the sake of argument that the kind of life you lead is a good one, how could we possibly arrange society so that the mass of men could lead it?" "That," they will conclude triumphantly, "is the problem which has to be faced."

Now I have some kind of an answer to these remarks, but first I should like to say that the word "problem" is one which I did not intend to use even once, partly because its monotonous reappearance is one of the striking signs of our general unhappiness. Every civilization has certain key words whose constant employment gives a clue to the dominant tone of that society, and our tendency to see everything in terms of "the problem" is one of the clues to ours. We have not only the problems of government and economics, which are, perhaps, problems in most societies; we have also the "problems" of culture, religion and even of recreation. Indeed, we have turned other, even less likely concerns into other "problems."

Consider, for example, the case of Love. It has been, in many times, many different things. It has been considered in some ages primarily as Sin. In others, it has been considered as perhaps the greatest of the mystical experiences. In still others, it has been merely a game or a diversion. But in ours alone it has become simply "the problem of sex." And the curious fact is that certain "problems" are rendered, as this one is, unsolvable by virtue of the very fact that we allow them to present themselves to us in the form of problems.

But to return to such answers as I can give. One, perhaps seemingly hardhearted, might be, of course, simply the denial that any one who finds himself fortunate is morally obliged to refuse to enjoy his good fortune because all are not equally fortunate. It might be argued that to refuse to accept happiness if everyone is not equally happy would not be a way of securing, even ultimately, happiness for everybody, but merely a way of making sure that misery becomes universal, since even the lucky will not permit themselves to enjoy their luck. Such perversity may seem a virtue to those who take certain attitudes, but it is perhaps not impertinent to point out that it has not always been so considered; that indeed, to Catholic theology it once was, and for all I know still is, a Sin—the sin of Melancholy which has been carefully defined as a stubborn refusal to be grateful for the good gifts of God.

But it is not really necessary to take this position, which many would find objectionable. The plain fact is that most people would not want my life. I am well aware of the fact that the majority of my acquaintances do not envy, but, rather, pity me. If I should take their inability to live in the country as "the problem" which I was obligated to solve, I should conduct a campaign to decentralize cities and to set the whole of a bitterly resentful population to catching trains with the commuters, whom the majority of them despise. Plainly, this is a case where the most applicable rule is not the Golden Rule, but that Brazen Rule proclaimed by Bernard Shaw: "Do not do unto others as you would that they should do unto you; their tastes may be different." And in my particular case I find that they usually are. The "problem" is made to vanish by the simple realization that it really isn't a problem at all.

I think that I shall not use the word again in the course of what I have reason, in experience, to hope will be a happy year. I am by no means disregarding the fact that I seem, to myself, to be in many ways singularly, if not quite uniquely, fortunate. That, indeed, is perhaps what this essay is about.

# Expressionism and Cubism

EDGAR LEVY

(*1950*)

EDGAR LEVY's paintings have been exhibited in the galleries and museums of this country for the past thirty years. He now teaches painting at Pratt Institute.

This article, which explores the origins and development of Expressionism and Cubism, is from a three-part series on modern art that Mr. Levy wrote for THE AMERICAN SCHOLAR. The other articles deal with "The Classical and Romantic Tempers" and "The Mystics."

IT IS RECOGNIZED that the line connecting Cubism with Cézanne is direct and unbroken. The roots of Cubism may be found in Cézanne's work and, reciprocally, the Cubists have demonstrated Cézanne's overwhelming importance by the vitality of their own accomplishment. Not so much may be asserted of Expressionism and Van Gogh. For though the Expressionists drew inspiration and courage from Van Gogh's painting, they were not strictly dependent on it, and have not focused attention on it as the indispensable source of their technique. If not Van Gogh, another equally convenient would have filled his place in the Expressionist hierarchy. Gauguin, for instance. Or Munch of Norway, or Ensor of Belgium. And without these, Expressionism would still have flourished, looking for precedent, if it felt it wanted precedent, to painters of remoter times, to El Greco, perhaps, or to Grünewald.

But it is precisely this want of necessity for formal sequence that is significant and characteristic of Expressionism. It stands for anarchy in art; its avowed aim is the unfettered expression of individual passions and of things private and inward, for which there can be neither objective style nor a treatment arrived at by community of effort. Perhaps the individualistic and Romantic temperament does not permit an awareness that such a style, perfected and ordered by many hands, is the very instrument of communication. In any case Expressionism's adoption of the broadest and most unlimited technical equipment—or should we say the most loosely formed and unrefined—signifies its impatience with objective statement and its desire for an extravagant range of freedom for subjective indulgence.

Whether the Expressionist believed that the material outcome of his soul-searching—the finished picture—was of value to the outside world, or whether he painted for himself alone, it is not important to determine. But let us suppose the extreme case of egocentrism—that he worked for his private satisfaction or, as Van Gogh did, to excrete the passions that he could not contain. In either case, by the mere act of painting he is caught up in compromise. The obscure combinations that are himself in an ultimate sense are surely not communicable. But in painting he is committed to transposing elements of these combinations to a level on which his own consciousness—the consciousness that is part and parcel of objective existence—will apprehend them. Therefore he must relate them to objectivity; he must find in them the resonances that are their universal properties, and lo! where has the unique, the sacred, the individualistic, flown? Thus every step the Expressionist takes toward making the content of his work more accessible brings him further from the Romantic ideal and closer to Classical logic. Romanticism is then seen to be a distinctly relative quantity in the history of art. It is for this reason that the older Romantics are less frenetic to our eyes than contemporary ones. Van Gogh, for example, seems almost tame compared to the Expressionists, simply because the passing of time has subdued the idiosyncratic features of his pictures in favor of their more general aspects—those details of color and design that have wider implications.

Something of the same may be said of the Expressionists themselves. The thirty-odd years that have elapsed since their first appearance have enabled us to see more clearly the few compositional and technical aspects they share with Western art as a whole. Within this broad context the Expressionists observed the minimum requirements of technique. Their brushwork was crude, if not brutal; their composition elementary; their color was brash and primary, as Van Gogh's seemed to his contemporaries.

Reviewing the movement historically, we note that it was antici-

pated by the group in Paris that around 1905 was derisively christened "Les Fauves," some of whose members were Matisse, Derain, Vlaminck, Dufy and Braque. But it was in Germany three
or four years later that the trend assumed the semblance of shape
and moment. Consistent with its undisciplined character, Expressionism did not form a single, unified group. Many individuals
and organizations are considered to have been party to it. "Die
Brücke" and "Der Blaue Reiter" are the two main groups to have
contained Expressionist membership. Oskar Kokoschka, Max Pechstein, Ernst Kirchner, Schmidt-Rotluff, Emil Nolde, are perhaps
the most well known individuals.

Of these men Emil Nolde was probably closest to the realization
of their ideal. In his paintings the impassioned energy of the Romantic soul takes violent and hysterical form. The sense of the
demonic is everywhere, and his subjects, their masklike faces barbarously painted and garishly colored, are reminiscent of a weird
and savage funerary rite. That the direction of the Expressionists,
as well as of many other Romantics, is death-tending and destructive is suggested, not by Nolde alone, but also by those on whom
Expressionism has called for spiritual and moral reinforcement:
by Van Gogh, by Munch, by Ensor. Perhaps no other Expressionist
displays this awful content more openly than Nolde, but it shows
itself to a considerable extent in all of them. The fullness of health
is not seen here—instead the craggy outlines of the skull are
sensed, madness looks out of the eyes, the glow of the flesh is not
that of abundance but of fever.

Returning to the technical features of Expressionism and asking
with what perplexities it confronts the viewer, we will answer that
there are none. Like the art of its great predecessor, Van Gogh,
Expressionism does not invent new instrumentalities, but uses
those that are already at hand. If we agree to accept its emotional
outpouring, we will find its technical basis extremely simple. It
employs the most elementary ways of representation, straining
and exaggerating them alarmingly, but not in any fundamental
manner changing them. It is enough that they be charged with a
content they can scarcely hold, which in its frenzied inward drive
threatens to overthrow and destroy them altogether. But as long
as the Expressionist chooses to remain intelligible (and, for all we
know, even when he withdraws into incoherence) his techniques
mean exactly what they appear to mean on the most primary level,
neither more nor less. They are the shrieking and agonized voice
of a shrieking and agonized message.

How powerful the urges are that produce such art, how close their appeal to the mind's eye, and how persuasive their beckoning, is attested by the enormous influence Expressionism has had on painting since 1910, an influence that has extended far beyond the places of its inception and has attracted dozens of painters in the United States. In France the tendency reached a zenith of fulfillment in the tortured paintings of Chaim Soutine and the more passively suffering figures of Georges Rouault, whose personal Expressionism preceded the German efflorescence by about five years. Nor has the artist of different temperament, drawn to the discipline and measure of Cubism, always been able to resist these impulses and eliminate an Expressionist fraction from his work. And there are many painters who, attracted in nearly equal degree to both polarities, turn now this way, now the other, or attempt to resolve the conflict within the frame of a single canvas. How much talent has been rendered sterile by this indecisiveness it is impossible to guess, but the effects of the dilemma may be studied in any one of our large group exhibitions. It is not too much to say that most of the problems, technical and conceptual, encountered by the present day artist are subsidiary to this one and will fall into place when once he decides this general question for himself.

To help both the artist and beholder out of this impasse, the nature of Cubism must be better understood and its method more widely available. Primarily, it should be recognized that this technique did not come about to serve the ends of science, literature, decoration, novelty, sensationalism or any claptrap aesthetic or system, but simply as the instrument of plastic sensibility. We have touched upon the term plasticity in a previous article and learnt that the artist attaches a special meaning to it, that of substantiality—the substantiality of visible things. Further inquiry into this subject will exhibit for us how plasticity has become a necessary function in the making of a Classicist art.

The concept of plasticity is neither new nor very ancient. Though indications of a plastic intent appear in diverse times and places, it may be safely asserted that it has been most peculiarly the property of the Western tradition in painting—the broad sweep that began with Duccio, Cimabue, and above all, with Giotto around the end of the thirteenth century—and has produced great works right into our own time. Before Giotto the muralists and mosaicists who worked under the sway of Byzantium contributed stunning decorations for the adornment of sacred buildings. But gorgeous as these were, their effectiveness was almost totally the result of two aspects of art with which plasticity has no concern: narration and decoration. The first of these has long been a matter of contention with artists and critics, but has finally been relegated to something of a secondary role in aesthetic discussions. If we feel impelled to invoke it—in dealing with Surrealism, for example—we will be justified in assuming that in general a negative attitude toward it is now taken for granted. Decoration, on the other hand, is still a powerful factor in the shaping of art forms and cannot be so lightly dismissed. However, it will be more convenient to postpone further examination of it till we take it up in relation to "Non-Objective" painting, in the later course of this inquiry.

Beginning with Giotto, painting was called upon to undertake a new and vital task. No painter since then has been able to avoid a declaration, in plastic terms and through commission or omission, of his attitude toward the material world. Those who, like Giotto and Classicist artists generally, wished to ally themselves with a point of view that recognized the objective character of this world, found in plasticity a prime method of celebrating its reality. For this reason, I think it profitable that to the two operations of technique already mentioned, a third should be added and the technical function of painting be thought of as threefold: as designed for narration, for decoration, and lastly, for *celebration*.

We have seen that a concern with plasticity was Cézanne's main technical occupation. And we know that his solution of the problems engendered by this concern hinged on the qualities of plane surfaces, on their capacity to fix and control the "solid and durable." It is not surprising that the Expressionists, involved with subjective affairs to the point of solipsism, paid little regard to plastic problems. But the Cubists, of quite another turn of mind, seized on Cézanne's discoveries and carried them forward to conclusions of their own.

Their attention concentrated, like Cézanne's, on the plane. After all, this is the ultimate visible unit; points and lines are hypotheses beyond the possibility of sight, and our depictions of them can only be used to indicate or bound. But the plane had such marvellous qualities; it was entrancing what could be done with it! It could be arranged in so many ways, each one as ravishingly plastic as the next. When it overlapped and cast a shadow, it became so tangible that the imagination might slip a finger behind it; when it was shaded skillfully and knowingly, it carried the eye back and forth in a most convincing sense of space. What was more logical, then, than to abstract from the subject one chose to paint, these delightful planes, and to exhibit them in such a way that the substantial nature of the subject became the object of emphasis? This is the central fact of Cubism. It was not part of its intention to destroy the subject or lose sight of its special character (though it was not interested in the merely circumstantial). On the other hand, it did generalize from the subject to the extent of making evident that it shared with a whole class of like subjects the solid quality of reality. It may be objected that this was Giotto's aim too, and Titian's and Ingre's, but that these men never denied the retinal image so bluntly as the Cubists did. However, it should be remembered that even in Cézanne's day the camera had largely freed the painter from the obligation of recording factual images of an instantaneous nature, and had left open the possibility of discovering visual relations that existed independently of the ephemeral. Pursuing this advantage, the Cubists were led to a procedure that has caused much confused explanation, but which has nevertheless been widely adopted. This is the combination of two or more planes—seen from different angles—into a single pictorial element. It is persistent in Picasso's work where, as often as not, a profile and a full face view combine in a single head. Or, a generally cylindrical object, a wine-glass for instance, is shown with the top as seen from above and the side as seen from eye level. There are variations of this device too numerous to mention, but the two which I have just described are typical instances, and have appeared in Cubist and Cubist-influenced painting for forty years or more.

The Cubists went further than this, and for a period, especially in the work of Braque and Picasso, around 1910, produced many pictures in which the planes were quite freely dissociated from their objects and redisposed on the canvas. To believe that these arrangements were arbitrary would be a mistake. The painter was bound by his relation to his subject; planes were chosen for their value in revealing the visual character of the subject and were displayed according to compositional demands of a particularly rigid kind. Consider, for a moment, the requirements such a construction made on its creator. He needed to select those planes from his subject that bore significance in the light of his visual relation to it. He was committed to emphasizing the decisive character of these planes, and therefore felt it necessary to present them in their most unvarying and revealing aspect. That would be frontally, or as nearly frontally as was consistent with the painting area in which they had to be confined. He also wished to show the quality of the subject and its relatedness to the space in which it existed. And this in addition to creating a satisfying and vigorous design, in accord with the tradition of which he knew himself a part. His over-all concern in painting was to communicate the complex of ideas generated by his visual experience, and he was thus constrained to invent a form which he believed held the possibility of such communication. A less arbitrary task or one less bound by considerations of a social nature would be hard to imagine.

After this austere period, which lasted several years and during which Cubism set the basic tenets of its technique, gentler and more playful impulses tempered the Cubist's work. Under the brushes of Picasso, Braque, Leger, Gris, and others in the decade from 1910 to 1920, the mechanisms of Cubism were consolidated and simplified, and witty practices that have had much influence on subsequent art first appeared.

But perhaps the most powerful painting instrument to appear in a new context since Cézanne is one that was adopted mainly by the Cubists and used with particular elegance by Picasso. This instrument is distortion.

That Picasso was early attracted by distortion is evidenced in pictures he made long before the invention of Cubism. As a very young painter he was strongly drawn to the work of Toulouse-Lautrec, whose sharp and acid vision veered close to caricature. But distortion of the sort that later became so striking a feature of Cubist painting—especially of Picasso's—was first encountered by Picasso and his friends in the form of African Negro fetishes and ceremonial masks, which came to their attention in 1906 or 1907. For two years or more, Picasso's painting reflected his contact with these deeply evocative sculptures. He put this interest aside while he was absorbed in the rigorous technical problems of Cubism, and it was not until these were explored that distortion again became a factor in his work.

To understand the Cubist's (again, particularly Picasso's) use of distortion, it is instructive to turn our attention to the Negro carvings already mentioned. We should note two apparently contrary facts: one, that the distortions are of an extreme nature extensively removed from normal anatomy; and, two, that nevertheless the finest of these figures possess a serenity to stand comparison with the purest manifestations of Classic sculpture.

Distortion of a very different kind is known to us. The Expressionists contorted limbs, heads and bodies in an orgy of destruction. That these distortions are brutal—if not downright sadistic —in their intent is hard to disbelieve in view of the painful reaction they induce. It is, in fact, a truism to connect such words as "tortured," "angry," "hysterical," with Expressionist work.

We may be able to clarify the differentiation between these two kinds of distortion by suggesting a redefinition for that purpose. The distortions in Expressionist art are distortions of degree—we might more correctly call them exaggerations. They seize on and enlarge or otherwise bring into prominence salient facts that already exist. This is like the easily accepted device of caricature. So, in Expressionism, the features that might contribute to the wanted effect were heightened in quite an obvious way. Bony contours, leering mouths, deeply set eye sockets; any gesture or contortion that would add violence, was emphasized. (It must be said that exaggerations are not confined to invidious uses. Italian primitive painters lengthened fingers and limbs to confer an ethereal grace. To convey the idea of power, Michelangelo broadened the shoulders and muscular development of the male figure.)

The contrary sort of distortion is one that transmutes an existing thing into something utterly different—a distortion of kind, bearing little or no resemblance to its original. It is possible to consider the animal-headed Egyptian deities as distorted in this way. We need not look far among examples of African Negro art to find figures—many from the Gabun region, for instance—in which the shapes of head and body are changed, not by a process of exaggeration, but by one of transmutation. The treatment of hands in certain modern paintings is another clear case of such distortion.

As we should expect, a great many African Negro pieces are distorted in the exaggerated, Expressionist way, reflecting perhaps cruel and hostile relationships between a tribe and its gods. But on the other side are those Negro sculptures that, though also distorted, are full of dignity and a supreme exaltation. How it is that virtues of high spiritual significance needed to be shown through the medium of such distortion is a subject worthy of much more exhaustive study than our present discussion will permit. It is not enough to say that they arise from an expert use of decorative factors such as symmetry, complexly achieved balance, satisfying curves, or from derivatives of style such as simplification, pose, etc., because their opposite numbers also employ these instruments. Whether the intention of the artist is to extol or to deprecate, when distortions are present in his work we cannot presume them to be unconnected with his aim or simply a matter of decoration.

It must be owned that it is our own mores we impose on these art forms when we distinguish between a distortion that extols and one that deprecates. For all we know, the cruel and (in our terms) hideous distortions were idealizations for the primitive sculptor. He may have admired the qualities they symbolized as much or more than those embodied in figures we find exalting instead of horrifying. The qualities we abhor translate themselves obviously into exaggerations, accenting elements that frighten and subdue. However, all transcendent values called for special treatment when they were to be represented, i.e., they needed to be shown in other than ordinary human forms. Therefore, not only violent but serene forces were expressed as distortions, but these latter were distortions in which the human form was qualitatively changed.

The primitive level of this attitude does not need to be labored. More sophisticated Negro peoples made sculptures in which distortion is hardly an ingredient. The great kingdom of Benin produced portrait heads that must have borne close resemblance to their patrician models. But these were a people secure in prosperity and authority; they were in control of outer circumstances to a much greater extent than their fellows.

The other African tribes also had in them the will to personify their ideals and were not to be deterred by hostile environment—by enemies, by disease, by ungrateful nature. So they gave to these ideals the appearance of the human form, distorting its features to place it on a level with the most potent and enduring forces they knew. So much skill, so much conviction, so much deep human feeling did the African Negro bring to this task that his cherished and well-wrought figures are now, many generations later, a lesson to humble our sophistries and a tribute to the greatness of the culture that created them.

But what is their relevance for modern art? How can we imagine our distortions to be as warranted, aesthetically and symbolically, as the Negro's? Psychology affords us an intimation. The unconscious source we call on for the raw material of our art is still as primitive as the African tribes were centuries ago. When immersed in a destructive and hostile climate, it, too, tends to draw strength from forces that would destroy it. The Expressionist, in fact, allies himself with these. But the artist who wishes to construct positive values also finds distortion a powerful and compelling instrument.

Why, it may be asked, is he enjoined from expressing himself in undisguised terms, in terms of regular human characteristics, of a physiognomy undistorted and universally admired? In less troubled times this is certainly possible. Have we, then, reason to feel that a situation now exists that inhibits the free communication of values of a glorified kind? Aside from the negative proof offered by the inanity and banality of official art, we must be cold indeed to every high humanistic impulse if we asserted otherwise. Drives to war, poverty, oppression and suppression are the order of the day. No wonder that the artist who undertakes to speak for the people, for humanity, finds in distortion a proper tool, tempered to eloquence by human misery.

In this spirit Picasso, in 1937, painted a great dedicated mural, "Guernica," to commemorate the tragedy suffered by the Spanish people at the hands of fascism. In it there is terror because the scene was terrible, not because the artist's brush brought terror to it. But it is exalted too, because it dispassionately records, above and beyond the horror of the day, the resiliency of man's creative will. Distortion and Cubism are the chief instruments of its effectiveness, and together demonstrate that a Classicist art has again found a way to epic statement.

# Snobs, Slobs and the English Language

## DONALD J. LLOYD

## ( *1951* )

Associate professor of English at Wayne State University, DONALD J. LLOYD is co-author of *American English In Its Cultural Setting* and an assistant editor of *Webster's New World Dictionary*.

In this article he insists that "the standard English used by literate Americans is no pale flower being overgrown by the weeds of vulgar usage: it is a strong, flourishing growth," not to be obstructed by the vigilance of linguistic sentries. In "The Retort Circumstantial," which follows, Jacques Barzun comments on the dangers of this growth and on what seem to him to be the fallacies of Mr. Lloyd's case.

THERE IS AT LARGE among us today an unholy number of people who make it their business to correct the speech and writing of others. When Winston Churchill says "It's me" in a radio address, their lips purse and murmur firmly, "It is I," and they sit down and write bitter letters to the New York *Times* about What is Happening to the English Language. Reading "I only had five dollars," they circle *only* and move it to the right of *had*, producing "I had only five dollars" with a sense of virtue that is beyond the measure of man. They are implacable enemies of "different than," of "loan" and "contact" used as verbs, and of dozens of other common expressions. They put triumphant exclamation marks in the margins of library books. They are ready to tangle the thread of any discussion by pouncing on a point of grammar.

If these people were all retired teachers of high-school English, their weight in the community would be negligible; but unfortunately they are not. They are authors, scholars, business men, librarians—indeed, they are to be found wherever educated people read and write English. And they are moved by a genuine concern for the language. They have brought us, it is true, to a state in which almost anybody, no matter what his education or the clarity of his expression, is likely to find himself attacked for some locution which he has used. Yet their intentions are of the best. It is only that their earnest minds are in the grip of two curious misconceptions. One is that there is a "correct" standard English which is uniform and definite and has been reduced to rule. The other is that this "correct" standard can only be maintained by the vigilant attention of everybody concerned with language—indeed, by the whole body of educated men and women.

The enemy these self-appointed linguistic sentries see lurking in every expression which stirs the correcter's instinct in them is something they call illiteracy—which is not a simple state of being unlettered, but something more. This illiteracy is a willful and obstinate disregard for the standards of civilized expression. It stirs anger in them when they think they see it, because it seems to them a voluntary ignorance, compounded out of carelessness and sloth. When they think they find it in men who hold responsible positions in the community, they feel it to be a summation of all the decline of the graces of culture, the last reaches of a great wave of vulgarity which is eroding the educated and literate classes. It seems to them to be a surge of crude populism; they hear in each solecism the faint, far-off cries of the rising mob. It is really a sort of ringing in their ears.

In view of the general agreement among the literate that a "correct" standard English exists, and in view of the vituperation directed at anyone suspected of corrupting it, one would expect some kind of agreement about what is correct. There is little to be found; the easy utterance of one educated man is the bane of another. "For all the fussiness about *which* and *that*," remarks Jacques Barzun in the *Nation*, "the combined editorial brass of the country have feebly allowed the word 'disinterested' to be absolutely lost in its original sense. One finds as careful a writer as Aldous Huxley using it to mean uninterested, so that by now a 'disinterested judge' is one that goes to sleep on the bench." And on the subject of what surely is a harmless word, *whom*, Kyle Crichton, associate editor of *Collier's*, is quoted in *Harper's*: "The most loathsome word (to me at least) in the English language is 'whom.' You can always tell a half-educated buffoon by the care he takes in working the word in. When he starts it I know I am faced with a pompous illiterate who is not going to have me long as company."

Probably only a cynic would conclude from the abundance of such comments that those who demand correct English do not know it when they meet it; but some students of language must have been led to wonder, for they have made up lists of disputed locutions and polled the literate on them. So far, the only agreement they have reached has to be expressed in statistical terms.

The latest of these surveys, a questionnaire containing nineteen disputed expressions, was reported by Norman Lewis in *Harper's* Magazine for March, 1949. Lewis sent his list to 750 members of certain groups chosen mainly for their professional interest in the English language: lexicographers, high school and college teachers of English, authors, editors, journalists, radio commentators, and "a random sampling of *Harper's* subscribers."

If we count out two groups on the basis of extremely special knowledge and interest—the college professors of English and the lexicographers—we find all the others accepting about half the expressions. The authors and editors (book and magazine) were highest with about 56 per cent, and the editors of women's magazines lowest with about 45. (The expression which was least favored was *less* in the sense of *fewer*—"I encountered *less* difficulties than I had expected"—but even that received an affirmative vote of 23 per cent.) The distinguished electors seem individually to have played hop, skip and jump down the column, each finding among the nineteen expressions about ten he could approve of. If any two fell on the same ten, it was merely a coincidence.

A person innocent in the ways of this controversy, but reasonably well-informed about the English language, noticing that the disputants ignore the massive conformity of most writers in most of their language practices, in order to quibble about fringe matters, might assume that they would welcome the cold light of linguistic science. This is a naïve assumption. In response to an attempt of mine to correct some of the misapprehensions I found in Mr. Barzun's article—among them his curious notion that "detached" and not "uninterested" was the original meaning of "disinterested"—he replied by letter that I represented a misplaced and breezy scientism, and that what I said struck him as "the raw material of 'populism' and willful resistance to Mind. . . . All dictionaries to the contrary notwithstanding, the word disinterested is now prevailingly used in the meaning I deprecated. . . .

The fact that an illiterate mistake may become the correct form
. . . is no reason for not combating it in its beginnings. . . ."
This rejection both of the professional student of language and of
the dictionary, when they disagree with the opinions of the writer,
has the effect of making each man his own uninhibited authority
on language and usage—an effect which I do not believe was exactly what Mr. Barzun had in mind.

What he did have in mind he stated clearly in one distinguished
paragraph:

> A living culture in one nation (not to speak of one world)
> must insist on a standard of usage. And usage, as I need not
> tell you, has important social implications apart from ele-
> gance and expressiveness in literature. The work of commu-
> nication in law, politics and diplomacy, in medicine, tech-
> nology, and moral speculation depends on the maintenance
> of a medium of exchange whose values must be kept fixed,
> as far as possible, like those of any other reliable currency.
> To prevent debasement and fraud requires vigilance, and it
> implies the right to blame. It is not snobbery that is involved
> but literacy on its highest plane, and that literacy has to be
> protected from ignorance and sloth.

It is a pity that these sentiments, so deserving of approval,
should receive it from almost all educated people except those
who really know something about how language works. One feels
like an uncultivated slob when he dissents—one of the low, inele-
gant, illiterate, unthinking mob. Yet as a statement about the
English language, or about standard English, it is not merely
partly true and partly false, but by the consensus of most professional students of language, totally false. It is one of those monstrous errors which gain their original currency by being especially
plausible at a suitable time, and maintain themselves long after
the circumstances which give rise to them have vanished. Mr.
Barzun's remarks are an echo from the eighteenth century; they
reek with an odor mustier than the lavender of Grandmother's
sachet. They have little relevance to the use of the English language in America in our day.

In actual fact, the standard English used by literate Americans
is no pale flower being overgrown by the weeds of vulgar usage: it
is a strong, flourishing growth. Nor is it a simple, easily describable
entity. Indeed, it can scarcely be called an entity at all, except in
the loose sense in which we call the whole vast sum of all the

dialects of English spoken and written throughout the world a single language. In this sense, standard American English is the sum of the language habits of the millions of educated people in this country. It is rooted in the intellectual life of this great and varied people. Its forms express what its users wish to express; its words mean what its users think they mean; it is correctly written when it is written by those who write it, and correctly spoken by those who speak it. No prim and self-conscious hoarding of the dead fashions of a superior class gives it its power, but its negligent use by minds intent on stubborn and important problems. There is no point in a tiresome carping about usage; the best thing to do is relax and enjoy it.

There are five simple facts about language in general which we must grasp before we can understand a specific language or pass judgment on a particular usage. It is a pity that they are not more widely known in place of the nonsense which now circulates, for they would relieve the native-born speaker of English of his present uncertainty, and give him a proper authority and confidence in his spontaneous employment of his mother tongue. They arise from a common-sense analysis of the nature of language and the conditions of its use.

In the first place, language is basically speech. Speech comes first in the life of the individual and of the race. It begins in infancy and continues throughout our lives; we produce and attend to a spoken wordage much greater than the written. Even the mass of writing which floods in upon us today is only the froth on an ocean of speech. In history, also, speech comes first. English has been written for only about fifteen hundred years; before this, it is of incalculable antiquity. In speech its grammar was developed; from changes in the sounds of speech, changes in its grammar come. The educated are inclined to feel that the most important aspect of language is the written form of it, and that the spoken language must and should take its standards from this. Actually, the great flow of influence is from speech to writing. Writing does influence speech somewhat, but its influence is like the interest a bank pays on the principal entrusted to it. No principal, no interest.

In the second place, language is personal. It is an experience and a pattern of habits of a very intimate kind. In the home, the family, the school and the neighborhood we learn the speechways of our community, learning to talk as those close to us talk in the give and take of daily life. We are at one with our nation in our easy command of the pitch, tune and phrase of our own home town. Language is personal, also, in that our grasp of it is no greater than our individual experience with it. The English we know is not that vast agglomeration of verbal signs which fills and yet escapes the largest lexicons and grammars, but what we have personally heard and spoken, read and written. The best-read man knows of his native language only a limited number of forms in a limited number of combinations. Outside of these, the wealth which a copious tongue has as its potential is out of his world, and out of everybody's, for no dictionary is so complete or grammar so compendious as to capture it.

The third fact about language is that it changes. It changes in its sounds, its meanings and its syntax. The transmission of sounds, words and meanings from generation to generation is always in some respects imprecise. Minute differences add up in time to perceptible changes, and changes to noticeable drifts. Difference in changes and in rates of change make local speech sounds, pitches, tones and vocabularies draw subtly and persistently away from one another. And all it takes to produce an identifiable dialect is sufficient segregation over a sufficient length of time.

The fourth great fact about language, then, is that its users are, in one way or another, isolated. Each has with only a few others the sort of familiar relationships which join them in one language community. Yet there are upward of two hundred million native speakers of English in the world. Obviously they cannot all be in close touch with one another. They congeal in nuclei—some stable, some transitory—which by a kind of double-action draw them together and enforce isolation of many more-or-less shifting kinds: the isolation of distance, of education, of economic levels, of occupation, age and sex, of hobbies and political boundaries. Any one of these will be reflected in language habits; any two or three will bring about, in one community, speech differences as great as those caused by oceans and mountain ranges.

The fifth great fact about language is that it is a historical growth of a specific kind. The nature of English is one of the absolutes of our world, like air, water and gravity. Its patterns are not subject to judgment; they simply are. Yet they have not always been what they are; like the physical world, they have changed with time, but always in terms of what they have been. *Boy loves girl* means something different from *girl loves boy*. It is futile for us to prefer another way of conveying these meanings: that is the English way, and we must live with it. Yet students of the language see in this simple pattern the result of a cataclysmic change, great and slow like the geologic upheavals that have brought old salt beds to the very tops of mountain ranges, and as simple. Each is what it is because of what it has been before.

Language as a social instrument reflects all the tides which sweep society, reacting in a local or surface way easily and quickly —as a beach changes its contours to suit the waves—but it offers everywhere a stubborn rock core that only time and massive pressures can move. The whim of a girl can change its vocabulary, but no will of man can touch its essential structure; this is work for the long attrition of generations of human use. Ever lagging a little behind human needs, it offers a multitude of terms for the things men no longer care about, but keeps them improvising to say what has not been said before.

Spoken English is, then, by its own nature and the nature of man, a welter of divergences. The divergences of class and place are sharpest in Britain, where the same dialects have been spoken in the same shires and villages for more than a thousand years. Although these can be heard in America by any traveler, no matter how dull his ear, they are relatively slight, for our language is essentially and repeatedly a colonial speech. Each of the American colonies drew settlers from various parts of Britain; each worked out a common speech based mainly on the dialect of its most influential group of immigrants (which differed from colony to colony) ; each remained in relative isolation from the others for about a hundred years. Then many colonists began to move to the interior: wave after wave of settlers traveled along rather distinct lines of advance until the continent was covered. Everywhere there was a mingling of dialects, with a composite speech arising, based mainly on the speech of the dominant local group. And so we have a Northern speech fanning out from the Northeastern states, a Midland speech fanning out from the Mid-Atlantic states, and a Southern speech in the land of cotton-raisers, all crossing and merging as the pioneers moved west. Local differences are greatest along the Atlantic coast.

Wherever our people settled, they worked out local ways of talking about the things of common experience, and found their own verbal symbols of class distinctions. Here and there are areas where foreign-speaking groups clung together and developed special exotically-flavored dialects, but otherwise most speech patterns in America can be traced back to the dialects of Britain. Everywhere there is a common speech used by the multitude which works with its hands, and a slightly different dialect spoken by the professional and leisure classes.

The standard English written by Americans is not, however, the written form of educated speech, which shows great local variation. Its spellings have only a rough equivalence to the sounds we make; its grammatical system, which has nationwide and even worldwide currency, had its origin in the educated speech of the Northeastern states, and before that in the dialect of London, England. The concentration of schools, colleges, publishing houses and print shops in early New England and New York had the same effect in this country as the concentration in England, for centuries, of political power, commercial activity and intellectual life in London: it established a written standard, native only to those who grew up near the Hudson River or east of it. Elsewhere in America this written standard has been a learned class dialect —learned in the schools as the property and distinguishing mark of an educated class. Like many of its spellings, it is itself a relic of the past, an heirloom handed down from the days when the whole nation looked to the schoolmasters of New England for its book-learning.

The present controversy about usage is simply a sign that times have changed. The several vast and populous regions of this country have grown self-sufficient and self-conscious, and have taken the education of their youth into their own hands. Where the young once had to travel to the East for a respectable education, they receive it now in local public systems of rapid growth and great size. From local schools they may go to local universities of fifteen to fifty thousand students, where they can proceed to the highest degrees. Yale University is overcrowded with some six thousand students; in the community colleges alone of California more than 150,000 are enrolled. Most of these young people take their diplomas and go to work among their own people. They form a literate class greater in numbers and in proportion to the total population than the world has ever seen before. Speaking the speech of their region, they mingle naturally and easily with its people. When they write, they write the language they know, and they print it, for the most part, in presses close at hand. Everywhere they speak a standard literate English—but with differences: a regional speech derived from the usages of the early settlers.

Standard written English is, after all, an abstraction—a group of forms rather arbitrarily selected from the multitude offered by the language as a whole—an abstraction which serves the peculiar needs of the intellect. It achieves its wide currency because the interests of its users are the common interests of the educated, which transcend frontiers and negate distances—law, literature, science, industry and commerce. It is the tool of intelligence. Any thinking person must use it, because only this form of the language provides the instruments of delicate intellectual discrimination. And it is not static. As the needs of the intellect change, standard English changes. Change is its life, as anyone can see who picks up a book written only a little time ago, or examines almost any old newspaper.

The common speech of the uneducated, on the other hand, is comparatively static. Though it varies greatly from place to place, it is everywhere conservative; far from corrupting the standard language, it follows slowly after, preserving old forms long ago given up by literate speakers. "Them things" was once standard, and so were "he don't," "giv," and "clumb" and "riz." Its patterns are archaic, its forms homely and local. Only its vocabulary is rich and daring in metaphor (but the best of this is quickly swiped by writers of standard English) . Seldom written because its speakers seldom write, it is yet capable of great literary beauties, uncomplicated force, compact suggestion, and moving sentiment. But it will not bear the burden of heavy thinking, and anyhow, heavy thinkers have a better tool to use. It is about as much danger to the standard language as an old house cat.

I have often wondered at the fear of common English and its speakers which the cultural aristocracy display, at their curious definition of illiteracy, and at the intemperance of their terms, which verges on the pathological. A Freudian should have a picnic with them. They use such epithets as *illiteracies, crudities, barbarisms, ignorance, carelessness* and *sloth.* But who is not negligent in language, as in the mechanics of driving a car? They mutter darkly about "inchoate mob feelings." They confess themselves snobs by denying that their attitudes are snobbish. The stridency of their self-assurance puzzles the mind.

We might better adjust our minds to the divergences of usage in standard written English, for time, space and the normal drift of culture have put them there. We need not raise our eyebrows at a different twist of phrase, but enjoy it as an echo of a way of life somewhat different from our own, but just as good. We could do more than enjoy these things; we could recognize that the fixed forms of the language which do not come to our attention were developed in the past. We have come too late for the show. It is the changing forms that evidence the life in our language and in our society; we could learn much about our people and their ways by simply and objectively observing them.

If there is one thing which is of the essence of language, it is its drive to adapt. In an expanding culture like ours, which is invading whole new realms of thought and experience, the inherited language is not wholly suited to what we have to say. We need more exact and expressive modes of utterance than we have; we are working toward finer tolerances. The fabric of our language is flexible, and it can meet our needs. Indeed, we cannot stop it from doing so. Therefore it would be well and wholesome for us to see, in the locutions of the educated which bring us up sharply as we read, not evidences of a rising tide of illiteracy (which they are not) , but marks of a grand shift in modes of expression, a self-reliant regionalism, and a persistent groping toward finer distinctions and a more precise utterance.

# The Retort Circumstantial

## JACQUES BARZUN

## *( 1951 )*

Words and language are to be used with precision and knowledge, JACQUES BARZUN replies to Mr. Lloyd. "The danger to English today is not from bad grammar, dialect, vulgar forms, or native crudity, but from misused ornaments. . . ."

Mr. Barzun is provost and dean of faculties at Columbia University.

MR. LLOYD'S ARTICLE is the culmination of a lively correspondence between him and me, in the course of which I feel sure that I repeatedly cut the ground from under his feet. Since from the outset he hadn't a leg to stand on, my efforts were bound to be useless, but we were both having such a good time that neither of us noticed his plight. At my suggestion he has consented to display his miraculous position in public, and I must therefore return to the charge. The public will judge.

It seems clear in the first place that by preaching the attitude of the mere recorder, the *registrar* of linguistic fact, Mr. Lloyd disqualifies himself for remonstrating with me or anybody else. I, as a writer, am his source, his document, his *raison d'être,* and he can no more logically quarrel with me than he can with a piece of papyrus. Nevertheless, I am willing to concede his human (and very modern) right to inveigh against my moralism in the tones of an outraged moralist.

What then does his objection come to? That in seeking to criticize certain tendencies in current literary English, I am usurping an authority I do not possess, and interfering with the natural evolution of the language. This is the prime fallacy in his case, which rests on a chain of reasoning somewhat as follows: English has greatly changed through the ages; many of these changes were resisted by purists; but the evolution was irresistible, and the result is something we now consider correct and natural. Hence Mr. Barzun's attitude is *contra naturam;* he is an old fogey, a snob, and an ignoramus who thinks he can set his face against the future only because he is blind to the past.

The truth is, of course, that one does not obtain "nature" by merely removing opposition, wise or unwise. Nor can we know what is inevitable until we have tried good and hard to stop it. The whole analogy with nature is false because language is an artificial product of social life, all of whose manifestations, even when regular, bear only a remote likeness to the course of nature. Being a social product, language is everybody's football, and that is precisely what gives me, as well as Mr. Lloyd, the right to push it this way or that by argument.

And here it is important to remember that resistance to change is by no means futile. The history of the language is not what the gallant liberals make out—a struggle between the dauntless Genius of English and a few misguided conservatives. It is a free-for-all. At this point it is usual for the advocates of the "Hands Off" policy to trot out the word "mob," which Swift attacked with several other curtailed forms, and pretend that it was ridiculous of the Dean to boggle at it, "in the light of what came after." Well, what came after is that we deodorized "mob," and abandoned altogether the other vulgarities he was deprecating: we no longer use *rep, pozz, phiz, hipps,* or *plenipo.* The future, in short, belonged as much to Dean Swift as to his opponents—and rather more if we count the hits and misses.

So much for the pseudo-naturalism of the linguistic registrars. Their vow not to judge among words and usages is a fine thing as long as it expresses a becoming sense of incapacity, but it must not turn into a union rule enforceable on those who have taken precisely opposite vows—namely, to exploit, preserve, and possibly enrich the language. This is the duty of the writer, it calls for judgment, and it brings us to that blessed word "disinterested," which seems to have acted on Mr. Lloyd like a whiff of mustard to the nose.

My simple and meritorious deed as regards "disinterested" was to draw attention to its widespread misuse as a duplicate of *uninterested.* Examples abound, and the fight against the plague may already be lost without the confusion being anything like over. Every piece of printed matter exhibits it, and nearly every conversation. Just the other day I heard this sentence, spoken to identify a stranger: "He is an impresario, but when it comes to art, he's completely disinterested." Did the speaker mean, X has no interest in art? Or: he is so much interested in it that money is no object? According to current usage this is impossible to determine without questioning the speaker. Not even his presumed degree of education will settle the matter, for the wrong use has affected all ranks.

At the phrase "wrong use," Mr. Lloyd twitched his non-existent leg, and with his hands made the motions of a man taking to earth in a dictionary. A few American, and especially collegiate, dictionaries do give the meaning "uninterested" as a second choice—which is a sufficient reason for me to view with a lack-luster eye Mr. Lloyd's naïve faith in lexicographers. The one work that seems relevant to the argument is the *O.E.D.*, which gives us the history of the word. It tells us that the meaning *uninterested* is obsolete and it lists five separate earlier forms, going back to the French of Montaigne, all connected with the idea of "removing the self interest of a person in a thing." As an English adjective, examples are given from 1659 to Dr. Livingstone in 1865, with the meaning: "not influenced by interest, impartial, unbiased, unprejudiced." My original remark was to the effect that nowadays the "disinterested judge" is probably taken to mean one who sleeps on the bench. My final remark is: As a writer concerned with the precision and flexibility of the language I use, I cannot regard the return to an obsolete and ambiguous form as useful or in any other way justified.

I now carry the war into the enemy's camp. If instead of complacently taking notes on the growing confusion, and protecting under pretext of "science" the vagaries of modern usage, Mr. Lloyd and his compeers would reflect upon their data, they might be able to safeguard the complex instrument of our speech by telling us when and why these deplorable losses occur, and how they might be repaired—loss of clarity and exactness at large, absolute loss of meaning in a word such as "disinterested" and in another such as "connive." Everyone has seen this last used as a synonym for "conspire" and "contrive"; I have heard it in the intransitive sense of "manage" about some trivial business. "How did you connive?" Hitherto, when you escaped from the concentration camp because the guard deliberately looked the other way, it was he who *connived* at your escape, no one else. Can it be that the action is obsolete and we no longer need the word?

These instances are not isolated, and I shall accept statistical refutation only from someone who can show that he reads each year more written matter than I, and hears a greater variety of local uses from a larger body of students.

Meantime, the generality which I hazarded, and which Mr. Lloyd assails as undemocratic and tainted with ethical feeling, is that with the rapid extension of educational opportunities, many persons of otherwise simple hearts are snatching at words half understood in order to bedeck their thoughts. Only the other day I read in a "literary" review about a distinguished American critic who was so full of insight that he could be called a *voyeur*. The writer meant *voyant*, if anything, but he could certainly be sued for slander before an educated court.

Foreign words are always treacherous, but what of the newspaper editorial which states that Mr. So-and-so's election is "highly fortuitous" (meaning "fortunate") , or the college dean who tells parents that his institution gives the students "a fulsome education"? Then there are those who believe that "to a degree" means "to a certain extent," instead of just the opposite. Have not the oil and drug companies been forced to change their labels to "flammable" because many users of their products took "*in*flammable" to mean non-combustible? At that stage, the issue ceases to be comic or inconsequential. With the tremendous output of verbiage by air and print to which we are all subjected, the corruption of meaning is rapid and extensive. We are at the mercy of anyone who thinks the sense of a word is discoverable by inspection, and whose misuse consequently liberates an echoing error in the minds of his peers.

To put it differently, the danger to English today is not from bad grammar, dialect, vulgar forms, or native crudity, but from misused ornaments three syllables long. The enemy is not illiteracy but incomplete literacy—and since this implies pretension it justifies reproof. There is no defense against the depredations of the brash except vigilance and no quarter given. I am certain that in this regard Mr. Lloyd, who writes with so much felicity and force, does exactly this in his capacity as a college teacher of English. Why then does he not square his precepts with his practice? I cannot answer for him, but to help his amputated philosophy to its feet, I want by way of conclusion to quote from a writer who, being anonymous and attached to both journalism and business, can hardly be suspected of flaunting pedantry and preciosity. The extract is from *Fortune* for November, 1950:

"Language is not something we can disembody; it is an ethical as well as a mechanical entity, inextricably bound up in ourselves, our positions, and our relations with those about us."

# Freud, Religion and Science

## DAVID RIESMAN

## ( *1951* )

Even before the publication of *The Lonely Crowd,* the
name of DAVID RIESMAN had become synonymous with creative and imaginative social science. Formerly on the faculty
of the University of Chicago, Mr. Riesman is now a member of
the Department of Social Relations at Harvard University.

Here he traces some of the many factors that caused the
pendulum shift in the relative positions of religion and
psychoanalysis in the United States during the thirties and
forties. An amplification of this essay can be found in Mr.
Riesman's book *Individualism Reconsidered,* Doubleday
Anchor edition, 1955.

WHEN FREUD ATTACKED religion as an illusion and defended a
scientific *Weltanschauung* in *The Future of an Illusion*
(1928) , he felt himself to be criticizing a great, vested institution
whose future might be dim but whose present was tenacious and
powerful. Sensitive to the charge that he was robbing people of
their faith, he pointed out that he had no such confidence his arguments would shake the faithful: who should know better than he
that people were capable of great "resistance" to unacceptable
thoughts? Indeed, Freud feared that he and his followers would
be the ones most likely to suffer from counter-blows if they attacked religion. He believed, moreover, that the churches (no
matter how small the enclave which, like some Vatican City, was
preserved against the inquiries of science) were still seeking to
put limits on the inquiries of science—to confine it, for example,
to the "material" universe while ruling the "soul" out of bounds.
It is my purpose in this article to trace a few of the many ironies
which have shifted the relative positions of religion and psychoanalysis in the intervening twenty years, particularly in the United
States.

# I

On the one side, a group of intellectual theologians and lay devotees of religion have made common cause with Freud—as they interpret him. They have claimed him as sharing their belief in man's demonic nature and need for unquestioning faith, and as sharing their scorn for the religious liberals who, it is alleged, are naïve enough to believe that man is naturally good, his life a feast of optimistic reason. They have compared Freud's stress on anxiety with the anxiety of the fear-and-trembling school of neo-orthodox theology, and they have found in Freud at least some metaphorical support for the doctrine of original sin.

A considerable violence, it seems to me, is done to Freud by this procedure. Freud is fundamentally an Enlightenment rationalist. As other nineteenth-century entrepreneurs took upon themselves the white man's burden of subduing foreign customs and procedures which seemed irrational from the standpoint of Ricardian economics, so Freud sought to subject to laws—for which he often used the term "economic"—all the seemingly irrational phenomena of sex, art and religion.

To be sure, Freud was not very sanguine about reason. He thought that to trust it might sometimes be to trust an illusion. But at least it was capable of disproof as an illusion, according to the canons of reason itself; and therefore it was superior to the illusion of religion, which did not offer itself to proof or disproof. If the individual could grow up and free himself of dependency on his father, so perhaps the human race might grow up and free itself of dependence on a father-surrogate, or God. Freud's toughness here is not the toughness of the neo-orthodox. In fact, he would tend to interpret their focus on anxiety as a sign of weakness, for he did not admire those who trembled in contemplation of the problems of living and dying; while he counseled resignation, it was the resignation of the Stoic—quite the opposite of the self-abasement which he felt religion inculcated.

True, there is some similarity between Freud's concept of original sin and that of modern Protestant orthodoxy. The similarity lies in the pessimism about the human enterprise which Freud shares with such a man as Reinhold Niebuhr. But the equally important difference is that Freud used his mocking concept of original sin as a democratizer of men: it pleased him to trace the innate symptoms of sex and aggression in the work of the high and mighty, while Niebuhr uses the concept to create a preferential position for those who recognize it and who proclaim man's intellectual and moral limitations. Moreover, pride, not humility, attracted Freud.[1]

This strange alliance between some themes in neo-orthodox religion and some themes in Freudian thought has come about in part because of a change since the thirties in the attitude of the intellectual *avant-garde* toward organized religion. Once the shock of Darwin's discoveries wore off, they were occasionally made to testify to the greater glory of God's handiwork; by the same token, Freud's discoveries have been made to testify to the lesser glory of men as against God. Many intellectuals, concerned with "turning to religion," find themselves in sympathy with any outlook which depreciates man.

## II

Just how far we have come can, I think, be seen if we look back at Ruth Benedict's *Patterns of Culture,* a book which appeared in 1934. There she discussed the problem of criticism of contemporary American institutions, and how such criticism might become more enlightened through anthropological and comparative studies. We have accustomed ourselves, she observed, to shedding our ethnocentrism when it comes to religion; nobody gets into trouble because he attacks religion. We have not done that, she goes on, however, with respect to our economic institution—that is, capitalism. It is here that we have remained ethnocentric, and an attack on this sacred institution may be dangerous for the attacker.

Today the situation appears very nearly to be reversed. The massed social pieties which were invested in the established eco-

---

[1] In correspondence, Dr. Niebuhr has pointed out that I have been unjust to him here, and I accept his criticism. Quoting Pascal's remark that "Discourses on humility are a source of pride to those who are proud," he declares: "I have again and again insisted that such are the powers of human self-deception that those who have what I believe to be a correct analysis of human nature may use it as a source of pride. . . . There is a sense of course in which everybody who strives for the truth gives implicitly a 'preferential' position to those who perceive the truth, as you do for instance, in your article. I cannot help but feel, though this may be quite unjust, that you had to make some critical remark like that in order to establish the preferential position of irreligion as against religion in the matter of truth, for it would be embarrassing to grant that any truth could come out of a religious position. . . ." Dr. Niebuhr referred me to statements in *Faith and History* and *The Children of Light and the Children of Darkness* to show how thoroughgoing a foe of pretence and arrogance, in and out of theology, he has been; I needed no references for his zeal on democracy's behalf.

nomic order in the pre-Roosevelt era now seem massed behind religion and nation. Provided one opposes communism (wherein both religion and nation are involved) , one need not defend capitalism; but one has to be—and, perhaps more important, feels one ought to be—considerably more respectful toward organized religion. The movies, with their extraordinary sensitivity to pressure, provide an excellent example. Today many movies are devoted to sentimental glorification of churchly figures. Conversely, our popular culture enjoys attacks on capitalism—Hortense Powdermaker points out, in her recent book on the movies, that businessmen are almost never presented in a favorable light in films. Psychoanalysts today join the general chorus of attack on our "competitive, money-mad culture," but have seldom continued, in the manner of Freud and Reik, to analyze, let alone criticize, religion.

Possibly, a psychoanalytic interpretation of this shift could help us to understand it. We might think of the image of the rebellious son who carries out a partial, not wholly successful, rebellion against his father. Because of his ambivalence and partial failure, the son feels guilty; because of his partial success, the father gives in; and there is a reconciliation on a new level. Similarly, the revolt against the Hoover economic order (or, more accurately, the radical change in economic conditions) carried out since 1934 has been partly successful—too successful to allow the "father" really to hope more than nostalgically for the restoration of "free enterprise." But father and son have come to terms on religion and nation, and the continuing and perhaps even increasing social anxieties and rigidities, displaced from economics, have found a new, "spiritual" fold. This shift today permits religious organizations—which in some ways seem to me to be more powerful than fifteen years ago—to feel themselves aggrieved by any scientific and intellectual tendency which is at all outspokenly irreligious. Such a tendency can then be attacked as an "attack on religion," without violating the code of fair play.[2] We can recall that when

[2] When I expressed this tentative view of the shift in power positions between "science" on the one side and "religion" on the other, in the course of my lecture, many in the audience questioned my interpretation. Some pointed to Blanshard's *American Freedom and Catholic Power* as evidence that the older Mencken attitude toward organized religion is still strong. A more important argument, in my opinion, was raised by those who contended that the *lack* of strong scientific attacks on religion today was caused, not by the strength of religion and the weakness of the scientific temper, but by its opposite: religion is no longer an issue which the young, emancipated by science, find worth arguing about. And to be sure, scientists now go their way with less worry than ever before about those theological issues which

the psychiatrist Brock Chisholm stated in a lecture to the Washington School of Psychiatry that the myth of Santa Claus was a swindle on children, the Canadian cabinet was forced to meet, and he very nearly lost his job as health minister.

### III

I may be mistaken—and certainly there are counter-tendencies which indicate the weakening of organized religion. But assuming that I am right, how are we to explain this alteration in the climate of discussion concerning religion? Obviously, in this article I can touch on only a few of the many factors involved. I have already referred to the increasingly sympathetic attitude toward religion taken among *avant-garde* groups. Intellectual anti-clericalism, like anti-clericalism in the labor movement, is out of fashion; and it is not surprising that psychoanalysts—even those "orthodox" in other respects—seem to have fallen in with the general trend, and either stick to their clinical work or claim religion as an ally.

To be sure, the *avant-garde* has little social power and less political influence. Nevertheless, it had power enough during the twenties to put religion on the defensive among those upper-class and upper-middle-class Catholics and other communicants who wanted to feel socially and intellectually accepted and up-to-date. Such people did not want to appear backwoodsy and bigoted. Today, however, it is "backwoodsy" to be anti-religious, and in fact I find among my students that only, on the whole, small-town, especially Southern, boys will go whole hog with Freud's view of religion. The revival of interest in religion (if not in church-going) among intellectuals means that many in the upper social strata who are affiliated with organized religion need no longer flinch in pressing the claims of religion and in attacking its few remaining outspoken foes. They can now accept without embarrassment the anti-scientific position of the devout of lesser social standing.

This alliance of the classes in defense of religion is facilitated by a development much more important in its bearing on our topic

---

developed in the great battles between science and organized religion from the sixteenth to the beginning of the twentieth century; the turmoil in which such a man as the biologist Gosse was caught by Darwinism is today hardly conceivable. But one reason for this "peace of Westphalia" is that religionists are at last resigned to leaving natural science alone—it is only philosophers, humanists and psychologists who, dealing with man, face even the possibility of jurisdictional dispute with organized religion.

than the altered mood of the *avant-garde*—namely, the rise in the social position of American Catholics in the last several decades. My friend and colleague, Everett Hughes, a very thoughtful and sympathetic student of church institutions and especially of Catholicism, has pointed out that one of the greatest sources of anxieties among middle-class Catholics is the problem of the relation between their church affiliation and their social mobility. Because they are mobile, these Catholics have looked for the definition of "good American" in the past largely to non-Catholics: to high-status Protestants, to Jewish intellectuals and mass-media opinion leaders, and (to a degree) even to the "leakage," as those are called who seep away from the Church. But as Catholics have increasingly moved into the managerial and professional classes, they have been able greatly to influence the definition of "good American," and have taken the lead, since they were among the "earliest arrivals" in the crusade against communism, in defining the "bad un-American" as well. At the same time, non-Catholic opinion leaders, for the reasons given earlier, do not define the middle- and upper-class style of life in such a way as to exclude good Catholics—save, perhaps, for the still differentiating and hence exceedingly anxiety-provoking issue of birth control.

Yet, while the Catholics have risen substantially, they have not yet gained full social security on the American scene—and the same, of course, is true of the Jews, whose "religious" revival deserves a chapter to itself. Consequently, they are not yet able to laugh off such criticisms of religion as, despite religious censorship of the mass media, continue to crop up. It is unlikely that, fifteen years ago, a high Catholic churchman would have dared to attack an Eleanor Roosevelt after the recent fashion of Cardinal Spellman; it is unlikely that, fifteen years hence, a high churchman will find such a polemic fitting and needful.

## IV

So far, I have stressed the tendencies to censor science and intellectual discourse that are implicit in the new "united front" of religionists and intellectuals. But in this same development there are liberating aspects. The seriousness with which religion is now taken has made an interest in it respectable among many scientists who would earlier have considered an irreligious attitude an essential mark of emancipation. While, as Lloyd Morris' account [3]

[3] In his book on James, in Scribner's *Twentieth Century Library*.

has recently shown, William James was considered by many of his professional colleagues to be a kind of nut for concerning himself with religious experience, especially of a mystical and sectarian sort, no such scorn would greet a similar student—for instance, Gordon Allport—today.

Indeed, Freud himself is in part to be thanked for this; by studying religion, he in a sense domesticated it for science (the anthropologists also, of course, did a great deal). His was a Promethean effort to rob religion of its mysteries, and even his ( as I think) false analogies between religion and neurosis sprang from his effort to treat religion in a way that science could manage. He made it possible for later psychoanalytically-oriented thinkers to feel at home with symbolism of a non-discursive sort, religious symbolism included.

But it is more than a joint concern for symbolism and ritual that today leads psychoanalysts, theologians and lay devotees of both psychoanalysis and theology to attempt communication with each other. One reason for such communication is, obviously, competition over who takes what troubles to whom; but this is not what I have in mind. Rather, I am interested in the increasing preoccupation with moral problems among analysts and among religious leaders. It may sound strange to speak of increasing concern for moral problems among religionists—we are apt to assume that this has always interested them. But we must not overlook the degree to which religion in the nineteenth century had become, for a great many people, a formal, often hypocritical shell. Church socials as the core of religious observances, moreover—as we can see by looking at Howells' novel, *A Modern Instance,* for example —did not begin their rise only with the twentieth century. Indeed, religion serves today, much more than in the preceding several generations, as a center for discussion of fundamental problems of value.

Meanwhile, by a quite different route, a similar development has overtaken the psychoanalysts. In his therapy, Freud rejected the notion that he was a moral or ethical guide; he thought that such a concept would lead to a concealed dictatorship, and that his job was done when he had helped the patient to find his own ego-ideals, free from compulsive obedience to, or flight from, a parental image. Actually, he could largely coast on the implicit ends of the nineteenth century, and assume that his patients were on the whole sensible people whose neuroses originated, not in a genuine moral conflict, but in over-obedience to the sexual restrictions which society preached but neither enforced nor expected people to live up to. Freud could easily find in such people—as in his wonderful analysis of the "private religion" of the German jurist Schreber—that their religion served as a reinforcement of their sexual inhibitions, and hence of inhibitions in all realms, qualified only by the "return of the repressed" within the religious system itself.

It seems to have been Jung who first realized, in the immediate generation of analysts after Freud, that this was neither the whole meaning of religion nor the whole reason why people came to psychoanalysts. His patients seemed to be mainly men of middle age who were "in search of a soul"—who asked the analyst: "What is the purpose of my life? What should I do with it?" Their neuroses seemed to be bound up with moral problems, problems of choice. Increasingly today, this new type of analytic work with people who are neither obviously ill nor seeking professional analytic training—people whose "symptom" is their *malaise,* their whole way of life—forces analysts to become concerned with problems of casuistry, of values, as part of the therapeutic task. Neurosis then appears, not so much as a conflict between "natural" libidinal demands and society's restraints, but as a conflict among moral strivings within the individual himself—though these, of course, reflect the conflicts within society. And, in terms of technique, the analyst's task may no longer lie in coaching sexual frankness—it is not so much their sex lives about which patients feel shame, but, more often, their tendencies to decent, humane or otherwise "soft" or gullible behavior. The analyst may have to help them confront repressed moral issues about which they ought to be, but are not consciously, troubled.

In two books, *Man for Himself* and *Psychoanalysis and Religion,* Erich Fromm has made an effort to grapple with these moral problems as they present themselves in analysis, within an evaluative framework that finds much in common with what he terms "humanistic" religion. He takes religion much more seriously as a source of illumination for psychotherapy than most psychoanalysts (including Jung) have hitherto done. At the same time, he employs the Freudian methods to understand the hold over men of both humanistic and "authoritarian" religion, and its value for them. Thus he regards himself, not incorrectly, as working in the tradition of Freud, but (like John Dewey) he regards as truly religious, certain elevated ethical attitudes and cosmologies that Freud, when he adverted to them at all, regarded as too highbrow to be given the name of religion. Freud, that is, criticized as an illusion precisely those religious forms that manifested human submission to a Father-god; Fromm, considering a wider ambit of religious experience, sees in it more of fundamental humanistic import—though it would do his treatment an injustice to see him as one of those analysts who regard religion as useful, not for morals, but for morale. Rather, he represents a number of contemporary analysts who are preoccupied with theological questions, not simply as Freud was—i.e., as "evidence" of human weakness and as sources of historical data—but on their merits and in their own terms. At the same time, theologians, turning the tables, can look to psychoanalytic developments for evidence concerning basic human needs and problems of an ethical and religious sort.

Such reconciliations, however, are not likely to get very far in the fear of criticizing religion which I have suggested is today the prevailing atmosphere. For if the onslaughts of organized religious groups succeed in putting psychoanalysis, along with other inquisitive sciences, on the defensive, psychoanalysis—far from joining in the possible creation of new, syncretistic religious patterns —will either leave religion alone, as too hot to handle, or will form expedient alliances and make expedient obeisances and denials of any claim to ethical and religious relevance. If, in other and more "emancipated" circles, psychoanalysis, in the form of a diluted popular Freudianism, can still put people on the defensive who would like to know how to live decent lives, they will look to analysis only for debunking clichés and for symptom-therapy, not for its moral illumination.

Indeed, if we are to get beyond such sterility and defensiveness on both sides, we must abandon the misleading notion that there is such a thing as pure science or pure religion. All thought—that of religion and psychoanalysis alike—is impure, or, as Freud would say, ambivalent; all thought must be constantly removed from its wrappings of this time or that place. This is true of Freud's views concerning religion, as their paradoxical uses traced here would seem to indicate. It is also true, I venture to say, not only of our religious inheritance as a whole, but specifically of our traditional religious way of dealing with the temerities of science.

No doubt, future developments in the relation between psychoanalysis and religion (including Fromm's attempt to break down this distinction and to develop new ones) will depend rather more on such larger issues of social structure as the fate of the Catholic middle class than on the success of the intellectual adventure of a handful of theologians and analysts. But religious and scientific advance must usually occur as relatively powerless movements within a precarious setting. Freud, like other innovators, started as a minority of one.

# Liberal Education and
# a Liberal Nation

## ARTHUR E. BESTOR, JR.

### (*1952*)

When this article was written in 1952, ARTHUR BESTOR launched his crusade against the so-called "life adjustment" policy of education in the public schools. The formation of the Council for Basic Education, of which Mr. Bestor was the first president, was a result of his plea for renewed emphasis on intellectual training in the curriculum. Mr. Bestor is professor of history at the University of Illinois.

WHEN IT IS so hard to pay for things we really desire, it is folly to pay for things we consider valueless. Yet this is what Americans appear to be doing with respect to higher education. We cheerfully send an ever-increasing proportion of the population through college and into graduate work, but we resent the university-trained man who attempts to bring his special qualifications to bear in the public service. We encourage society (which is ourselves) to pay for his education, but when it is paid for, we deny that it has any value for society in terms of either expert knowledge or maturity of judgment.

It was a magnificent thing to have offered college training at public expense to veterans, but this was rather a gesture of gratitude to the G.I. than a reaffirmation of faith in the social value of higher education. Few Americans thought of the program as a great investment in the intellectual advancement of the nation. And when the question of draft deferment for college students came up for discussion a year ago, few Americans showed that they took seriously the danger it was designed to prevent—the danger that a halt in the steady flow of men trained in the fundamental scholarly and scientific disciplines might impoverish the nation intellectually, slow down its technological progress, or weaken its leadership. In planning industrial mobilization, we insisted that there be as little impairment as possible of every resource essential for civilian life—*except* independent and original scientific investigation, fundamental scholarship and higher education. The sky was the limit on expenditures for military technology last year, but when the National Science Foundation recommended a mere fourteen million dollars for fundamental scientific research, Congress at first planned to cut the appropriation by ninety-eight per cent, and finally compromised on a sum of three and a half millions.

Having apparently ceased to believe that the fundamental disciplines of science and scholarship have any real value for society, Americans seem almost anxious for their investment in higher education to be wasted. They furnish funds from gifts and taxes, and then, as alumni or citizens, demand in return for their support the kind of commercialized campus athletics that is steadily corrupting and even wrecking the educational institutions they have built. It is as if they bought shares in a factory and then, as stockholders, forced the management to turn the assembly line into a steeplechase.

We are willing to waste not only our material resources, but even the most precious of our human ones. We will make heavy sacrifices to send our children to college, but we will not be bothered with urging them to take seriously the intellectual tasks involved. We are happy to play Santa Claus by indulging them in a good time, and we never dream we are shirking parental responsibility if we smilingly acquiesce when our sons rate extra-curricular frivolities higher than serious academic effort, or when our daughters insist that the college's most important diploma is one to be worn on the third finger of the left hand. To put the matter bluntly, we treat higher education as something delightful but hardly meaningful to the recipient, and distinctly valueless to society. The college or university has become, to our minds, merely a respectable branch of the luxury-purveying trade. Like the club car on a passenger train, it dispenses the amenities of life to persons bound on serious errands elsewhere.

Now, public opinion is not so perverse as to adopt such a view without cause. It is not that Americans are ignorant of the traditional claims of higher education. Rather, they refuse to take these claims seriously when they witness the gap between profession and performance. This gap is not the public's fault. Responsibility for it rests squarely upon university administrators and college faculties. The former have sponsored, and the latter have tolerated, programs, practices and attitudes in the colleges that make a mockery of the ideal of liberal education. Given these flourishing academic heresies, the public has good reason to doubt that universities and colleges are fostering among their students that breadth of view, that critical objectivity and that balanced judgment for which higher education has supposedly stood.

The first of these heresies, and perhaps the easiest to see through, is the assumption that any kind of educational program, provided only that it adds up to the requisite number of hours, is the equal of any other as a means of liberal education. This is one of the evil legacies of the free-elective system into which the college curriculum disintegrated at the end of the nineteenth century. That curious educational cafeteria put precisely the same value on courses in the older fundamental disciplines, on courses in the newer sciences (which certainly deserved recognition), and on courses in fields that had no conceivable claim to scholarly or scientific standing.

A multitude of such pseudo-subjects were introduced, not because they could advance fundamental knowledge, but because they might prepare groups of students for certain specified jobs. A liberal education, of course, has always been a preparation for life, including the making of a livelihood. But in preparing a man for his future profession or vocation, liberal education made a fundamental distinction. With one aspect of vocational training it had as little as possible to do. To practice any profession successfully, one must know something about how the profession operates, about the ordinary situations that one must encounter from day to day, about the short cuts that are legitimate and necessary, about the human relations involved. These are the tricks of the trade, and they are learned most rapidly and effectively in actual practice. Apprenticeship, combined perhaps with a brief period of instruction, can be relied on to provide an intelligent man with what he needs in this respect. To dilute a program of liberal education with courses in matters like these, devoid as they are of intellectual content, should have remained unthinkable.

There is another reason for excluding such types of instruction —their relative ineffectiveness. The popular sneers at book-learning are not really directed at learning in the liberal sense. They result directly from the bumbling inefficiency shown in real life by students who have learned so-called "practical" subjects from a book, under an instructor who has perhaps never practiced the trade he purports to teach. It is not the liberally educated man who becomes a laughingstock. It is the journalism major who can't write a sentence that any editor would print, the speech major whom no one would want to listen to in a public hall, the home economics major who can't run her own house, the education major who knows less about the subject she teaches than the parents of her own pupils, the commerce major who can't carry on a business as effectively as the clerk who dropped out of high school.

Liberal education is based upon something very different from such ineffectual teaching of the tricks of a given trade. It is based on the conviction that a good teacher needs to know a great deal more than methods of teaching, a good librarian a great deal more than cataloguing and routine book selection, a good newspaperman a great deal more than the quirks of journalistic writing. And liberal education concentrates upon the great deal more. It believes that a man's real value in his profession is measured by what he brings to it over and above the knack that anyone can pick up. This is not a gratuitous assumption; it is a conclusion derived from our knowledge of what has made men useful and humane and great in the past. It is a conclusion supported by rational considerations as well, for scholarship and science are nothing else than tremendously powerful intellectual tools, applicable to the solving of the widest variety of problems, including the problems that confront a man in his public and professional life.

The debasement of higher learning began when persons who repudiated this concept of liberal study began to worm their way upward into colleges and graduate schools. An example in point can be drawn from the field of pedagogy, now usually miscalled education. Normal schools a century ago provided a necessary short cut into the teaching profession at a time when genuine standards of liberal education for teachers could not be sustained. Faced with a sharply limited period of instruction, the founders of normal schools had no choice but to pass on the tricks of the trade as effectively as they could, offering in addition such a smattering of general study as time would allow. There was nothing culpable in this bowing to necessity. The betrayal of liberal education occurred when these institutions were allowed to expand into four-year colleges without sloughing off their old habit of thinking in terms of mere pedagogical technique. Society had reached the point where it could demand of its future teachers a really adequate period of preparation. It expected them to be liberally educated men and women, exemplifying in their own lives the value of that knowledge and disciplined intellectual power which it was their high calling to impart to others. But both society and the teachers themselves were defrauded. Though more years of training were required, the pedagogical locusts devoured the harvest. They juggled requirements so that most of the newly allotted time had to be wasted in intellectually sterile courses in methods of teaching or in watered-down surveys of the liberal arts and sciences, surveys which offered the "content" (whatever that might mean) without the intellectual discipline.

The next downward step was the bestowing of advanced degrees in education, so-called. Printed in the university catalogue, the offerings of departments and colleges of education could be made to look like genuine graduate courses. But they lacked the two things needful: a definable body of knowledge to provide substance, and a distinctive method of investigation to serve as the basis for rigorous training in intellectual processes. Fancy terminology could not alter the fact that these supposedly advanced courses were simply dressed-up versions of the old normal school instruction in tricks of the teacher's trade. Professors of education did not offer to deepen a student's understanding of the great areas of human knowledge, nor to start him off on a disciplined quest for new solutions to fundamental intellectual problems. They did not believe in preparing him for professional activity by enlarging the store of information and insight upon which he could draw in meeting practical problems. Instead, they merely undertook to pass on to young men and women the little ingenuities that make a profession easier to practice.

When doctorates began to be offered in a field as empty of intellectual content as this, other professions and trades were encouraged to do likewise. Librarians who were also scholars were in demand, and a Ph.D. in history or English literature or economics or biology was a valuable added asset. But library schools soon expanded their courses in the techniques of librarianship until they were in a position to send out graduates with a doctorate in library science. But this new-fangled degree no longer signified that a man was *both* a librarian and a scholar. It meant merely that he had spent more time than his undoctored colleague in learning the tricks of the trade. The law of diminishing returns was treated as repealed, and three years of this sort of thing were considered twelve times as valuable as three months.

One occupation after another sought this dubious academic

recognition—journalism (now beginning to be rechristened "mass communications"), business, physical education, hotel management and the rest. For years, responsible administrators and boards had been seeking men with disciplined intellectual training over and above their professional skill, and had learned to accept the Ph.D. as a symbol of this. A fraud—the term is not too harsh—was perpetrated upon them by these new doctorates, which signified no tested grasp of a recognized field of knowledge, no special command of the tools of intellectual investigation, no proven ability to advance science or scholarship.

Genuine professional training—as given, for example, in engineering, law and medicine—is something completely different from this. It does not replace liberal education, but builds upon it. Educational standards in these genuinely learned professions have risen steadily over the years. This has meant a constantly lengthened period of training. But how has the added time been spent? Primarily in two ways. An education in the liberal arts and sciences—the four years required for a bachelor's degree—has been made the prerequisite for admission to professional training in one after another of the leading professional schools. And more and more thorough work has been required in the basic disciplines—physiology, bacteriology, mathematics, chemistry, history, as the case might be—which the profession undertakes to apply in practice. The specialized scientific training has sometimes unduly crowded the liberal arts, but leaders of the various professions have ordinarily taken a strong stand against the sacrifice of either. And they have certainly never been tempted to ape the professional educators by frittering away precious time upon endless courses in bedside manner, in how to set up a law office in a small town, in the psychology of engineer-client relationships.

The contempt which the new vocationalists feel for science and scholarship is nowhere more clearly revealed than in their disregard of the varying educational requirements of different professions and occupations. If the profession of medicine requires graduate training leading to the doctorate, if fundamental research in physics requires the kind of training represented by the Ph.D., then the job of writing advertisements for the radio should have its program of graduate training culminating in a doctorate too. One is reminded of Gilbert and Sullivan's "Gondoliers," where equality was achieved by granting exalted titles to everyone, "the Lord High Bishop orthodox" ranking with "the Lord High Coachman on the box." To paraphrase a bit:

*The Ph.D. who rules the state—*
*The Ph.D. who cleans the plate—*
*The Ph.D. who scrubs the grate—*
*They all shall equal be!*

Since higher education itself is endangered by this nonsense, it is high time for scholars to declare what Emerson said it was the scholar's duty always to declare, "that a popgun is a popgun, though the ancient and honorable of the earth affirm it to be the crack of doom."

Scholarship and science are threatened today not only by outsiders to whom liberal education represents an alien ideal, but equally by men in the recognized disciplines in the colleges who misunderstand and misinterpret what it stands for. The other great heresy I wish to discuss is the notion that traditional programs of liberal education are primarily concerned with communicating information. Our quiz programs are a symptom of this widespread misconception. The fallacy can be illustrated by a difference in terminology—a difference trivial at first glance, but in the end portentous. What I have hitherto called the fundamental disciplines—history, chemistry, mathematics, philosophy and the like—have become, in the jargon of the educators, "subject-matter fields." But a discipline is not the same as a subject-matter field. The one is a way of thinking, the other an aggregation of facts.

The scholarly and scientific disciplines won their primacy in traditional programs of liberal education—and deserve to retain it in all sound programs—because they represent the most effective methods which men have been able to devise, through millennia of sustained effort, for liberating and then organizing the powers of the human mind. It is nonsense to say that they occupy their position in intellectual life because some clique of men have agreed to confer an arbitrary prestige upon them. The reverse is true. It is the disciplines that have conferred prestige—and more than prestige, power—upon mankind. The disciplines represent the various ways (and thus far the only ways) which man has discovered for achieving intellectual mastery and hence practical power over the various problems that confront him. He lives in a world of quantity and relationship, and he has put four thousand years of ingenuity into creating the mathematical tools with which he handles quantity and relationship. He knows that his present is influenced by his past, and through continuous trial and error he has shaped the historical techniques that provide the maximum reliable knowledge of this aspect of his environment. He works every day with matter, and he has subdued matter to his purposes by sorting out its various characteristics in his mind and eventually creating the sciences of physics and chemistry, which have grown more useful to him in proportion as they have grown more abstract and theoretical. There is nothing arbitrary or fortuitous in any of this. The older disciplines have emerged, and newer ones are emerging, as responses to man's imperious need for that wide-ranging, precise, yet generalized comprehension which means power: power over himself and over all things else.

It is this concentrated intellectual power for which the scholarly and scientific disciplines are respected. A man is educated in them that he may gain the powers which they confer. Note, however, one curious thing: to be given only the *results* of the exercise of this species of power is to be given nothing. A man may be given wealth or he may inherit social position, each the product of another's exertions, but thereafter he can exercise whatever power appertains to either. But if a man is given merely the answer to a complex mathematical calculation, or the narrative which results from a critical investigation of historical sources, he shares in no slightest way the power of the mathematician or the historian. Some poor inert formula, some poor inert fact, is all that is left in his hand.

Liberal education, in other words, is essentially the communication of intellectual power. That it cannot be communicated by someone who does not possess it—by a teacher who is not also a scholar—is self-evident. But neither can it be communicated by scholars and scientists if they pay too much attention in their classes to what they have learned and too little to how they learned it. Academic courses which teach men to perform mathematical computations but not to think mathematically, to manipulate laboratory apparatus but not to think scientifically, to remember dates but not to think historically, to summarize philosophical arguments but not to think critically—these advance no man toward liberal education. Courses may bear the respected labels of academic disciplines and yet be, in reality, no more than the subject-matter fields about which the educators prate. To be perfectly honest, we must admit that higher education has lost repute because so many offerings in the liberal arts and sciences have failed to provide the intellectual discipline which they promise. So much must be conceded to the various practitioners who would replace the liberal studies by a curriculum purely vocational. But the answer, surely, is not to abandon the ideal of disciplined intelligence in favor of an educational program which even on the surface offers nothing to liberate and strengthen men's minds. The answer is not to banish the scholarly and scientific disciplines but to hold them rigorously to their task.

The test of every course and of every program is the extent to which it trains a man to think for himself and at the same time to think painstakingly. Originality and rigor, imagination and discipline—these are not pairs of mutually exclusive qualities. They are qualities that must be welded together in a liberal education. The aim is expressed most broadly and clearly in the requirement laid down for the highest university degree: that a student shall make an original contribution to knowledge. I am aware of the paltry substitutes that are frequently accepted—dissertations which show merely that the candidate has read his sources or his dials faithfully, and has performed his critical or his statistical manipulations in approved fashion. The real questions are too rarely asked, I know, but they are at least implicit in the requirement. Has the student developed in the process of doing research the penetrating mind that will make him more than an accredited technician? Does he see the world bristling with unsolved problems: historical problems if he is an historian, biological problems if he is a biologist? Does he seize with a kind of instinct upon the ones that are crucial to the determination of even larger issues? Does his imagination range over all the possible, and even the impossible, avenues to a solution, before he selects the most promising? Having chosen, does he possess the ingenuity to construct, as they are required, the little bridges and the narrow but necessary stairways that will enable him to cross successfully the unforeseen obstacles lying between him and his destination? And does he, finally, possess the toughness of intellectual fiber to carry through a hard task to a really definitive conclusion? If the answers are affirmative, then the student has done more than make a contribution to knowledge. He has given assurance that he can think and act with power and precision when completely new problems confront him. To him has been communicated not merely factual information and craftsmanship, but intellectual discipline.

This is not the ideal of graduate instruction alone. It is, or it should be, the ideal of liberal education at every level. It can direct the first steps in instruction, and it can guide a man's quest for knowledge to the end of his life. A man whose formal education has strengthened these qualities in him is equipped for life in the present and in the future as no vocational training could possibly equip him. His is a disciplined mind. And because his mind is disciplined, the man himself is free.

To preserve freedom in the parts of the world where it still lives, we as a people are ready to make the terrible human sacrifices that military effort requires. We are willing to mobilize our industry in all its branches. We recognize the necessity, and we see with reasonable clarity the means. What we do not recognize so clearly is the necessity of producing the free men who are to rebuild and inhabit the world we seek to preserve. The disillusionment that creeps over us at times usually finds expression in the query, "What are we fighting for?" The answers we give are often hollow and bombastic or sentimental and trivial. Our orators preach vaguely about the democratic way of life; our advertisements describe lovingly the pleasant routines and the familiar recreations we should all be sorry to lose. But what we really need is a fervent belief in the importance of human life lived on its highest plane. Then we shall know that we are fighting for a world in which there is opportunity for the fullest development by every man and woman of his or her capacity for disciplined thought, for artistic creation, and hence for enduring satisfaction. Then we shall have faith once more in liberal education as both an indispensable means and an ultimate end.

# Life and the World It Lives In

## PAUL B. SEARS

## ( *1952* )

In this simple and concise statement, PAUL B. SEARS, botanist and ecologist, sets forth his belief that a permanent and intelligent order for mankind cannot be achieved until we realize that the great scientific laws that govern our technology apply equally to the living landscape of which we are a part.

In 1950, Dr. Sears established at Yale University one of the country's first graduate programs of research and instruction in the conservation of natural resources.

S INCE THE SCIENTIST is our source of information in the present instance, a few memoranda concerning him seem in order. To begin with, he is a scientist because he wants to be and, like the rest of us, rests heavily on intuition and aesthetic impulse. Scientific activity is basically what our ecclesiastical friends might call an "act of faith," for the scientist is moved by a profound belief that the universe of our experience is a consistent universe. Without that conviction, I doubt if he would have either the courage or inclination to persist in the intricate and exacting labors which are the price of verified knowledge. Do not be deceived by his skepticism—it is the safeguard of his basic confidence.

His code requires him to test and verify continually, with the aid of his five senses, those phenomena which interest him. But he must continually seek to probe beyond their limits, by means of induction, deductions and inferences that seem most reasonable in the light of what he already knows. Ceaselessly and fruitfully he tests the ideas thus formed; in the course of time, unnoted planets appear where calculation shows they should be, and the invisible atom is put to work.

But he cannot always advance from the safe ground of previously organized knowledge. He must, at times, attack exceedingly complex problems, knowing in advance that many of their details must await later solution, and being content meanwhile to verify their larger aspects. It happens, for example, that the chemistry of carbon, whose compounds are so prevalent in living organisms as to give rise to the name "organic" chemistry, could not for generations be made intelligible in terms of the relatively simpler inorganic chemistry. Students still complain that the subject reminds them of a project in learning the dictionary. But the chemists did not wait until all the necessary ground had been cleared in fundamental theory. They went ahead making tremendous progress and developing an extremely useful branch of knowledge long before they were able to explain it in detail.

What is true of organic chemistry is infinitely more true of the study of living organisms, plants and animals. We simply have to get on with the subject the best we can, knowing that it will be a long time, if ever, before we can resolve in detail many of the phenomena with which he must deal. After all, we have good precedent in the higher mathematics, in which we are accustomed to designating complex entities by symbols, treating them as wholes and establishing important relationships concerning them, without stopping first to analyze and resolve each complex entity into all of its factors.

Such, in essence, is certainly the method we have to follow in the subject known as ecology, which deals with the relations between life and environment. It is with these relations we deal when we concern ourselves with the conservation of natural resources, and with planning for the present and future welfare of mankind. My own business for years has been the study of the ecology of plants and animals, and I have found that you cannot pursue it very far without discovering that man is involved, too. He is inseparably a part of the living landscape and subject to the great laws which govern it.

And I have discovered, as have others before me, that there is little hope of intelligent and permanent order for mankind until people realize that they are inescapably subject to the great scientific laws which govern the universe. We accept these laws readily enough in machine design, industrial chemistry and the electrical arts. But we often—perhaps generally—act as though they did not apply to the landscape of which we are a part.

Few problems in modern education seem to me more important than this: to develop in the mind of the student, not merely a casual glimpse, but an integrated picture of the universe of physical reality. What this could mean as a background to great decisions! How few statesmen possess it! Jan Smuts, Thomas Jefferson, Chaim Weizmann, to a degree Theodore Roosevelt can be named—beyond that meager list, the search falters.

Because the intelligent application of knowledge depends upon the values that people cherish and toward which they work, it seems in order to glance backward briefly. Among the many factors which have made modern science possible, it is important to recognize the great creative contribution of the Jewish people. In the midst of very difficult conditions of belief and practice, they postulated the idea of a single Deity who ruled through universal law and who respected His own laws. Without this belief and the confidence which it inspires, I do not see how the foundations of modern science could have been laid.

Science also owes an inestimable debt to the Greek belief in the right of free inquiry, to the Roman instinct for order and clear communication, and to the restless curiosity of such irrepressible individuals as Galileo. But it has continued to owe much to that hunger, manifest in every great religious system, for some semblance of certainty about the cosmos. I know of no faith which has not its basis in some kind of conception of the universe.

Until about a century ago, the idea of Special Creation was prevalent. This is the idea that all species of plants and animals were created in the beginning as they are today. We think of it now only as religious dogma. Dogma it certainly was, but we must not forget that it was also the simplest, most plausible explanation possible in view of the evidence then at hand. It was Darwin's great merit, not that he originated the idea of organic evolution, for he did not, but that for the first time he made it a reasonable scientific hypothesis.

Special Creation had been subjected to increasing strains as soon as men began to travel widely and explore all the continents. Further strain came from the finding of fossil remains of extinct animals, and the explanation of geological change by familiar processes. But the final *coup de grâce* came as a result of the travels and explorations of the young British naturalist whom I have just named. After he had examined the natural history of South America and its islands, the old idea was no longer adequate to explain what he had seen.

He found that the farther apart animals of the same group lived, the less they resembled their closest relatives. For example, in the islands off the coast, there are not many kinds of birds, but there are the finches. Some of these finches are seed-eaters, as are those we know. Others have become insect-eaters. One type has developed a short, powerful chisel bill like the woodpecker. This finch will climb the bark of a dead tree and peck away until it unearths an insect. Then, lacking the useful tongue of the woodpecker, it will take a thorn and employ it as we would a nutpick to get the hidden morsel out so it can be eaten.

Evidently, while all of these island finches were closely related, they had been separated from their kin on the mainland so long that they had become thus differentiated. These and many other instances Darwin observed and thought about for years, but the answer eluded him until one day he chanced on the work of a British clergyman: "An Essay on Population," by Malthus.

Malthus knew that all kinds of life, including our own, have a tremendous capacity for increase, whereas food supply is finite. He knew that, in fact, populations never increase in theoretical fashion over any very long period of time. This had certainly been true of Europe since the Norman Conquest. Such disasters as the Black Death and the Thirty Years' War had clearly operated to keep the population down. Reflecting on the situation, Malthus decided that, while population always tends to increase beyond the limits of subsistence, the Three Horsemen—War, Pestilence and Famine —tend to hold it within those limits.

In this principle, Darwin immediately saw a clue to his great riddle. Granting that a high proportion of organisms is being eliminated in each generation, might there not be some principle that determined which survived and which did not? Darwin had long since observed that no two plants or animals are precisely alike, and that the tendency to variation is universal. From this he reasoned that some variations are better fitted to the environment than others, and so tend to survive, while those less fitted are lost. The outcome of this train of thought was his theory of Natural Selection.

The statement of this theory was a terrific jolt to traditional thought, but that is a story in itself. Our interest is in the fact that, for the first time, a wholly reasonable alternative to the doctrine of Special Creation was offered, and that environment now came into the picture as an inescapable element in the process of life.

Meanwhile, however, other interesting things had been happening. That merry but intelligent monarch, Charles II, had been "mightily amused" (actually, I suspect, irritated) that the scientists of his Royal Society at Gresham College were wasting their time "doing nothing but the weighing of air." Yet within a century, their efforts had paved the way to the discovery of oxygen and the eventual demonstration that plants and animals are dependent upon materials and energy from earth, air, water and sun. Not only that, but it was further proved that these constant interchanges are very precise and orderly, and the very basis of material existence.

In other words, it was shown that the individual cannot survive apart from the material world. Every breath represents an interchange with it, and every transformation is as much to be accounted for as the transactions in a bank. It is impossible, except as a matter of temporary convenience, to think of any living body in any sense apart from the world around it. When, added to this, Darwin had shown how essential the environment had been in the long pageant of past life, it became forever clear that we and our fellow creatures are inseparably a part of the universe in which we live.

To me it is not a depressing thought, but rather a magnificent one, that the materials of our bodies are merely ours on loan. We have no permanent right to them. They have been used by countless generations of plants and animals before us, and countless generations will have need of them after we are gone.

What is true of the precise transformations of material is likewise true of the flow of energy, with the sobering difference that energy from the sun ultimately seems to become unavailable, being finally dissipated as heat after its course of use is run. In a universe without vegetation, this dissipation happens rather promptly. But where green plants are present, they are able to store it for themselves and other organisms. It is the profit and loss account of this storage and use transaction which determines the net worth of our adventure here on earth in material terms. And it is very much to our interest to see that storage is as efficient as it can be, and use as economical as possible. Success will depend, to some degree, upon our industrial pattern, but even more largely upon our skill and care in utilizing the land.

Incidentally, our understanding of the energy budget owes much of its beginning to the work of a brilliant young Yankee, Harvard graduate and loyalist named Benjamin Thompson. He later became Count Rumford and had, I suspect, much to do with the later municipal and industrial efficiency of Germany. It was while he was supervising the machining of cannons in a royal European arsenal that he studied the relation of heat and work, supplying information which was later utilized by physical scientists in establishing the principle of the conservation of energy. This, with the principle of conservation of matter, is really basic to that art of wise husbandry which we call Conservation with a big "C."

To get at the problem from a different perspective, that of time and process, a simple illustration will help. Let us take a book, say *American Men of Science,* in an edition of two thousand pages. If each page is given the value of a million years, the volume may represent the approximate age of the earth, around two billion years. In the first half of the book, there would be little record, though probably some, of living things. Most of their story comes in the second thousand pages. Taking the oldest assignable age of man as the skeletal remains and associated charcoal of Peking Man, their record would not exceed the last page, while recorded history would be a fraction of the last line of that last page.

Viewing the human adventure in terms of this immense perspective should be a rather sobering experience. Instead of regarding the world as casually thrown together for our own convenience, we should realize the tremendous momentum of the organization which has preceded us, and which so largely must condition our activities unless we wish to join the long procession of extinct forms. In particular, we should understand the imperative pattern which life has developed in relation to the transformation of materials and the flow of energy.

The carbon compounds made by green plants, used by them and by animals, require energy in the making. That energy is stored in them and, with the materials which they contain, can be used to sustain life as the compounds are broken down. The breakdown may be complete, releasing all of the energy at once. This happens when wood burns, or sugar is oxidized to give energy to a growing plant. More often, however, the breakdown is a gradual, step by step process. This is what happens when sugar ferments to form alcohol. There is much energy left in the alcohol, as there is some in the vinegar which is a further step in the breakdown of alcohol.

A similar phenomenon occurs in autumn when the leaves change color and fall to the ground, there to undergo slow decomposition to their original raw materials of earth and atmosphere. As in the forest floor, so in the prairie, the field, the sea, or the manure pile, we observe the familiar proteins, fats and carbohydrates slowly releasing their energy as they break down.

At each step in this slow release, there is an opportunity, technically a *niche*, for particular forms of life to sustain themselves, as pigs do from the garbage of a farm kitchen, or flies from the droppings of animals, or molds from rotting fruit. One wave of life follows another as the process continues, until it is complete.

In the long course of time, this means that the rich variety of organic life establishes a close interdependence. And as time goes on, it seems likely that unless an organism in its niche establishes some fairly useful function (technically a *role*) in its relation to the whole system of which it is a part, it is likely to be eliminated. No doubt it was some adumbration of this fact which lay at the base of the old, egocentric idea that everything on earth was put here for our good.

At any rate, it is nonsense to speak of a solitary plant or animal. The web of life is seamless. The tigers space themselves "one to a hill," as the Indians say, each in terms of the territory claimed by his neighbors, and so do the wide-spaced cacti of the desert, whose shallow roots determine the zones of competition. Even the sweet songs of birds in the spring are less the outpourings of hearts bursting with love than warnings to fellow robins and larks to keep their proper distance.

What is true within the species is certainly true between species. The termite eats wood, but cannot digest it without the microscopic organisms which live in the body of the termite. Hatch termite eggs under sterile conditions, and the young will starve in a bath of sawdust. The corn which keeps millions from starvation is equally dependent upon us, and it has been stated that the last maize plant would not survive the last farmer more than a few years. Truly the web of life is seamless, and we are a part of it.

Thus has the world community of living things shaken down into a grand working order through the ages. But more than this, we can see the innumerable smaller communities which compose it, each in turn moving in the same direction, toward relatively greater order and efficiency, until circumstances set a limit to the process.

We are familiar with the characteristics of the human pioneer —tough, hardy, self-reliant. We are less familiar with the fact that his toughness is a perishable quality, not always well adapted to success in a highly organized and civilized community for which he is the indispensable precursor. He is likely to sense this himself, and get nervous when too many neighbors move in, too close for his comfort. And the very traits which made him a success in his proper role of pioneer are likely to be serious liabilities at a later stage in community life.

The analogy holds in nature. The pioneer plants and animals which first move in and occupy vacant ground do so very efficiently. But they cannot continue to hold it against all comers. They cannot endure the shade which they create, nor can their young come up beneath it. I suggest that you sometime examine a birch or pine wood, for both represent a pioneer stage, and look for young birches or pines. You are not likely to find them. Instead, you will see spruces, or maples, or beech trees taking over. And you would eventually, if you lived long enough, see that space occupied and dominated by plants and animals all sensitively interrelated and capable of maintaining themselves indefinitely, unless struck by some such cataclysm as fire, climatic change or man.

In terms of energy, what happens is that the community develops toward what our friends in physical chemistry would call a steady state. This is a condition in which a system maintains itself while using the flow of energy through it in reasonably efficient manner to accomplish work. The phenomenon is not mentioned here as a mere biological curiosity. Rather, it is the prototype and example of the kind of process which we must use as our model as we develop our relationships among our own kind, and between ourselves and the world of nature of which we are inescapably a part. As we succeed in doing this, we build toward permanence. As we violate this great principle, we go down into physical failure and cultural disintegration. History affords sufficient evidence on this score.

But it is better to emphasize the positive side. History and contemporary life afford us encouraging instances of human communities that have made peace with their environments, maintaining themselves in stable and efficient order. The ancient and beautiful terraces of the Igorots between Manila and Baguio exemplify this, and so in our own country does the landscape occupied by the thrifty Amish and Mennonites in Pennsylvania.

Increasing numbers of individuals, with the aid of modern science and capital, are following this pattern on land which they control. This is the secret of grass-farming, exemplified on the holding of a New York financier near the Delaware Water Gap, and more picturesquely on Malabar Farm, where the irrepressible Louis Bromfield holds forth. Bromfield is a farmer, and a good one. I have watched his farm from its beginning, and you can believe what he writes about it. As he says, he has taken nature for his model, developing stabilized communities of plants which are in equilibrium with the animals and the human occupants. He uses legumes to convert the nitrogen of the air into proteins, and feeds minerals to his animals by way of the soil and vegetation.

Such are the possibilities, and such is the necessity, if our civilization is not to follow those disastrous examples of the past which have long since worn out their welcome on the fertile earth.

# Christian Gauss

## HIRAM HAYDN

### (1952)

One of the founders of THE AMERICAN SCHOLAR, Christian
Gauss served on its Editorial Board for nineteen years.
His strong conviction that a vital and uncompromising
scholarship would be well received by the reading public
was an influential factor in guiding the magazine through
its formative years.

This editorial was written after Dean Gauss's death in
November, 1951.

THROUGH ALL THE MANY TRIBUTES printed after the death of
Christian Gauss runs one refrain. Almost without exception,
there is reference to his courage in support of unpopular causes in
which he believed and—if only by subsequent inference—his integrity. I should like to explore what seems to me the precise nature of that courage and that integrity.

Since I knew him for only eight years, there are probably others
who are much better qualified to pursue such an exploration. Yet
I had the opportunity, during those years, to see him fairly often
in the act of having to make a difficult decision, and I have a very
vivid memory of those times.

Invariably, he would listen in silence to the account of the problem and consider the choices that lay before him. Invariably, when
those present had finished what they had to say, and sat there,
waiting in some eagerness for him to speak, he would break his
silence with a sigh.

After three or four such occasions, that heavy sigh became for
me a symbol. A symbol, all at once, of genuine reluctance, genuine
integrity, a genuine sense of responsibility. Christian Gauss was a
gentle and peace-loving man. He had none of that indiscriminate,
suspect zeal of the professional "do-gooder," none of the pride of
those who seem to be proving something to themselves when they
"stand up to be counted." He had (to the best of my knowledge)

nothing left undiscovered that he wanted to prove to himself or to anybody else. He wished, sometimes desperately, that he might be left alone to pursue the personal interests from which he was always being called to this or that duty.

For that was the point: he did not enjoy alienating others or taking a lonely or unpopular stand, and that heavy sigh represented all his reluctance. Yet the social duty, the responsibility of integrity, were real to him, and the sigh also meant that his decision was made.

Surely this is becoming increasingly rare in our age of specialization and organization, self-division and anxiety. Yet just as surely this is what it means to be a man: to weigh the evidence, to see clearly the disadvantages to oneself and to sigh over them, and then, with unpretentious courage and honesty, moved by an unfailing sense of man's commitment to other men and to truth, to act on the basis of what one feels to be right—the action wedded to the conviction, all of one piece.

We who loved him have lost his visible presence. If we can, even in small measure, attain to his integrity, we have not lost him.

HIRAM HAYDN

# Christian Gauss as a Teacher of Literature

## EDMUND WILSON

## ( *1952* )

EDMUND WILSON studied with Christian Gauss at Princeton University. It was in this association that Mr. Wilson acquired his conception of literary criticism—a history of man's ideas and imaginings in the setting of the conditions that have shaped them. This portrait, which was written several months after Dean Gauss's death in 1951, later became a part of Mr. Wilson's *The Shores of Light,* a literary chronicle of the twenties and thirties.

WHEN Christian Gauss of Princeton died on November 3, 1951, I was asked by the Princeton *Alumni Weekly* to write something for a set of tributes that were to appear in the issue of December 7. I sent the editor, who wanted a column, only part of what I had written in response to this request, and even this was much cut before it was printed. I have now further elaborated my original memoir, and I am including it here to serve as a sort of prologue, for it indicates to some extent the point of view from which I started off in my criticism of the twenties.

I have been asked to write about Christian Gauss as an influence on my generation at Princeton. Since we knew him as a teacher of literature only—I was in the class of 1916, and he did not become dean of the college till 1925—I shall speak mainly of this side of his activity.

As a professor of French and Italian, then, one of the qualities that distinguished Gauss was the unusual fluidity of mind that he preserved through his whole career. A teacher like Irving Babbitt was a dogmatist who either imposed his dogma or provoked a strong opposition. Christian Gauss was a teacher of a different kind—the kind who starts trains of thought that he does not himself guide to conclusions but leaves in the hands of his students to be carried on by themselves. The student might develop, extend them, transpose them into different terms, build out of them constructions of his own. Gauss never imposed, he suggested; and his own ideas on any subject were always taking new turns: the light in which he saw it would be shifted, it would range itself in some new context. It bored him, in his course on French Romanticism, to teach the same texts year after year; and with the writers that he could not get away from, he would vary the works read. With the less indispensable ones, he would change the repertory altogether. If Alfred de Vigny, for example, had been featured in the course when you took it, you might come back a few years later and find that he had been pushed into the background by Stendhal. Christian would have been reading up Stendhal, and his interest in him would seem almost as fresh as if he had never read him before. He would have some new insights about him, and he would pass these on to you when you came to see him, as he was doing to his students in class. I know from my own experience how the lightly dropped seeds from his lectures could take root and unfold in another's mind; and, while occupied in writing this memoir, I have happened to find striking evidence of the persistence of this vital gift in the testimony of a student of Romance languages who sat under Gauss twenty years later, and who has told me that, in preparing his doctor's thesis, he had at first been exhilarated by an illusion of developing original ideas, only to find the whole thing in germ in his old notes on Gauss's lectures. But though his influence on his students was so penetrating, Gauss founded no school of teaching—not even, I suppose, an academic tradition—because, as one of his colleagues pointed out to me, he had no communicable body of doctrine and no pedagogical method that other teachers could learn to apply. If one went back to Princeton to see him, as I more or less regularly did, after one had got out of college, one's memory of his old preceptorials (relatively informal discussions with groups of five or six students) would seem prolonged, without interruptions, into one's more recent conversations, as if it had all been a long conversation that had extended, off and on, through the years: a commentary that, on Christian's part, never seemed to be trying to prove anything in any overwhelming way, a voyage of speculation that aimed rather to survey the world than to fix a convincing vision. In his role of the least didactic of sages, the most accessible of talkers, he seemed a part of that good eighteenth-century Princeton which has always managed to flourish between the pressures of a narrow Presbyterianism and a rich man's suburbanism. It is probable that Christian was at home in Princeton as he would not have been anywhere else. He was delightful in the days of his deanship, in the solid and compact and ample yellow-and-white Joseph Henry house, built in 1837, where there was always, during the weekends, a constant going and coming of visitors, who could pick up with him any topic, literary, historical or collegiate, and pursue it till someone else came and the thread was left suspended. Though by this time so important a local figure, he seemed always, also, international. He had been born of German parents in Michigan, and German had been his first language. In his youth he had spent a good deal of time in France. He had no foreign accent in English, and, so far as I was able to judge, spoke all his languages correctly and fluently; but French, Italian and English, at any rate, with a deliberate articulation, never running the words together, as if they were not native to him. One did not learn a bad accent from him, but one did not learn to speak the Romance languages as they are spoken in their own countries. On the other hand, the very uniformity of his candid tone, his unhurried pace and his scrupulous precision, with his slightly drawling intonations, made a kind of neutral medium in which everything in the world seemed soluble. I have never known anyone like him in any academic community. He gave the impression of keeping in touch, without the slightest effort—he must have examined all the printed matter that came into the university library—with everything that was going on everywhere, as well as everything that had ever gone on. It used to amuse me sometimes to try him out on unlikely subjects. If one asked him a question about the Middle Ages, one absolutely got the impression that he had lived in Europe then and knew it at firsthand.

This extreme flexibility and enormous range were, of course, a feature of his lectures. He was able to explain and appreciate almost any kind of work of literature from almost any period. He would show you what the author was aiming at and the methods he had adopted to achieve his ends. He was wonderful at comparative literature, for his reading had covered the whole of the West, ancient, medieval and modern, and his memory was truly Macaulayan (an adjective sometimes assigned too cheaply). He seemed to be able to summon almost anything he wanted in prose or verse, as if he were taking down the book from the shelf. (He told me once that, in his younger days, he had set out to write something about Rabelais and had presently begun to grow suspicious of what he saw coming out. On looking up Taine's essay on Rabelais, he found that he had been transcribing whole paragraphs from it, his unconscious doing the work of translation.) He was brilliant at revealing the assumptions, social, aesthetic and moral, implicit in, say, a scene from a romantic play as contrasted with a scene from a Greek tragedy, or in the significance of a character in Dante as distinguished from the significance of a character in Shakespeare. I remember his later quoting with approval A. N. Whitehead's statement, in *Science and the Modern World,* that, "when you are criticizing the philosophy of an epoch," you should "not chiefly direct your attention to those intellectual positions which its exponents feel it necessary explicitly to defend. There will be some fundamental assumptions which adherents of all the variant systems within the epoch unconsciously presuppose. Such assumptions appear so obvious that people do not know what they are assuming because no other way of putting things has ever occurred to them." Gauss had always had a special sense of this. But he was interested also in individuals and liked to bring out the traits of a literary personality. His commentary on a poem of Victor Hugo's—*Le Mendiant* from *Les Contemplations*—would run along something like this: "A poor man is passing in the frost and rain, and Victor Hugo asks him in. He opens the door *'d'une façon civile'*—he is always democratic, of course. *'Entrez, brave homme,'* he says, and he tells the man to warm himself and has a bowl of milk brought him—as anybody, of course, would do. He makes him take off his cloak—*'tout mangé des vers, et jadis bleu'* —and he hangs it on a nail, where the fire shines through its holes, so that it looks like a night illumined by stars.

> *Et, pendant qu'il séchait ce haillon désolé*
> *D'où ruisselaient le pluie et l'eau des fondrières,*
> *Je songeais que cet homme était plein de prières.*
> *Et je regardais, sourd à ce que nous disions,*
> *Sa bure où je voyais des constellations.*

"This sounds impressive, but what does it mean? Not a thing. We have not been told anything that would indicate that the old man is full of prayers. It is a gratuitous assumption on the part of Hugo. That the cloak with its holes reminded him of a heaven with constellations has no moral significance whatever. Yet with his mastery of verse and his rhetoric, Victor Hugo manages to carry it off. —I don't mean," he would add, "that he was insincere. Rather than live under Louis Napoleon, he went into voluntary exile—at considerable personal inconvenience—for almost twenty years. He lived up to his democratic principles, but he was always a bit theatrical, and he was not very profound."

I include such reminiscences of the classroom in the hope that they may be of interest in putting on record Gauss's methods as a teacher, for the work of a great teacher who is not, as Gauss was not, a greater writer is almost as likely to be irrecoverable as the work of a great actor. Not that Christian was ever in the least histrionic, as some of the popular professors of the time were. On the contrary, for all the friendliness of one's relations with him outside class when one eventually got to know him, his tone was sober and quiet, his attitude detached and impersonal. This was partly due to shyness, no doubt; but the impression he made was formidable. He would come into the classroom without looking at us, and immediately begin to lecture, with his eyes dropped to his notes, presenting a mask that was almost Dantesque and levelling on us only occasionally the clear gaze that came through his eyeglasses. When he made us recite in Dante, he would sometimes pace to and fro between the desk and the window, with his hands behind his back, rarely consulting the text, which he apparently knew by heart. In the case of some appalling error, he would turn with a stare of ironic amazement and remonstrate in a tone of mock grief: "You thought that barretry was the same as banditry? O-o-oh, Mr. X, that's too-oo ba-a-ad!" This last exclamation, drawled out, was his only way of indicating disapproval. His voice was always low and even, except at those moments when he became aware that the class was falling asleep, when he would turn on another voice, loud, nasal, declamatory and pitilessly distinct, which would be likely to begin in the middle of a sentence for the sake of the shock-value, I think, and in order to dissociate this special effect from whatever he happened to be saying—which might be something no more blood-curdling than a statement that André Chénier had brought to the classical forms a nuance of romantic feeling. When this voice would be heard in the class next door—for it penetrated the partition like a fire-siren—it always made people laugh; but for the students in Gauss's own room, it seemed to saw right through the base of the spine and made them sit forward intently. When it had had this effect, it would cease. He was never sarcastic and never bullied; but the discipline he maintained was perfect. Any signs of disorder were silenced by one straight and stern look.

Nevertheless, though Christian's methods were non-dramatic, he had a knack of fixing in one's mind key passages and key facts. His handling of Rousseau, for example, was most effective in building up the importance of a writer whom we might otherwise find boring. (In this case, he *has* left something that can be used by his successors in his volume of *Selections* from Rousseau, published by the Princeton University Press—though, as usual with Gauss's writing, the introduction and notes have little of the peculiar effectiveness of his lecture-room presentation.) He would start off by planting, as it were, in our vision of the panorama of history that critical moment of Rousseau's life which, since he did not include it in the *Confessions,* having already described it in the first of his letters to M. de Malesherbes, is likely to be overlooked or insufficiently emphasized (compare Saintsbury's slurring-over of this incident and its consequences for Western thought, in his *Encyclopaedia Britannica* article) : the moment, almost as momentous as that of Paul's conversion on the road to Damascus, when Jean-Jacques, then thirty-seven, was walking from Paris to Vincennes, where he was going to see Diderot in prison, and happened to read the announcement that the Academy of Dijon was offering a prize for the best essay on the question, "Has the progress of the arts and sciences contributed to corrupt or to purify society?" Such an incident Gauss made memorable, invested with reverberating significance, by a series of incisive strokes that involved no embroidery or dramatics. It was, in fact, as if the glamor of legend, the grandeur of history, had evaporated and left him exposed to our passing gaze, the dusty and sunstruck Jean-Jacques—the clockmaker's son of Geneva, the ill-used apprentice, the thieving lackey, the vagabond of the roads—sinking down under a tree and dazzled by the revelation that all the shames and misfortunes of his life had been the fault of the society that had bred him—that "man is naturally good and that it is only through institutions that men have become wicked." In the same way, he made us feel the pathos and the psychological importance of the moment when the sixteen-year-old apprentice, returning from a walk in the country, found for the third time the gates of Geneva locked against him, and decided that he would never go back.

Christian admired the romantics and expounded them with the liveliest appreciation; but the romantic ideal in literature was not his own ideal. In spite of his imaginative gift for entering into other people's points of view, he was devoted to a certain conception of art that inevitably asserted itself and that had a tremendous influence on the students with literary interests who were exposed to Gauss's teaching. Let me try to define this ideal. Christian had first known Europe at firsthand as a foreign correspondent in the Paris of the late nineties, and he had always kept a certain loyalty to the "aestheticism" of the end of the century. There was a legend that seemed almost incredible of a young Christian Gauss with long yellow hair—in our time he was almost completely bald—who had worn a green velvet jacket; * and he would surprise you from time to time by telling you of some conversation he had had with Oscar Wilde or describing some such bohemian character as Bibi-La-Purée. It was rumored—though I never dared ask him about this—that he had once set out to experiment one by one with all the drugs mentioned in Baudelaire's *Les Paradis Artificiels*. He rather admired Wilde, with whom he had talked in cafés, where the latter was sitting alone and running up high piles of saucers. He had given Christian copies of his books, inscribed; and Christian used to tell me, with evident respect, that Wilde in his last days had kept only three volumes: a copy of Walter Pater's *The Renaissance* that had been given him by Pater, Flaubert's *La Tentation de Saint Antoine* and Swinburne's *Atalanta in Calydon*. And it was always Gauss's great advantage over the school of Babbitt and More that he understood the artist's morality as something that expressed itself in different terms from the churchgoer's or the citizen's morality; the fidelity to a kind of truth that is rendered by the discipline of aesthetic form, as distinct from that of the professional moralist: the explicit communication of a "message." But there was nothing in his attitude of the truculent pose, the defiance of the bourgeoisie, that had been characteristic of the fin de siècle and that that other professor of the Romance languages, Gauss's near-contemporary, Ezra Pound, was to sustain through his whole career. How fundamental to his point of view, how much a thing to be taken for granted, this attitude had become, was shown clearly in a conversation I had with him, on some occasion when I had come back after college, when, in reply to some antinomian attitude of mine, or one that he imputed to me, he said, "But you were saying just

---

* I learn from Mrs. Gauss, who has shown me a photograph, that the realities behind this legend were a head of blond bushy hair and a jacket which, though green, was not velvet.

245

now that you would have to rewrite something before it could be published. That implies a moral obligation." And his sense of the world and the scope of art was, of course, something very much bigger than was common among the aesthetes and the symbolists.

Partly perhaps as a heritage from the age of Wilde but, more deeply, as a logical consequence of his continental origin and culture, he showed a pronounced though discreet parti pris against the literature of the Anglo-Saxon countries. In our time, he carried on a continual feud—partly humorous, yet basically serious—with the canons of the English department. I remember his telling me, with sly satisfaction, about a visiting French professor, who had asked, when it was explained to him that someone was an authority on Chaucer, "*Il est intelligent tout de même?*" Certain classical English writers he patronized—in some cases, rightly, I think. Robert Browning, in particular, he abominated. The author of *Pippa Passes* was one of the very few writers about whom I thought his opinions intemperate. "That Philistine beef-eating Englishman," he would bait his colleagues in English, "—what did he know about art? He writes lines like 'Irks care the crop-full bird? Frets doubt the maw-crammed beast?' " When I tried to find out once why Browning moved Christian to such special indignation, he told me, a little darkly, that he had greatly admired him in boyhood and had learned from him "a lot of bad doctrine." He said that the irregular love affairs in Browning were made to seem too jolly and simple, and insisted that the situation of the self-frustrated lovers of *The Statue and the Bust* had never been faced by Browning: If "the end in sight was a vice," the poet should not have wanted to have them get together; if he wanted them to get together, he ought not to have described it as a vice, but, on the other hand, he ought to have foreseen a mess. "He is one of the most immoral poets because he makes moral problems seem easy. He tells you that the good is sure to triumph." He would suggest to you an embarrassing picture of a Browning offensively hearty—"not robust," he would say slily, "but robustious"—bouncing and booming in Italy, while the shades of Leopardi and Dante looked on, as Boccaccio said of the latter, "*con isdegnoso occhio.*" The kind of thing he especially hated was such a poem as the one, in *James Lee's Wife*, that begins, "O good gigantic smile o' the brown old earth.". . . Of Byron—though Byron's writing was certainly more careless than Browning's—he had a much better opinion, because, no doubt, of Byron's fondness for the Continent as well as his freer intelligence and his experience of the ills of the world. He accepted Byron's love affairs—he had nothing of the prig or the Puritan—because Byron knew what he was doing and was not misleading about it. As for Shakespeare, though Christian was, of course, very far from the point of view of Voltaire, there was always just a suggestion of something of the kind in the background. He knew Shakespeare well and quoted him often, but Shakespeare was not one of the authors whom Christian had lived in or on; and he always made us feel that that sort of thing could never come up to literature that was polished and carefully planned and that knew how to make its points and the meaning of the points it was making. He was certainly unfair to Shakespeare in insisting that the Shakespearean characters all talk the same language, whereas Dante's all express themselves differently. For Christian, the great poet was Dante, and he gradually convinced you of this in his remarkable Dante course. He made us see the objectivity of Dante and the significance of his every stroke, so that even the geographical references have a moral and emotional force (the Po that finds peace with its tributaries in the Paolo and Francesca episode, the mountain in the Ugolino canto that prevents the Pisans from seeing their neighbors of Lucca) ; the vividness of the scenes and the characters (he liked to point out how Farinata's arrogant poise was thrown into dramatic relief by the passionate interruption of Cavalcanti) ; and the tremendous intellectual power by which all sorts of men and women exhibiting all sorts of passions have been organized in an orderly vision that implies, also, a reasoned morality. No Englishman, he made us feel, could ever have achieved this; it would never have occurred to Shakespeare. Nor could any English novelist have even attempted what Gustave Flaubert had achieved—a personal conception of the world, put together, without a visible seam, from apparently impersonal descriptions, in which, as in Dante, not a stroke was wasted. He admired the Russians, also, for their sober art of implication. I remember his calling our attention to one of the church scenes in Tolstoy's *Resurrection,* in which, as he pointed out, Tolstoy made no overt comment, yet caused you to loathe the whole thing by describing the ceremony step by step. This non-English, this classical and Latin ideal, became indissolubly associated in our minds with the summits of literature. We got from Gauss a good many things, but the most important things we got were probably Flaubert and Dante. John Peale Bishop, who came to Princeton intoxicated with Swinburne and

247

Shelley, was concentrating, by the time he graduated, on hard images and pregnant phrases. Ezra Pound and the imagists, to be sure, had a good deal to do with this, but Gauss's courses were important, too, and such an early poem of Bishop's as *Losses*, which contrasts Verlaine with Dante, was directly inspired by them. Less directly, perhaps, but no less certainly, the development of F. Scott Fitzgerald from *This Side of Paradise* to *The Great Gatsby*, from a loose and subjective conception of the novel to an organized impersonal one, was also due to Christian's influence. He made us all want to write something in which every word, every cadence, every detail, should perform a definite function in producing an intense effect.

Gauss's special understanding of the techniques of art was combined, as is not always the case, with a highly developed sense of history, as well as a sense of morality (he admirably prepared us for Joyce and Proust). If he played down—as I shall show in a moment—the Thomist side of Dante to make us see him as a great artist, he brought out in Flaubert the moralist and the bitter critic of history. And so much, at that period, was all his thought pervaded by the *Divine Comedy* that even his own version of history had at moments a Dantesque touch. It would not have been difficult, for example, to transpose such a presentation as the one of Rousseau that I have mentioned above into the sharp concise self-description of a character in the *Divina Commedia:* "I am the clockmaker's son of Geneva who said that man has made man perverse. When for the third time the cruel captain closed the gates, I made the sky my roof, and found in Annecy the love Geneva had denied" . . .

With this sense of history of Christian's was involved another strain in his nature that had nothing to do with the aestheticism of the nineties and yet that lived in his mind with it quite comfortably. His father, who came from Baden—he was a relative of the physicist Karl Friedrich Gauss—had taken part in the unsuccessful German revolution of 1848 and come to the United States with the emigration that followed it. The spirit of '48 was still alive in Christian, and at the time of the first World War an hereditary hatred of the Prussians roused him to a passionate championship of the anti-German cause even before the United States declared war. Later on, when Prohibition was imposed on the nation, the elder Gauss, as Christian told me, was so much infuriated by what he regarded as an interference nothing short of Prussian with the rights of a free people that he could not talk calmly about it, and, even when dean of the college and obliged to uphold the law, the American-born Christian continued in public to advocate its repeal, which required a certain courage in Presbyterian Princeton. It was this old-fashioned devotion to liberty that led him to admire Hugo for his refusal to live under the Second Empire, and Byron for his willingness to fight for Italian and Greek liberation. "Everywhere he goes in Europe," Christian would say of Byron, "it is the places, such as the prison of Chillon, where men had been oppressed, that arouse him." When he lectured on Anatole France, he would point out the stimulating contrast between the early France of *Sylvestre Bonnard,* who always wrote, as he said, like a kindly and bookish old man, and the France who defended Dreyfus, made a tour of the provinces to speak for him and remained for the rest of his life a social satirist and a radical publicist. In the years when I was at Princeton, Gauss called himself, I believe, a socialist; and during the years of depression in the thirties, he gravitated again toward the Left and, in *A Primer for Tomorrow* (1934), he made some serious attempt to criticize the financial-industrial system. In an inscription in the copy he sent me, he said that my stimulation had counted for something in his writing the book. But I was never able to persuade him to read Marx and Engels at firsthand: he read Werner Sombart instead; and I noted this, like the similar reluctance of Maynard Keynes to look into Marx, as a curious confirmation of the theory of the Marxists that the "bourgeois intellectuals" instinctively shy away from Marxist thought to the extent of even refusing to find out what it really is. Yet Christian had read Spengler with excitement—it was from him that I first heard of *The Decline of the West*—immediately after the war; and he never, in these later years, hesitated, in conversation, to indulge the boldest speculations as to the destiny of contemporary society.

He was a member of the National Committee of the American Civil Liberties Union, and he made a point, after the second war, of speaking to Negro audiences in the South. On my last visit to Princeton when I saw him, in the spring of 1951, he talked to me at length about his adventures in the color-discrimination states— how the representatives of some Negro organization under whose auspices he had been speaking had been unable to come to see him in his white hotel, and how, as he told me with pride, he had succeeded, for the first time in the history of Richmond, in assembling—in a white church, to which, however, he found the Negroes were only admitted on condition of their sitting in the back pews—a mixed black and white audience. As he grew older, he became more internationalist. He foresaw, and he often insisted, at the end of the first World War, that nothing but trouble could come of creating more small European states, and, at the end of the second war, he was bitterly opposed to what he regarded as the development of American nationalism. He complained much, in this connection, of the intensive cultivation, in the colleges, of American literature, which had been carried on since sometime in the middle thirties with a zeal that he thought more and more menacing to sound international values. I did not, on the whole, agree with him in disapproving of the growth of American studies; but I could see that, with his relative indifference to English literature, he must have conceived, at the end of the century, an extremely low opinion of American. He took no interest in Henry James and not very much in Walt Whitman. He told me once that Henry Ford had said, "Cut your own wood and it will warm you twice," not knowing that Ford had been quoting Thoreau. For Christian, the level of American writing was more or less represented by William Dean Howells, the presiding spirit of the years of his youth, for whom he felt hardly the barest respect. It was absolutely incredible to him—and in this I did agree with him—that *The Rise of Silas Lapham* should ever have been thought an important novel. "It wasn't much of a rise," he would say. Yet the "renaissance" of the twenties—unlike Paul Elmer More—he followed with sympathetic, if critical, interest.

Christian Gauss was a complex personality as well as a subtle mind, and one finds it in some ways difficult to sort out one's impressions of him. I want to try to deal now with the moral qualities which, combined with his unusual intellectual powers, gave him something of the stature of greatness. In some sense, he was a moral teacher as well as a literary one; but his teaching, in the same way as his criticism, was conveyed by throwing out suggestions and dropping incidental comments. In this connection, I want to quote here the tribute of Mr. Harold R. Medina, the distinguished Federal judge, from the symposium in the *Alumni Weekly*. It expresses a good deal better than anything I was able to write myself, when I drafted this memoir for the first time, the penetrating quality of Gauss's power, and it is interesting to me in describing an experience that closely parallels my own on the part of an alumnus of an earlier class—1909—who was to work in a different field yet who had known Christian Gauss, as I had, not as dean of the college, but as teacher of literature.

"Of all the men whom I have met," Mr. Medina writes, "only four have significantly influenced my life. Dean Gauss was the second of these; the first, my father. From freshman year on I had many courses and precepts with Dean Gauss and during my senior year I was with him almost daily. He attracted me as he did everyone else; and I sensed that he had something to impart which was of infinitely greater importance than the mere content of the courses in French Literature. It was many years after I left Princeton before I realized that it was he who first taught me how to think. How strange it is that so many people have the notion that they are thinking when they are merely repeating the thoughts of others. He dealt in ideas without seeming to do so; he led and guided with so gentle a touch that one began to think almost despite oneself. The process once started, he continued in such fashion as to instil into my very soul the determination to be a seeker after truth, the elusive, perhaps never to be attained, complete and utter truth, no matter where it led or whom it hurt. How he did it I shall never know; but that it was he I have not the slightest doubt. His own intellectual integrity was a constant example for me to follow. And to this precious element he added another. He gave me the vision of language and literature as something representing the continuous and never-ending flow of man's struggle to think the thoughts which, when put into action, constitute in the aggregate the advance of civilization. Whatever I may be today or may ever hope to be is largely the result of the germination of the seeds he planted. The phenomena of cause and effect are not to be denied. With Dean Gauss there were so many hundreds of persons, like myself, whom he influenced and whose innate talents he developed that the ripples he started in motion were multiplied again and again. In critical times I always wondered whether he approved or would approve of things I said and did. And this went on for over forty years."

"To instil into my very soul the determination to be a seeker after truth . . . no matter where it led or whom it hurt." I remember my own thrilled response when, in taking us through the seventeenth canto of the *Paradiso*, Christian read without special emphasis yet in a way that brought out their conviction a tercet that remained from that moment engraved, as they say, on my mind:

> *E s'io al vero son timido amico,*
> *Temo di perder viver tra coloro*
> *Che questo tempo chiameranno antico.*

—"If to the truth I prove a timid friend, I fear to lose my life [to fail of survival] among those who will call this time ancient." The truth about which Dante is speaking is his opinion of certain powerful persons, who will, as he has just been forewarned in Heaven, retaliate by sending him into exile—a truth which, as Heaven approves, he will not be deterred from uttering. Another moment in the classroom comes back to me from one of Christian's preceptorials. He had put up to us the issue created by the self-assertive type of romantic, who followed his own impulse in defiance of conventional morality and with indifference to social consequences; and he called upon me to supply him with an instance of moral conflict between social or personal duty and the duty of self-realization. I gave him the case of a problem with which I had had lately to deal as editor of the *Nassau Lit*, when I had not been able to bring myself to tell a friend who had set his heart upon contributing that the manuscripts he brought me were hopeless. "That's not an impulse," said Christian, "to do a humane thing: it's a temptation to do a weak thing." I was struck also by what seemed to me the unusual line that he took one day in class when one of his students complained that he hadn't been able to find out the meaning of a word. "What did you call it?" asked Christian. "Didn't you call it something?" The boy confessed that he hadn't. "That's bad intellectual form," said Christian. "Like going out in the morning with your face unwashed. In reading a foreign language, you must never leave a gap or a blur. If you can't find out what something means, make the best supposition you can. If it's wrong, the chances are that the context will show it in a moment or that you'll see, when the word occurs again, that it couldn't have meant that." This made such an impression on me that—just as Mr. Medina says he has been asking himself all his life whether Christian would approve of his actions—I still make an effort to live up to it.

I love to remember, too, how Christian began one of his lectures as follows: "There are several fundamental philosophies that one can bring to one's life in the world—or rather, there are several ways of taking life. One of these ways of taking the world is not to have any philosophy at all—that is the way that most people take it. Another is to regard the world as unreal and God as the only reality; Buddhism is an example of this. Another may be summed up in the words *Sic transit gloria mundi*—that is the point of view you find in Shakespeare." He then went on to an explanation of the eighteenth-century philosophy which assumed that the world was real and that we ourselves may find some sense in it and make ourselves happy in it. On another occasion, in preceptorial, Christian asked me, "Where do you think our ideals come from—justice, righteousness, beauty and so on?" I replied, "Out of the imaginations of men"; and he surprised me by answering, "That is correct." This made an impression on me, because he usually confined himself to a purely Socratic questioning, in which he did not often allow himself to express his own opinions. I felt that I had caught him off guard: what he had evidently been expecting to elicit was either Platonic idealism or Christian revelation.

It was only outside class and at secondhand that I learned that he said of himself at this time that his only religion was Dante; yet it could not escape us in the long run that the Dante we were studying was a secular Dante—or rather, perhaps, a Dante of the Reformation—the validity of whose art and morality did not in the least depend on one's acceptance or non-acceptance of the faith of the Catholic Church. Christian would remind us from time to time of Dante's statement, in his letter to Can Grande, that his poem, though it purported to describe a journey to the other world, really dealt with men's life in this, and we were shown that the conditions of the souls in Hell, Purgatory and Heaven were metaphors for our moral situation here. The principle of salvation that we learned from Dante was not the Catholic surrender to Jesus—who plays in the *Divine Comedy* so significantly small a role—but the vigilant cultivation of *"il ben del intelletto."*

Some of those who had known Christian Gauss in his great days as a teacher of literature were sorry, after the war, to see him becoming involved in the administrative side of the University. I remember his saying to me one day, in the early stages of this, "I've just sent off a lot of letters, and I said to myself as I mailed them, 'There are seventeen letters to people who don't interest me in the least.'" But the job of the Dean's office did interest him—though it seemed to us that it did not take a Gauss to rule on remiss or refractory students. He had never liked repeating routine, and I suppose that his department was coming to bore him. He made, by all accounts, a remarkable dean—for his card-catalogue memory kept all names and faces on file even for decades after the students had left, and the sensitive feeling for character that had been hidden behind his classroom mask must have equipped him with a special tact in dealing with the difficult cases. His genius for moral values had also a new field now in which it could exercise itself in an immediate and practical way, and the responsibilities of his office—especially in the years just after the war, when students were committing suicide and getting into all sorts of messes—sometimes put upon him an obvious strain. Looking back since his death, it has seemed to me that the Gauss who was dean of Princeton must have differed almost as much from the Gauss with whom I read French and Italian as this austere teacher had done from the young correspondent in Paris, who had paid for Oscar Wilde's drinks. The Gauss I had known in my student days, with his pale cheeks and shuttered gaze, his old raincoat and soft flat hat, and a shabby mongrel dog named Baudelaire, which had been left with him by the Jesse Lynch Williamses and which sometimes accompanied him into class—the Gauss who would pass one on the campus without speaking, unless you attracted his attention, in an abstraction like that of Dante in Hell and who seemed to meet the academic world with a slightly constrained self-consciousness at not having much in common with it—this figure warmed up and filled out, became recognizably Princetonian in his neckties and shirts and a touch of that tone that combines a country-club self-assurance with a boyish country-town homeliness. He now met the college world, unscreened, with his humorous and lucid green eyes. He wore golf stockings and even played golf. He interested himself in the football team and made speeches at alumni banquets. Though I know that his influence as dean was exerted in favor of scholarships, higher admission requirements and the salvaging of the Humanities—I cannot do justice here to this whole important phase of his career—the only moments of our long friendship when I was ever at all out of sympathy with him occurred during these years of officialdom; for I felt that he had picked up a little the conventional local prejudices when I would find him protesting against the advent in Princeton of the Institute for Advanced Study or, on one occasion, censoring the *Lit* for publishing a "blasphemous" story. One was always impressed, however, by the way in which he seemed to have absorbed the whole business of the University.

We used to hope that he would eventually be president; but, with the domination of business in the boards of trustees of the larger American colleges, it was almost as improbable that Christian would be asked to be president of Princeton as it would have been that Santayana should be asked to be president of Harvard. Not, of course, that it would ever have occurred to anyone to propose such a post for Santayana, but it was somehow Characteristic of Christian's career that the idea should have entered the minds of his friends and that nothing should ever have come of it. There appeared in the whole line of Christian's life a certain diversion of purpose, an unpredictable ambiguity of aim, that corresponded to the fluid indeterminate element in his teaching and conversation. He had originally been a newspaper correspondent and a writer of reviews for the literary journals, who hoped to become a poet. He was later a college professor who had developed into a brilliant critic—by far the best, so far as I know, in our academic world of that period—and who still looked forward to writing books; I once found him, in one of his rare moments of leisure, beginning an historical novel. Then, as dean, in the late twenties and thirties, be came to occupy a position of intercollegiate distinction rather incongruous with that usually prosaic office. Was he a "power" in American education? I do not believe he was. That kind of role is possible only for a theorist like John Dewey or an administrator like Charles W. Eliot. Though he was offered the presidency of another college, he continued at Princeton as dean and simply awaited the age of retirement. When that came, he seemed at first depressed, but later readjusted himself. I enjoyed him in these post-official years. He was no longer overworked and he no longer had to worry about the alumni. He returned to literature and started an autobiography, with which, however, he said he was unsatisfied. In October of 1951, he had been writing an introduction for a new edition of Machiavelli's *Prince,* and he was pleased with it when he had finished. He took Mrs. Gauss for a drive in the car, and they talked about a trip to Florida. He had seemed in good spirits and health, though he had complained the Saturday before, after going to the Cornell game, where he had climbed to one of the top tiers of seats, that he was feeling the effects of age—he was now seventy-three. The day after finishing his introduction, he took the manuscript to

255

his publisher in New York and attended there a memorial service for the Austrian novelist Hermann Broch, whom he had known when the latter lived in Princeton. While waiting outside the gates for the train to take him back to Princeton, with the evening paper in his pocket, his heart failed and he suddenly fell dead.

One had always still expected something further from Christian, had hoped that his character and talents would arrive at some final fruition. But—what seems to one still incredible—one's long conversation with him was simply forever suspended. And one sees now that the career was complete, the achievement is all there. He has left no solid body of writing; he did not remake Princeton (as Woodrow Wilson in some sense was able to do); he was not really a public man. He was a spiritual and intellectual force—one does not know how else to put it—of a kind that it may be possible for a man to do any of those other things without in the least becoming. His great work in his generation was unorganized and unobtrusive; and *Who's Who* will tell you nothing about it; but his influence was vital for those who felt it.

> Chè in la mente m'è fitta, ed or m'accora,
>   La cara e buona imagine paterna
>   Di voi, quando nel mondo ad ora ad ora
> M'insegnavate come l'uom s'eterna. . . .

# Cézanne Today

## MAURICE STERNE

### ( *1952* )

MAURICE STERNE, who died in 1957, was a painter and sculptor whose work was exhibited in the principal cities of Europe and America, including the Metropolitan Museum, the Museum of Modern Art and the Tate Gallery of London. His memoirs are to be published within the next several years. In this article, Mr. Sterne assesses Cézanne and the critical evaluations of him, ranging from condemnation in his own time to adulation in the present.

To BE MISUNDERSTOOD and ridiculed was the common lot of the masters of the nineteenth-century French Renaissance, but only Cézanne aroused hatred. He became the symbol of everything that was anathema to his contemporaries, the target of bitter recrimination. The public, the critics, even his fellow artists joined in unanimous attack. But it is significant that hardly a single voice questioned his honesty and his sincerity.

Now, almost half a century since his death, a mighty chorus of adulation has replaced the one of condemnation. One encountered only gushing enthusiasm over his recent exhibition at the Metropolitan Museum. Cézanne was the chief topic at cocktail, dinner, luncheon parties—the invisible guest of honor. Posters in buses urged one to attend the show; a heroine of a radio murder mystery possessed ruby-red lips and Cézanne-blue eyes!

To one of my generation, who had to learn by the slow, painful process, since there were no teachers to teach us, this sensational success was truly amazing. Evidently the present generation has been taught a far easier way to appreciate the master. Still, I wonder whether the direct approach is not preferable to the new streamlined, often erroneous versions of interpreters.

The spectacular success of the Van Gogh exhibition in these

galleries about two years ago did not surprise me. His appeal is direct. His dramatic life, his poverty, his heartbreaking struggle for recognition, his madness and tragic death had been widely publicized and aroused morbid curiosity. And he is more in harmony with our time, our jitterbug civilization that demands a violent kick from a work of art, or a slushy antidote for its shock.

Painting, unless executed in frenzy, has become boring. Anyone can behold a bush on a lawn. To see it burst into flickering, crackling flames at the touch of a magic brush like Van Gogh's is a sight not beheld since Genesis. Its sinister yellow, orange, green-blue, violet hues and sulphurous odor suggest a volcano in eruption. But how Cézanne, whose art is so difficult to fathom, could meet with such spontaneous appreciation, I could not understand. I began to doubt the genuineness of the response.

I first heard of Cézanne in 1904 when I arrived in Paris. I must not fail, I was told, to see the Salon d'Automne, where Puvis de Chavannes, the most successful and famous painter of his era, was honored with a one-man show. Another gallery was devoted to a comparatively obscure painter called Paul Cézanne. This was unfortunate. The outcry against Cézanne dimmed the rather feeble lustre of Puvis; and the critics in their violent denunciation of the master of Aix found little space for exultation over the immaculate art of the master of those lovely murals at the Pantheon.

Go and see Puvis; you will learn something, I was told. And don't forget to look at Cézanne—you will have a good laugh. I visited both many times. I did not learn anything from Puvis and I did not laugh at Cézanne. I was too horrified and upset for laughter. But I noticed something strange. The more I saw of Cézanne, the more Puvis shrank in stature. Yet Cézanne still remained a mystery I could not fathom.

Intrigued and perplexed, I wondered who this painter was who could disturb me so deeply. A second-rate Impressionist, I was told, who was welcomed to their exclusive group not because of affinity with their theories but because he was a fellow rebel against entrenched official academism. Others informed me that he was a paranoiac with delusions of grandeur, a hopeless amateur with no talent and little training. But there were a few so-called eccentrics who claimed that he was the new beacon on the horizon and had already become a chef d'école.

This first encounter took place in Paris almost fifty years ago. The century was still in swaddling clothes, and I was struggling with poverty, a stubborn coal stove and smoky kerosene lamp. But by far the most strenuous struggle was against preconceived, deeply rooted traditional art standards, that so often interfere with an open mind and heart in our approach to the art of others, especially when it happens to be radically different from our own.

Cézanne was the Gordian knot I felt I must untie because his art attracted and repelled me. I was not equipped with a keen-edged sword and could not, like Alexander, cut it. Patiently I proceeded to untie the knot, and it took me many years before I more or less succeeded. This became obvious when I discovered that Cézanne, unlike his contemporaries, did not possess a master key that could open all locks. Each painting was a new problem and required an individual solution.

My second round with the master took place at Vollard's little shop on the Rue Lafitte. My friend Leo Stein, who was interested in my art education, introduced me to Vollard, who was very obliging and showed us half a dozen canvases, two of which I liked: a very early portrait and a landscape with nudes. I had recently come from Italy, where during a stay at Florence I first perceived the importance of the tactile sense in visual art. These two canvases by Cézanne seemed to possess it in a higher degree than anything else I had seen in contemporary painting. Manet, Renoir and Degas were certainly not devoid of it, but did not have it in such intensity. Those figures, hurled against the background with utter disregard for surrounding space, were alive in spite of the listless, airless world around them because of the intensity of his tactile perception. But I was still blind to his later, far greater period, from which Vollard had a large number of paintings.

My third encounter took place at the 1905 Salon d'Automne, where again a room was devoted to Cézanne. I visited that show many times but made no progress. Late one afternoon I found two elderly men intently studying the paintings. One, who looked like an ascetic Burmese monk with thick spectacles, was pointing out passages to his companion, murmuring "magnificent, excellent." His eyes seemed very poor, and he was very close to the paintings. I wondered who he could be—probably some poor painter, to judge by his rather shabby old cape.

Suddenly a pompous, portly personage appeared on the threshold. His gray Van Dyke beard, his well-fitting clothes, the wide black ribbon from which hung a gold pince-nez, his red button of the Legion of Honor—these proclaimed him a successful artist. He paused at the door, fussed with his beard, put on his pince-nez and rushed from one painting to another. He was in a state of extreme indignation. Suddenly losing all self-control, in a shrill voice he shouted, "I protest against such *cochonnerie* being shown to the public. I protest against such vile daubs that idiots call art. I protest, I protest!" His face was so purple that I feared the poor man would have a stroke. The two visitors turned sharply and faced him. "You, Monsieur Degas!" he gasped. "What the devil are you doing here?" Without a word, Degas (the man with the thick spectacles) and his companion hurriedly left.

I was shocked and astonished when I learned that the man in the cape was Degas—that the painter I held in the highest esteem was an admirer of what appeared to me to be uncouth daubs. Suddenly this dramatic scene appeared comical, and I burst into laughter. The aesthetic protestant looked at me ferociously and hastened out. He must have misunderstood. How could he know that I laughed at myself, for I was indeed in a quandary.

I learned the identity of the apoplectic gentleman. He was a well-known painter, a perfect specimen of the conquering hero who marches on from success to success to ultimate failure, so different from the master he attacked, who marched from failure to failure to ultimate triumph. This man was a synthesist who adopted the essential rudiments of his betters and by dilution made them palatable to a cultured, well-mannered public. I was familiar with his work; it was neither good nor bad. Technically, it was immaculate. But if there is one thing that is worse than bad art, it is bad art well done. He belonged to that small group called "progressive." They are productive but not creative, full of ambition for glory, material success and greed for power. When these are gratified, when the gold medal has been won at the Spring Salon and the coveted red ribbon of the Legion of Honor gleams in the lapel, they rest on their laurels. Poised safely in the center, they swiftly sway from left to right and from right to left within a tiny prescribed area, like a pendulum, without creative direction. They produce respectable, well-mannered "art"—lively but not really alive. They cater to a fairly large cultured public, are prize winners, chairmen of juries and arbiters of the fate of their betters. The extreme right and the extreme left at least follow directions—backward or forward—but the center is automatic and lifeless.

Those words of Degas—his "magnificent, excellent"—cut deep. When I mentioned this episode to a friend, a young painter who had won the Prix de Rome, he shrugged his shoulders. His only comment was "Chacun à son goût."

What right has a painter to have taste! Only a layman can indulge in this dubious luxury. The painter must have judgment and perception in his approach to the art of others. That dramatic scene in the Cézanne room was indeed a crisis in my life. The painter I respected most turned out to be an admirer of the painter I disliked—and the painter I respected least agreed with me! This was not only puzzling, it was humiliating!

The next day I decided to look at the rest of the exhibition, but did not find much of interest. I was soon back in the Cézanne room. It was late. I consulted my watch and found that it had stopped. I opened the lid, examined the works, gave it a sharp tap—and it became alive. The mechanism which in a static state was purely decorative suddenly turned into a functioning organism. And when I looked at the paintings on the wall I realized that I really had not seen them. Like my watch, they too now took on life. Those houses and trees, roads, hills, and Mount St. Victoire in the distance played relative parts in the drama, like any functioning mechanism or living organism. In mathematics the sum is equal to all its parts; in aesthetics the sum is always one. If it is less than one or more than one, the problem has not been solved. Looking at these pictures, I felt that if any single part were different, no matter how right in itself, it would be wrong; for then the aesthetic mechanism would cease to function.

There is a similitude between the biological, the mechanical and the aesthetic. It consists of parts that must "work" in unison, and the importance of each part is in its performance of a definite function. This collaboration is disrupted when some artery or pivot or color breaks down and declares its independence. Then our attention is diverted from the general to the particular; then the body or the machine or the painting has ceased to be a completely integrated organism.

The violent blows delivered me by Degas and my Ingersoll watch helped to lift the curtain that had obstructed the view of a heretofore undiscovered aspect of art and of nature. Until then I had been a conscious critic and unconscious devotee (quite a common ailment). Is there some universal truth in all genuine art that exerts a subtle appeal to our instinct in spite of our "better" judgment?

There has been too much emphasis on Cézanne's emotionalism and his abstraction. *What* aroused his emotion, *why* his art is abstract, has hardly been given serious consideration. Cézanne was a realist who observed reality not only with his eyes, but with his body and soul too: a realist who penetrated within his motif. How could a public (this includes both the artist and the critic) brought up on the superficial notion that realism consists of the depiction of obvious appearances be expected to possess the inner eye to see at a glance an image it took the artist sometimes many weeks to project, and the outer eye a lifetime to evolve?

To Cézanne the appearance was not a point of arrival; it was a point of departure, a journey not away from the motif, likely to turn into a joy-ride by oneself (so freely indulged in at present), but a journey of exploration into the hidden secrets that reality may hold. In common with the pure scientists, the pure artists attempt to bring into the light what is still hidden in darkness. Because they embody truth, they strive for affirmation with the creative forces of which they are microcosms. When they succeed in projecting an aural or visual pattern suggestive of the energy and rhythm of these causes that gave them form, they are quite rightly proclaimed "genius."

Cézanne was a realist; he was also a mystic who could identify himself with reality. Unlike the religious mystic who identifies reality with himself, his identification is not abstract but corporeal. Cézanne *became* the plate of apples or the landscape, or whatever he happened to be painting. This is the main reason he had to have his motif constantly before him. It took him some time to penetrate his subjects in depth, and even longer to break through the shell of his ego—a Herculean task when the person happens to be a profound individual. If, in spite of his intentions, the patterns were not entirely free from the taint of individualism, it was not his fault. His main objective was to create an image as closely as possible in accordance with his visual experience. The emotions which the motif evoked were incidental. His only interest was in the *noun;* his only purpose, to present it in all its significance. His emotions were *adjectives* of little interest to him. His paintings are not epigrams or lyric poems: they are epics moving in austere blank verse. His art suggests a tree with roots moving downward in the earth, the trunk reaching skyward and the limbs branching out in every direction.

And this is not supposed to be realism, according to the aesthetes! Is it because they have cut the umbilical cord that throughout the ages has held art to nature? Reared on synthetic concoctions called "aesthetics," served from precious containers, they are bound to be contemptuous of the old-fashioned method of nursing, so dear to the realistic painter who finds the taste of the milk

and the breasts of Mother Nature far more attractive and nour-
ishing.

Of course Cézanne is bound to appear abstract to the layman
who only looks at, seldom sees and never has insight into reality.
If he could develop as much insight into nature as he exercises in
his perception of art, he might discover why all artists, the best and
the worst, have always worshipped nature, derived their inspiration from it, been too intent upon its transmutation to bother with
the nature of its interpretation. They are discoverers, not inventors; creators, not producers; nature worshippers, not self-idolators.

"Yet all that is I see," said the queen to Hamlet when her son
beheld his father's ghost; but Hamlet saw, heard and spoke to him.
To Hamlet, no less than to Shakespeare, the ghost was real. If the
queen mother and critics cannot see visions, it is not the visions'
fault.

Of course Cézanne was emotional. But his ecstasy was always
contingent upon the degree of his reaction to a visual experience.
This reaction, in spite of his keen penetration within his subject,
did not interfere with his sensitive response to nature's changes of
expression.

The contribution made by the Impressionists is of lesser importance in their individual works than in its influence on their more
gifted contemporaries. Had Cézanne not been cognizant of their
refreshing new vision, he might have continued in the direction
indicated in his earliest period, when he indulged in violent chiaroscuro and projected form in airless space. The Impressionists
brought the outdoors, fresh air and sunlight, into his studio
gloom. Out the window went his old palette with its somber blacks
and acid greens; a new palette with radiant chromatic hues took
its place, like a rainbow after a storm. His traditional rendition of
form by means of chiaroscuro was discarded, and a new art of
modeling form in space by color emerged. Cézanne took full advantage of their precious gift and was ever conscious of the debt
he owed them. Endowed with a tactile sense unsurpassed by the
greatest masters of the past, Cézanne was not, like Monet, interested solely in nature's momentary expression, in her changing
moods, in the transitory, but more in what is basic in substance and
character—what is underneath the façade.

It is surprising that one with so keen a sense of plastic form had
never visited Italy, where he could have seen the greatest triumphs
of tactile perception in the works of Masaccio, Giotto, Piero della
Francesca and Michelangelo. Was it because he feared that greater

intimacy with these masters might interfere with his newly acquired vision? His art has the body of sculpture, the containment of space of architecture, and the spirit of painting fused in one. The Impressionists gave him a new direction. He broke the ties with the past, but his roots remained firmly planted in the earth. And it is these sturdy roots nourished by the past, no less than the sunlight and oxygen supplied by the Impressionists, that brought such immortal fruit from the tree of intuitive wisdom.

But he was not a solitary giant. We must not forget that Renoir and Degas also had the good fortune to live in this glorious nineteenth-century Renaissance. They too had a tactile sense and had been affected by the Impressionists, but their sense of form was of lesser intensity. Renoir was more sensitive to the movement of light; his rhythm is more flowing, Cézanne's staccato. Renoir painted his women like dancing trees, Cézanne like rocks resting on the earth.

A tactile perception of deepest intensity combined with a sensitive reaction to the subtleties of the ever-changing aspects of nature is Cézanne's greatest contribution. And it is possible that he esteemed the latter more than the former, because he was born with the first and took it for granted, whereas he had to earn the second. We are likely to attach greater value to what we have acquired than to what we have inherited. He was born with the vision of a sculptor and gradually developed the more abstract visual sensitivity of a painter.

At first, there was conflict between the two. This is apparent in his first period, when his intense reaction to concrete forms found expression in exaggerated presentation of their plastic reality. Figures are projected on the canvas to shift for themselves, with no attempt at co-ordination with the surrounding spaces; independent units in a somber vacuum. He was still the sculptor in the round in paint.

When he realized that the pictorial plane must be free of "holes," that the intervening spaces between concrete objects moving in depth must possess form no less significant than concrete form, his painting took on the character of sculpture in bas-relief. And some of his finest canvases were painted in the second period. Nonetheless, he strove for a more perfect pictorial effect, to render tri-dimensional reality without sacrificing the bi-dimensional character of the pictorial plane. He did not realize how hopeless this was. It can be achieved in black and white when the effect is limited to two contrasting tones without intermediary grays. To render it in color is utterly impossible, because our reaction to color is not positive but relative. Since colors take on their individual character through optical illusion, our reaction is purely spatial. Hence his constant cry, "I cannot realize." No one ever did or ever will realize aesthetically what is contrary to our perception of natural phenomena. But he tried persistently, and in spite of his failure, he succeeded far more than he realized; for in his striving for a flat bi-dimensional plane, he shrank the spatial depth to its utmost limitations and obtained architectonic space pictorially far more satisfying than anyone had before him, with the exception of Giotto, whose contraction of the pictorial plane without the sacrifice of concrete form was no less noteworthy.

The prevalent notion that the picture should never transcend its bi-dimensional character, with which the younger generation is obsessed, might be valid in a formless, spaceless universe of spectral silhouettes. But how anyone with the tactile sense of a Cézanne, who often pointed out that all forms can be reduced to the cone, the cylinder and the cube, to whom even the intervening spaces between concrete forms were transcribed into complementary formal values, should constantly strive for it, is incomprehensible. And yet we should be thankful that he did. It is not only what the creative artist succeeds in expressing but what he perceives beyond his horizon, what he cannot materialize in visual images, what his creative antennae can *almost* touch, that is of equal importance.

As he grew older, he shrank more and more from human contact; his motifs replaced human relationships. They became his constant companions, always together, either whispering secrets or fighting ferociously. Sooner or later he would reach the boundaries of human perception. Convinced that his motif had betrayed him, that it had kept some inner truth from him, he abandoned it in disgust and, in a fit of desperate frustration, cried, "I cannot realize." He would often leave a particular painting behind to rot in the field.

All this became clear to me only when I had suddenly seen his paintings as a whole, free from the deficiencies one is bound to find in new forms when one's approach has been too much influenced by the old. As long as our reaction to so-called revolutionary art is dominated by taste cultivated by tradition, we are bound to be shocked by the new, and its positive values appear negative.

What are the "defects" I found so objectionable at first? They were both "aesthetic" and what is called "spiritual." Spiritually

I resented his superficial rendition of character. After all, human physiognomy is not a rock or an apple; man is supposed to have a soul, as was shown by the great masters of the Renaissance and by Rembrandt. Cézanne's portraits as significant interpretation of character are quite unimportant.

But Cézanne was not the only painter of this period whose interpretation of "spiritual" values was very superficial compared with the great masters of the past. These artists were far more interested in what is called "pure aesthetic values." Manet's men and women are rather dull middle-class folk; Renoir's, pretty little things full of charm; Degas' laundresses and dancers, typical bourgeois one sees on Paris streets.

During the nineteenth century in France, there was a shift of interest among progressive artists from the spiritual, or illustrative, to the aesthetic. A keen insight into natural phenomena supplanted the prevalent concentration on psychological content; and the more the artists pursued this new direction, the more the general public, including connoisseurs, critics and the majority of the artists, persisted in evaluating a work of art according to their deeply rooted conviction that above all it must enhance the spirit. Instead of looking for God in man's image, painters found Him in apples and flowers and trees and hills and valleys. If we expect to find in Cézanne what we have learned to appreciate in Rembrandt, we are sure to be disappointed. It would be just as unfair to demand from Rembrandt what only Cézanne has given us.

Unfortunately, the important fact that truly great painters did not have to dematerialize the body in order to enhance the soul was overlooked. Giotto, Masaccio and Michelangelo did not have to sacrifice the body as a burnt offering to the spirit. They revealed that the spirit can and does dwell within the body of man, that the one enhances the other, that the two are inseparable while we are still alive. The astral plane of the soul they wisely left to the future. Nonetheless, when we compare the masterpieces of the Renaissance with even the finest works of the later periods, we are impressed with the difference in spiritual content. The old masters reveal far deeper penetration of character. Only supermen could have had so deep a perception of complex human nature. And it was not because their sitters, apart from external trappings, were different from our contemporaries. Had Lászlo painted Raphael's *Pope Julius II* or Titian's *Pope Paul III*, these pontiffs would look quite different. Had Dürer portrayed the English mid-Victorian aristocracy, he would have revealed depths of character Sargent never dreamed they possessed.

The complex psyche of man that has always been the chief source of interest to the creative artist, though still found in literature, has entirely vanished from the visual arts. In vain we look for visual images of a Hamlet, a Mona Lisa or an Ivan Karamazov on the canvases of the last few centuries. Only in Daumier is there any spiritual affinity with the masters of the past.

There is neither progression nor retrogression in art. Who can say that Michelangelo was "better" or "worse" than Phidias, Cézanne greater than Poussin or Chardin or Delacroix? They are different. Each has his personal message that we might appreciate if we could rid ourselves of preconceived notions as to what is good or bad, better or worse. There is no "bad" painting. When it is "bad" it is not painting.

We should approach the artist from his—not our—point of view. What he has achieved is a direction one can follow. But what he has failed to achieve is nonetheless a direction that should lead to as yet unexplored potentialities. Only the director has a definable beginning and a definite end. The momentum he projects is without the one or the other.

The direction indicated by Cézanne is still awaiting further progression. Undoubtedly his influence on the art of the first half of this century has been remarkable, but on the whole deteriorative rather than constructive. Or is it too "constructive"? That fatal remark of his that all forms can be reduced to the cone, the cylinder and the cube has put too great an emphasis on construction. A couple of gifted adolescents took up the battle cry and invented cubism. Not what Cézanne says with his brush, but what he said with words was readily understood, while the wisdom in his paintings is still a mystery only too often misunderstood and misinterpreted. To quote Goethe: "Every great idea as soon as it appears exerts a tyrannous influence. Hence the advantages that it produces are all too soon transformed into disadvantages."

That fatal dictum about the geometric basis of form had a sinister effect on the Cubists. A principle, instead of being a means to an end, became an end in itself. Again I quote Goethe: "Hypotheses are scaffoldings which precede the building and which one takes down when the building is finished. They are indispensable to the workman, but he must not mistake the scaffolding for the building."

It would almost seem as if Goethe had foreseen the Cubist movement in which the painter incorporated the scaffolding in the finished building: an attempt to introduce the element of time, the prerogative of aural art, in the visual art that is projected in space. I understand that the two are regarded as having become synonymous. This may be true in the realm of mathematics or metaphysics—but the painter must face concrete reality and comprehend the distinction between them.

By introducing the processes that have led to the final image, the Cubists have proudly shown what they thought about form with utter disregard of what they have felt and perceived. The result is a vulgar exhibition of newly acquired knowledge not unlike that of a parvenu who shows off his unfamiliar riches. No wonder Braque and Picasso soon abandoned this abortive impasse. Only a few, with souls of plumbers, have stuck to it and stuck in it.

That dictum of Cézanne has been familiar as a principle to visual artists for ages. It is most apparent in Egyptian sculpture and Renaissance painting. The Cubists adopted this ancient precept and, under the influence of African sculpture that had just invaded the Latin Quarter, succeeded in inventing a brand new style: cubism, Parisian twentieth-century baroque—the florid, flamboyant curves so characteristic of the earlier style transformed into sharp angles, interrupted planes, over-rationalized analysis, forming a geometric pattern consistent with our technological age. Its main claim to fame is that it initiated the present malady: invented art.

Of course all worth-while artists are not only discoverers; they must also be *inventive,* but never inventors. The inventive faculty is stimulated when the well-known technical means appear inadequate. Then the artist will search for some mode to express his personal reaction. Only as a means to an end is it of any importance. When an end in itself, it can be at best mildly amusing, as is manifested in the latest movement called "accidentalism."

What are the aesthetic "defects" that interfere with a more spontaneous appreciation of Cézanne's superb art? First, his style; second, his drawing; third, his distortion; fourth, his lack of finish; fifth, his perspective; sixth, his color; seventh, his chiaroscuro. I will analyze these so-called defects for the benefit of those who are both attracted and repelled but find it difficult to respond fully because of these "shortcomings."

His style, a highly individual hand which is hard to decipher, is the first obstacle. A painting, unlike a literary or musical script, cannot be copied, printed or typed; it always must remain the author's original manuscript. The painters of the past took great pains with their penmanship because they were more cognizant of their public. Cézanne was too engrossed with the projection of an image to pay any attention to the manner of its execution. Consequently we must learn to read his hand before we can expect to understand the content. Only then do the crotchety accents, the indeterminate lines make any sense, and only then is what at first appeared like vacillating scribble transformed into symbolic graphic recordings of forms moving in space. In the throes of creation there was no time to worry about whether his efforts would convey a message or whether it could be understood.

When this first hurdle has been successfully cleared, new obstacles arise: his "faulty" drawing, ugly distortion and lack of finish. These are really closely linked and need not be considered separately. True, his drawing has not the perfection of an Ingres, with its classical, lyrical rhythm, its immaculate purity; or the precise incision of Degas, who wielded his crayon with the skill of a master surgeon. Cézanne's contours have a double function with a single purpose: to render concrete form effectively, impressionistically, not only as it is, but as it appears, by conjoining it with surrounding space. Those rugged accents emphasize form where its plasticity is essential, or lose it in space; they indulge in a delightful game of hide-and-seek. The flowing, rhythmic contours so freely indulged in by painters who attribute too much importance to the decorative were anathema to Cézanne. He loathed the "artistic" because he worshipped reality. He could not have more than one deity at a time, and his motif was the only one for the time being.

His drawing has more affinity with Rembrandt's, not as we know it from his paintings or etchings, but from those amazing, rapid sepia sketches unparalleled in the history of Western art. They reveal the Dutch master at his best, reaching the highest degree of abstraction, when the means employed were utterly unconscious in his impatience to project a visual image of a concept of the mind and heart.

But even more than his drawing, Cézanne's distortion, especially of the human body, aroused indignation and severe criticism. In a tree or an apple it is often not even noticed, but if one dares to deform the "sacred" human being, we take it as a personal insult! Is it because we like to identify ourselves with a pictorial image and would rather it be a bland Apollo Belvedere or a Madonna by Raphael? In art as in life we have certain standards of beauty, and too great a divergence from these ideals is likely to interfere with our aesthetic enjoyment. It is easy to understand how Cézanne's disregard of this time-honored canon outraged even his most ardent admirers.

Only when I realized that his distortion was not due to his inability to draw "correctly" or to optical imperfection, but to reasons purely compositional—only then did I comprehend that his malformations were in reality transformations. When seen separately, an arm or a leg or a torso appears disfigured; but seen as a whole, the separate units, as if swayed by a centripetal force, renounce some degree of their identity for the sake of the unity of the composition. He had to sacrifice the "beauty" of the part for the sake of the whole.

Throughout the ages painters have shown far greater latitude in color and chiaroscuro than in their interpretation of form. Form was something one had to respect; one could cheat a little, but one must not get too impertinent. Cézanne was not the first to distort; he only went further, and for a good reason. Sensitive to spatial reality no less than to corporeal, and perceptive of the elemental power of movement, he fused the three; and as a painter his chief interest was in appearances, not individual characteristics. Consequently all objects had to conform to his over-all composition, and even human beings had to renounce their long-enjoyed priority. It is possible that he might have preferred to avoid distortion; but Cézanne, in his modesty, always believed that the picture's will, not his, should prevail.

Of all the changes in our standards of aesthetic values, none is more startling than our concept of when a painting is "finished." This problem has preoccupied the painter throughout the ages. We might have had many more masterpieces had the painters of the past listened to their consciences, trusted their eyes, and not had their ears cocked to the voice of the public. Now and then a Hogarth or a Turner or a Constable revolted against this concept of the public, and in a moment of freedom let the horse take the bit between his teeth and run away. What a pity they did it so seldom!

The concept of "finish" is based on a traditional notion that painting is a sister art of architecture and is subject to the same laws. As a matter of fact, their only kinship consists in that both are visual arts.

Since painting is essentially an abstract projection of an image, it is more closely related to music and literature. True, architecture has often been called "frozen music," but the painter is not interested in frozen objects. His main endeavor is to suggest the pulsation and rhythm of reality in fluid movement. Architecture is petrified, a static rock; painting, the surf washing over its surface. As long as one demands from a painting the attributes of a building, a painting devoid of minor details seems "unfinished." Only when we grasp the difference between material "finish" and spiritual completion can we fully appreciate Cézanne's amazing accomplishments. For he was not a *maker* of paintings; he was a *creator* whose chief aim was to project a graphic image of a visual, spiritual and emotional experience evoked by his motif. When he succeeded in its presentation according to his abilities, then the painting was finished, in spite of its unfinished appearance.

His "faulty" perspective? As a matter of fact, he was a master of pictorial perspective as it had been rendered throughout the ages prior to the discoveries made by Piero della Francesca and Paolo Ucello, whose scientific studies had, on the whole, a detrimental effect on painting. Their mental contribution displaced instinct, and the painter had to make sure he was right, whereas formerly he had *felt* that he was right. It was fortunate indeed that Giotto, the last of the classicists and the first of the Renaissance moderns, did not live a century later; he then might have been influenced by those *quattrocento* discoveries. Then his infallible pictorial perspective, so lyrical, so faultless, would have lost its architectonic rhythm. And this was not Giotto's contribution; it was a heritage from the past—from classical tradition.

I never could understand why the pre-Giotto painters are called "primitives." Primitives? They were the last of a glorious school, if anything too sophisticated and over-stylized. And Cézanne's perspective is of this tradition. There is nothing faulty about it; it is merely a question of the point of view. Instead of conceiving the picture from his eye level, it is seen from above, from a certain elevation. When the picture plane tilts upward diagonally, the ground plane must soon reach the upper edge of the frame. When objects are seen from an elevation, their dimensions do not undergo any violent diminution; when seen from the ground level, they grow smaller and smaller, and a greater depth is achieved— so destructive to the architectural picture plane, which should always retain its relative depth consistent with the bi-dimensional proportions of the painting.

The outstanding colorists of the past aimed at boundaries of color saturation, achieving a sumptuous richness. They soon reached ultimate perfection because of the limitation inherent in pigment. The paintings of Titian, El Greco, Rubens, Delacroix and others gleam like precious jewels. To explore color in the upward direction was futile: Cézanne turned in the opposite direction and explored it downward. This had been attempted by Poussin, Chardin and others, but had never been brought to such consummate perfection. When he sacrificed jewel-like saturation, his color range gained enormously in depth. When this became evident, I found that his color, which had seemed muddy, turned into a pattern of infinite variety of hues and nuances never before seen in art, but constantly before our eyes in nature. It also eliminated my objection to the ruminant surface of his paintings. Cézanne was deeply sensitive to form, and the only way he could project it in space was by breaking up the larger masses into smaller component parts as they move in light in the third dimension. And this in turn can be rendered only by means of neutral nuances of infinite variety.

As for chiaroscuro, his sin is one of omission rather than of commission. Chiaroscuro, as an aesthetic element of design so evident in his first period when it played so dominating a role in the overall pattern, became less and less important as his interest in color deepened. Even in his best canvases it only renders good service by emphasizing forms in their movement in the space. As an aesthetic element, it contributes little to the pictorial pattern of the composition. In old age, the greatest masters became more and more fascinated by the dramatic possibilities of chiaroscuro; we can see this in the last works of Michelangelo, Titian, Rembrandt, Daumier and others. Cézanne, too, fell under its spell; and in his third or last period, there is a reawakened interest in chiaroscuro. But he did not live long enough to bring it to greater fruition. Technically, he also reverted to his first period, again indulging in heavy impasto so characteristic of his earliest efforts.

As a painter I wonder what effect the Cézanne exhibition will have on our younger generation. It could be very salutary if he were taken, not as a model, but as an example. He has been called "the father of modern art." If he is, then the legitimacy of his children is questionable. What kinship can there be between a father whose very soul was intertwined with nature, and the new school of non-objectivists, who have cut loose from the cumbersome ties that inhibit their self-expression? If they are his offspring, then they must suffer from the notorious Oedipus complex and, with pencil, brush, chisel or mallet, are bent on the murder of their outmoded parent. At the moment the prospect is rather glum, for pure abstraction has become the ultimate purpose. There is little likelihood that the avant-garde, as long as it persists in its present direction, can learn anything from his art.

Had non-objective painting been instigated by some orthodox sect with an irresistible urge for graphic expression, who in their piety would not break the commandment "Thou shalt not make thyself a graven thing, nor the likeness of anything that is in heaven above, or in the earth beneath, nor of those things that are in the waters under the earth," there might be excuse for it, if not on aesthetic, then on moral grounds. But its adherents can be found among all creeds: they form a new hierarchy of self-worshippers, devotees of the only deity worthy of worship—oneself. They suffer from inflammation of the ego, not unlike an ingrown toenail that finds its way inward when it cannot move outward. But since the pain is abstract, it really does not matter.

The master of Aix never worried whether his art was abstract or not; he was too preoccupied with the interpretation of his motif. I understand that in Europe there is a movement back to nature, but here we are still passionate adherents of what was up-to-date some time ago in more advanced Europe and is passé there today. The American art student, because of the extraordinary availability of the reproductive processes, has become too pervious to the multitudinous influences of the diverse arts from all over the globe. He is disoriented and makes desultory efforts in every direction. And he is encouraged by the critic who, cognizant of the errors of judgment committed by his past colleagues who condemned what they could not understand, is now likely to commit the same errors in reverse.

In art as in science, ours is the experimental age. When successful, it reveals new horizons. Extensive experiments are being conducted in laboratories, and intensive ones in the studios of artists —who have much more fun, since the artist, unlike the scientist, has no test or criterion to settle once for all whether his experiment is successful or should go down the drain. Only his conscience can answer it. Judging by the pigmentary effusions that have found their way by hook or crook outside the artistic laboratories, his conscience is often caught napping.

Cézanne was not a nihilist; there is no interim between the past and the present. He was both an innovator and a resurrector of worth-while values which had been lost sight of. He had much in common with Johannes Brahms. Both were rebels and deeply traditional; both resurrectors of elemental values that had been dissipated in the stagnant pools of academism or ignored in the feverish haste of the avant-garde; both quick to benefit from contemporaries, but borrowing no more than they could assimilate.

Cézanne was deeply perceptive of his inheritance—a basic tactile sense that is timeless—and keenly conscious of what he had acquired: a color concept introduced by the Impressionists that then seemed temporal. The cultural interval between these extremes had little interest for him.

It is precisely this lack of polish, his utter disregard of good manners, that a cultivated public, with an exaggerated belief that above all the artist must learn to behave himself, resented most. As a matter of fact, he was preoccupied with matters more important than his manners. And it was his disregard of etiquette that interfered with a more sensitive response to what is so vital in his art: the eternal primitive flame that keeps on burning long after the fire of the creator of the flame has burned itself out and only a handful of ashes remains.

# Thomas Wolfe in Berlin

## H. M. LEDIG-ROWOHLT

## ( *1953* )

HEINRICH MARIA LEDIG-ROWOHLT is general manager and a
partner in Rowohltverlag of Hamburg, one of Germany's
leading publishing houses. It was this firm that in 1930 first
published Wolfe's *Look Homeward Angel* in the German
language. Mr. Ledig-Rowohlt met and formed a close friendship with Thomas Wolfe in 1938, when the author came to
Berlin upon an invitation from Mr. Ledig-Rowohlt's father.

IN HIS POSTHUMOUSLY PUBLISHED NOVEL, *You Can't Go Home
Again,* Thomas Wolfe wrote: "Lloyd McHarg was, of course,
one of the chief figures in American letters, and now, at the zenith
of his career, when he had won the greatest ovation one could win,
he had seized the occasion, which most men would have employed
for purposes of self-congratulation, to praise enthusiastically the
work of an obscure young writer who was a total stranger to him
and who had written only one book."

Lloyd McHarg is of course none other than Sinclair Lewis, who
had so highly praised Wolfe's first novel, *Look Homeward, Angel,*
at the Nobel Prize award in Stockholm in 1930. Furthermore,
he had drawn his German publisher's attention to the young
writer's work, and Ernst Rowohlt had eagerly accepted Wolfe's
novel after another important Berlin house had just turned it
down. The last feature editor of the Berlin *Vossische Zeitung,* Dr.
Monty Jacobs, took a chance and ran it as a pre-publication serial.
The experiment was a success: it was the swan song, as it were, of
old Auntie Voss. When the book appeared, it was enthusiastically
received by all the serious German reviewers who were covertly
opposed to cultural *Gleichschaltung,* and Ernst Rowohlt took the
opportunity of inviting Wolfe to Berlin. (In the winter of 1934
Wolfe was on the run, as it were, from the American publication

275

of his new novel, *Of Time and the River;* he had fled to London, where he met Sinclair Lewis for the first time.) So it was in the spring of 1935 that I first met him.

It was a bright, peaceful summer, in the days when we still considered Berlin a busy metropolis. Wolfe had unexpectedly stopped off at Hanover—pursuing some amorous adventure, he told me later with a secret smile—and he arrived in Berlin a day late. I had accepted an invitation to a reception for a well-known foreign correspondent at the American Embassy, and had left a message at the office that Wolfe should just come along. Martha Dodd, the daughter of Ambassador William Dodd, had already been primed for his arrival. The animated conversation was suddenly interrupted by the appearance of a gigantic, embarrassed man who was introduced as the expected writer. I shall never forget the scene: the dark, imposing head towering above all the guests, the almost coquettishly deferential modesty of the giant who was soon the center of the party, and who was blushingly putting himself out to say something friendly all the time and to brush aside any compliments.

Thomas Wolfe did not bestow his friendship lightly. But soon the two of us were affording a queer sight on the Kurfürstendamm between Uhlandstrasse and the Gedächtniskirche: the boyish, happy giant (for a joke, a press photographer put a traffic cop under his arm) and my own slight figure. I soon got to love him as a big brother, and apparently he returned my affection. As he liked to speak only what he called his "cab-driver's German" to simple folk, for whose fates and faces he had an unquenchable curiosity, I was obliged to summon up all my English, which he was later to reproduce with such phonographic exactness. We had as yet no hint of the dangerous uniformity hidden behind Berlin's happy, summery busyness. After New York, Wolfe enjoyed its restful quiet, and from day to day he became more open. One afternoon, in the garden of the Alte Klause, he described how he had got involved in a real *Oktoberfest* fight in Munich and how he, the giant, had thought his opponent dead and how, bleeding from many wounds, he had mistaken the police hospital for a prison hospital. Vividly and with grotesquely exaggerated humor, he described his qualms of conscience and his mental distress, very much as this episode appears later in the *Oktoberfest* section of his novel *The Web and the Rock.*

Our conversations that summer remained predominantly unpolitical. The enthusiastic press he got from stand-pat German

friends transfigured all Berlin for him. But he kept uneasily referring to the lack of news from New York about the success of his
book *Of Time and the River,* which Scribner's had published in
March. He longed for the relief, the liberation of a big success. In
Brooklyn in 1929, he had furtively bought at a kiosk the newspapers with the first reviews of *Look Homeward, Angel.* As he
crossed the streets he had counted the passing cars (an odd or even
number decided whether the criticism was favorable or unfavorable). He had not read the papers in the street, but had hurried
home, anxiously avoiding stepping on the lines between the pav-
ing stones for fear of bad luck. There was something comical and
touching in the way he described his shyness of criticism, and with
that mighty fist that had nearly cost some Bavarian thickhead his
life, he furiously thumped on a little marble table in the Romanische Café, because critics in the United States had declared that
he was just copying from life, and merely from his own life, at that.

Had the big gamble come off this time? "I think the real discovery of America is still ahead of us," he was to say in his last
book.

And he, the mason's son from Asheville, North Carolina, who
had fled from his own eulogies, from America to Europe, was now
in Berlin longing to discover and conquer America.

Night was his time, the North his longing. We climbed up to
my little foxhole of an attic flat on the Kurfürstendamm, in which
he looked grotesque and gigantic. He leaned against the mantel-
piece or squeezed out into the little roof garden, enjoying the sea
of city lights under the starry sky and raving about New York.

And later, when we sat on the other side of the Kurfürstendamm, under the lime trees whose leaves looked Schweinfurt-
green in the artificial light, he told me how, back home in the little mountain town of Asheville, he had heard the trains going
north in the nighttime, and how they had always tempted him to
go north too, into the darkness of the big cities, into the atmosphere of murder and prostitution. One day he would write the
novel of a night express: he would describe the rush of the night-
black streams, the singing of the rails in the clear-sounding darkness, the roar of wheels over bridges and past houses, the manifold echo in the changing landscape. And I had the impression
that those very trains were scurrying by like shadows across his big
broad face. He was proud to be a child of simple folk, and he told
me of his brothers and his boyhood friends, till almost in dismay
I realized that practically all the characters in his books were

really alive. One was now an automobile agent, another was a teacher. They had their own existence and at the same time they lived in him.

He talked while the traffic in the summery Kurfürstendamm night gradually went to sleep. He drank one glass of Moselle after another and went on telling me about his mother, who kept a little boardinghouse (for that reason, he didn't like to stay in boardinghouses) ; about the difficulties facing a writer when he tries to write of his own life and experiences; about how shocked the people of Asheville had been over his first novel, and how upset the kindly reader at Scribner's, who suffered from angina pectoris (when Wolfe had put him into a short story the poor man became the laughingstock of New York literary circles and, as a consequence, had nearly been driven to suicide). And suddenly he asked sharply how we, Ernst Rowohlt and I, would react to such a literary portrait. Rather embarrassed, I said that we would never be so upset as the Scribner's reader, but that we would feel honored to pose as models for literary reality. At the time I didn't know his habit of memorizing the day's conversations and putting them down of a night, word-perfect and sound-perfect, and I certainly didn't foresee that two years later I might easily have been victimized because of this habit. Anyway, I declared, we were probably not interesting enough for portraits of that kind. Thomas Wolfe laughed.

We left the restaurant, and he showed me how, when he was a newsboy, to save time he would throw the papers a considerable distance into his clients' gardens and would excitedly listen for the slap of the paper against the door. With a few quick gestures he skillfully folded the thick Sunday edition of the *Berliner Tageblatt* into a little package which he threw with sure aim right across the Kurfürstendamm straight into the little garden of my house. "Slap" it went, quite clearly in the still of the night, and he laughed like a youngster whose trick has come off.

One unforgettable night, we were in a small artists' *Lokal* in the Kleiststrasse—painters, writers, and young women such as one always finds in that sort of company. Suddenly Thomas Wolfe stood before us, gigantic and beaming, his black hair disheveled. He greeted us loudly, let himself fall into an armchair which groaned under him, and with a wide and jovial gesture he declared to us modest beer-drinkers, "Let's all have some wine—I'm rich!" He was not drunk. He had at last received the awaited letter from New York, and he was intoxicated by the sensational success of his novel *Of Time and the River*. The great gamble that had caused him such anxiety had come off: the American journals published eulogies set out big, with his picture on the front page.

"I'm rich!" said he who was putting up at the Hotel am Zoo with a shabby suitcase and always wore the same dark-brown suit. He was as happy as a child, enjoyed his drinks, seemed like a man set free. We wanted to celebrate the event, so we set off in a big party to the Taverne, the favored *Lokal* of foreign journalists in the Courbièrestrasse. Martha Dodd was there, also in a party. We sat down at the next table, and I wondered why she didn't ask us over. It turned out that she was with Donald Klopfer of Random House, and Klopfer refused to sit at the same table with Germans. I felt as if someone had knocked me on the head: how could a foreigner not distinguish between Germans and Nazis, as we could! For the first time it occurred to me that I was identified with the Nazis, and for the first time I became aware of the gulf that—already, in the summer of 1935—separated us from the rest of the world. I wasn't going to let Klopfer's argument pass: I went over to him and introduced myself. We exchanged a few words about William Faulkner, an author our two houses had in common. But it was a brief and forced conversation, even though Klopfer bit back his feelings enough to shake hands with me. I was upset when I came back to our table, and our former good mood would not return again.

When the party at the neighboring table broke up, Martha whispered furtively to us to come along to coffee at the Embassy. It was some while before we got away from the others, and we arrived as day broke. In the spacious hall we stood like guilty schoolboys. Above us on the broad staircase stood Martha Dodd, ostentatiously holding Wolfe's new book, *Of Time and the River*. Rather pathetically she reproached him with destroying his talents as a writer by excessive drinking. Wolfe foamed with rage. Furiously he stormed up the staircase, snatched from her the thick volume that had sealed his fame as a writer, ripped it out of its cover, tore its thousand pages with his bear's paws, and threw the little bits like a shower of confetti out of the window into the steel-blue morning of the Tiergarten. Martha Dodd was terrified at this outburst of rage and cried, "How can a writer do a thing like that!"

But Wolfe didn't seem to hear. Hadn't he put America's "sober bitter colours" into words as Whitman once had, and hadn't he the success he had longed for in black and white in his pocket?

With giant strides he stormed through the great room, cursing and swearing, and overwhelming with grim recriminations the unhappy girl, who had thrown herself sobbing on the couch. I was helpless. The tension got on my nerves. Eventually I tried to turn the scene into comedy, and began turning somersaults backward and forward over the soft carpet until Wolfe noticed.

He understood immediately. He rushed over to me, embraced me so heartily, so extravagantly that he nearly crushed me in his strong arms: "Henry, you're a great sport, you're wonderful!"

Martha smiled also. The wicked mood was dissolved. Wolfe sat down by her, quietly begging her forgiveness. I shall never forget how the two of them later stood by the very window out of which he had just thrown the fragments of his book, with the dawn sky behind them above the high treetops of the Tiergarten, and the birds just beginning to sing.

We decided to drive out to the Havel and have breakfast there somewhere. The car was waiting at the door, and in the garden the bits of the torn-up book still lay. I picked up a handful and put them in my pocket as a keepsake (I still have them). We drove out to the Grunewald. The freshness of the early summer morning did us good. As we passed the gloomy Grunewaldsee, on whose moor-dark surface the ancient firs were mirrored, two white swans flew up in the shadowy morning stillness, and, simultaneously with their majestic flight, a curious, guttural animal cry of delight came from Wolfe's throat. Joy and ardor played on his powerful face. He who loved the big city above all lived in a mythical harmony with nature. In the Schloss Marquardt the comfortable yellow chairs were still standing on the tables, and instead of waiters, the cleaners had taken charge. For all that, a corner was assigned to us. In a joking mood, Wolfe tore a colored cloth off the table, wrapped it round him with a bold gesture, Indian-fashion, and sat down announcing, "I'm Sitting Bull!" We had a cheerful, noisy breakfast, and returned to town dead tired.

It was still a peaceful summer, though one day Martha Dodd came back from Munich indignant to report that a Jew had been beaten there in the open street and that she had saved him in her car.

Only occasionally did our conversation touch on the murky political situation and on the "Dark Messiah," as Wolfe was later to call Hitler. His political skepticism was still glossed over by joy at his literary success; and besides, he loved Berlin more than any other European capital. He felt how genuine the response was which his mighty figure and his childish lack of affectation awakened everywhere, whether among cab drivers, trolleymen, salesgirls or waiters, or even among German writers, who treated him with respect.

As soon as my work in the office allowed, I would pick him up from the Hotel am Zoo, where a smart little bellhop enjoyed his special affection. Quite often I found him in his hotel room, reading the big Webster's dictionary he always took with him on his travels, reveling in the abundance of the English language and enriching his own vocabulary. He told me about his way of working, and how he would force himself to reconstruct from memory certain rooms in Paris and London, certain people, conversations and situations, down to the slightest detail; how often an overwhelming stream of nostalgic memories would reveal to him the peculiar characteristics of America—how differently the locomotives whistled there and the trains thundered over the bridges—indeed, how it was only when he came abroad that the image of America had first become close to his heart, and how he had needed this spatial distance to realize properly the literary truth of his existence.

Our conversations at that time knew no political restrictions: he was already then that "citizen of humanity" that he called himself in a letter shortly before his death. For everyone who came into contact with him in Berlin, he was the embodiment of that free world that we in Hitler's prison were longing for more and more. He was aware of this, and our response was for him the confirmation of his enormous power.

At night we strolled like two dissimilar brothers through Berlin's West End. I still see him at Anne Menz's on the Augsburgstrasse, eyeing the handsome waitress behind the bar and winking comically and rubbing his knife and fork together like a butcher's knife and steel: "She's a fine piece, I'll cut a slice of her." I see him embracing the trees of the Kurfürstendamm with panic ardor and praying for a big woman appropriate to his size.

The North was his longing. I could not keep him, though I seriously doubted if he would ever return to Germany. He longed for the North, for big handsome women. So one morning he left for Copenhagen. I did not feel happy at the station. I felt that the most important things between us still remained unsaid. I walked by him, ran by him, stayed behind, waved, and did not notice that my face was distorted by the pain of parting and wet with tears. Only later was I to read that Wolfe had noticed it all too well.

In the Olympic summer of 1936, under a provocative forest of swastika flags, Berlin had once again resumed the appearance of an international metropolis. On July 3 we received a letter from Wolfe, posted in New York on June 22, in which he wrote: "I am working hard and getting a lot done; but I confess I am sometimes tempted to get on a fast ship and come over to pay you all a visit, and perhaps see something of the Olympic games. North German Lloyd has written me several letters and suggested that I could earn part or most of my passage over if I could write an article for a travel magazine which they publish; and if you and Ernst could sell a few copies of *Von Zeit und Strom,* may be, I could take you all up and down Kurfürstendamm or to Schlichters'; but get thee behind me, Satan—the idea is too tempting—I had my fling last year, perhaps it is better now that I keep at work."

Meanwhile, *Of Time and the River* had appeared in Hans Schiebelhuth's translation. It promised to be a big success with the critics. But despite enthusiastic reviews, only about four thousand copies were sold up to the beginning of the war. As *Look Homeward, Angel* had sold eight to nine thousand copies, and we had not enough foreign currency to pay him his royalties, I cabled Wolfe that same day to come and use up his money in Berlin.

Three weeks later he was with us, telling us in the old extravagant way how my telegram had torn him away in the middle of his work. That same evening he had impetuously gone down to the docks, and it wasn't till he got there that he discovered he hadn't enough money for the journey.

That evening he was to go to the Embassy, where a reception in honor of Charles Lindbergh was taking place. He skipped around the office in delight, but suddenly he fell into deep despair: he had no clean dress shirt. I calmed him down: nothing could be simpler —we would buy one. It hadn't occurred to me that the Berlin shops of 1936 no longer catered to the measurements of the Potsdam Guard of 1736. Desperately we ran along the Tauentzienstrasse shortly before closing time. It was the same scene in every shop: humbly Wolfe would bend down to let the obliging shopgirl measure his neck; then would follow shrugs of regret that no dress shirt of this titanic size was in stock. Wolfe's temper got worse and worse. This seemingly hopeless hunt was calculated to bring to mind again all the infuriating trouble his size had been causing him for years.

He complained of the miserable rainy day that made him see everything as gray on gray; he cursed the provincialism of Berlin and he cursed Hitler—fortunately in an American that neither the new gentlemen of the Tauentzienstrasse nor the walls of the former Jewish firms understood.

At last we landed up near the Wittenbergplatz in an elegant shop where they took Wolfe for a famous athlete. Again the same humility on the part of the grumbling giant, again the salesgirl's polite shrug, till at last the urgency of our requirements sank into the manager's skull, and he decided to violate a normal dress shirt. Immediately the despair of the giant to whom the world could offer nothing made to measure changed to high glee. Before his eyes a shirt was cut down the back; the sleeves marked for suitable insertions; the excessive size noted down; the starched front, at least, preserved; the whole ingenious patchwork to be delivered at his hotel in time. In his excess of gratitude he wrote his name in the pompous visitors' book which was daily displayed in the shopwindow throughout the Olympic games, and which hitherto had featured only international sporting stars. So beside the healthy bodies, a healthy mind proudly stepped: "With sincere thanks for help in urgency. Thomas Wolfe, writer."

Cheerfully we walked back along the Tauentzienstrasse, and Thomas Wolfe, who was known on both sides of the Atlantic as the Homer of modern America, sang in a stentorian voice a lot of frivolous nonsense which—like the previous curses—none of the astonished passers-by understood.

Because of the Olympic games, the German press was allowed to publicize certain international figures and events. In the office we naturally made good use of this on Wolfe's behalf, though he made no secret of what he thought of Hitler's activities. Patiently and modestly he submitted to many stupid questions. An interview with a big daily paper was arranged for August 6, to take place in Wolfe's hotel room. The interviewer appeared in the company of a newspaper artist, a big handsome blonde who was obviously to Wolfe's fancy. He answered the journalist's questions absent-mindedly, while the artist sat by quietly, seeming to fix in her mind every movement of his lively features. "Berlin?" was an inevitable question. "Wonderful," declared Wolfe superficially, with an admiring glance at the blonde. "If there was no Germany, it would be necessary to invent one. It's a magical country. I know Hildesheim, Nuremberg, Munich, the architecture, the soul of the place, the glory of its history and its art. Two hundred years ago my forefathers emigrated from southern Germany to America." Perhaps fleeing from that glorious history . . . ?

I was relieved that this particular promontory had been safely rounded, and I recounted—with Wolfe only supporting me absently—the episode of the Munich *Oktoberfest* in 1928, and finally the incident of the dress shirt. With this interview, I believed I had been of service to Wolfe the writer, and was rather surprised to be confronted with Wolfe the man, who questioned me enthusiastically about the handsome blonde and seemed delighted with her imposing appearance. I took the whole thing as a passing fancy, and still did on the next day when we sat in the Café Bristol, listening to the radio transmissions from the Olympic Stadium, with Wolfe shouting enthusiastically when the United States won a new medal.

I bought the paper, calmly skipped through the interview, and handed it to Wolfe. He did not read it. True to his custom, he put it in his pocket to read in his hotel room. Next day he was extremely angry and indignant; the blonde's drawing had offended him deeply. He found himself disfigured beyond recognition. He declared with comical pride that in his mother's opinion he was the most handsome of her boys, and suddenly, after a furious glance in the mirror, he asked me in German: "Habe ich ein Schweinsgesicht?" I laughed, but there was no consoling him. Eventually, in all seriousness he declared the blonde had been bribed by the Gestapo. Lately he had come across so many frightening details about the National Socialist regime that he, too, began to suffer under the weight of personal mistrust and political suspicion. Perhaps to divert himself and to forget the big blonde, he wanted to take a trip to Potsdam. I explained that I was not a qualified guide to Potsdam, but he insisted. We brought my wife along, but though we made every effort to cheer Wolfe up, the excursion was an utter failure. At odds with himself, he quarreled with us too; he seemed to have eyes for nothing, and finally he asked just why we were dragging him around all this sober royal Prussian pomposity.

Not until evening did the celebrated Potsdamer Stangenbier and all kinds of sausage specialties make him more peaceably disposed. Even so, on the way back to the station, he would stop for a minute or two by a shopwindow or some mirrored advertising display, and comically craning his neck, he would angrily and thoughtfully compare his handsome, mighty head with the "Schweinsgesicht" with which the artist had given the lie to his mother's opinion.

Throughout this visit the "Dark Messiah" was the recurring subject of our conversations. Wolfe had observed him from the American Embassy box at the Stadium. From Martha Dodd, he got to know more of his deeds and methods than we Germans officially knew. He feared still greater mischief to come, and he realized bitterly that everywhere the men of good will were being oppressed by the men of power, and that Hitler was unleashing nothing but evil in the world.

By these conversations, I came to realize to what a great extent we were being affected by the lack of freedom, and how powerless the individual was. I spoke of the temptation to escape from political pressure by fleeing abroad; I talked insistently to Wolfe, trying to encourage him to write a great novel by which he as a writer, not as a political propagandist, should appeal to the conscience of mankind. He smiled: just because he loved mankind above everything, he would be obliged to be political in such a book. I begged him, for daily he experienced what a source of encouragement his books were to German readers. He had an obligation to these Germans, who were appealing to him. But as soon as he attacked the German government, all his books would be banned in Germany! He understood what I was trying to say, that I was not speaking as a profit-seeking publisher, but as an incorrigible idealist who, in Germany's isolation, did not want to miss the comfort of his books—in short, as that "strange saint" who was later to figure in his account of this summer.

He shook his head. "A man must write what he has to," he declared later in that same account. "A man must do as his convictions order him." I was silent and sad. Between us was already opening the gulf that separated Germany from the democratic countries, and across it we were greeting each other fraternally for the last time. I thought of the many friends who were already no longer within reach.

I was melancholy and depressed, and, though even inside the American Embassy we had to be cautious before the servants, there, behind locked doors, I spoke of my personal troubles and of how under the National Socialist despotism it was becoming increasingly difficult to lead one's private life without interference. Wolfe consoled me, and at the same time he was horrified.

Through my own example it became particularly clear to him how much the tyranny of National Socialism forced us to abandon our individual rights, and how much we Germans were being driven into lonely waters where there was scarcely any communication with each other—became clear to him, and to many Americans who barely nine months later were to become acquainted with all the "highly treasonable" details of our talks.

A big party was given in Wolfe's honor, in Rowohlt's private flat on Rankestrasse, and all literary folk who were still of free opinion were invited, but it showed very clearly to what an extent the tree of our literature was already stripped of its leaves. All the great names of German letters had emigrated. Instead, the unfortunate woman artist was there.

I feared the worst, but Wolfe was soon very intimate with the stately blonde. His rage over the "Schweinsgesicht" was forgotten. He hardly spoke to anyone else, and he left the party in her company. I did not take this flirtation very seriously, and so I was rather surprised next day when Wolfe announced, with comically defiant earnestness, that he and the blonde artist were going off to the Tyrol together. I said nothing against it. For the moment at least, he seemed to be under the influence of some great passion. Wolfe went off, and returned to Berlin alone at the beginning of September. He was cross and disappointed, and I gathered from random remarks that he had left his blonde traveling companion standing in some Alpine meadow and come back. I asked no questions, but I thought I deduced from his allusions that everything essentially feminine irresistibly attracted and at the same time repelled him. He spoke of bitter experiences in New York, of importunate and ambitious women who had caused him much anger and had sharpened his mistrust.

I do not know whether he ever again saw this woman whom he had loved very much for a short time; neither do I know whether some political reason lay behind their disagreement. The only remarkable thing is that this experience apparently left in Wolfe some poisoned sting. He was irritable and oversensitive; he wanted to get away, to go home via France, but the homeward journey was delayed time and again by currency difficulties. He no longer made any secret of his animosity toward Germany and National Socialism. His mistrust was nourished when Rudolf Grossmann wanted to make a portrait of him for *Querschnitt* and arrived with a man unknown to me, who invited Wolfe to visit a labor camp. Wolfe got out of the invitation, and I later advised him to keep away from anything that could in any way be used as Nazi propaganda.

The poisoned atmosphere must have seemed completely impenetrable to him when we met a literary man in the Romanische Café, whom we nicknamed "The Prince of Darkness." He made the priggish remark about Hemingway that he was stuck and showed no signs of developing any more; and, moreover, he permitted himself to make tactless remarks about Wolfe's brown hat. Wolfe was furious. I told him a number of details about the man, who was absolutely no Nazi and who emigrated shortly afterward. But the tragedy was slowly dawning on Wolfe. "It was the creeping paralysis of mistrust that crippled and infected all relations between men and peoples," I was later to read in his book. "It was a poison against which there was no antidote, and from which no salvation was to be found." I tried to explain this latent condition: I wanted to make him understand how careful one had to be, even with literary friends—with the result that Wolfe was soon suspicious of us too. He thought it improbable that, despite all the literary reverberations, so few copies of his books had been sold. Though officially the "creeping paralysis of mistrust" between us had subsided, it went on smoldering underground.

After Wolfe had missed his ship several times, partly through his own fault, partly through delay over the granting of currency, we went on a spree in the old way for the last time. Wolfe seemed to be the prey of some inexplicable uneasiness, and the drunker he got, the more touchy he became. Suddenly the "Schweinsgesicht" worried him again. Then the question of royalties came up, without our managing to bring any light to that dense thicket of misunderstanding. Wolfe used his early-morning departure as an excuse to hurry away. I was helpless and unhappy. I went after him, and found him in a bar in the company of a doubtful girl and a silly youngster. He was furious that I had tracked him down: "Why do you spy on me?" But I wouldn't let him chase me away, for I was afraid that in his irritable mood he might say something indiscreet and miss his train. We drank some more, and in the street he started a quarrel. Eventually I left him in a drunken rage. This time I had no tears. Our parting seemed as absurd as everything else around me. The creeping poison seemed to have destroyed our friendship too. Dead tired, I staggered to bed and slept well into the bright day. In the afternoon I found a note from him at the office: "Never mind our trouble. Love to both of you. Tom."

A friendly post card from Paris followed, then a sparse correspondence, and finally many of our letters remained unanswered. Early in 1937, Martha Dodd returned to Berlin after a visit to the United States. She rang one afternoon and asked me to see her. She talked of New York and of Wolfe, about whom she was worried. I figured in his new novel; that was why she had rung me. Flattered, but somewhat anxious too, I lightly passed it off. She remained terribly serious: the way in which Wolfe had presented me and my conversations was rather dangerous for me personally; I had better read it for myself. And she handed me a copy of the *New Republic,* which was lying on the table.

Right on the front page was a bold reference to Thomas Wolfe's new novel about "Nazi Germany." The published extract was called "I Have a Thing to Tell You." I feared the worst. This was the phrase with which I had begun all my "atrocity stories," all my discourses on the political situation. I read on, and went alternately hot and cold with shock. In this short story, which is included word for word in his last novel, *You Can't Go Home Again,* Thomas Wolfe had worked over all our conversations with phonographic exactness, with a few deviations, of course, from reality. He had brought together his visits of both summers, 1935 and 1936, and had set them in the Olympic summer, so that the furious ill-humor of 1936 was dampened or even neutralized by the easy, cheerful mood of 1935. For all that, any careful observer must have been able to reconstruct the reality of it down to the last detail.

Though I appeared as a librarian under the name of Franz Heilig, and spoke a dry, schooled-on-Shakespeare English, all my personal circumstances were described exactly. Reading it took my breath away and brought the tears to my eyes. Wolfe had spitted me with his pen, had given a merciless X-ray picture of me with all the constraint, all the inner contradictions that the tactical juggling of those years involved and that he, as an American, simply could not understand. If these facts became known, if some unfriendly contemporary revealed the secret of Franz Heilig, then my fate was sealed. I was confused and shattered.

The latent fear in which we were living then became a naked terror. Martha Dodd took a serious view of it, for she knew that the New Republic was read and "gutted" in Goebbels' Propaganda Ministry. She advised me to leave Germany, with her help, as quickly as possible.

I needed time to think. Rowohlt calmed me down and tried to belittle the whole affair, and as he was curious about his own literary portrait, he proposed that I should first of all translate the text. After a restless night, during which I destroyed many valuable letters and souvenirs, or at least hid them before the Gestapo pounce, I set to work; and as I translated, I was again moved by the human greatness that spoke out of every line of Thomas Wolfe. "Not as a political propagandist, but as a writer," I had implored him some nine months before. Here indeed, a writer had seized on an outstanding political situation, had "written what he had to write," and had made his appeal to the conscience of mankind. We who had spent two summers with him were clay in his hands. He had shaped the clay and had brought it to life with the spirit of an objective truth of which we, with our prejudices, were hardly capable.

I was not offended like the Scribner's reader, though I was placed in a far more dangerous position than ever he was. I was faced with a movingly objective image of myself. I understood what Thomas Wolfe had not directly expressed. I understood too, now, why he no longer wrote to us, why he did not dare to send us news. I understood how imperceptibly and how fatefully our view of the world, of life and of ourselves had threatened to become changed and falsified under the pressure of National Socialism. I thought everyone must recognize who Franz Heilig was. I could no longer sleep peacefully. Every ring at the door of my flat made me start up in fright. I was afraid, and still I stayed in Germany. Later, I heard that "I Have a Thing to Tell You" caused quite a stir in the United States. Luckily for me, the fragment remained unknown in Germany for the time being, until Will Vesper referred to its publication in the New Republic. I thought my last hour had come indeed when Gestapo officials appeared at the office one afternoon. Crazy ideas of escape chased through my head—excuses, intellectually intricate counterarguments. But their visit was "only" concerned with the confiscation of the book Die Grüne Front, which had attacked the reactionary German agrarian policy. They wanted to know what had become of its author, Erwin Topf.

It did not occur to the Gestapo to look for the original of Franz Heilig. But Franz Heilig was often close by me—long after Thomas Wolfe's early death in September, 1938, which shook me

289

more than the events of Godesberg and Munich that sealed the fate of Germany.

Amidst the later desolation I recalled the ominous ending of "I Have a Thing to Tell You," which I knew by heart: "There-fore," he thought, "old master, wizard Faust, old father, of the ancient and swarm-haunted mind of men, old earth, old German land with all the measure of your truth, your glory, beauty, magic, and your ruin; and dark Helen burning in our blood, great queen and mistress, sorceress—dark land, dark land, old ancient earth I love—farewell!"

# The Turn of the Tide

## H. M. TOMLINSON

### ( *1953* )

An English writer and a master of sensitive and colorful nar-
ratives about the sea, the late H. M. TOMLINSON is best
known for *The Sea and the Jungle, Tidemarks* and *Gallions
Reach,* a novel. This essay is from *A Mingled Yarn,* a volume
of autobiographical writings published in 1953 to commemorate Mr. Tomlinson's eightieth birthday.

AT THE LOWEST OF THE EBB of a spring tide, just where the
smooth sands of Burra are so saturated that their polish in-
verts the sky, and on a day when a flat sea makes no division between land and water, some dark hummocks appear. They are not
uncovered except at low water of a spring tide, but then they are
plain, though of no height; that dark area in the miles of shining
and immaculate strand is then as notable as would be a ship
ashore.

Visitors seldom trouble to go down to see what the nondescript
markings are. It is too far. They keep to the ridge of blue-grey
boulders which protects the land from the breakers of storms.
From those boulders to the sea is a long descent into windy space,
when the tide is out, even on a fair day of summer. It is too far
down into an empty but brilliant world. The people who are making holiday keep to the ridge, which shelters the village; it is
easier and more natural to stroll the other way, down the hither
side of the boulders, and up the street, to the shops and houses and
the assurance to be had from seeing other people about. There is
nothing to windward, before the turn of the tide, but the glinting
of the Atlantic.

When we were young it surprised us to see that distant blemish
on the polish of the sands at low water. What was it? It was as
though the sea had left one of its secrets ashore, in daylight,

291

though whether it was in the water or really at the edge of the beach it was impossible to say. It was a flaw in a mirror. Yet nobody appeared to notice it. Nobody was curious. Nobody suggested an exploration. And certainly it was strange and a little fearful, all that air and light to seaward. It was vast and bright and without sound, and perhaps we were better off where we were, on the boulders, which were solid and heavy, with much that was curious secreted in their damp crevices. Out beyond our foothold the world did not seem real or safe—so much space and so shimmering a brightness. Even the sands were shining, and shivered in a breeze like the skin of a bubble. If we trod on it, that bubble might burst, and down we should go to the clouds, which we could see floated below the beach as well as above it. Out there the air quivered. That world was too far and radiant to be safe. It did not look like the earth at all, but only the wide silence beyond the earth. If a wave moved in, it was only a brief shadow; it broke, and you could not hear it. It only glittered for a second. If we went down into that light, we might be like that white gull, which was soaring there for a moment, then turned with a flash and was not there.

Next morning we saw that more of the dark area was uncovered by the edge of the sea. Without saying where we were going, and without even telling each other what we wanted to know, two of us idled away and somehow found ourselves looking for shells nearer and nearer to the great light. Presently, when we glanced back, we saw we were sundered. If anyone had signaled to us from the boulders, we should not have known who it was. It might not have been for us. The ridge of rocks appeared to be of no account now. There did not seem enough of it to keep the sea from the land. If our friends were still resting upon it, they were only markings we could not make out. We were alone. But the bubble on which we walked did not burst. It only darkened around our feet at every step we took, as though we were not heavy enough to break the film. We had left the solid ground, and must go on. The sea was nearer and plainer. The horizon stood above us. In a little while these sands, which were the sea-floor, would be claimed again.

The black markings, when we reached them, appeared to be of no importance at all. We had come to a patch of tough and darkened clay. The sea had smoothed it, rounded its corners, varnished it here and there with a green glaze. It was pitted with the holes of a boring shellfish. We saw the white shells in places, sticking out from holes like double razors. Rills and gushes of the tide made islands of these hummocks, and between them were deep pools. It was a curious place, exposed and lonely, and the pools were alive with shrimps. In one tank of glass a cuttlefish, just as we arrived, shot through like a gleam of blue light. He vanished somehow, though we could not see where he had gone; he had spread among the vague colors at the deep bottom of the pool. But while we were still trying to find him, we noticed what we thought was a black leg-bone sticking from the clay by the edge of the water. We tried to get it out, but it was brittle, and snapped. It was not a bone, but a root of a tree.

What was a root doing there? Then we saw the clay was full of black bones. On its wet surface the roots coiled about as they do in life, which was very puzzling, for how could they have grown there? The clay was full of roots.

So our first guess, that a tree afloat had foundered there years ago, would not account for it. We took our spades and dug into it, and then found we could part the stiff black paste into layers as thin as paper, for it was like a mass of pressed leaves. It *was* of leaves. We found the familiar outline of an oak leaf, just as one does in the old soil in the shadow of a wood. While wondering over that, pulling a lump of the rubbish to pieces to see what was inside it, we found a hard, round object—why, of course, though it might have been a carving in ebony, it was a hazelnut! Had all this stuff grown where we saw it?

We looked back to the ridge of boulders. It was a mile away. It was too distant to make out anyone on it, or even what it was. Only the old church tower on the hill behind it was recognizable, and the houses. There was no forest, we knew, for many miles inland. Then the first impulse of the returning tide began to send thin layers of water in arcs up to our feet. The pool with the cuttlefish became agitated and thick with sand. Nothing like a forest was near us. The water was becoming noisy. It was time to go.

What did this discovery mean? Leaves and nuts and shellfish, yet the sea, too, which drove us away! How could such things be together? Oak roots and a cuttlefish! Things had got mixed. The sea was where the land used to be.

We did not talk about it on our return journey to the rocks and our friends. It is not easy to understand, when you begin to see that the sea and the land can change places. How long does it take? Does it take more than a lifetime? The queer shimmering of the wet sands before us in wind and light helped the suggestion that the earth was not so solid as we had thought it, and that strange things could happen and nobody know it. I remember that our elders were not very interested in our discovery. They were talking of other things. What was this old forest? There were no hummocks to be seen then. The tide was rolling over them, in so short a while. We might have been mistaken; but I had the hazelnut in my pocket, though that was not much to show for so great a change. Our elders, in fact, were talking of a piece of good fortune which had come to somebody. It concerned that field behind the rocks on which we were sitting. It had been bought, that field, for next to nothing. Somebody had got it, and was going to build a house there. Could there be a better place? An excellent site, somebody remarked. So near to the beach, and sheltered from the wind. Its value would increase as this secluded little hamlet became better known, as it deserved to be.

How long ago was that morning? It does not seem long ago. That hazelnut still survives, and as I look at it on my desk, I can see the wet sand darkening round our feet as we walk in the sun. As who walks? Where are the people who sunned themselves that day on the rocks? They all cannot meet again. When last year I was on those rocks, in a glance the world appeared as it did yesterday, or years ago. There were the hummocks. The boulders were in place. That light out beyond might have been the eternal light; it had not ceased to quiver, as though alive and immortal, and even the gull reappeared in a flash as I watched. Perhaps the ridge of boulders did not seem to be as high as when we first knew it, but there could be more than one reason for that.

Yes, our memory was at fault. When I looked round, there was the scene which had given us, long ago, the happiness of abiding tranquillity. That immense gulf of brightness assured us still of a changeless and radiant peace. The clouds were the same clouds. Those waves, advancing in leisurely ranks, falling along the strand in deliberation, were the same waves. The transient arcs of thin glass, rimmed with foam which the tide impelled over the sands, were so familiar that they could have been there all the time, more lasting than the works of men.

"Well," said my companion, "then this will be the field which someone was lucky enough to buy. Must be, I think. There was no other."

Yes, it was the field, what was left of it. Whoever the man was, he had built his house, but it was the worse for the weather. He had ceased to live in it. When? He had made a garden, but the ridge of boulders had invaded it. Rocks were scattered before his dilapidated porch. The tops of the garden pales projected, in places, only just above the stones. The invasion was real and deep; part of the roof of the house was blown awry.

There could be no doubt about it. This was the place. There used to be a row of cottages opposite that field, with a path between; and there they were still, though changed. The path was not to be seen. Boulders filled the end of the little street which had been kept so neat. The row of cottages had shrunk, but I could not guess by how much. At the seaward end of the row, the dead turf of old gardens was hanging from a little cliff of crumbling sand. One cottage, at least, had gone. On the wall above us a rag of faded wallpaper fluttered, and a firegrate beside it was high out of reach, with all the Atlantic before it, but no floor.

# Three American Philosophers

## GEORGE SANTAYANA

## ( *1953* )

GEORGE SANTAYANA, distinguished philosopher and poet, died in Rome in September, 1952. This manuscript was found among his papers.

THE ARTICLE in the November issue of *Humana* on *Spirito e Orientamento della Filosofia in America*, excellent on its general theme, prompts me to add something concerning the *special characters*, backgrounds and doctrines of the three persons considered.

It is only John Dewey who genuinely represents the mind of the vast mass of native, sanguine, enterprising Americans. He alone has formed a philosophic sect and become a dominant academic influence. He inherits the Puritan conscience, grown duly practical, democratic, and positivistic; and he accepts industrial society and scientific technique as the field where true philosophy may be cultivated and tested.

Dewey is a native of Vermont, the most rural and retired of the New England States, where philosophy was represented in his youth mainly by popular preachers; but his critical mind at once rejected all that seemed myth or dogma, and adopted the general outlook of Hegel, whom he still praises for his breadth of view. This initial attachment is important because it explains how society and history may be regarded as composing the reality ultimately to be appealed to in philosophy; the physical world and the individual mind may then be dismissed as conventional and specious units, what Hegel called abstractions. For Hegel, society and history composed the "Phenomenology of Spirit"; but Spirit is not mentioned by Dewey, and the panorama of the world remains the ever-varying subject matter of knowledge, a panorama floating and growing in its own medium.

In middle life, Dewey passed to Chicago where he founded his school of pragmatic or instrumental logic; the atmosphere could not have been more radically practical and realistic. But the value of pure disinterested speculation was duly acknowledged, because out of its apparently most useless flights important practical results may follow unexpectedly, as from the relativity of Einstein or the splitting of the atom.

Later, passing to New York, Dewey became a leader also in humanitarian and political movements, even far away from America, in China or in the Russia of Trotsky. From the centre of capitalist and imperialistic America he seemed to diffuse a contrary purely humanitarian influence; yet with a special qualification. Luxury and inequality were indeed to be deprecated: on the other hand, ignorance and poverty were to be extirpated all the world over. To remain simple peasants from generation to generation was not to be allowed. The whole world must be raised to American standards.

I think we may fairly say that in Dewey, devotion to the distinctly modern and American subject matter of social experience has caused him to ignore two prior realities which the existence of that experience presupposes. One reality is the material world in which this experience arises and by which its development is controlled. The other reality is the transcendental spirit by which that whole dramatic process is witnessed, reconsidered and judged. His system therefore may be called a social moralism, without cosmology and without psychological analysis.

In William James, on the contrary, who jointly with Dewey was the apostle of pragmatism, psychological analysis was the high court of appeal. His breeding and background were those of a man of the world and largely European, his education irregular, and his interests manifold. At first he wished to be a painter, then studied medicine, finally from medicine, or as a part of it, turned to psychiatry and psychology. In general philosophy he resisted the systematic Germans and followed the British empiricists, then represented by J. S. Mill. But there was another interest, contrary to a dry empiricism, which inwardly preoccupied him. His father was one of those independent American sages, in the style of Emerson and the Transcendentalists of New England, who possessed inarticulate profound insights and browsed on the mystic wisdom of all ages and countries. The son too had an irresistible intuition of spiritual freedom and, his wife being a Swedenborgian, was especially drawn to the study of psychical revelations. Ultimately he wrote his *Varieties of Religious Experience*—by far his most influential book—in which he showed his strong inclination to credit supernormal influences and the immortality of the soul.

All this, however, was a somewhat troubled hope which he conscientiously tested by all available evidence; and his most trusted authorities were often French, Renouvier and later Bergson; thus the textbook in psychology which we had under him in 1883, at Harvard, was Taine's *De l'Intelligence*. It was only much later that he produced the sensational theories by which he is known, at least by hearsay, all the world over: his *Pragmatism,* in which the reality of truth seemed to be denied, and his article entitled "Does Consciousness Exist?" where he answered this question in the negative.

In that article James takes an important, if not the final, step in the phenomenalistic analysis of experience. If we reject matter with Berkeley and spirit with Hume, we have only data or phenomena with which to compose the universe. But the immense extent and dark detail of nature, as science conceives them, are not data for human beings; if we are to credit science, as pragmatism should, we must therefore admit that the world is composed of phenomena that are self-existent; and those that fall within the magnetic field of our action will form our minds, while the rest, equally self-existent, will compose the rest of the universe. Things and ideas, on this view, are of the same stuff, but belong to different sequences or movements in nature. This system has been worked out later by Bertrand Russell and the school of "Logical Realists" or "Logical Analysts," and if it were found tenable would give William James a high place among modern philosophers.

As for me, it is only by accident that I am numbered among American philosophers. I cannot be classed otherwise, since I write in English and studied and taught for many years at Harvard College, near Boston. My mother's older children by her first marriage were Americans on their father's side; and that fact caused my father to take me to Boston to be educated. But in feeling and in legal allegiance I have always remained a Spaniard. My first philosophical enthusiasm was for Catholic theology; I admired, and still admire, that magnificent construction and the spiritual discipline it can inspire; but I soon learned to admire also Hellenistic and Indian wisdom. All religions and moralities seem to me forms of paganism; only that in ages of ripe experience or of decadence they become penitential and subjective. When a student my *vade mecum* was Lucretius; and of modern philosophers I never intimately accepted any except Spinoza, and in a measure Schopenhauer, if we may take "Will" to be a metaphorical substitute for the automatism of nature, as when he says that the Will to Live of a possible child causes young people to fall in love. I cannot understand what satisfaction a philosopher can find in artifices, or in deceiving himself and others. I therefore like to call myself a materialist; but I leave the study and also the worship of matter to others, and my later writings have been devoted to discovering the natural categories of my spontaneous thought, and restating my opinions in those honest terms. It is essentially a literary labour, a form of art; and I do not attempt to drive other people to think as I do. Let them be their own poets.

# America and Art

## LOUIS KRONENBERGER

## ( *1953* )

Deft writing and astute perception are the hallmarks of Louis
Kronenberger's drama, literary and social criticism. In this
article, which later appeared in his book *Company Manners,*
Mr. Kronenberger censures Americans for exalting the synthetic and thereby betraying the desire and ability to create.

THE COMPELLING FACT ABOUT ART IN AMERICA is that it is not
organic. It has almost no share in shaping our life; it offers,
rather, compensation for the shapelessness. And just because we
prescribe a certain amount of art for ourselves as a kind of corrective—being "deficient" in art as we might be in calcium or
iron—we regard it less as ordinary nourishment than as a tonic,
something we gulp rather than sip, regard with esteem and yet
suspicion, and either require to be made up with a pleasant taste
or exult in because it tastes unpleasant. The American feeling, or
lack of feeling, for art has been immemorially easy to satirize,
whether at the one extreme of Babbittry or at the other of Bohe-
mia. All the same, for whatever reasons, such feeling has long been
part of the American character—which is to say that the American
bent, the American genius, has honestly moved in other directions.
Like the Romans and the Germans, we are not an artistic people.
This may be partly the result of our so long being able to reach
out, rather than having to turn inward; of our possessing a vast
continent to traverse, subdue, explore, develop, grow rich on, so
that there was no husbanding or skilled handling of resources,
no modifying what we started with or were saddled with into
something gracious and expressive. A race, like an individual,
develops a style in part through what it has uniquely, in part
through what it has too little of. French prose owes its dry, neat
lucidity to the same things that produced a general lack of magic
in French poetry; French women owe their chic, I would think,

to their general lack of girlish beauty. Americans have suffered from overabundance—from not needing to substitute art for nature, form for substance, method for materials. At the very point where a patina might begin to appear, or mellowness to suffuse, we have abandoned what we made for something newer, brisker, shinier; and with each such act, we have become a little less "artistic" in our approach. But of course there is more to it than that. An artistic people—the French, the Chinese, the ancient Greeks—is one whose necessities are made the comelier by its dreams, but whose dreaming is equally controlled by its necessities: the two are integrated, are never so harshly at odds that the dreaming must serve as a lurid compensation. With an artistic people, a kind of good sense regulates both its acquisitive side and its aspiring one; and from deprecating excess on a large scale, it eventually does so in small ways as well. Hence the design of existence stands forth more powerfully than the décor; and because design, unlike décor, affects a whole society, the national traits and instincts and responses get beyond cost or size or class, and equally characterize the rich and the poor, the cultivated and the unlettered. There is always a sense of bone structure about an artistic people—think of the Spaniards—a touch of severity, of economy. There is, I suppose, something rather classic than romantic—a sense of the ancestor as well as the individual.

An artistic people need not (and very likely will not) be profoundly poetic or mystical, as the English and the Germans are. It is plainly because the English and the Germans lead such double lives, because one extreme must almost atone for the other, because dreaming grows out of repressions or helps to stamp out reality, that two nations so given to vulgar instincts and material aims should be capable of such splendid intensities—intensities which, for all that, do constitute excesses. And we too, as a people, are driven to compensate; are so excessively aspiring for being so excessively acquisitive; come back to God through guilt or satiety; go on binges with Beauty because it is no part of our daily life—and we somehow think the extent of the undertaking will make up for the quality. Our magnates are always giving away millions not too shiningly acquired; our aging plutocrats leave a spendthrift order for art like the flashy sports who buy their women ten dozen American Beauty roses. Nothing amuses or appalls us more than a gangster's funeral with its carloads of flowers and wreaths; and nothing teaches us less. The gangster's funeral is actually the model for Broadway's super-musicals, for the murals on civic architecture, for Florida's luxury resorts; and the gangster's funeral is itself a late development, the descendant of the Newport "cottage"—the only difference being that at Newport conspicuous waste was confined to living, where in Chicago it specialized in death.

But it is not just the excesses born of wealth that have failed to make us an artistic people. After all, corsairs and conquistadors are the ancestors of *most* cultures; and French châteaux and Italian palazzi of even the best periods stress sheer display quite as much as they stress beauty. We may just come near enough to being an artistic people to explain why we *are* not and perhaps *cannot be* one. We are an inventive and adaptive people; and thus our whole effort, our whole genius, is to modify rather than mold, to make more efficient rather than more expressive. We are dedicated to improvement—to improving our minds and our mousetraps, our inventions and our diets. We are so dedicated to improvement that we neither ask nor care whether a thing needs to be improved, is able to be improved, or, qualifying as an improvement, will necessarily seem like a benefit. We never seem to wonder whether we may not be complicating things by simplifying them, or making them useless by so constantly making them over. But the ability to invent, the desire to improve, may partly spring from our having got so much later a start than other civilizations—from our being at a log-cabin and homespun stage when Europe had long achieved silks and marble, and then lagging for so long behind them. We first were made competitive from a sense of our marked inferiority to others; we then became, from our sense of our natural wealth and resources, competitive among ourselves; and we are now, of course, inventive *because* we are competitive: last year's model must be disparaged so that this year's model can be sold. But no matter how genuine was the original impulse, or how sheerly commercial it is today, inventiveness has become ingrained in our practice, and our source of constant pride; and even among the best of us—unless we are extremely vigilant—it is now an influence on our taste. Abroad, avant-gardism expressed the crying need among old cultures for new forms and feelings; here, we often seem to be breaking with tradition before establishing it; here, experiment has a gadget air, a will-to-invent about it, as often as a sense of rebellion or release. This gadget aspect crops up everywhere, in the most unexpected places. Thus, our highbrow criticism is constantly inventing and amending a vocabulary

—one that somehow will seem a special, up-to-the-minute possession of critics, exactly as the latest models in cars or television
sets will seem a special, up-to-the-minute possession of prosperous
suburban life. The actual character, too, of our present-day
literary jargon—so much of it psychiatric and sociological—is
that of a profoundly inartistic, indeed, an aesthetically quite
barbarous yet irrepressibly inventive people. Take just one simple example. In the entire language I doubt whether there exists
an uglier word, or one less needed for the use it has been put to,
than the word *sensitivity*. One special and particular meaning
could be allowed it—the sensitivity, let us say, of a photographic
plate to light. But even among critics with a historical sense and a
cultivated ear, it has almost completely ousted the two words that
for centuries so happily shouldered, and so neatly divided, the
burden: *sensibility* and *sensitiveness*. But the whole highbrow
vocabulary, the whole need for new spring-and-fall models in
literary language—*subsume* one year, *mystique* the next, *exfoli-
ate* the year after—exhibits our national need to adapt and
amend and apply at any cost, with no great concern for the
urgency, and perhaps even less for the rightness, of the words
themselves. And even more indicative than their original "coinage" is the indecent speed with which they become almost unbearable clichés; even more, also, than their coinage itself is the
fact that they are so uniformly pretentious, so very rarely picturesque. If only critics would read Dr. Johnson for his wisdom
and not for his choice of words. We are inartistic, indeed, in our
very approach to art.

We have never as a people regarded art as something to live
with, to freely delight in, to call by its first name. Perhaps this
derives from something beyond an inventive streak that keeps us
restless, or an awe that makes us uncomfortable: perhaps had we
had more opportunity to live with art, we might have acquired a
more relaxed attitude toward it. It has never been on our door-
step; we have had to go in search of it, go doubly in search—as
much to discover what it is as where it is. The journeys have had
a little of the air of pilgrimages; the works of art, a great deal of
the sanctity of shrines. The whole burden of our criticism, our
constant cultural plaint, is how scant, and impure, and imperfect,
and isolated art in America has been—which, inevitably, has conditioned our approach to it. We insist on strong, emphatic, un-
mistakable reactions; we either swoon or snub, analyze at tedious
length or dismiss with a mere wave of the hand. We go at art, in

other words, not like casual, cultivated shoppers, but like a race of antique-shop dealers for whom everything is either magnificently authentic or the merest fake; and the result—though of course there are other reasons, too—is that we cannot take art in our stride. So belated and uneasy an approach has made us about art what Prohibition made my whole generation about wine: either frank, unblushing ignoramuses or comically solemn snobs. Different levels of Americans reveal very different attitudes toward art; but what is perhaps most significant is that they all reveal one marked kind of attitude or another. They either tend to hold back lest they commit howlers; or to go into raptures lest they be taken for clods; or to pooh-pooh the whole business lest they seem longhaired and sissified; or to purse their lips and utter pronunciamentos lest they seem just vulgarly susceptible or humanly responsive.

If classifying them as fence-straddlers or as poseurs or as philistines or as prigs is to simplify and even travesty the matter, it may yet help account for the fact that we are not a people for whom, at any level, art is just a natural and congenial aspect of existence. The very "uselessness" of it—the fact that art, like virtue, is its own reward; again, the very magic of it—the fact that it cannot be reduced to a formula or equation; the utter arrogance of it— the fact that money cannot buy it nor American salesmanship or elbow grease achieve it: these are, at the very outset, reasons for mystification and distrust. *Its* kind of arrogance, or refusal to be won on extrinsic terms—as of a high-mettled, beautiful girl whom no suitor can win on the strength of his bank account, his family background, or his sober, industrious habits—seems improper, even unethical, to a people who can respect putting a high price on something, who can approve and even enjoy a hard tussle till things are won, but who can no more understand than they can approve that something is beyond negotiations, is just not to be bought. Art to them is not a high-mettled girl, but an extremely unreasonable woman. Art's kind of magic again—art's refusal to be achieved through laboratory methods, through getting up charts or symposiums or sales conferences, through looking at smears under the microscope—its magic seems behind the times, almost downright retarded, to a people with a genius for the synthetic. Art's kind of uselessness, finally—its non-vitamin-giving health, its non-pep-you-up modes of pleasure, its non-materialistic enrichment—quite genuinely confuses a people who have been educated to have something to show for their efforts, if only a title or a medal or a diploma. Art, for most

Americans, is a very queer fish—it can't be reasoned with, it can't be bribed, it can't be doped out or duplicated; above all, it can't be cashed in on.

Someone, Max Beerbohm perhaps, once defined a Bohemian as a person who uses things for what they're not intended—a window drapery, let us say, for a ball dress, or a goldfish bowl for a soup tureen. And this just a little defines the American sense of the artistic. We must endow everything with a new twist, an added value, an extra function. We literally cannot let well enough alone; hence we very often make it worse—and never more, perhaps, than when we also make it better. The new element, the new effect, the new use to which an art form is put, very often has to do with achieving something more tractable or palatable or painless or time- or labor-saving; with offering, at the very least, old wine in new bottles, and much more to our satisfaction, old wine in plastic containers or ice cream cones. Thus we have Somerset Maugham re-edit and abridge the classics; we get a present-day version of Buckingham's *The Rehearsal,* a Negro *Juno and the Paycock,* a *Cherry Orchard* laid in Mississippi; we have Mr. Orson Welles telescoping five of Shakespeare's plays into one; we have something written for the piano performed on the violin, something intended for men taken over by women. We're not, to be sure, the only nation that does such things; but I think we're the only nation that feels a compulsive urge to do them. Where the Germans have a particular genius for ersatz, for substitutions, we have one for new twists and gimmicks, new mixtures and combinations. We simply *have* to tamper: if we don't cut the words, we must add to the music; if we don't change the story, we must shift the locale. Nowhere else, surely, can there be such a compulsion to make plays out of books, musicals out of plays, *Aida*'s into *My Darlin' Aida*'s; to insert scenes, delete characters, include commentators; to turn gas stations into cathedrals, or churches into dance halls. Out of Plato and Berkeley we get transcendentalism; out of transcendentalism we concoct Christian Science; and then, almost immediately, Jewish Science out of Christian. Many nations have discovered the devil in dancing, but we are perhaps the first to find God through calisthenics. And no doubt we create from all this the illusion that we are notably experimental in the arts, ever seeking new forms, contriving new functions, establishing new perspectives. But, even ignoring the material or commercial side of it all, our contrivance of so many artful blends and twists and variants is really our avoidance of art itself, exactly as our craving for sensations argues a distaste for, or fear of, experiences. Our whole artistic effort, if it does not parallel, then at least involves our genius for concocting the mixed drink and for putting the packaging ahead of the product. The result—from which almost all of us suffer more than we realize—is a kind of vulgarization, and one that can take place at high levels no less than at low ones. Our stressing significance in art rather than intensity, our present search for symbolic figures and concealed meanings and multiple levels: isn't this part of our compulsion to introduce something new, add something extra, offer something unprecedented? Does it not bear witness, also, to our intellectual ingenuity rather than our aesthetic responsiveness? Hasn't the new multi-level *Pierre* or Confidence Man a kinship with the new split-level house, or the concealed meanings with the concealed plumbing, or the indirect approach with the indirect lighting, or the taste for knotty problems with the taste for knotty pine? I do not think I am being anti-intellectual when I say that in America the intellect itself is being over-used and misused in the world of art, where—after all—the most thoughtful elucidation avails nothing without the right, pure, instinctive response; for in art the reverse of Wordsworth's saying is also true and immensely important: in art, there are tears that do often lie too deep for thoughts.

Given our inventiveness, such endless and manifold vulgarization is inevitable. No race can make an idea go farther than we can. We get the last ounce of derivable income from it: we carry it, indeed, to distances that virtually obscure the original starting point. From the classic sandwich made with bread, we evolve the triple-decker made with ice cream; from the first motel, that could hardly have competed with a bath house, we are now contriving structures that will outdo—if not soon outmode—the Ritz. And quite beyond our double-barreled desire to make things profitable as well as attractive, all this technical skill and inventive cleverness must in the end conspire as much against our creative instincts as against our artistic ones. A nation that can so marvelously concoct must less and less feel any need to create. We are developing a genius for rewrite at the expense of one for writing, for stage directors who will do the work of dramatists, for orchestrators who will do the work of composers. Everything today must carefully and exactly conform to public taste, yet offer a new wrinkle into the bargain—we insist on what might be called a kind of Murphy-bed of Procrustes.

The effect of this vulgarization is almost sure to be pervasive and permanent. There is something disarming, often indeed unnoticeable, about vulgarization itself. Sheer vulgarity quickly stands self-condemned, hence tends quickly to correct itself. Or where it persists—as representing something congenial to a particular social milieu or human type—it is so blatant as to isolate itself and proclaim its own quarantine. So long as what is "wrong" can be quickly spotted, and thereafter vividly contrasted with what is "right," whether or not it continues to exist, it can no longer triumph. The most insidious aspect of vulgarity, I would think, concerns not those to whom its appeal is obvious and immediate, but those, rather, whom it gradually and imperceptibly manages to win over, those who in the beginning are partly superior to it and who only by habituation sink to its level. A vulgarity that can thus contaminate won't often, it seems clear, be of a primitive or glaring sort; it will be, rather, a worm in the apple, a sort of Greek bearing gifts. In the world of art, such vulgarity may boast that it does far more good than it does harm, that it makes many people respond to what they might otherwise pass by. I'm not speaking of the out-and-out popularization, but rather of such things as the movie version of *Henry V* or Stokowski's arrangements of Bach—of things offered under the auspices of culture and aimed at reasonably cultured people. This form of vulgarization will by no means altogether misrepresent or even too greatly discolor. And though a severe taste may resist or reject it at once, a fairly sensitive taste—what I suppose is most conveniently called a middlebrow taste that, if left alone, might come to appreciate Bach or Shakespeare "neat" —will not resist or reject the adulteration, will soon, in fact, come to prefer and eventually to require it.

Vulgarization isn't always a matter of making things pleasanter to the taste, or easier to swallow; it can also consist—which can constitute the highbrow maneuver—in making them more difficult and abstruse, rather resembling the homely girl who goes out of her way to accentuate her homeliness. It is as possible to defeat the primary end of art, the sense of beauty, by minimizing it as by rouging it up. Short cuts represent one kind of vulgarization, labyrinths represent another. The highbrow procedure, if we were to raid the vocabulary that accompanies it, might be called counter-vulgarization. It constitutes, in any case, no cure or corrective for the middlebrow ailment, but rather a different kind of disease; and though its very lack of cheap allure will cause it to render art far less of a disservice than the rouge-and-syrup process, it is yet equally a barrier to our becoming an artistic people. What with art being something, on the one side, that slides smoothly down our gullets and on the other, something to be chewed long after any flavor is left, we can seldom any longer, I think, get the fine, sharp, vivid, simple first experience of art that must be the preliminary to any more complex one. Something is always doused over it or drained out of it, hiding the flavor or heightening it, removing gristle or adding lumps; or the thought or look of the thing, before we even bite into it, conditions us. A man can no longer even read, let us say, the "Ode to a Nightingale" without the slightly guilty or, at any rate, self-conscious feeling that it is "romantic poetry."

As a result of the vulgarizing effort to make things palatable and of a counter-vulgarization that renders things parched, there is being beggared out of existence a high yet workable cultural ideal, a climate in which a *sense* of art can flourish. And it seems to me that the lack of a proper climate for art is a much more serious shortcoming in America than the small number of works of art themselves. Culture—in the old-fashioned, well-rounded sense of something civilized and civilizing alike—has not simply failed as a reality in America, but is fast fading as an ideal. Such a culture stands in relation to formal education as good wine to the grape: it is a fermentation, a mellowing, a very special and at the same time wholly characterizing element; and it permeates society in terms of its sensibilities no less than its art. One can, of course, all too easily exalt such a culture as a way of disparaging much that is essential and even healthful in modern life; and one can sigh for it on a sentimental basis, in stand-pat terms. All the same, any way of life that lacks its best qualities can scarcely be looked upon as cultivated at all; at any rate, no amount of education or knowledge or skill can begin to mean the same thing. And actually the climate I desiderate is no more than a salubrious, breeze-swept temperate zone; it is not forbidding, nor oppressively patrician, nor strenuously democratic. A cool, dry judgment is mingled there with gusto and generous appreciation; the people there are no more mired in the past than running wild in the present; its tone is altogether urbane without being even faintly genteel; it boasts neither untouchables nor sacred cows; it displays a constant corrective irony and perhaps not overmuch virtue; and everyone there is just sufficiently wrongheaded and prejudiced and inconsistent to be attractively human.

# Alaskan Summer

## Leaves from a Candid Journal

### F. FRASER DARLING

### ( *1953* )

In 1952, F. FRASER DARLING, British author and ecologist, visited Alaska with A. Starker Leopold to appraise the wildlife situation there on behalf of the Conservation Foundation. These notes, excerpted from the diary that Dr. Darling kept at that time, were incorporated into his book *Pelican in the Wilderness*.

JUNE *1, 1952*. We have left the Olympics and the Cascades behind and the busyness of the straits of water between Seattle and Vancouver, the weather has faded out the landscape and we just sit for hours in the DC4, five abreast, waiting to reach Alaska down there where the sun isn't shining. My stomach tells me we are descending, the sun goes as we bump into the clouds—oh misery—and then a rift discloses a mountainous landscape of the kind I know well, for here are the West Highlands of Scotland all over again, acid rocks, an acid vegetation, the drowned coastline and not only the evidence of glaciation but glaciers as well.

We crocodile out of the plane at Juneau and look around. It is the same forlorn scene as if I were looking across from Ballachulish to Kingairloch. The rain is the same, the temperature is the same, the latitude is almost the same, and doubtless many of the problems of Juneau as a human habitat are the same.

Thirteen miles into Juneau, passing a tidal grass flat where 20 or 30 Guernsey cows are grazing. They look better than most cows I have seen stateside, and the good Swedish barn expresses a confidence in the future. My colleague Starker Leopold and I share a room at the Baranov, $10. It is an excellent hotel, and I marvel to myself as ever at the American capacity to do things well in out-of-the-way places.

We stroll downtown to get some late lunch and go into a dive complete with soda fountain and juke box. Good choice of food and a cheerful woman serving it; our change in silver dollars. Sunday being a day we could have to ourselves, Starker and I walk uphill into the forests of Sitka spruce and hemlock. My education in Alaska had begun. Here was a coniferous forest as it should be, not sterile-floored and black-dark like a spruce plantation in Britain, but a place of beauty and grace, softened by a rich shrub and field layer—a branching *Vaccinium* new to me, a rose-colored *Rubus* and a wild strawberry. Beauty and ecological repose are one.

The birds are new, but Starker knows them—the varied thrush, chestnut-breasted and black-collared; the blue grouse booming in the great spruces; and a lovely little warbler newly come, greenish with black head and eye-stripe. Life was good once more and seemed to be continuing from last Sunday afternoon when I had had tea at home 7,500 miles away in an old English rectory garden where the nightingale sang as if to wish me Godspeed. But now there was no sun and we had climbed to the snowline.

*June 3.* Chicagoff Island today. We flew in yesterday and joined the U.S. Fish & Wildlife Service patrol ship *Grizzly Bear,* and have cruised around these forested coasts, going ashore from time to time. What wealth this forest is! Alaska, as America's last frontier, is in an interesting situation. The philosophy and practice of conservation are practical politics now, and Alaska has the chance no other new country has had, to put conservation into practice *before* the catastrophes of exploitation. Everywhere else the idea has come afterwards and the journey back is long and hard. There are plenty of people itching to get their claws into these southeast Alaskan forests, but the federal government is doing a fine job of holding tight, and where a logging concession is being made, as down at Ketchikan, the contract is being tied up on conservation principles so that the forest shall be a continuing resource.

Cribbage is Alaska's card game. Yes, I have played it; taught by my grandfather, but a long time ago. All right, I succumb to the engineer-cook-steward's persuasion, and take three games off him. Aha! we've heard of that British capacity for understatement. Not at all; I was brought up to being dealt five cards, throwing out two to the crib. Here you are dealt six cards and keep four to play with. It makes it too easy.

We put in at a little shack and a smokehouse near a salmon trap: "Burns is the name, Richard Burns, born in Georgia," says the old bachelor. "If you guys like to go over there and see a Canada goose's nest by an otter's den, I'll get my teeth in so's I can talk to you, and I'll pick you some young rhubarb." The cairn of rocks near the goose's nest was an otter town and must have held a dozen of these playful creatures, evidently to the delight of the gentle Mr. Burns.

The old man was picking red sweet stalks of rhubarb about as thick as a pencil. "I'm not really a fisherman, but I'm watchin' and figgerin' it out. Guys around here don't tell you much and I have to learn my own way. If I'm doin' sump'n and I sees a fella smilin', I knows I'm doin' it wrong someways, so I watches out on that pretty doggone careful next time."

*June 7.* In Anchorage after 800 miles through clouds and rain. Cleared a little as we came down low to fly across the Copper River flats, which are miles and miles of gravel braided by innumerable channels of the river. I was going to say it was desolation, but not so, for down there was a mother bear and her two cubs scooping salmon out of the water—salmon, the main export of Alaska to the value of a hundred million dollars.

A double room has been booked for us at a first-class hotel, $14 a night. We are in a boom town of nearly 30,000 people pressing into accommodation fit for about half that number. Yet the town spreads its unsightly squalor over many miles of country, shacks, hovels and super-apartment buildings. There is a hurdy-gurdy below our window, blaring Strauss waltzes far into the night. The town is full of hard-faced types talking contracts and dollars, and the dust is frightful. Everywhere is gravel and huge earth-moving machines and the air weeps dust. No rain here and what a lovely country! If you get out of the dust the air is fragrant with the opening balsam poplar, *trichocarpa.* But round any corner you may be invited into Alf's Place or Dinning Rooms (how true, for the juke box penetrates as far as the dust).

*June 8.* A 20-mile walk today up the Eagle River which flows down a great glacial valley covered in woods of balsam poplar, birch, willow, aspen and black spruce in the muskeg. The moose are numerous and obviously overbrowsing the willow. Predatory animals are being killed out and the Eagle River valley is closed to moose shooting. The two notions don't add up.

\* \* \*

*June 10.* A day of days in the life of a naturalist. The sun was bright at 3.0 o'clock this morning in McKinley Park, at almost Latitude 64°N. We motored far into the Park, reaching an altitude of 4,100 feet on Sable Pass. Here the mountains were yellow, with harlequin snowfields, an entirely new landscape for me; yet holding a bird I knew well, the rock ptarmigan, sitting white on the snow, its crimson eye-ceres like little flowers.

How often have I wished to see the Highlands of Scotland as they were 10,000 years ago, a relatively short time after their emergence from the Quaternary ice! That vision has been granted now, with the ptarmigan before me on the snow as a sweet and living link in time and space. I look across the Toklat River and see a flat expanse of gravel two miles wide between the mountains. Here was a highland strath of 10,000 years ago, waiting for its capping layer of finer alluvium before the grass and trees could flourish. And the higher winter temperature, of course. That too will come in its own time and then Alaska will be ready for Western civilized man. At the moment she is too new and cannot stand the wear which man given to aggregation is attempting to put upon her. Alaska is too tender yet.

The mother grizzly bear with her two cubs playing in a snowfield make sheer delight; a big lump and two little lumps, but in movement how supple and fluid. The mother sees us but does not bother. Then the cubs see us but have no innocent lack of fear. Instead, they scuttle to the lee of the vast bulk of their mother. What now? The seconds tick by and four little ears appear above the back of Mama, four little eyes and two little noses. We are under observation from the age-old safety of the maternal skirt.

The caribou beginning to move across the Park help to dispel the illusion of linear time from my mind. We have lost them at home these thousand years and all we can do is raise in wonder a blackened antler from the bog.

Since long before Alaska was reality to me, I had longed to see the white Dall sheep. Its cousin the Bighorn was familiar already, but the whiteness which is not albinism has its own beauty. Expectancy did not prepare me for what I saw in that first flock of ewes and lambs. These were sheep in the heroic mould. Their faces were gentle but not sentimentally silly as in so many domesticated breeds. Each step they took was beautiful to watch, their muscles showing and not hidden by wool or fat. Later I was close to some full-grown rams and felt that the Dall sheep were indeed sheep in the ideal of the philosopher, occupying the niche to which they have evolved, the hard, high ground of short, sparse herbage. (That habitat is not unlimited in Alaska, and as I traveled over so much of the country in the four months I was in the Territory, I felt that any great increase in numbers could neither be expected nor was to be desired. Wild sheep, like any others, do best when they are not stocking their range to capacity. It is almost certain that the high numbers of the 1920's took their natural consequence in the crash of the early 1930's.)

The humbler members of this great fauna of the Park took up much of our time. Who can stay a smile at the busy, hay-making pika? Then a small porcupine walked across the gravel near tufts of withered grass and as he moved, and the wind moved the stalks of the grass, you saw how like were the grass and the little northern porcupine.

*June 15.* We are free of the nightmare environment of Anchorage and have flown through Rainey Pass and down the Kuskokwim River to Bethel. The railway from Seward to Fairbanks, and latterly the Alaska Highway, have taken away the former importance of the great rivers of Alaska as highways. Bethel doubtless had a reason for being there when the Kuskokwim was the road. Now, there would seem to be none, but Bethel goes on, a collection of poor shacks on piles to keep them out of the water—for the river floods the site after the breakup—two or three stores, a hospital, and an air strip over the river. You can't say Bethel has been left high and dry in the march of progress; rather has it been left behind in a slough of despond, with a tuberculosis rate around 30 per cent of the native population. The heaps of empty cans on vacant lots apparently have prestige value for those who sling their refuse on these cairns of the new age. The squalor of Anchorage is short-term and there is determination to overcome it, but in Bethel it is normality, past, present and future. Point Four could start right here.

I got out of the village after a few boss shots, for the swamp is so close about, and got on to the wide tundra northwards where, a couple of miles from Bethel, I found a little knoll quite two feet higher than the rest. There I sat in the evening sunshine enjoying the sweet air. The terrain was as much like the great northern bog of the Outer Hebrides as anything I could imagine, except that on this knoll there was a willow bush three feet high and a dwarf birch a foot or so. The sheep of the Outer Hebrides would never have left such succulence unbrowsed. The pipits sang their little song like our pipits, and there was the long-spurred lark trilling also. I heard a willow ptarmigan in the distance calling as do our red grouse, and a snipe drummed high above. His drumming is a little higher pitched than ours, but his chick-chacking when he comes to earth is just the same.

We spent the night in a shack kept by a half-breed. His wife sold ice cream and fizzy soft drinks and played the juke box. There was nothing wrong with the *spirit* of their hospitality and because of that I would have smiled through a lot worse, and our night's doss was only $2.50 apiece.

Next morning as we were about to fly off the river in the Fish & Wildlife Widgeon, a young half-breed came to the water's edge to talk to me; a fine clean-cut youth he was, whose farthest journey in his life had been to Anchorage. He had a good, eager intelligence; "I read and read," he said, "but I can't get it all sorted out."

"Tell me about your Queen. How is she different from President Truman?"

I tried to explain the principles of monarchy as we understood it, spiritually and constitutionally. The passage of royal blood through 1,500 years impressed him.

Next the socialized medicine: would our new government throw it out? I told him it was accepted in principle by all parties and would certainly not be thrown out, though there could well be modification.

"We have bits of it here among the natives of Alaska, but it doesn't get to the root of the trouble. What's the good of hospitals if you leave folk living in these conditions?"

He pointed to three separate shacks. "In each of those there's someone about to keel over from tuberculosis."

I was sorry to leave that boy.

Two hours' flying from Bethel and we are watching the ice floes on the Kashunuk River, which leads to the Bering Sea. Dave Spencer, pilot-biologist, is completely unhurried as he looks down wondering where he can make it. We are in an area of low tundra as big as mainland Scotland, empty of men except for a very few Eskimo families. This immensity of flatness is something new to me, but more dramatic still are the thousands of geese here for the nesting. The day and night are never quiet for their cacophonies—emperors, cacklers, whitefronts and brants. This is one of the great goose nurseries of the world, unknown till the Fish & Wildlife Service found it a few years ago. The geese are not all, for there are trillions, almost, of phalaropes, sandpipers, turnstones and other waders. And the sandhill cranes, the flight, call and behavior of which exercise a strange fascination. (Three months later, at Big Delta in the interior, I saw 300 of them as a flock ready to migrate. They rose higher and higher till the sun shone golden on their undersides; then they took up a treble V formation and flew away southeastwards.) I saw two Arctic hares here, about as big as a gazelle and probably faster.

*June 20.* We flew from the Kashunuk River tundra across part of the Bering Sea to Nunivak Island yesterday. Here are 1,200 square miles of dry basaltic tundra carrying a population of 225 Eskimos, 4,000 reindeer and 75 musk oxen. Administration is a credit to the United States and the Alaskan Native Service. The main "industry" is the reindeer herd, the increase of which is slaughtered, processed and frozen in a most modern corral and handling plant. The resident engineer-*cum*-administrator was Fred—how different from the notion of a British Colonial Service native commissioner, but Fred had what it takes for the job. You could see how the folk trusted him, and the children adored him. Fred was a fine man, from whom you could get reliable knowledge on archaeology and folklore, who could get the most out of a work team, who would never spare himself. The United States might well pick out its Freds, if Nunivak is to be the pattern of native administration, whether Eskimo or Indian, in Alaska or Arizona.

The Eskimo has emerged from the Stone Age as a superb craftsman. Here on Nunivak you can examine an everyday sealing outfit on the tiny bone-runnered sledge which is carried on the front of the kayak; you can look closely at the construction of the kayak, for the beautiful frames are at this season stripped of skin and set up on stands, and you can turn over in your hands some pieces of ivory carving as sweet to the touch as a Chinese jade. The Eskimo's hands can take hold intelligently of 20th-century engineering, and in the Arctic there are Eskimo foremen responsible for hundreds of thousands of dollars' worth of diesel equipment, doing a fine job. Nunivak islanders get immense sport out of buying the highest-powered outboard engine and fitting it to the lighest, slimmest dory that would float if you wiped it underneath with a damp sponge. There are two speeds, all-out and stop, and as the outfit hydroplanes over the water at high speed, the Eskimo smiles happily.

The reindeer situation on Nunivak is a microcosm of what has happened all over western Alaska. Carrying capacity of the range was misjudged and techniques were not advanced enough to see that the deer were eating themselves out while yet increasing their numbers. That is one of the tragedies of pastoralism the world over: deterioration of the range and the condition of the animals do not keep in phase; then suddenly the herds crash. Wolves and poachers, sometimes where they do not exist, are blamed rather than the plain fact of a beaten-up range. There is no lichen range left on Nunivak, so a very much reduced herd must continue to live on dwarf willows and sedges.

*June 25.* We flew over Bristol Bay on the first day of the salmon-fishing season. There must have been a thousand boats down there, large and small, and as we learned later, they trailed 87 miles of drift net of 8½-inch mesh. We had also flown over a large forest fire north of Dillingham; how shocking it is from above! Wildfire is one of the curses of Alaska and has taken its course over 80 per cent of forested land since the white man went in. Wildfire empties a country of caribou quicker than the rifle, for the lichen goes; but fire favors willow growth, which is moose feed.

*June 28.* Grounded at King Salmon, which is the administrative nerve-center of the fishing. The Fish & Wildlife salmon-fisheries men are troubled. The fish are not going up the rivers to seed the spawning beds, and it is probable those 87 miles of net are catching pretty well the whole run. Dave Spencer has flown the rivers to see if the fish were coming, but no. The Fish & Wildlife men are getting jumpy. (We learned later that the Service stopped all fishing for two or three days—during which time the air went blue!—and a good run of fish got into the rivers, ensuring the future generation.) This most valuable natural resource is down to half what it was in fish; only the increased price has kept up the value. Conservation research is going full blast and is yielding excellent results, but as one wise guy insists, "We don't want research; we want fish." So it isn't dead easy for the Fish & Wildlife Service.

*June 30.* Kenai, an old Russian settlement: a man calls to ask if we will come and help search for a two-year-old child who has strayed from a homesteader's tent in the forest. Dave, Starker and I drive 7 miles on a brand-new gravel road. At the very end of this is a pathetic bundle of household chattels, and back in the forest is a tent round which the man and his wife had been clearing when the baby girl had disappeared. The Marshal of Kenai gets out of an-

other car, armed and wide-hatted. A beet-faced drunk falls out of a
third car and calls for some method in the search. He rolls away
unmethodically. Fifty men appear from nowhere, it seems, and the
Marshal strings us into a line well over half a mile long, and we
are to sweep round the locus of the tent. It is a bit of a job getting
all these rugged individualists working together, but we go ahead
through dense, wet undergrowth. After getting round perhaps 10°
of our circle we come to a trail and halt to re-form our line. Then
just as we are about to start again (I am nearer the peripheral end
of the line) there is a shout at the extreme end, "We've got her,"
and 300 yards to my left I see a child in a man's arms. She is upright, so I know she is alive. She had got almost a mile into the
forest in two hours. We wave handkerchiefs to two small airplanes
and they wobble to show they understand. And now an ugly
little man with 10 days of a beard walks up with the child. He is
her father. But the child is of extraordinary beauty—large brown
eyes, fine features, very small. Blissfully ignorant, abjectly clad, she
smiles happily, talks in her own way and pokes an exquisite finger
into that beard. The little runt himself is in ecstasy, seeing nothing, saying nothing, just striding ahead. This surely is his moment
of beauty, for he found her. Bearded sourdoughs, cheechakos, construction men, engineers, bums and biologists come near, their
faces all silly.

"Well, Goddammit miss if you haven't started soon enough going away from home! What the hell you'll be doin' at 17 damned
if I know," and such pleasantries. The princess' court and its out-
riders proceed, till a bedraggled woman comes along, crying hys-
terically. Her relief is uncontrolled as she reaches the child. The
retinue of 50–100 men suddenly becomes a group of individualists
who happened to be walking that way. Those behind the family
walk by as if it did not exist. It must be left alone in its moment of
reunion. When we get back to the hub of operations, there is the
little pile of things in the rain and that awful poke of a tent which
must be these poor folks' home till they build their cabin. They
are homesteaders; the Lord have mercy on them. The Marshal
and two or three other braves with rifles stand by the bedding,
point their guns into the air and fire six rounds to call in the
stragglers. The hunt is done.

*July 4.* Manifestations of the blessings of this day in Kenai have
been restricted to sporadic explosions of fireworks and slightly
heavier boozing than usual. I spend the day reading in Dave's and

the Marshal's library. There is a lot of thrilling stuff about Alaska from the days of early possession by the United States when many eager men went forth to explore. This period continued till the advent of the airplane and bush flying, since when little has been hidden, though it is far from being understood. That is the present phase of exploration here, trying to understand. It is impossible not to get excited about what there is to be done.

*July 16.* I take my picture of the sun shining on the pack ice at midnight, Point Barrow. Suppose every greenhorn does that. A 6-foot-high cone of chopped-up freshly killed walruses is not pretty. The indignity seems greater than when a carcass is skinned and slung on a spandrel, for there is not the repose of individual death. As leads appear in the pack, the Eskimos are going forth in their umiaks to the walrus hunting. The whole of the walrus is used some way or other, but the quarry is so large and strong in life that the hunting tends to be wasteful. Many dead and wounded animals sink before they can be secured.

*July 31.* In the Romanzoff Mountains: this is one of the remotest spots on earth, at the northeast end of the Brooks Range, yet we have a large tent and have had cornflakes and fruit juice for breakfast. I cannot get any notion that we are exploring. The airplane is the key to Alaska and is a most romantic thing in what it achieves here, but it destroys much of the earlier romance of travel. We have flown here from Umiat on the Colville River and have come through vast areas of spiry mountains and undulating Arctic prairie, sometimes feeling we could touch the Dall sheep as we passed them on a mountain side, and being thrilled by the close-massed herds of caribou grazing the glacial valleys or moving toward the Arctic Ocean. These few weeks in the Arctic are the climax of our journey, and for me the Arctic third of Alaska is the best. Perhaps this is because it is the least touched by Western man and therefore the least spoiled. It is an eternal regret to me that there are so few places on earth where man improves on nature. Civilizing man as an ecological climax-breaker almost makes civilization a contradiction in terms. This is the ecologist's and the conservationist's biggest job, to remove the contradiction; how can we civilize without laying waste the planet? Not only has the answer to be found, but we have a big loan to pay back to the planet which has subsidized our existence since the dawn of civilization. We have not lived on the earth's free income, but on her accumulated capital, and she is beginning to complain.

Here in Lake Peters, a glacier-water lake at 2,900 feet, from which the ice went only 10 days ago, there are lake trout or char weighing up to 22 pounds. These monsters are swallowing mere 3-pounders whole. We are eating the monsters.

*August 21.* Wainwright: have flown here from Kotzebue and Cape Lisburne today. The Cape is a quite horrific limestone headland which juts into the Chukchi Sea opposite Siberia. There was a 40-mile-an-hour wind and the temperature at freezing. But the sun shines here at Wainwright and the wind is only a strong breeze. As we come to rest on the beach, a horde of brown, solemn faces are at the windows of the little airplane, gazing awestruck at an Englishman *in extremis*. They recover their smiles as rapidly as he does his peristaltic equilibrium.

Wainwright is a small Eskimo village set in a great expanse of low, flat tundra. The small modern school is in the charge of a young couple from New York State devoted to their job, the sort who will give of their utmost from idealism and who have taken the trouble to get an anthropological training. The impression I have brought away from their little house is of springtime growth and flowers. How was it done? Uncle Sam, be kind to them.

Counted 84 snowy owls on the trip of 100 miles to Barrow. They sit on the ridges of the frost polygons, visible for miles on the tundra. Many of them have not bred this year because the snow did not melt soon enough to lay bare the harvest of lemmings on which they feed.

*September 12.* Receiving the academic hospitality of the University of Alaska at Fairbanks. I am happy here in the eagerness of young folk. Some things are still raw, but the specialist graduate schools are second to none. I liken this place to a Renaissance university: so many of us are poor, God knows where many of us sleep, individuality is almost percussive, and the élan is something older institutions have lost, I think. Here it sweeps you forward in its enthusiasm.

The fine, dry, clear atmosphere of the interior, playing on the fading foliage of the woods, makes the fall a lyrical time. Could time stand still on these days! In another month I shall be back in the old rectory garden, the nightingale gone and only the robin singing.

# A Glimpse of Incomprehensibles

## GEORGE W. CORNER

## ( *1954* )

In this address, originally presented at Swarthmore College, GEORGE W. CORNER of the Rockefeller Institute tells how a professional anatomist reconciles his sworn duty to study the human body and mind as a physical mechanism with the realization that the human intellect and emotions transcend the operations of any ordinary machine. This essay, which was written while Dr. Corner was director of the Department of Embryology of the Carnegie Institution of Washington, was included in his volume of autobiography and selected essays, *Anatomist at Large*.

O NE OF THE MOST INTERESTING PROJECTS now under way at our laboratory is an experimental study of the behavior of uterine muscle. Dedicated as we are to the study of embryology, we are bound to consider the environment in which the embryo lives, and in particular that remarkable muscular organ, the uterus, in which everyone has his first home. A visitor who steps into the rooms of Dr. Arpad Csapo, the leader of this particular research, sees him facing a mass of apparatus, tubing and wires, all of which is focused upon a small vial housing a strip of rabbit's uterus, three centimeters long. This bit of living tissue is kept at body temperature in physiological salt solution. It is supplied with oxygen and with energy in the form of dextrose. Its environment is thus made as much as possible like that within the intact animal. One end of the strip is fastened to a lever, so that when it contracts, as any involuntary muscle will do of its own accord when so prepared, its rhythmic contractions are recorded on a drum. Watching the lever move up and down, watching the muscle itself shorten and then relax, the fascinated observer realizes with a start that what he is watching is an engine, as much an engine as those which run our motorcars. Like them it has its own firing system by which the energy on which it operates is turned into mechanical work by a kind of explosion. Dr. Csapo chooses to supplant this natural "spark-plug" mechanism by mild electrical shocks from a mechanical timer; thus gaining somewhat smoother timing, he finds that he is indeed running an engine in the most literal sense. The experiment becomes quantitative, like an engineer's test of any steam or gasoline engine. The energetics of operation can be calculated. The work done is precisely related to the amount of contractile protein in the sample and of the fuel used. The strength of the contractions (i.e., isometric tension) can be predicted from the size and physiological state of the muscle sample, and Dr. Csapo has even found a way, by the use of the ovarian hormones, to alter the mechanical performance in much the same way as when the pressure of steam supplied to a steam engine or the rate of carburetion of a gasoline motor is changed.

Thus far I have spoken only of isolated muscle tissue under fully controlled laboratory conditions; but we know also from very recent experiments by Dr. Brenda Schofield that the whole uterus, in the rabbit's body, operates on the same principle and would behave as uniformly except that it is affected by other complex regulatory factors, such as the nervous system and the ovarian hormones.

The nerves of the uterus apparently come into play chiefly for regulatory purposes on critical occasions; that is to say, the impulses they carry co-ordinate one part of the uterus with another when the fertilized eggs are to be received and accurately positioned in the uterus, and again when the infants are to be delivered. These nerve impulses are known to consist of ionic reactions; they and the blood flow that transports carbohydrate fuel to the uterus, in fact all the operative controls, are physicochemical processes. The whole organ must be regarded as a mechanism, no less than the isolated strip, although the intact uterus *in situ* is of course a more complicated mechanism and less uniform in its activity under experimental observation.

The investigator, silently for hours watching and controlling these experiments, inevitably asks himself, Is not then the whole rabbit also a mechanism, and if so, why not the man who watches? His muscles and nerves and brain that devised the experiment, his curiosity that asked the questions, the energy that drives him to answer them—is not all this the product of biochemical reactions under fixed laws of the physical world?

This is an old question, as old as philosophy itself, to which in the past an answer has often been given one way or the other by scientist or theologian. It was put again to me, not long ago, by one of America's eminent scholars. This friend of mine, a professor of literature, has a doctor son who works alongside us; perhaps it was the younger man's enthusiastic talk of biophysics that disturbed the father. Perhaps also the professor, who is expert in the history of eighteenth-century thought, is still irked by the brash statements of mechanistic philosophy given two centuries ago by men like La Mettrie, author of books entitled *Man a Machine* and *Natural History of the Soul*. At any rate, he asked me in all seriousness whether the advance of science and particularly of human biology does not threaten to reduce all human activity to physico-chemical terms and thus to destroy the humanities and do away before long with the arts and all learning, except physics.

In reply to the professor's question, I say in the first place that we anatomists, physiologists and biochemists are for practical reasons bound to work on the assumption that the animals and parts of animals we study are indeed mechanisms. We must try as hard as we can to bring all animal and human behavior under observation and measurement. If the premature acceptance of non-physical "vitalistic" forces leads us to abandon physical and chemical investigation, we shall only wander in a no man's land of conjecture.

In the second place, the progress of these sciences brings into the realm of materiality much that was once thought to be immaterial. One example of this will suffice. The phenomenon of vision was a great enigma to the ancients. Aristotle himself cried out in wonderment, "Who would believe that so small a space [as the eye] could contain the images of all the universe? What skill can penetrate such a wonderful process? This it is that leads human discourse to the consideration of things divine!" Since then we have marched steadily toward understanding human seeing as a physical and chemical activity. In Aristotle's time and in the Middle Ages, all existing knowledge was encompassed in a vague concept of the eye as the lantern of the soul. What we now call the lens was believed to be the central receptor of things seen, passing visual images inward to the soul itself. That the eye is a camera working on strict optical principles, and the retina its photoreceptor, became clear in the seventeenth century. In another hundred years, discovery of the optic nerve-fibers made known that the brain is involved in the process of vision. The actual areas of the brain concerned in seeing, and the exact pathways from the retina to the cortex, were worked out in the nineteenth century; the biochemistry and biophysics of nerve conduction are the work of our own age. In view of all this progress toward a physico-chemical concept of the visual process from eye to brain cortex, should the biologist be thought too daring if he now expects that biophysics will one day explain the conversion of cortical optic responses into conscious thought, and trace all the channels over which they reverberate throughout the body, causing the seer to stare or tremble or soar in ecstasy at what he sees?

We are indeed daring, I admit, when we predict that conscious-ness will be explainable in physico-chemical terms, but nowadays even those who doubt the possibility of such understanding usually base their doubts not on grounds of vitalism or of piety, but on a materialistic argument involving a sort of uncertainty principle which states that a thinking machine is necessarily incapable of perceiving how it thinks.

Meanwhile, experimenters are attacking the citadel of the mind, the subconscious mind at least, by the study, for example, of conditioned reflexes. A clear description of one such investigation appeared in a recent number of the *Scientific American,* in an article by Professor Liddell of Cornell University on his experi-mental production of anxiety-states in sheep and goats. By the simplest physical means, namely the continuous administration of slight painless electrical shocks on a monotonously regular sched-ule, he produced long-continued disorders of emotional behavior. Again, anyone who has observed the effect on human patients of drugs like desoxyamphetamine has seen how high-level mental phenomena, that is to say, elaborate apprehensions, conscious fears, and disorders of judgment, can be altered for the time being by a physical agent that can only be hastening or retarding, some-where in the brain, some such purely biophysical action as the passage of ions across the borders of specific nerve cells.

Rather, however, than carry this line of argument for the ma-terial nature of human thought to the length of saying outright, with La Mettrie, that man is a machine and even his highest ac-tivities are the product of physical reactions, let us go back and look again at the small living mechanism with which we started, the muscle strip studied by my colleague. Simple as it seems, this little engine is actually much more complicated than a man-made motor. It is not made of metal, but mostly of complex, unstable proteins. It is not able to burn ordinary hydrocarbons like wood, coal or oil, but only one very special and elaborate substance, adenosine triphosphate. It has to make this fuel for itself from sugar brought by the blood stream, stepping up the chemical structure through at least a dozen enzyme processes until it has built what it can burn. It is not controlled by a throttle but by ion-movements across a semi-permeable barrier membrane. I have by no means stated all the complexities; if we could look inside this muscle when in action, we would see in each of its microscopic cells more ions, atoms, molecules and larger aggregates going systematically about their business than all the people and automobiles in the city of Philadelphia. I once made a calculation that one cell of an endocrine gland, the corpus luteum, produces in one day more than a thousand billion molecules of its internal secretion.

The muscle machine is not only very complex; it is also very unstable. It runs well only within a narrow range of temperature; 60 degrees centigrade will cook it; one crystal of cyanide will stop it quicker than a monkey wrench in a crankcase. The protein molecules of which it is chiefly composed are held in a precarious state of teetering equilibrium by interacting tensions, like the gymnasts in a human pyramid. Such is life at the level of the cell. At the level of the organs—heart, lungs, liver—and at the level of the body, life consists of the interaction of such complex and unstable, therefore sensitive, tissues and their co-ordination by equally complex and unstable tissues such as nerves and blood vessels. At the level of the mind, the structure in which thinking is done is no less complicated. Dr. Karl Lashley, in a pioneering essay "In Search of the Engram," on the physiological basis of learning, closely estimated the number of nerve cells in the visual apparatus of the white rat from retina to brain cortex, and got a total of thirteen millions. With these neurones the rat is able to retain (says Lashley) scores, perhaps hundreds of visual habits involving discrimination of complex figures. The rhesus monkey has about a hundred times as many visual neurones; man, we may conjecture, a thousand times thirteen millions. A student reading his textbooks instantly distinguishes any one of ten thousand patterns presented by the printed words before him.

This enormous, overwhelming, almost inconceivable complexity of the human structure and mental function forces us, if we are to be materialists, into materialism of a new sort. When La Mettrie said that man is a machine, a machine to him meant something like a clock or the primitive Newcomen steam engine. He must have realized that the human machine is more complicated than that, but still it was to him figuratively a thing of cogs and levers. If, however, I say that man is a machine, I have to think of an apparatus much more complicated than the biggest electronic computing machine, and also much less stable, much more sensitive than any piece of man-made automatic hardware. The difference between old and new concepts of the living machine is so great, so fundamental that twentieth-century scientific materialism is bound to be very different from that of the past. My variety of it, you may say when I finish, is not materialism at all.

Mention of electronic calculating machines brings us to the most recent aspect of mechanistic thought, the kind of analysis called cybernetics. This stems from the observation of certain similarities between electronic circuits and the structure and functioning of the nervous system. Not only is the transmission of the nerve impulse analogous to the electric current; not only are the synapses or nerve junctions analogous to electrical connections, and the primary reflex arc merely a doorbell circuit; more than that, something much like feed-back wiring and regenerative circuits can be seen in the brain, suggesting the existence of stages of amplification like those of a radio set. On the contrary, some of the mental activities of men and animals can be imitated by machines built on these principles: for example, simple remembering, simple discriminations, even choice between alternatives simply presented. Some of these operations are fairly impressive. Everyone has heard what the great computing machines can do, for example, in solving complicated differential equations in a fraction of a second. When a wartime committee under my direction was studying devices for the blind, the engineer Zworykin of the Radio Corporation of America built us a machine that recognizes the individual letters of a printed alphabet and calls them off vocally. Another less serious engineer made a mechanical bug that knows when it is hungry for more juice in its little battery, trots off to the proper socket, connects itself and gets a recharge. If there is radio interference in the neighborhood, I suppose the gadget might develop a simple sort of nervous prostration like Professor Liddell's sheep and goats.

This jest of mine reflects the feeling of conservative anatomists and physiologists that cybernetic concepts fall far short of explaining the workings of the nervous system, partly, I admit, because we have by no means worked out a complete description of the animal machine for engineers to imitate. There are a lot of circuits and connections still to be traced. Yet the parallel onward march of neurology, biophysics and electronic engineering makes it probable that all the operations of the animal mind result from the flow of electrical charges, that is to say, the transfer of ions in the cells of the body. When an experimenter produces neurosis in the sheep, or (to take a more agreeable example) when a hunting dog is conditioned to stand and point to a pheasant, I have no difficulty in supposing that the whole conditioning process occurs entirely on the material level. If asked whether I suppose this to be true also of more complex mental performances involving intricate choice of alternatives on the basis of a large stock of stored information, say, a fullback running through a broken field or Shakespeare writing a sonnet, I have to say I do not know. Even what I just said about the hunting dog is a hypothesis. We biologists are bound to work on such hypotheses, even if we do not expect that a good sonnet will ever be written by a man-made machine.

But suppose, just for the argument, that it is so, that all the higher activities of the mind—all that raises man above the unreflective beast and leads him to create arts, sciences and humane learning—suppose that this is entirely the result of ionic shifts in our cells for which we may some day calculate the equations: what then? Do we scrap our libraries and colleges? Is my humanist friend whose question started me on this essay to discontinue teaching the history of literature and philosophy?

What I now reply is not the utterance of mystics or metaphysicians; it is the word of the histologist looking up from his microscope, the physiologist from his oscillograph. We see that the human thinking mechanism, if it is a mechanism, is utterly complex and multifariously sensitive beyond any conceivable instrument of metal and glass, and therefore its individual reactions will always be in large part unpredictable. Let me reinforce this statement by quoting again Karl Lashley, one of the most thoughtful of our neuropsychological experimenters. In his essay on the mechanism of learning, he writes:

> The trace of any activity is not an isolated connection between sensory and motor elements. It is tied in with the whole complex of spatial and temporal axes of nervous activity. The space and time coordinates can, I believe, be maintained by . . . rhythmic discharges which pervade the entire brain, influencing the organization of activity any-

where. Within a functional area the cells acquire the capacity to react in certain definite patterns. . . . The characteristics of the nervous network are such that when it is subjected to any pattern of excitation, it may develop a pattern of activity, reduplicated throughout an entire functional area by spread of excitations. . . . All the cells of the brain must be in almost constant activity, either firing or actively inhibited. . . . The learning process must consist of the attunement of the elements of a complex system in such a way that a particular combination of cells responds more readily than before the experience.

The mental patterns of learning and of directed response, of which Lashley writes, are set up in an apparatus which in man consists of billions of neurones, interconnected through innumerable channels. The organ in which these patterns are stored is subject to excitation from outside through five senses, each of them so critically sensitive that a touch, a whiff of odor can suddenly revive a whole chapter of the past—one chapter for me, another for you; one syllable heard may set off a torrent of emotion or activity. The mechanism is also sensitive to stimulation from within itself by stored memories, by organic sensations, by local subthreshold fluctuations of physical states throughout the body. Surgeons sometimes have an opportunity to stimulate the brain directly, in a patient who is conscious and co-operative during an operation under local anesthesia. Dr. Wilder Penfield thus found that electrical stimulation at a single point of the cortex can elicit elaborate memories of things seen or heard. A big electronic computer has a bank of keys like a pipe organ; who can estimate the number of keys to the human mind, within the body and on the surface of its sensorium, through which impulses are thrown into one circuit or another, to start who knows how many oscillations in the next circuit, and the next? Nervous and mental operations involve, however, more than mere spread and flow of impulses. There are slowing and blocking resistors; there are shunts and diversions. There are circuits that operate to cut out other circuits, or to cut them in, or steady their oscillations. The elements of these circuits, moreover, are not copper wires, metal switches and electronic tubes. The conducting threads, as well as the whole organism they interconnect, are made up of elaborate and unstable chemical substances, very critically responsive to changing conditions.

Their hookup into a vast network is also unstable and critically responsive. Integration of an organism so that this multiplex system will behave in a measurably constant way calls for all sorts of internal controls—the homeostatic regulators that Walter Cannon wrote about—and in higher animals on the behavioral level it demands intensive habit formation by experience, training and education. Even when such patterning of response is well established, the richness of internal communication is so great that a small resistance here, a sudden surge of mental current there, in the network may channel the impulses in a new direction.

It is these uncertainties that create individual differences in behavior and capacity. They direct and redirect for good or bad whatever is passing through our heads. They must in some way account for the mystery of original thinking and artistic composition. They will forever keep education from being a routine business.

The complexity of human thought and behavior is of course nothing new; my point is that science has caught up with that fact and now perceives that the bodily mechanism possesses a similar order of complexity and therefore may be assumed capable of conducting very complex and subtle operations. A recent experiment illustrates perfectly what I am trying to say. One subject of Liddell's investigation at Cornell was a nursling goat, three weeks old. When it was given the routine treatment of painless but unceasingly recurrent electric shocks, it developed the usual neurosis. This animal was one of twins. The other of the pair of kids was subjected to the same experimental treatment, except that its mother was left with it in the large stall where it lived during the period of exposure to emotional trauma. This second kid did not become neurotic at all. The presence of its mother had done something inside the little animal that kept its nerves from jangling. If its unprotected brother's neurosis was a mechanistic disturbance, from which the twin was protected by the comforting presence of a mother, then—at least in the case of these particular goats, under experiment by Liddell in a barn near Cayuga Lake—it looks as if the benefit afforded by the nanny's presence was also a biophysical phenomenon. But the scientist must admit that a mechanism that needs its mother is indeed a special kind of mechanism.

By such means as this, by the intercommunication of companionship, of mood, of sympathy and solace, individuals are integrated into still more complex organizations of flock and herd, family, tribe and race. In this gift of communication, living organisms greatly excel the machines. We have all been astonished by Von Frisch's discovery of the signal-language of honeybees. Certain man-made automatic control systems perhaps approach that achievement of the bees; but at a higher level how infinitely varied is the ability of human beings to transmit complex eddies of thought and emotion to one another!

Thus we have just about reached a truce in the old quarrel between vitalism and mechanism. Both sides perceive that whatever our respective hypotheses may be about the way things work inside us, we too are creatures subject to repeated shocks, born to trouble, yet capable of adjustment. More complexly organized even than other creatures, we can go beyond mere mental adjustment, on to new accomplishments and achievements; but all the more do we need the influences that come through human kinship and the experience of our race, all that is learned at a mother's knee and at the feet of alma mater, and in the world of arts and letters.

When I mentioned the experiments at Cayuga Lake, some readers may have thought of a shepherd who once tended flocks beside another inland sea, who experienced in his own person both frustration and adjustment, and who being a poet saw the parallel between his own trials and joys and those of his sheep. Lifting his eyes to heaven, he said as of a greater Shepherd, "He leadeth me beside the still waters, He restoreth my soul." I have not chosen to carry, here, my concept of the new mechanistics into the field of religion. Science and theology tend to get heavy-handed with each other when discussing this subject. La Mettrie was banished and his books were burned because of his materialism. I think I do not risk any such fate because of mine. The biologist realizes that the mechanism is so sensitive to outward influences, and to stimuli so subtle that current science is not able to define the limits of its sensitivity; and therefore, while in the laboratory he must base his own working hypothesis upon what he can see and measure, he will not in the present state of knowledge banish from the company of scholars any man whose personal hypothesis, or faith, takes him all the way with the highhearted old scientific humanist Sir Thomas Browne, who bade us, "Have a glimpse of incomprehensibles; and thoughts of things which thoughts but tenderly touch. Lodge immaterials in thy head; ascend into invisibles; fill thy spirit with spirituals, with the mysteries of faith, the magnalities of religion, and thy life with the honour of God."

Biophysics will not soon measure the wave length of exaltation like that; but even so, we shall go on exploring the body and brain. Let not my learned friend be troubled; if and when all the circuits are traced, when the last equation is written for the ionic movements that run the works in eye, ear, nerve, muscle and viscera, the mechanism, however fully we then understand it, will still be complexly excitable and still sensitive to all the subtleties of a subtle universe. New combinations of neurones will go on being formed. Individuals will still be unpredictable. Patterns of behavior will still have to be established by training and education. Human history will not cease being made nor poetry to be written. If all the nerve cells are to be kept firing in the most effective sequence, some of the keys of the human mechanism will still have to be operated by the professors of languages and literature, by artists and by philosophers.

# Irwin Edman

## HIRAM HAYDN

### (1954)

A man of reason and sensibility, IRWIN EDMAN remained an
unfaltering optimist throughout his life, equally stalwart in
his belief that truth is the only master worth serving. During
his fourteen years as a member of the AMERICAN SCHOLAR
Editorial Board, he brought a grace and wit to the magazine
that left their mark long after his death in 1954.

WHEN A TRUE VOICE is stilled, one little relishes chirping in its
place—even in tribute. And so, wanting somehow to express
here our sense of loss and our thanks to Irwin Edman, I turned to
his own words, written a few short weeks before his death and
printed in this issue in the department called *Under Whatever
Sky,* which has been his in every number since its inception in the
Spring of 1945.

And there I found (as you will find), to my surprise, intimations
of what has happened. Nothing could be more inappropriate, in
writing of that dry, bubbling intelligence, spring of wit and irony
and true sensibility, than to attribute to it sentimental forebod-
ings, mystical or intuitive apprehensions of a morbid kind. Nor do
I mean anything of the sort—but rather simply that in these pages
you will find illusions and references to death that suggest, at the
least, that he had turned his face in that direction and fixed there
his clear, perceptive gaze.

He writes of first things and last, first times and last, and says
how seldom one realizes at such occasions their significance: "Nor,
as a matter of fact, with respect to either personal or public events,
does one often remotely know that this is the end. One leaves a
friend in perfect health and the next day one hears he is dead."
And a little farther on in his column, he quotes Edna St. Vincent
Millay's address to Persephone over a friend who has just died:

> Say to her, "My dear, my dear,
> It is not so dreadful here."

When I turn back to the very first column he wrote for THE AMERICAN SCHOLAR, I read his endorsement of the feeling that "serenity can come only from seeing events in that light of eternity which is commonly called philosophy." It is my simple conviction that Irwin Edman thought and lived in that light.

He was "a master of the ready word"; he loved and practiced the intellectual quip, the ironic twist, the epigram, the gay and charming turn of phrase. An apt parodist, with an extraordinary memory and the gift of the raconteur, he could often make a half-hour's monologue delightful. Yet, as he once wrote, "The true master can in a few words speak volumes"—and the quick but courteous retort, the brief gay sally, were equally characteristic of him.

Still, for some curious reason, many people assume that such a man, such a mind, may not be profound. I have heard professional philosophers and others drag in this tired comment, "Edman is light and popular; he is not a serious philosopher or scholar." This is a facile and, I think, foolish judgment. But a sour puritanical dislike of the lighthearted is a part (thank God, not a decisive part) of the Anglo-American heritage.

Only those who, like Irita Van Doren, have known him long and cherished him have the true measure, I believe. She writes, "He had the most extraordinary gift for making difficult and abstruse matters clear and simple to the layman." His writing, his teaching, his conversation—all illustrate this gift.

No true friend of Irwin Edman's can blink the fact that he was not, in the conventional sense, a devout or pious man. Yet I think of him as a genuinely religious man of a humanistic faith, and one who stood courageously by this faith in the face of whatever disapproval, opposition or danger.

Moreover, in this last installment of *Under Whatever Sky*, he concludes his account of first and last times with these words: "I have good authority for believing that in larger matters it is simply world without end." And therefore I feel, as it were, his amused blessing when I say that I am sure he will not need Persephone to comfort him. For fourteen years he sat among us, dispensing challenge, cheer and wisdom; and I more than half-believe that he sits now at a higher board, with Socrates and Voltaire and Montaigne, perhaps with his old loved masters, Santayana and Dewey. I think I can see them rise as he comes, and they are saying "Welcome."

HIRAM HAYDN

# The Pseudo-Conservative Revolt

## RICHARD HOFSTADTER

## ( *1954* )

In this article, RICHARD HOFSTADTER, a capable historian of the American intellectual and political heritage, describes what he calls pseudo-conservative dissent. Parading as conservatism, this dynamic new force, in actuality, is a relentless demand for conformity, directly opposed to the liberal dissent of the thirties. Mr. Hofstadter, who received a Pulitzer Prize in 1955 for *The Age of Reform,* is a professor of history at Columbia University.

TWENTY YEARS AGO the dynamic force in American political life came from the side of liberal dissent, from the impulse to reform the inequities of our economic and social system and to change our ways of doing things, to the end that the sufferings of the Great Depression would never be repeated. Today the dynamic force in our political life no longer comes from the liberals who made the New Deal possible. By 1952 the liberals had had at least the trappings of power for twenty years. They could look back to a brief, exciting period in the mid-thirties when they had held power itself and had been able to transform the economic and administrative life of the nation. After twenty years the New Deal liberals have quite unconsciously taken on the psychology of those who have entered into possession. Moreover, a large part of the New Deal public, the jobless, distracted and bewildered men of 1933, have in the course of the years found substantial places in society for themselves, have become home-owners, suburbanites and solid citizens. Many of them still keep the emotional commitments to the liberal dissent with which they grew up politically, but their social position is one of solid comfort. Among them the dominant tone has become one of satisfaction, even of a kind of conservatism. Insofar as Adlai Stevenson won their enthusiasm in

1952, it was not in spite of, but in part because of the air of poised and reliable conservatism that he brought to the Democratic convention. By comparison, Harry Truman's impassioned rhetoric, with its occasional thrusts at "Wall Street," seemed passé and rather embarrassing. The change did not escape Stevenson himself. "The strange alchemy of time," he said in a speech at Columbus, "has somehow converted the Democrats into the truly conservative party of this country—the party dedicated to conserving all that is best, and building solidly and safely on these foundations." The most that the old liberals can now envision is not to carry on with some ambitious new program, but simply to defend as much as possible of the old achievements and to try to keep traditional liberties of expression that are threatened.

There is, however, a dynamic of dissent in America today. Representing no more than a modest fraction of the electorate, it is not so powerful as the liberal dissent of the New Deal era, but it is powerful enough to set the tone of our political life and to establish throughout the country a kind of punitive reaction. The new dissent is certainly not radical—there are hardly any radicals of any sort left—nor is it precisely conservative. Unlike most of the liberal dissent of the past, the new dissent not only has no respect for nonconformism, but is based upon a relentless demand for conformity. It can most accurately be called pseudo-conservative—I borrow the term from the study of *The Authoritarian Personality* published five years ago by Theodore W. Adorno and his associates—because its exponents, although they believe themselves to be conservatives and usually employ the rhetoric of conservatism, show signs of a serious and restless dissatisfaction with American life, traditions and institutions. They have little in common with the temperate and compromising spirit of true conservatism in the classical sense of the word, and they are far from pleased with the dominant practical conservatism of the moment as it is represented by the Eisenhower Administration. Their political reactions express rather a profound if largely unconscious hatred of our society and its ways—a hatred which one would hesitate to impute to them if one did not have suggestive clinical evidence.

From clinical interviews and thematic apperception tests, Adorno and his co-workers found that their pseudo-conservative subjects, although given to a form of political expression that combines a curious mixture of largely conservative with occasional radical notions, succeed in concealing from themselves impulsive tendencies that, if released in action, would be very far from conservative. The pseudo-conservative, Adorno writes, shows "conventionality and authoritarian submissiveness" in his conscious thinking and "violence, anarchic impulses, and chaotic destructiveness in the unconscious sphere. . . . The pseudo-conservative is a man who, in the name of upholding traditional American values and institutions and defending them against more or less fictitious dangers, consciously or unconsciously aims at their abolition." [1]

Who is the pseudo-conservative, and what does he want? It is impossible to identify him by class, for the pseudo-conservative impulse can be found in practically all classes in society, although its power probably rests largely upon its appeal to the less educated members of the middle classes. The ideology of pseudo-conservatism can be characterized but not defined, because the pseudo-conservative tends to be more than ordinarily incoherent about politics. The lady who, when General Eisenhower's victory over Senator Taft had finally become official, stalked out of the Hilton Hotel declaiming, "This means eight more years of socialism" was probably a fairly good representative of the pseudo-conservative mentality. So also were the gentlemen who, at the Freedom Congress held at Omaha over a year ago by some "patriotic" organizations, objected to Earl Warren's appointment to the Supreme Court with the assertion: "Middle-of-the-road thinking can and will destroy us"; the general who spoke to the same group, demanding "an Air Force capable of wiping out the Russian Air Force and industry in one sweep," but also "a material reduction in military expenditures"; [2] the people who a few years ago believed simultaneously that we had no business to be fighting communism in Korea, but that the war should immediately be extended to an Asia-wide crusade against communism; and the most ardent supporters of the Bricker Amendment. Many of the most zealous followers of Senator McCarthy are also pseudo-conservatives, although there are presumably a great many others who are not.

The restlessness, suspicion and fear manifested in various phases of the pseudo-conservative revolt give evidence of the real suffering which the pseudo-conservative experiences in his capacity as a

[1] Theodore W. Adorno et al., *The Authoritarian Personality* (New York, 1950), pp. 675–76. While I have drawn heavily upon this enlightening study, I have some reservations about its methods and conclusions. For a critical review, see Richard Christie and Marie Jahoda, eds., *Studies in the Scope and Method of "The Authoritarian Personality"* (Glencoe, Illinois, 1954), particularly the penetrating comments by Edward Shils.

[2] On the Omaha Freedom Congress see Leonard Boasberg, "Radical Reactionaries," *The Progressive*, December, 1953.

citizen. He believes himself to be living in a world in which he is spied upon, plotted against, betrayed, and very likely destined for total ruin. He feels that his liberties have been arbitrarily and outrageously invaded. He is opposed to almost everything that has happened in American politics for the past twenty years. He hates the very thought of Franklin D. Roosevelt. He is disturbed deeply by American participation in the United Nations, which he can see only as a sinister organization. He sees his own country as being so weak that it is constantly about to fall victim to subversion; and yet he feels that it is so all-powerful that any failure it may experience in getting its way in the world—for instance, in the Orient—cannot possibly be due to its limitations but must be attributed to its having been betrayed.[3] He is the most bitter of all our citizens about our involvement in the wars of the past, but seems the least concerned about avoiding the next one. While he naturally does not like Soviet communism, what distinguishes him from the rest of us who also dislike it is that he shows little interest in, is often indeed bitterly hostile to such realistic measures as might actually strengthen the United States vis-à-vis Russia. He would much rather concern himself with the domestic scene, where communism is weak, than with those areas of the world where it is really strong and threatening. He wants to have nothing to do with the democratic nations of Western Europe, which seem to draw more of his ire than the Soviet Communists, and he is opposed to all "give-away programs" designed to aid and strengthen these nations. Indeed, he is likely to be antagonistic to most of the operations of our federal government except Congressional investigations, and to almost all of its expenditures. Not always, however, does he go so far as the speaker at the Freedom Congress who attributed the greater part of our national difficulties to "this nasty, stinking 16th [income tax] Amendment."

A great deal of pseudo-conservative thinking takes the form of trying to devise means of absolute protection against that betrayal by our own officialdom which the pseudo-conservative feels is always imminent. The Bricker Amendment, indeed, might be taken as one of the primary symptoms of pseudo-conservatism. Every dissenting movement brings its demand for Constitutional changes; and the pseudo-conservative revolt, far from being an exception to this principle, seems to specialize in Constitutional revision, at least as a speculative enterprise. The widespread latent hostility

---

[3] See the comments of D. W. Brogan in "The Illusion of American Omnipotence," *Harper's*, December, 1952.

toward American institutions takes the form, among other things, of a flood of proposals to write drastic changes into the body of our fundamental law. Last summer, in a characteristically astute piece, Richard Rovere pointed out that Constitution-amending had become almost a major diversion in the Eighty-third Congress.[4] About a hundred amendments were introduced and referred to committee. Several of these called for the repeal of the income tax. Several embodied formulas of various kinds to limit non-military expenditures to some fixed portion of the national income. One proposed to bar all federal expenditures on "the general welfare"; another, to prohibit American troops from serving in any foreign country except on the soil of the potential enemy; another, to redefine treason to embrace not only persons trying to overthrow the government but also those trying to "weaken" it, even by peaceful means. The last proposal might bring the pseudo-conservative rebels themselves under the ban of treason: for the sum total of these amendments might easily serve to bring the whole structure of American society crashing to the ground.

As Mr. Rovere points out, it is not unusual for a large number of Constitutional amendments to be lying about somewhere in the Congressional hoppers. What is unusual is the readiness the Senate has shown to give them respectful consideration, and the peculiar populistic arguments some of its leading members have used to justify referring them to the state legislatures. While the ordinary Congress hardly ever has occasion to consider more than one amendment, the Eighty-third Congress saw six Constitutional amendments brought to the floor of the Senate, all summoning simple majorities, and four winning the two-thirds majority necessary before they can be sent to the House and ultimately to the state legislatures. It must be added that, with the possible exception of the Bricker Amendment itself, none of the six amendments so honored can be classed with the most extreme proposals. But the pliability of the senators, the eagerness of some of them to pass the buck and defer to "the people of the country," suggests how strong they feel the pressure to be for some kind of change that will give expression to that vague desire to repudiate the past that underlies the pseudo-conservative revolt.

One of the most urgent questions we can ask about the United States in our time is the question of where all this sentiment arose. The readiest answer is that the new pseudo-conservatism is simply

4 Richard Rovere, "Letter from Washington," *New Yorker*, June 19, 1954, pp. 67–72.

the old ultra conservatism and the old isolationism heightened by the extraordinary pressures of the contemporary world. This answer, true though it may be, gives a deceptive sense of familiarity without much deepening our understanding, for the particular patterns of American isolationism and extreme right-wing thinking have themselves not been very satisfactorily explored. It will not do, to take but one example, to say that some people want the income tax amendment repealed because taxes have become very heavy in the past twenty years: for this will not explain why, of three people in the same tax bracket, one will grin and bear it and continue to support social welfare legislation as well as an adequate defense, while another responds by supporting in a matter-of-fact way the practical conservative leadership of the moment, and the third finds his feelings satisfied only by the angry conspiratorial accusations and extreme demands of the pseudo-conservative.

No doubt the circumstances determining the political style of any individual are complex. Although I am concerned here to discuss some of the neglected social-psychological elements in pseudo-conservatism, I do not wish to appear to deny the presence of important economic and political causes. I am aware, for instance, that wealthy reactionaries try to use pseudo-conservative organizers, spokesmen and groups to propagate their notions of public policy, and that some organizers of pseudo-conservative and "patriotic" groups often find in this work a means of making a living —thus turning a tendency toward paranoia into a vocational asset, probably one of the most perverse forms of occupational therapy known to man. A number of other circumstances—the drastic inflation and heavy taxes of our time, the dissolution of American urban life, considerations of partisan political expediency—also play a part. But none of these things seem to explain the broad appeal of pseudo-conservatism, its emotional intensity, its dense and massive irrationality, or some of the peculiar ideas it generates. Nor will they explain why those who profit by the organized movements find such a ready following among a large number of people, and why the rank-and-file Janizaries of pseudo-conservatism are so eager to hurl accusations, write letters to congressmen and editors, and expend so much emotional energy and crusading idealism upon causes that plainly bring them no material reward.

Elmer Davis, seeking to account for such sentiment in his recent book, *But We Were Born Free*, ventures a psychological hypothesis. He concludes, if I understand him correctly, that the genuine difficulties of our situation in the face of the power of international communism have inspired a widespread feeling of fear and frustration, and that those who cannot face these problems in a more rational way "take it out on their less influential neighbors, in the mood of a man who, being afraid to stand up to his wife in a domestic argument, relieves his feelings by kicking the cat." [5] This suggestion has the merit of both simplicity and plausibility, and it may begin to account for a portion of the pseudo-conservative public. But while we may dismiss our curiosity about the man who kicks the cat by remarking that some idiosyncrasy in his personal development has brought him to this pass, we can hardly help but wonder whether there are not, in the backgrounds of the hundreds of thousands of persons who are moved by the pseudo-conservative impulse, some commonly shared circumstances that will help to account for their all kicking the cat in unison.

All of us have reason to fear the power of international communism, and all our lives are profoundly affected by it. Why do some Americans try to face this threat for what it is, a problem that exists in a world-wide theater of action, while others try to reduce it largely to a matter of domestic conformity? Why do some of us prefer to look for allies in the democratic world, while others seem to prefer authoritarian allies or none at all? Why do the pseudo-conservatives express such a persistent fear and suspicion of *their own government,* whether its leadership rests in the hands of Roosevelt, Truman or Eisenhower? Why is the pseudo-conservative impelled to go beyond the more or less routine partisan argument that we have been the victims of considerable misgovernment during the past twenty years to the disquieting accusation that we have actually been the victims of persistent conspiracy and betrayal—"twenty years of treason"? Is it not true, moreover, that political types very similar to the pseudo-conservative have had a long history in the United States, and that this history goes back to a time when the Soviet power did not loom nearly so large on our mental horizons? Was the Ku Klux Klan, for instance, which was responsibly estimated to have had a membership of from 4,000,-000 to 4,500,000 persons at its peak in the 1920's, a phenomenon totally dissimilar to the pseudo-conservative revolt?

What I wish to suggest—and I do so in the spirit of one setting forth nothing more than a speculative hypothesis—is that pseudo-

[5] Elmer Davis, *But We Were Born Free* (New York, 1954), pp. 35–36; cf. pp. 21–22 and *passim.*

conservatism is in good part a product of the rootlessness and heterogeneity of American life, and above all, of its peculiar scramble
for status and its peculiar search for secure identity. Normally
there is a world of difference between one's sense of national identity or cultural belonging and one's social status. However, in
American historical development, these two things, so easily dis-
tinguishable in analysis, have been jumbled together in reality,
and it is precisely this that has given such a special poignancy and
urgency to our status-strivings. In this country a person's status—
that is, his relative place in the prestige hierarchy of his community—and his rudimentary sense of belonging to the community—
that is, what we call his "Americanism"—have been intimately
joined. Because, as a people extremely democratic in our social institutions, we have had no clear, consistent and recognizable system of status, our personal status problems have an unusual intensity. Because we no longer have the relative ethnic homogeneity
we had up to about eighty years ago, our sense of belonging has
long had about it a high degree of uncertainty. We boast of "the
melting pot," but we are not quite sure what it is that will remain
when we have been melted down.

We have always been proud of the high degree of occupational mobility in our country—of the greater readiness, as compared with other countries, with which a person starting in a very
humble place in our social structure could rise to a position of
moderate wealth and status, and with which a person starting
with a middling position could rise to great eminence. We have
looked upon this as laudable in principle, for it is democratic, and
as pragmatically desirable, for it has served many a man as a stimulus to effort and has, no doubt, a great deal to do with the energetic and effectual tone of our economic life. The American pattern of occupational mobility, while often much exaggerated, as in
the Horatio Alger stories and a great deal of the rest of our mythology, may properly be credited with many of the virtues and
beneficial effects that are usually attributed to it. But this occupational and social mobility, compounded by our extraordinary mobility from place to place, has also had its less frequently recognized drawbacks. Not the least of them is that this has become a
country in which so many people do not know who they are or
what they are or what they belong to or what belongs to them. It
is a country of people whose status expectations are random and
uncertain, and yet whose status aspirations have been whipped up

to a high pitch by our democratic ethos and our rags-to-riches mythology.[6]

In a country where physical needs have been, by the scale of the world's living standards, on the whole well met, the luxury of questing after status has assumed an unusually prominent place in our civic consciousness. Political life is not simply an arena in which the conflicting interests of various social groups in concrete material gains are fought out; it is also an arena into which status aspirations and frustrations are, as the psychologists would say, projected. It is at this point that the issues of politics, or the pretended issues of politics, become interwoven with and dependent upon the personal problems of individuals. We have, at all times, two kinds of processes going on in inextricable connection with each other: *interest politics,* the clash of material aims and needs among various groups and blocs; and *status politics,* the clash of various projective rationalizations arising from status aspirations and other personal motives. In times of depression and economic discontent—and by and large in times of acute national emergency—politics is more clearly a matter of interests, although of course status considerations are still present. In times of prosperity and general well-being on the material plane, status considerations among the masses can become much more influential in our politics. The two periods in our recent history in which status politics has been particularly prominent, the present era and the 1920's, have both been periods of prosperity.

During depressions, the dominant motif in dissent takes expression in proposals for reform or in panaceas. Dissent then tends to be highly programmatic—that is, it gets itself embodied in many kinds of concrete legislative proposals. It is also future-oriented and forward-looking, in the sense that it looks to a time when the adoption of this or that program will materially alleviate or eliminate certain discontents. In prosperity, however, when status politics becomes relatively more important, there is a tendency to embody discontent not so much in legislative proposals as in grousing. For the basic aspirations that underlie status discontent are only

[6] Cf. in this respect the observation of Tocqueville: "It cannot be denied that democratic institutions strongly tend to promote the feeling of envy in the human heart; not so much because they afford to everyone the means of rising to the same level with others as because these means perpetually disappoint the persons who employ them. Democratic institutions awaken and foster a passion for equality which they can never entirely satisfy." Alexis de Tocqueville, *Democracy in America,* ed. by Phillips Bradley (New York, 1945), Vol. I, p. 201.

341

partially conscious; and, even so far as they are conscious, it is difficult to give them a programmatic expression. It is more difficult for the old lady who belongs to the D.A.R. and who sees her ancestral home swamped by new working-class dwellings to express her animus in concrete proposals of any degree of reality than it is, say, for the jobless worker during a slump to rally to a relief program. Therefore, it is the tendency of status politics to be expressed more in vindictiveness, in sour memories, in the search for scapegoats, than in realistic proposals for positive action.[7]

Paradoxically the intense status concerns of present-day politics are shared by two types of persons who arrive at them, in a sense, from opposite directions. The first are found among some types of old-family, Anglo-Saxon Protestants, and the second are found among many types of immigrant families, most notably among the Germans and Irish, who are very frequently Catholic. The Anglo-Saxons are most disposed toward pseudo-conservatism when they are losing caste, the immigrants when they are gaining.[8]

Consider first the old-family Americans. These people, whose stocks were once far more unequivocally dominant in America than they are today, feel that their ancestors made and settled and fought for this country. They have a certain inherited sense of proprietorship in it. Since America has always accorded a certain special deference to old families—so many of our families are *new* —these people have considerable claims to status by descent, which they celebrate by membership in such organizations as the D.A.R. and the S.A.R. But large numbers of them are actually losing their other claims to status. For there are among them a considerable number of the shabby genteel, of those who for one rea-

---

[7] Cf. Samuel Lubell's characterization of isolationism as a vengeful memory. *The Future of American Politics* (New York, 1952), Chapter VII. See also the comments of Leo Lowenthal and Norbert Guterman on the right-wing agitator: "The agitator seems to steer clear of the area of material needs on which liberal and democratic movements concentrate; his main concern is a sphere of frustration that is usually ignored in traditional politics. The programs that concentrate on material needs seem to overlook that area of moral uncertainties and emotional frustrations that are the immediate manifestations of malaise. It may therefore be conjectured that his followers find the agitator's statements attractive not because he occasionally promises to 'maintain the American standards of living' or to provide a job for everyone, but because he intimates that he will give them the emotional satisfactions that are denied them in the contemporary social and economic set-up. He offers attitudes, not bread." *Prophets of Deceit* (New York, 1949), pp. 91–92.

[8] Every ethnic group has its own peculiar status history, and I am well aware that my remarks in the text slur over many important differences. The status history of the older immigrant groups like the Germans and the Irish is quite different from that of ethnic elements like the Italians, Poles and Czechs, who have more recently arrived at the point at which they are bidding for wide acceptance

son or another have lost their old objective positions in the life of business and politics and the professions, and who therefore cling with exceptional desperation to such remnants of their prestige as they can muster from their ancestors. These people, although very often quite well-to-do, feel that they have been pushed out of their rightful place in American life, even out of their neighborhoods. Most of them have been traditional Republicans by family inheritance, and they have felt themselves edged aside by the immigrants, the trade unions, and the urban machines in the past thirty years. When the immigrants were weak, these native elements used to indulge themselves in ethnic and religious snobberies at their expense.[9] Now the immigrant groups have developed ample means, political and economic, of self-defense, and the second and third generations have become considerably more capable of looking out for themselves. Some of the old-family Americans have turned to find new objects for their resentment among liberals, left-wingers, intellectuals and the like—for in true pseudo-conservative fashion they relish weak victims and shrink from asserting themselves against the strong.

New-family Americans have had their own peculiar status problem. From 1881 to 1900 over 8,800,000 immigrants came here, during the next twenty years another 14,500,000. These immigrants, together with their descendants, constitute such a large portion of the population that Margaret Mead, in a stimulating analysis of our national character, has persuasively urged that the characteristic American outlook is now a third-generation point of view.[10] In their search for new lives and new nationality, these im-

---

in the professional and white-collar classes, or at least for the middle-class standards of housing and consumption enjoyed by these classes. The case of the Irish is of special interest, because the Irish, with their long-standing prominence in municipal politics, qualified as it has been by their relative nonacceptance in many other spheres, have an unusually ambiguous status. In many ways they have gained, while others, particularly insofar as their municipal power has recently been challenged by other groups, especially the Italians, they have lost some status and power. The election of 1928, with its religious bigotry and social snobbery, inflicted upon them a status trauma from which they have never fully recovered, for it was a symbol of the Protestant majority's rejection of their ablest leadership on grounds quite irrelevant to merit. This feeling was kept alive by the breach between Al Smith and FDR, followed by the rejection of Jim Farley from the New Deal succession. A study of the Germans would perhaps emphasize the effects of uneasiness over national loyalties arising from the Hitler era and World War II, but extending back even to World War I.

[9] One of the noteworthy features of the current situation is that fundamentalist Protestants and fundamentalist Catholics have so commonly subordinated their old feuds (and for the first time in our history) to unite in opposition to what they usually describe as "godless" elements.

[10] Margaret Mead, *And Keep Your Powder Dry* (New York, 1942), Chapter III.

migrants have suffered much, and they have been rebuffed and made to feel inferior by the "native stock," commonly being excluded from the better occupations and even from what has bitterly been called "first-class citizenship." Insecurity over social status has thus been mixed with insecurity over one's very identity and sense of belonging. Achieving a better type of job or a better social status and becoming "more American" have become practically synonymous, and the passions that ordinarily attach to social position have been vastly heightened by being associated with the need to belong.

The problems raised by the tasks of keeping the family together, disciplining children for the American race for success, trying to conform to unfamiliar standards, protecting economic and social status won at the cost of much sacrifice, holding the respect of children who grow American more rapidly than their parents, have thrown heavy burdens on the internal relationships of many new American families. Both new and old American families have been troubled by the changes of the past thirty years—the new because of their striving for middle-class respectability and American identity, the old because of their efforts to maintain an inherited social position and to realize under increasingly unfavorable social conditions imperatives of character and personal conduct deriving from nineteenth-century, Yankee-Protestant-rural backgrounds. The relations between generations, being cast in no stable mold, have been disordered, and the status anxieties of parents have been inflicted upon children.[11] Often parents entertain status aspirations that they are unable to gratify, or that they can gratify only at exceptional psychic cost. Their children are expected to relieve their frustrations and redeem their lives. They become objects to be manipulated to that end. An extraordinarily high level of achievement is expected of them, and along with it a tremendous effort to conform and be respectable. From the standpoint of the children these expectations often appear in the form of an exorbitantly demanding authority that one dare not question

[11] See Else Frenkel-Brunswik's "Parents and Childhood as seen through the Interviews," *The Authoritarian Personality*, Chapter X. The author remarks (pp. 387–88) concerning subjects who were relatively *free* from ethnic prejudice that in their families "less obedience is expected of the children. Parents are less status-ridden and thus show less anxiety with respect to conformity and are less intolerant toward manifestations of socially unaccepted behavior. . . . Comparatively less pronounced status-concern often goes hand in hand with greater richness and liberation of emotional life. There is, on the whole, more affection, or more unconditional affection, in the families of unprejudiced subjects. There is less surrender to conventional rules. . . ."

or defy. Resistance and hostility, finding no moderate outlet in give-and-take, have to be suppressed, and reappear in the form of an internal destructive rage. An enormous hostility to authority, which cannot be admitted to consciousness, calls forth a massive overcompensation which is manifest in the form of extravagant submissiveness to strong power. Among those found by Adorno and his colleagues to have strong ethnic prejudices and pseudo-conservative tendencies, there is a high proportion of persons who have been unable to develop the capacity to criticize justly and in moderation the failings of parents and who are profoundly intolerant of the ambiguities of thought and feeling that one is so likely to find in real-life situations. For pseudo-conservatism is among other things a disorder in relation to authority, characterized by an inability to find other modes for human relationship than those of more or less complete domination or submission. The pseudo-conservative always imagines himself to be dominated and imposed upon because he feels that he is not dominant, and knows of no other way of interpreting his position. He imagines that his own government and his own leadership are engaged in a more or less continuous conspiracy against him because he has come to think of authority only as something that aims to manipulate and deprive him. It is for this reason, among others, that he enjoys seeing outstanding generals, distinguished secretaries of state, and prominent scholars browbeaten and humiliated.

Status problems take on a special importance in American life because a very large part of the population suffers from one of the most troublesome of all status questions: unable to enjoy the simple luxury of assuming their own nationality as a natural event, they are tormented by a nagging doubt as to whether they are really and truly and fully American. Since their forebears voluntarily left one country and embraced another, they cannot, as people do elsewhere, think of nationality as something that comes with birth; for them it is a matter of *choice*, and an object of striving. This is one reason why problems of "loyalty" arouse such an emotional response in many Americans and why it is so hard in the American climate of opinion to make any clear distinction between the problem of national security and the question of personal loyalty. Of course there is no real reason to doubt the loyalty to America of the immigrants and their descendants, or their willingness to serve the country as fully as if their ancestors had lived here for three centuries. None the less, they have been thrown on the defensive by those who have in the past cast doubts upon the fullness of their Americanism. Possibly they are also, consciously or unconsciously, troubled by the thought that since their forebears have already abandoned one country, one allegiance, their own national allegiance might be considered fickle. For this I believe there is some evidence in our national practices. What other country finds it so necessary to create institutional rituals for the sole purpose of guaranteeing to its people the genuineness of their nationality? Does the Frenchman or the Englishman or the Italian find it necessary to speak of himself as "one hundred per cent" English, French or Italian? Do they find it necessary to have their equivalents of "I Am an American Day"? When they disagree with one another over national policies, do they find it necessary to call one another un-English, un-French or un-Italian? No doubt they too are troubled by subversive activities and espionage, but are their countermeasures taken under the name of committees on un-English, un-French or un-Italian activities?

The primary value of patriotic societies and anti-subversive ideologies to their exponents can be found here. They provide additional and continued reassurance both to those who are of old American ancestry and have other status grievances and to those who are of recent American ancestry and therefore feel in need of reassurance about their nationality. Veterans' organizations offer the same satisfaction—what better evidence can there be of the genuineness of nationality and of *earned* citizenship than military service under the flag of one's country? Of course such organizations, once they exist, are liable to exploitation by vested interests that can use them as pressure groups on behalf of particular measures and interests. (Veterans' groups, since they lobby for the concrete interests of veterans, have a double role in this respect.) But the cement that holds them together is the status motivation and the desire for an identity.

Sociological studies have shown that there is a close relation between social mobility and ethnic prejudice. Persons moving downward, and even upward under many circumstances, in the social scale tend to show greater prejudice against such ethnic minorities as the Jews and Negroes than commonly prevails in the social strata they have left or are entering.[12] While the existing studies in this field have been focused upon prejudice rather than the kind

[12] Cf. Joseph Greenblum and Leonard I. Pearlin, "Vertical Mobility and Prejudice" in Reinhard Bendix and Seymour M. Lipset, eds., *Class, Status and Power* (Glencoe, Illinois, 1953), pp. 480–91; Bruno Bettelheim and Morris Janowitz, "Ethnic Tolerance: A Function of Personal and Social Control," *American Journal of Sociology*, Vol. IV (1949), pp. 137–45.

of hyper-patriotism and hyper-conformism that I am most concerned with, I believe that the typical prejudiced person and the typical pseudo-conservative dissenter are usually the same person, that the mechanisms at work in both complexes are quite the same,[13] and that it is merely the expediencies and the strategy of the situation today that cause groups that once stressed racial discrimination to find other scapegoats. Both the displaced old-American type and the new ethnic elements that are so desperately eager for reassurance of their fundamental Americanism can conveniently converge upon liberals, critics, and nonconformists of various sorts, as well as Communists and suspected Communists. To proclaim themselves vigilant in the pursuit of those who are even so much as accused of "disloyalty" to the United States is a way not only of reasserting but of advertising their own loyalty—and one of the chief characteristics of American super-patriotism is its constant inner urge toward self-advertisement. One notable quality in this new wave of conformism is that its advocates are much happier to have as their objects of hatred the Anglo-Saxon, Eastern, Ivy League intellectual gentlemen than they are with such bedraggled souls as, say, the Rosenbergs. The reason, I believe, is that in the minds of the status-driven it is no special virtue to be more American than the Rosenbergs, but it is really something to be more American than Dean Acheson or John Foster Dulles—or Franklin Delano Roosevelt.[14] The status aspirations of some of the ethnic groups are actually higher than they were twenty years ago —which suggests one reason (there are others) why, in the ideology of the authoritarian right wing, anti-Semitism and such blatant forms of prejudice have recently been soft-pedaled. Anti-Semitism, it has been said, is the poor man's snobbery. We Americans are always trying to raise the standard of living, and the same principle now seems to apply to standards of hating. So during the past fifteen years or so, the authoritarians have moved on from anti-Negroism and anti-Semitism to anti-Achesonism, anti-intellectualism, anti-nonconformism, and other variants of the same idea, much in the same way as the average American, if he can manage it, will move on from a Ford to a Buick.

[13] The similarity is also posited by Adorno, *op. cit.*, pp. 152 ff., and by others (see the studies cited by him, p. 152).

[14] I refer to such men to make the point that this animosity extends to those who are guilty of no wrongdoing. Of course a person like Alger Hiss, who has been guilty, suits much better. Hiss is the hostage the pseudo conservatives hold from the New Deal generation. He is a heaven-sent gift. If he did not exist, the pseudo-conservatives would not have been able to invent him.

347

Such status-strivings may help us to understand some of the otherwise unintelligible figments of the pseudo-conservative ideology—the incredibly bitter feeling against the United Nations, for instance. Is it not understandable that such a feeling might be, paradoxically, shared at one and the same time by an old Yankee-Protestant American, who feels that his social position is not what it ought to be and that these foreigners are crowding in on his country and diluting its sovereignty just as "foreigners" have crowded into his neighborhood, and by a second- or third-generation immigrant who has been trying so hard to de-Europeanize himself, to get Europe out of his personal heritage, and who finds his own government mocking him by its complicity in these Old-World schemes?

Similarly, is it not status aspiration that in good part spurs the pseudo conservative on toward his demand for conformity in a wide variety of spheres of life? Conformity is a way of guaranteeing and manifesting respectability among those who are not sure that they are respectable enough. The nonconformity of others appears to such persons as a frivolous challenge to the whole order of things they are trying so hard to become part of. Naturally it is resented, and the demand for conformity in public becomes at once an expression of such resentment and a means of displaying one's own soundness. This habit has a tendency to spread from politics into intellectual and social spheres, where it can be made to challenge almost anyone whose pattern of life is different and who is imagined to enjoy a superior social position—notably, as one agitator put it, to the "parlors of the sophisticated, the intellectuals, the so-called academic minds."

Why has this tide of pseudo-conservative dissent risen to such heights in our time? To a considerable degree, we must remember, it is a response, however unrealistic, to realities. We do live in a disordered world, threatened by a great power and a powerful ideology. It is a world of enormous potential violence, that has already shown us the ugliest capacities of the human spirit. In our own country there has indeed been espionage, and laxity over security has in fact allowed some spies to reach high places. There is just enough reality at most points along the line to give a touch of credibility to the melodramatics of the pseudo-conservative imagination.

However, a number of developments in our recent history make this pseudo-conservative uprising more intelligible. For two hundred years and more, various conditions of American development

—the process of continental settlement, the continuous establishment in new areas of new status patterns, the arrival of continuous waves of new immigrants, each pushing the preceding waves upward in the ethnic hierarchy—made it possible to satisfy a remarkably large part of the extravagant status aspirations that were aroused. There was a sort of automatic built-in status-elevator in the American social edifice. Today that elevator no longer operates automatically, or at least no longer operates in the same way.

Secondly, the growth of the mass media of communication and their use in politics have brought politics closer to the people than ever before and have made politics a form of entertainment in which the spectators feel themselves involved. Thus it has become, more than ever before, an arena into which private emotions and personal problems can be readily projected. Mass communications have aroused the mass man.

Thirdly, the long tenure in power of the liberal elements to which the pseudo-conservatives are most opposed and the wide variety of changes that have been introduced into our social, economic and administrative life have intensified the sense of powerlessness and victimization among the opponents of these changes and have widened the area of social issues over which they feel discontent. There has been, among other things, the emergence of a wholly new struggle: the conflict between businessmen of certain types and the New Deal bureaucracy, which has spilled over into a resentment of intellectuals and experts.

Finally, unlike our previous postwar periods, ours has been a period of continued crisis, from which the future promises no relief. In no foreign war of our history did we fight so long or make such sacrifices as in World War II. When it was over, instead of being able to resume our peacetime preoccupations, we were very promptly confronted with another war. It is hard for a certain type of American, who does not think much about the world outside and does not want to have to do so, to understand why we must become involved in such an unremitting struggle. It will be the fate of those in power for a long time to come to have to conduct the delicate diplomacy of the cold peace without the sympathy or understanding of a large part of their own people. From bitter experience, Eisenhower and Dulles are learning today what Truman and Acheson learned yesterday.

These considerations suggest that the pseudo-conservative political style, while it may already have passed the peak of its influence, is one of the long waves of twentieth-century American history and not a momentary mood. I do not share the widespread foreboding among liberals that this form of dissent will grow until it overwhelms our liberties altogether and plunges us into a totalitarian nightmare. Indeed, the idea that it is purely and simply fascist or totalitarian, as we have known these things in recent European history, is to my mind a false conception, based upon the failure to read American developments in terms of our peculiar American constellation of political realities. (It reminds me of the people who, because they found several close parallels between the NRA and Mussolini's corporate state, were once deeply troubled at the thought that the NRA was the beginning of American fascism.) However, in a populistic culture like ours, which seems to lack a responsible elite with political and moral autonomy, and in which it is possible to exploit the wildest currents of public sentiment for private purposes, it is at least conceivable that a highly organized, vocal, active and well-financed minority could create a political climate in which the rational pursuit of our well-being and safety would become impossible.

# Psychoanalysis and Morality

## NORMAN KELMAN

## ( *1955* )

The author of numerous articles in the field of psychoanalysis and child development, NORMAN KELMAN is a training
analyst and lecturer for the American Institute of Psychoanalysis. This article explains how absolute standards of morality which promise ultimate fulfillment paradoxically result in just the opposite.

ALL STATEMENTS REGARDING MORALITY rest on assumptions, explicit or implicit, concerning human nature. In the different
schools of psychoanalysis, and among individual analysts, one finds
the same variety of assumptions that one may find among other
students of the problem. If one starts with the notion that man can
be wholly understood mechanistically, then morality, if it is considered at all, becomes a question of social engineering. Or, paradoxically, a leap is made to include some higher realm of absolute
values which somehow or other influence man the machine.

There are some who base their concepts on the thesis that man
is essentially evil and, were it not for an imposed set of curbs or
sanctions, derived from an armed truce, would be unable to live
communally. This point of view emphasizes the instinctual ani-
mality of man and tends to consider his artistic, creative, spiritual
aspects as "merely" sublimations of his baser drives.

Another approach assumes that human nature contains both
good and evil, and the moral task for man, if he is to achieve harmony, is to arrange conditions and codes to assure the supremacy
of the good.

And then there are those, biologically and humanistically
rooted, who start with man as a growing, existential being. For
these analysts, man is born, like Adam, without knowledge of either good or evil. But in the process of growth, of living in rela-

tionship with others and with that which transcends him, he creates his own moral values. When he is free and rooted in his own being, he is able to discover, even to create alternatives, and to choose, with experience, between them. It will be evident that this last point of view, generally stemming from the psychoanalytic work of Karen Horney, is the approach of this article.

It would be a convenient simplicity if at the onset we could state a definition of morality and then elaborate it in detail. Perhaps from this beginning one could speak of the source of the good, the meaning of evil, the ways by which the good can be achieved. This would make for a neat package, easy to codify into slogans and sanctions. But to do so would be to leave out the creator and the object of morality, and hence the essential flavor. Therefore, while failing to provide a precise definition, we may better obtain a feeling of the meaning and purpose of morality by noting the conditions under which questions of a moral nature arise.

Morality becomes a matter of increasing interest and study when people experience their lives to be in some measure unsatisfactory, vulnerable, without meaning. We may question and doubt, or proclaim and defend, our values when we are threatened. And our questions may go to the roots of our being, to the very meaning of life itself. New knowledge and new experiences in themselves are not responsible for the questioning of our moral values, although they provide some of the data for the questions. Perhaps, at first, distress over the new and strange may cause us to re-examine our data; we may then discover our first estimate of them to be incorrect, or we may come to recognize them as familiar, after all, under a new guise. However, it may require a threat to our values before we are able to mobilize ourselves and review more carefully the disturbing evidence. But in the face of stubborn facts and continuing disturbance, we must sooner or later question our point of view, our goals and our values.

We may ask, what do we mean by totalitarianism or democracy? What do we really mean by equality and love, by friendship and brotherhood? What do we mean by good or evil or God? We ask about the subject matter of values—is this or that good? And then we ask, what is goodness itself? These become an individual's concern when he experiences the impoverishment of his own life. They are of especial import to the community when people question institutional forms, governments, codified rules or the less tangible customs and manners. As in the case of an individual's values, the questioning or doubting of an institutional form does not necessarily mean that it is wrong or inadequate. Viable people and viable communities are open to new knowledge and experiences, however strange. And in the process of digesting the new, we may be stirred beyond our taste buds to our guts.

Affirmatively, then, morality is a creation of man and an attribute of his nature. It arises from his relationship to himself and to others, persons as well as things—to his community, his history and his universe—in his growing, in his being and becoming himself. The stuff out of which morality is created is the joint and accumulated wisdom of our artists and scientists, our statesmen and our sages, our mystics and our philosophers, you and me. It is recorded on our farms and in our schools, on the walls of our galleries, in our laws and customs. It is distilled and set down in the Bible and in the legends which are part of the heritage of every community. It is a living, growing thing which aids man in the conduct of daily intercourse, offering guidance, purpose and meaning to life.

No matter what the particular standards of morality, the forms by which they are expressed or the conditions under which they are to be achieved, their purpose is the fulfillment of man's potentials now or in the hereafter. This is so when the values to be discovered or created are absolute, whether they are to be achieved under the authoritarian aegis of the church or the state, or by direct communion with deity. Our becoming more perfectly what we can be is also the goal when our values are relational and to be achieved by human experience and intercourse.

Psychoanalysis is concerned with people who feel themselves unfulfilled, or more accurately, who feel they are being emptied. This feeling becomes evident even though the introductory problem that the patient brings to therapy be marital discord, difficulty in work, an ungovernable temper, anxiety or the many physical symptoms of psychological import. And in the course of psychoanalytic therapy, there is always a reorientation of values. The patient comes to realize that the inner code of values under which he has been living is impossible of achievement because it is composed of conflicting parts and authoritarianly demanding of absolute perfection. He comes to know that he is draining himself of life; that he can do otherwise only if he ceases to demand of himself goals beyond human capacities. Psychoanalysis then affords an opportunity to study in intimate detail the creation of moral values in their ultimate habitation, the living, growing human being.

This is not to imply that patients undergoing psychoanalysis are immoral or amoral by the usual surface application of generally accepted moral codes. Some of course are. But the vast majority represent a good cross section of the population in the values they strive for and, in many instances, force themselves to achieve. An analogy may be the best way to illustrate this point. A man's garb may be eminently correct. In variety and style, in color and texture, in function and taste, it may be impeccable. Yet he seems stiff or awkward or in some other intangible way not quite "put together." He and his clothes seem to fit, yet, like a country boy in the big city for the first time, he is subtly or grossly a stranger. By contrast there is the person who fits—his clothes, his terrain, his own skin. He walks with grace, his arms and legs go with the rest of himself. He is, in a word, authentic. In terms of morality, about the first man one must write that he is "honest," "friendly," "loving." In describing the second person, one leaves off the quotation marks. His values are intimately a part of himself and they fit because they have a belongingness and a flexibility that comes, as with the comfort of an old shoe, from experience and wear.

If moral values are to serve for the enrichment of life and not merely as the watchdogs or guardians of behavioral harmony, they must really belong to a man. They must be owned, not borrowed or forcibly applied by fear. In the process of analytic therapy, the reorientation of values involves more than a change in content of morality. The return of vitality to the person results in a humanizing of his values. Honesty is no longer a mere slogan, and friendship and love cease to be masks. He is friendly and he does love, and he can honestly discriminate. He can say "yes" and he can say "no."

The distortion of values or the ill-fitting quality of so many "moral" people is related to a feature characteristic of all patients. Regardless of symptoms or other personality differences, the neurotic person is in some degree alienated from himself and others. This is essentially the very situation referred to by Kierkegaard and other Existentialist philosophers as man's estrangement from himself and the ground of his being. It is the condition extensively explored by Ortega y Gasset in the *Revolt of the Masses*. It is the crux of the struggle against the evils of modern technical civilization and the totalitarian state. It accounts for the paradox that the Mass Man, the conformist, is the man most isolated from his fellows, despite his common uniform and clichés. The recollection of the Storm Troopers, a visit to Roseland and the glassy-eyed jivers, or to many mass cocktail parties will convince one of this.

A dream of one patient will illustrate some of the dynamic conditions of this alienation. He dreamed that he was cast up on an island, which, on awakening, he felt to be Majorca. Making his way toward the south end of the island, he found a community of people that seemed to have all the essentials of life. It was clean, and the people seemed to be active in some work, intellectual and physical. There was an adequate state of nutrition and no obvious disease. However, while there was no hostility among them, there was also no friendliness. The whole atmosphere was flat, gray, flavorless. He, a newcomer, was not noted with friendliness or hostility; he was neither feared nor welcomed. Then he became aware, with no particular indication how, that in the north of that island was an area and community of thriving, luxuriant growth. He knew that there was a place of joy and creativeness, of excitement and variety. Without clear evidence, but with a feeling of inner knowing, he became aware of an impenetrable barrier between the two parts of the island. He had no idea what the barrier consisted of, whether it was man-made or a natural feature of the terrain, whether it was guarded and desired by the north community or not. As he related the dream, he described his feelings as being neutral, neither eager for the richness of the one community nor despondent at finding the flavorless group; not grateful for his survival of the sea or frightened by the fate that almost overtook him. Yet his voice, as he spoke, indicated a yearning for the good life he knew existed, and at the same time betrayed a feeling of hopelessness that he could ever achieve it.

Some of the features of this dream and the manner of its being related will indicate a particular patient's difficulty and illustrate some generalizations for us all.

First, what stands out is the fact that so much of the dream was described in negative or neutral terms: no hostility, no friendliness, not feared, not welcomed, not grateful, not anxious, no eagerness. The south was flavorless, flat, i.e., without depth and richness. Here are reflected the relative barrenness and impoverishment of a personality, and, it will be noted, all in a smoothly functioning community. How like the desired and, unfortunately, too often achieved streamlinedness of family relations, where the nursery looks more like an aseptic operating room than a place for play. Three other significant factors are: he is an isolated being, noted and noting, an observer, almost a camera, but practically unrelated to others; he does nothing to establish communication; and, most important, he accepts the impenetrableness of the barrier without exploring, experimenting, endeavoring or reflecting. This detachment and paralysis are part of his feeling of hopelessness—a hopelessness of achievement. Whether or not the barrier in the dream in fact exists as impenetrable, the noninvolvement of this man makes it an operational fact. In a more humorous way, but just as true, was the condition of another patient, a young boy of thirteen, who said: "I'll cross that bridge when it comes to me."

John Dewey has emphasized the importance of reflection and experimentation in dealing with morality. This, as I understand it, includes the taking into one's self of one's feelings, thoughts and hopes. It includes being active, not only to achieve, but to change one's focus and point of view—to vision, touch and smell, to add pain and suffering. This patient only peripherally betrayed, by the quality of his voice, his yearning for the good life and his feeling of hopelessness, and so could not yet effectively question his values. Actually, he was still very much involved in attempting to see the source of his dissatisfaction as lying outside himself. He blamed his wife, the economic system, the hostility of others for his difficulties. He was striving to add to his bank account and the externals of his life to overcome his underlying insecurity. Instead of presenting himself to himself and others, he held out his academic degrees, his job, his car and his status. Externally successful, he was alienated from the vital, responsible person he could be. Being aware neither of his yearning nor of his hopelessness, it is no wonder that, in the dream, he could not be active, challenge the barrier.

There are some further indications in the dream, brought out in the analytic work, which bear on the dynamics of the patient's condition and on the problem of morality. Ordinarily, this person associated the north with barrenness and the south with fertility. In the dream the reversal of this order was an indication of some inner distortion. The moral life, the good life, has characteristics which differ from those of the south, in the idiom of the dream. The southern community was smoothly functioning, without conflict and hostility, while in the north it was likely that some friction obtained and sparks sometimes flew. But the essential difference could best be described in terms of flavor, depth, richness, joy, growing, creating. Somewhere, only dimly perceived, this man knew that life could be more fulfilling, that for some at least it could have meaning beyond mere functioning and sterile serenity.

As he mulled the dream over, he began to wonder if the land to the north might be Eden, a land of eternal plenty and harmony. Here was a further clue to this man's moral difficulty. He was considering the good life in absolute terms. The metaphors of the Bible and this person's dream suggest a problem. Adam, responding to his own flesh, disobeyed an absolute mandate of an absolute God and was banished. Cain, exploring his own resources, dared to try his creativeness by plowing the fields instead of dutifully tending the Lord's flocks like Abel, and had his offering rejected. So this man, alienated from himself yet dimly aware of human possibilities, feels himself rejected, an outsider, guilt-ridden, doomed to exist only in barrenness. He too was failing to meet standards set in absolute terms, standards set by himself.

At this moment we are not seeking historical, genetic causes for the patient's present condition, but rather are interested in the factors that perpetuate his impoverishment. His inner moral code, by which he attempts to live, is rigidly authoritarian. He *should* love his wife and his child—is it not the role of a husband and a father to love? He *should* love his neighbors—are we not all brothers? He *should* be at least civil and accommodating at all times. He *should* also be firm and strong—is this not the role of a man? But what is he to do when his wife would like his attention, his child wants to be taken on his lap, and a neighbor knocks to ask a favor?

It is one of the facts of our being that we are temporal and spatial. We cannot be in two places at the same time. But we would have to be, were we to live up to the rigid, absolute code we so often adopt. Feeling obliged to satisfy everyone, this man variously rushed from one person to another in the effort to live up to his code. He had to streamline himself to keep to a minimum any friction and consequent loss of time. But efficiency to the degree demanded by his standards could never work. He had to blind himself to others' wants, deny within himself his impulse to be helpful, and gradually narrow and numb himself. Yet mutual helpfulness is an essential for the moral life. So a kind of formal helpfulness, with a pretense of interest, took the place of genuine, wholehearted mutuality. It even became impossible for him to accept the help of another, since then his own driven sense of obligation would rear up. Thus another facet of the good life was sacrificed.

Little by little, warmth, tenderness, discrimination vanished— to be replaced by a flavorless mass of pretense. A personal interest in creative writing which needed a measure of aloneness and concentration had to be thrust aside. When he did grant himself time alone, he was so often occupied with holding in check his feeling that someone was demanding his presence, or so burning with anger at feeling an obligation to be doing something for others, that little could ever reach the paper.

How immoral such a need to be attentive to all wishes can be is demonstrated in this pathetic family scene. Home from his office, he sits with his child on his knee, open book in his right hand, "reading" the bedtime story the child asked for, while in his left hand he holds his mail and silently scans through his letters. Could there be any greater lack of morality? He cannot really take in any more than the words of the letters, and he deprives himself of the joy of being with his child. He experiences only a pretext of participation, and cheats himself and his youngster of the presence and enrichment of a human relationship. He is almost a machine, certainly a poor expression of a person. And yet he proudly boasts of his agility, "After all, the boy doesn't seem to mind, and I know the story by heart."

The importance of self-awareness and human relatedness to morality is illustrated in an episode that has particular significance for teaching and learning. This involved a father's taking his seven-year-old son out in a rowboat. The boy had for some time been able to pull an oar with the boat anchored in shallow water, but now he was eager for a try in the deep sea. As he pulled the oars, it was evident to his father that he was angling or feathering the oar so that only a small surface was exposed to the water. For the father, the forward speed was negligible, but evidently speed was not a value for the son. The former, offering his advice as to what would be good to do to achieve greater speed, suggested that he hold the oars more perpendicularly to the surface of the water. "If I do that, Daddy, my arms aren't strong enough and we don't get anywhere," the boy said, and demonstrated. To be sure, as he pulled, the boat remained still and he practically lifted himself out of the seat. Value for him came through experience—of his own strength or limits, his testing and experiment. The father, at first taking into account only his own values, had ignored or failed to value correctly the boy's strength. But through communication and a willingness and ability to share values and knowings, each could demonstrate his way and his values.

It is the current condition of any person who is estranged from himself, whether in a totalitarian state or a democracy, that he lives under an inner dictatorship that demands absolute fealty to absolute values. Genetically, this arises when one is in fact subjected to rigid authoritarian codes, whether harsh or benevolent in quality. As long as freedom and human relatedness are minimized, some measure of life is destroyed or perverted. A child is then in fact alone, isolated in a hostile world, and, if he develops any of his potentials at all, they tend to be those that make for expediency. He may develop his intellect to a marked degree when he discovers that this will help him in gaining security. He may limit his physical explorations, because these bring only scolding criticism when the room is too messy for his meticulous parent. And so, hypertrophy of one resource goes along with atrophy of another. In the process of doing this, he deadens or distorts so much of himself that he becomes a partial being, an excluding, not including or embracing, person.

He seeks, for instance, human companionship, but he fails to be spontaneous and affectionate. He is able to entertain his friends with his erudition, but he is awkward and insensitive when it comes to the tender intimacies. And so he often finds himself more and more lonesome, baffled that others value so little what he values. He becomes a frightened person, and, out of fear, he seeks some answer to allay all his anxieties. He may seek in some external institution or in some philosophy the final answer and the ultimate cause to affirm his meaning. And within himself he creates an idealized image of absolute perfection. These efforts would in themselves be of no great harm were they merely goals, stars to give him direction. But, bred of fear, they are not standards assumed freely and used humanely as guides. They become instead a stern Moloch. They make of a person a mean thing who must clamor and blindly rebel to be heard, or who must submit meekly. As long as he lives, he cannot err without self-contempt; he cannot disagree without fear of reprisal. If he rebels blindly, he becomes a headless conglomerate of passion. If he fails to struggle, he submits and becomes bland and tasteless, like the community on the island. If he withdraws from life, not simply as a social recluse, but with a formal sociability, he withdraws from his own juice and sap, from the vital stuff of self.

The moral problem of today has been studied under many aspects, as indeed it must be if we are to guide ourselves intelligently. Students of the human community have seen the problem in terms of nationalism and the conflict of power. Others have correctly recognized the massive pressure toward conformity and the fear of differentness. Some have defined the difficulty in the Promethean terms of man's reaching beyond himself and being unable to control the product of his initiative, science. Man, some say, has become again a beast, aiming at the destruction of his brothers. The essential problem, others say, is that we have become estranged from God, and hence have lost our meaning and our spiritual sanctions.

Psychoanalysis, dealing as it does with the individuals who compose the community, cannot offer any all-embracing formulation of these problems. However, men do make laws, change them, enforce them, rebel against them. Men do cast the votes which unleash destruction or direct their delegates to negotiate. Men are prejudiced or compassionate. Men hate or love, close themselves off or are open to learning and growth. Certainly, whatever we can know of the intimate elements of human nature can add to the understanding, and perhaps the resolution, of the problems studied under any other aspect.

Analytic experience demonstrates that as a person is able to free himself of an absolute morality he becomes more mutually related to others. His life becomes both richer and humbler. He is able to give more and he can receive more. Imagination, often hypertrophied to create a life that cannot be lived in actuality, can be freed for effective use as one tool among many. Now it can be free to take in the poetry and music that enrich life and to project action which can add to our knowledge and resources.

Briefly stated, the experience of this approach is that a living morality is identical with self-realization. But does self-realization not lead man to egocentricity or selfishness? Does this not make man arrogant and asocial? Does it not make him irreligious and more kin to the flesh than to the spirit? Analytic experience shows quite the contrary. Under the heel of authoritarian rule, either inner or outer, we tend to become objects, functions, unreflective and unrelated. When we are close to ourselves, we are able to relate to other people as people, not as things. And out of this human relationship, we are able to experience our relationship with that which transcends us.

A dream of one patient, beginning to free himself from the inner alienating dictatorship of neurosis, gives eloquent testimony to this. Functionally conforming to accepted good values, he egocentrically considered other people as commodities. Now, becoming aware of a cramping loneliness, he dreamed that he was confined alone in a small room. He moved from wall to wall, from corner to corner. Then, with increasing panic, he rushed about in greater and greater disorganization. Then he began to feel and know that if he could cry, weep, he could find his way out. This was a person able to act, to explore, but too much concerned with the physical expression of unreflective action, with power. Now he was beginning to know that tears, suffering, honestly felt and expressed, had a freeing power. He was coming to realize what Sartre and the modern Existentialists, in their attempt to free man for humanism, seem not to know. There *is* an exit, not through a leap of faith into the abyss, but by man's tapping his own resources, his own vital juices. This is not to elevate tears and suffering to a moral plane to the exclusion of other elements. To do so would be no different from the overvaluing of action, force, intellection or love. Morality in its essence must be inclusive, not exclusive, of one's self, of all of which this self consists, of others and the mysteries which transcend us. This is a spirituality that is humble and, coming out of experience, is owned and assented to. It is not an ill-fitting adaptation, arising from fear.

But a morality based on self-realization, while inclusive in quality, is not without discrimination. If it were, the particular person, who is after all the focus of morality, would be lost. For example, it is said that man stands against nature, or that the artist is in conflict with nature. Logically, this ensues if we mistake a condition of differentness or contradiction as conflict. Psychologically, it obtains when we ourselves grant a sameness to ourselves and the nonhuman universe. For there is a difference between a condition and a self-conscious agent. If we say that we are better than dogs who swill their food from the ground while we eat from china, are we ennobling ourselves or do we not demean ourselves by this comparison? When we see a statue, made of stone which had no interest in being or not being a statue—or anything else, for that matter—do we ennoble the sculptor by saying that he conquered nature, he outwitted the stone? Is this not similar to the belief that speaks of God as beneficent or angry? When man can feel his own strength, he can be humble and rich, aware of the ground of his own being and his fellow's being. At the same time, he can be aware of nature as uninterested in him, yet able to feed or crush him.

It is moral and enriching to distinguish human life from nonhuman life and the living from the non-living. Differences in kind do not predicate superiority or inferiority—whether in terms of status, prestige or vanity. And out of this grosser distinction, may we not be able to make the more immediate and finer ones? May we not be able to see that human life is not measured by geography, that values are not a matter of number—even of majorities of votes or guns? And, whether we like it or not, men in community must take some responsibility for judging their fellows. Will we not judge with greater humility and love when, in our discrimination, we can recognize the other in particular as well as in general?

Absolute standards of morality which promise ultimate fulfillment paradoxically result in just the opposite. Under such a standard man makes of himself a thing among things, all variety and differences erased. And this can take mathematical or religious form in which individuality and uniqueness are merged and blurred. Then, like the pilot in the stratosphere, we can guide ourselves only by instrument. It is out of the relations of people whose values are relational, grounded in differences, that we have the possibility for an including, creating and moral community. This is a morality that can include justice, law and love, that lives and grows with the human beings who create it.

# Jehovah's Witnesses as a Proletarian Movement

## WERNER COHN

## ( *1955* )

The growth and influence of one of America's most publicized religious sects is analyzed by WERNER COHN in a well-documented study of Jehovah's Witnesses. Mr. Cohn is assistant professor of sociology at the University of British Columbia.

O F ALL THE NUMEROUS SMALL RELIGIOUS SECTS in this country, that of the Jehovah's Witnesses is possibly the best known. Its members are seen proclaiming the Kingdom of God on the street corners of all our cities and towns; the United States Supreme Court has had occasion to consider the Witnesses over and over again since the First World War; international Witness conventions, held in New York's Yankee Stadium in 1950 and again in 1953, have astounded the press and the public by their huge attendance and their superb organization; and the Witnesses, partly as a result of such aggressive slogans as "Religion is a Snare and a Racket," have often been the object of intense hostility and mob violence.

The most usual immediate response toward the Witnesses touches also, in my opinion, that which is sociologically most important about them: people feel that here is something very "curious." Whether one is attracted toward them or has one's hostility aroused, one cannot help noticing that the Witnesses are *different* and that they do not seem to fit into the patterns of our everyday lives. As I will try to show, the Witnesses are actually separated by an almost airtight spiritual barrier from the rest of American society; the organization is truly a universe unto itself.

A close study of the Witnesses has convinced me, now, that the organization is typical of a certain sociological type which I call "proletarian," which includes not only the radical religious sects but also such other fanatical movements as the traditional German youth movement *Wandervögel* (literally "roaming birds") and some of the Zionist youth groups. Most important of all, it also includes the Nazi and Communist movements. Following Toynbee, I use the term "proletarian" to describe a movement which lives in, but is not of, a given society. I take this to be the original meaning of the word in our modern languages. When Marx described the working class as "proletariat," he wished to indicate that it lives and works in, but does not partake of capitalist society. He spoke of the worker's "alienation" from the conditions of his work; he advocated a workers' organization that would function within, but look beyond the present society. A radical version of this precept is the program of all proletarian movements.

I should emphasize in the beginning that their common quality of being proletarian does not make very different groups identical in other respects. In my own estimation of them, there is a tremendous difference between Zionist youth groups, which arouse my interest and sympathy, and the totalitarians, whom I abhor. While I believe that totalitarianism is an extreme consequence of all proletarian movements, I also realize fully that one cannot judge things simply by the extreme consequences to which they might lead.

It is not difficult, now, to recognize a proletarian movement intuitively by its aura of social estrangement: these movements do not participate in the charitable, religious or political activities of the community—they have a profound distrust for social institutions. They might, of course, utilize institutions; the Communists utilize parliamentary institutions and trade unions, and Jehovah's Witnesses utilize the courts to protect their organization. But utilization is not participation. The distinction is perhaps best illustrated by the Communist role in the European parliamentary institutions. Non-Communists who participate in these institutions deal with legislative proposals as important in their own right; proletarians, on the other hand, can deal with such matters only as maneuvers to further aims which are essentially outside parliamentary competence.

Still on the level of an intuitive recognition of the proletarian character of fanatical movements, we invariably find a number of "separation rites"—demonstrative practices by which the proletarians set themselves apart from everyone else. For one thing, there is always a peculiar jargon of the proletarian group; Arthur Koestler, in *The God That Failed,* tells the story of how the Gestapo was able to spot German Communists by the way they turned a phrase even when speaking about the most non-political subject, and I myself shall never forget a fellow-traveling acquaintance who remembered the title of Ribble's classic *The Rights of Infants* as *The Democratic Rights of Children.* "Zionese," the jargon of extreme Zionist youth groups, mixes Hebrew phrases with English in such a manner that the language becomes altogether unintelligible to the outsider, as in this passage from a journal published by one of them, Hashomer Hatzair: "And so, the moshavot ended, the tents folded, the songs died out in the machaneh, and against the darkness of the night a shura at attention was silhouetted. . . . The degel came slowly down. . . ." Jehovah's Witnesses, finally, boast that their "ability to speak a 'secondary language' . . . unites them far more effectively and completely than a language such as English unites all English-speaking peoples."

I

Examination reveals that, despite their many obvious differences, the ideologies of the various proletarian groupings show the most striking resemblances: invariably they emphasize eschatology. A cataclysmic end of the world, with a millennium following, is prophesied by all the movements.

The proletarians, of course, are not alone in holding eschatological views. All believing Christians do, and, as I have indicated, all the denominations that issue from Marx do too. But it is the radical sectarians among the Christians, and the Communists among the Marxists, who *emphasize* eschatology. This "doctrine of the last days" is central to proletarians (and only peripheral to non-proletarians) because it says, in effect, that nothing that is going on now is really very important, except insofar as it destroys the status quo; it allows proletarians to reject responsibility for, or interest in, any of the affairs of "this world."

Proletarian eschatology typically contains a particular esoteric knowledge system, a doctrine of rejection of the world, and a description of the millennium. It is these elements to which I refer collectively as the proletarian ideology.

Esoteric knowledge is most familiar to us in its Communist and Nazi forms; the Communist view that dialectics form a super-

365

science and invalidate "bourgeois" science and the Nazis' theories on race are the most immediate examples. Proletarians feel that they—and they alone—have access to certain facts and to a body of knowledge which are infinitely superior to the common sense of the larger society: its truths are by definition esoteric since they are not accessible to anyone outside the proletarians' universe.

All religious belief, in a certain sense, partakes similarly of the esoteric, since it always requires a believer's faith to appreciate the truly religious; and it is also probably true that ultimately elements of faith are necessary for an acceptance of what is now known as the "scientific method." But there are degrees, not only of reasonableness itself, but also of the proletarian tendency. As will be shown later, our social structure everywhere has proletarian elements; and as everyone knows, the most reasonable has its unreasonable sides. But the fact remains that there is a fundamental area of common assumptions, that is to say, a *common sense*, which is accepted alike by American Protestants and Catholics, by Democrats and Republicans, and (for a European example) by all the Anglicans and Catholics and Nonconformists and Laborites and Conservatives in England—and that Jehovah's Witnesses and other proletarian groups stand outside this common sense.

The esoteric belief subscribed to by the Witnesses is especially instructive for a study of proletarian movements in general. It has all the essential qualities of proletarian ideology without evoking the tense emotional reactions which nowadays make objective discussion of the totalitarians so difficult.

According to Witness doctrine, the Kingdom of God began in 1914. Since then, God and Satan have shared in the rule of the world, as they will continue to do until some time in the near future. This joint rule is very unstable and will terminate after the coming battle of Armageddon, at which time Satan will be defeated in a bloody war and the theocratic millennium will begin.

Human beings are divided into two classes: the "heavenly class," consisting of 144,000, and the "other sheep," consisting of all the rest. The heavenly class will share governmental power with Jesus during the millennium; it will reside in heaven, and from there direct the theocracy. Many of the other sheep will perish during the battle of Armageddon; the rest—presumably those who accept the teachings of Jehovah's Witnesses—will live on this earth forever. "Millions now living," say the Witnesses, "will never die."

Most of the heavenly class died during previous generations, and they will have to be resurrected immediately after the battle of Armageddon. But there are some—estimated by the Witnesses to number 20,221 as of 1952—who are still living and functioning in the Witness organization. This "remnant" will ascend from the earth directly to heaven after Armageddon.

Witness esoteric knowledge is quite exact when it comes to dates and figures. It has definitely established that Adam was created in the fall of 4025 B.C. The year 1914—the beginning of the Kingdom—was arrived at by the most painstaking computations. A short quotation will give the flavor of this research:

> From Genesis 7:11, 24, 8:3, 4, we learn that five months are exactly 150 days, thirty days to a month, thus giving us 360 days for a year according to Bible reckoning. Further, in Revelation 12:16 we have a time period of 1,260 days, which in verse 14 is also referred to as being "a period, periods (that is, two periods) and a half a period of time," or three and a half times. So our seven times or years would be seven times 360 days or twice 1,260 days for a total of 2,520 years.
>
> . . . Since those nations began trampling Jerusalem underfoot in 607 B.C., then 2,520 years later, or A.D. 1914, would mark the coming of him whose right it is and the restoration of sane, divine dominion over mankind.

I have purposely selected this passage because it contains so much that is typical of all proletarian ideology. First, there is the close, mathematical reasoning; the argument is presented in a manner that appeals to our most rational faculties. Second, the argument is completely esoteric, for ordinary reasoning power alone is of no help in trying to understand it. For those equipped with no more than the common sense (i.e., for those lacking the esoteric insights), the passage contains at least two unbreachable barriers: (1) The word "periods" that appears in Revelation 12:14 is immediately followed by the Witness interpolation "that is, two periods." But if we do not take it for granted that "periods" means "two periods," the whole calculation topples. (2) The date 607 B.C. is not entered in any of the standard secular or religious histories as the year in which "nations began trampling

Jerusalem underfoot," so far as I can tell after considerable research. The date is unique to Witness historians; they do not bother to discuss just how it was arrived at, but flatly attack all criticisms of their historical method with the remark that they "are not called upon to harmonize these [chronological computations] with the tangled records of secular history."

The proletarian doctrines of rejection are almost identical in the various groups. Everything in this world is wicked; the values of society are superficial, hypocritical, false; in fact, there are no meaningful ideological differences in the world except those that exist between the inside (the given proletarian movement) and the outside (everyone else). Furthermore, the present order is doomed, and will presently be replaced by a new and absolutely perfect one. Obviously no interest should be taken in any of the affairs of this world, since such affairs are destined for an early, complete and violent termination.

To Jehovah's Witnesses, the worldly institutions—governments, religions, international organizations—are all involved in a vast Satanic conspiracy against the Kingdom. The United Nations is described as a "many-membered beastly association of nations," as "the disgusting thing of Matthew 24:15 and Daniel 11:31." The government of the United States, that of Russia, the various Protestant denominations, and especially the Roman Catholic Church —all these are "tools of Satan" without any important differences among them. After a simple change of its terms, this doctrine becomes identical with that of the Communists, to whom democratic liberalism and nazism are twin aspects of the same capitalist evil; it becomes identical also to Nazi doctrine, which saw no essential difference between believing Catholics and Communists, between democrats and bolshevists.

The proletarian doctrine of rejection is in a sense—certainly in a formal sense—the very core of proletarianism itself. As I use the term here, proletarianism *means* isolation from the world and spiritual detachment from society and its institutions. But as we shall see again and again, proletarians have more than a merely formal opposition to worldly institutions; theirs is a deep-going alienation from the ways of the world, which expresses itself most revealingly in their contempt and mistrust of the ordinary and everyday concerns of society.

Along with a fanatical rejection of the present world, the proletarians present us with visions of a millennium. The Nazis referred to the "Thousand Year Reich"; the Communists invoke "Socialism." "The New World" is the millennium as predicated by Jehovah's Witnesses. The Witnesses describe their utopia as follows:

Then, with the end of worldly warfare, freedom in the full sense of the word sets in. Freedom from fear will be there, for no more will atomic or hydrogen bombs or the devilish demonic heavens hang like a threatening cloud over the people. Gone will be the need for armed troops . . . or even a local police force. . . . Lawlessness and vice, together with casualty-producing accidents, fires and floods, will be things of the old-world past. Neither will there then be millions of unemployed or displaced persons wandering aimlessly from one city to another. . . .

Famine and drought, together with rationing and black marketing, will cease for all time. . . . The terrestrial globe, free of those who ruin the earth, takes on a new appearance, developing into a place of Edenic grandeur. . . . Then even the beasts of the field will be at peace with one another and their guardian, man.

The visible part of the new world will be a diseaseless "new earth." . . . Aches and pains will die out, as radiant health, unmarred by cancer, influenza, or even a toothache, implants itself in every soul. . . . This means the vanishing of old age, with its wrinkled skin, its gray hair, its feebleness. It means that vigorous, energetic youth, so fleeting today, will be the eternal lot of every faithful human. . . . No dream is this, nor propaganda scheme to solicit for a man-made "better world," but it is the truth.

These utopian visions interest me mainly because they reveal the more subtle and the less conscious difficulties which the proletarian finds in this world. The New World is seen without such everyday hazards as accidents, fires, disease—without even a toothache. It is such things, however, that reality is inevitably made of, and the Witness vision of a world without any kind of grief suggests an underlying inability to come to terms with the risks and dangers inherent in life itself. Freud, in *Totem and Taboo,* had already touched upon the real core of proletarianism when he declared that "the rejection of reality is at the same time a secession from the human community."

The most astounding of all passages that I have seen in the literature of Jehovah's Witnesses deals with survival after Armageddon. It compares the fate of the righteous with that of the rest of humanity:

> The survivors of this "war of the great day of the Almighty" will be his lovers, the New World Society. After the battle they will go forth and look upon the carcasses of those whom Jehovah has slain, unburied, the food of worms that will not die or cease from swarming over the odious carcasses until they have eaten the bones clean, the food of fire mixed with sulphur that will not be extinguished until it has completed the consumption of all remnants of the carcasses. . . .

Those who happen to be outside the "New World Society" (i.e., the Witness organization) clearly do not have much to hope for. But even the survivors of the terrible battle of Armageddon must watch their step! Those that are found wanting in obedience will be executed:

> those refusing to keep the Kingdom sabbath [i.e., honor the millennium] by faith and by ceasing from selfish works of sin and false religion will be executed by the Lord of the sabbath and be destroyed eternally.

Speaking even of the children who will be born during the millennium, the Witnesses warn that:

> Every child, reared in the discipline and authoritative advice of Jehovah, will have full opportunity for life through Christ the King. Any not desiring to serve Jehovah will be executed, rightly.

The meaning of the proletarian secession from society lies largely in the escape from the conflicts and ambiguities of reality. Proletarian ideology seeks to end these by forbidding all controversy, and the proletarian's millennial dreams can be interpreted, I think, as fantasy fulfillments of the wish to abolish all the difficulties inherent in ordinary life.

The totalitarians have explored the more horrendous possibilities of proletarianism by acting out these fantasies. Their concentration camps became the grounds where the supposedly unfaithful were "slain," while the righteous were able to "go forth and look upon the carcasses." And not only were the unfaithful slain and executed, but they were destroyed "eternally"; the totalitarian history books do not mention them, for their names have never really existed.

Proletarian ideology fights a constant battle to abolish reality; but the battle now is full of compromises. So long as the movement cannot transform society in the image of its own fantasies, the stubborn material demands of reality intrude at every turn. Once society has been transformed into a totalitarian universe, however, reality can be abolished to a very significant extent. Since men can be made to believe ideology in preference to truth, many of the demands of science and consistency can be overcome. Since terror can be made almost absolute, the most primitive sadistic fantasies can be acted out upon prisoners in concentration camps. And since, above all, fanaticism can take the place of self-interest, grandiose and fantastic military campaigns can be carried out without the benefit of military science. These are the extreme consequences of proletarian ideology.

## II

Proletarian organizations show highly interesting similarities in organizational structure. In her *Origins of Totalitarianism,* Hannah Arendt describes most of these features as they appear in the Nazi and Communist movements; I shall try, with special attention to Jehovah's Witnesses, to show here how her observations might be applied to all proletarian movements. The features to which she directs attention—specifically, irregularity of organizational form, the "onion" form of organization, and underlying mystification—seem to be not only characteristic of the totalitarians, but natural concomitants of proletarianism as such. One more such concomitant is charismatic leadership, which I shall also consider.

The proletarian principle of irregularity rejects all formal organizational structure. Proletarians do utilize these structures, but only for purposes of hiding the actual authority relationships; the classical case is the file clerk in the totalitarian embassy who gives orders to the ambassador. The irregularity in the totalitarian countries becomes most obvious by the fact that the various ostensible lines of command are ill-defined and have a tendency to become tangled. Not only is there a constant rivalry between such structures as army, party and state (or party and espionage machines in the Communist movements outside of Russia), but the line of command within any one of these is unstable and varies from moment to moment. And then there are personal cliques everywhere, cutting across all other allegiances. The result of this kind of arrangement is a situation in which no individual can ever be sure of his status for long; the highest official can become a slave laborer overnight.

Youth-movement organizations are perhaps the prototype of proletarian irregularity. In its revolt against parent domination, the youth movement presents the youthful charismatic leader as the only acceptable guide for the adolescent. And while a youth movement often shares many characteristics with such adult-sponsored "youth-serving" groups as the American Boy Scouts or Young Judea, the charismatic quality of "youth leading youth" constitutes an invariable distinction. The youth-movement leader has grown up in the movement and perpetuates the spirit of defiance against authority and regularity; the youth-serving leader, on the other hand, is appointed by the adult authority, is generally paid for his efforts, and tends to give the youth-serving organization a stamp of subservience to authority and of regularity.

As in totalitarian organizations, the principle of irregularity is carefully covered by formal trimmings among Jehovah's Witnesses. Witnesses have three distinct legal corporations: the Watchtower Bible and Tract Society, the Watchtower Bible and Tract Society Incorporated, and the International Bible Students' Association. But all three corporations have a total membership of only about 500, whereas there are over 150,000 Witnesses in the United States. Supposedly there are no membership rolls of rank-and-file Witnesses, though the organization keeps very exact statistics of the number and the activities of these people. The work of each Witness is carefully controlled and directed by a central authority; this authority is very real, but it is in no way accounted for by any formal plan of organization.

The top Witness leader—at present N. H. Knorr—is the president of the three legal corporations; he has no other official title. His actual status in the organization, however, is no more defined by his title than was Stalin's. And neither can the status of the secondary Witness leadership be measured by titles. I have found that the most reliable method of establishing the standing of any particular Witness leader is to observe how often his name is mentioned in the Witness publications, and to see how closely it is connected with that of Knorr.

Proletarian groups typically consist of various layers of differing degrees of initiation. At the center are the leader and the elite, at the periphery is the casually associated individual, the sympathizer, the fellowtraveler; in between are the ordinary members, who are again stratified according to how far they have gone—or how far they have been permitted to go—into the proletarian universe. This structural characteristic of proletarian organization is called the "onion" form.

The onion form has a direct relationship to the esoteric knowledge of the movement; since the requirements of everyday life make it necessary to maintain a certain minimum of common sense, the proletarian core surrounds itself with layers that increasingly compromise with ordinary reality. While for the Communist elite the products of "bourgeois" science are unacceptable, the Communist movement has a place for "innocents" and "progressives" who are allowed to play with the community's common sense and even with the common science. But these outer peels of the onion do more than merely protect the inner ones from the unfriendly environment of common sense; they also have the function of creating a special aura which, as it emanates from the husk of the proletarian movement, can give rise to social regions in which differences between the common sense and the movement's esoteric knowledge—between sense and non-sense—become obliterated. Such regions have at various times existed in some parts of the liberal sections of the American academic world and in some parts of the European labor movement.

The onion form of Jehovah's Witnesses is almost an exact duplicate of that of the totalitarians. There are the leader and the elite that surround him; there are various classes of field officials, and various classes of rank-and-file members. Some of these classes are institutionally recognized—there are "pioneers," "special pioneers" and "company publishers" (the lowest grade)—though the stratification system as a whole is neither institutionalized nor at all stable. It will be remembered that though there were various official strata of Nazi members—the S.A., the S.S. and its various special formations, among many others—the total stratification system of the Nazis depended on the momentary relative standing of party, state, police and army, as well as on identification with a particular personal clique. The Witnesses' arrangement is similar.

Witnesses publish two kinds of periodicals. One, *The Watch-*

373

*tower,* deals with the esoteric knowledge system and is almost incomprehensible to outsiders. The other, *Awake,* gives the impression of an interest in the everyday affairs of the world. *The Watchtower,* printed on good bond paper, is the technical journal of the insider; *Awake,* printed on cheap newsprint, is for the sympathizer. Witnesses do not try to hide their opinion that the contents of *Awake*—while necessary to hold the interest of the innocents—are ultimately of an order inferior compared to those of *The Watchtower.* This attitude is typical of proletarians on all levels toward the thinking of those whose place in the onion is more peripheral than their own.

In addition to the marked irregularity of all proletarian organizational life and its onion form, there is an invariable tendency toward deliberate mystification. This is perhaps most obvious in the peculiar addiction to exact statistics from which most of the groups seem to suffer. Historians of Nazi Germany were surprised to find a wealth of Nazi statistics on such matters as the number of Jews killed on any one day, and the number of gold fillings in the teeth of these Jews. The production statistics from the Soviet Union are equally fascinating; while a multitude of exact figures and percentages are presented by the government, they give no important clues to the realities of Soviet economic life.

Jehovah's Witnesses have an equal interest in numbers and exact statistics which is matched only by the exactness with which they tabulate the history of the universe (Adam's creation took place "in the fall of 4025 B.C."). In reporting on their 1953 convention in Yankee Stadium, the Witnesses present figures of attendance, broken down for each day, and for "stadium proper," overflow, and the Trailer City which the Witnesses had established in New Jersey. Looking up the figures for the sessions I attended, I was interested to learn that those present at the morning session of the eighth day numbered 72,469 persons in the stadium and an "overflow" of 14,368. Now there were no tickets, ticket-takers or turnstiles of any sort at the stadium, and, like everyone else in sight, I walked in and out of the stadium several times during the session without molestation. I saw nobody counting with hand-counters. While anyone experienced with large crowds could certainly have ventured an estimate of the attendance, one would need truly to have had divine inspiration to come up with a figure like 72,469. Furthermore, Witnesses do not stop at a mere reporting of the figures; various percentages and increases are computed. The increase of total attendance of the first day of the convention over the first-day attendance at the 1950 convention, to pick a convenient example of Witness statistical science, amounted to exactly 47,113.

The most amazing example of Witness statistics that I have seen, however, is the report of Witness activities for the year 1953. Two and one-half pages of closely printed figures are presented, informing us, among other things, that in the United States a total of 12,978,943 pieces of literature were sold during 1953, and that in Sierra Leone the Witnesses spent a total of 28,772 hours working for the "Society." Similar figures are given for countries all over the world, including such far-off places as Israel (21 Witnesses there), Senegal, Hong Kong, Okinawa, Southern Rhodesia and Swaziland. But the truly striking thing about these figures is that they could all have been published in the January 1, 1954, issue of *The Watchtower*—I received my copy a few days before New Year's Day. The accompanying article, it is true, sometimes refers to the "1953 service year," but no indication is given that this is different from the calendar year; more often than not, the article uses the phrase "during 1953" when discussing the figures.

These three typical proletarian mechanisms—irregularity, onion form and mystification—are indications of the proletarian's instability and his profound distrust of order. In the same way in which the proletarian's eschatology serves to place him outside the concerns of ordinary men, so do the proletarian organizational principles separate him from the responsibilities of everyday life. To have an orderly, rational organizational life within the proletarian movement would be self-defeating, for all the social responsibilities against which the proletarian revolts on the outside would then crop up right at home in the form of humdrum organizational housekeeping.

The complete lack of inner order and organization, to be sure, frequently shows itself in very desperate attempts at precision and superb organization. The exactness in dates and in statistics illustrates this tendency; but this exactness is really all a house of cards —the figures which are later so carefully tabulated and manipulated with all the sophistication of modern statistical techniques are simply invented to begin with. And, thus, all the exaggerated efforts at achieving exact order merely result in compounding the disorder. The fanatic is typically doctrinaire: what are absolute certainties on the surface can hide the tremendous underlying uncertainties he feels.

As in all cases of an essential separation from the community's common sense, of course, proletarians find it necessary to make certain substantial compromises with reality. They run business enterprises, deal with money, come to temporary agreements and understandings with other social forces. But these compromises with reason—always relegated to the outer layers of the onion—are but subordinate parts of a larger pattern that is dominated by fanatical disorder and complete contempt for reason.

What has here been discussed as the principle of irregularity in proletarian organization is in many ways similar to what is technically known as charismatic leadership, an arrangement whereby leaders have followers not because of any formally acquired status, but because of a personal "gift of grace." A man like Father Divine is a good example of a charismatic leader. He is followed not for any tangible achievement or any special preparation; his followers, rather, attribute a very personal and extraordinary power to him —one that cannot be duplicated by anyone else. Charismatically led groups, through their rejection of institutional stability, are thus certainly irregular. But the question is whether it is necessary for all irregular groups—e.g., proletarian movements—to have charismatic leaders.

The classical interpretations have made a great deal of the personal importance of Hitler and Stalin in the totalitarian movements; some writers have even held that the worship of leaders constitutes the core of the totalitarian phenomenon, and that, once the totalitarian leader dies, the movement that has been connected with his name will necessarily crumble.

Quite aside from the fact of the post-Stalinist existence of communism—which by itself is enough to refute this view—it seems to me that one would seriously (and perilously) underestimate the social importance of proletarianism if one were to limit it to the reach of personal magnetism. Proletarian movements have found means—notably the apparatus of organization and esoteric ideology—of transferring the charm of the charisma from the person of the leader to the movement as a whole. As will be shown, it is certain social conditions and certain kinds of personalities that determine the existence of proletarian movements; the charismatic leader alone certainly does not.

While proletarian movements can exist without such personages, there is, nevertheless, a basic ambivalent attraction to charismatic leaders from within these movements. On the one hand, this type of leader threatens the very existence of the movement by his inescapable quality of being mortal; on the other hand, there is a great psychological need on the part of the proletarian for such a person. Jehovah's Witnesses—and apparently the Communists too—now have an arrangement whereby there is a charismatic leader in principle though not in practice. The name of Knorr is constantly mentioned in connection with all Witness activities, and he is spoken of as if he were the equivalent of the early leaders of the organization, who really did exercise charismatic powers. But when Knorr appears in public, Witnesses greet him with no more than a polite applause; his speeches are carefully read by him, and verbatim printed versions are distributed the moment he finishes. There is absolutely none of the real excitement that surrounded the early leaders, none of the ecstasy with which followers greeted Hitler.

The dilemma of needing a charismatic leader and not being able to afford one is the sort of thing Marx called an "internal contradiction"; it remains a source of potential crisis for any proletarian movement. How well a given group can deal with this danger depends in large measure on how much need there is for the movement within the society in which it functions. Where the surrounding society is well integrated, all the internal troubles of the proletarians have a tendency to multiply. Where the society is beset by forces of disintegration, the proletarian movement can overcome its own difficulties much more easily.

### III

It is interesting, finally, to look at the social and psychological origins of proletarianism.

It has been frequently noted that there is an adolescent quality about proletarian movements: there is a romantic selflessness that has contempt for the grownup's concern over economic security; there is an all-important "cause" whose internal life takes the place of family relationships. It does not surprise us, therefore, that youth movements—the organs of adolescent social revolt— are a prototype of all proletarian movements in psychological atmosphere and organizational structure. The untranslatable German word *bündisch* expresses these adolescent qualities; it is a term, interestingly enough, which the Nazis took over from the *Wandervögel*. If we had to summarize the psychological origins of proletarianism in a single phrase in English, that phrase would be "adolescence fixation."

If we borrow a term now from Durkheim, *anomie*, we also can identify the main social conditions that foster proletarianism: material insecurity, a lack of spiritual cohesion among the various elements that make up society, and a feeling that social disputes can no longer be arbitrated through a common governmental institution. Perhaps the most striking recent example of these conditions is the Weimar Republic, in which setting all proletarian movements flourished. The *wandervögel* became a mass movement in the early days of Weimar; the Nazis grew spectacularly in the late twenties and early thirties (partly because they knew how to utilize *Wandervögel* traditions) ; and the German Communist party became the largest outside of Russia.

We may generalize, I believe, that both adolescence fixation and anomie are causal conditions for proletarian movements. Their relative importance seems to vary inversely. Where—as in England and the Scandinavian countries—anomie is at a minimum, the proletarian movements are small and are composed of individuals whose personal difficulties loom exceptionally large; where social anomie is dangerously acute—as it was in the Weimar Republic and is now in France and Italy—the rank and file of proletarian movements are not restricted to the emotionally disturbed. But even in these countries, we have evidence that the proletarian inner elites consist almost exclusively of perpetual adolescents.

I cannot close without warning that in actual life the proletarian cannot be as neatly distinguished from the non-proletarian as it might appear in this article. For the sake of simplicity, I have dealt mainly with groups in which proletarianism has been brought to an extreme; this is particularly true of Jehovah's Witnesses and of the totalitarian movements. But if we stop to consider that emotional immaturity comparable to that of adolescents is not restricted to members of proletarian movements, and that elements of anomie exist not only in Europe but also in this country (especially, I would say, in the South) , it should not surprise us to find potential proletarian leaders and followers in a great many places indeed.

Ultimately, the roots of all proletarian movements lie in contemporary society. We might speak of the proletarian's desire to secede from the community, but we know that this desire is always conditioned by spiritual and material deprivations. The strength of proletarian movements within a country is a good barometer of the cohesion and permissiveness of its social structure. Instead of merely hating and despising these movements, we might take them as a challenge to reorder things so that none will need to take flight into proletarian fantasies.

# The Possibilities of Heroism

## DAVID DAICHES

## (*1955*)

Critic and essayist DAVID DAICHES here explores the changing concepts of the hero in recent English and American
novels. He soundly supports his contention that the possibilities of heroism have been vastly diminished, first by prudence, and now by knowledge. Mr. Daiches, who has taught
both in this country and in England, is university lecturer in
English at Cambridge University.

FOR A LONG TIME literature depended on heroes, but in our time
it has had to learn to live without them. Heroes are not necessarily good people; they are, however, people of moral stature,
people who command our moral attention whether their acts are
right or wrong. The equation of physical prowess with moral
stature often occurs in certain early phases of literature; in English literature one thinks of Arthur and his knights, though by the
time Malory came to handle these stories the relation between
prowess and virtue had become less simple, and the heroic key
was modulated into elegy—a sure sign of the decay of one kind of
heroic ideal in literature. The hero had a heroic destiny, whether
tragic like that of Oedipus or epic like that of Aeneas, and his
destiny was bound up with those aspects of his character which
gave him moral stature and physical courage. Only the folk tradition, in its iconoclastic wisdom, occasionally protested against the
assumption that destiny is determined by quality of personality,
and threw up stories of feckless younger sons or irresponsible
paupers who achieved a hero's reward through sheer luck. A more
sophisticated age, looking for substitutes for conventional heroes
in whom it can no longer believe, will turn with relief to these
fools and paupers, as Yeats did in his later poetry or, on a different level, Kingsley Amis did in his novel, *Lucky Jim;* for Yeats,

379

the fool symbolizes the paradox of ultimate wisdom; for Amis, the hero as clown is a commentary on the fatuity of the world.

Prudence and knowledge are the enemies of heroism, and the hero in modern literature has succumbed to a series of attacks, first by the former and then by the latter. Too intimate a knowledge of a hero inevitably reduces his stature. No man is a hero to his valet—or to his psychoanalyst. Oedipus remains a hero so long as he is not simply suffering from an Oedipus complex; once we learn to explain him in terms of repressed hopes and fears, traumatic childhood experiences, or a vitamin deficiency in infancy, he may remain *interesting* (indeed, he will gain a new kind of interest) but he loses *stature*. As for prudence, that is always the ultimate destroyer of a heroic age. Arthur's knights remain heroic because nobody (at least, nobody before Mark Twain) stands outside their world to question the prudence of their exploits. Don Quixote is less fortunate; standing between the feudal period and a more modern commercial age, he is exposed to the voice of prudence, which reduces his chivalry to folly. Yet his is a noble folly; he is ridiculously deluded, but the delusion of a man who prefers to live in a lost heroic world rather than face the realities of a contemporary prudential one has something admirable about it—or so we can afford to feel once that lost world is so far away as to be no longer a threat to our modern self-interest. Don Quixote is a transitional figure, seeking the "crowded hour of glorious life" in a civilization which has only recently given up that sort of thing. As we leave the feudal age farther and farther behind and move through commercial toward industrial civilization, we note the emergence of a new kind of hero, the prudential hero, of whom Robinson Crusoe is the first important example in English literature. The hero whose motives are prudential rather than selfless, or who seeks safety rather than glory, can never appeal to the imagination as the older species of hero could (Ulysses is perhaps an exception, but I have not space to explain why I think he manages to retain his heroic appeal in spite of his cunning self-interest); and romantic attempts to revive the older hero provide an interesting testimony to man's reluctance to accept prudence as an ideal. The romantic historical novel is an attempt to create a world in which the old kind of hero is still possible; and the genre is still with us, though not respectable. The other way was to find new kinds of heroes—men of good heart, like Tom Jones and Mr. Pickwick; Ulysses as businessman, like Scott's Baillie Nicol Jarvie; incomplete personalities who are completed and improved by experience, like (in very different ways) Pendennis and Gwendolyn Harleth; reformers, like Felix Holt; victims of fate, like Tess, or of society, like Ernest Pontifex; and many other varieties. The novelist survived the age of prudence. He even found ways of making prudence heroic, and where he could not do that he found new ways of giving stature to his characters. A character could even achieve a certain symbolic stature by being kicked around long enough, not like patient Griselda, who was after all demonstrating moral virtue, but like a mere football illustrating the wayward athleticism of fate.

The story of the fictional hero in the age of prudence is fascinating. Even when the prudential hero—the Robinson Crusoe or Samuel Smiles type—was finally found out by the Victorians as a hypocrite or a villain, a large number of new heroic types survived. Knowledge has proved a more fatal enemy. *Tout comprendre c'est tout pardonner* says the French proverb, "To understand all is to forgive all"; but it is also to reduce all characters to a dead level of interest. Anglo-American fiction of the last ten years has tried hard to come to terms with psychological and other kinds of knowledge. The problem was posed by the novelists of the 1920's; in the thirties and early forties the pressure of public affairs deflected the novelists from the problem altogether. They have returned to it recently with interesting results.

Before discussing some of these results I must try to make the problem explicit. New psychological knowledge posed problems for novelists concerned with the presentation of character; it also troubled those who were concerned with the moral pattern of their work. We know, or we think we know, so much about psychological conditioning, about the psychosomatic aspects of illness, about the relationship of childhood frustrations and adult vices, that we are in danger of being unable to pass any moral judgment on individuals. This man committed rape or murder, but we know that he saw something terrible in the woodshed when he was three, was brought up in a slum without orange juice and cod-liver oil, was bullied by a drunken stepfather, had his emotions and instincts warped in this way or that; how, then, can we blame him for what he was eventually driven to do? If our moral judgments are to be dissolved in psychological understanding, how can we pattern a tragedy or create in literature characters who have true stature? Certainly, a behaviorist psychology—using this term in the widest sense—leaves little room for an appraisal of personality as such; and without an appraisal of personality as such, why should Hamlet's death be any more significant than that of Polonius?

That is one aspect of the problem. Another is that the more we know about the individual consciousness, the more complex and lonely it appears; and the less revealing of our true selves are those public gestures that the need to attempt to communicate with others forces on us. The eighteenth- and nineteenth-century novelists for the most part saw their characters publicly, as it were; saw their fate adequately reflected in changes of fortune or social status; allowed them to experience nothing that was not both communicable by themselves and capable of being symbolized by some publicly visible action. The great theme of the English novel in the nineteenth century was the relation between gentility and morality; but the English novelist of the twenties was concerned with the relation between loneliness and love. Consciousness is the sum of one's previous private emotional history; we are each the prisoner of our own subconscious; how, then, is communication possible? Not only the artist, but all individuals are alienated from society—Leopold Bloom as much as Stephen Dedalus, Mrs. Dalloway as much as Septimus Warren Smith. We seek rituals of communication in parties and pubs: one aspect of modern man as seen by novelists and short-story writers is symbolized by the *New Yorker* cartoon which showed a bartender offering a microphone to a customer and saying, "If you will record your troubles into the machine, sir, I will listen to them as soon as I have a moment."

The novelists of the twenties sometimes tried to solve the problem by limitation of the context: at most you could, in E. M. Forster's terms, be a member of the "little society" as opposed to the deceptive "great society." For Forster, as for D. H. Lawrence, the "great society" is always the enemy. It is not a question of how to reform the great society, as it was in Dickens— "O, reform it altogether." Lawrence's concern was with how individuals could fully realize themselves as individuals as a preliminary to making true contact with the "otherness" of another individual. That was as far as you could go. But the contemporary novelist cannot even go so far as that. The hero of L. P. Hartley's novel, *The Go-Between,* is a boy moving about in a world of adults and creating out of his own responses to that world something which exists only in his own mind. In America, the hero of Salinger's *Catcher in the Rye* moves in a world to whose conventional gestures he finds himself unable to make any public response whatsoever.

The number of recent novels and short stories dealing with children and adolescents moving about in worlds half-realized indicates the degree to which the question of loneliness and love has come to haunt the modern imagination: the child in a grown-up world is the proper symbol of man in society, surrounded by the public masks of others just as he himself presents to others his own public mask. In the 1920's you found salvation—if you were lucky—in the little society; in the 1950's the little society is no better than the great society; you are as lonely in a bar as in a ballroom. You can grow out of the problem by becoming more of an extrovert, like the heroine of *A Member of the Wedding* at the end of the story; but the problem will be waiting for you around the next corner.

Knowledge thus dissolves value in explanation and substitutes inevitable loneliness for communion. The dissolution of value makes heroic stature impossible; but what about loneliness? Is not one kind of hero essentially the lonely man? He is, when his loneliness results from his being above his fellows: it is Oedipus' paternal attitude toward his people that dooms him to isolation. But if all the others are lonely too, and lonely in the same way—if we are all members of the lonely crowd—loneliness cannot confer heroic status. One way out is to make your loneliness into a Bohemian glory, give Stephen Dedalus enough to drink and give him a taste for practical jokes—combine him with Buck Mulligan, in fact—and you get someone like Joyce Carey's artist Jimson. But Jimson's Bohemian heroics are not wholly convincing: they do not belong, we feel, to our world. Another way is to see man not within society but against nature. Here Hemingway's *The Old Man and the Sea* is interesting, for Hemingway is a secret society man from way back, seeking in his earlier novels to find a select heroic environment to set against the shoddiness of modern urban life. The trouble with *Across the River and into the Trees* is that, in his perennial search for heroism in the modern world, Hemingway was incautious enough to try to combine the stoical and the matey, the Suffering Servant and the bar fly, as though one could have at the same time the dignity of isolation, the cameraderie of the really *tiny* secret society (you, your girl and the barkeeper) and the comfort of confession. In *The Old Man and the Sea* he is content with a wholly elemental situation, narrated with a ritualistic precision. The old man has the boy, but on his ordeal he is alone with the big fish. Man's truest communion is not with his own kind, but with the inhuman forces of nature which he both fights and loves. You get back your hero this way, it is true, but at the cost of abandoning the depth and complexity that modern literature has worked so hard to attain. The recent tendency to approximate literature to myth—myth being literature as emblem rather than as exploration—involves a kind of surrender, an admission of inability to cope adequately with the richness of modern knowledge; but it has its compensations.

The American writer—haunted, I suspect, by that same yearning for a lost heroic way of life that we find so magnificently expressed in Mark Twain's *Life on the Mississippi,* with its contrast between the old days of river heroism and the new railroad age—has been more reluctant to give up the hero than the British. Even the toughest American prober into the jungle of human history, society and psychology—even Faulkner himself—insists on a moral pattern, on a meaning, on at least a potential heroism, even if he has to inflate his language in order to suggest it. The British have been more content to accept what might be called the "anti-hero." The early novels of Aldous Huxley presented him often, and he is a staple figure in the novels of Evelyn Waugh. This kind of hero is related to the hero as victim whom we find in Butler's *Way of All Flesh.* But we are asked to laugh at him—as we laugh at Paul Pennyfeather in Waugh's *Decline and Fall*— rather than to pity him, even though the laughter has masochistic overtones. Idealism emerges as mere ignorance, innocence as a dangerous lack of sophistication, with the virtuous anti-hero the complacent tool of sophisticated vice, as Paul Pennyfeather finds himself (without knowing what it is all about) organizing the white slave traffic. If you try behaving like an old-fashioned hero, as the hero of *Men at Arms* does when he goes on an unauthorized and dangerous private raid on the enemy coast, you will find yourself court-martialed and demoted. This can be hilariously funny in the hands of a witty and skillful writer like Waugh. Interest is sustained by a gallery of nostalgic eccentrics who are sometimes funny (like Apthrope in *Men at Arms*) and sometimes pathetic. We feel this most in *Brideshead Revisited,* in whose first chapter the nostalgic note swells out as never before in Waugh's novels. Here the cruelly farcical coincidences of many of the earlier novels give way to suggestions of a lost world lying dimly behind the feverish gestures of valueless modern life. Religion, the old Catholic religion, is presented in Waugh's later novels not as a living source of spiritual values which can redeem the modern wasteland, but as what might perhaps be called the stiff upper lip of the soul; it gives the believer dignity of bearing, like wearing evening dress in the jungle. Thus religion provides aristocratic gestures to shore against the ruins (quite Hemingway-like, really). This is an odd use of religion in fiction, but perhaps no odder than the more serious use of it made by Graham Greene, another Catholic novelist, who seems concerned with showing the essential incompatibility between human decency and theological virtue: the decent thing is, literally, damnable, or if not absolutely damnable, it is (like the hero's behavior in *The Heart of the Matter*) only doubtfully exempted.

Waugh is a satirist, but knowledge can dissolve blame as well as praise. Angus Wilson's *Hemlock and After* moves from satire to diagnosis, and in the end we know all and cannot blame anybody. Sheer malice, accompanied by brilliant wit, can create a sort of a world—witness Mary McCarthy's *Groves of Academe*—but you must have more than wit and malice to convince the reader of that world's importance. Swift was passionately concerned about man, and his villains are the anti-types of potential heroes; but we have the impression that Mary McCarthy doesn't give a damn for *la condition humaine* anyway, which may not be true, of course, but which makes her hero-less novel somewhat dreary in the last analysis. Randall Jarrell's *Pictures from an Institution*, another academic satire, is all done with mirrors, the author creating a character who wisecracks about the other characters; and this would seem a good way to achieve some success with a hero-less world; but old-fashioned heroism emerges in spite of Mr. Jarrell's satiric intentions, and there is a discrepancy between what he knows and what he esteems. *Lucky Jim*, a very different English academic novel, is based on sheer nihilism, and the clowning hero stands for nothing but himself, the fortunate fool, which is funny but not satisfying.

Can a man be seen as a hero if we know him better than he knows himself? Can the individual come to terms with his loneliness and achieve moral stature in spite of—or because of—his isolation, which he shares with his fellows? These seem to me to be the themes with which the Anglo-American novel in the last decade or so has been most fruitfully concerned. In the last analysis, the question is: What has civilization done for us? The modern novelist, unlike some of his predecessors, does not know the answer; but he has achieved some searching ways of posing the question.

# The Present Human Condition

## ERICH FROMM

### (1955)

ERICH FROMM has long emphasized the need for the social and cultural orientation of psychoanalysis, in contrast to orthodox Freudianism. Dr. Fromm, in this article, which is more fully developed in his book *The Sane Society*, stresses that man must acquire a sense of self in both his human and spiritual life if he is to function effectively.

AT THE CLOSE OF THE MIDDLE AGES, Western man seemed to be headed for the final fulfillment of his keenest dreams and visions. He freed himself from the authority of a totalitarian church, the weight of traditional thought, the geographical limitations of our but half-discovered globe. He built a new science which eventually has led to the release of hitherto unheard-of productive powers, and to the complete transformation of the material world. He created political systems which seem to guarantee the free and productive development of the individual; he reduced the time of work to such a level that man was free to enjoy hours of leisure to an extent his forefathers had hardly dreamed of.

Yet where are we today?

The danger of an all-destructive war hangs over the head of humanity, a danger which is by no means overcome by the spirit of Geneva prevalent at the time of this writing. But even if man's political representatives have enough sanity left to avoid a war, man's condition is far from the fulfillment of the hopes of the sixteenth, seventeenth and eighteenth centuries.

Man's character has been molded by the demands of the world he has built with his own hands. In the eighteenth and nineteenth centuries, man's character orientation was essentially exploitative and hoarding. His course through life was determined by the desire to exploit others and to save his earnings to make further profit from them. In the twentieth century, man's character orientation is essentially a receptive and a marketing one. He is receptive in most of his leisure time. He is the eternal consumer; he "takes in" drink, food, cigarettes, lectures, sights, books, movies—all are consumed, swallowed. The world is one great object for his appetite, a big bottle, a big apple, a big breast. Man has become the suckler, the eternally expectant—and the eternally disappointed one.

If "privately," individually, modern man is a consumer, he is "publicly," in his active participation in his society, a trader. Our economic system is centered around the function of the market as determining the value of all commodities, and as the regulator of each one's share in the social product. Neither force nor tradition, as in previous periods of history, nor fraud or trickery govern man's economic activities. He is free to produce and to sell; market day is judgment day for the success of his efforts. Not only are commodities offered and sold on the market; labor itself has become a commodity, sold on the labor market under the same conditions of fair competition. But the market system has reached out farther than the economic sphere of commodities and labor. Man has transformed *himself* into a commodity, experiences his life as capital to be invested profitably; if he succeeds in this, he is "successful," and his life has meaning; if not, "he is a failure." His "value" lies in his salability, not in his human qualities of love and reason or in his artistic capacities. Hence his sense of his own value depends on extraneous factors, his success, the judgment of others. Hence, he is dependent on these others, and his security lies in conformity, in never being more than two feet away from the herd.

However, it is not only the market which determines modern man's "public" character. Another factor, though one closely related to the market function, is the mode of industrial production. Enterprises become bigger and bigger; the number of people employed by these enterprises as workers or clerks grows incessantly; ownership is separated from management, and the industrial giants are governed by a professional bureaucracy which is mainly interested in the smooth functioning and in the expansion of their enterprise, rather than in profit per se.

What kind of man, then, does our society need in order to function smoothly? It needs men who co-operate smoothly in large groups; who want to consume more and more, and whose tastes are standardized and can be easily influenced and anticipated. It needs men who feel free and independent, who do not feel subject to any authority or principle or conscience, yet are willing to be commanded, to do what is expected, to fit into the social machine without friction—men who can be guided without force, led without leaders, be prompted without any aim except the one to be on the move, to function, to go ahead. Modern capitalism has succeeded in producing this kind of man; he is the automaton, the alienated man. He is alienated in the sense that his acts and forces have become estranged from him; they stand above and against him, and rule him rather than being ruled by him. His life forces have flowed into things and institutions, and these things, having become idols, are not experienced as the result of his own efforts, but as something apart from him which he worships and to which he submits. Alienated man bows down before the works of his own hands. His idols represent his own life forces in an alienated form. Man does not experience himself as the active bearer of his own forces and riches, but as an impoverished "thing," dependent on other things—things outside himself, into which he has projected his living substance.

Man's social feelings are projected into the state. Just because he has made the state the embodiment of his own social feelings, he worships it and its symbols. He projects his sense of power, wisdom and courage into his leaders, and he worships them as his idols. As a worker, clerk or manager, modern man is alienated from his work. The worker has become an economic atom that dances to the tune of automatized management. He has no part in planning the work process, in its outcome; he is hardly ever in touch with the whole product. The manager, on the other hand, is in touch with the whole product, but he is alienated from it as something concrete and useful. His aim is to employ profitably the capital invested by others; the commodity is the abstractified embodiment of capital, not something which, as a concrete entity, matters to him. The manager has become a bureaucrat who handles things, figures and human beings as mere objects of his activity. Their manipulation is considered to be a concern with human relations, when actually one deals with the most inhuman relations—those between abstractified automatons.

Our consumption is equally alienated. It is determined by the advertising slogans, rather than by our palates, eyes or ears.

As a citizen, then, modern man is willing even to give his life for his fellow men; as a private individual, he is filled with an egotistical concern for himself. The meaninglessness and alienation of work result in a longing for complete laziness. Man hates his working life because it makes him feel a prisoner and a fraud. His ideal becomes absolute laziness, in which he will not have to make a move, where everything goes according to the Kodak slogan: "You press the button; we do the rest." This tendency is reinforced by the type of consumption necessary for the expansion of the inner market, leading to a principle which Huxley has very succinctly expressed in his *Brave New World*. One might epitomize the way many of us today have been conditioned from childhood with: "Never put off till tomorrow the fun you can have today." If I do not postpone the satisfaction of my wish (and I am conditioned only to wish for what I can get), I have no conflicts, no doubts; no decision has to be made; I am never alone with myself because I am always busy—either working or having fun. I have no need to be aware of myself as myself because I am constantly absorbed with consuming. I am a system of desires and satisfactions; I have to work in order to fulfill my desires, and these very desires are constantly stimulated and directed by the economic machine.

We claim that we pursue the aims of the Judaeo-Christian tradition, the love of God and of our neighbor. We are even told that we are going through a period of a promising religious renaissance. Nothing could be further from the truth. We use symbols belonging to a genuinely religious tradition, and transform them into formulas serving the purposes of alienated man. Religion becomes a self-help device for increasing one's own powers for success. God becomes a partner in business. The "Power of Positive Thinking" is the successor of "How to Win Friends and Influence People."

Love of man is a rare phenomenon too. Automatons do not love; alienated men do not care. What is praised by love experts and marriage counselors is a team relationship between two people who manipulate each other with the right techniques, and whose love is essentially a haven from an otherwise unbearable aloneness, an egotism à deux.

What, then, can be expected from the future? If one ignores those thoughts produced by our wishes, one has to admit, I am afraid, that the most likely possibility is still that the discrepancy between technical intelligence and reason will lead the world into an atomic war. The most likely outcome of such a war is the destruction of industrial civilization and the regression of the world to a primitive agrarian level. Or, if the destruction should not prove to be as thorough as many specialists in the field believe, the result will be the necessity for the victor to organize and dominate the whole world. This could be realized only by a centralized state based on force, and it would make little difference whether Moscow or Washington would be the seat of government.

But, unfortunately, even the avoidance of war does not in itself promise a bright future. In the development of both capitalism and communism as we can visualize them in the next fifty or a hundred years, the process of automatization and alienation will proceed. Both these systems are developing managerial societies in which inhabitants are well fed and well clad, having their wishes satisfied, and not having wishes that cannot be satisfied; automatons, who follow without force, who are guided without leaders, who make machines that act like men and produce men who act like machines; men whose reason deteriorates while their intelligence rises, thus creating the dangerous situation of equipping man with the greatest material power without the wisdom to use it.

In spite of increasing production and comfort, man loses more and more the sense of self, feels that his life is meaningless, even though such feeling is largely unconscious. In the nineteenth century the problem was that *God is dead;* in the twentieth century the problem is that *man is dead.* In the nineteenth century inhumanity meant cruelty; in the twentieth century it means schizoid self-alienation. The danger of the past was that men became slaves. The danger of the future is that men may become robots. True enough, robots do not rebel. But given man's nature, robots cannot live and remain sane. They become "golems"; they will destroy their world and themselves because they cannot stand any longer the boredom of a meaningless life.

What is the alternative to war and robotism? Most fundamentally, perhaps, the answer could be given by reversing Emerson's phrase: "Things are in the saddle and ride mankind," and saying: "Put mankind in the saddle so that it rides things." This is another way of saying that man must overcome the alienation which makes him an impotent and irrational worshiper of idols. This means, if we remain in the psychological sphere, that he must overcome the marketing and receptive orientation which dominates him now, and emerge into the mature, productive orientation. He must acquire again a sense of self, he must be capable of loving, and of making his work a meaningful and concrete activity. He must emerge from a materialistic orientation and arrive at a level where spiritual values, love, truth and justice truly become of ultimate concern to him. But any attempt to change only one section of life, the human or spiritual one, is doomed to failure. In fact, any progress which occurs only in one sphere is destructive of progress in all spheres. The gospel concerned only with spiritual salvation led to the establishment of the Roman Catholic Church; the French Revolution, with its exclusive concern with political reform, led to Robespierre and Napoleon; socialism, insofar as it was only concerned with economic change, led to Stalinism.

Applying this principle of simultaneous change to all spheres of life, we must think of those economic and political changes which are necessary in order to overcome the psychological fact of alienation. We must retain the industrial method. But we must decentralize work and the state so as to give them *human* proportions, and permit centralization only to an optimal point which is necessary because of the requirements of industry. In the economic sphere we need co-management of all who work in an enterprise to permit their active and responsible participation. The new forms for such participation can be found. In the political sphere, we must return to the town meeting by creating thousands of small face-to-face groups which are well informed, which discuss, and whose decisions are integrated in a new "lower house." A cultural renaissance must combine work education for the young, adult education, and a new system of popular art and secular ritual throughout the whole nation.

Just as primitive man was helpless before the natural forces, modern man is helpless before the social and economic forces created by himself. He worships the works of his own hands, bowing to the new idols, yet swearing by the name of the God who commanded him to destroy all idols. Man can protect himself from the consequences of his own madness only by creating a sane society which conforms with the needs of man, needs which are rooted in the very conditions of his existence: a society in which man relates to man lovingly, in which he is rooted in bonds of brotherliness and solidarity, rather than in the ties of blood and soil; a society which gives him the possibility of transcending nature by creating rather than by destroying; one in which everyone gains a sense of self by experiencing himself as the subject of his powers rather than by conformity; one in which a system of orientation and devotion exists without man's needing to distort reality and to worship idols.

Building such a society means taking the next step; it means the end of "humanoid" history, the phase in which man has not become fully human. It does not mean the "end of days," the "completion," the state of perfect harmony in which no conflicts or problems confront man. On the contrary, it is man's fate that his existence is beset by contradictions which he is impelled to solve without ever solving them. When he has overcome the primitive state of human sacrifice, be it in the ritualistic form of the Aztecs or in the secular form of war; when he has been able to regulate his relationship with nature reasonably instead of blindly; when things have truly become his servants rather than his idols—he will be confronted with the truly human conflicts and problems. He will have to be adventuresome, courageous, imaginative, capable of suffering and of joy, but his powers will be in the service of life, and not in the service of death. The new phase of human history, if it comes to pass, will be a beginning, not an end.

# This Literary Generation

ROBERT LANGBAUM

*( 1955 )*

Because the present literary generation aspires to domesticity and order as its parents aspired to freedom, it has been labeled "unoriginal," "academic," "silent." ROBERT LANGBAUM, a member of this new literary generation, accounts here for its character and pathos. Associate professor of English at the University of Virginia, Mr. Langbaum is author of *The Poetry of Experience* and numerous literary and political articles.

EVEN BEFORE World War II was over, everyone was speculating about the character of the new literary generation; and the speculation continues—with publishers positively prospecting for the new Hemingway, the new Fitzgerald, the new Faulkner, and with any number of alert critics ready to pounce upon whatever new trends are in the making to turn them into literary history. I wonder if any literary generation has ever been so awaited, so encouraged, even compelled, to be original, to display its character. The result is that the new generation, the generation that fought the war and is now in its thirties and early forties, still seems, to everyone's dismay including its own, to have no character. Nobody has said this outright, but it is implied by the words used to describe the new generation—words like *conservative, academic, conformist, other-directed* and, best of all, *silent*. The Silent Generation is, I think, the name which will stick. Now no one could be more dismayed by all this than the new generation itself, as I, a member of it, can testify; for no one could be more interested in learning what the character of the new generation is going to be than we are.

The trouble is that the older literary men were expecting a new Lost Generation and have never forgiven us for not being original in their manner. I remember a talk Malcolm Cowley gave a few years ago before a college literary society, in which he chided the young writers as timid, conventional prigs who were taking university jobs for the sake of economic security. He told amusing anecdotes of his own youthful days of wild, hand-to-mouth existence, and spoke of the interesting characters he had known—of Hart Crane and the odd things he did before he went mad and committed suicide, and of Scott Fitzgerald who, the last time Cowley saw him, was on the wagon, drinking tumblers of water which he finally confessed were gin. Somewhere the tone had changed, the amusing anecdotes had turned into something else. The change made us feel, in Browning's words, "chilly and grown old." We felt the passing of time and the gulf separating us from that period.

Not that we were indifferent to its romance. The nostalgia for the twenties has been a phenomenon of the past decade—a dialectic of comparison having been established between the two postwar decades, with the thirties a mere bridge making little appeal at the moment to our imagination. If the nostalgia proceeds from the regret of the older people for the youth they have lost, it proceeds also from the regret of the young people for the youth they have missed. For we shared, I suppose, the expectation of the older people that we would repeat the experience of the Lost Generation; but we found ourselves, once the war was over, somehow too old for an experience involving so much exuberant irresponsibility. John Aldridge, in *After the Lost Generation,* his study of the new novelists, tells how he and his literary friends thought they were going to participate in a brilliant postwar period of revolt and innovation, but came to realize soon after the war was over that the new age had not arrived and was not going to. In the same way, one might add, the new Hemingway and the new Fitzgerald, the novelists we were waiting for who would speak for this generation as the novelists of the twenties spoke for theirs, have not arrived and may not be going to. Instead we have what is on every side being attacked as an age of criticism.

Malcolm Cowley, for example, has since published his attack on the present period in his book, *The Literary Situation,* where he calls it "the new age of the rhetoricians"—comparing it to the last period of classical culture when creative activity was relegated to the past, and literary effort was devoted to establishing an authoritative canon of great works and classifying and reclassifying, analyzing and reanalyzing them with ever more tortuous subtlety and ingenuity. The same attack has been made with even greater violence by younger critics like Randall Jarrell, Irving Howe, John Aldridge. In fact, the rhetoricians themselves are the first to agree with their attackers, to sigh "all too true and all too sad" as they turn back to their textual analyses. It is not their fault that they are thrust into the limelight by the absence of a creative literature powerful enough to keep them subsidiary.

If more criticism is being written than before, it is because more is being read. The serious young writer is tempted to write criticism because it sells more easily and brings faster prestige than poetry or even short fiction. He may also turn to criticism after having failed in his first attempts at fiction—after having found that he cannot in fiction escape the manner of his immediate predecessors, that he cannot invent a fable to express what is different about the new period; whereas he can express the difference by taking off in criticism from other men's fables. For the same reason, the reader of the literary quarterlies is likely to turn first to the critical articles, and may not even get around to the one story the issue carries. That is because he does not expect to find anything new in the story, but is almost certain to find something new in at least one or two of the articles. Indeed, if the talk one hears is any indication, the tendency to skip the fiction in magazines may be spreading to readers of the *New Yorker, Harper's* and the *Atlantic* as well.

Connected with the question of the new generation's character is the question of whether fiction is losing its old pre-eminence. "Is the novel dead?" has been the subject of a running debate these last ten years, a debate which may have reached its climax in England the summer before last with a newspaper controversy involving several famous names. The complaint against the new novels is that they are either not new or, if new, without general relevance. In other words, there has not yet emerged from them a set of characters and situations, a rhythm of speech, a code of manners, a point of view, which catch or create the style of this age as the novelists of the twenties both caught and created the style of theirs. To say the new generation has no character is to say that the new novelists have been unable—whether through their fault or ours—to show us our style, our sense of ourselves.

It is their style we envy the twenties, its consistency and their acute awareness of it. The age is all of a piece: the stripped prose of the novels and the cool forlornness of the young people in the novels, their drinking, their speeding in motorcars, their movement in novel after novel toward a wanton and elegant self-

destruction—these things have their counterpart in the life outside the books: in the jazz, the new clothes for women, the new
tough, informal sophistication, the new pathos of understatement.
Both in and out of books these things, which we have inherited,
were for them signs of their difference from the prewar generation, signs of their allegiance to a code uniting the young against
the old—a code demanding that its adherents at any price, even
the price of self-destruction, not be hypocrites and sentimentalists
like the Victorians.

There, in the rebellion against the Victorians, we see why the
twenties had style and we do not. The twenties still had the Victorian grannies and aunties around to shock. Typical of the pos-
ture they could assume was the well-known remark of Harold
Ross that he was not editing the *New Yorker* for "the old lady
from Dubuque." Nowadays, alas, the old lady from Dubuque
reads the *New Yorker,* drinks martinis before dinner and is probably under analysis. She was, in fact, a flapper in her time—which
is why the *New Yorker* has lost its kick and the old lady's children
haven't got a point of view to call their own. Implicit in the fiction
of the twenties is an age group and social class which could be
identified with respectability and convention, and against which
the protest of the young, their unconventional behavior and assertion of the meaninglessness of life, took on moral significance.
There is no such given bulwark of respectability in the new fiction.
The old are as "unconventional" as the young, often more so; and
the well-to-do are notoriously more dissolute and often more politically radical than the poor.

I am reminded in this connection of a story in the *New Yorker*
a few years ago by a new writer, Hortense Calisher. The story is
about a good-looking, sensitive, Ivy League young man, the kind
who in a Fitzgerald story would have gone in for a career of
cutting-up. But this is a young man of the fifties who, with sober
and long-suffering composure, takes care of an ex-flapper mother
in her peregrinations between Greenwich Village, where she
drinks, and the sanatorium in Greenwich, Connecticut, where she
recovers. At the apartment of a Bohemian, homosexual older
man, our hero meets the man's daughter, a demure young woman
who has spent her life shuttling between her "interesting" father
and a mother who has married and divorced some four or five
times. The two young people strike up an immediate understanding. "For they were," the author says in the end, "the same age,
whatever that was, whatever the age was of people like them."

The story establishes perfectly the relation between the two post-war generations, the responsibility forced upon the young by the irresponsibility of the old. It also suggests a new literary pathos, the pathos of a generation that never was young—that, starting where its parents left off, aspires to domesticity and order as its parents aspired to freedom.

You will not find this pathos, however, in many new novels. Most of them still carry on with the pathos of youthful self-destructiveness, with protest and aggressive unconventionality. But since the protest does not, in the new setting, have an adequately represented object in respectability and convention, it takes on an automatic, compulsive quality which may, if the story comes off, give the protest a surrealistic or symbolic look, but which more often gives it the look of a tired literary convention. This is how, since Hemingway, young people in novels act: they drink, they are promiscuous, they say profound things in monosyllables, they don't give a damn—just as in the Victorian novels of the Byronic tradition the young men were reputedly wicked but always chivalrous, and the young women susceptible but chaste. It is as though the older novelists had bequeathed to us, in their picture of the First World War and the decade that followed it, a kind of literary country where our novels go on taking place regardless of their ostensible setting.

We have not been "capable," says Leslie Fiedler in last Summer's issue of *Partisan Review,* "of seeing around the great literary platitudes of the twenties."

> We have lived for thirty years in the world of someone else's dreams: a compulsive world in which Lieutenant Henry forever declares his private peace, Sherwood Anderson eternally walks out of his office, the Artist forever leaves the world of Puritanism and Respectability for the utopias of Bohemia or Expatriation. To be sure, we do not all relive the legendary pattern, or even believe it; but we have been unable to imagine our choices in any other image.

Mainly in critical writing, like this piece of Fiedler's, have we been given such liberating awareness and even shown the possibility of new choices. This may be why we talk of the decline of the novel and turn to social, psychological and literary discussion, to criticism in the widest sense, for that novelty of accent, that experience of breaking through the received to the actual truth which we used to look for in the novel. Does any novel speak so distinctively of and for the past decade as, say, *The Lonely Crowd* of Riesman, Glazer and Denney, or Lionel Trilling's *Liberal Imagination?*

In a symposium published in *Partisan Review* in 1952, a large group of American intellectuals agreed that the intellectuals have since the war terminated their exile from American life, that they now find America as good a place as Europe and perhaps a better one for the thinker and artist. The symposium made a neat parallel with Harold Stearns' symposium of 1922, called *Civilization in the United States,* in which thirty American intellectuals agreed that America was no place for the life of intellect and art— thus giving at least one signal for that trek to Paris which was to figure so brilliantly in our cultural history. Reading the earlier symposium today, however, one finds that American life is still, despite certain improvements, very much as described there. Why, then, the return from exile, the switch from negation to affirmation?

The question is related to the question one asks about so many new novels, about so fine and honest a novel for example as Norman Mailer's *The Naked and the Dead.* Why, since we recognize as true Mailer's account of the sordidness of the war and of the American society which made his characters what they are, why are we not moved to greater indignation and compassion? The answer to both questions is, I think, that the fight against the bourgeois or Philistine sins, as these are defined by Mailer and the 1922 symposium, has been won on the *literary* front, even if we still commit them. That is, our vision has already been organized by the ideas Mailer draws on; so that we recognize in his novel what we have been taught to see with our old eyes, whereas literature at its best gives us new eyes. The return of the intellectuals from exile is merely a recognition of what has been achieved. But their new affirmative attitude is less an acquiescence to things as they are, than an attempt to define new issues, new objects for attack. To take one example: *The Lonely Crowd,* since it denies the relevance of many old issues, looks affirmative; yet there emerges from it, in the figure of the "other-directed" man, an object for as much critical attack as was launched in the twenties against the Philistine.

Certainly the contributors to the 1952 symposium did not relinquish the modern assumption that the intellectual's role is to criticize and that great literature is to be equated with what they called "critical nonconformism." One of the questions they considered was whether it would be possible, in the face of the new affirmative attitude, to maintain the American literary tradition of critical nonconformism. A few (Mailer was one) thought the new affirmative attitude not much more than a "sellout"; but most thought that critical nonconformism would have plenty to do to improve the quality of our culture by taking up new issues.

It is not easy to see why criticism should at present care more conspicuously than fiction for new issues—unless it is that we have, through critical effort, to free ourselves from an old myth before we can make a new one. I sometimes think, in my more savage moments, that the real purpose of our age of criticism is to kill off our immediate predecessors in literature by understanding them, by tucking their dreams away in the pigeonholes of abstract discourse so we can get on with our own. A kinder interpretation of the same phenomenon is to say we have come to the point where we must pause to count the cultural riches of the modern period, to master a whole canon of modern classics before we can make our contribution.

For our age of criticism differs from the Alexandrian model at least in this: that we are not interested in old literature, but almost exclusively, too exclusively, in modern literature and what bears on modern literature. Nor are we only interested in explicating texts, but in bringing literature into such combination with the ideas and facts of the time as to create a new unity—a unity wrought by our very best critics with so much passion and imagination that their writing is not merely ancillary to literature but a literary genre in its own right. What we are really trying to do— and only this can explain the seriousness with which we read and write criticism—is to create out of the modern movement in literature a secular spirituality, a new tradition to give meaning to our culture. Even the so-called New Criticism, which is considered narrowly technical, has in its exploration of symbolic language no lesser purpose than to establish the validity of poetic statements of spiritual perception by showing them to be of another order of truth from scientific statements of fact.

We are doing two things with our critical effort. We are using modern literature as a source of revelation for the values we are trying to organize into a new tradition, at the same time that we are sifting out the cant of modernism. The double endeavor is understandable if we consider that modernism has removed us from the older orthodoxies, leaving only itself as a source for values; and that modernism, a movement of revolt, has itself become an orthodoxy with its own absurdities and hypocrisies. (Only think of the highly respectable professors who beam contentedly as the bright-eyed faces before them take it down in notebooks that ours is an age of despair, a wasteland, et cetera.) The concern with what is to be believed, rather than what is not to be believed, is understandable in a generation that is not *lost* because it has had the experience of fighting a war it believed in and has gone on believing in. Such a generation cannot give its respect to an attitude of merely naive revolt. For having seen revolutionary slogans used to support oppression, and having sustained the contradiction between its hatred of the war as a personal experience and its belief in the necessity of the war, it remains sensitive to complexities.

It is our sensitiveness to complexities that renders us *silent*—that, with a high ideal of taste of the absolutely first-rate in life and art, which may finally prove to be our distinguishing virtue. If we read fewer new novels, we read plenty of slightly older ones, and our respect for The Novel as an idea increases steadily—just as poetry is read, by those who read it at all, with greater seriousness than ever before. It may be that our rigorous demands on art, our overriding concern with masterpieces has, as Randall Jarrell points out, discouraged the creative efforts of the finer spirits among us (the grosser would not be affected). Malcolm Cowley complains, for example, that the young poets and novelists write with one eye on the critics. Yet such virtues as ours, if they bear fruit, should bear the finest. Perhaps this generation, unlike the last, will age well. Perhaps our writers, derivative in their precocious work, will find their own manner (Saul Bellow's *Augie March* is a step in this direction) and produce their best work in maturity. Perhaps, after all, we have been these last ten years in a state of suspension, waiting to see whether the Bomb is going to fall or not—whether we must let our silence speak for us as the only ultimate expression of despair, or whether we can release that joy wherein lies, I firmly believe, the spring of our originality if only circumstances allow us to tap it.

# The Flowering of Latter-Day Man

MAX LERNER

(*1955*)

A perceptive and effective writer, journalist and teacher, MAX
LERNER is the author of *America as a Civilization* and other
books in the area of social theory. In this article, Mr. Lerner
finds pathos in latter-day man because, living amidst an encompassing sense of doom, he can obtain neither personal fulfillment nor a sense of community with others.

IF MAN TODAY IS DOOMED FOR TOMORROW he shows a strange up-
welling of energy and bounce. Surely history offers no parallel
to the paradox of a prevailing sense of doom accompanied by far-
reaching ferment in technics and thought, culture and society. If
man is candidate for a corpse, then the about-to-be corpse is showing the most heterodox stirrings of vitality.

I have been finishing a difficult book on America as a civilization,
and through the decade since I began the book I have made little
headway with the problem of where this civilization is moving—
and along with it the world whose destiny is linked with its own.
There is little question in my mind that America's situation is also
the world's. While I find the concept of American "uniqueness" a
useful one, that uniqueness lies not in the differences of America
in nature and destiny from other civilizations, but in the wide
margin of its lead in technology and power, and the fact that it has
therefore become the carrier for many world changes. It prefigures
in its cultural style and personality traits many of the emerging
trends and traits elsewhere. The American is thus an archetypal
man, not in the Jungian sense of reaching back to a prehistoric
past and a racial unconscious, but in the quite different sense of
reaching into the common future of technical man and his society.

Thus when I speak of "latter-day man," I speak of the type I
know best—the American—while implying at the same time that

what I say is roughly true of other peoples as they enter and pass through similar experiences of technology and culture.

What is there of the latter day, we may ask, in latter-day man? Here the exuberance of American standards of living and the stock-market boom is dismally deceptive. Throughout the world there is the feeling of having experienced much, perhaps too much —wars and revolutions, and the incineration of millions, and the preparations for the radioactive poisoning of still more millions. This is a weary feeling, of having almost reached the ultimate in the Faustian bargain of man's mastery over nature and having glimpsed in atomic power more of mastery and also more of death than man is ready to face.

The old apocalyptic vision of mankind going to its death in an orgy of revolutionary class-conflict no longer has much validity. The classic revolutionary impulse, from the Gracchi to Lenin, is played out, because under modern conditions revolutions can only be successful through wars and can only lead to wars—and war has become the Medusa-head that turns us all to radioactive stone.

I do not say that we have seen the end either of revolutions or of Communist struggle. When in Asia, I saw enough to convince me that the colonial-nationalist thrust toward self-assertion will not be arrested until it has used up its energy. The African movements are waiting in the wings to take the stage in the next act. But I do say that a sense of limits has been imposed on all of these movements, including the Communist, perhaps especially the Communist, which was not there earlier. It is the fear of embroiling their region, their cause, and the world in the most destructive of wars. In that sense Marxism has become archaic in its ultimate power-aspects, since the essence of it was the impersonal march of history—over the bodies of men and empires, if need be —toward a predestined goal. That impersonal march is now banned by a self-imposed tabu.

What remains, then, of the revolutionary impulse? The struggle for nationalist self-realization by pressures short of destructive war. What remains of the Communist impulse? The struggle for mastery of as many of the nation-states as possible by methods short of destructive war. What remains of the capitalist democratic impulse? Similarly, the struggle to maintain its power and to fulfill its inner purposes and possibilities by means short of destructive war. What has happened to the world is strangely reminiscent of the "love-rack" in James Cain's novels, when two people who had once loved each other are caught in a common guilt of a committed crime. In the world's case it is not a love-rack but a hate-rack, with two systems that had hated each other now finding themselves caught in the common guilt of an about-to-be-committed crime from which they recoil. Thus they are unwillingly imprisoned in a brotherhood they do not feel but from whose protective embrace they dare not break.

If there is this sense of bounds, it is for the first time in the history of the modern nation-state. In their wars and revolutions men have been overpassing the bounds that divide the human from both the godlike and the satanic. J. L. Talmon, in his writings on the "totalitarian democracy" of the French revolutionary epoch, and Hannah Arendt, in her book on totalitarian imperialism, have fixed upon the same dramatic paradox: the movements that overpassed the bounds into the bestial always were linked with some idea—democracy, freedom, nationalism, race, progress—which started with the fire of idealism in it. The Nazi crematoria, the Russian purge-trials and extermination camps, the Chinese mass liquidations, were all the logical outcome of passionate ideas that set no bounds to themselves and had no bounds set to them. One can say the same about the Japanese officer-elite that started the Asiatic war and about the highly idealistic American civilians, including Truman and Stimson, who felt that the transcending law of survival empowered them to end the war with atomic death. Today, whether out of guilt or out of some sense of innocence that never faltered through all the planetary turmoil, we are carefully putting some of the young Japanese girls through operation after operation in facial surgery, in an effort to repair what the bombs have disfigured. The Russians are releasing some of their political prisoners and returning Nazi war prisoners, and the Germans have been paying some restitution to Israel for the property taken from their Jewish victims.

If all this seems difficult to reconcile, consider the case of the H-bomb. Insofar as there is objective ground for fearing the physical doom of humanity, the H-bomb is it. We know little of whatever scruples the Russians may have had in moving toward the manufacture of the H-bomb. We do know, since ours is a free country, that American scientists faltered for a moment in the face of the apocalypse of death. Even Teller, who led the group that pushed its doubts aside, has written how he and his colleagues sighed with relief when they found that the fusion bomb would not set the whole earth on fire. The demands of defense and patriotism, however, drove scientists and administrators on, whatever camp they were in, and the division of labor enabled them to leave the ethical questions to the philosophers who specialize in such matters.

This then is at least part of what we mean by the latter-day mood of latter-day man. He has looked into the future and it doesn't work. He has caught a glimpse of what man could do to man if and when he follows to their logical conclusion the institutions of war, nationalism and science. The glimpse has made him sadder, if not wiser. He has been through the Promethean phase of stealing fire from the gods and letting the brands burn as they will. He is faced by the unshatterable fact that he is not God and cannot act as if he were, lest he turn all the planets into a hell. Very late in his latter-day phase he has learned at least one bound that he cannot overpass without committing suicide—the bound of atomic war and radioactive devastation. I don't say that he has learned yet to hold himself this side of the thin line that divides him from suicide, but he has at least had to face the consequences that will flow from not holding himself back.

One could make out a pretty strong case for the proposition that there is a crisis in the condition of society which is as grave as the crisis of survival wrought by the H-bomb. One finds a widespread belief, especially among younger sociologists who seem to have been born old, that there is a "New Society" in which almost everything is degenerate and that America is its forerunner and carrier.

It is a New Society in which the automatic factory and the electronic eye are the symbols of an automatism of the spirit, in which the sources of genuine creativeness in the arts have dried up and popular culture casts its pall of deadly mediocrity over everything, in which government planning and control (even when held to a minimum) are bound to bring an Orwellian nightmare, in which men's minds are swayed by synthetic appeals provided by the public-relations firms ("engineers of consent"), in which the ranks of the sexual deviants have been swelled, in which alcoholism and drug addiction gain constantly, in which the family has crumbled, the old heroism is gone, honor is only a name and loyalty is something checked upon by hunters for dangerous thoughts.

The truth is that the crisis of society is real, and that in some respects I have mentioned (but by no means all) the sickness is palpable. One could spin out the indictment and multiply the counts, and what would remain is that the New Society is indeed a new one, and that men have been cast out of their old securities to stand on their own feet and make their own way, and have not yet discovered how to do it. When Graham Wallas, almost a half-century ago, described the new "Great Society" that was taking shape around him, he was drawing the implications of the Great Technology which was reweaving the social structure after its own image. He saw the intricate and fragile web of communication, and the division of labor which was projected from the factory into the society, and the new techniques for molding men's minds by the power of suggestion. Today, almost fifty years later, the process Wallas saw and described has been stretched so much farther that new concepts and dimensions are needed to grasp it.

The current tendency is to stress its pathology, to talk of its psychosis, and in fact—by making the focus of analysis the idea of the alienation of man from man—to deny that it is a society at all rather than an unhappy collection of atomistic and about-to-be-atomized individuals. Yet it seems a better approach to start with the fact that it is some kind of society, to ask what kind and what is its central principle.

I suspect that the clue lies again, as with Wallas, in the Great Technology, whose changes in America have been so rapid and continuous that Russell Davenport used for them the Trotzkyist phrase "Permanent Revolution." In America, at any rate, the technology is approaching a high degree of automation, which is to say that the basic problem of production has been solved. The problem of distribution, about which the Marxists thought there would be unresolvable class-conflicts, has worked out better than the theorists had expected. Man has been released—not only his time, but his energies and longings as well—for modes of cultivation and expression for which neither he nor his instruments and institutions are ready. The hackneyed way to say it is that he has been released for "leisure." The truer way would be to say that he has been released for thinking about what he shall do with his release. The New Society is new mainly in the sense that it is cluttered up with the new gadgets—automation, the big media of communication and entertainment, the new wealth and consumers' goods, the new ways of bridging space and filling time—which mark the end and beginning of an era. Actually it is a society that still is trying to use the old social forms for the new purposes now at hand.

The pathos of latter-day man in the New Society is that he hungers for personal fulfillment and for a sense of community with others, and he has been unable to attain either. Much of the reason for the spread of mental disease is that, with the problems of making a living less and less pressing, hungers have been awakened for making a *life* before the social means and the social wisdom have been found for satisfying them. I wish one could say that the psychosis of modern life had a single cause, for then one could prescribe a single cure for it. There is not even the solace of finding a good, whopping, satisfying historical parallel with even, let us say, imperial Rome in its stage of decline, degeneracy and collapse. Alas, not even the diatribes against the contemporary American family can draw much sustenance from the parallel. The problem in Rome was an aversion to marriage: the problem in America is a mysterious propensity for it. The problem in Rome was a declining birth rate: the problem in America is the "baby boom," not so much among the ignorant and feckless as among the literate and hopeful. It is true that the American family is a kind of child-oriented anarchy, that marriages come too early and divorces too frequently; but whatever its faults, they derive from the effort to use the principle of democracy within the structure of family authority, and to seek uncompromisingly within the family the happiness that latter-day man longs for. Surely neither of those propositions could have been made about Rome.

I use the family as illustration. Equally I could use the moral codes, sexual behavior, the quest for education and "culture," the idea of happiness. The point is certainly not that we have achieved the good society or the sane society or the happy one or the holy one or the rational one or the cohesive one or the fulfilled one. The point I am making is that latter-day man—if America is to be judged as the test—is trying to make an enormous leap. All along he has been *homo faber,* and in our generation he is reaching the heights of his skill as the fabulous artificer. But he has come to the end of that story, and now he wants to make a leap even riskier than the Daedalian one—the leap from *homo faber* to *homo felix,* from a concern with commodities to a concern with his own personality and its happiness, from adventures among markets to adventures among meanings.

It is in this sense that I speak of the "flowering" of latter-day man. He lives amidst an encompassing sense of doom, he has seen and experienced enough to make him weary of the garment of the earth and the tent of heaven and the body of his own flesh; within his New Society he is surrounded by automatism, battered by sounds and images hurled at him as a target, pressured toward conformity; he wanders lonely as an alienated cloud, roaming over a wilderness of commodities; he scarcely knows what to do with the wealth that his own contrivance has placed in his hands, and he is aghast at the destructive power he holds in his grasp. Yet amidst it all a surprising number of people are buoyant and hopeful, wanting more than anything else to pour meaning into the new molds of abundance that technology offers. This era of alienation, automation and looming radiation is exactly the time when more people are more eager than ever to learn how to get more enjoyment and meaning out of more life.

It is easy to mock them for their eagerness and perhaps their naïveté, or to mourn over their failures, but neither of these is the point. The question is not how wise or sophisticated they are, nor how much of that elusive commodity of "happiness" they are achieving. The massive fact is also the paradoxical one that such a flowering of energy and eagerness is taking place in so bleak an era. It may even lead us to ask whether a generation so intent on meanings and the discovery of identity in the individual life may not even manage the miracle of finding a way to nail down controls over atomic death.

# The Judgment of the Birds

## LOREN C. EISELEY

## *(1956)*

LOREN C. EISELEY, now provost of the University of Pennsylvania, was formerly its chairman of the Department of Anthropology. Since his undergraduate years, a dual curiosity in science and literature has enabled Mr. Eiseley to capture the timeless mystery of the earth and its creatures. The unique qualities of his writing are apparent in the selected essays and lectures in *The Immense Journey* and *The Firmament of Time*.

IT IS A COMMONPLACE OF ALL RELIGIOUS THOUGHT, even the most primitive, that the man seeking visions and insight must go apart from his fellows and live for a time in the wilderness. If he is of the proper sort, he will return with a message. It may not be a message from the god he set out to seek, but even if he has failed in that particular, he will have had a vision or seen a marvel—and these are always worth listening to and thinking about.

The world, I have come to believe, is a very queer place, but we have been part of this queerness for so long that we tend to take it for granted. We rush to and fro like mad hatters upon our peculiar errands, all the time imagining our surroundings to be dull and ourselves quite ordinary creatures. Actually, there is nothing in the world to encourage this idea, but such is the mind of man, and this is why he finds it necessary from time to time to send emissaries into the wilderness in the hope of learning of great events or plans in store for him that will resuscitate his waning taste for life. His vast news services, his world-wide radio network, he knows with a last remnant of healthy distrust, will be of no use to him in this matter. No miracle can withstand a radio broadcast, and it is certain that it would be no miracle if it could. One must seek, then, what only the solitary approach can give—a natural revelation.

Let it be understood at the outset that I am not the sort of man to whom is entrusted direct knowledge of great events or prophecies. A naturalist, however, spends much of his life alone, and my life is no exception. Even in New York City there are patches of wilderness, and a man by himself is bound to undergo certain experiences falling into the class of which I speak. I set mine down, therefore: a matter of pigeons, a flight of chemicals, and a judgment of birds, in the hope that they will come to the eye of those who have retained a true taste for the marvelous and who are capable of discerning in the flow of ordinary events the point at which the mundane world gives way to quite another dimension.

New York is not, on the whole, the best place to enjoy the downright miraculous nature of the planet. There are, I do not doubt, many remarkable stories to be heard there and many strange sights to be seen, but to grasp a marvel fully, it must be savored from all aspects. This cannot be done while one is being jostled and hustled along a crowded street. Nevertheless, in any city there are true wildernesses in which a man can be alone, and the marvel can happen in a hotel room or on the high roofs at dawn.

One night, on the twentieth floor of a midtown hotel, I awoke in the dark and grew restless. On an impulse I climbed upon the broad old-fashioned window sill, opened the curtains and peered out. It was the hour just before dawn, the hour when men sigh in their sleep or, if awake, strive to focus their wavering eyesight upon a world dissolving into shadows. I leaned out sleepily through the open window. I had expected depths, but not the sight I saw.

I found I was looking down from that great height into a series of curious cupolas or lofts that I could just barely make out in the darkness. As I looked, the outlines of these lofts became more distinct because the light was being reflected from the wings of pigeons who, in utter silence, were beginning to float outward upon the city. In and out through the open slits in the cupolas passed the white-winged birds on their mysterious errands. At this hour the city was theirs, and quietly, without the brush of a single wing tip against stone in that high, eerie place, they were taking over the spires of Manhattan. They were pouring upward in a light that was not yet perceptible to human eyes, while far down in the black darkness of the alleys it was still midnight.

As I crouched half asleep across the sill, I had a moment's illusion that the world had changed in the night, as in some immense snowfall, and that if I were to leave, it would have to be as these other inhabitants were doing—by the window. I should have to launch out into that great, bottomless void with the simple confidence of young birds reared high up there among the familiar chimney pots and interposed horrors of the abyss.

I leaned farther out. To and fro went the white wings, to and fro. There was no sound from any of them. Man was asleep and this light for a little while was theirs. Or perhaps I had dreamed about man in this city of wings—which he could surely never have built. Perhaps I, myself, was one of these birds dreaming unpleasantly for a moment of old dangers far below as I teetered on a window ledge.

Around and around went the wings. It needed only a little courage, only a little shove from the window ledge to enter that city of light. The muscles of my hands were already making little premonitory lunges. I wanted to enter that city and go away over the roofs in the first dawn. I wanted to enter it so badly that I drew back carefully into the room and opened the hall door. I found my coat on the chair, and it slowly became clear to me that there was a way down through the floors, that I was, after all, only a man.

I dressed then and went back to my own kind, and I have been rather more than usually careful ever since not to look into the city of light. I had seen, just once, man's greatest creation from a strange inverted angle, and it was not really his at all. I will never forget how those wings went round and round, and how, by the merest pressure of the fingers and a feeling for air, one might go away over the roofs. It is a knowledge, however, that is better kept to oneself. I think of it sometimes in such a way that the wings, beginning far down in the black depths of the mind, begin to rise and whirl till all the mind is lit by their spinning and there is a sense of things passing away, but lightly, as a wing might veer over an obstacle.

To see from an inverted angle, however, is not a gift allotted merely to the human imagination. I have come to suspect that it is shared by animals, though perhaps as rarely as among men. The time has to be right; one has to be, by chance or intention, upon the border of two worlds. And sometimes these two borders may shift or interpenetrate and one sees the miraculous.

I once saw this happen to a crow.

This crow lives near my house, and though I have never injured him, he takes good care to stay up in the very highest trees and, in general, to avoid humanity. His world begins at about the limit of my eyesight.

On the particular morning when this episode occurred, the whole countryside was buried in one of the thickest fogs in years. The ceiling was absolutely zero. All planes were grounded, and even a pedestrian could hardly see his outstretched hand before him.

I was groping across a field in the general direction of the railroad station, following a dimly outlined path. Suddenly out of the fog, at about the level of my eyes, and so closely that I flinched, there flashed a pair of immense black wings and a huge beak. The whole bird rushed over my head with a frantic cawing outcry of hideous terror such as I have never heard in a crow's voice before, and never expect to hear again.

He was lost and startled, I thought, as I recovered my poise. He ought not to have flown out in this fog. He'd knock his silly brains out.

All afternoon that great awkward cry rang in my head. Merely being lost in a fog seemed scarcely to account for it—especially in a tough, intelligent old bandit such as I knew that particular crow to be. I even looked once in the mirror to see what it might be about me that had so revolted him that he had cried out in protest to the very stones.

Finally, as I worked my way homeward along the path, the solution came to me. It should have been clear before. The borders of our worlds had shifted. It was the fog that had done it. That crow, and I knew him well, never under normal circumstances flew low near men. He had been lost all right, but it was more than that. He thought he had been high up, and when he encountered me looming gigantically through the fog, he had perceived a ghastly and, to the crow mind, unnatural sight. He had seen a man walking on air, desecrating the very heart of the crow kingdom, a harbinger of the most profound evil a crow mind could conceive of— air-walking men. The encounter, he must have thought, had taken place a hundred feet over the roofs.

He caws now when he sees me leaving for the station in the morning, and I fancy that in that note I catch the uncertainty of a mind that has come to know things are not always what they seem. He has seen a marvel in his heights of air and is no longer as other crows. He has experienced the human world from an unlikely perspective. He and I share a viewpoint in common: our worlds have interpenetrated, and we both have faith in the miraculous.

It is a faith that in my own case has been augmented by two remarkable sights. As I have hinted previously, I once saw some very odd chemicals fly across a waste so dead it might have been upon the moon, and once, by an even more fantastic piece of luck, I was present when a group of birds passed a judgment upon life.

On the maps of the old voyagers it is called *Mauvaises Terres*, the "evil lands," and, slurred a little with the passage through many minds, it has come down to us anglicized as the "Badlands." The soft rustling of moccasins has passed through its canyons on the grim business of war and flight, but the last of those slight disturbances of immemorial silences died out almost a century ago. The land, if one can call it a land, is a waste as lifeless as that valley in which lie the kings of Egypt. Like the Valley of the Kings, it is a mausoleum, a place of dry bones in what once was a place of life. Now it has silences as tangible as those in the moon's airless chasms.

Nothing grows among its pinnacles; there is no shade except under great toadstools of sandstone whose bases have been eaten to the shape of wine glasses by the wind. Everything is flaking, cracking, disintegrating, wearing away in the long, imperceptible weather of time. The ash of ancient volcanic outbursts still sterilizes its soil, and the colors in that waste are the colors that flame in the lonely sunsets on dead planets. Men come there but rarely, and for one purpose only, the collection of bones.

It was a late hour on a cold, wind-bitten autumn day when I climbed a great hill spined like a dinosaur's back and tried to take my bearings. The tumbled waste fell away in waves in all directions. Blue air was darkening into purple along the bases of the hills. I shifted my knapsack, heavy with the petrified bones of long-vanished creatures, and studied my compass. I wanted to be out of there by nightfall, and already the sun was going sullenly down in the west.

It was then that I saw the flight coming on. It was moving like a little close-knit body of black specks that danced and darted and closed again. It was pouring from the north and heading toward me with the undeviating relentlessness of a compass needle. It streamed through the shadows rising out of monstrous gorges. It rushed over towering pinnacles in the red light of the sun, or momentarily sank from sight within their shade. Across that desert of eroding clay and wind-worn stone they came with a faint, wild twittering that filled all the air about me as those tiny, living bullets hurtled past into the night.

It may not strike you as a marvel. It would not, perhaps, unless you stood in the middle of a dead world at sunset, but that was where I stood. Fifty million years lay under my feet, fifty million years of bellowing monsters moving in a green world now gone so utterly that its very light was traveling on the farther edge of space. The chemicals of all that vanished age lay about me in the ground. Around me still lay the sheering molars of dead titanotheres, the delicate sabers of soft-stepping cats, the hollow sockets that had held the eyes of many a strange, outmoded beast. Those eyes had looked out upon a world as real as ours; dark, savage brains had roamed and roared their challenges into the steaming night.

Now they were still here or, put it as you will, the chemicals that made them were here about me in the ground. The carbon that had driven them ran blackly in the eroding stone. The stain of iron was in the clays. The iron did not remember the blood it had once moved within, the phosphorus had forgotten the savage brain. The little individual moment had ebbed from all those strange combinations of chemicals as it would ebb from our living bodies into the sinks and runnels of oncoming time.

I had lifted up a fistful of that ground. I held it while that wild flight of southbound warblers hurtled over me into the oncoming dark. There went phosphorus, there went iron, there went carbon, there beat the calcium in those hurrying wings. Alone on a dead planet, I watched that incredible miracle speeding past. It ran by some true compass over field and wasteland. It cried its individual ecstasies into the air until the gullies rang. It swerved like a single body; it knew itself and, lonely, it bunched close in the racing darkness, its individual entities feeling about them the rising night. And so, crying to each other their identity, they passed away out of my sight.

I dropped my fistful of earth. I heard it roll, inanimate, back into the gully at the base of the hill: iron, carbon, the chemicals of life. Like men from those wild tribes who had haunted these hills before me seeking visions, I made my sign to the great darkness. It was not a mocking sign, and I was not mocked. As I walked into my camp late that night, one man, rousing from his blankets beside the fire, asked sleepily, "What did you see?"

"I think, a miracle," I said softly, but I said it to myself. Behind me that vast waste began to glow under the rising moon.

I have said that I saw a judgment upon life, and that it was not passed by men. Those who stare at birds in cages or who test minds by their closeness to our own may not care for it. It comes from far away out of my past, in a place of pouring waters and green leaves. I shall never see an episode like it again if I live to be a hundred, nor do I think that one man in a million has ever seen it, because man is an intruder into such silences. The light must be right, and the observer must remain unseen. No man sets up such an experiment. What he sees, he sees by chance.

You may put it that I had come over a mountain, that I had slogged through fern and pine needles for half a long day, and that on the edge of a little glade with one long, crooked branch extending across it, I had sat down to rest with my back against a stump. Through accident I was concealed from the glade, although I could see into it perfectly.

The sun was warm there, and the unseen murmurs of forest life blurred softly away into my sleep. When I awoke, dimly aware of some commotion and outcry in the clearing, the light was slanting down through the pines in such a way that the glade was lit like some vast cathedral. I could see the dust motes of wood pollen in the long shaft of light, and there on the extended branch sat an enormous raven with a red and squirming nestling in his beak.

The sound that awoke me was the outraged cries of the nestling's parents, who flew helplessly in circles about the clearing. The sleek black monster was indifferent to them. He gulped, whetted his beak on the dead branch a moment, and sat still. Up to that point the little tragedy had followed the usual pattern. But suddenly, out of all that area of woodland, a soft sound of complaint began to rise. Into the glade fluttered small birds of half a dozen varieties, drawn by the anguished outcries of the tiny parents.

No one dared to attack the raven. But they cried there in some instinctive common misery, the bereaved and the unbereaved. The glade filled with their soft rustling and their cries. They fluttered as though to point their wings at the murderer. There was a dim, intangible ethic he had violated, that they knew. He was a bird of death.

And he, the murderer, the black bird at the heart of life, sat on there, glistening in the common light, formidable, unmoving, unperturbed, untouchable.

The sighing died. It was then I saw the judgment. It was the judgment of life against death. I will never see it again so forcefully presented. I will never hear it again in notes so tragically prolonged. For, in the midst of protest, they forgot the violence. There, in that clearing, the crystal note of a song sparrow lifted hesitantly in the hush. And finally, after painful fluttering, another took the song, and then another, the song passing from one bird to another, doubtfully at first as though some evil thing were being

414

slowly forgotten. Till suddenly they took heart and sang from many throats joyously together as birds are known to sing. They sang because life is sweet and sunlight beautiful. They sang under the brooding shadow of the raven. In simple truth they had forgotten the raven, for they were the singers of life, and not of death.

I was not of that airy company. My limbs were the heavy limbs of an earthbound creature who could climb mountains, even the mountains of the mind, only by a great effort of will. I knew I had seen a marvel and observed a judgment, but the mind which was my human endowment was sure to question it and to be at me day by day with its heresies until I grew to doubt the meaning of what I had seen. Eventually darkness and subtleties would ring me round once more.

And so it proved until, on the top of a stepladder, I made one more observation upon life. It was cold that autumn evening and, standing under a suburban street light in a spate of leaves and beginning snow, I was suddenly conscious of some huge and hairy shadows dancing over the pavement. They seemed attached to an odd, globular shape that was magnified above me. There was no mistaking it. I was standing under the shadow of an orb-weaving spider. Gigantically projected against the street, she was about her spinning when everything was going underground. Even her cables were magnified upon the sidewalk and already I was half-entangled in their shadows.

"Good Lord," I thought, "she has found herself a kind of minor sun and is going to upset the course of nature."

I procured a ladder from my yard and climbed up to inspect the situation. There she was, the universe running down around her, warmly arranged among her guy ropes attached to the lamp supports—a great black and yellow embodiment of the life force, not giving up to either frost or stepladders. She ignored me and went on tightening and improving her web.

I stood over her on the ladder, a faint snow touching my cheeks, and surveyed her universe. There were a couple of iridescent green beetle cases turning slowly on a loose strand of web, a fragment of luminescent eye from a moth's wing and a large indeterminable object, perhaps a cicada, that had struggled and been wrapped in silk. There were also little bits and slivers, little red and blue flashes from the scales of anonymous wings that had crashed there.

Some days, I thought, they will be dull and gray and the shine will be out of them; then the dew will polish them again and drops will hang on the silk until everything is gleaming and turning in the light. It is like a mind, really, where everything changes but remains, and in the end you have these eaten-out bits of experience like beetle wings.

I stood over her a moment longer, comprehending somewhat reluctantly that her adventure against the great blind forces of winter, her seizure of this warming globe of light, would come to nothing and was hopeless. Nevertheless, it brought the birds back into my mind and that faraway song which had traveled with growing strength around a forest clearing years before—a kind of heroism, a world where even a spider refuses to lie down and die if a rope can be spun on to a star. Maybe man himself will fight like this in the end, I thought, realizing that the web and its threatening yellow occupant had been added to some luminous store of experience, shining for a moment in the fogbound reaches of my brain.

The mind, it came to me as I slowly descended the ladder, is a very remarkable thing; it has gotten itself a kind of courage by looking at a spider in a street lamp. Here was something that ought to be passed on to those who would fight our final, freezing battle with the void. I thought of setting it down carefully as a message to the future: *In the days of the frost, seek a minor sun.*

But as I hesitated, it became plain that something was wrong. The marvel was escaping—a sense of bigness beyond man's power to grasp—the essence of life in its great dealings with the universe. It was better, I decided, for the emissaries returning from the wilderness, even if they were merely descending from a stepladder, to record their marvel, not to define its meaning. In that way it would go echoing on through the minds of men, each grasping at that beyond out of which the miracles emerge and which, once defined, ceases to satisfy the human need for symbols.

In the end I merely made a mental note: One specimen of Epeira observed building a web in a street light. Late autumn and cold for spiders. Cold for men, too.

I shivered and left the lamp glowing there in my mind. The last I saw of Epeira, she was hauling steadily on a cable. I stepped carefully over her shadow as I walked away.

# Our Documentary Culture

## MARGARET MEAD

*( 1956 )*

A spirited and imaginative anthropologist, MARGARET MEAD is particularly well known for the field trips she has conducted to study primitive cultures. Associate curator of ethnology of the American Museum of Natural History, she writes here on one of her favorite subjects, youth, and discusses the consequences of our self-conscious reflexive response to a "world of semitruths and manipulated backgrounds and faked shadows within which young people find the images on which to model their lives."

O NE OF THE FAMILIAR EXPERIENCES of any field worker is the combined rejection and acceptance of frequently repeated clichés—the simultaneous recognition that what people are saying does not make sense as it stands, but nevertheless does make sense, slightly transposed. Almost automatically one finds oneself pigeon-holing phrase after phrase under a little label marked "hold for further clarification," as when people say that a large house is too small or a small house too large, that a silent wife is too talkative, that a short distance is a long one, that a prolific writer has never published anything. They are quite obviously not saying what they seem to be saying, and quite as obviously are trying to say something. The clues which convince us are the lack of correspondence with reality, on the one hand, and a kind of monotony, on the other, as the phrases recur, dully, inappropriately, like a pulse beat which should be below the level of consciousness but is not.

It is within such a context that I have come, during the last year, to place the statement that today's youth is characterized by something called "conformity"—a condemnatory phrase originating among intellectuals in their late forties or older, which is replacing yesterday's cliché that youth was looking only for "security." To anyone who has paid reasonable attention during the last thirty years, this statement is untrue at the simple, descriptive level. There is today less blind, unquestioning acceptance of class or regional standards, more sense of choice and planning among styles of work and styles of life, more upstanding resistance to parental expectations that each generation should transcend the social level of the last, more willingness to reject values which were unquestioned in the last generation—such as the evident desirability of a college education—than there was twenty-five years ago. Young people pick and choose their way in a maze which extends from Saudi Arabia to Japan, in which consumption values are balanced against achievement values with clarity and information. Whether to enter the services first or later, when to marry and when to have a first baby, whether to work for a big company or a small one, whether or not to try for a stint overseas, whether to live in the same suburb with the other men in the office or in a different one—these are all articulate choices. Planning and selection have replaced unquestioning acceptance of parental values or the equally unquestioning counteracceptance which led a certain portion of each college generation to become doctrinaire freethinkers, radicals, pacifists, two generations ago.

Yet the phrase is repeated too often and is responded to with too much anxiety by the harried young, who have replaced their 1940 response to their elders' condemnation, "*Ought* one to have a conscience?" with the question, "Are we *too* conforming?" The disappointed and nostalgic middle-aged intellectuals are talking about something. But what?

I think the answer lies not in any conformity itself, which is less rather than greater, but in the quality of such conformity as there is. It is not that more young men who aspire to be junior executives consider what ties they shall wear—a time-honored piece of behavior on the part of those who wish to succeed in business—but that they are more conscious that as they do or do not wear a given tie they are dressing more or less in accordance with a possible career line. Similarly, the young people—or the middle-aged, for that matter—who hesitate to sign petitions on behalf of apparently good causes headed by names that have been associated with many, possibly too many, good causes, do not hesitate out of a simple conformity to the majority opinion around them but out of a sophisticated knowledge of how such petitions have been and may again be used. As willing as ever to die for a good cause, if necessary, they are far less willing to lose a chance to work overseas in a UN agency because they have uncritically let some slogan and the pressuring of some overeager roommate get their name into carefully plotted bad company. Granted that the consequences of the United Front —and the prefigurative consequences of the next United Front— have crippled our use of some of our more cherished institutions, it does no good to belabor youth who have discovered the petitions can become not a means to attain good social ends but a means for compromising and immobilizing the generous and the uncritical liberal. Only those who equate lack of political sophistication with goodness—probably a safe criterion for value in those over sixty —can regard as conformity the refusal to put one's name on an open-ended list.

Ours has always been a culture within which one staked out membership in a given group from the outside in. Clothes and manners came before more tangible signs of membership: peasant girls from the Carpathians wore high-heeled shoes before they knew a dozen words of English; the rebellious daughters of clergymen bobbed their hair before, not after, they read their first articles in Freudian psychology. Through our lighted, uncurtained windows opening on our hedgeless lawns, we have invited the passing world to see the outward and visible signs of some newly acquired social grace, political stance or psychological sensitivity —whether these are symbols of acceptance of America, the city or a new class position, or whether they are symbols of rebellion against such majority choices. Unlike people in older societies, to whose behavior it would be mere nonsense to attach the term "conformity," because the word itself implies some consciousness, some choice of nonconformity, Americans for the most part have always acted with a slight degree of self-consciousness. For every enclave in which choice was not yet known—whether it was the sterile, embittered gentility limited to a family line within which unmarried sons and daughters withered in the old house they could neither leave nor support, or the pitiful ignorance of any alternative possibility which, as late as the beginning of World War II, made the sons of miners into miners in remote Pennsylvania towns and tied the children of sharecroppers to cotton or tobacco, hookworm and despair—such helpless and unconscious conformity has been felt to be un-American and has been given perhaps a disproportionate place in our national literature for just that reason. But, in general, Americans are people who were able to break the rules of the Old World and were willing to learn the rules of the New, to learn new manners out of a book as easily as new rules for baking a cake or cutting out a dress. True, the new rules tend to be observed with the obsessive insistence of new converts. And one hears, with both amusement and understanding, the passionate rebellion of the daughter of a successful peasant, now residing in a middle-class suburb and going to a good college, who rages against the "bleak conformity" of American life as compared with the magnificent diversity and assumed freedom of the individual existing in a Europe she has never seen and would be unable to tolerate for twenty-four hours were she to participate in that life from the inside instead of admiring the changing regional styles in architecture—and faces—as depicted in cinema travelogues.

If this has been so, if American culture has always been stamped with the self-conscious conformity of the convert, the immigrant, the learning of adulthood rather than the automatic acceptance of childhood, what increase in self-consciousness can be invoked to explain the present trend which so revolts our systematically and recurrently revolted critics of the American scene? Any attempt to assay what is happening is bound to be over-selective, to miss some of the important threads in the pattern—if only because David Riesman or Holly Whyte may have done them recent justice or injustice. But I would tentatively suggest as one explanation the growth of the "documentary" approach.

In using the term "documentary," I risk offending one of the values of the late 1930's, when the documentary film was seen as a medium of social truth which would free us from the sham fictions of Hollywood. It is true that a great deal of fire and imagination and vivid social criticism went into the documentary movement; yet, despite the difference in position, it remained, I believe, in essence the same approach as that of *Life* magazine—a compromise between actuality and art in which a new order of irreality was introduced. The documentary, as I use the term here, includes a film, a set of still pictures, a reportorial article, a "life history," and any contrived and constructed attempt to replicate some aspect of life in which the actors or characters are taken from real life. The farmer in the film is a farmer, the miner is a miner, and the miner's children are the children of *that* miner; but now they are posed in attitudes, perhaps once their own, mimicked or distorted for the occasion by producer, photographer or reporter. Sometimes, of course, there is even more distortion; one real actor is introduced for the most difficult part or, as those with easily titillated minds whispered, the members of the "little family" in *Chang* were unrelated to each other. But the point against the documentary can be made clearly enough even when the most exacting rules are observed, when the actors are all taken not from those trained to the theater but from those who live the scene which is being portrayed, or when—as in all but one of *Ten Soviet Portraits*—every word the types speak is taken from an interview, and nothing is fabricated except the coincidence of scattered verbatim texts in the mouth of a single type mouthpiece.

The novel, the short story, the drama create life through the disciplined imagination of the artist, committed both to his form and to an artistic truth which must not be—like life—stranger than fiction; and today photography, both still and moving, makes possible a record of actuality more meticulously, immediately and fleetingly accurate than art would wish to be. The documentary falls in between. The men and women are "real," they are who they are said to be, ennobled by no art or artifice; but the postures they take are attitudes imposed upon them not by a Stanislavsky, but by the script which has been agreed upon by a magazine staff working on a story line, or by a group of people with a message about technical change, man's exploitation of man or—for these are equally documentaries—the invigorating effect of the free enterprise system. When the aim is social criticism, the film maker seeks out the type case of overt misery; when it is social self-glorification, the kitchen sparkles as only an American kitchen can. And the "characters" move stiffly—posed, pushed, retaken, robbed of spontaneity, without skill—through their lines.

In most of the human civilizations of which we have any proper record, youth has drawn either on art or on life for models, planning to emulate the heroes depicted in epics, on the shadow-play screen or the stage, or those known human beings, fathers or grandfathers, chiefs or craftsmen, whose every characteristic can be studied and imitated. As recently as 1910, this was the prevailing condition in the United States. If he came from a nonliterate background, the recent immigrant learned to speak, move and think like an American by using his eyes and ears on the labor line, in the homes of more acculturated cousins, by watching the other school children, or by absorbing the standards of the teacher, the foreman, the clerk who served him in the store. For the literate and the literate children of the nonliterate, there was art—the story of the frustrated artist in the prairie town, of the second generation battling with the limitations of the first. And, at a simpler level, there were the Western and Hollywood fairy tales which pointed a moral but did not, as a rule, teach table manners.

With the development of the countermovement against Hollywood, with the efflorescence of photography, with *Time-Life-Fortune* types of reporting and the dead-pan *New Yorker* manner of describing the life of an old-clothes dealer in some forgotten street or of presenting the "accurate," "checked" details of the lives of people whose eminence gave at least a sort of license to attack them, with the passion for "human documents" in Depression days—a necessary substitute for proletarian art among middle-class writers who knew nothing about proletarians and middle-class readers who needed the shock of verisimilitude—a new era in American life was ushered in, the era in which young people imitated neither life nor art nor fairy tale, but instead were presented with models drawn from life with minimal but crucial distortions. Doctored life-histories, posed carelessness, "candid" shots of people in their own homes which took hours to arrange, pictures shot from real life to scripts written months before—supplemented by national polls and surveys which assured the reader that this bobby-soxer did indeed represent a national norm or a growing trend—replaced the older models.

With the speed of modern life, it is difficult for art to keep up, and American young people are impatient of settings in which the traditions of a forgotten way of life or even the fashions of yesterday make the characters unreal. The simpler fairy tales of popular art, the Cinderella theme, the Horatio Alger stories, have been skitted too often to serve. So today's adolescents turn to the weekly picture magazines, to the documentary films, to the real life stories of public men and women, trying to model their career lines after people whom they do not know personally but whom they have been led to believe they may come to know through pictures, through "verbatim" interviews, through broadcasts and telecasts. Uninformed by the imagination or the disciplined skill of the artist or writer and unillumined by the point-for-point correspondence with actuality of the genuinely unposed picture, these stereotyped, semiposed, semidoctored accounts come to have the quality of a cliché. The postures, the clothes, the accents used by the young people—who like young people everywhere are and must be looking for models—ring hollow and sound off-key to the adult spectators, especially to the fastidiously literate spectator who despises television, listens only to music over the radio, and has never learned to care for the picture magazine or science fiction, although, of course, there is Ray Bradbury. The echo of a partially contrived sound is there and, coming as it does from a world with whose values the critics are largely unfamiliar, it is only thin echoes that they hear as they exclaim over the increase in conformity.

This increase in self-conscious reflexive response to partly accurate, partly contrived pictures of what young executives, career girls, Americans overseas or exurbanites do, think, say, feel, what they read, eat, wear and believe, may indeed have lamentable consequences, although they are not the consequences which are immediately prophesied by the critics.

Perhaps the most serious possibility is in the absence of any ideal beyond the imputed norm of behavior for one's own class, age, sex and level of education, or the imputed norm for the class into which one wishes to move. There has always been in the United States a curious paradox between the belief in a world in which any man could be President and the actual narrow range of competition in which most people compete only with those very close to them, with brothers rather than with fathers and uncles, and very seldom hope to get out of their own league. As the Cinderella story and the Horatio Alger myth are repudiated and the fictionalized hero is replaced by a creature constructed from a market survey and illustrated by a photograph, there comes to be a corresponding narrowing of ambition and a shortage of imaginative models for change. As long as one can check one's knowledge of foreign events, preference in books, church attendance and satisfaction in marriage on a scale and can find oneself in the upper percentiles, there is a theoretical satisfaction, although in actuality it is dust and ashes. Americans who grew up believing you should hitch your wagon to a star, or even those who were reared by people who courted such a belief, find the rope slackening in their hands even while statistics, posed photographs and rating scales show them to be successful, contented and well adjusted.

Television seemed to be a medium which would defeat this predigesting of models. Perhaps it is for this reason that there has been such rabid and critical fury over any broadcast in which a public relations firm is believed to have arranged the setting or to have inserted homey remarks about dogs. Yet, television is the closest we have come to actuality since politicians stumped the country and could be seen closely. The possibility of a genuine break-through from the documentary to the actual is there and may—no one is quite sure yet—again be betrayed. But the fact

423

that it can be as much betrayed by a cameraman who seems to be on one's own side as by a public relations firm which is known to be on the other, has, as yet, hardly been taken into account. Television is still not the proper concern of most intellectuals, who now can find reasons for preferring the once despised radio broadcast. Yet, it may well be that if we are to return to a world in which character is dignified by art, it will be by way of a medium in which it is impossible to lie face to face. Successful fiction like *Death of a Salesman, The Caine Mutiny, The Blackboard Jungle* or *The Man in the Gray Flannel Suit* reflect the middle world of the documentary, and myth replaces character. The themes, handled by writer and producer in print, film and on the stage, remain the same as the "heroes" and "heroines" shift and change in a way that would not be possible with the novel of character. Like all myths, the theme overshadows those who embody it, just as in the weekly picture magazine or in the picture of "Miss Subways" the careful detail of name and address serves to emphasize that each picture is a synthetic type made out of a real person.

It may also be suggested that this reflexive state in which we live is a kind of stepchild of some of the most important developments of the last quarter-century—of increased awareness of ourselves as individuals with a partly forgotten past, as members of a culture many of whose values are unformulated but nonetheless real. It would be easy to blame our present state on an exaggerated self-consciousness which has destroyed both innocence and spontaneity. But it may also be blamed upon those who have used the tools which have been developed by the therapist, the teacher and the research scholar as implements of manipulation within a system which they despised and hated, often quite unfairly, but from which they continued to draw a livelihood. The frustrated novelist who sells his soul to an advertising agency or a public relations firm, the frustrated liberal who condones the use of sensational sex stories to sell a politically liberal newspaper, the cynical reformer who thinks the only way to get members of Congress to do a good deed is to offer them bad rationalizations—these are among the people who, out of disillusion, self-contempt, and contempt for their employers and their audiences, have helped to construct this world of semitruths and manipulated backgrounds and faked shadows within which young people find the images on which to model their lives—and so seem to their elders to be "conforming."

# The Meaning of Bandung

## SAUNDERS REDDING

### (1956)

As the first international conference of colored peoples, the Bandung Conference of 1955 represented more than one half of the world's population. Pointing to the relevance of this conference, SAUNDERS REDDING, professor of English at Hampton Institute, defines the surging growth of color-nationalism as the new and decisive influence in international relations. In 1952, Mr. Redding was sent to India by the State Department to interpret American life.

WHEN THE PRESENT CENTURY was just two years old, a young scholar, brooding over the problem that was to occupy him the rest of his long life, wrote, "The problem of the twentieth century is the problem of the color line." No doubt many who read that sentence thought that it referred generally to America and specifically to the South. But W. E. B. DuBois' mind, well stocked with knowledge and sharpened by insight, moved in a much wider compass. In two years of foreign study and travel he had talked with South African and Indian colonials in England, and with African tribal chiefs in France and Belgium; and while he was a student in Germany one of his warmest acquaintances was an Asiatic "refugee" from the Straits Settlements. Already, too, DuBois was dreaming of an organization that would unite all the colored peoples of the world. Such an organization came into being in April, 1955, in an Indonesian city named Bandung, of which few people of the West were aware until then.

But there was another matter of which most Westerners were and even now are not aware, or—even more disturbing—pretend not to be aware. The delegates to the conference at Bandung were there because of a conviction that *the problem of the twentieth* *century is the problem of the color line.** Although the American press alone sent seventy reporters (jocosely described as "the largest delegation to Bandung") and the British press, including Canada and Australia, sent thirty, no American and no British newspaper easily available on this continent gave this conviction the preponderant weight it had in the thinking at Bandung. The *Christian Science Monitor* did remark that "the West is excluded. Emphasis is on the colored nations of the world." But this is not quite the same as saying, as it might in truth have done, that emphasis is on the color problem in the world, and that it was this that made the Asian-African Conference "perhaps the greatest historic event of our century." Of the half-dozen or so book-length essays about the Bandung Conference, only the one by Richard Wright gave due weight to the central truth—and that book has been largely ignored.

What Western newspapers did not neglect to emphasize was the diversity of those gathered. And, indeed, there were great and basic differences. The twenty-eight nations nominally comprised four orientation blocs—neutralism, communism, socialism and democracy—and if the great divisive factor in the world is differences in ideology, as the West claims, then the Bandung Conference should not have been held at all. Surely, too, the jingo nationalism plangent in all the countries arching over the Indian Ocean from the Tasman Sea to the South Atlantic increased the divisive potential.

And as great as were the differences of a political kind, the diversities of a cultural and historical kind were greater. They ran the scale from animal worship to ancestor worship; from polygamy to polyandry; from practical classlessness to theoretically rigid caste; from industrial competence to agrarian stagnation. Indonesia has nearly the highest illiteracy rate in the world; Japan, the lowest. The people of Africa speak a hundred different dialects. The people of India speak a dozen different mother tongues and passionately resist the idea that Hindi should be the tongue of all. The language problem was so pervasive at Bandung that English, which is not the language of any of them, was made the official language. In India there is a militant resurgence of orthodox Hinduism. Egypt, Iran, Iraq, Saudi Arabia and Syria are Muslim, and Pakistan was established as an Islamic theocracy. In Nkrumah, the Gold Coast has a leader who relies heavily on the methods of fascism. There were two Vietnams at Bandung, represented by the

* All italics in the article are the author's.

426

same ethnic strain, but one is Communist and the other is not. In short, the Asian-African nations that met at Bandung seemed to be, as the London *Times* said, an assemblage of "self-irritants." The London *Times* spoke the West's conscience, the West's fear, the West's hope. It is a conscience made painfully tender by the recognition of the jinni that six hundred years of cant and incantation have at last conjured up. It is a fear aroused by the reflected knowledge of that jinni's potential for evil. "The first international conference of colored peoples in the history of mankind," President Sukarno called it—and so it was, representing more than half the population of the earth, an awesome thing to contemplate. In *Cry, the Beloved Country*, Msimangu, a native, says, the "great fear is that when they are turned to loving we shall be turned to hating." It is a fear that it is hard to live with, and it was therefore quite in the nature of things that the Western press should reflect less of the truth that aroused that fear and more of the delusions that sustained hope. Certain Western spokesmen reacted quite normally by pumping out propaganda designed to make the Asian-African Conference appear something other than it was—the organization of a new bloc, perhaps a new power bloc, that had been forming in the world for a quarter of a century.

Even before the delegates could assemble, their intentions were variously misconceived and misinterpreted. The New York *Times* said that the mission of the Conference was "to see that peace would prevail in the world." Like other sober-minded people, the delegates doubtless did want peace to prevail, but as a matter of cold fact this was the least and last of the intentions set forth in the official invitation. The first intention was "to promote goodwill and cooperation *among the nations of Asia and Africa; to* explore and advance *their* mutual as well as common interests." The second was "to consider social, economic and cultural problems and relations of the *countries represented.*" The third intention was "to consider problems of *special interest to Asian and African peoples*, for example, problems . . . *of racialism and colonialism.*" The fourth was "to view the position of Asia and Africa and *their peoples* in the world today." And finally, almost an appendix not really necessary to complete the text, was the intention "to view the contribution they can make to the promotion of world peace and cooperation."

Although the New York *Times* thought that world peace was the mission of the Conference, its chief on-the-spot correspondent,

Tillman Durdin, took care to remark, "Rivalries, cross-currents and animosities abound . . . at Bandung," and, inferentially because of them, "Bandung seems to promise very limited achievements." Many influential metropolitan dailies—the St. Louis *Post-Dispatch*, the Louisville *Courier-Journal*, the Norfolk *Virginian-Pilot*—suspected some ulterior Communist motive cooked up by Chou En-lai and naïvely abetted by Nehru, who was suddenly—in the pages of the American press—"peevish" and "unpredictable," and altogether something less than the "friendly, decisive and pro-Western" figure he had been before. While there was much talk to the effect that Nehru and Chou would influence the Conference to promote their Five Principles of Peaceful Coexistence—principles, it was widely hinted, which were somehow Machiavellian—there was on the other hand a rainfall of predictions that the Conference would resolve into a struggle between Nehru and Chou for dominance among the colored peoples of the world: *Time* took this view, and so did *U.S. News and World Report*.

On April 20, the New York *Times* printed excerpts from the Conference's opening speeches, and the next day various sectors of the American press followed its lead. The excerpts were carefully selected for their anti-Communist slant, and the *Times* commented editorially: "The Bandung conference . . . attended by some of the major participants for the purpose of indicting the West for its *alleged* 'colonialism, racism and imperialism,' has started with a dramatic turnabout which dispels any notion that Asia and Africa speak with one voice." The exculpating "alleged" is a Swiftian stroke that deserves remarking, but it is more important in the present context to point out that the excerpted speeches plainly misrepresent the truth, while the editorial itself is just as plainly a misinterpretation of fact. Reading in full those opening speeches, one is thunderously impressed that all of them laid primary emotional and intellectual emphasis upon the West's racism and colonialism. And why not? This and their hatch of attendant evils—poverty, ignorance, personal indignity—had brought the delegates together in the first place.

President Sukarno of Indonesia bore down heavily on this theme: "My heart is filled with emotion. This is the first international conference of colored peoples in the history of mankind. . . . All of us are united by more important things than those which superficially divide us. We are united by a common detestation of colonialism. . . . We are united by a common detestation of racialism." He quoted, with some bitterness, "the saying of a diplomat from abroad. 'We [of the West] will turn this Asian-African Conference into an afternoon tea party.' " Chou's main speech echoed Sukarno's emphasis, but what the American press chose to quote was from his supplementary remarks, remarks which were a defense of Red China.

Even the speeches of Sir John Kotelawala of Ceylon, and Carlos P. Romulo of the Philippines, both widely trumpeted in the Western press as "putting blame where blame belonged" (on communism), were abstracted to avoid mention of the blame they also put on racialism and colonialism. Romulo was especially eloquent, if repetitious: "I have said that besides the issues of colonialism and political freedom, all of us here are concerned with the matter of racial equality. This is a *touchstone,* I think, for most of us assembled here are the people we represent. . . . We have known . . . the searing experience of being demeaned in our own lands, of being systematically relegated to subject status not only politically and economically and militarily—but racially as well. Here was a stigma! . . . To bolster his rule, to justify his own power to himself, the Western white man assumed that his superiority lay in his genes, in the color of his skin. . . . I think that over the generations the deepest source of our own confidence in ourselves had to come from the deeply rooted knowledge that the white man was wrong, that in proclaiming the superiority of his race, qua race, he stamped himself with his own weakness and confirmed all the rest of us in our dogged conviction that we could and would reassert ourselves as men. . . ."

And there was more, much more, but practically none of it was printed in the Western press.

Perhaps it was the knowledge (known to the press but kept from the Western public) of the underscoring of this theme that led the *Times* to remark editorially, "There was—and there still is—the possibility that some of the delegates would be so busy flogging a dead horse that they would not see a live tiger." The live tiger, of course, was communism. Although Kotelawala, Romulo, Iraq's Mohammed al-Jamali and Pakistan's Mohammed Ali all pitched into him with zealous wrath, the tiger was much more alive in the Western press than at Bandung. Chou, indeed, was as mild as May. A nonwhite correspondent reported, "Communism at Bandung was conspicuous for its shyness, its coyness, its bland smile and glad hand for everyone. Chou En-lai . . . moved among the delegates . . . listening to all arguments with patience, and turning the other cheek when receiving ideological slaps."

Meanwhile, however, Western voices had sounded off ominously about a Red China build-up for a strike at Matsu, Quemoy and Formosa. Admiral Robert B. Carney, CNO, had been quoted in the Manchester *Guardian,* the Paris edition of the *Herald-Tribune, Le Monde,* and in the New York *Times:* "They [the Chinese Reds] probably will initiate the attack on Matsu in mid-April. The significance of the timing is that it would tie in with the Afro-Asian conference in Bandung."

On the day the Conference opened, Secretary Dulles reported to President Eisenhower "a greatly intensified build-up of offensive air power by the Chinese Reds opposite Formosa." Naturally disturbed by this information, the President, speaking as if in an aside to Bandung, expressed his fear that "peace is now in grave jeopardy" and reminded the Asian-African leaders that they had "an opportunity, at a critical hour, to voice the peaceful aspirations of the peoples of the world. . . . Such an influence, if it prevailed, would open a new era of social and economic development for the Asian-African peoples." But this was not all. The distinguished American journalist Felix Belair reported that the President was "redesigning" the aid bill for Asia so as "to lure friends for the United States" at the Bandung Conference.

On April 23, the day before the Conference closed, the West's final appraisals began. "Official Washington has recovered from its apprehensions over the Asian-African conference at Bandung. The meeting is being assessed as a useful exercise in international relations, rather than as a disaster for the West, which many senior officials feared it would be. In an open contest for the good opinion of millions . . . Communist China and neutral India have so far failed to dominate the proceedings." And as if to round out the record of the West's exculpations and misinterpretations of the ultimate meaning of Bandung, the New York *Times* said, on April 24: "The choice of participants seemed arbitrary at some points. It was supposed to be largely geographic in its delineation. But even this delineation was not exact. It was Asian and African but was not inclusive in respect to either continent."

And, of course, the choice of participants *was* arbitrary, but it was not arrived at through caprice. South Africa was not invited. Australia complained that she should have been invited. Why these countries were excluded becomes clear immediately one understands the basis of choice.

The basis was race. This was the fact that the Western press, reacting for the Western public, wished neither to see nor to permit

itself to believe. It is not an easy thing to contemplate. It is the
thing that caused Western "apprehensions over the Asian-African
conference," the thing that wore the look of "disaster for the
West." The unity of the colored peoples of the world is a new fact
and a great change. Though it has been coming for fifty years—
but with accelerated pace only in the last twenty-five—the change
has come before the West has had time to change to meet it. So it
presents itself in terrible aspect, wearing a face recognizable in
the mirror of the Western conscience—the face of racism. Hoping
to exorcise by adjuration, by denunciation and by threat, Westerners turned away. But not before a premonitory moment of reality
had permitted a hasty glimpse or two.

On January 1, 1955, the Toronto *Globe and Mail* noted point-
edly, "What is significant about the call to Bandung is that the
common plight of Asians and Africans has been recognized and
proclaimed—in Asia." And on the very day this appeared, *Newsweek* let out a yawp of alarm. After quoting Kaiser Wilhelm II's
ominous, forty-two-year-old words—"Everybody knows what must
come to pass between Asia and the West, the yellow and the white.
. . . All the world understands that the gravest crisis in the destiny of the earth's population is at hand"—*Newsweek* went on to
say that Wilhelm was "right in foreseeing a crisis that now threatens in a more virulent form than he envisaged—an Afro-Asian
combination turned . . . against the West."

But if neither the turning away nor the fear that caused it need
have been, certainly the denunciations and the veiled threat
should not have been. The fact that they were, sharpened the
charges ("Washington feared and tried successively to condemn,
ignore and sabotage the conference") made at Bandung and repeated throughout the Afro-Asian world. Never did a more ironic
situation develop than the one in which U.S. Congressman Adam
C. Powell, accredited as a correspondent, felt impelled to deny this
blanket charge while admitting in the very next breath that
Thruston B. Morton, Assistant Secretary of State, had cabled him
denying that "the relationship [of the U.S. Government] to the
Bandung Conference would warrant" a message of greeting and
friendship. A message of a kind had already gone out, but it was
the wrong kind, and no one at Bandung missed the careful timing
and the purpose of announcing two billions in aid to Asia. If our
government's relationship to Bandung did not warrant a friendly
greeting, then the purpose of the announcement was not only very
clear but very nasty: at worst it was bad faith; at best, bad man-

ners. America's intellectual and emotional wires were crossed, and she might have succeeded in short-circuiting into existence the very racism she fears. This fear is in part—and perhaps in greater part—a projection of the West's own conscience, although the point should not be labored here. What should be is that if an Afro-Asian combination threatens the West, America can do much to reduce the threat.

The time has only recently passed when American statesmen and world statesmen had to think first and solely of their own national self-interest. We went to Yalta and to Potsdam with this in mind: we would have been criminally foolish had we not. A quick succession of French premiers pledged themselves not to the saving of Europe, but to the saving of France. Churchill's "I did not become His Majesty's Prime Minister in order to preside over the dissolution of the British Empire" still reverberated against the mountain peaks of the world. In this clear and dangerous time, America posed herself a simple question: What do we want in Europe? The answer was relatively easy to come by, for most of Europe seemed to want what we wanted and what, without much searching of the soul, (indeed, we believed, in order to save our soul) we could help her have. Europe wanted financial aid. She wanted to rebuild her industries, to restore her economy, and to reassume her dignity as a congeries of independent nations. She wanted, or thought she wanted and said she wanted—and we certainly wanted it for ourselves and for her—security against the creeping, evil power of international communism, which she and we had every right to fear. These were relatively simple matters, and America went about the business of accomplishing them with relative simplicity. She could do this with uncomplicated directness—and almost wholly on the strength of her national wealth—because she was dealing with peoples who did not have to prove anything, except their loyalty to democracy; with people who were known, who shared the same Greco-Roman cultural heritage, the same material outlook, the same aspirations and fears.

But America—and the West—should have known in April, 1955, that the same question could not even be asked in regard to Afro-Asia. The peoples there suspected that it had already been asked too often, and once more would be too much. Nosing around the periphery of the Middle East or being perceptive about France's unlearned lessons in Indochina and Algeria, Britain's in Iraq, or Spain's in Goa should have taught that. There must be a new question, and though the answers to it will be as simple in their humanistic terms as the answers in Europe were in their materialistic terms, they will be much harder to apply by a people—the Western people—who for close to seven hundred years have established policies of international behavior on the assumption that the probation of races is over and done and, as W. E. B. DuBois pointed out, "that the backward races of today . . . are not worth saving." The assumption must erode quickly if the new question is to be understood and its new answers applied, and if a new and dangerous racism—a potential at Bandung—is not to come into being. "The reality of race was there," says Richard Wright, "swollen, sensitive, turbulent." But its meaning was not racism—then. Its meaning was that race-nationalism was the unifying principle, the cohesive element. Its meaning was that Bandung created and confronted the West with the most important reality in twenty-five years of time just passed—and with a new question: What do the Afro-Asian peoples want?

And the answers were also at Bandung, on the tongues of men representing more than half the population of the earth. Yield us our true self-consciousness as men, the Afro-Asian peoples said. We want to be co-workers in the kingdom of culture. We want economic aid, surely, and a share of the world's resources. But most of all and first of all, we want the acknowledgment of our human equality.

# Joseph and His Brothers

## A Comedy in Four Parts

### MARK VAN DOREN

### (*1957*)

One of America's leading literary figures, MARK VAN DOREN, recently retired as professor of English at Columbia University, was awarded a Pulitzer Prize in 1940 for his *Collected Poems*. He is equally well known for his work in fiction, criticism and biography. His first play, *The Last Days of Lincoln*, was published in 1959.

To SAY THAT MANN's *Joseph and His Brothers* is primarily a comic work is to say no more than the author himself said in his foreword to the new edition of 1948. He called it then "a humorous song of mankind," an "epic undertaking" in the spirit of Goethe rather than of Wagner, a narrative written "playfully," with many "pleasantries" in it which he hoped would "cheer those who come after us," though with "pathos" in it, too, which at some later time might still be touching. He spoke of it, that is to say, as a comic poem of vast proportions. And so it is. Its "seventy thousand calmly flowing lines"—someone else might say its twelve hundred continuously intelligent pages—make up a modern masterpiece with which there are few things to be compared, though Marcel Proust's *Remembrance of Things Past* is surely one of those. That equally vast work depends equally with *Joseph and His Brothers* upon our sense of time; or, if you prefer, upon our sense of eternity; or, if you insist, upon our sense of the present moment. For when we have succeeded in giving ourselves to the present moment we are as near to eternity as we shall ever get. Eternity is not a lot of time; it is no time at all, and so is this moment that passes before we know it has come—except that we do know some moments when they come, and it is these and only these from which we learn.

The comic genius loves to speculate about such matters. It has not always done so as explicitly as in the two outstanding cases of Proust and Mann; but then ours is an explicit age which struggles to be conscious of everything, so that we are not surprised when Mann discusses at length a number of things that Chaucer, say, could take for granted. The comic genius has never been more alive than it was in Chaucer, but it does not appear that he thought he needed a theory of time, or at any rate a statable one which in effect would constitute his subject matter. Neither, of course, does Mann think simply that; his subject matter after all is never anything but Joseph and his father and his brothers, and the wonderful world of Egypt where he spent his most brilliant years, just as in *The Magic Mountain,* Mann's other masterpiece which deals with time, the subject matter is whatever the persons of the story talk about when their excellent brains catch fire in the cold solitude of an Alpine sanatarium. Yet it is true that Mann must think out loud as he writes, and what he thinks about is the bottomless well of time which threatens, if looked into deeply enough, to obscure every individual character and countenance—even those of Joseph himself—and to silence every event so that we who come long after may have doubts that it occurred, or in any case that it made much noise in the universe it could not manage at the end to alter. The famous prelude to the work, called "Descent into Hell," might have been called instead "Descent into Time." The genius of story can never dispense with time, but the genius of comic story stands in a peculiar relation to that commodity. It both believes in it and it does not. Tragedy believes furiously, even obsessively, in time; time always presses there, leaving the hero unfree to act in the wise way he might if he had the leisure. Comedy, on the other hand, relaxes and disperses time, spreads it out or draws it thin so that it looks a little like eternity. It is not eternity, and it cannot ever be; but enough of it will establish the perspective that comedy likes and indeed must have. Only, given the maximum perspective, movement comes to a stop and men are reduced to resembling one another so closely, even so absurdly, that merely man is left, or, to put it abstractly, human nature.

Perhaps it was human nature that Mann lived with during the sixteen dreadful years, between 1926 and 1942, when he was composing *Joseph and His Brothers.* One could also say that he lived with Joseph, the individual upon whose image he had settled. But the image enlarged while he studied it, as did the image of every other person in the tale, so that at last he had before him something like the whole spectacle which human life provides when nothing operates to distort it. In the Germany of these years it was outrageously distorted, and there were those who said it would never regain its ancient shape. Here, though, was that very shape; and Mann has testified to the satisfaction he derived from contemplating its breadth and depth. "It was my refuge, my comfort, my home," he says, "my symbol of steadfastness, the guarantee of my perseverance in the tempestuous change of things."

Yet he would have done substantially as he did in any case. Mann's genius was entirely comic; which is to say that it was contemplative, discursive, skeptical, tender, mocking and loving all at once. It was contemplative because it desired the oldest and the widest view of things, somewhat as they are, supposing man can know this, in their eternal aspect. It was discursive because man's mind is most at home in conversation, in endless talk that considers, measures, analogizes and compares. No reader of Mann needs to be told how irresistibly he was drawn to language, and how much pleasure he took in imitating the various dialects of thought. The comic genius is among other things a mimic; so in America, where Mann wrote the fourth section of his epic, it was natural for him not merely to see a parallel between Joseph the Provider and Roosevelt the prophet of abundance, but also to adopt so many idioms of the time and place as to incur the charge that he no longer wrote in German, though of course he did, to the enrichment of that none-too-lively language. *The Magic Mountain,* like any pure comedy, tends to be all conversation; and if this is not quite true of the Joseph books, it is nevertheless true that what his people say to one another, and what Mann says about them as he converses with his reader, can be understood as carrying most of the burden. Nor can one miss the fact that Joseph's own gift, his distinguishing art, is the wonderful way he has with words, so that he entrances all who come within the sound of his voice or—the same thing—the reach of his mind. When he read aloud to Potiphar, it was as if he were creating a new beauty in the text. The intellect of any person is perhaps most swiftly revealed by the way he reads a page he has never seen before. Potiphar knew the pages by heart, but never had they sounded like this. "Joseph read . . . capitally," we hear, "was fluent, exact, unaffected, moderately dramatic, with such natural command of words that the most involved literary style had a happy conversational ease. Literally he read himself into the heart of the listener; and when we seek to understand his swift rise in the Egyptian's favor we must by no means leave out of account these reading hours." He knew his way among intricate phrases as Hamlet, speaking to the players, knew his; no mind, no tongue, has ever been more nimble than that. But this was Hamlet in his comic aspect: his original aspect, which tragedy, as Ophelia divines, has already overwhelmed and lamentably deformed. -

The genius of Mann is skeptical in the finest sense of an often misapprehended term. It was not that he believed nothing; he believed everything; he liked ideas, and could live with all of them at once. No sooner did one start up in his brain than another came to reinforce, illuminate or check it. This was why he could turn so soon from tenderness to pathos, and why he could mock the very man he loved the most. These transformations of his mood will bewilder anyone who does not comprehend how serious at last the comic spirit is. Nothing in man is more serious than his sense of humor; it is the sign that he wants all the truth, and sees more sides of it than can be soberly and systematically stated; it is the sign, furthermore, that he can remember one idea even while he entertains another, and that he can live with contradiction. It is the reason, at any rate, that we cannot take seriously one whose mind and heart have never been known to smile. The gods do not weep; they smile. Eternity is something like the sun.

The comic spirit has a perfect sense of time, as of a good comedian we say that he has perfect timing. The comic spirit knows that time both does and does not exist; it can look like sheer illusion, though the illusion is one in which comedy will luxuriously live. Comedy takes its time, as truth and history do. The good storyteller is never in a hurry, nor do we want him to be; his digressions, his elaborations, his hesitations, his gestures, are in the end more interesting than the action he unfolds; we do not, in fact, want him to reach the end, for then we shall no longer hear his voice or relish with him the way he looks at life, of which the story at hand is but one illustration. While it was being told it amply sufficed our hunger for understanding; it replaced all other stories, was, in effect, story itself, was poetry in the flesh. It treated of only a few people and things, and it treated them in some present moment which absorbed us so that we forgot the rest of time. Yet it had also something to do with the rest of time, which hung about it like a haze, beautifying and validating its apparently random, its artfully accidental details. "The form of timelessness," says Mann, "is the here and now." He can say this because he knows how to see Joseph and Jacob as men who lived both long ago and now. They lived so long ago that if time were altogether and simply real they would have no identity today; their figures, their faces, would be woefully indistinct, and the thoughts they had would be mere puffs of desert dust. But time is not that real; Joseph and Jacob can exist not only again but yet; because they existed so intensely in their moment they live always, in all moments. These things are forever happening. History, with a monotony that comedy loves rather than deplores, repeats itself ad infinitum. All thoughts, all things, all men, are simultaneously true, as somehow in God's mind they are. The mind of comedy is not that great, but it is the greatest possession of the one creature made in God's image—unless, as Mann playfully suggests, man was the maker of God: in the person of Abram was none other than His father. But in that case it would still be true that the greatest thing in man is his power to know and remember many things at once, to master time, to be in a word the receptacle of the comic spirit.

Any story that is worth telling can be told either briefly or at length. Ideally, these alternatives are absolute: the teller takes no time at all, or else he takes an infinite amount of it. Since neither of those miracles is possible, the narrative artist must be content with a choice between abridgment and amplitude. Mann certainly did not abridge the story of Joseph. His work is forty-five times as long as the section of Genesis which deals with the hero alone, and fifteen times as long as the section which covers in addition, as Mann himself does, the careers of Abraham, Isaac and Jacob. This is amplitude indeed, and there have been those who wondered whether Mann did not achieve too much of it for any earthly purpose. The answer ought to be clear. His purpose was comic, and comedy takes its time. It insists upon leisure, of which it is confident that there cannot be too much. Also, it is addicted to talk, its own and others', and entertains itself with as much of that as the subject suggests, or as we shall listen to. The subject of Joseph suggested everything to Mann; nothing he knew or thought was alien to it, and no idea was irrelevant. So for sixteen years, with major and minor interruptions, he happily spun his web until it draped like a silken veil the whole figure of the world.

Even Genesis had lingered over the story as it did not in the cases of Abraham, Isaac and Jacob. There was something special about Joseph even then and there; he had nothing of the patriarch about him, and in after times his name dropped out of the Bible. God appeared to Moses as the God of three great men, not four.

Joseph had saved the race in Egypt, but he was never to be honored as one of its founders. He was not simple enough for that. Neither in a sense was Jacob, yet Jacob's name lived on as one of the never-to-be-forgotten three. Jacob for one thing did not become an Egyptian; he never became anything but what he was, so that when Joseph met him in the Land of Goshen there was a fantastic difference between the two figures: the younger one brilliant with linen and gold, the older one as plain as the wagon seat on which he had ridden all the way from Israel, through dust and among the remnant of his herds. It was not easy for the father to recognize his son in the splendid prince he saw step out of a chariot; nor, when the time came to talk, did he hesitate to say some things that may have sounded bitter to the young man whose mind was full of the glittering deeds he knew he had done. "God has . . . given you back, but yet not quite, for he has kept you too. . . . He has elevated and rejected you both in one, I say it in your ear, beloved child, and you are wise enough to be able to hear it. He has raised you above your brothers just as in your dream—but He has raised you in a worldly way, not in the sense of salvation and the inheritance of the blessing. . . . You are blessed, my dear one, . . . blessed with blitheness and with destiny, with wit and with dreams. Still, it is a worldly blessing, not a spiritual one. . . . Through you salvation is not to reach the peoples and the leadership is denied you. . . . You are not like the fathers, my child, for you are no spiritual prince, but a worldly one." This is Mann writing, not the author of Genesis, but it is what the whole Bible means in spite of its silence on the subject. The Bible is silent like the patriarchs; Mann, like Joseph, is eloquent as civilization and comedy are eloquent. He is even loquacious, for there is nothing he would rather do than put into words what simple men suppose cannot be said, or for that matter has no need to be said.

There can be no comedy about patriarchs. They come before civilization is in flower, and comedy is the finest of the flowers. They are the foundation, for the most part hidden from sight; it is the cornice, the gables and the roof. Or, to change the figure once again, they are the blood and it is the complexion. Mann's Joseph is all grace, all light, all intellect at its highest. He can do anything except be the silent, tremendous man each one of his ancestors was. In Egypt he remembers the faith of his fathers, and characteristically gives a lucid account of it whenever asked. But it is not a part of him; it is not in his bones as it is in the bones of Jacob.

If anything, he understands it too perfectly; it is one of the works of art he knows like a connoisseur; it is outside of him, and he can leave it there when he likes. He leaves it there during his sundry flirtations with other faiths and other deities: Tammuz, Ashtaroth and Osiris. What Mann calls "the soul's love-affair with matter" fascinates him if anything too much. There was a youthful moment when he almost worshipped the Moon and subscribed to its cult. "As a cult," says Mann, "it was vague, confused, and prone to degenerate—calculated to alarm the careful father—but just on that ground intoxicating, because mental and physical emotions were therein so enchantingly mixed." Egypt, the Kingdom of the Dead and therefore the embodiment of all that Jacob had taught him to abhor, was not visited by Joseph voluntarily; Jacob's other sons, the red-eyed sons of Leah, sent him there; but once there he again became the connoisseur of customs, in this case exquisite ones which the artist in him could not but admire. He did no more than admire and master this new way of life; he remained faithful to his fathers, and said so often enough; yet none of his fathers could have done what he did—could have become more Egyptian than any son of Egypt, and worn its manners like so many jewels. It is impossible to imagine Isaac, for example, flattering, as Joseph did, the guide who was about to take him in to his first audience with Pharaoh. Isaac would never have been there in the first place; but supposing that he was, and supposing that the guide asked him whether he knew how to salute the god, it could never have occurred to him to smile and say: "I wish I did not, for it would be pleasant to learn it of you." This was flattery, and it was mockery too; it came from the top of Joseph's mind that touched the stars.

Joseph is material for comedy precisely because he is civilized. Both comedy and tragedy depend on civilization for their power. The stories of the patriarchs belong perhaps in neither category; they are too primitive, possibly they are too important, to be classified at all. They simply exist and tell themselves, as seeds germinate in the ground. The first fathers were, to be sure, the heroes of great stories; they were this side of God in whose life there are no events; but they were nowhere near as far away from absolute simplicity as Joseph was. Joseph was secular; he could believe anything and everything; he was advanced; he was free; and his only illusion was that he had none. He had several concerning himself, the chief of these being that there was no real difference between him and Jacob. Even at the end he was not too certain as to what the difference was that Jacob had tried his best to put into words.

This supremely intelligent man did not, that is to say, know everything. And just there is the point at which he becomes available for comic treatment. The stupid person who knows nothing is of no interest to the comic spirit. The brilliant person who nevertheless is blind to something as visible as the ground before his feet— he is the one upon whom wit delights to sharpen its knives. And so with Joseph in Mann's case. Loving his hero as he loved himself, Mann still could mock him because he was not God. And in the same breath he could adore him. He lavished upon him all the understanding that he had, all the elaboration of which his wit was so abundantly capable. His marvelous reconstructions of the Egyptian court, intricate perhaps beyond any imagination but his, and ornate as only he could delicately achieve ornateness—witness for example the entrance of Nefertiti, "with swaying tread, faintly smiling, her eyes cast down, the long, lovely neck thrust anxiously out: the bearer of the seed of the sun"—still do not match the work he did inside Joseph's mind, where recess upon recess opens, as it were, into the very caverns of genius. And this work is endless; it fills a fearsome multitude of pages; nor was any of it done in Genesis. It is all Mann, all modern and all comedy.

Mann's method of amplification is simple in one sense: it is the method of filling in, of stuffing interstices with matter he thinks belongs there. The Biblical narrative is famously bald; it leaves almost everything to the imagination, after, of course, giving the imagination great work to do. Mann cannot be said to desire that nothing be left for his own reader to imagine; he too gives him work, and it can be a life's work if one chooses to do it; but the reader in this case has ideas to contemplate rather than actions to complete. And the ideas are Mann's. Claiming to know in full detail what the people of the ancient tale said to one another in this crisis or that, he supplies conversations which themselves are food for the soul, so delicate and deep they are. The colloquies between Jacob and his favorite son explore the entire field of filial and paternal feeling. What Pharaoh said to Joseph tells us more about Egypt than the archaeologists can. And what Potiphar's wife confessed to him in her third-year agony of love is the climax of a whole fine novel of which she has been the distinguished heroine —though in Mann's opinion Joseph has not been its distinguished hero. He gives us that opinion—it has to do with Joseph's vanity —just as he always lays bare for us the process of his own thought. We are continuously in his confidence; the book could, in fact, be described as a conversation between the author and the reader, or

441

rather as a monologue which the reader is expected to overhear. But the method is not so simple as all that. Sometimes it involves the addition of circumstances and deeds, the outright invention of narrative details, none of which we could have worked out for ourselves unless our talent and our scholarship had been identical with Mann's. And the richest number of these is to be found in the Potiphar section, which Mann himself called "the artistic zenith of the work." Potiphar's household becomes a fascinating world all by itself. The dwarves, the parents of the master, the eunuch master and his tragic wife—these are the central figures, and each one of them is a triumph of creation, yet they are surrounded by others still, in a busy and beautiful house which for the time being absorbs our entire attention. And none of this is in the Bible. Perhaps it did not need to be, but we do not think of that; and even if we did we would find nothing that contradicted or violated the primitive fable. It is simply that Mann has moved us up close enough for us to be able to see what happened in this household day by day—it may be minute by minute—during the three years it was a part of human history. There is the day, for instance, of the ladies' party, when Potiphar's wife, incapable any longer of bearing alone the crushing burden of her love for Joseph, invites her friends to come and eat oranges with her. Each of them is given a little, sharp knife with which to open the precious fruit; each starts to do so at the moment when Joseph appears to pour the wine; and down each snow-white wrist runs a stream of crimson blood. For so much beauty, so suddenly entering the hall, has captured each lady's eyes that her knife knows not where it should cut. And this was exactly as Mut had planned it when she told Joseph he must come in among them at such and such a moment. It is an unforgettable moment; nor did Mann need to invent it. His scholarship, which surely was enormous, found it for him in the Koran, in seventeen Persian poems, and in "countless renderings by pencil and brush." Those are the sources he reveals to us; but if we have access to none of them we can go to Louis Ginzberg's *Legends of the Jews* for a version graphic enough.

Not that Mann inserts the episode of the ladies' party with a flourish of narrative trumpets or with any brave show of art. Here also he is true to the comic tradition of storytelling, which plays down the narrative art. It says that history is more interesting than fiction; so history is what it pretends to write. Chaucer has his "author" whom he merely follows; Cervantes has his Arabian biographer whom he merely translates. The comic artist will not ad-

442

mit that he has invented anything; the truth is enough for him—
Mann says "the facts"—and all truth is as old as the hills anyway;
there can be no new stories, just as there can be nothing new under
the sun; see the Bible as to that. Every man knows everything; except, of course, that some men forget what they know, or do not
wholly realize it, and so commit the only sin that comedy is designed to deal with, namely, folly. Folly is not a fatal sin, though
there are those who unaccountably grow fond of it in themselves;
therefore it either can be cured or can be rendered harmless as a
spectacle at which we wiser ones may smile. It is rendered harmless by understanding: the fool's understanding at last, or if this
is not to be expected, then ours; and probably too that of several
other persons in the story. The essence of comedy is its love of
understanding. That is why it goes in so heavily for talk—or
rather, we hope, lightly: deliciously and lightly. The dialectic of
comedy may seem queer, but it is dialectic nevertheless; and they
are right who credit Plato with having perfected both philosophy
and comedy in his matchless dialogues. Now it would be saying too
much, if not too little, to say that the essence of tragedy is misunderstanding. The errors of tragic heroes are too vast to be so trivi-
ally dismissed. Yet they do misunderstand their situations and
themselves; and in the rush of events which their own blindness
accelerates they do dreadful things which with more time and
light they would never have done. Tragedies are dark and short;
more light, more time, more talk, would make literally all the difference in the world; but those blessings are not available.
Whereas they are the very stuff of comedy, which, like John Tan-
ner, keeps on talking though the heavens fall. But, in fact, they do
not fall. In comedy there is neither the midnight of utter confusion nor the sudden blaze of a belated dawn. In comedy the hour is
always noon.

And nothing much happens then. The action of any comedy is
less interesting—certainly less memorable—than the discussions
it contains. A tragedy whose plot cannot be remembered in the
strict order of its events is no tragedy at all; the events create their
own order, from which there is no escape, or else they have no
meaning for the mind. This must have been what Aristotle meant
when he said the soul of a tragedy was its plot; the action was everything. In comedy there is action too, or we should have no
story; but it is most interesting for what can be said about it before
and after it is done, which throws still further light upon the fact
that comic poets underplay their plots and take no responsibility

443

for them in the first place. By the same token they are indifferent to dramatic or narrative effects; they ignore the conventional devices for securing such effects; they lean over backwards to avoid melodrama, which to be sure they may approach as a possibility, but which they would rather parody than embrace.

So Mann in his great comedy refuses to make what tragedy would make, and what the Bible did make, out of certain recognition scenes. The recognition scene is essential to tragedy, which lives on such bursts of feeling as it perfectly provides. There was an opportunity for Mann to contrive a meeting between Joseph and Mut-em-enet after Joseph came home from prison. But he discusses the possibility only to reject it. Romancers, he says, have tried their hands at such a scene, and the result is "Persian musk," is "attar of roses," which is to say, sweet nonsense. For one thing, "it has nothing to do with the facts." For another, their story was done. And even the recognition scenes which he is bound to accept because they come down to him and are a part of his duty—those between Joseph and his brothers at the climax and between Jacob and Joseph at the very end—he deliberately muffs, and here and there even mocks. Of course they are moving; but Mann does not want them to break our hearts, and he knows how to keep them from doing so. He wraps them in talk; the principals murmur to each other even while they weep; dialectic still holds the center of the stage. And as for the weeping, what would a tragic poet have to say of one who in the immortal scene between Joseph and his brothers transmogrifies the Biblical "he wept aloud" into: "His nose began to prickle inside, he sniffed a little, and his eyes all at once ran over"? Granted, on a later page—much later, for the scene is long—we are told that "glittering tears ran down his cheeks." This, to be sure, is more like drama; yet even there we are forced to suspect that the tears of Joseph *would* glitter, since everything about him shines. Nor at the moment when the great scene was preparing had the author kept us in suspense as to whether it would happen. The comic artist cares nothing for suspense, which indeed is never so indispensable to narrative as commonly it is thought to be. It is at best a second-rate device for generating interest where no interest naturally exists. At least this is true if it consists of no more than the artificial withholding from us of some information we need for understanding and would normally have. When it consists of telling us that a given thing will happen but letting us wait to see how it happens, and precisely when, it is a powerful because it is a natural narrative tool. And

444

it is thus that Mann uses it, and confides to us that he does. "Joseph's suspense was great," he writes on one occasion; "on this point depended his future relations with the brothers. We, of course, are in no suspense: we know all the phases of the story by heart. . . . So in our wisdom we may smile at him." Such, remarks Mann on an earlier occasion, is the advantage of having an old story to retell. "If I were here a mere inventor of tales, what I have to tell would certainly expose me to the reproach of drawing too long a bow, and presuming far too much upon a credulity which after all has its limits. Luckily, such is not my role. I rest upon the traditional facts, which are not less sound because some of them ring as though they were newly minted. Thus I am in a position to state what I have to tell in an assured and tranquil tone that in the face of all doubts and reproaches carries conviction." A tragic poet who stopped his story to address his audience thus would instantly break his spell and lose all power to convince. For the comic poet there is no spell; or if there is one and its name is truth, it is just in this offhand way that he invokes it.

The truth about Joseph is, of course, a complicated thing which it is the main business of the book to convey. Mann's hero is perhaps not different from the one we meet in Genesis, nor is his father altered from the ancient Jacob; nor for that matter is their relation to each other built here upon ground which the original text did not at least lay out. But Mann's refinements are as many as they are marvelous. The brilliance and beauty of Joseph have few parallels in the fiction of the world. And the vanity. The problem was to make the vanity palatable, and it was solved by suggesting, not indeed in so many words, that it was like the vanity of a golden mirror which can no more help being what it is than a bright person can help being bright. Joseph might have bitten off his tongue, as Potiphar's poor wife all but did; yet he did not; he kept on saying with it the most fascinating and impudent things; and we are as glad of this as Jacob was, or Benjamin, or even the ten sullen half-brothers who in spite of themselves adored the speaker of them at the same time that they wanted to kill him, or at least to remove him from their sight forever. It was Jacob, however, who resisted Joseph least; which is a mild way of saying that he committed the sin of idolatry by elevating him to the rank of favorite son, somewhat as he had committed that same sin by loving Rachel for herself and not in God. Mann is willing to say that the doting father was the chief source of his son's misery, if misery it was. Perhaps it was never that; for the pits into which this youth

445

was cast, first in the desert and then in Egypt, yielded in every case an experience he could dramatize; and there was no exercise he loved more. In no crisis of his life did he die so that he might be reborn. He does not look to us at the end like one of those truly great men of whom it can be said, not that they have lived a lot but that they have died a lot—have been, we sometimes say, in hell. No, in some amazing way he has not been touched by the bonfires he walked through. For one thing, though he would deny this, he has never ceased to assume that others must love him more than they love themselves. The assumption had been wrong both in the case of his brothers and in that of Mut-em-enet, and now he knows that it was wrong. Yet he has not changed in the secret depths of his heart where he still knows that he is like nobody else. "Have you ever heard the voice of self-denying love?" Jacob asks him this in the Land of Goshen, and the question answers itself. When on the last page of the book Joseph insists to his brothers that they are to forgive him, not he to forgive them, he speaks in the character he has enjoyed from the beginning. "If it is a question of pardon between us human beings, then it is I myself must beg for it, for you had perforce to be cast in the villain's part so that things might turn out as they did." The hero's part had been so naturally his that he still needs no rehearsing in it.

Not that we love him less because all this is true. The triumph of Mann is that we love on every page the hero he himself loves this side of idolatry. Idolatry in Mann would have destroyed his comedy, since comedy admits no gods that are made of earth. That he resisted the sin, tempted though he surely was, is a triumph more stupendous still. The sign of his resistance is the impression of Joseph he leaves with us at last: the impression of one whose understanding is so fine that the light in his mind almost puts out the stars—yet not those stars at which his great-grandfather Abraham, that wonderful old man, stared without speaking a single word. "One can easily be in a story," Mann has Joseph say, "and not understand it." Joseph understood everything in his story except himself. His light never shone altogether inward, producing perfect silence.

# Machiavelli's *Prince*:
# Political Science or Political Satire?

## GARRETT MATTINGLY

### *(1958)*

GARRETT MATTINGLY's interpretation of Machiavelli's *The Prince* as political satire radically departs from the traditional approach to the work as a handbook of advice on the use of political power. Professor of European history at Columbia University, Mr. Mattingly is the author of studies in fifteenth- and sixteenth-century diplomatic history, including *The Armada*.

THE REPUTATION of Niccolò Machiavelli rests on a curious paradox, a paradox so conspicuous and so familiar that we have almost entirely forgotten it. After the collapse of the Florentine republic, which he had served faithfully for fourteen years, Machiavelli relieved the tedium of exile and idleness by taking up his pen. He wrote poems—verse, at least—and tales and plays, including one comedy which is a classic. But mostly he wrote about politics. He was mad about politics. He says in one of his letters that he had to talk about it; he could talk of nothing else. So, in short discourses and political fables, in a history of Florence, in a treatise on the art of war and, notably, in a series of discourses, nominally on the first ten books of Livy, he strove to pass on to his fellow countrymen the fruits of his experience, his reading and his meditation. These are solid works, earnest and thoughtful, often original and provocative. Scholars who have read them usually speak of them with great respect. But not many people ever look at them, and most of those who do have had their curiosity aroused by the one little book which everyone knows: *The Prince*.

*The Prince* is scarcely more than a pamphlet, a very minor fraction of its author's work, but it overshadows all the rest. Probably

447

no book about politics was ever read more widely. Certainly none has been better known to people who have never read it. Everyone knows that Machiavelli recommended hypocrisy and ingratitude, meanness, cruelty and treachery as the traits proper to princes. Everyone recognizes "Machiavellian" as an adjective for political conduct that combines diabolical cunning with a ruthless disregard for moral standards. But *The Prince* obsesses historians and political philosophers who know a good deal more about it than that. Its burning prose still casts a lurid glow over the whole landscape of Renaissance Italy: historians who ought to know better call the whole period "the age of Machiavelli" and describe it as if it were chiefly characterized by the kind of behavior on which *The Prince* dwells; and philosophers, undertaking to describe Machiavelli's political thought, after carefully apprising their readers of the greater weight and complexity of the *Discorsi* and his other writings, end up by choosing half or more of their quotations from one slender volume. But *The Prince* is a short book, and most people remember short books better than long ones. Moreover, *The Prince* is easily Machiavelli's best prose. Its sentences are crisp and pointed, free from the parenthetical explanations and qualifying clauses that punctuate and clog his other political writings. Its prose combines verve and bite with a glittering, deadly polish, like the swordplay of a champion fencer. It uses apt, suggestive images, symbols packed with overtones. For instance: A prince should behave sometimes like a man, sometimes like a beast, and among beasts he should combine the traits of the lion and the fox. It is studded with epigrams like "A man will forget the death of his father sooner than the loss of his patrimony," epigrams which all seem to come out of some sort of philosophical Grand Guignol and, like the savage ironies of Swift's *Modest Proposal*, are rendered the more spine chilling by the matter-of-fact tone in which they are uttered. And this is where the paradox comes in. Although the method and most of the assumptions of *The Prince* are so much of a piece with Machiavelli's thought that the book could not have been written by anyone else, yet in certain important respects, including some of the most shocking of the epigrams, *The Prince* contradicts everything else Machiavelli ever wrote and everything we know about his life. And everyone who has studied the subject at all has always known this.

The history of Machiavelli's literary reputation underlines the paradox. His other political works were received on publication much as they have been received ever since, respectfully but without undue excitement. However, when *The Prince* was published in 1532, five years after its author's death, it achieved an enormous *succès de scandale*. As word of its appalling doctrines spread, all Europe hummed with a chorus of disapproval. For two centuries, to call one's political opponent a disciple of Machiavelli was about the worst thing one could say of him. The cynical immorality of the maxims in *The Prince* horrified even so unscrupulous a young rascal as Frederick the Great of Prussia—or at least he said they did.

Then, as the modern spirit of nationalism dawned, the image of Old Nick began to change. Appropriately enough, it was Herder who first declared that *The Prince* was neither a satire nor an iniquitous guide for political criminals, but an objective study of sixteenth-century Italian politics, offered by a patriot as a service to his country. People began to point out that if Machiavelli recommended behavior of which one could not really approve, he did it for the sake of a united Italy. Some of his councils were shocking, truly, but only bitter, dangerous medicines would suffice for his corrupt age. So, from being a sort of Byronic diabolist, Machiavelli gradually became a hero, and then a saint of the Italian Risorgimento. Villari's solid volumes proving that Machiavelli was a Florentine patriot, and perhaps even an Italian one, are the chief monument to this nineteenth-century hero-image.

In the twentieth century the image changed again, partly, perhaps, because of difficulties in the nationalist explanation, but mostly, I suspect, because of a change in the prevailing climate of opinion. Kossuth and Garibaldi were being shouldered aside by Darwin and Pasteur, and from being a patriot whose exaggerations were forgivable because of his devotion to torn and trampled Italy, Machiavelli became the passionless, objective scientist, the perfect mirror and analyst of his time. Machiavelli's "objectivity" and "realism" had been praised in the nineteenth century and even earlier by a few people, mostly by philosophers like Herder and Fichte and Hegel, who did not bother to check up on him; but it was Sir Frederick Pollock who, about 1910, first conferred on Machiavelli the proud title of "scientist." As far as I know he has held it to this day, the dissenters being mainly belated exponents of the nationalist-patriot school. In his *Myth of the State* Ernst Cassirer enshrined the current image in an eloquent passage describing Machiavelli watching political behavior and drawing conclusions from it with the passionless detachment of a chemist in a laboratory.

449

There is a certain superficial plausibility about this view. Since so much of *The Prince* does harmonize with the rest of Machiavelli's thought, and since it is so quotable, the temptation to explain away the discords is hard to resist. And often Machiavelli did say that he wanted to show things as they really are instead of as they ought to be, and often he did try to do so, not only in his state papers, where dispassionate, objective reporting was expected of him, but also in the *Discorsi* and other works in which the literary tradition was different. He tried; he did not always succeed. To insist that republics are always juster, wiser and more trustworthy than princes, as Machiavelli frequently does in the *Discorsi*, seems a judgment as much charged with subjective emotion as its reverse would be. And, in the year 1520, to dismiss firearms as unimportant in war seems slightly unrealistic even for a cloistered scholar, and rather more so for a man who had been more than a decade the secretary of war of an embattled republic. Yet usually he did try to be objective, and that is why *The Prince* is so serious a stumbling block. The notion that this little book was meant as a serious, scientific treatise on government contradicts everything we know about Machiavelli's life, about his writings, and about the history of his time.

In the first place, this proposition asks us to believe that Niccolò Machiavelli deliberately wrote a handbook meant to help a tyrant rule the once free people of Florence. The Machiavelli were an old Florentine family, noted for their devotion to the republic. In the two centuries before Niccolò was born they had given Florence twelve *gonfalonieri* and fifty-four priors. In the fifteenth century, Niccolò's great-granduncle Girolamo won himself a place in the hearts of the people by suffering imprisonment, torture, exile and death in defense of their liberty. Another Machiavelli, Francesco, was remembered for a public speech in which he said, "It is freedom that makes cities and their citizens great. This is well known. Tyranny makes only desolation. For tyrants must always fear good citizens and try to exterminate them." Nearly a century later, Niccolò made this assertion one of the central theses of his *Discorsi,* thus prolonging the family tradition in which he was brought up. We know more about his youth now than we did until a few years ago when the diary of Niccolò's father, Bernardo, was found and published. It is not unlike the diaries of many other of the pious, thrifty, hard-working, rather puritanical Florentine petty bourgeoisie who were the backbone of the city's greatness. Bernardo was almost poor and, in those days of Medici domination, without public honors. But he was proud of his family, a firm but affectionate father, anxious to bring up his son to good Latin letters and a devotion to republican principles. Poor as he was, Bernardo had a small library of classics, including, the diary shows, a Livy, which by the time Niccolò was seventeen had to be rebound. To his wife, Bartolomea de'Nelli, the authoress of a number of hymns, *laudi sacre,* Bernardo probably left their son's religious education, but he himself would have seen to it that Niccolò learned the history of his *patria,* how Florence was the citadel of freedom and the guardian of Italian liberty, and the share his own family once had in this glorious heritage.

In the 1470's it was still possible to believe that this heritage was not lost. The constitution of the city was still republican, and though the Medici enjoyed an influence that republicans like Bernardo might regard as sinister, and though the young Medici did not mask their power with the same care their grandfather had used, they were still in form and law just scions of the leading family of a free commonwealth. In fact, as the popular wrath against the Pazzi conspirators proved, most Florentines, particularly the *popolo minuto,* the "little people," still thought of the Medici as the guardians of their liberties both against foreign domination and against the selfish designs of the oligarchs. It was only slowly, in the 1480's, that most Florentines began to realize the attrition of their freedom. When Niccolò was twenty-five they rebelled, and Piero de Medici rode out of the city gates, never to return. Four years later Niccolò Machiavelli was appointed chancellor of the second chancery, and shortly thereafter secretary to the Ten of War. For the next fourteen years he served the Florentine republic with furious, dedicated zeal. He has left the proof of his devotion in the record of his activities and in the state papers in which he spun endless schemes for the defense and aggrandizement of the republic, and constantly preached the same to his superiors. One characteristic quotation is irresistible. The subject is an increase in the defense budget that Machiavelli's masters were reluctant to vote. He reminds them with mounting impatience that only strong states are respected by their neighbors and that their neglect of military strength in the recent past has cost them dear, and he ends with anything but detached calm: "Other people learn from the perils of their neighbors, you will not even learn from your own, nor trust yourselves, nor recognize the time you are losing and have lost. I tell you fortune will not alter the sentence it has pronounced unless you alter your behavior. Heaven will not and cannot preserve those bent on their own ruin. But I cannot believe it will come to this, seeing that you are free Florentines and have your liberty in your own hands. In the end I believe you will have the same regard for your freedom that men always have who are born free and desire to live free."

Only a man who cared deeply for the independence of his city would use language like this to his employers. But Machiavelli gave an even more impressive proof of his disinterested patriotism. After fourteen years in high office, in a place where the opportunities for dipping into the public purse and into the pockets of his compatriots and of those foreigners he did business with were practically unlimited (among other duties he acted as paymaster-general of the army), Machiavelli retired from public life as poor as when he had entered it. Later he was to refer to this record with pride, but also with a kind of rueful astonishment; and, indeed, if this was not a unique feat in his day, it was a very rare one.

For fourteen years Machiavelli served the republic. Then, in 1512, the militia he had counted on so much ran like rabbits at the first sight of the Spanish veterans. There was the bloody sack of Prato, and the republic collapsed before his eyes. The Medici, Cardinal Giovanni and his brother Giuliano, came back behind the Spanish pikes, and while the new government was still unsettled there was a plot to murder them. Two young men named Capponi and Boscoli were arrested. One of them tried to get rid of a paper on which was a short list of names. They were the names of prominent republicans, some of whom had already fled. One was that of Niccolò Machiavelli.

Machiavelli had not fled. Dismissed from office, he still lingered in Florence. He was arrested, imprisoned and interrogated under torture. Four turns of the rack were usually enough to break a man, body and spirit. Niccolò endured six, and well enough to congratulate himself afterward not just on his survival but on his courage. He admitted nothing, and since nothing could be proved against him, he was released with no further punishment than the loss of his offices, a ruinous fine, and exile to his tiny estate seven miles from the gates of Florence, there to eat his heart out in loneliness and boredom.

Machiavelli emerged from prison in mid-March, 1513. Most people believe that *The Prince* was finished by December. I suppose it is possible to imagine that a man who has seen his country enslaved, his life's work wrecked and his own career with it, and has, for good measure, been tortured within an inch of his life should thereupon go home and write a book intended to teach his enemies the proper way to maintain themselves, writing all the time, remember, with the passionless objectivity of a scientist in a laboratory. It must be possible to imagine such behavior, because Machiavelli scholars do imagine it and accept it without a visible tremor. But it is a little difficult for the ordinary mind to compass.

The difficulty is increased by the fact that this acceptance of tyranny seems to have been a passing phase. Throughout the rest of his life Machiavelli wrote as a republican and moved mainly in republican circles. In 1524 two of his closest friends and patrons, Zanobi Buondelmonti and the poet Luigi Alamanni, were involved in another conspiracy against the Medici and fled. Much later Machiavelli's name was connected with this conspiracy too. The accusation came too late to do him any harm, and nothing was proved. Of course it does not prove anything either that when the Medici were finally driven out again in 1527, Buondelmonti and Alamanni began working at once to bring their old friend back to the service of the restored republic. But the facts do seem to indicate a singularly consistent life, except for one aberration.

The notion that *The Prince* is what it pretends to be, a scientific manual for tyrants, has to contend not only against Machiavelli's life but against his writings, as, of course, everyone who wants to use *The Prince* as a centerpiece in an exposition of Machiavelli's political thought has recognized. Ever since Herder, the standard explanation has been that in the corrupt conditions of sixteenth-century Italy only a prince could create a strong state capable of expansion. The trouble with this is that it was chiefly because they widened their boundaries that Machiavelli preferred republics. In the *Discorsi* he wrote, "We know by experience that states have never signally increased either in territory or in riches except under a free government. The cause is not far to seek, since it is the well-being not of individuals but of the community which makes the state great, and without question this universal well-being is nowhere secured save in a republic. . . . Popular rule is always better than the rule of princes." This is not just a casual remark. It is the main theme of the *Discorsi* and the basic assumption of all but one of Machiavelli's writings, as it was the basic assumption of his political career.

There is another way in which *The Prince* is a puzzling anomaly. In practically everything else Machiavelli wrote, he displayed the sensitivity and tact of the developed literary temperament.

He was delicately aware of the tastes and probable reactions of his public. No one could have written that magnificent satiric soliloquy of Fra Timotheo in *Mandragola*, for instance, who had not an instinctive feeling for the response of an audience. But the effect of the publication of *The Prince* on the first several generations of its readers in Italy (outside of Florence) and in the rest of Europe was shock. It horrified, repelled and fascinated like a Medusa's head. A large part of the shock was caused, of course, by the cynical immorality of some of the proposals, but instead of appeasing revulsion and insinuating his new proposals as delicately as possible, Machiavelli seems to delight in intensifying the shock and deliberately employing devices to heighten it. Of these not the least effective is the way *The Prince* imitates, almost parodies, one of the best known and most respected literary forms of the three preceding centuries, the handbook of advice to princes. This literary type was enormously popular. Its exemplars ran into the hundreds of titles of which a few, like St. Thomas' *De Regno* and Erasmus' *Institutio principis christiani* are not quite unknown today. In some ways, Machiavelli's little treatise was just like all the other "Mirrors of Princes"; in other ways it was a diabolical burlesque of all of them, like a political Black Mass.

The shock was intensified again because Machiavelli deliberately addressed himself primarily to princes who have newly acquired their principalities and do not owe them either to inheritance or to the free choice of their countrymen. The short and ugly word for this kind of prince is "tyrant." Machiavelli never quite uses the word except in illustrations from classical antiquity, but he seems to delight in dancing all around it until even the dullest of his readers could not mistake his meaning. Opinions about the relative merits of republics and monarchies varied during the Renaissance, depending mainly upon where one lived, but about tyrants there was only one opinion. Cristoforo Landino, Lorenzo the Magnificent's teacher and client, stated the usual view in his commentary on Dante, written when Niccolò Machiavelli was a child. When he came to comment on Brutus and Cassius in the lowest circle of hell, Landino wrote: "Surely it was extraordinary cruelty to inflict such severe punishment on those who faced death to deliver their country from slavery, a deed for which, if they had been Christians, they would have merited the most honored seats in the highest heaven. If we consult the laws of any well-constituted republic, we shall find them to decree no greater reward to anyone than to the man who kills the tyrant." So said the Italian

Renaissance with almost unanimous voice. If Machiavelli's friends were meant to read the manuscript of *The Prince* and if they took it at face value—an objective study of how to be a successful tyrant offered as advice to a member of the species—they can hardly have failed to be deeply shocked. And if the manuscript was meant for the eye of young Giuliano de Medici alone, he can hardly have been pleased to find it blandly assumed that he was one of a class of whom his father's tutor had written that the highest duty of a good citizen was to kill them.

The literary fame of *The Prince* is due, precisely, to its shocking quality, so if the book was seriously meant as a scientific manual, it owes its literary reputation to an artistic blunder. And if it was meant for a Medici prince, it has at its core an even more inexplicable piece of tactlessness. For to the Medici prince, "to a new prince established by fortune and the arms of others," Machiavelli offers Cesare Borgia as a model. There was just enough truth to the suggestion that Giuliano de Medici owed his principate "to the arms of others"—after all, it was the Spanish troops who overthrew the republic as it was French troops who established Cesare in the Romagna—to be wounding. There was just enough cogency in the comparison between the duke of Valentinois, a pope's son, and the duke of Nemours, a pope's brother, to make it stick. These things merely heightened the affront. A Medici, of a family as old and as illustrious as any in Florence, a man whose great-grandfather, grandfather and father had each in turn been acknowledged the first citizen of the republic and who now aspired to no more than to carry on their tradition (or so he said) was being advised to emulate a foreigner, a Spaniard, a bastard, convicted, in the court of public opinion anyway, of fratricide, incest and a long role of abominable crimes, a man specially hated in Tuscany for treachery and extortion and for the gross misconduct of his troops on neutral Florentine soil, and a man, to boot, who as a prince had been a notorious and spectacular failure.

This almost forgotten fact lies at the heart of the mystery of *The Prince*. We remember what Machiavelli wrote about Cesare in his most famous work, and we forget what Cesare was. But in 1513 most Italians would not have forgotten the events of 1503, and unless we assume that Machiavelli himself had forgotten what he himself had reported ten or eleven years before, we can scarcely believe that his commendation of the Borgia was seriously meant. If we take *The Prince* as an objective, scientific description of political reality, we must face contradiction not only by what we know of Machiavelli's political career, of his usual opinions and of his literary skill, but also by the facts of history as reported by, among others, Machiavelli himself.

Let us take just a few instances, the crucial ones. Relying on assertions in Chapter Seven of *The Prince*, most historians in the past hundred years have written as if the Borgia had restored peace and order in the Romagna, unified its government and won the allegiance of its inhabitants. Part of the time this must have been going on, Machiavelli was an envoy in the duke's camp. Although he does warn the signory repeatedly that Valentino is a formidable ruffian, daring, unscrupulous and of unlimited ambition, he never mentions these statesmanlike achievements—nor do any of the other reports from observers in the area, Spanish, French, Venetian, Sienese; nor do any other contemporary sources. All the indications are quite contrary. The most probing recent study of Valentino's career, Gabriele Pepe's *La Politica dei Borgia*, sums the matter up by saying that the duke did nothing to end factional strife and anarchy in the Romagna; he merely superimposed the brutal rule of his Spanish captains on top of it.

We can make a concrete check on a related instance. After saying in Chapter Thirteen that the duke had used first French troops, then mercenaries under *condottieri* captains and then his own men, Machiavelli comments, "He was never esteemed more highly than when everyone saw that he was complete master of his own forces." But in the *Legazione*, Machiavelli never once refers to the military capacity of the duke or praises the courage or discipline of his army. Instead, as late as December 14, 1502, he writes from Imola of the troops under Cesare's own command: "They have devoured everything here except the stones . . . here in the Romagna they are behaving just as they did in Tuscany last year [of their passage then, Landucci had noted in his diary that none of the foreign armies that had crossed Tuscany in the past seven years had behaved so abominably as these Italians under the papal banner] and they show no more discipline and no less confusion than they did then." There is no subsequent indication that Machiavelli ever changed his mind.

Nowhere is *The Prince* more at odds with the facts of history or with Machiavelli's own previous judgments than in the famous concluding passage of Chapter Seven on which any favorable opinion of Cesare's statecraft must be based. The passage in *The Prince* reads: "On the day Pope Julius II was elected, the Duke told me that he had thought of everything that might happen on the death of his father and provided for everything except that when his father died he himself would be at death's door. . . . only the shortness of the life of Alexander and his own sickness frustrated his designs. Therefore he who wants to make sure of a new principality . . . cannot find a better model than the actions of this man." Could Machiavelli have believed this in 1513? He certainly did not believe it in 1503. He did not even record then that Cesare ever said anything of the sort; and though it would not be unlike some of the duke's whimperings, he could not have said it on the day of Julius II's election, when he was boasting to everyone that the new pope would obey him. In any case, Machiavelli would have believed what, in *The Prince,* he said the duke said, as little as he believed the bluster that, in 1503, he actually reported. By November of 1503, nobody could have believed it. In fact, even in August, when Alexander VI died, at the age of seventy-two after a papacy of eleven years (not such a short life and not such a short reign), most people in Rome, including all of the ambassadors whose reports survive and most of the cardinals with whom they had talked, felt sure Cesare was finished. He had always ridden on his father's shoulders, and he was hated, feared and despised even by most of the faction who had stood by the old pope. No one trusted him, and there was no one he could trust. No pope would dare support him, and without papal support his principate was built on quicksand. He had never, in fact, faced this eventual predicament, and he did not face it when it arose. It is true that he was ill in August with a bout of malaria, but not too ill to stall the election and then maneuver the choice of the old and ailing Pius III, thus delaying an unavoidable doom. Julius II was not elected until November. In all those months and even after the election, Italy was treated through the eyes of its ambassadors to the spectacle of the terrible Borgia duke writhing in an agony of indecision, now about to go to Genoa to raise money, now ready to start for an interview with the king of France, now on the point of leading his troops back to the Romagna, but in fact hovering about the curia, plucking the sleeves of cardinals and bowing and smiling to envoys he used to bully, sometimes swaggering through the streets with the powerful armed guard he felt he needed to protect him from the vengeance of the Orsini, sometimes shaking beneath bedclothes with what might have been fever and might have been funk. We catch a glimpse of him at midnight in the chamber of Guidobaldo de Montrefeltre, the duke of Urbino, who had been newly restored to his former estates by the loyalty of his subjects, and to his former rank of *gonfaloniere* of the Church by the new pope. There Cesare kneels on the floor, sobbing in pure terror, begging the old friend whom he had betrayed and robbed, with incredible meanness, not just of his duchy, but of his books and his antique medals, not to kill him, please not to kill him, to leave him at least his life, until Guidobaldo, beyond any feeling about this curious monster, says he does not wish to kill him; he only wishes him to go away.

Shortly thereafter Cesare slinks off to Naples and imprisonment, followed by the scornful laughter of Italy. For nothing is more absurd than the great straw-stuffed giants of carnival, and when such a giant has for a season frightened all Italy, the laughter is that much the louder. Machiavelli was one of the ambassadors in Rome. He knew all this as well as anyone. One can read in his dispatches his growing impatience with the duke, his growing contempt for Cesare's wild talk, aimless shifts of plan, alternate blustering and whining. "The duke, who never kept faith with anyone," he wrote, "is now obliged to rely on the faith of others." And later, "The duke, who never showed mercy, now finds mercy his only hope." Later in his historical poem, *Decennali*, Machiavelli made his distaste for the Borgia clear enough. Did he really mean to propose him in 1513 as a model prince? Was he writing as a friend of tyrants or as a dispassionate scientific observer when he said he did?

There is, of course, an alternative view, never predominant and now hopelessly old-fashioned, but one that was once held by some quite respectable people. The earliest explicit statement of it I know comes from Alberico Gentili, an Italian who lectured on the civil law at Oxford in the reign of Elizabeth I. Speaking of his fellow countryman, Gentili wrote, in part: "He has been much calumniated and deserves our sympathy. He was, indeed, a praiser of democracy (*Democratiae laudator*) and its most zealous champion. Born, educated and honored with office in a republic, he was a supreme foe of tyrants. It was his purpose not to instruct tyrants but to reveal their secret machinations, stripping them bare before their suffering people. . : . he aimed to instruct [those] people under the pretext of instructing the prince, hoping that thus his teaching might be tolerated." Toward the end of the seventeenth century, Baruch Spinoza, without, I think, ever having read Gentili, expressed a similar opinion, and nearly a hundred years later Jean Jacques Rousseau concurred. In the course

458

of those centuries before violent nationalism had blurred men's vision, enough writers must have identified *The Prince* as a satire so that Herder felt compelled to begin his defense by indignantly repudiating this view.

Perhaps nobody should be rash enough today to call *The Prince* a satire, not in the teeth of all the learned opinion to the contrary. But when one comes to think of it, what excellent sense the idea makes! However you define "satire"—and I understand that critics are still without a thoroughly satisfactory definition—it must include the intention to denounce, expose or deride someone or something, and it is to be distinguished from mere didactic condemnation and invective (when it can be distinguished at all) by the employment of such devices as irony, sarcasm and ridicule. It need not be provocative of laughter; I doubt whether many people ever laughed or even smiled at the adventures of Gulliver among the Yahoos. And though satire admits of, and in fact always employs, exaggeration and overemphasis, the author, to be effective, must not appear to be, and in fact need not be, conscious that this is so. When Dryden wrote, "The rest to some faint meaning make pretense / But Shadwell never deviates into sense," he may have been conscious of some overstatement, but he was conveying his considered criticism of Shadwell's poetry. And when Pope called "Lord Fanny" "this painted child of dirt that stinks and stings," the language may be violent, but who can doubt that this is how Pope felt? Indeed the satirist seems to put forth his greatest powers chiefly when goaded by anger, hatred and savage indignation. If Machiavelli wrote *The Prince* out of the fullness of these emotions rather than out of the dispassionate curiosity of the scientist or out of a base willingness to toady to the destroyers of his country's liberty, then one can understand why the sentences crack like a whip, why the words bite and burn like acid, and why the whole style has a density and impact unique among his writings.

To read *The Prince* as satire not only clears up puzzles and resolves contradictions; it gives a new dimension and meaning to passages unremarkable before. Take the place in the dedication that runs "just as those who paint landscapes must seat themselves below in the plains to see the mountains, and high in the mountains to see the plains, so to understand the nature of the people one must be a prince, and to understand the nature of a prince, one must be one of the people." In the usual view, this is a mere rhetorical flourish, but the irony, once sought, is easy to discover,

459

for Machiavelli, in fact, takes both positions. The people can only see the prince as, by nature and necessity, false, cruel, mean and hypocritical. The prince, from his lofty but precarious perch, dare not see the people as other than they are described in Chapter Seventeen: "ungrateful, fickle, treacherous, cowardly and greedy. As long as you succeed they are yours entirely. They will offer you their blood, property, lives and children when you do not need them. When you do need them, they will turn against you." Probably Machiavelli really believed that this, or something like it, happened to the human nature of a tyrant and his subjects. But the view, like its expression, is something less than objective and dispassionate, and the only lesson it has for princes would seem to be: "Run for your life!"

Considering the brevity of the book, the number of times its princely reader is reminded, as in the passage just quoted, that his people will overthrow him at last is quite remarkable. Cities ruled in the past by princes easily accustom themselves to a change of masters, Machiavelli says in Chapter Five, but "in republics there is more vitality, greater hatred and more desire for vengeance. They cannot forget their lost liberty, so that the safest way is to destroy them—or to live there." He does not say what makes that safe. And most notably, with savage irony, "the duke [Borgia] was so able and laid such firm foundations . . . that the Romagna [after Alexander VI's death] waited for him more than a month." This is as much as to put Leo X's brother on notice that without papal support he can expect short shrift. If the Romagna, accustomed to tyranny, waited only a month before it rose in revolt, how long will Florence wait? Tactlessness like this is unintelligible unless it is deliberate, unless these are not pedantic blunders but sarcastic ironies, taunts flung at the Medici, incitements to the Florentines.

Only in a satire can one understand the choice of Cesare Borgia as the model prince. The common people of Tuscany could not have had what they could expect of a prince's rule made clearer than by the example of this bloodstained buffoon whose vices, crimes and follies had been the scandal of Italy, and the conduct of whose brutal, undisciplined troops had so infuriated the Tuscans that when another band of them crossed their frontier, the peasants fell upon them and tore them to pieces. The Florentine aristocrats on whom Giovanni and cousin Giulio were relying to bridge the transition to despotism would have shared the people's

460

revulsion to Cesare, and they may have been rendered somewhat more thoughtful by the logic of the assumption that nobles were more dangerous to a tyrant than commoners and should be dealt with as Cesare had dealt with the petty lords of the Romagna. Moreover, they could scarcely have avoided noticing the advice to use some faithful servant to terrorize the rest, and then to sacrifice him to escape the obloquy of his conduct, as Cesare had sacrificed Captain Ramio. As for the gentle, mild-mannered, indolent Giuliano de Medici himself, he was the last man to be attracted by the notion of imitating the Borgia. He wanted no more than to occupy the same social position in Florence that his magnificent father had held, and not even that if it was too much trouble. Besides, in the days of the family's misfortunes, Giuliano had found shelter and hospitality at the court of Guidobaldo de Montrefeltre. Giuliano lived at Urbino for many years (there is a rather charming picture of him there in Castiglione's *Il Cortegiano*), and all his life he cherished deep gratitude and a strong affection for Duke Guidobaldo. He must have felt, then, a special loathing for the foreign ruffian who had betrayed and plundered his patron, and Machiavelli must have known that he did. Only a wish to draw the most odious comparison possible, only a compulsion to wound and insult, could have led Machiavelli to select the Borgia as the prime exemplar in his "Mirror of Princes."

There is one last famous passage that reads differently if we accept *The Prince* as satire. On any other hypothesis, the final exhortation to free Italy from the barbarians sounds at best like empty rhetoric, at worst like calculating but stupid flattery. Who could really believe that the lazy, insipid Giuliano or his petty, vicious successor were the liberators Italy awaited? But if we have heard the mordant irony and sarcasm of the preceding chapters and detected the overtones of hatred and despair, then this last chapter will be charged with an irony turned inward, the bitter mockery of misdirected optimism. For before the Florentine republic had been gored to death by Spanish pikes, Machiavelli had believed, as he was to believe again, that a free Florentine republic could play the liberator's role. Perhaps, since he was all his life a passionate idealist, blind to reality when his desires were strong, Machiavelli may not have given up that wild hope even when he wrote *The Prince*. If he had not, then the verses at the end take on a new meaning, clearer perhaps to his contemporaries than they can be to us.

461

*Virtù contro a furore*
*Prenderà l'arme, e fia il combatter corto;*
*Chè l'antico valore*
*nell'italici cor non è ancor morto.*

The antique valor Petrarch appealed to was, after all, that of republican Rome. Perhaps that first sharp combat was not to be against the barbarians.

However that may be, we must agree that if *The Prince* was meant as a satire, as a taunt and challenge to the Medici and a tocsin to the people of Florence, then it must have been recognized as such by the Florentine literati and by the Medici themselves. If so we have the solution to two minor puzzles connected with this puzzling book. A rasher ruling family than the Medici might have answered the challenge by another round of torture and imprisonment or by a quiet six inches of steel under the fifth rib. But brother Giovanni and brother Giovanni's familiar spirit, cousin Giulio, though in fact they were aiming at exactly the kind of despotism that Machiavelli predicted, hoped to achieve it with a minimum of trouble by preserving for the time being the forms of the republic. It would not do, by punishing the author, to admit the pertinence of his satire. So the Medici did nothing. But they were not a stupid family, and they cannot have been very pleased. This would explain some puzzling things: why, for example, the ardent republicans among Machiavelli's friends, like Zanobi Buondelmonti, were not alienated by *the Prince,* and why the former republicans in Medici service among his correspondents, like Vettori, for instance, refer to it so seldom and with such muffled embarrassment. It would also explain why, among all the manuscripts of *The Prince* dating from Machiavelli's lifetime (and it seems to have had a considerable circulation and to have been multiplied by professional copyists), we have never found the copy which should have had the best chance of preservation— I mean that copy, beautifully lettered on vellum and richly bound, presented with its dedication to the Medici prince. Not only is it absent from the Laurentian library now, there is no trace that it was ever there. There is no evidence that it ever existed. Probably Machiavelli figured that the joke was not worth the extra expense.

# Equality

## America's Deferred Commitment

### C. VANN WOODWARD

### (1958)

With the dispassionate clarity of the true historian, C. VANN WOODWARD, a professor of history at Johns Hopkins University, suggests that the Civil War aim of equality was as revolutionary for the North as it was for the South.

This article later appeared in a book of Mr. Woodward's essays entitled *The Burden of Southern History*.

NOW THAT THE DRIVE IS ON to give accustomed cant about equality some basis in fact and to deliver on promises nearly a century old, the temptation is strong to pretend that we have been in earnest all along. Such a pretense, successfully maintained, might stiffen resolution, put the forces of resistance further on the defensive and, in general, further a good cause. Before we become so deeply committed to the pretense that we believe it ourselves, however, it would be well to look soberly into the curious origins of the commitment to equality during the Civil War and into its subsequent abandonment.

The North had a much more difficult time defining its war aims than the South. The aims of the South were fixed and obvious from the start—the establishment and the defense of independence—and they remained constant until rendered hopeless. The North moved gradually and gropingly toward a definition of its war aims. Its progress was obstructed by doubt and misgiving and characterized by much backing and filling. The debate and the outcome were shaped by the course of the war itself, by military necessities, foreign propaganda needs and domestic morale demands, as well as by the exigencies of party politics and political ambitions.

As the North progressed toward the framing of war objectives, America was inched along from right to left. It moved from hesitant support of a limited war with essentially negative aims toward a total war with positive and revolutionary aims. The character of the war changed from a pragmatic struggle for power to a crusade for ideals. The struggle took on many aspects of an ideological war, and in some minds became a holy war, fought and financed and supported by men who could feel themselves instruments of divine will.

It was far different at the outset. Lincoln was inaugurated President of a slaveholding republic. He had been elected on a platform firmly pledging him to the protection of the institution of slavery where it existed; and in his first inaugural address, while not abandoning his moral views of slavery, he explicitly denied that he entertained any "purpose, directly or indirectly, to interfere with the institution of slavery in the states where it exists." Not only had he no purpose, but he declared he had "no lawful right" and, indeed, "no inclination to do so." He assured the people of the South that their property was not "in any wise endangered by the now incoming administration." His emphasis was upon the negative aim of preventing secession and the disruption of the Union.

Four and a half months later, after blood had been shed and the war was in full swing, Congress took a hand in defining war aims. On July 22, the House adopted, with only two negative votes, a resolution declaring that "this war is not waged . . . [for the] purpose of overthrowing or interfering with the . . . established institutions of those States, but to . . . maintain . . . the . . . States unimpaired; and that as soon as these objects are accomplished the war ought to cease." The Senate backed this sentiment up with a similar resolution, also adopted by a nearly unanimous vote. At this stage, so far as both President and Congress were able to formulate war aims, this was a war of narrowly limited objectives and no revolutionary purpose. It was to be a war against secession, a war to maintain the Union—that, and nothing more.

This negative phase did not last long. No mood lasted very long in the flux and change of the Civil War. Five months later the House voted down a motion to reaffirm the resolution of limited war aims. Already the movement was under way to extend those aims from mere union to embrace freedom as well. The second war aim was not attained by a stroke of Lincoln's pen, as Lincoln was the first to admit. It was forced by events, by necessities; and those events and necessities first took the shape of thousands of pitiable fugitive slaves crowding into the Union lines. Their path toward freedom was tedious and rugged and filled with obstacles. Thousands wavered between freedom and slavery for years and were never quite sure when freedom came, or even if it did. The majority only began their struggle for freedom after the war was over.

Freedom as a war aim was arrived at by a long succession of piecemeal decisions. There were orders by field commanders, some countermanded, some sustained; there were acts of state legislatures; and there was a long succession of bits and driblets of emancipation enacted by Congress, which did not get around to repealing the Fugitive Slave Act until June of 1864. And always there was the embarrassed and reluctant dragon of emancipation, the invading army. "Although war has not been waged against slavery," wrote Secretary Seward to Charles Francis Adams in 1862, "yet the army acts . . . as an emancipating crusade. To proclaim the crusade is unnecessary. . . ."

The crusade was eventually proclaimed, though the proclamation was not the President's. Lincoln never wanted to turn the war into a moral crusade. It is not necessary to retrace here the painful steps by which Lincoln arrived at his numerous decisions upon slavery and emancipation. It is sometimes forgotten, however, how often he deprecated the importance of his Proclamation of Emancipation. He characterized it as a war necessity, forced by events, ineffectual, inadequate and of doubtful legality. It is plain that his heart was in his plan for gradual emancipation, which he repeatedly but unsuccessfully urged upon Congress and proposed as a constitutional amendment. This was an extremely conservative plan for gradual and voluntary emancipation over a period of thirty-seven years, to be completed by 1900, to be administered by the slave states themselves, and to be assisted by the federal government with compensation to the slaveowners and foreign colonization of the freedmen. Support was not forthcoming, and war developments underlined the impracticality of the plan.

When Lincoln finally resorted to the proclamation he presented it as a war measure, authorized by war powers and justified by military necessity. Again and again he repeated that it was a means to an end—the limited Lincolnian end of union—and not an end in itself, that union and not freedom was the true war aim. Yet freedom had become a second war aim anyway, and for many the primary war aim. In spite of the fact that the proclamation

465

emancipated no slaves it had a profound effect upon the war—more effect upon the war, in fact, than upon slavery.

For one thing, it helped to elevate the war to a new plane. It was still a war for union, but not a war for union with slavery as before. It was no longer merely a war against something, but a war for something, a war for something greatly cherished in American tradition and creed—a war for freedom. What had started as a war for political ends had, by virtue of military necessity, undergone a metamorphosis into a higher and finer thing, a war for moral ends. What had commenced as a police action had been converted into a crusade. Some abolitionists professed disappointment in the proclamation, but so ardent a believer as Theodore Tilton was in "a bewilderment of joy" with the new spirit "so racing up and down and through my blood that I am half crazy with enthusiasm."

The great majority of citizens in the North still abhorred any association with abolitionists, but they were now free to share the forbidden transports of the despised radicals at no cost to their reputation whatever. Conservative, humdrum, unheroic millions could now sing "John Brown's Body" in naïve identification with the demented old hero and partake vicariously and quite inexpensively of his martyrdom. An aura of glory descended upon the common cause that sometimes lifted men out of themselves, exalted them, though it seems to have inspired civilians and noncombatants more often than soldiers. It could endow men with a sense of moral superiority and divine purpose that enabled them to regard the enemy with a new indignation and righteousness. It emboldened them to make messianic pronouncements with no apparent self-consciousness. The exuberant religiosity of the age was tapped for war propaganda and yielded riches. How otherwise could men, with no consciousness of blasphemy, lift their voices to sing, "As He died to make men holy, let us die to make men free"?

Before he issued the proclamation Lincoln had written privately that he was holding the antislavery pressure "within bounds." He could no longer make that boast with assurance, for after the edict of January 1, 1863, antislavery sentiment could not always be kept in bounds. As Professor Randall put it, "The concomitants of emancipation got out of Lincoln's hands. He could issue his proclamation, but he could not control the radicals." The "concomitant" of the second war aim of freedom was a third—equality.

No sooner was the Union officially committed to the second war aim than the drive was on for commitment to the third.

It cannot be said that this drive was as successful as the movement for freedom, nor that by the end of the war the country was committed to equality in the same degree it was to freedom. There was no equality proclamation to match the one for emancipation. The third war aim never gained from Lincoln even the qualified support he gave to abolition. Without Presidential blessing the commitment was eventually made, made piecemeal like that to freedom, and with full implications not spelled out until after the war, but it was made.

The formal commitment to the third war aim would never have been possible had the abolitionist minority not been able to appeal to more venerable and acceptable doctrine than their own. It would be preposterous to credit the abolitionists with surreptitiously introducing the idea of equality into America. The nation was born with the word on its tongue. The first of those "self-evident" truths of the Declaration of Independence was that "all men are created equal." Back of that was the heritage of natural rights doctrine, and back of that the great body of Christian dogma and the teaching that all men are equal in the sight of God.

There were, of course, less disinterested inducements in operation. If freedom was in part a military expedient, equality was in part a political and economic expedient. Equality of the franchise for freedmen was deemed essential to Republican supremacy, and Republican supremacy was deemed essential by influential classes to protect the new economic order.

Equality was not only a political and economic expedient; it was also a psychological and religious one. For fulfillment of abolitionist purposes it was almost a necessity. Abolitionists had grounded their whole crusade against slavery on the proposition that it was a "sin." It is not sufficient simply to abolish a sin. It has to be expiated and the sinner purified. Purification and expiation involve penance and suffering. Equality had a punitive purpose: the infliction of a penance of humiliation upon the status of the sinner. For those with an uncomplicated interest in sheer vengeance upon a hated foe, equality had punitive uses of a simpler sort.

Even with all these resources at their command, however, the radicals could never have succeeded in their drive for the formal commitment to equality had it not been launched upon the mounting tide of war spirit and had the war not already been converted into a moral crusade. A moral crusade could only be justified by high moral aims, even if those aims were embraced by the great majority as an afterthought, by many with important mental reservations, and by others as expedients for extraneous ends having nothing whatever to do with the welfare of the freedmen.

So far as the abolitionist minority was concerned, the association of freedom and equality, as Jacobus tenBroek has demonstrated, was rooted in three decades of organized antislavery agitation. Antislavery congressmen carried this association of aims into the framing of the Thirteenth Amendment. The debates over the question in the Senate in the spring of 1864, and in the House of Representatives in January, 1865, contain evidence that the framers aimed at equality as well as emancipation. Both aims were assumed by the opponents as well as the sponsors of the amendment during the debate. As one of the supporters, William D. Kelley of Pennsylvania, put it: "The proposed Amendment is designed . . . to accomplish . . . the abolition of slavery in the United States, and the political and social elevation of Negroes to all the rights of white men." His broad construction of the amendment was echoed with variations by numerous supporters. They did not include enfranchisement among the rights of Negroes, but they specifically and repeatedly mentioned equal protection of the laws, safeguard for privileges and immunities, and guarantee against deprivation of life, liberty and property without due process of law. The main ground of opposition to the amendment was this very aim of equality. A constant complaint of opponents was that the amendment would not only free the Negroes but would "make them our equals before the law."

The broad construction of the Thirteenth Amendment to include equality as well as freedom was not sustained when put to test, and the radicals themselves abandoned the interpretation. But they did not abandon their aim of equality; instead, they increased the scope of it. Responding to provocation of Southern aggression against Negro rights and to inducement of political gains as well, they proceeded to make equality as much the law of the land as freedom. In the Civil Rights Act of 1866, they gave sweeping protection to the rights of Negroes as citizens, guaranteeing them "full and equal benefit of all laws and proceedings for security of person and property, as is enjoyed by white citizens," regardless of any law to the contrary. When the President vetoed the bill, they passed it over his veto. When doubt was cast upon its constitutionality, they enacted most of its provisions into the Fourteenth Amendment. When the South balked at ratification, they stipulated adoption of the amendment as a condition of re-admission to the Union. Later they extended federal protection to the Negro franchise by the Fifteenth Amendment. They re-enacted the Civil Rights Act, implementing protection of voters, and followed that by another bill to implement rights established by the Fourteenth Amendment. To crown the achievement, they passed still another Civil Rights Act in 1875, which provided sweepingly that "all persons within the jurisdiction of the United States shall be entitled to the full and equal enjoyment of the accommodations, advantages, facilities, and privileges of inns, public conveyances on land or water, theaters, and other places of public amusement, subject only to the conditions and limitations established by law and applicable alike to citizens of every race and color, regardless of any previous condition of servitude."

Thus, by every device of emphasis, repetition, re-enactment and reiteration, the radical lawmakers and constitution-amenders would seem to have nailed down all loose ends, banished all am-biguity, and left no doubt whatever about their intention to ex-tend federal protection to Negro equality. So far as it was humanly possible to do so by statute and constitutional amendment, Amer-ica would seem to have been firmly committed to the principle of equality.

And yet we know that within a very short time after these im-posing commitments were made they were broken. America re-neged, shrugged off the obligation, and all but forgot about it for nearly a century. The commitments to the war aims of union and freedom were duly honored, but not the third commitment. In view of current concern over the default and the belated effort to make amends, it might be of interest to inquire how and why it ever occurred.

Equality was a far more revolutionary aim than freedom, though it may not have seemed so at first. Slavery seemed so formidable, so powerfully entrenched in law and property, and so fiercely defended by arms that it appeared far the greater obstacle. Yet slavery was property based on law. The law could be changed and the property expropriated, but not so inequality. Its entrench-ments were deeper and subtler. The attainment of equality in-volved many more relationships than those between master and slave. It was a revolution that was not confined to the boundaries of the defeated and discredited South, as emancipation largely

469

was. It was a revolution for the North as well. It involved such unpredictable and biased people as hotel clerks, railroad conductors, steamboat stewards, theater ushers, real estate agents, and policemen. In fact it could involve almost anybody. It was clear from its start that this revolution was going to require enthusiastic and widespread support in the North to make it work.

Was there any such support? Who were the American people so firmly committed to this revolutionary change and what degree of enthusiastic support were they prepared to lend it? For one thing, among the supporters of the Union were the people of the border area, which included not only Kentucky, Missouri and West Virginia, but also the southern parts of Ohio, Indiana and Illinois. This area embraced a white population approximately equal to the number of whites in the Confederate States. And if Maryland be added, as I think it should be, the area included considerably more white people than the Confederacy. Most of these people were still living in slave states during the war, and many of their attitudes and habits were not very different from those of people in states to the south. Their enthusiasm for the third war aim was a matter of some doubt.

What of the Republican party itself, the party responsible for enacting the commitment to equality? During the war it was, of course, exclusively a sectional party, a party of Northern people. Its membership was heavily recruited from the defunct Whig party, and the new party never shook off its Whiggish origins. Many of its members, to use Lincoln's phrase, disliked being "unwhigged." The essence of Whiggery was accommodation and compromise, compromise of many kinds, including the old type of sectional compromise. Before Reconstruction was over, Republicans were again seeking out their old Whig friends of the South with proffered compromise that would leave the solution of the race question in Southern hands.

Lincoln was fully aware of the limited moral resources of his party and his section of the country. He knew that there were limits beyond which popular conviction and conscience could not be pushed in his time. Whatever his personal convictions—and he may, as one historian has maintained, have been entirely color blind—yet when he spoke as President of the United States or as leader of his political party, he spoke with measured words. And he did not speak in one way to Negroes and another to whites. To a delegation of Negro leaders at the White House he said: "There is an unwillingness on the part of our people, harsh as it may be, for you free colored people to remain with us." He expressed deep sympathy for the wrongs done to them as slaves. "But even when you cease to be slaves," he said, "you are yet far removed from being placed on an equality with the white race. . . . The aspiration of men is to enjoy equality with the best when free, but on this broad continent not a single man of your race is made the equal of a single man of ours. . . . I cannot alter it if I would. It is a fact . . . It is better for us both, therefore, to be separated." This idea of separating the races led Lincoln to support the most impractical and illusory plan of his entire career, the plan for colonizing the freedmen abroad or settling them in segregated colonies at home.

What were the sentiments of the Federal army, the army of liberation, about the issue of equality? That great body included eventually more than two million men. There appears to have been a lower proportion of men from the upper income and social classes in the Federal than in the Confederate army. But there were men of all kinds and all views. Among them were officers and enlisted men of deep and abiding conviction, dedicated spirits whose devotion to the moral aims of the war was borne out in their conduct and in their treatment of slaves, freedmen and Negro soldiers.

Unfortunately it cannot be said that soldiers of this turn of mind were typical of the army sentiment, or even that they were very numerous. They seem, on the contrary, to have been quite untypical. "One who reads letters and diaries of Union soldiers," writes Professor Bell I. Wiley, who has indeed read many of them, "encounters an enormous amount of antipathy toward Negroes. Expressions of unfriendliness range from blunt statements bespeaking intense hatred to belittling remarks concerning dress and demeanor." Many of the Union soldiers brought their race prejudices with them from civilian life. Sometimes these prejudices were mitigated by contact with the Negro, but more often they appear to have been intensified and augmented by army experience. Men who endure the hardships and suffering and boredom of war have always sought scapegoats on whom to heap their miseries. And in the Civil War the Negroes who crowded into Union lines were made to order for the role of scapegoat. The treatment they often received at the hands of their liberators makes some of the darkest pages of war history. Another shameful chapter is the treatment of the 200,000 Negroes who served in the Union army. Enlistment of Negroes in the first place appears to have been

471

strongly opposed by the great majority of white troops. And even after their battle record proved, as Dudley T. Cornish says, "that Negro soldiers measured up to the standard set for American soldiers generally," they continued to be discriminated against by unequal pay, allowances and opportunities. These inequalities lasted throughout the war. It would seem at times that the army of liberation marched southward on its crusade under the banner of White Supremacy.

One is driven by the evidence to the conclusion that the radicals committed the country to a guarantee of equality that popular convictions were not prepared to sustain, that legal commitments overreached moral persuasion. The lag between conviction and commitment could be illustrated by many more examples than space allows. Such examples would include race riots and violent labor demonstrations against the Negro that broke out during the war in Cleveland, Cincinnati, Chicago, Detroit, Buffalo, Albany, Brooklyn and New York. The tendency would also be illustrated by the neglect, exclusion or hostility that craft unions and national unions exhibited toward the Negro during the war years and afterward. Further illustration could be drawn from the measures adopted by Western states to discourage freedmen from settling and working within their boundaries or going to school with their children. One should also recall that between 1865 and 1868, by legislative or popular vote, Negro suffrage was rejected by the states of Wisconsin, Minnesota, Connecticut, Nebraska, New Jersey, Ohio, Michigan and Pennsylvania. The Republican party thought it advisable to assure the people of the North in a plank of its platform of 1868 that while Negro suffrage had already been imposed upon the Southern states, where it was "demanded by every consideration of public safety, of gratitude and of justice," the question of Negro suffrage in the Northern states "properly belongs to the people of those states."

In concentrating upon the North as a source of illustration of this moral lag in equality, I have certainly not intended to suggest that it was peculiar to the North. I have taken agreement for granted that the lag was even greater in the South and that resistance to fulfillment of the commitment was in that area even more widespread, stubborn and effective. It has been my intention, however, to suggest that the lag was not peculiar to the South.

When such a lag develops between popular convictions and constitutional commitments, and when that lag cannot be conveniently rationalized by statutory or amendatory procedures, it becomes the embarrassing task of the Supreme Court of the United States to square ideals with practice, to effect a rationalization. The justices in this instance examined the words of the Fourteenth Amendment and, by what Justice Harlan in a famous dissenting opinion called "subtle and ingenious verbal criticism," discovered that they did not mean what they seemed to mean at all, nor what their authors thought they meant. By a series of opinions beginning in 1873, the court constricted the Fourteenth Amendment by a narrow interpretation that proclaimed that the privileges and immunities we call civil rights were not placed under federal protection at all. In effect, they found that the commitment to equality had never really been made.

The Union fought the Civil War on borrowed moral capital. With their noble belief in their purpose and their extravagant faith in the future, the radicals ran up a staggering war debt, a moral debt that was soon found to be beyond the country's capacity to pay, given the undeveloped state of its moral resources at the time. After making a few token payments during Reconstruction, the United States defaulted on the debt and unilaterally declared a moratorium that lasted more than eight decades. The country was only nominally spared the formality of bankruptcy by the injunctions of the Supreme Court that cast doubt upon the validity of the debt. In the meantime, over the years, interest on the debt accumulated. The debt was further augmented by the shabby treatment of the forgotten creditors, our own Negro citizens.

Then in the middle of the twentieth century, conscience finally began to catch up with commitment. Very suddenly, relatively speaking, it became clear that the almost forgotten Civil War debt had to be paid, paid in full, and without any more stalling than was necessary. As in the case of the commitment to emancipation during the Civil War, amoral forces and pressures such as the exigencies of foreign propaganda, power politics and military necessities exercised a powerful influence upon the recommitment to equality. But also as in the case of emancipation, the voices of conscience, of national creed and of religious conviction played their part. In the second instance, the demands of the Negroes themselves played a more important part in the pressure than before. Equality was at last an idea whose time, long deferred, had come about.

Once again a lag had developed between popular conviction and constitutional interpretation. Only this time the lag ran the opposite way and it was the Constitution that lagged behind conviction. Again it proved unfeasible to close the gap by statutory or amendatory procedures. And again it became the embarrassing task of the Supreme Court to effect an accommodation, a rationalization. Once more the justices scrutinized the words of the Fourteenth Amendment, and this time they discovered that those words really meant what they said, and presumably had all along. The old debt that the court had once declared invalid they now pronounced valid.

Although this was acknowledged to be a national debt, in the nature of things it would have to be paid by a special levy that fell with disproportionate heaviness upon one section of the country. The South had been called upon before to bear the brunt of a guilty national conscience. It is now called upon a second time. One could hope that the South's experience in these matters might stand it in good stead, that having learned to swallow its own words before, it might do so again with better grace, that it might perform what is required of it with forbearance and humility. I do not know. I can only admit that present indications are far from reassuring.

There is no apparent prospect of early compliance or of easy solution. The white South is resisting, and a reactionary part of it is defiant. The resistance is stubborn. A minority could become nasty and its defiance brutish. Already the patience of the rest of the country is running out. There is an outraged sense of frustration and a demand that there be no more faltering. The taunts and jeers of our foreign adversaries are a provocation, and so are the partisan rivalries of politicians. The demand for stern measure and the use of armed force is growing. An example has already been set, and more could follow. The center of resistance has not yet been seriously challenged, and when it is, the prospect is likely to grow even darker. These are facts that no one can contemplate soberly without a sense of foreboding.

We are presently approaching the centennial anniversary of the Civil War. Simultaneously we are approaching the climax of a new sectional crisis. It is a crisis that divides the country along much the same old sectional lines, over many of the same old sectional issues. It would be an ironic, a tragic coincidence if the celebration of the anniversary took place in the midst of a crisis reminiscent of the one celebrated.

The historian who, in these circumstances, writes the commemorative volumes for the Civil War centennial would seem to have a special obligation of sobriety and fidelity to the record. If he

474

writes in that spirit he will not flatter the self-righteousness of either side. He will not picture the North as burning for equality since 1863 with a hard, gem-like flame. He will not picture the South as fighting for the eternal verities. He will not paint a holy war that ennobled its participants. And he will try to keep in mind the humility that prevented the central figure in the drama from ever falling in with the notion that he was the incarnation of the Archangel Michael.

# Thornton Wilder:
# The Notation of the Heart

## EDMUND FULLER

### (*1959*)

This appraisal of Thornton Wilder as one of the greatest American writers of the twentieth century was prompted by EDMUND FULLER's belief that Wilder possesses those fundamental qualities so lacking in modern novelists: true compassion, blended of sympathetic perception and clearly defined values; broad scholarship; a passion for the beauty and integrity of the English language. Mr. Fuller is the author of a number of books, including two novels and *Man in Modern Fiction*.

THORNTON WILDER has to his credit one of the greatest novels (*The Bridge of San Luis Rey*) and one of the greatest plays (*Our Town*) in this century's American writing. The rest of his body of work is consistent in quality. Success has visited him: he is a Pulitzer Prize winner in both fiction and drama; his plays have had packed houses; one of the novels was a best-seller. Yet, proportionate to his achievement, this man's stature is singularly overlooked or taken for granted. Until quite recently three of his five novels, all of them among the best American writing, had been out of print for years, and even *The Bridge* was not in hard covers.

He has had his due more among the drama critics than among those who study the art of prose fiction. In the books that talk of the contemporary American novel, where a fixed set of names is bandied about among a fixed set of critics, Wilder seldom is discussed. Malcolm Cowley is a notable exception, having written an excellent essay as Introduction to *A Thornton Wilder Trio* (1956), which brought back into print the first three novels.

### 476

This curious general neglect is partly because literary critics tend to inherit their subjects, passed along from one group to their successors. Within the contemporary field, one echelon seldom has the imagination to study someone whom the preceding echelon has ignored. Due to a socioeconomic accident, Wilder was slighted by most critics practicing in the thirties and, accordingly, has not received attention since that time to any extent commensurate with his importance as a novelist.

The strange public history of *The Bridge of San Luis Rey,* its abrupt drop from acclaim to neglect, is worth pausing to examine. The book became a best-seller and a Pulitzer Prize winner. Malcolm Cowley remarks, wrongly I believe, that this success is "still a little hard to understand, for the best qualities of *The Bridge* are not those usually regarded as being popular." It "exactly fitted the mood of the moment, and nobody knows exactly why."

Public response often is surprising and hard to explain. The stylistic excellences and subtleties of thought and observation in this novel are not mass commodities. Yet greatness, which this book possesses, is never in itself a bar to popularity, given other viable elements. Shakespeare was a mass artist, and a substantial number of fine books make the best-seller list.

*The Bridge* is short and wonderfully lucid reading, with a simplicity hardly suggesting its extensive substrata. The question that the fall of the bridge thrust upon humble Brother Juniper: "Either we live by accident and die by accident, or we live by plan and die by plan"—in short, whether the events of life are chance or design—presents itself intensely, even agonizingly, at some time in almost every life. Thus it is that the Marquesa de Montemayor sometimes would be "dizzy with despair, and . . . would long to be taken from a world that had no plan in it." Consciously or unconsciously, from the French existentialists to the beat generation, this is a major psychic problem of the hydrogen age. The unlettered and the educated alike ponder the question in their own terms. It is a problem that presents itself as much amidst plenty as at any other time, which is why the book spoke to the anxieties beneath the boom of the flush twenties.

Another basis of the book's appeal is that its characters are sufficiently strange, colorful and remote to be fascinating, yet they are so universally human in their qualities that we can identify ourselves with them. Its original success and its re-emergence are gratifying, but not mysterious.

The book's abrupt eclipse (which engulfed all of Wilder's early novels) is a peculiar story. When the depression struck, the dreary wave of "social" novels, "protest" novels, "proletarian" or Marxist novels was ushered in and caused a corresponding literary depression, both in creation and criticism. What was possibly the best single book of that genre, *The Grapes of Wrath*, does not survive the passing of its topicality as well as *The Bridge* survives its temporary, circumstantial eclipse. I am one of many who came of age in the early thirties, heard *The Bridge* spat upon as bourgeois, escapist, popular pap, and had to find it for myself after depression and war had passed and writers had again discovered that the problems of man are not narrowly topical, or uniquely and exclusively centered on the masses, on workers or even on soldiers.

Wilder is unique among modern American novelists for possessing in the highest degree certain qualities currently undervalued and hence desperately needed among us. No one of his countrymen rests his work upon such an understructure of broad scholarship, cultivation and passion for the beauty and integrity of the English language. This equipment, rare in our time, gives tone to his work, especially the novels, and yet brings with it no taint of pedantry. To find work equally rich in allusion and grounded in humane learning, we must turn to English-born Aldous Huxley, although Wilder employs these attributes even more gracefully and unobtrusively than he. In a period when literary honors are bestowed often upon the craftless, the semiliterate and uncultivated, and in which the Yahoo has become hero, we need to recall that we have Wilder working among us. He helps to redeem the time.

He is notable for his versatility. Although he is not the only man writing both the novel and the play, no one else has written both at such a level of excellence, in such a marked diversity of modes, or in such form-renewing and form-extending ways as mark his work in the two media.

Wilder is a conspicuous exception to the common generalization that American writers tend to be youthful, writing of and from youth and immaturity, failing to mature in art as they age in years. He juxtaposes his always mature vision of life and character to our predominantly adolescent literature, while his range is greater than that of those established men who are most nearly his peers. There is an immense spread between the sophistication of *The Cabala* and the homely simplicity of *Our Town*, and Wilder is comfortably at home in both.

He is neither compulsive in his choice of material and method nor conditioned by some warped piping from a private clinical world. His view of life and behavior is broadly encompassing and humanely compassionate in the only true compassion, which is blended of sympathetic perception and clearly defined values.

He has the highest development and conscious control of style— having no close rival among Americans in this respect—yet he spelled out the limits of style in *The Bridge,* in a passage about the Conde's relish for the famous letters of the Marquesa de Monte-mayor (which are like those of Mme. de Sévigné) :

> . . . he thought that when he had enjoyed the style he had extracted all their richness and intention, missing (as most readers do) the whole purport of literature, which is the notation of the heart. Style is but the faintly contemptible vessel in which the bitter liquid is recommended to the world. The Marquesa would even have been astonished to learn that her letters were very good, for such authors live always in the noble weather of their own minds and those productions which seem remarkable to us are little better than a day's routine to them.

It is in this "whole purport of literature . . . the notation of the heart" that Wilder's genius is felt, and the flexible grace and individuality that attend his work in both his chosen media proceed from that "noble weather" of his own mind.

The novels are dazzlingly epigrammatic—a word that often carries with it a suggestion of glibness that does not fit this work. The epigram is a stylistic device, a perfectly shaped single thought, calculated to arrest attention and then, at its best, to start thought moving in a fresh direction. Such ability to shape and state things is sometimes given to shallow minds who waste it on minor witticism. In Wilder this gift is coupled with penetrating perception and wisdom. It helps him to communicate the depth and sharpness in which he sees character, motivation and impulse, and the significance that he discerns in things.

Wilder's work is permeated by a profound mystical and religious sensibility—too mature to war upon or sneer at orthodoxy, too creative to fit snugly in its confines. His vision and celebration of man is harmonious with Christian humanism. He gives us a *creature,* touched with the divine image, but scarred and maimed somewhat in his human state, perishable in his flesh and eternal in his soul; a creature variously perverse and responsible, despicable and indomitable, vulgar and rarefied. The separateness of these attributes remains blurred in Wilder's work as it is blurred in the creature and in the creature's self-understanding. Applying here some words from the Foreword to his first volume of short plays, *The Angel That Troubled the Waters,* "there has seldom been an age in literature when such a vein was less welcome and less understood."

He has been publishing and producing intermittently since 1926, and there is no reason to suppose that we have heard the last from him. His productive years, to date, span the time from his twenties to his late fifties, so he has been walking in step with his century. The reference of his work is always universal, regardless of its period identification. In times of depression and war he has not occupied himself with the obviously topical that commands attention sometimes to the temporary exclusion of all else. His nearest approach to the topical—the perennial topicality of the catastrophic—was in *The Skin of Our Teeth,* cast in such imaginative terms as to baffle literal minds.

Wilder is absorbed, always, with one or more of what, in *The Ides of March,* Caesar calls "the first questions which one puts to life itself." Or, as in *The Woman of Andros,* "How does one live? . . . What does one do first?" His answer is: one loves, if one can.

Of the master ideas or themes, threaded through and through the whole body of Wilder's work, certainly that of love is foremost. He is concerned with identifying its nature and its kinds, the modes of its operation, and the follies and waste associated with it. His is a conspicuous depth of insight at a time when many novelists have lost, or repudiated, the knowledge of love, offering violences, abuses and perversions of the body as substitutes for love rather than as violations or corruptions of it. In such modes, even the nature and meaning of simple passion itself are distorted, and the limited range of passion is unremarked.

In one of the most luminous passages of *The Bridge,* Wilder looks into the secret heart of the Perichole, who is marred by smallpox and convinced that love is forever lost to her.

This assumption that she need look for no more devotion now that her beauty had passed proceeded from the fact that she had never realized any love save love as passion. Such love, though it expends itself in generosity and thoughtfulness, though it give birth to visions and to great poetry, remains among the sharpest expressions of self-interest. Not until it has passed through a long servitude, through its own self-hatred, through mockery, through great doubts, can it take its place among the loyalties. Many who have spent a lifetime in it can tell us less of love than the child that lost a dog yesterday.

One of his three-minute plays, exercises in that compression that Wilder prizes so highly and has mastered so well, the play that lends its title to a whole volume, *The Angel That Troubled the Waters* (1928), contains the words: "In Love's service only the wounded soldiers can serve."

In the polished and precocious first novel, *The Cabala* (1926), two of his characters, Astrée-Luce and the Cardinal, reach a terrible spiritual impasse. When they

. . . discovered that they were living in a world where such things could be forgiven, that no actions were too complicated but that love could understand, or dismiss them, on that day they began their lives all over again.

The failure to love is the failure to realize life. Wilder is pained at how we fumble love, fail in realization, often through no worse a sin than perennial human blindness—that proverbial blindness that is never so great as in those who will not see.

So in that poignant scene of *Our Town* in which the dead Emily ventures to return to live over again her twelfth birthday (a scene anticipated in *The Woman of Andros*), there comes the girl's anguished cry, "Let's look at one another." And a moment later, ". . . it goes so fast. We don't have time to look at one another . . . I didn't realize. So all that was going on and we never noticed." Then follows the great question and answer:

> EMILY: Do any human beings ever realize life while
> they live it?—every, every minute?
> STAGE MANAGER: No. (*Pause*) The saints and poets, maybe—
> they do some.

It is the waste of love and life that pains Chrysis, the woman of Andros: "She did not realize that this wasting of love in fretfulness was one of the principal activities on the planet."

The crowning of this theme of love is in *The Bridge*. Nothing but burning rewards the gentle Juniper for his naïve attempt to

481

fathom the secrets of God and "surprise His intentions in a pure state." Unresolved though it must necessarily remain, this question of chance or design gives shape to the novel, from the opening chapter, "Perhaps an Accident," to the closing one, "Perhaps an Intention." Yet if Juniper's search for "an intention" fails, Wilder still develops subtly for us the possibility of an intention of some kind on the part of One who moves in a mysterious way, in a design infinitely more intricate than the too simple equation the monk had sought (like Job) between a man's moral qualities and the things that happen to him.

Whether it is the reason for the event or not, there is indeed a sense in which, as Juniper had speculated, each of the five lives lost made up a perfect whole when the bridge fell. The Marquesa, Pepita, Esteban, Uncle Pio and even, in a special sense, the boy Jaime, who must venture out to face the world with the burden of epilepsy—each had been through a crisis of decision and commitment, or moral self-realization and responsibility, and above all, a crisis of love. Accordingly, perhaps, now each can be permitted release—for death is often so viewed by Wilder, without negating his affirmation of life.

If any intention underlies the fall of the bridge, it cannot involve only the lives ended—it must involve also the lives remaining. So it is that Captain Alvarado, the Perichole, the daughter of the Marquesa, and Mother María del Pilar, all are enlarged in grace and comprehension. It is of the love of God toward man that the Abbess speaks, saying to herself, "Now learn, learn at last that anywhere you may expect grace."

The true burden of the book is disclosed in its final line:

There is a land of the living and a land of the dead and the bridge is love, the only survival, the only meaning.

This is the bridge that does not fall.

Human life as Wilder shows it is a web of folly, faith and tenacity. The folly is always present—a constant in the human character. As Dolly Levi says, in *The Matchmaker,*

. . . there comes a moment in everybody's life when he must decide whether he'll live among human beings or not—a fool among fools or a fool alone.

In *Our Town,* the Stage Manager reflects:

Wherever you come near the human race, there's layers and layers of nonsense. . . .

Folly, both of the lighter and the grimmer orders, is threaded through that fantastic synopsis of the race's history, *The Skin of Our Teeth,* summed up in Sabina's cry,

> We're all just as wicked as we can be, and that's the God's truth.

But Wilder is a gentle, not a savage, observer of folly. He blends folly with faith in the extravagant, picaresque, evangelical adventures of George Brush, the hero of *Heaven's My Destination* (1935). This fourth novel is startlingly different, in manner, method and material, from the other novels. Its tone is that of his plays, and I have wondered if, at some stage in its gestation, it may have hovered between the two forms. It is high parody, in somewhat the vein, and with the same deceptive simplicity, as *Candide* or *Joseph Andrews.* There is even a touch of the Sinclair Lewis of *The Man Who Knew Coolidge.*

George, who is a textbook salesman and evangelist extraordinary, is the innocent fool, in the kindliest sense of both the noun and the adjective. He is striving to be the fool in Christ, sowing the inevitable amazement, consternation and wrath that must ensue when Christ's fool runs at large among the worldly wise. This, in dark tones, was the concept underlying Dostoevsky's *The Idiot.*

Wilder's George is also "the perfectly logical man," fulfilling conviction in action, practicing his preaching. To understand him it is necessary to observe the quotation from *The Woman of Andros* that Wilder uses as a text in the front matter of *Heaven's My Destination:* "Of all the forms of genius, goodness has the longest awkward age."

For all the sophistication that underlies the creation of George Brush—indeed, that was essential to it—Wilder loves this innocent and will not consent that we should do otherwise. His is the awkward age of a true goodness. Simple, it is; stupid, it is not. Nor is it easy. George suffers his own bitter crises of faith, and his occasional cry of "I don't want to live" is a genuine anguish. Among the most subtle and interesting devices of the book is the unseen figure called Father Pasziewski, seemingly comic in his context, but who becomes, through the simple bequest of a silver spoon, the instrument to free George from his darkest night of the soul. In this border terrain of folly and faith, Wilder sounds a cautionary note to the George Brushes of the world through Judge Carberry:

Go slow; go slow. . . . The human race is pretty stupid.
. . . Doesn't do any good to insult'm. Go gradual.

Reflecting the perennial tension between faith and reason, we
are told that Astrée-Luce, in *The Cabala,* has "goodness without
intelligence." Her frustration is that "Sainthood is impossible
without obstacles and she never could find any." Yet this wholly
nonintellectual woman is capable of "remarkable penetrating
judgments, judgments that proceeded from the intuition without
passing through the confused corridors of our reason."

The Cardinal Vaini, in the same book, who makes a grave
miscalculation as a spiritual director in dealing with her, has his
own soul crisis after being retired to Italy from his lifetime work
in China.

Living is fighting and away from the field the most frightening
changes were taking place in his mind. Faith is fighting, and
now that he was no longer fighting he couldn't find his faith
anywhere.

It is this same Cardinal, by the way, in Wilder's early anticipation
of the modern dilemma of blurred values in the midst of an
advanced technology, who says, with wry reservations about the
attainments of the age:

You want me to compliment you because you have broken
the atom and bent light? Well, I do, I do.

But whether the follies of man be those of the subtle mind or
the simple, or even those of the wicked, there is an amazing tenacity in the creature. It is this tenacity that is celebrated in *The
Skin of Our Teeth* (1942), one of the most wildly creative, antic
and imaginative plays of the modern theater. It stunned to befud-
dlement its early audiences, but it has captured increasing command over playgoers ever since, here and abroad, as the appalling
march of modern society has made us more and more sensitive to
the threatened chaos. Wilder has observed, correctly, that it plays
best in times of crisis. He says, by the way, that it is heavily in-
debted to *Finnegans Wake,* which is apparent, and is perhaps
sufficient rebuke to me for an abiding prejudice against that work.

The play pours out for us, in tumbling fantasy, the total, sprawl-
ing, blundering chronicle of Man. We see it in a multiple vision
which superimposes the Pleistocene, the Flood and the ages since,
upon present-day New Jersey.

484

Mr. and Mrs. Antrobus (the pun is inescapable) , the complaining but durable Sabina, and the children, including the troublesome Cain (re-named Henry, but the same boy) , are indomitable. Mrs. Antrobus, at the end, amidst the wreckage of war, cries to her husband:

> . . . the only thought we clung to was that you were going to bring something good out of this suffering. In the night, in the dark, we'd whisper about it, starving and sick.—Oh, George, you'll have to get it back again. Think! What else kept us alive all these years? Even now, it's not comfort we want. We can suffer whatever's necessary; only give us back that promise.

George Antrobus says:

> All I ask is the chance to build new worlds and God has always given us that. And has given us voices to guide us, and the memory of our mistakes to warn us.

He turns the leaves of a book.

> We've come a long ways. We've learned. We're learning. And the steps of our journey are marked for us here.

As in this play, so in all his work Wilder delights in making free with time and space, as well as all sequences and juxtapositions of history. He treats time not so much in the Greek way, as cyclic, but as if all time is always still present. We might call it the simultaneity of all time. He translates the Marquise de Sévigné from seventeenth-century France to eighteenth-century Peru, to reincarnate her as the Marquesa de Montemayor. He gives us the dying John Keats in twentieth-century Rome, and embodies there, in *The Cabala*, certain of the Olympian gods in latter-day decline, and calls up the shade of Virgil. In *The Ides of March*, we find the extraordinary, bedridden American playwright, Edward Sheldon, on the isle of Capri, metamorphosed into the fearfully maimed Lucius Mamilius Turrinus. This most intimate friend and confidant of Caesar, once well favored of the gods but now brought low, is, like Sheldon, mentor and dispenser of wisdom to a host of talents more fortunate than himself.

Applying this free movement as a playwright, Wilder has helped to liberate the stage of our period from the strait jacket of the box set. He discusses this aspect of his intentions in the Preface to

*Three Plays* (1957), which is a valuable, brief essay on the relationship of things to themes in the theater.

Certain of his one-act plays are preparatory studies for the major dramatic works. They test the essential "round" pattern that characterizes *Our Town* and *The Skin of Our Teeth,* the spirit of which might be vulgarized as "here we go again." Thus the short plays are a valuable study in the development of technique and idea, as a set of variations in music may be seen sometimes as part of the growth of a work.

*The Long Christmas Dinner* telescopes ninety years into a single meal, as *The Skin of Our Teeth* traverses all the ages of man in three acts. The latter play's procession of planets and hours has a trial run in *Pullman Car Hiawatha.* And in this, and in *The Happy Journey to Trenton and Camden,* plain chairs are made to serve as whatever setting is needed. *Pullman Car Hiawatha* also has a versatile, chatty Stage Manager, all in anticipation of *Our Town.* The pullman car stops at "Grover's Corners," but the long later play relocates this from Ohio to New Hampshire. The emotional final sequence of *The Happy Journey* resembles in tone the intimate home scenes of *Our Town.* Finally, in *Pullman Car,* a dead young woman makes an itemized good-bye speech to persons and places anticipating Emily's tender good-bye to the world and Grover's Corners.

In speaking of these experiments in time and space, Wilder defined the purpose that informs all of his work in all media—the attempt "to capture not verisimilitude but reality." This is pregnant with counsel for an over-literal age of letters, bogged down often in the narrowest naturalism, or worse still and even more prevalent, pseudo naturalism. Wilder's is that truer realism, unconfined in its means, seeking, as he said of *Our Town,* to "find a value above all price for the smallest events in our daily life." He achieved this aim uniquely in that play.

Wilder has a deep affinity for the ancient world; and apart from much allusion to it in all the works, he has turned to it for time and place in two of his novels. He did this first in the gentle, lyric, lovely *Woman of Andros,* set on the isles of Greece in that time when "the land that was soon to be called Holy prepared in the dark its wonderful burden."

It is in *The Ides of March* (1948) that we get his most ambitious image of the ancient world, in the most intricately constructed and ambitious of all the novels. Its spaciousness of concept creates a sense of a much larger work, physically, than it is in fact.

Nowhere is his self-avowed "passion for compression" more successfully operable.

Here he takes his familiar liberties with time sequence and literal, factual matters, but he gives us a sense of a living Rome and a living Caesar. Through the difficult and adroitly practiced device of imaginary letters and documents, he evokes the most complex Caesar that I know in any work of art. This Julius' closest relative is Shaw's—that is, both are created in indifference to historical actuality as idealizations of a point of view (a device of the classical historians as well, as witness Herodotus' famous dialogue between Solon and Croesus). These Caesars have in common a detached, deliberative calm, and the relationship of each of them to Cleopatra is dominated primarily by a "passion for teaching." Yet Shaw's Caesar is a one-dimensional cartoon, withal brilliant, while Wilder's is complexly human with the special dimensions of genius.

Caesar's reflections on Roman society cut sharply into our own.

. . . the ostentation of vulgarity has become a political factor with which I must deal. The plebeian world is ameliorable in itself, but what can I do with a plebeian aristocracy? . . . it's now smart to talk pure *pleb*.

The book is rich in its meditations upon liberty and rule, freedom and responsibility, interest and disinterest in public actions. The dual study of Caesar and Catullus (wholly as fanciful as Solon and Croesus) puts before us the statesman vis-á-vis the poet. Catullus is, in a sense, one face of this Caesar who says

. . . one of the things in this world that I most envy is the endowment from which springs great poetry. To the great poets I ascribe the power to gaze fixedly at the whole of life and bring into harmony that which is within and that which is without them.

Is this not the transcendent aim of the great statesman?

I think there is only one solitude greater than that of the military commander and of the head of state and that is the poet's—for who can advise him in that unbroken succession of choices which is a poem? It is in this sense that responsibility is liberty; the more decisions that you are forced to make alone, the more you are aware of your freedom to

487

choose. I hold that we cannot be said to be aware of our minds save under responsibility. . . .

*The Ides of March* is a text so rich that it requires exploration rather than reading.

Wilder's love of the ancient world, however, is not a flight from the modern one. He has been wise about that from the first. The returning American narrator of *The Cabala* is advised by Virgil, as he leaves Rome: "The secret is to make a city, not to rest in it."

Perhaps, finally, with Wilder, after love comes beauty as the second great theme. He said, in the Foreword to *The Angel That Troubled the Waters,* speaking of religion as a subject in art, ". . . in these matters beyond logic, beauty is the only persuasion." He has made it the instrument of his own persuasion in all matters. This may be what has shaped his style. The stamp of taste and the sure sense of the precise and subtle gradations of meaning that come with mastery of language and that are the essence of beauty in the written word are firmly in his possession.

And with beauty comes praise. Praise of life is constant with him. He knows the sometime kindness of death. He has the vision of something beyond death. He can remark the pain of living, as he gives words to the shade of Virgil:

Are you still alive? Alive? How can you endure it? All your thoughts are guesses, all your body is shaken with breath, all your senses are infirm and your mind ever full of the fumes of some passion or another. Oh, what misery to be a man. Hurry and die!

Yet, like a descant over all his melodies, is the note of praise, and the thirst to hear things praised, sounded at the most painful times.

One of the dead, a woman, in the poignant dual vision of the famous graveyard scene in *Our Town,* is reminded of childbirth, and remarks, with almost a laugh,

I'd forgotten all that. My, wasn't life awful
(*With a sigh*)
—and wonderful?

Emily herself, retreating from the pain of her return on her twelfth birthday, ends her cry of farewell to all people, places and things of life, with:

Oh, earth, you're too wonderful for anybody to realize you.

In *The Cabala*, the narrator visits the bedside of the dying poet (Keats transposed) . He wounds the suffering man unintentionally by a casual slur upon Chapman's Homer, and so

discovered that he was hungry for hearing things praised . . . the poet wanted before he left the strange world to hear some portion of it praised.

Again, in *The Ides of March*, Caesar at the bedside of another dying poet, Catullus, observes:

I am no stranger to deathbeds. To those in pain one talks about themselves, to those of clear mind one praises the world that they are quitting. There is no dignity in leaving a despicable world and the dying are often fearful life was not worth the efforts it had cost them. I am never short of subjects to praise.

Thornton Wilder, wise observer and celebrant of life, speaks in the dying courtesan, Chrysis, of Andros, as she is making "the most exhausting of all our adventures . . . that journey down the long corridors of the mind to the last halls where belief is enthroned." As she goes this course, she reflects:

I have known the worst that the world can do to me, and . . . nevertheless I praise the world and all living.

So, likewise, does Wilder, in the total body of this humane notation of the heart that is his work. In his shrewd, sometimes caustic observation of *genus homo* and his history, we find one of the most searching, balanced and mature visions of ourselves as Man that any American writer offers us.

# The Limits of Analysis

## A. ALVAREZ

## ( *1959* )

This article by A. ALVAREZ, written for a special issue of THE
AMERICAN SCHOLAR devoted to contemporary poetry, under-
scores the need for two essential elements in criticism: judgment and intelligence. Mr. Alvarez is the drama critic of the
*New Statesman* and poetry reviewer for the *Observer*.

I INTENDED TO CALL THIS ESSAY "A Paraphrase of Heresy." But a
tour of the New Criticism is no longer necessary. In scholarly
company Criticism (with a capital *C*) is no longer a fighting word.
*The Explicator,* which began, in the best tradition of scruffy little
magazines, as a revolutionary battlefield, all war cries and fighting
footnotes, has become just another scholarly paper. Yesterday's
critics have become today's contributors to P.M.L.A.

What, in short, has happened in the last thirty-odd years is not
that the old Dry-as-Dusts have disappeared, but simply that they
have been replaced by Dry-as-Dusts of another style. Perhaps this
was inevitable; the pressures of academic life sooner or later bring
down everything to plain method. For method is impersonal, almost an abstraction. It reduces to clear teachable elements the
huge complexity of disciplined response and choice with which the
reader otherwise needs to re-create for himself each poem.
Method, of whatever brand, is always easier to teach than discrimination. The scholars substituted for the work of art the multitudinous details of its background; the critics replaced it with
the details of their own technical process. Landscape or physiology? Either way the life of the work is hardly touched.

Granted all this is old hat. Granted, too, the technical revolution was necessary. In *Practical Criticism* I. A. Richards demonstrated blindingly enough that undergraduates who were, in theory, both specialists in literature and, the reputation of Cambridge

490

being what it is, sophisticated representatives of their breed, were simply unable to read. The subsequent critical revolution restored at least that *sense of analysis* without which good criticism is impossible. For the sense of analysis is a token of sanity in all the varied critical fringes of literature. It guarantees that each judgment, each detail of interpretation, each generalization, is based on observation and argued from it. The critic is not simply exploiting his sensitivity in order to rewrite the poem in his own simpler terms. For example:

> . . . that miracle of the summer air, airy and glittering as the nets of the summer light and early dew over the strawberry beds—a poem so airy that it might have been woven by the long fingers of the sylphs in their dark and glittering Indian gauzes, floating like a little wind among the jewelled dark dews on the leaves of the fruit trees—this flawless poem . . . et cetera, et cetera.

The subject of that, believe it or not, is *The Rape of the Lock*. It is, of course, not criticism at all. It is simply a literary travelogue of a kind that no one now bothers with, apart from a few elderly members of literary circles and poetry societies scattered here and there in the interior. "Fine writing" has been left to the light essayists; it is no longer the final criterion of the excellence of critical prose. Back in 1930, in the first chapter of *Seven Types of Ambiguity*, William Empson wrote:

> Critics, as "barking dogs," . . . are of two sorts: those who merely relieve themselves against the flower of beauty, and those, less continent, who afterwards scratch it up.

The scratchers have carried the thirty years since then. Criticism has ceased to be a questionable skill—a self-conscious parading of sensitivity had gone a long way to destroy such residual respect as the nonspecialist still had for the art—it has become instead an arguable one. Its opinions can be challenged on the evidence produced, its reasons are susceptible to other reason. There is no longer an impassable barrier between being sensitive to poetry and being intelligent.

There is, however, a difference between being intelligent and simply using one's wits, and a difference again between the latter and the mere fitting of a ready-formed technique to whatever material appears; a difference, in short, between a sense of analysis and analysis as an end in itself. Without a sense of analysis no good criticism is possible, although there might well be good critical theory. On the simplest level, the sure touchstone of a critic is the maxim: "By his quotations shall ye know him." The influence of Matthew Arnold and T. S. Eliot, for instance, is as much in what they quoted as in what they said. The critical case remains unproved without exact lines to back it up. And it is impossible to smell out the quotations without a peculiarly shrewd idea of the weight and mechanics of the language; without, that is, a sense of analysis. So it goes back as far as good criticism, as far at least as Dryden. Until the appreciators and the journalists moved in, the question was simply the extent to which the analysis was put down or left implicit.

But now, in the time of the dissectors, the question is of the use it is put to. Consider, for example, Doctor Johnson on the famous lines of Denham:

> O could I flow like thee, and make thy stream
> My great example, as it is my theme!
> Though deep, yet clear; though gentle, yet not dull;
> Strong without rage, without o'er-flowing full.

The lines are in themselves not perfect; for most of the words, thus artfully opposed, are to be understood simply on one side of the comparison, and metaphorically on the other; and if there be any language which does not express intellectual operations by material images, into that language they cannot be translated. But so much meaning is comprised in few words; the particulars of resemblance are so perspicaciously collected, and every mode of excellence separated from its adjacent fault by so nice a line of limitation; the different parts of the sentence are so accurately adjusted, and the flow of the last couplet is so smooth and sweet, that the passage, however celebrated, has not been praised above its merit. It has beauty peculiar to itself, and must be numbered among those felicities which cannot be produced at will by wit and labour, but must rise unexpectedly in some hour propitious to poetry.

The analysis has embroiled the doctor in comments about the function of language that are both misleading and wrongheaded: "If there be any language which does not express intellectual operations by material images, into that language they cannot be translated." "There is, of course," Professor I. A. Richards tartly replied, "no such language." But although Johnson's conclusions may be faulty, his reasons are not. The analysis is there only as part of a genuine critical response: the feeling that the lines are better than anything Denham, on the evidence of the rest of his work, could ever reasonably have been expected to do. That is why the doctor devotes his last sentence to explaining the mechanics of the poetic fluke—which has, at other times, been called inspiration. He analyzed, in fact, because he was unable to believe that a poet as undistinguished as Denham could turn out lines so good that were not also faulty. The analysis is there to serve the purpose of the judgment and, like the generalizations, is dictated by it.

The difference between this and New Critical analyses is not that the doctor is wrong and the analysts, on the whole, are right; it is instead that Johnson is, to use the fashionable word, *organic* and they are not. And he is organic—his analysis, generalizations and judgment are all part of a single process—because his concern is, first and last, with the poetry. He writes what I would call primary criticism: criticism that, as rationally, deliberately and lucidly as possible, gives a sense of what the poetry is like. This means it describes not only the mechanics of the verse, the interaction of the various complex elements: meter, imagery and the rest; it also judges the work and sets it down within some scale of values. The values may never be set out formally, but they are everywhere implied in the critic's tone, reasons and choice of works.

Secondary criticism, on the other hand, is concerned more with its own processes than with the work of art. This makes for a queer unrelatedness between its major and minor premises, its generalizations and local analyses. For example, off and on for seven years I have been working on a book on the Metaphysicals, yet in that time I have never once come across a seventeenth-century Metaphysical poem that fits Professor Cleanth Brooks's definition:

> The Metaphysical poet has confidence in the powers of the imagination. He is constantly remaking his world by relating into an organic whole the amorphous and heterogeneous and contradictory. Trusting in imaginative unity, he refuses to depend upon non-imaginative classifications, those of logic and science.

It is an odd statement in itself; it becomes odder when you remember Donne's open, steady contempt for aesthetic values unrelated

493

to the more active, skeptical intelligence; but it is oddest of all as a critical response to the extraordinarily tough, dialectical movement of Donne's verse, the continual pertinacity of his argument. Now that we have got over the shock of the conceits, it is remarkable how small a part, in cold blood, they contribute to the effect of Donne's work, and how subordinate they are to the remorseless and insistent logical movement. They are themselves part of the world of "logic and science." If anything, they are there as a kind of aesthetic disinfectant: to prevent the work from sounding too "poetical." Professor Brooks, in fact, is generalizing not from Donne's poems but from Eliot's essays on the Metaphysicals. And Eliot was more concerned to find traditional precedents for Symbolist devices than to define, in any disinterested way, a particular seventeenth-century style. There are, after all, only two ways in which a poet can criticize his own work: the first is to rewrite it later, which was the way of Crashaw, Wordsworth, Keats, Tennyson and Yeats; the second is to pretend that you are writing about someone else, which is what Lawrence did with the novels of Hardy, and what Eliot did with the Metaphysicals. There is nothing in the least questionable about Eliot's practice. But it is odd that Professor Brooks should have made the same mistake after so painfully picking apart so much seventeenth-century verse.

The reason is that the business of secondary criticism is to show above all how neatly the machinery can be set in motion and the wonders it can perform with such slim material. Fundamentally, this great rumbling of critical engines seems to me to be covering up a certain nervousness. It is as though the analysts were unsure of the value of the work they discuss, and so had instead to affirm at every point the soundness and verifiability of their method: "Poetry," they seem to say, "may be marginal, antisocial nonsense, but we can at least write about it as thoroughly and unsentimentally as if it were the latest A.E.C. report." I once read a paper by a professor of philosophy designed apparently to spread the message of the New Criticism to his colleagues. Its subject was the method of Professor Brooks and its title was a paradox: "Criticism without Evaluation." The theme was roughly that positive philosophers could now begin to respect criticism since it had at last been purged of all personal taint. The analysts had reduced the skill to "the explication of the various constituents of the work of art. . . . And because they have correctly understood the organic character of these constituents, they have stressed in their critical exegeses the functional role of the various constituents." By this

494

token, the business of the critic is no more personal than that of the analytical statistician, or even, to risk a minor blasphemy, that of the positive philosopher himself. The logical inconsistency of the position hardly matters. (Who is to choose which elements to stress? Who is to decide about the primacy of the "organic character" of a poem? And so on. The personal elements are not so easily exorcised.) What is odd is the fact that Professor Brooks never, to my knowledge, tried to correct the interpretation. Of course, no one is to blame for his admirers; but, as James said of Gautier's essay on Baudelaire, "One must, in some degree, judge a man by the company he keeps. To admire Gautier is a mark of excellent taste. But to be admired by Gautier we cannot but regard as somewhat compromising." Similarly, Professor Brooks would no doubt never have voluntarily gone out so far and precariously along the limb. But there he is.

He looks odd there because he is above all an educationalist. His achievement is to have reduced the immensely complex discoveries of modern criticism to formulas and methods simple enough for the needs of university freshmen. And this, after all, is something. But it is something rather more than is suggested by his philosophical protagonist. For by reducing criticism to impersonal descriptive analysis he has reduced the critic to the status of grammarian, who teaches literature, or literary analysis, simply as a useful way of "training the mind." Literature, in fact, dwindles to a kind of dead language, like school Latin and Greek, justified only by the degree to which it supports the pedagogical technology. We are back, by another way, to the position Robert Graves found in Oxford after the First World War:

> At the end of my first term's work I attended the usual college board to give an account of myself. The spokesman coughed and said a little stiffly: "I understand, Mr. Graves, that the essays that you write for your English tutor are, shall I say, a trifle temperamental. It appears, indeed, that you prefer some authors to others."

At Oxford, where the methods of analysis have still hardly penetrated, one-third of the syllabus for a Bachelor of Arts degree in English is made up of Anglo-Saxon, Middle English and Modern Philology, a less daring method still of ensuring some element of "mind training." Both brands of professor, in short, distrust literature. For the English it is merely so much gentleman's relish, one of the amusements of gracious living, like port and six-course dinners, never to be defined or discussed, only to be surrounded, for professional purposes, by a few well-chosen facts.

The American methodologists, on the other hand, seem to distrust literature for precisely the reasons Englishmen like it: for its accretion of triviality. They seem afraid that some successful administrative pragmatist may one day demand straight out, "What is the *use* of all this poetry? And why do you, a grown man with a college education, devote your life to it?" The reply to this is simple: "If you can ask those questions, you couldn't even begin to understand any answer I gave you." But the analysts never make it. Instead, they first make their position worse by insisting on the absolute independence of aesthetic criteria from all others; they then, in a kind of triumphant reversal, show how their peculiar brand of critical automation produces organization men who are shrewder, less sentimental, more analytically wary than those who come out of any other educational mill. The best mechanical grooms for the mechanical brides are the products of the most rigorous aesthetic technology. It is for this reason, I suppose, that academic critics insist on a vocabulary of technical terms that never at any point touches those used naturally of human behavior. The discipline must be invulnerable, uncorrupted by life. And it doesn't matter a jot, apparently, that literature is *simply* human behavior crystallized into its finest, sharpest, most translucent form.

They are, of course, hardly fair to the students whom they subject to this technology. For the undergraduates, presumably, have come to literature for education, not for mere technique. That is, they have come to have their own judgment and experience developed, measured and affirmed by vital contact with what Matthew Arnold called "the best that is known and thought in the world." The professor who fails to encourage this kind of creative response shelves his responsibility as a teacher and becomes merely a specialist.

Teaching, however, is not my subject here. The critic, either as a professor or as a man of letters, has other responsibilities: to himself and to his position in society. Fundamentally, the fault of *merely* technical analysis is much the same as that of *merely* appreciative criticism, for all that one exploits is a method and the other a trick of sensitivity. Both are too easy; both, essentially, are at best middle-brow. The sensitives, of course, have never pretended their work had any truck with intelligence. The case of the analysts is less obvious. It is not so much a question of the com-

496

plexity of their work—most of them know how to attain at least the appearance of considerable difficulty—it is a question of attitude. For the complexity of the analysts is simply a matter of technique. They go at the work of art, explicate it fold upon fold, for the sake only of their method. The process is mechanical and is judged, like any other technology, for its usefulness.

Genuine criticism, on the other hand, is never, in any obvious sense, useful. For it is not concerned with conventional values. On the contrary, its value depends precisely on the distance it keeps from the conventional. Everyone knows that the function of criticism is to serve literature; but it does not follow from this that criticism is therefore servile. What the professor is in theory, the critic is in practice: an intellectual. He is, I mean, someone to whom ideas are emotionally important, who responds to experience by thinking for himself. This, I take it, is what makes Donne the first properly intellectual poet. The intellectual thinks by virtue of what he is in himself, not because he happens to know the accepted technique. It is the business of the pedagogues to be useful, but it is the business of the critics to be lucid. Perhaps this is what Matthew Arnold meant in his essay on "The Function of Criticism at the Present Time": The course of literary criticism, he wrote, "is determined . . . by the idea which is the law of its being; the idea of a disinterested endeavour to learn and propagate the best that is known and thought in the world, and thus to establish a current of fresh and true ideas." In his "disinterested endeavour" to come to terms with the nature of a work of art, the critic also extends and substantiates his own values. The essence of his job, in fact, is judgment. The artist creates his own moral world out of his intuitions into the nature and significance of his experience; the critic does the same out of his intuitions into the nature and significance of the work of art. Both are concerned with a morality that is continually flexible and continually open to fresh impulses. Both are also concerned to make their intuitions, of no matter how obscure a nature, as lucid as possible. For it is lucidity, not complexity, that is the final token of intelligence and honesty.

The two essential elements of primary criticism, then, are judgment and intuitive pertinacity. The business of the intellectual is to be true to his own lights, not to find excuses for popular tastes. He can safely leave conventions to the administrators. The one demand that can be reasonably made of the critic is that he be original. In the last analysis, it doesn't matter if he is right or wrong, bigoted or generous, narrow-minded or catholic, provided he says his own say, gets his own feelings straight and sets up his own standards for inspection and, if necessary, for disagreement; provided, that is, he creates his own moral world with as much intelligence as he can muster. And this is the most fundamental form of commitment; it is not a matter of political dogma or accepted standards, but of the life of the man linking creatively with the life of the work. Apart from the artist, the literary critic is perhaps the only intellectual left who is concerned more directly with life than with abstractions. Hence he is an intellectual in the proper sense of that term: not just a man with an adroit, well-trained intellect, but a man who is qualified above all by the subtlety and depth of his human intelligence. That, as I understand it, is what Eliot meant when he disposed, offhand, with the whole problem of critical method: "The only method," he said, "is to be very intelligent."

# Reflections on Mass Culture

## ERNEST VAN DEN HAAG

## ( *1960* )

ERNEST VAN DEN HAAG has long been interested in mass culture. He believes that whatever hope America nurtures for high culture has been diminished by concessions to egalitarian thinking, concessions which are difficult to avoid. Mr. van den Haag teaches social philosophy at New York University and at the New School for Social Research. He is the author of *The Fabric of Society* (with Ralph Ross), *Education as an Industry* and numerous articles.

B Y AND LARGE, people seriously concerned with mass culture fall into three groups. There is first a nucleus of artists and literary men, supported by a few theoreticians. They fell isolated, alienated, submerged and pushed aside by mass culture; their hopes are dim and they detest it. The literati and the theoreticians are opposed by another group—the practical men, who have decided it is their duty to work for the mass media in spite of the opulent salaries pressed on them. Sedulously aided by academic fellow travelers, they resolutely defend popular culture and their own *sacrificium intellectus*.

The third and largest group stays squarely in the middle, although for motley reasons. Most sociologists are located here; they have been taught that to be anywhere else, particularly when cultural matters are involved, is unscientific. Besides, many of them lack the trained sensibility that would discriminate between, say, English prose and their own writing. Liberal philosophers, on the other hand, have investigated the impossibilities of justifying value judgments for so long that they regard anyone criticizing mass culture for moral or aesthetic reasons as bold but naïve. There is no evidence, they seem to say, for practically any view; hence, let's close our eyes and discuss methodology.

499

With all that, liberal philosophers seem to stress, somewhat unilaterally, the lack of evidence for negative views of mass culture. Perhaps they feel uneasy with rejections of mass culture because of political fears—misplaced ones, in my opinion. They seem unable to free themselves from the suspicion that a rejection of mass culture implies a rejection of the masses (although the contrary is no less logical) and is, therefore, antidemocratic. However, this is a *non sequitur*. One might think little of the cultural capacity of the masses but not therefore of their political capacity.* But even if one thinks little of their political competence, one might still feel that there is no reason why they should not suffer, benefit and possibly learn from its use (and no more is needed to argue for democracy). Finally, although one might be somewhat pessimistic about the masses, one might be even more so about the political capacity of restricted groups. At any rate, neither mass culture nor objections to it seem to promote specific political views: fascists and communists, as often as liberals, favor mass culture, although they occasionally borrow some phrases from its opponents.

Historians, who of all men might be expected to discern the uniqueness of mass culture, seldom do. When they pay heed to mass culture as a historical phenomenon, they seem to take the wrong cue. Thus, Stuart Hughes recently observed, in a perceptive paper, that "our students yawn over the classics" because they have "very little to do with their own lives." He implies that we might as well forget about the classics. This seems odd. Students have always yawned over the classics—only, in times past, teachers were not so sensitive to their own popularity rating nor so eager to entertain their students as to be willing to drop the classics. They dropped some yawning students instead and kept the interested ones. An immature mind cannot understand the classics; and it matures, in part, by learning to understand them—or, at least, to know them so that they may be understood later. Students brought up in an age of rapid technological change may be convinced that literature, like machinery, is subject to obsolescence—a conviction some teachers share or dare not oppose enough to crack the shell. Perhaps this is what makes the classics seem irrelevant.

Yet the classics, if truly classic, cannot be irrelevant, for they deal with subjects relevant to the universal human predicament in

---

* Conversely, I have not found cultivated people to be politically very sagacious. (I'd prefer to entrust my political destiny to farmers or workers rather than to professors as a group.)

ways to be re-experienced perennially. Of course, it is possible that we have become irrelevant to the classics: if our lives have lost all meaning, then no literature worthy of that name can be meaningful to us. For it is the possible meaning of human life that classic literature explores; and we cannot be interested without any experience of meaning and style in our own lives. If we have no such experience, then entertainment bereft of meaning—diversion from boredom, time killing, mass culture—is all that remains. In this case, the relevant must become irrelevant, and only what is irrelevant to begin with can be absorbed. But I'm not yet willing to give up altogether. Under favorable conditions, the study of literature helps us see the possibilities of man's career on earth.

While some are ready to yield to those bored by high culture, others are convinced that the mass media can serve, indeed do serve, to bring high culture to the masses, and that in doing so they justify their existence or, at least, render an important service. Popular magazines may have authors such as Norman Vincent Peale, the argument goes, but don't they also publish an occasional uncensored article by Bertrand Russell? They do. However, a piece by a major philosopher does not make a philosophical magazine out of *Look*—it may make a popular journalist out of the philosopher. In the stream of, at best, diverting banalities, the worth-while piece tends to disappear without impact. It may seduce a Russell to lower his standards and write more such pieces, becoming less worth while and more acceptable in the process. It won't lure *Look* readers into the *Principia Mathematica*. Mass culture can be decorated with high culture pieces without being otherwise changed.

Note further that Russell's opinions are not offered to *Look* readers because of their intrinsic merit; they are offered because they are *his* opinions. Russell is by now a public figure, which means that he can be published without being taken seriously. Had I written the same words, I could not have broken into *Look*, precisely because people might have taken the utterance seriously instead of gobbling it up with the rest of the fare, while captivated by the utterer's fame.

Not everybody defends the mass media as vehicles that bring elements of high culture to the masses. Some depict the culture of the masses, articulated by the mass media in their normal offerings, as superior to high culture to begin with. Thus, one of mass culture's most faithful admirers, Mr. Gilbert Seldes, recently explained that he thinks more highly of Charlie Chaplin than of Marcel Proust because the former has brought more happiness to more people than the latter. Now happiness is hard to measure, and I am not sure that it makes sense to compare the feeling of a person reading Proust to that of another seeing Chaplin. We may grant, however, that more persons have been amused and diverted by Chaplin than by Proust. Still more people are made happy or are diverted by whiskey, apple pie, penicillin, Marilyn Monroe or, perhaps, by a movie that Mr. Seldes and I might agree is thoroughly bad. In short, making people happy is a criterion only if that is what one sets out to do—and I doubt that this was Proust's purpose or the purpose of any serious writer. Surely more persons enjoy Rodgers and Hammerstein than Bach—more enjoy Liberace than Glen Gould. By definition, popular culture is enjoyed by more people than high culture. Mr. Seldes' view would sanction the elimination of art in favor of entertainment—high-class entertainment, at best.

And this is precisely what I am afraid of. Mass culture demands entertainment and so extravagantly rewards those who provide it with money, prestige and power that serious artists become isolated—and tempted. To be sure, such tendencies have always existed; but now they prevail. The strength of the offerings of mass culture, compared with those of art, has risen immensely, and the dividing line has been blurred.

The chances for the values of mass culture to be internalized in childhood also have greatly increased, so that what I have described as temptation is not felt to be such, but, on the contrary, as the due reward for well-directed, talented efforts. The view held by Mr. Seldes in all innocence is widely accepted by less articulate persons. It is a very basic American view, a naïvely pragmatic and philanthropic view that refuses to recognize what cannot be tangibly measured in terms at once hedonistic and altruistic.* The measurement for art thus becomes the number of people made happy—and as soon as this becomes the end of art, art ends.

The answer to those who oppose pessimistic views on mass culture lies here. They argue that there is no evidence that the masses are culturally worse off. (I suspect they are far from well off, but

---

* When the Puritan American heritage collided with the more hedonistic attitudes of later immigrants, an interesting fusion resulted. Pleasure, the Puritans implied, is bad; sacrifice, good. The immigrants wanted to pursue happiness. The resulting attitude is: the pleasure sacrificed and given to others is all right, as is the happiness shared and given. What is bad becomes good if it is not enjoyed by oneself but produced for others.

comparisons are nearly impossible.) As far as the elite is concerned, they ask what prevents it from being as creative as ever? Why can't it coexist with mass culture? Haven't there always been several coexisting levels of culture? Can't we have a pluralistic society?

This reasonable argument overlooks the historically most distinctive and important characteristic of mass culture: the dominant power of the mass of consumers over production, public opinion and prestige. The elite in the past was sufficiently isolated and protected from the masses (which, properly speaking, did not exist as such) to be able to cultivate its own garden. And the mass market (hardly in existence) had nothing much to offer. Further, power, income and prestige distribution being what they were, the masses had no desire to impinge on the culture of the elite; on the contrary, they made room for it. At any rate, if they had a wish to participate or encroach, they had no way of making their demands felt and of articulating them. (Even political revolutions, before Hitler, were led and inspired by members of the elite.) But this has changed. We all now cultivate cash crops in market gardens. Mass culture is manufactured according to the demands of the mass market. No *independent* elite culture is left, for mass culture is far too pervasive to permit it. Cultivated individuals and islands of high culture remain, of course. But they are interstitial and on the defensive even when admired and respected; indeed, then more than ever, for they easily may be "taken up" and typecast. The intellect when alive is not part of our social structure, nor does it have its own domicile.

A convinced egalitarian may ask, So what? No more elite, no more high culture; but the great majority of people—who never belonged—have what they wish. To be sure, most people never were, are not now, and are unlikely ever to be interested in high culture. Yet, it does not follow that high culture is unimportant. Its importance cannot be measured by the number of people to whom it is important. Political issues may be decided by majority vote (or, at least, by letting the majority choose who is to decide them). This is surely not a good way, but nevertheless, I think, the best available.

However, the analogy between political issues and cultural issues (or, for that matter, moral ones) is inappropriate. Political issues, by whatever means they are decided, require collective action. Taxes cannot be levied only on those who feel they benefit proportionately from a pattern of public expenditure, or on individuals who are willing to vote for them. With art and literature it is otherwise, or it was. They could be cultivated by intellectual elites, without mass participation. This is becoming less possible every day. Mass culture threatens to decide cultural issues by a sort of universal suffrage. This is a threat to culture, not an occasion for rejoicing. For once cultural issues are regarded as indivisible, the majority view will prevail—and the majority prefers entertainment to art. Yet, unlike properly political matters, cultural ones do not require collective action, but rather that the mass of people and the law do not interfere. Culture cannot be created by political actions, although it can be destroyed by them. (The support of social groups is required, of course, but not that of society —or of masses—except inasmuch as it makes the existence of the social groups possible.) There would never have been any serious art, philosophy or literature if a majority vote had decided whether a given work was to be created and presented.

Yet, even if these things are important only to a few people, they are the best and most important people, the saving remnant. Actually, these things and these people are important even to those who ignorantly sneer at them. Such feelings as love; such experiences as wit, beauty or moral obligation; or styles of congress, housing and living—all, however degenerate they may become, are brought into existence and elaborated by artists and intellectuals. Without them, life is formless. With them, there is, at least, a paradigm. The most common of human experiences and the most trite still depend on artists and intellectuals to become fully conscious and articulate. Even the silliest entertainer and his public are part of, or are parasites of, a long line of creators of cultural expression—artists, philosophers, writers, composers, et cetera. For as Bernard Berenson suggested, "Popular art is always a derivation from professional individual art." Just as the technician depends on pure scientists he may never have heard of, so civilized nations in general depend on the creators of cultural expression— intellectuals and artists. The relation of the cultural elite to the masses may be compared to the relation of the saints and the cloistered to the faithful at large. Or, the cultural elite may be compared to the playwrights and the actors on stage, whose words, actions, costumes and settings are of significance to the spectators across the footlights, even though they are but spectators.

Although few people become outstanding mathematicians, scholars and artists, or understand what these are doing, society must permit those who cultivate such activities their separate existence or cease to be civilized. And the loss and degeneration of civilization injures everyone—the living and the unborn generations for whom we should hold in trust their rightful heritage. It is not enough, either, to permit some individual specialists to go their way. We need an intellectual and artistic elite (joined, of course, by merit) supported by a necessarily restricted and therefore discriminating public, both with reasonably continuous traditions. If this elite is not allowed autonomy and self-cultivation, if instead it is induced to follow mass tastes and to cater to them, there can be no cultural creation. We may parasitically ring a few changes on the culture of the past; we may find ways to entertain ourselves; but we won't have a style and an experience of our own.

I should not object to cultural pluralism—to mass culture coexisting with high culture—if it were possible. (Folk culture is long dead—although many people don't know a zombie when they see one.) A universally shared high culture is, of course, absurd and self-contradictory. This may sound snobbish, but I didn't make the world; I'm merely describing it. Talents as well as intelligence and sensitivity to various values are differentially distributed. We are lucky if 1 or 2 per cent of the population can be creative in any sense and 15 to 20 per cent can cultivate some sensibility. The remainder benefits indirectly.

The trouble with mass culture is that in various direct and indirect ways it tends to make the existence of high culture impossible. In our eagerness to open opportunity to everybody, we have greatly diminished the prizes available to anybody. Good wine is hard to cultivate when it is habitually diluted and we are brought up to be indiscriminate. We might do well to abandon the sterile and injurious attempts to "improve" mass culture, for its main effect is to debase high culture by "bringing it to the masses." What we must do is to bring some gifted people—not masses—to high culture. We must concentrate on finding ways to save and transmit high culture independently of the culture of mass society. My own view is pessimistic. I should like nothing better than to be proved wrong.

# John Dewey's Legacy

## CHARLES FRANKEL

### *( 1960 )*

With precision and vigor, CHARLES FRANKEL evaluates John
Dewey the man and the philosopher, removing the barnacles
"progressive educationist" and "life adjuster" which have
been attached to Dewey. The author of numerous studies in
contemporary social philosophy, Mr. Frankel is a professor of
philosophy at Columbia University.

EVEN DURING HIS LIFETIME John Dewey suffered the unfortunate fate that the gods seem to reserve for those who become
too influential in philosophy. He disappeared as an individual and
became a symbol. Plato, it will be remembered, fought in his letters to preserve the image of his poor singular self, and insisted
that what he had taught could not be condensed into a doctrine.
Even Karl Marx felt the need to remind his friends wistfully that,
after all, he himself was not a Marxist. And it is difficult now to
remember that John Dewey was a man, not an institution, a philosopher and not a social movement.

For more than two generations the mention of this unassuming
man's name has been less an invitation to the discussion of his
philosophy than a signal for the start of large debates about the ail-
ments of the modern world. To be for Dewey has been to be for
progress, reason and enlightenment. To be against him has been
to be for God, the ancient values of our civilization and the triumph of spirit over matter. To himself Dewey must have seemed
to be what any philosopher who is not self-deceived must seem to
himself to be—an individual, working ultimately in solitude,
plagued by doubts, impatient with his deficiencies, and taking a
chance on such ideas as he might happen to have. But to his admirers Dewey was and is a representation of all that is most hopeful in American civilization. And to his detractors he was and

remains a paradigm of some of the worst ills of our society. Indeed, even those for whom Dewey's name is not a battle cry find it difficult to approach his work with detachment. For whatever Dewey's influence may really have been, his ideas are in the air and his name has echoes. He stood astride an era in American thought with which we are still busy making our peace. To read Dewey's works is to be forced to ask what we ourselves, facing our own problems, really think about progressive education, the welfare state, the moral implications of science, the meaning of liberalism, or almost any one of the other contemporary issues around which intellectual controversies rage. Even when we turn to aspects of the present scene with which Dewey cannot be associated —the vogue of Zen Buddhism or existentialist theology at one extreme, the influence of linguistic philosophy on the other— Dewey's image comes to mind, teasing us to decide whether we have fallen from grace or have finally begun to recover our senses. For Dewey stands there as a palpable presence, a possible alternative. To know where we stand toward Dewey's ideas is to find out, at least in part, where we stand with ourselves.

It may be good to be reminded, therefore, as the Dewey centennial celebrations have recently done, that he was born a hundred years ago. For he lived so long and vigorously, he remains so inextricably associated in the public mind with what is "new" and "progressive," and he is still so substantial a figure among us, that it is easy to forget that he grew up in a world very different from our own. Indeed, the problems that gave Dewey's thought the shape it retained throughout his life were different in fundamental ways from the problems we face.

Dewey was born before Lincoln was President. He was fifty-five years old when the long peace of the nineteenth century collapsed into permanent war, revolution and tension. When he was a graduate student at Johns Hopkins, the most speculative of philosophies, idealism, dominated the university scene, and not the most antispeculative of philosophies, logical empiricism. The great idea that had to be absorbed into Western thinking was the theory of evolution. Socialism was a mere ideal, communism in Russia unthinkable, fascism unimagined. And Freud was unheard of, Kierkegaard forgotten, and the Orient a reality only to exotics.

In the law and social thinking Dewey was faced by the principles of Social Darwinism and the doctrine of "natural rights" applied to the behavior of impersonal corporations. In economics he saw unbridled competition on one side, and insecurity and indignity for masses of men on the other. In politics he had to worry about a state that did too little, not a state that did too much. In the schools there was political patronage, antiquarianism and a discipline so senseless that children might even be prohibited from turning their heads in class. And in American intellectual life generally Dewey had to wrestle, not so much with the slick vulgarity that troubles us today, but with prudishness, gentility, and conceptions of culture and the good life to which only a few in a democratic and industrial age could hope to aspire.

What does a man who grew up in such a world, and whose basic ideas were shaped as answers to such problems, have to say to us? The question is all the more pertinent because Dewey was so honestly and eagerly a creature of his time. And it becomes more insistent when we examine the curious equipment that Dewey brought to his philosophical tasks.

To begin with, he wrote badly—almost, indeed, as though it were a matter of principle. Most of his books were unorganized and repetitious, many of his arguments imprecise and incomplete. At times his sentences have vigor and bite. At other times we enter a sentence of Dewey's and find ourselves in a trackless thicket, from which we emerge at the other end scratched, shaken and relieved. In Dewey's hands even individual words play tricks on us, snarling when we expect them to purr, evaporating when we expect them to stand for something solid. Dewey did not invent his own system of notation, but he did not write in ordinary English either. With some help from his long apprenticeship in German idealism, he made ordinary English over into an artificial tongue.

To be sure, there was a purpose behind this semantic mayhem. Dewey had a sense of the nuances of terms and a shrewd Yankee judgment about their ambiguities. He saw, or thought he saw, that many words we habitually use—including words like "experience," "reality," "true" and "good," which are fundamental in building our conception of the world and our place in it—have quite the wrong meanings attached to them as a result of their historical careers. He wanted to squeeze the wrong meanings out of these words and attach new and better meanings to them. So he used the words not as they are ordinarily used, but as he thought they ought to be used, and he frequently gave old terms new depth and power in the process.

Unfortunately, however, he did not always remember that his readers needed to be warned about what he was doing. And he frequently replaced an old ambiguity simply with a new and more troublesome polyguity. Surely, for example, it is confusing to remark, as Dewey once did, that his book *Experience and Nature* might just as easily have been called *Culture and Nature,* and that the title would not have changed its meaning with this change in its terms. Whatever the reasons may have been, Dewey wrote tortuously, inexactly, carelessly.

Nor is it only Dewey's prose that we must take into account in considering his deficiencies. It must also be said, I think, that Dewey regularly ignored important ideas and issues that were clearly relevant to the themes he chose to discuss. He wrote about logic, but he was largely indifferent to symbolic logic and the revolutionary work of Bertrand Russell and Alfred North Whitehead. He devoted much of his time to questions about the growth of personality and the education of children. But even though he continued to pay attention to these questions after 1920, he did less than disagree with Freud: he virtually ignored his existence.

Perhaps most disconcerting of all, Dewey repeatedly claimed that his ideas were supported by the logic of science and pleaded continually for the use of scientific method in all fields. But the examples of scientific thinking that Dewey offered and analyzed were only rarely examples of scientific thought at its theoretical or system-building levels. They were much more often examples taken from practical life—a doctor diagnosing a disease, an engineer planning a bridge. Compared with Russell, Whitehead, Morris Cohen or even Josiah Royce—to mention only a few of his distinguished contemporaries in philosophy—Dewey's knowledge of the sciences, and particularly of mathematics and the physical sciences, was secondhand.

Dewey had, to be sure, an original and powerful insight into certain issues. He is clearly one of those most responsible for helping us to recognize the constructive and creative aspects of scientific thought and the difference that scientific habits of mind make in any culture that accepts them. But in the history of the interpretation of science there are men like Francis Bacon or Voltaire, who look at science from the outside, seize on some one of its features, and then go on to explain to the nonscientist the general difference that science can make in human attitudes or in standards of right reason. There are, on the other hand, men like Descartes or Immanuel Kant, who understand science from the inside, and who deal, so to speak, with some of its professional problems of logic and method as well as with its general relation to other styles of life and thought. Dewey falls somewhere between these two groups. He was neither so clear and dramatic, nor quite so superficial, as Bacon or Voltaire. But he did not have the precise grasp of details or the informed authority of Kant or of other philosophers in the American tradition like Charles Peirce.

In fact, there is rather generally a curious remoteness about Dewey, a habit of talking around a subject without coming to close grips with it. He showed this trait even when he dealt with subjects about which he knew a good deal. Much of his philosophic writing, for example, consists of criticisms of the great historical traditions in philosophy. There are few historians of philosophy at work today, however, who would not regard the picture that Dewey drew of his philosophic ancestors as slanted and inaccurate. Again, although Dewey's central interest was in social affairs, one cannot find anywhere in his work a direct, systematic examination of major social philosophies—for example, competitive capitalism, socialism, anarchism, syndicalism, guild socialism—that were competing for men's allegiance in his day.

In short, although Dewey argued that philosophy must be a guide to the solution of concrete, practical problems, he repeatedly left his readers guessing what he himself thought about such issues. He was a man of rugged courage who was not afraid to take sides in public controversies. But in his writing he regularly stopped at just the point where we are anxious to see, if only in outline, the kind of practical, positive program he thought his ideas implied. He was a social reformer whose position toward socialism in America, even in the thirties, was unclear. He was a writer on morals who never discussed questions of sexual morality. He was an innovator in education whose views about progressive education are still a legitimate subject for debate. He was modest and had good sense, and this may explain why he was unwilling to pontificate in areas where no man, and least of all a philosopher, can be sure of himself. But it cannot explain the difficulty there is in determining where Dewey stood, simply as one man among other men, on many of the issues that he himself raised for discussion.

What, then, remains? Why did Dewey make the stir that he did? What did he leave that was important, and that we can choose to forget only at a great loss to ourselves?

The answer can be found, I think, only if we are prepared to look at Dewey from a point of view that is not habitual in philosophical circles today. He did not have some of the qualities that a professional philosopher ought to have. He was not an elegant thinker and not always a disciplined one. But he had a quality which can make the difference between a merely skillful philosopher and a first-rate original mind. In his own cheerful, unaggressive way he was a visionary.

It is not easy to think of this quiet, patient man in this way. He was easygoing, unimpassioned and temperate. He did not go in for flights of fancy or bursts of indignation, or indulge in the consolations of paradox and irony like those other visionaries of his generation, Shaw and Russell. He simply kept going, year after year, sticking to his guns, insistent, indefatigable, and always returning—the sure mark of a visionary—to the same basic theme.

And it was a distinctive theme, which the comparison with Shaw and Russell highlights. Shaw was fundamentally disturbed, as he once remarked, by stupidity; it was the direction of life by a consistent view of things that excited him. In Russell's work there are the twin visions of certainty in intellectual matters and justice in the arrangement of human affairs. But while Dewey did not like stupidity and injustice, what basically disturbed him was the decline of any human being's life into a state of passivity. It seemed to him to be the denial of the human birthright.

There is a sentence in Karl Marx's *Capital* which, with appropriate alterations, suggests what Dewey thought the basic human problem of his day was. Under capitalism, Marx wrote, the advance of technology and the accumulation of capital, far from helping the worker, "mutilate the laborer into a fragment of a man, degrade him to the level of appendage to a machine, destroy every remnant of charm in his work and turn it into hated toil. . . ." Dewey could not speak with the scorn and bitterness of a Hebrew prophet. Moreover, he thought too steadily in terms of the individual's day-to-day experience to believe that an abstract change in the law of property would be enough to change a man's relation to his work. He would have asked whether factories were still organized in an authoritarian manner or whether the economic revolution had been imposed without the consent of those affected. And he would have looked at other areas where human behavior is governed and human personality is shaped or misshaped—for example, at philosophies that suggest that the answer to men's problems can be found simply by consulting fixed principles, or at educational systems that make submissiveness the child's central experience in the classroom.

But Dewey would have agreed that it was the "mutilation" of the individual, the imposition upon him of an external, mechanical routine, which was the basic moral problem of industrial society. He would have thought, indeed, that it had been the moral problem of all major forms of social organization that had ever existed. And he would have felt an immediate sympathy, it may be suspected, with the direct language, the immediate and aesthetic language, that Marx employed in this passage. For the program of reconstruction in philosophy, morals and society which Dewey proposed can be understood only if we see that Dewey took the daily experience of individuals more seriously than he took anything else, and that he ultimately evaluated everything as an instrument for the enrichment of such experience.

This is the heart of Dewey's philosophy, I suggest, and the ultimate meaning that is to be attached to calling him a "pragmatist" or "instrumentalist." What Dewey wanted to see diffused throughout human life, and what he thought that democracy, science and technology could diffuse, were qualities that we find best exemplified in the arts—spontaneity, self-discipline, the involvement of the personality, and the marriage of individuality and order, the delightful and the meaningful. His enemies were routine, drill, external dictation and the ready-made in ideas; and the targets he attacked were social arrangements, educational methods of philosophical systems that seemed to promote such qualities.

Oddly enough, this philosopher who wrote so badly, whose thinking seems so homely and prosaic, and who is remembered for his glorification of science, had essentially a poet's vision of the possibilities of human life. He wished to see men's environments so ordered that the life of art was possible for all. His ideal was a world in which individuals lived with a sense of active purpose, exerting their individual powers, putting their mark on their environments, sharing their experiences, and making their own contribution to the common enterprises of humanity. He did not seem to think that this was a utopian ideal—or perhaps he did not care if it was. For he was convinced that it could be more closely approximated in the modern world than it had ever been before, and it was the only ideal which could give our power and wealth some meaning beyond themselves.

"Democracy," Dewey once wrote, and he said the same thing in one way or another again and again, "is belief in the ability of human experience to generate the aims and methods by which further experience will grow in ordered richness." It is an odd definition, and a dark one. But it becomes clearer when we put it alongside a remark he made in his book on aesthetics, *Art as Experience*. "Ultimately," Dewey wrote, "there are but two philosophies. One of them accepts life and experience in all its uncertainty, mystery, doubt and half-knowledge and turns that experience upon itself to deepen and intensify its own qualities—to imagination and art. This is the philosophy of Shakespeare and Keats."

It is a long way from the poetry of Shakespeare and Keats to a philosophy of democracy, but Dewey had a way of bringing distant things together. And the bridge by which he made such transitions was his theory of human experience—his conception of human life in its ideal form. He rejected any philosophy that seemed to cut human life or society to a pre-arranged form. He preferred philosophies that liberated men from leading strings and allowed them to take control of their own lives. And so he framed his moral philosophy, his educational theory and his conception of democracy not primarily in terms of abstract ideals or institutional arrangements, but in terms of the diffusion throughout a society of this distinctive sort of personal experience.

This is the vision that stands behind the freshness and power of John Dewey's insights. With this vision he turned logic, the history of philosophy, and even that most abstruse and apparently artificial of philosophical subjects—the theory of knowledge—into subjects with moral and cultural significance. He connected theory not only to practice but to a coherent image of what human life might be. And he made philosophy what it has always been when it has been most vigorous—a commentary on things outside itself and a challenge to men to make up their minds about the terms on which they are willing to conduct their business in this world. Underneath the difficulties of his language and the technicalities of his arguments Dewey's vision, it seems to me, is the source of the excitement and the sense of importance that his work communicated, and still communicates, to others.

Despite the looseness and occasional tedium of John Dewey's books, they have, then, an inner dynamism. There is a coherent theory of experience that propels them. This theory is best formulated in *Art as Experience*, the most revealing of Dewey's books, I think, and the one to which too little attention is paid. But it also controls Dewey's thinking in his books on education, morals, democracy and science. What was this theory? To what

513

notions about human culture did it lead Dewey? How did it affect his philosophy of education and of science? These are the questions to which we must turn.

There are for Dewey two extremes between which our experience moves. At one extreme we live by habits, which include, of course, habits of mind and feeling as well as habits of motor behavior. Without habits our lives would be unendurable: every action that was not instinctive would call for a decision. And so long as we do not meet new situations in which our habits come a cropper, our lives move smoothly. But they also move without awareness on our part, without questions, without self-consciousness.

At the other extreme from the life of habit, there is the sudden break in our routine activity, the event so new and different that we are startled into noticing it. This is what it means, in Dewey's special language, to have a "sensation." It is not a mere feeling, like the feeling of being tickled or the seeing of a brown patch of color. It is to be aroused by the unusual, to have the kind of experience in which "sensational" journalism specializes. And just as an individual is passive when he is wholly a creature of habit, he is also passive when he is overcome by sensation. It is something that happens to him, that plays over him, and that he may enjoy because it releases him from routine and returns an edge to his consciousness. But he cannot do anything about it except notice it. The moment that he can fit it into his own normal pattern of life and work it ceases to be merely sensational. It becomes something he can use, grist for his intellectual mill. It stops being a "sensation" and becomes something he can make sense of.

But these extremes of routine and shock between which so much human experience oscillates suggest what it is to have "experience" in the ideal sense. We have "an experience" when our habits are interrupted, when novelty intrudes, and when we master this novelty by developing the ideas that allow us to fit it into a new pattern of successful action. We have experiences, in short, when we solve problems. And the point of successful problem-solving for Dewey is not simply that it allows us to return to the even, habitual tenor of our ways, but that it provides us with those moments in which we are most intensely conscious of our surroundings, most aware of our own purposes, and most cognizant of the relation between our surroundings and our purposes. To have an experience is to have a story to tell. It is to move in an orderly way from a blocked purpose through a series of exploratory actions to a conclusion in which our purpose is realized or at least intelligibly defeated. Experience, in this sense, is its own reward. It is a means to having other experiences, but it is also—although Dewey did not like the expression—an end in itself. And in terms of this view of experience, the problematic is more interesting than what is settled, and taking risks and acting deliberately on hypotheses is to be preferred to the illusions of safety and certainty.

Dewey, it is plain, was using the word "experience" in his own way. Moreover, his theory of experience was not quite what he made it seem. Until the end of his life Dewey retained the habits of a not quite reformed philosophical idealist. He did not believe that there is a clear distinction to be made between descriptions of the facts and judgments of value, and he presented his theory of experience as though he were giving an account of the growth of experience out of habit and sensation. He admitted that human experience in fact contained many moments that were merely passages to something else and had no intrinsic worth of their own, and that there were other moments that were just dead ends. But instead of deploring these facts on explicit moral or aesthetic grounds he preferred to suggest that they were somehow instances of experience nipped in the bud, cut off before it had come to full development.

But the notion of "development" always contains an implicit standard of what is normal or desirable. We want a ten-year-old boy to grow, for example, but at some point we should also like to see him stop growing. Dewey, I believe, would have helped his readers immeasurably, and would have avoided much unnecessary controversy, if he had presented his theory of experience for what it was. It was not a psychologist's account of the laws that govern human perception or motivation, or a sociologist's account of the relation of the individual's attitudes and behavior to his culture, class or social role. It leaned on such facts (or on guesses about such facts). But its purpose was not description for its own sake; its purpose was to describe a kind of experience that sometimes occurs and that Dewey thought ought to occur more frequently, and to show the conditions under which such experience may be blocked or realized. Facts are not irrelevant to it; but appeal to facts alone will not suffice to justify it. We also have to share Dewey's implicit ideals.

Once we adopt these ideals even provisionally, however, a new landscape opens before us. For Dewey employed his notion of ideal experience to develop a remarkably trenchant and comprehensive critique of Western philosophy and culture. The views of human experience that had prevailed in the past were not, to his mind, transcripts of unchanging truths about the human scene. They were reflections of specific social conditions, and of conditions that need no longer exist. Men had lived in a world which for the most part they could not control. So they had looked to pure reason to provide them with a refuge, and had used philosophy to paint a picture of another and better world—a "real" world behind phenomena—where everything was permanent and safe. Even more to the point, men had lived in a social world rigidly divided into separate classes. The great majority had done manual work; a tiny minority had enjoyed leisure and "culture." So the practical, the useful, the material, had been denigrated; the contemplative and the useless had been the things to admire.

In short, such conditions had created, Dewey believed, the traditional philosophical "dualisms," the sharp divisions that philosophers had characteristically set between mind and matter, reason and the senses, values and facts. In Dewey's view intelligence, when properly understood, is the activity of a biological creature, caught in mid-passage by some block to his habits or interests, and seeking and finding new habits that will be effective in place of the routines that do not work. In such a view of intelligence there is no place for separating the work of thought and the work of the senses, the movements of the mind and the effective manipulation of the physical environment. All are phases of the same activity and all support one another. In such circumstances, mind and matter, reasoning and sensing, are effectively one, and philosophical dualisms that place them in separate categories merely reinforce attitudes and habits of behavior that prevent men from having experience in its ideal form.

Once more, of course, all this raises questions. But before we turn to these questions, it is important to see what we can easily fail to see. In a sense, Dewey's ideas suffer from their very sanity: we may not recognize how fresh and radical they were. For Dewey's conception of intelligence restored men to a view of themselves that the most powerful traditions in Western philosophy and religion had tended to obscure.

If Dewey was right, then the mind is not a mysterious ghost in the machine of the body. It is simply one type of physical disposition and activity. If Dewey was right, there is no world of eternal ideas, and no order of original, pure perceptions, to which our ideas must conform. Our ideas derive their meaning from the uses we give them in specific contexts of language and inquiry. And if Dewey was right, our thinking does not normally fall into neat, military divisions marked "thinking about facts" and "thinking about values." Accordingly, moral insight is not the special prerogative of the humanities or religion or metaphysics; and if men in these fields have opinions about either facts or values, these opinions must meet the same tests that beliefs in any other field must meet.

But questions remain. There are questions, for example, about the accuracy of Dewey's account of the philosophical past, and questions, as well, about the lengths to which Dewey's fear of "dualisms" led him. To argue, for instance, that thinking about values is not independent of thinking about facts is one thing. But to say that a value judgment cannot be distinguished from a judgment about the facts is quite another. Yet this is what Dewey sometimes seems to suggest. But perhaps the greatest question raised by Dewey's theory of experience and culture, which is to say his notion of right experience and right culture, is the implicit value judgment that it involves. "Ideas are worthless," Dewey wrote, "except as they pass into actions which rearrange and reconstruct in some way, be it little or large, the world in which we live." Surely it can be agreed that a life devoted exclusively to the mental rehearsal of possibilities would be a thin and cold affair; and it can also be agreed that a society which does not use its ideas to guide its behavior will be blind or reckless in what it does. But the kind of play of the mind that is sheer play, that does not involve an irritable reaching after decisions and programs, seems to me to have a place in any calendar of the virtues that is circumspectly drawn.

No doubt Dewey did not mean to deny this value utterly. Passages certainly can be found in his books where he tries to make a place for it and emphasizes its importance in enriching experience and in bringing it the qualities of humor and compassion. But I do not think that even his stanchest defenders will say that he did not emphasize doing and acting even more, or that it was not characteristic of him to be impatient with thought for thought's sake. He spoke for men in a rising democracy, energetic, busy, committed. But a democratic culture will be richer if it can also find a place for the disengaged mind and for a kind of thinking that is not necessarily a prelude to action.

This element of distortion in Dewey's point of view seems to me to affect his views on both science and education. His most important contribution to the philosophy of science is undoubtedly his "instrumentalist" theory of ideas. Although he owed this theory in large part to Charles Peirce, he developed and applied it with an originality that was his own. Very briefly, this theory holds that an idea is an instrument by which we move from situations in which we do not know what to think or how to act to situations in which our perplexities are dispelled. Ideas are leading principles, rules which tell us what observations to make and what inferences to draw from our observations. The truth of an idea, therefore, is a matter of its effectiveness in leading to successful predictions and to actions in which our purposes are realized—in short, its effectiveness in dealing with the particular problem that it was created to solve.

The instrumentalist theory is an immensely liberating one. It explains the function of fundamental scientific ideas like the theory of the atom and tells us what we mean when we call such ideas true even though we cannot directly observe the objects whose structure they purportedly describe. And it can be used—Dewey, in fact, did use it with great success—to dispel a host of perennially disturbing problems. In moral philosophy, for example, it has traditionally been thought that we cannot rationally determine how we ought to behave unless we have some abstract definition of "good" and "right" with which to work. But Dewey argued that our moral dilemmas arise only in definite situations where individual or social interests are blocked. What we do in such circumstances is to work out some plan of action that will eliminate the specific conflict that is troubling us. And we test this plan, not by its agreement with some general definition of "the good," but by its feasibility and its consistency with other values we actually hold. Particularly when Dewey dealt with the logic of our practical judgments he exhibited, it seems to me, a shrewd, close grasp of the facts and a stubborn resistance to traditional intellectual follies—two qualities, it must be confessed, that are not entirely usual among philosophers.

But Dewey had the defect of this virtue. As one of his early essays, "The Logic of Practical Judgment," states explicitly, he believed that scientific thinking could be made to fit the model of practical judgment. At the very least, this is an overstatement. For while it is true that many fundamental scientific ideas have an instrumental function, it is a gross simplification (as Dewey himself sometimes recognized) to say that they are tools for manipulating the environment. Their acceptance in a scientific system depends equally on purely intellectual considerations such as economy, elegance and the possibility of connecting them with other systems. Moreover, Dewey's insistence that thinking always remakes and reforms the materials on which it works makes it difficult to find a place for the clearly primary objective of the theoretical science— namely, to understand a world whose structure does not depend on what we think or do about it. Dewey repeatedly failed to distinguish between facts as they exist and those beliefs about the facts that have the warrant of science at some particular time. But unless this distinction is kept clearly and uncompromisingly in mind we cannot explain what Dewey himself thought the hallmark of scientific thinking—its openness to correction by further evidence.

Dewey's view of science, indeed, has something a little dated about it. It seems to be the view of a man whose fundamental ideas about science had been formed before the rise of modern physics, which, for all its practical and ominous usefulness, describes a world that transcends almost all our practical and habitual expectations. When Dewey argued that "scientific method" or "scientific habits of thought" should be diffused throughout society, what did he mean by these elusive phrases? The science that played the greatest role in Dewey's thinking was biology; and what he meant by "the scientific attitude," I would suggest, was primarily the evolutionary attitude—a recognition that nothing is exempt from change, that new circumstances require new ideas and institutions, and that we should measure the worth of these ideas and institutions not in terms of allegedly eternal truths, but in terms of their contribution to the control of the human environment and the satisfaction of human interests. He was right to have believed that if such an attitude could be generally diffused in a society, a remarkably liberating revolution would take place. And he would be equally right to say, as he surely would today, that some appreciation of the intellectual significance of contemporary science should be regarded as a necessity for all educated men in our society. But the view of science and scientific method which he held is not one which is likely to warn us about the extrarodinary difficulty of this task.

And so we come, by a quite natural transition, to Dewey's philosophy of education. I must be brief, and I speak with the diffidence that befits any discussion either of Dewey or of education. Dewey's philosophy of education, as Sidney Hook has argued, rests on two pillars—first, a commitment to democracy and a belief that the habits developed in the classroom are as important to a student's effective participation in democracy as the facts and ideas he acquires; second, a belief that the content and methods of instruction should be governed by the best scientific knowledge available. To this certain other propositions may also be added. Teaching is effective only when the student's perspective is taken into account and only when his active interest and participation in the work of the classroom is aroused. Further, since we do not understand facts or ideas until we know how to use them, the student must be provided with facts and ideas in contexts in which he can put them to use and test them out for himself.

Any teacher can report how easy it is to forget these principles in everyday practice, and yet they may seem too obvious to constitute a significant educational philosophy. But if they do seem obvious, this is a measure of Dewey's achievement. For they were not at all obvious when he first began to write on education. In 1892, for example, Joseph Rice made a survey of American schools in thirty-six cities. He told the story of a teacher in Chicago who, after asking a question, would say, "Don't stop to think. Tell me what you know!" In New York, Rice asked a school principal whether students were allowed to turn their heads. The man replied, "Why should they look behind when the teacher is in front of them?" This is the sort of thing that Dewey was thinking about when he emphasized that teachers teach students and not only subjects, that a spirit of inquiry should animate the classroom, and that play too has its educational uses. It is grossly untrue to say that Dewey had insufficient respect for the intellectual goals of education. His philosophy was not an attempt to make the schools more frivolous. It was an attempt to return the schools to seriousness.

But Dewey, unhappily, did write vaguely. In the hands of eager disciples, his language, never an adequate instrument for the communication of ideas, has been converted into a jargon that hides them. Moreover, as Dewey himself pointed out late in life in his little book *Experience and Education*, his philosophy of education had merely been an attempt to emphasize neglected issues in education. But many of his admirers have taken a matter of emphasis for the whole story. Although I remain diffident, I cannot forebear saying that the results have frequently been bizarre.

I can mention only one issue, an issue raised by Dewey's emphasis on "the practical." It has led, I would suggest, to a mistaken conception of the kind of thing that needs to be done to involve a student actively in the learning process. Dewey was right to think that a student will master an idea only when he has had a chance to use it for himself. But it is wrong to conclude that the student can learn the use of important ideas by focusing primarily on homely problems within the round of his daily experience. If ideas have a direct bearing on such issues, that is all to the good. The alert teacher will exploit the opportunity. But we learn the distinctive function of an important idea when we see it at work, not simply reorganizing the world we have known, but leading to other worlds we might never have imagined otherwise. Accordingly, unless the student's attention to things outside his ordinary world is deliberately engaged, and unless his perceptions are liberated from domination by the familiar, the school will not have done its job.

Although Dewey would undoubtedly have agreed with this truism, I believe that he must bear some of the responsibility for the tendency of those who espouse his educational philosophy to forget it. For there is a repeated error into which Dewey falls in his educational philosophy, and in his philosophy in general. He wished passionately to show that the everyday practical experience of men could have an ideal dimension. But he slid from this idea to the quite different one that a man's—or a child's—experience must always have a practical dimension.

And yet these criticisms do not touch the heart of what John Dewey succeeded in doing. He thought that philosophy was an instrument by which a society criticizes itself, throwing off the ideas that block its development and finding the possibilities within itself that it might work to realize. He set himself to this task and performed it with a quiet, steady passion, magnanimously, imaginatively, without nostalgia for the past or regret for the comforting dogmas that had to be sacrificed. And he put his finger on the two main issues of his day—the steady growth in the importance of science and the struggle to extend democracy—and revealed their moral meaning, their possibilities for our day-to-day experience.

Dewey helped men to see that science meant something much more than an increase in their power to control their environment. He showed that science challenged inherited forms of authority and offered an alternative way by which men could stabilize their lives. And despite all his emphasis on practical manipulation and control, Dewey also showed that science represented a revolution in the human imagination, extending human horizons and making men aware of remote and unfamiliar things.

So he brought science to the same test that he brought everything else—its impact on men's immediate experience; and he taught men to value science for what it could do to enhance the meanings they found in their everyday lives.

He transformed the theory of democracy in a similar way. "The one thing in the world of value," Emerson once wrote, "is the active soul." This was the central point of Dewey's theory of experience, and it is the source of his conception of democracy. Only in a society in which the lines between classes are fluid and in which men freely mingle and communicate with one another, Dewey believed, can active souls be generated everywhere. And so he saw that democracy could mean something much more than a political form. It could mean a change in the quality of a culture, an opportunity for men to experience more and to live more intensely.

Without vanity or pretentiousness, John Dewey made himself a spokesman for the best hopes of his generation. And to our generation he leaves the image of a man of unforced courage and honesty, living by choice in the mainstream of events, and yet rising above events to a coherent vision of what men might make of themselves. He helped us to see farther and to move more freely. It is to him as much as to anyone that we owe what belief we have that our own place in history can be an opportunity and not a fatality.

For Product Safety Concerns and Information please contact our EU
representative GPSR@taylorandfrancis.com
Taylor & Francis Verlag GmbH, Kaufingerstraße 24, 80331 München, Germany